stripped:
depeche mode

stripped:
depeche mode

JONATHAN MILLER

OMNIBUS PRESS

LONDON / NEW YORK / PARIS / SYDNEY / COPENHAGEN / BERLIN / MADRID / TOKYO

Exclusive Distributors:
Music Sales Limited,
8/9 Frith Street,
London W1D 3JB, UK.

Music Sales Corporation,
257 Park Avenue South,
New York, NY 10010, USA.

Macmillan Distribution Services,
53 Park West Drive,
Derrimut, Vic 3030,
Australia.

To the Music Trade only:
Music Sales Limited,
8/9 Frith Street,
London W1D 3JB, UK.

Every effort has been made to trace the copyright holders of the photographs in this book but one or two were unreachable. We would be grateful if the photographers concerned would contact us.

Typeset by Galleon Typesetting, Ipswich
Printed in Great Britain by Creative Print & Design, Wales.

A catalogue record for this book is available from the British Library.

www.omnibuspress.com

Contents

Introduction

From Ultrapop To Stadium Rock

The story of Depeche Mode is an unlikely tale of how, against all odds, four Essex lads achieved fame, fortune and that elusive musical nirvana of longevity and respectability while remaining loyal to their integrity and indie roots. It involves charismatic frontman Dave Gahan, outwardly quiet, yet genuinely gifted songwriter Martin Gore, and self-confessed non-musician Andy 'Fletch' Fletcher. The fourth – no longer a member – is Vince Clarke, synth Svengali and, when it comes to writing hits, a man with the Midas touch, whose parallel career must be considered as part of this same story. His replacement – Alan Wilder, a Londoner by birth – was equally integral in shaping the sound of Depeche Mode's world breakthrough.

Depeche Mode first stormed the UK singles chart in the early Eighties with infectious slices of fresh-faced, one-fingered synth pop like 'Just Can't Get Enough' and 'See You'. Light, bright and upbeat, they offered a refreshing contrast to the doom-laden paranoia that had served fellow synthesiser enthusiast Gary Numan so well. By chalking up two number one singles and two number one albums in a three-month period of 1979, Numan had become the UK's fastest rising synth star, opening the floodgates for the wave of early-Eighties synth-based acts that followed. Among these hopefuls were Depeche Mode, whose then-principal songwriter Vince Clarke christened his catchy compositions 'U.P.' or 'Ultrapop' while his fellow synth-playing cohort Andy Fletcher once crowed, "We're going to be The Beatles of the indies!"

With the benefit of hindsight, the irony of Fletcher's prophetic words would surely not be lost on the man today: from Basildon beginnings to globetrotting stadium superstars, teenage bubblegum synth popsters to popular late-thirty-something 'serious' musicians, clean-cut to drug-fuelled and back again, Depeche Mode have done it all, and survived – quite literally so in the case of vocalist Dave Gahan.

Having sold a staggering 40 million albums and performed to some six million people over 20 years, who'd have guessed they'd still be releasing multi-million-selling albums of dark, yet somehow uplifting songscapes that have become their latter-day trademark? It nearly wasn't so – on more than one occasion.

For Depeche Mode are no strangers to pop's undulating currents. They were written off as early as 1981 when, dissatisfied with the promotional and touring circus, Clarke unexpectedly departed immediately following the release of the band's lightweight début LP, *Speak & Spell*. While he wasted little time in finding success with Alison Moyet in Yazoo and longevity with Erasure, Gahan and remaining synth players Fletcher and Martin Gore refused to be beaten. The latter promptly took over songwriting duties while classically trained keyboard virtuoso Alan Wilder filled Clarke's on-stage shoes and soon proved indispensable in the studio.

Confounding fans and critics alike, Depeche Mode admirably reinvented themselves over the coming years, finally attaining world domination status on the 101st and final concert of their *Music For The Masses* world tour in front of a 70,000-strong audience at Pasedena's Rose Bowl in California on June 18, 1988. It was often claimed that, after The Beatles, Depeche Mode were the most popular pop/rock outfit in the Soviet Union! Clearly their appeal knows no political bounds.

What goes up must come down. Following 1993's 'difficult' *Songs Of Faith And Devotion* album, the 158-show trek to over two million fans took its toll in more ways than one, not least Wilder's 1995 dramatic departure, put down to "dissatisfaction with the internal relations and working practices of the group". Doom merchants again predicted Depeche Mode's disbandment, not least because of Gahan's substance abuse. They were almost right.

Gahan, Gore and Fletcher only just managed to regroup as a trio under the watchful production gaze of Bomb The Bass dance maverick Tim Simenon – Depeche Mode having inadvertently influenced a new generation of global electronica in its dazzling array of guises (techno, house, trance, trip-hop, *et al*). 1997's chart-topping *Ultra*, shifted over four million copies worldwide, and spawned 'Barrel Of A Gun' – the group's highest UK hit single in several years. A tough act to follow, but Depeche Mode showed no sign of letting up, tentatively touring – only 65 dates this time out – in support of their well-earned *The Singles 86>98* compilation, albeit mindful of recent excesses and 'near misses'.

Come 2001, a revitalised Depeche Mode were back in the studio, firing on all cylinders. Chosen to helm what became the *Exciter* album was producer Mark Bell, co-founder of LFO, a Warp Records signing dubbed as one of the most influential techno acts of the early Nineties. At the time of writing, three million copies had been sold following Depeche Mode's 83-date North American and European tour.

Exciter itself is testament to the teamwork behind Depeche Mode's enviable endurance – in this case Bell's production skills and Gore's songwriting talent, a talent rightly recognised with the May 1999 presentation of an award for International Achievement by the British Academy of Composers & Songwriters. Mute Records founder Daniel Miller, the man who sealed a deal with Depeche Mode with a simple handshake – no written details, no formal contracts – back in 1980, made that presentation.

To evoke a cliché – what is the secret of Depeche Mode's success? Perhaps fellow British electropop pioneer Thomas Dolby is in a better position to answer: "When a Depeche Mode song comes on the radio, I know instantly it's them – even if it's a brand-new release or an obscure album cut I've never heard before. Even in the overcrowded world of electronic music, where we all have more or less the same tools at our disposal, Depeche Mode consistently stands out. They just have a sound that's completely unique, and hard to put your finger on . . ."

Jonathan Miller
Whitley Bay, September 2002

For Emma and Megan . . .

PART I

Basildon Bygone Daze

"Sometimes I feel, all of a sudden, I'm going to wake up, and then I'm going to be doing my old job, with a synthesiser in a suitcase, going to a small little place in Canning Town. So it does seem like a real dream, and it's gone very, very fast!"

— Andy Fletcher, 2001

1

Basildon Bonding

"I really hated Basildon. I wanted to get out as quickly as I could. I think being in a band was an escape. There was very little to do. It's one of those places where you go drinking because that's your only option."

— Martin Gore, 2001

They may think otherwise, relaxing in luxurious mansions in exotic locations around the world, but the Depeche Mode story does begin in the peculiarly ordinary Essex town of Basildon.

Located some 30 miles east of Central London, this unassuming area is one of several so-called 'New Towns' originally created as a direct result of the 1946 New Towns Act, designed to ease the capital's chronic housing problem in the aftermath of the Blitz. The brainchild of Minister of Town & Country Planning, Lewis Silkin, the legislation gave Clement Atley's post-Second World War Labour government the power to compulsorily designate any area of land on which a New Town development could be considered beneficial to the national interest.

Silkin himself chaired a public meeting at Laindon High Road secondary school on September 30, 1948, to debate the proposed plan for the creation of a 50,000-population New Town. By 1951 – the year Basildon New Town welcomed its first 'new' residents – the district's population had trebled to 34,000 residents since the 1931 census.

The name Basildon is of Saxon origin, as immortalised in British playwright Arnold Wesker's critically acclaimed community production, *Beorhtel's Hill*, commissioned to celebrate the town's fortieth anniversary, in 1989. Wesker's play was a fascinating document of London's East Enders who became the first Basildon New Town settlers. Originally, a different breed of Londoner had taken to the wilds of Essex. As the London, Tilbury & Southend Railway system opened up the area from the mid-1850s onwards, the surrounding cheap land gave rise to the erection of sub-standard 'shacks' which were connected by unmade roads with no services. One company selling land at Pitsea and Vange, between 1901 and 1906, reputedly lured potential purchasers with free champagne lunches and rail tickets!

Yet the Basildon from which the New Town inherited its name – and from where Depeche Mode would emerge – was little more than a tiny village in the Forties, a mere pinprick on the Essex map. Its development heralded great change as the existing towns of Laindon and Pitsea with their all-important respective London rail links were effectively fused together. Amazingly, Basildon would not be blessed with its own railway station until 1970, though this apparent oversight did little to stem the rapid population influx.

As former 'Basildonian' and lifelong friend of Vince Clarke, Robert Marlow, observes: "All the people that came to Basildon were strangers. My family were from Wales – my mother was Welsh, my father came from Bishop's Stortford in Hertfordshire. So it was all about resettlement – there were no roots, as such. I never felt like there was any sense of community, as it were. And I think that's why anybody who lived there in the Sixties and Seventies probably had their little cliques or gangs, whereas in other areas, people often had established family living nearby. Anthropologically speaking, it's quite interesting."

If Gypswyk sounds like a strange street name then the Basildon Development Corporation, charged with overseeing the New Town's construction, could conceivably be forgiven as they strove to transform the area into a thoroughly modern town; building and naming hundreds of new streets in rapid succession. With a population exceeding 120,000, today Basildon has over 1,200 street names – and rising.

By 1981 those streets were well on their way to completion, and pop's fresh-faced, one-fingered synth pop phenomenon, Depeche Mode were already putting Basildon on the musical map. Indeed, when Depeche Mode first achieved front cover status in the August 22, 1981 issue of *New Musical Express*, the group's diplomat Andy Fletcher was keen to point out, "It's got an electoral role of 107,000 and that's not including kids. That's the biggest in the country, and next time it has got to be split up into Basildon East and West."

Basildon New Town has since achieved a degree of notoriety, representing a barometer reading of British general election results. This largely stems from an early announcement that MP David Amess had held it for the Conservatives in 1992, the first indication that Neil Kinnock's Labour party was not about to defy the opinion polls and oust John Major's government. Basildon's relative prosperity under Thatcherism – during which a high proportion of its local authority housing had been sold to occupiers – would live to fight another day.

Basildon, it would seem, is something of an anomaly – in more ways than one. According to Robert Marlow: "The sound of Basildon came out of the bricks!"

The Martins were but one of literally thousands of families who warmed to the promise of low-cost housing and good employment prospects. East Enders Dennis and Rose Martin married late in life. Their eldest son, Vincent, was born in South Woodford, on July 3, 1960.* Vince remembered his father as being "a bit of a wheeler and dealer". Dennis was actually a tic-tac man,† specialising in greyhound racing, while Rose worked as a seamstress. In 1965, the couple were able to move their growing family into a brand-new, comparatively spacious, four-bedroomed local authority house at 44 Shepeshall, Basildon.

For young Vince, older sister Carol, and younger brothers, Michael and Rodney, Basildon's pristine countryside was nothing short of revelatory with its numerous planned park and woodland areas in which to roam and play.

Vince Clarke: "It was great. We had a fine time. There were a lot more green areas back then than there are there now. We had three areas – the woods, the hill and the trees. Everything was based around those places. When you're a little kid they're very, very big."

Boys will be boys, and brothers Michael and Rodney were swiftly initiated into Vince's gang for elaborate games of bows and arrows, crab football, and other popular pastimes in the nearby woods. Carol kept her distance, an unspoken arrangement that apparently suited both parties. "We hated our big sister, and of course she hated us."

In Basildon, *circa* 1965, the sun evidently shone brightly on Vince Martin. As he would one day reflect in adulthood: "It was quite a straightforward,

* In 1980, as Depeche Mode prepared to release their first record, Vince Martin adopted the stage surname, Vince Clarke. For the purposes of this book, all direct quotes are attributed to Vince "Clarke".
† Tic-tac being the secret and complex sign language used by bookmakers at racecourses to indicate movements in the price of a horse, or, in Dennis' case, usually a dog.

normal family background. We all got on, pretty much." From the age of five, Vince attended Laindon's Bluehouse County Infant School, on Leinster Road.

Vince Clarke: "I enjoyed infant and junior school because they were quite small schools. So I felt like I was a bit of a big fish in a small pond. Then when I went to Laindon High Road, I was a small fish in a big pond, and I hated it."

The youngster joined the 5th Basildon Boys' Brigade, whose junior section met on a weekday evening at Janet Duke Primary School in Markhams Chase, Laindon. Unbeknownst to Vince, Alison 'Alf' Moyet, his future musical partner in synth duo Yazoo, was attending school there.

Vince Clarke: "Boys' Brigade was *fantastic*! It was like a youth club; you went there to play table tennis, basically. The only thing you had to do was go to church on Sundays, which was OK. But you put up with that for the good stuff. We went camping and we went on canal boat trips. It was just a brilliant experience for us all."

Vince made friends with another Basildon boy brigadier, Rob Allen, who lived around the corner from the Martins, at 3 Gypswyk.

Robert Marlow:* "Vince and I always get mixed up as to whether we were six or seven, or seven or eight when we met up at Boy's Brigade – certainly it was very early. And, of course, Andy Fletcher was part of that as well."

The lanky, strawberry blond Andrew John Fletcher, born in Nottingham on July 8, 1961, was another new kid on the Basildon block. York Shipley, a Nottingham-based refrigeration and cooling equipment manufacturer, had moved his father, John, to work at their new Basildon-based factory. Andy later admitted: "It was a job for a house. If you could get a job, you could get a house."

In the event, 101 Woolmer Green, a modern three-bedroom mid-link villa on a pedestrian-only street within walking distance of Shepeshall, would be the Fletcher family's south eastern destination. Younger sisters, Susan and Karen shared a bedroom while Andy, a keen footballer and life-long Chelsea supporter, had a room to himself. Like Vince Clarke, his

---

* When signed to Vince Clarke's short-lived Reset Records label in the Eighties, Rob Allen followed his mentor's lead and adopted the stagename, Robert Marlow, as he is now known. For the purposes of this book, all direct quotes are attributed to Robert Marlow.

earliest Basildon memories paint a pretty picture: "When I was growing up we had fields, cricket, football, countryside."

Andy's Basildon schooling began at Chowdhary, on Markhams Chase, a mere three-minute walk from his new home. Former neighbour and lasting friend, Rob Andrews recalls: "I lived 20 yards from 'Fletch', we shared the same area at the bottoms of our gardens and so played together from an early age. We had pretty separate lives at junior school – our one-year age difference counted then!"

Despite Chowdhary's adjacency to Shepeshall, Vince Clarke was at a loss to explain why he attended different schools to his future Depeche Mode bandmate. Boys' Brigade, and ultimately the church, would form the backbone of their bonding.

Although young Fletcher was regarded as a "good boy", former Markhams Chase resident Linette Dunbar fondly recounted meeting Andy on her way home from Girls' Brigade. "He asked me if I was wearing navy knickers, or something to that effect. I cried all the way home to my mum."

Andy Fletcher: "I became involved in the church by accident when I was eight. Dad suggested I join the Boys' Brigade so I could play football."

Such was Andy's enthusiasm for the game that his father was stirred into establishing and managing Central Boys Football Club, a team made up mainly of 5th Basildon Boys' Brigade members. Former player Chris Sheppard remembers Andy as being "something of a good footballer but was, and probably still is, a misguided Chelsea fan!" John Bowden was in that same Boys' Brigade, but "only for the football". News of John Fletcher's team evidently spread fast amongst Basildon's up-and-coming soccer converts.

"Everybody in the Boys' Brigade was into football," says Vince, "well, not necessarily *into* football, but we played because an inter-Boys' Brigade football thing was going on, so you'd invariably be roped in. I was always a sub."

Yet another local lad, Norman Webb, whose father was the Captain of the 5th Basildon Boy's Brigade at Janet Duke Primary School, remembered this football team's formation coinciding with a move to the Senior Boys' Brigade at St Paul's Methodist Church on Ballards Walk. Vince Clarke is adamant he was 11 when this change occurred, as his parents separated around the same time. "My mum remarried pretty quickly soon after she split up with my father," he would recall. Vince's family then moved around the corner to a three-storey council house at

59 Mynchens, a bizarrely named cul-de-sac within spitting distance of St Paul's Methodist Church, the proximity of which would not be lost on the Basildon boy.

The Senior Boys' Brigade's new-found association with St Paul's didn't escape Robert Marlow: "Neither Vince nor I were particularly good at football, but we used to go along and have a dabble. It was great. I suppose what went along with that – and now it's a very non-trendy thing to say – was that we got involved with the church. We had to go every week to Bible classes on a Sunday; that was part of the Boys' Brigade regime."

One-time attendee Chris Sheppard shed further light on this regime: "Part of the deal with the Boys' Brigade was to attend St Paul's, the local church, and you were marked for attendance. If you went missing regularly you ran the risk of being dismissed from the Brigade. Every four weeks or so, there was a full parade, where everyone donned full uniform to attend the service."

Andy Fletcher was well versed in the drill, much to his chagrin: "The most embarrassing thing was attending parades in Bas [Basildon] wearing full BB [Boys' Brigade] uniform. That period shaped my moral beliefs and attitudes."

But where there's praise there's often song, as Robert Marlow concurs: "Going to the church was quite musical in itself. You went to the Boys' Brigade thing on a Friday and did your saluting and marching, then on a Tuesday night it would just be games – snooker and table tennis; all the usual churchy stuff. But they had an old piano there, and I'd been having piano lessons since I was about five or six. Eventually, Vince brought his guitar along to Boys' Brigade and we'd just jam."

Despite a year's age gap that translated to two years' difference at their respective schools, music would play a defining role in the enduring friendship between Rob Allen and Vince Martin.

Vince readily admits to having no interest in music at all as a child, "though I thought I was quite musical; I could pick out tunes on the piano." Surprisingly, tinkling the ivories would not be responsible for kick-starting his musical education but rather bowing the strings. Upon starting his dreaded Laindon High Road Comprehensive schooling, Vince began Saturday morning violin lessons. For that he had his mother to thank: "My mum liked listening to music and got us all into music. She *made* us do music lessons! Carol did the clarinet, flute, violin and piano;

Michael did the piano; and Rodney did the flute. It seemed quite appealing at the time — for about two weeks, and then it became a complete bore." As for his instrument of choice: "No one was doing violin, so I thought I'd do it and be a bit odd, I suppose."

Karen Shorter, who was in the same year as Vince Martin throughout their time at Laindon High Road, remembered him as being "a very smiley chap and very friendly — basically, a well-adjusted happy sort of person." In observing that Laindon High Road was not the greatest of schools, she also noted that Vince's crowd were of a more quiet and studious disposition than her own. "He seemed the type that should have gone to a more academic school."

This corresponds with Vince's subsequent explanation as to why he attended this 1928-vintage school, when the considerably newer Nicholas Comprehensive on Leinster Road, Basildon, was closer. "My sister went to Laindon High Road, and, at that time, it was a better school. Actually, it was still a Grammar school the year before I arrived and then it became one of the first Comprehensives in the country. It went from being quite a good school to quite a terrible school."

Rivalries ran high and there were regular fights between the two schools. Admittedly, Vince conceded that there were "a couple of decent teachers" during his five-year tenure, but for someone who confessed to feeling "like a small fish in a big pond" this was not a good sign. "I learnt very early that I didn't like being in a place someone told me to be, or doing something someone told me to do. It was an injustice, as far as I was concerned, being made to go to school. So I spent a lot of time not going — bunking off."

Karen Shorter's recollection of Vince's violin lessons in the school's Great Hall hardly suggests a musical career in the making. "I have to say, he didn't seem great — I would never have put him down as writing all those great songs and being so musically gifted."

Clearly, Vince and the violin were not made for each other, and following a two-year uneasy partnership, they went their separate ways. Instead, Vince turned to guitar, convinced that the instrument "sort of makes a horny sound".

An art teacher at Laindon High Road, remembered only as Mr White, was to become his new musical mentor, making an impression on the sheltered schoolboy if only because of his long hair and beard. Vince can't remember why he borrowed one of the school's acoustic guitars to attend Mr White's evening guitar classes, but professes to still owning song sheets to Sixties classics like Bob Dylan's 'Blowin' In The Wind' from those formative lessons.

Former Laindon High Road pupil Paul Cornhill, who recalled Vince as being "a quiet lad at school", claimed the future synth Svengali started a guitar club of his own at the school. "I attended out of curiosity. I later took up the guitar and still own *The Beatles Complete* which he inspired me to buy having seen the copy he owned. I guess he was as big a Beatles fan as I was."

Vince Clarke: "I learned guitar at those classes, and then Rob, who'd always been playing piano, and myself started mucking about together."

For Rob Allen, whose family had, by now, bought a more upmarket Basildon property at 312 Falstones (still within walking distance of Vince's Mynchens abode) memories of those refreshingly naive times remain vivid.

Robert Marlow: "Vince used to come round my house and we'd sit up in the back bedroom, plotting and scheming – typical schoolboy stuff. We started playing guitar together – terrible versions of 'Get Back' by The Beatles and 'Pinball Wizard' by The Who. I remember jumping around in my bedroom wanting to be Pete Townshend! We really did want to be pop stars; that's *definitely* what I wanted to be – ever since I saw Marc Bolan on *Top Of The Pops* singing 'Children Of The Revolution'."

If Vince Martin harboured any similar aspirations, he played them close to his chest. Rob thought his mate's painfully shy and sensitive persona influenced his musical outlook. "Vince was more reticent, because of his taste. He was into singer/songwriters – he loved Simon & Garfunkel – and he was a big fan of Pink Floyd, because of the atmospheres. Around that time I used to go round his house on a Saturday night, when his parents were out, and we'd watch old horror movies. We'd make ourselves fried egg sandwiches, turn the lights off, light a joss stick, then listen to *Ummagumma* – all that weird and wonderful stuff like 'Set The Controls For The Heart Of The Sun' – or Hawkwind's *Space Ritual*. Then we'd watch the horror film; that would be the pinnacle of the evening."

Since the Martin family didn't own a record player – nor, indeed, a radiogram until Vince was 13 years old – it was at Rob's place that the duo made their first tentative compositional steps. "As well as having a piano, we had a Hammond-like organ with a rhythm machine on it," Marlow reminisced. "That was where we first started hearing those *boom-boom-tschak, boom-boom-tschak*-type sounds."

"The drum machine thing came from when I first heard OMD,"

10

Clarke revealed, describing the duo's bedroom-based *modus operandi* as follows: "There'd be something in the charts, and we'd listen to the record and work out the chords. We'd also get two magazines – *Words* and *Disco 45*, which was a bit like an early *Smash Hits* – so we'd have the words to the song, which we'd then write the chords above. We didn't *perform* to other people, as such; it was more just a case of us mucking about."

Yet Rob Allen was hedging his musical bets.

Robert Marlow: "I met Martin Gore for the first time through school when we were in a play together; we did *My Fair Lady* in 1974/75. Fletcher and him were in the year above me at Nicholas, because, although we're the same age, I was born later, in October 1961. Martin wasn't really churchy, he was just really studious – what you might call a swot."

Depeche Mode's future chief songwriter, Martin Lee Gore, was born on July 23, 1961, and grew up at 16 Shepeshall, together with younger sisters Karen and Jacqueline. The Gore family had relocated from Dagenham, Essex, where his stepfather David worked at Ford's car plant, as did his telephonist mother, Pamela.

Martin Gore: "I didn't want to leave school. I felt secure there." Fellow Nicolas Comprehensive pupil, Mark Bargrove trailed a couple of years behind Martin, whom he described as "a very quiet, unassuming, polite lad." A 16th birthday party invite from mutual friend Mark Crick, who in 1981 would design the sleeve artwork for Depeche Mode's début single, yielded an unexpected result that left an indelible imprint on Bargrove. "After much alcohol had been drunk, I remember Martin stunning the room into silence in the early hours with an acoustic guitar, accompanying himself in a faultless rendition of Don McLean's 'American Pie'."

Robert Marlow: "Martin was one of the most painfully shy people I've ever met – until he had a drink." This impression ties in with Vince Clarke's account of first sighting his future bandmate: "I was walking home from somewhere and Martin was unconscious in the bushes just outside his house, sitting in his own vomit, having been to the school disco."

Martin Gore: "My interest in pop music stemmed from a couple of things. Firstly, I was heavily into the teen mag *Disco 45*. I had hundreds of them and used to read all the song words. I can still remember all those lyrics, though I haven't got a good memory for anything else. A friend taught me a few guitar chords and we started to write songs."

Robert Marlow: "Martin lived round the corner – in between my

11

house and Vince's house – in Shepeshall, so I used to go round there and up to his bedroom where he was really into Sparks. Like me, he was more into glam rock. I used to have a tape we made of us playing 'Blockbuster'! He had a sort of Bontempi organ, which he'd play, and I'd play fuzz guitar – I had a distortion box I used to carry around with me.

"I'd progressed from my £5 Spanish guitar to an electric, a white Jedson Strat copy, which cost about £25 – *and* I had a 9.5W amplifier! It made enough of a racket that my mum used to switch off the electricity!"

In keeping with this Damascus-style conversion, Rob had taken to customising his school uniform. "We were all starting to dress – as much as you could at school – in a sort of punk fashion: plastic sandals, straight trousers, sunglasses and trying to make your tie as tight as possible. I remember getting sent home for wearing a German iron cross on my school blazer! Of course, some of those teachers back in the Seventies still remembered the war."

Such behaviour secured Rob Allen a brief foray into the burgeoning world of punk, courtesy of The Vandals, a previously all-girl band fronted by upcoming vocalist Alison Moyet.

Robert Marlow: "She was in the year above me at school; one day she came up to me and said, 'You play guitar, don't you? You're doing a gig on Saturday!'"

A couple of brief rehearsals took place at fellow Vandal Kim Forey's house at 12 Gladwyns, in readiness for the big night. "Alison had written these songs, which were fairly easy, two-chord numbers," Marlow recalled. "One was called 'I'm In Love With My Guitar' which had a kind of reggae, skanky beat."

Rob took to the stage for the first time with Alison, Kim and Sue Padchett, at Southend's rather salubrious – at least for an angry-sounding punk band – Grand Hotel.

Robert Marlow: "Because the art school was nearby, all these posy people and punks came along. It was the first time I'd ever played through a big amplifier, so there was all this screeching going on. At no point was I able to hear what Alison sounded like, and it wasn't until Vince later played me a portastudio demo that he'd made of 'Only You' that I found out. He said, 'Guess who that is?' I told him I didn't have a clue, and he said, 'It's Alison!' That was bizarre."

Punk's opening salvo had left Alison cold, if not token male Vandal, Rob Allen. Robert Marlow: "All of a sudden, round here we were quite the thing – because of Alison's voice. I thought it was because of my guitar playing, but obviously it wasn't! We were influenced by X-Ray Spex, The Clash and the Pistols – the whole punk thing."

Vince Martin and Andy Fletcher were still deeply committed to a Christian youth fellowship at St Paul's Methodist Church at the time. "Vince and I were born-again Christians from the age of 11 to about 18," admits Andy. "We used to go to Greenbelt every year from the age of 11, which is a massive Christian rock festival. We had an active social life that revolved around the church seven days a week. Me and Vince were into the preaching side – trying to convert non-believers. Vince was number three in the local hierarchy. On Saturdays, there was a BB [Boys' Brigade] coffee bar where I'd try to preach to the yobs. Of course, we got stick for our beliefs."

That they did. Former Nicholas Comprehensive pupil Brian Denny – now Foreign Editor on British Marxist newspaper the *Morning Star* – sheepishly admitted to once snowballing "the Christians attending the church on Ballards Walk."

Vince Clarke: "We preached in the streets and all sorts of places like coffee clubs. We were terribly into it. Everybody would go to Greenbelt. We had trips to London to these big kind of Christian revivalist-type things at the Albert Hall. We used to go on holidays; it was all very youth orientated."

Central to these events was a fellow named Chris Briggs, whom Vince Clarke recalled as being "*very* influential to us all – he's a preacher now. He was a really excellent listener. The youth fellowship was a sort of sideline to the Methodist church we went to, and he was the leader. We were kind of the revolutionaries of the church, because the Methodists were quite staid. We were going to go out and save everybody – almost like Pentecostals within the Methodists!"

In keeping with this remark, Rob Allen is adamant that he saw Vince walking around Basildon College Of Higher Education, wearing a long grey coat with 'Jesus Saves' emblazoned across its shoulders. Religion undeniably made its mark on Allen's own life.

Robert Marlow: "Growing up through your teenage years, you're looking and searching for things, aren't you? And, I suppose, that was what Fletch, Vince and other peripheral people like Rob Andrews were doing."

Music was integral to the Christian fellowship at St Paul's in more ways than one, as Andy Fletcher confirmed: "That was where we learned how to play our instruments and sing – we learned our trade, I suppose."

With Rob Allen otherwise engaged with Martin Gore, Vince Martin resumed his musical pursuits at church: "I was involved with another guy called Kevin Walker – he's a preacher as well. We formed a little group, a folk duo, playing guitar and singing. He wrote most of the stuff; we did a couple of covers, and then I started writing songs – I don't know why or how."

The songs were undemanding, yet from the outset, Vince Clarke's ear for a melodious tune was evident: "They were happy-clappy, kind of like nursery rhymes – simplistic stuff, but always melodic."

Kevin Walker also played drums in a rock band called Insight, together with fellowship leader Chris Briggs. They played The Who's 'I Can't Explain' alongside obscure religious covers, though as Vince Clarke was at pains to point out, these were "contemporary religious songs, with a folk kind of feel". Insight regularly performed at St Paul's social evenings and those of other related churches in their locale, undoubtedly impressing receptive teens Vince Martin and Andy Fletcher. Before long, Andy, too, was expressing an interest in all things musical.

Andy Fletcher: "Vince and I had a group when we were 16 called No Romance In China which tried to be like The Cure. We were into their *Three Imaginary Boys* LP. Vince used to attempt to sing like Robert Smith."

Vince confirmed The Cure influence: "We wanted to be The Cure. I've got a CD copy of my first demo, which is surprisingly like The Cure."

Clarke is certain that No Romance In China, "the first band that I was in with a name that ever performed," was a four-piece outfit, comprising himself on lead guitar and vocals, Andy Fletcher on bass, moonlighting Vandal guitarist Sue Padgett, plus drummer Pete Hobbs. That said, No Romance In China only ever performed once – at The Double Six public house on Basildon's Whitmore Way.

Vince Clarke: "They had a jam night on Wednesdays. There was a drum kit in there already set up and you just went on and did your songs. We only did about three or four numbers. We wrote our own songs; we didn't ever do any covers."

Rob Andrews agreed that No Romance In China was "pretty much a guitar band" but cannot remember Sue Padgett ever being part of its line-up. By 1979, Andy Fletcher was musically active, a move that perplexed Gary Smith, another childhood chum of Rob Andrews and former friend of Vince Martin, "because . . . how can I put it? Andy was not really that musically orientated."

All of which begs the question: were No Romance In China actually any good? Probably not – if Basildon journalist Mat Broomfield is to be believed. "Andy was awful on guitar! No one really knew Vince, but he was very serious about being a musician – a bit like John Lennon being the driving force in The Beatles."

Broomfield recalls seeing Vince Martin, Andy Fletcher and possibly Pete Hobbs practising after Boys' Brigade at their old Ballards Walk haunt in an eight-foot-square storeroom amongst a load of jumble sale bags. Broomfield also claims that Andy Fletcher's habitual habit of shirking Boys' Brigade duties by nipping off to the toilet with a newspaper earned him the rather appropriate, if crude, nickname of 'bogroll'!

Robert Marlow: "Me and Andy once went to see The Damned in London. Fletch wore this railway jacket with British Rail buttons on it! I remember getting on the train, and there were these couple of girls from Basildon. I can't recall their names now, but I can clearly remember Fletcher saying, 'Oh, wasn't it good the other night at church, Rob?' So there I am sitting there, smoking my cigarette, trying to look cool in front of these birds, and he's harping on about church and Boys' Brigade!"

However, Vince Martin was quick to spot the potential in his bass-playing protégé: "Fletcher was really quite good; he bought himself a bass guitar and I kind of showed him how to play it. He was very keen and enthusiastic – very eager to listen and learn. And that's really how Depeche Mode started; it was just me and Fletch."

2

Romancing The Synth

"[Andy] Fletcher's school friend Martin Gore bought a synth, so we got him in the band because he had a keyboard. Then we decided that we couldn't play guitars – we were crap at it – but we could get away with playing synthesisers, because you only needed two fingers."

– Vince Clarke, 2001

While Vince Martin and Andy Fletcher were taking their first tentative musical steps, Martin Gore had likewise been active. Still a student at Nicholas Comprehensive, he regularly played guitar in a band called Norman & The Worms. As reported by Steve Taylor in Depeche Mode's first feature interview for the teen bi-monthly *Smash Hits* (dated July 9–22, 1981), "Martin, who still goes to Methodist church once a month, was the guitarist in a middle-of-the-road West Coast orientated band which played 'nice songs'."

That Norman & The Worms were not referred to by name is perhaps understandable, though it's interesting that Taylor made mention of 19-year-old Martin's church-going escapades – at Vince and Andy's regular Basildon meeting place, St Paul's Church on Ballards Walk.

"Martin just used to come along for the singing," was Fletcher's recollection. "I suppose I thought I'd convert him."

Martin Gore has since professed to be an atheist on more than one occasion, prompting *Uncut* magazine's Stephen Dalton to shrewdly observe, "but an enduring curiosity about spirituality still runs through his blasphemous beats and devotional lyrics."

Blasphemy was far from Norman & The Worm's agenda, with the responsibility for singing those "nice songs" resting on one Phil Burdett's shoulders. It would be many years before the still painfully shy Gore was prepared to step into the limelight with his own vocals. Gore's church association resulted in misgivings from some quarters as to where Norman

16

& The Worms were coming from, musically or otherwise. Vince's friend, Gary Smith voiced his classmates' concerns: "At the time they struck us as coming from very Christian families. I don't know how into it they all were, but we always assumed the band was a Christian-type, folksy affair. From my angle, that's what they were branded as. I saw them a couple of times, but we didn't flock to see them."

Paradoxically, Christianity was not Phil Burdett's bag, but rather the blues: "My brother liked blues music, mainly, because he's 11 years older than me. He had all these records that I'd listen to – those that weren't blues were West Coast acoustic stuff. That's all I thought existed. When I wanted to get a band together when I was 13 or 14, my first thought was to form a blues band, because I already knew loads of blues songs – it's easy to play . . . *badly*! It was only when I started listening to chart stuff that I realised there was other stuff."

Gore was partly responsible for expanding Burdett's musical horizons. "When I first met Martin, he was always talking about music, which kind of surprised me. I thought somebody like him – he was a bit of a swot at school – would just like what was in the charts and that's it."

In fact, Gore's fixation with all things of a popular music nature began before he met Burdett. "I fell in love with music at about the age of 10 when I found a bag of records in my mother's cupboard – it was her old 45s, all old rock'n'roll stuff – and I just felt this immediate passion for it; there was something [there] that moved me."

Inevitably, Gore soon began buying records of his own. Gary Glitter was an early favourite – and would remain so for quite some time. "I was a Gary Glitter fan up until a very late stage," Martin confessed to Stephen Dalton. "I remember when he brought out 'Remember Me This Way', and having to sneak into town and make sure no one I knew was around when I snuck into the record shop door and quickly got it in a bag and ran out again! David Bowie was a massive influence. The first album I ever owned was *Ziggy Stardust*. I used to love Bryan Ferry."

The inquisitive pop fan could only remain passive for so long.

Phil Burdett: "Martin was something of a natural. I taught him some chords, and he picked it up really quickly. Then we thought we'd write some stuff; I wrote a couple of things that were probably pretty awful, but one of the songs that Martin wrote at that time was later recorded by Depeche Mode – that was 'See You'; we used to do a version of that, sort of a mid-tempo acoustic ballad, because we were both writing our material on acoustic guitars."

By the time Norman & The Worms took to gigging, Gore and Burdett had progressed to electric guitars while their ranks had swelled to include drummer Pete Hobbs, who had briefly played in No Romance In China (featuring Vince Martin). Burdett joked that Hobbs played drums for every band in South East England, and described an early band outing. "We did a Basildon rock festival which was the only gig we did where we had a full set with a mixture of our own stuff and other people's. We did the *Skippy* theme tune, which has since become something of a legend. I think that might have been because Martin could do the noise!"

Martin Mann, future husband of Vince Martin's one-time girlfriend Deb Danahay, recalls Norman & The Worms entering a talent contest at The Castlemaine public house on Basildon's Maine Road.

"I don't know why they decided to go in for it. Norman & The Worms were probably just trying to be a contemporary pop/rock band, but it wasn't a pub for them, really; it was more of a family pub, but it was – and still is – renowned for live music. They used to have local bands and local crooners – people who wanted to get up and have a sing-song. Those were the days before karaoke, of course. What I can remember from that night is that Phil Burdett had a stinking cold and he was sticking Vicks Sinex up his nose to try and clear his nasal passages – he began their set by saying, 'I dedicate this number to Vic Sinex!' They didn't win."

In fact, according to Rob Andrews, Norman & The Worms lost out to a Tom Jones impersonator, "despite the will of the crowd".

When Norman & The Worms eventually disbanded, Phil Burdett went on to become a singer/songwriter of some repute in the Southend folk scene, with several albums to his credit.

Robert Marlow: "Phil's a local geezer who's got a voice that's a bit like Van Morrison. He made some albums, had some success with that, and he's still plugging away at it."

Meanwhile, Vince Martin was having similar experiences. "Me and a few of my mates got together this gospel-folk thing, and we entered a talent competition," he told *Future Music*. "At that age you really believe you're the bees knees, and with the guitar you can make a nice sound almost as soon as you pick it up, so we thought we were brilliant. You sit there planning all the things you're going to buy as soon as you're famous . . . all from a local talent show. And, of course, we were awful. Didn't come anywhere in the end."

It's possible that Vince actually performed alongside his future bandmate, Martin Gore at Norman & The Worms' Castlemaine gig, as he recalled being "allowed to perform with Norman & The Worms – I played bass for one gig. I think I probably borrowed [Andy] Fletcher's bass."

With the demise of No Romance In China, following their one-off public performance at The Double Six, Vince formed a duo with 'subsonic pupil' Andy Fletcher, having invested in "a crappy Stratocaster copy". Accompanied by "one of those Selmer Auto-Rhythm drum boxes with the little pitter-patter beats that you put on top of your home organ," Vince and Andy confidently christened their latest quest for pop stardom, Composition Of Sound.

Vince Clarke: "That's kind of when I started thinking more seriously about doing music properly. I'd spent loads of time working in crappy jobs trying to buy a decent guitar – a Fender Strat, or something – and a Marshall stack, because I was under the impression that the more expensive equipment you bought, the better you would sound."

By now Vince had left Laindon High Road Comprehensive with a respectable five O levels to his name – not bad considering he still "hated it. It was an injustice, as far as I was concerned, being made to go to school." Somewhat predictably, he shared a similar attitude to work. "My first job was in a yoghurt factory, shifting cans of milk, for £21 a week after tax," Clarke recalled to *Future Music* in 1995. "Then I worked for Sainsbury's for six months, stacking shelves, followed by a stint at Kodak, some packing at Yardley's and delivering letters for the Post Office. Oh, and I did some time with the Civil Service and worked in the wages department for British Rail. In fact, Sainsbury's was the longest time I spent working in one job before I started doing music properly. I think the one thing that made me want to get into music was because I hated working. I hated having to go to work – it seemed like such an injustice!"

Robert Marlow: "Vince has always been a bit of an outsider – *painfully* shy in those days, painfully sensitive. I remember the first time we went to a party in London – this was when I lost my virginity – and he was really upset and walked off home with the hump because I'd slept with this woman who was a friend of a friend's mother."

Such behaviour could, of course, be partly attributed to the religious turmoil that was engulfing Vince during this period, as he explained: "I think most people fell away from the whole church thing. You used different *reasons* to justify it at the time. Upon reflection, it was all about the

19

fact that suddenly we'd have these talks about feeling guilty and shit. And when you're a teenager, discovering sexuality and women, that's not what you need to hear. Some people got very high and mighty – myself included, probably, but you're so impressionable at that age. You think you can change the world – we really did believe that."

This high and mighty attitude extended to career opportunities, as Marlow confirmed: "I remember having the police turning up at my parent's door one day asking if we'd seen him, because apparently he'd been reported missing from work. I think that might have been the British Rail job in Fenchurch Street; he'd gone off at lunchtime and decided he wasn't coming back. He'd think, 'I'm pissed off; this is not what I want; I'm going!' And he would walk home from wherever he was.

"[Another] time he worked for a lemonade delivery company called Alpine Drinks. They had this fleet of three-tonne lorries, and they used to employ a driver and a driver's mate – bearing in mind that Vince was only 18, his mate couldn't have been any more than 16. But Vince had a bit of a prang, and that was it! He parked the van up, told the boy to 'fuck off' and walked home. But the thing was, he then called on me, saying, 'Put your leather jacket on, we're going to get my wages.' He would always bitch on after these debacles, so I would say, 'Bollocks! You only touched somebody's car!' But the drinks people used to shout and tell him off; they didn't sound like they were very nice people.

"That's where [Vince] was different – maybe different to the rest of us – because he had a much bigger inner life, a much bigger sense of what could be done – much more *ambitious*, in a way. And also he had the nous to actually connect the cerebral stuff to 'How am I going to get this? How can I do this?' Whereas most of us sit there and dream, don't we? 'I can play guitar; I'm a fairly good-looking bloke; I think I'll be a pop star!' Well, that kind of thinking would never enter Vince's mind. He would just think: 'Right, I've got to get from Step A to Step B,' or whatever. He's ever the pragmatist."

Pragmatic or political, for now 'Step A' involved temporarily suspending Composition Of Sound in favour of another musical collaboration with Rob Allen.

The Vandals had by now disbanded because, according to Rob, "all the girls wanted boys, and it all got to be a bit messy. So Vince and I formed another group, which was my band really, called The Plan. He played guitar and I'd conned my mum into buying me a synthesiser. I'd been listening to a lot of Ultravox with John Foxx – songs like 'Saturday Night In The City Of The Dead' and 'The Man Who Dies Everyday', songs that had sounds that you could only get on a synthesiser. So I got my mum to take out a hire purchase agreement on a Korg 700 – a *fantastic* synth! It was all silver toggles with colour coding on them, and it had these great big traveller-type switches for the VCOs [Voltage-Controlled Oscillators] and stuff, so you could stand there and sway about as you opened and closed the filter, or whatever. Vince has got one now, the jammy sod, because he *collects* these things!"

Vince Clarke: "Rob got his synth first; he was the first person I knew who bought one, but his family had bought their own house – they were quite posh, you see. What happened was that Gary Numan did 'Are 'Friends' Electric?' So suddenly we were all turned on to synthesisers. That was what sparked off The Plan."

Like many, Rob Allen was completely taken aback by Numan, when tuning into *Top Of The Pops*, one fateful evening in May 1979. Tubeway Army's soon-to-be-number one hit single 'Are 'Friends' Electric?' was quite unlike anything he'd heard before. By chalking up two number one singles ('Are 'Friends' Electric?' and 'Cars') and two number one albums (*Replicas* and *The Pleasure Principal*) during a three-month period in 1979, 21-year-old West London ex-punk Gary Numan briefly became an icon for a generation of synthesiser fans, including Allen, who took to bleaching his own hair and accordingly acquired the nickname 'Tube'. (Coincidentally, in autumn 1984, Beggars Banquet chose to release a collection of previously shelved Tubeway Army recordings as *The Plan*!)

The Plan rehearsed in nearby Rayleigh, where drummer Paul Langwith's father owned a sandblasting factory. Scarf wearing became a temporary requirement because dust from the sandblasting came through the walls! Whether this look would have been permanently adopted can never be known as The Plan's début performance – set for January 1, 1980 at Barons nightclub, attached to The Elms pub, Leigh-on-Sea – failed to materialise, because, according to Robert Marlow, "there was a big fight the week before, so they closed it down."

Meanwhile, Andy Fletcher was putting his own musical plan into action. According to an early Depeche Mode Information Service bio, Fletcher had previously played in a band called The Blood. Vince Clarke remains sceptical as to this group's existence, however. "It's the kind of thing Fletcher would do, but, knowing him, it was more a figment of his imagination! He probably had a concept, but I'm not sure if The Blood ever performed; I'm not sure who was in it – apart from himself!"

Former Nicholas Comprehensive pupil Chris Sheppard remembered seeing Fletcher quite regularly "as we used to travel home on the same late night bus after he had been playing at a Basildon pub. He was always lugging a guitar around with him." Could these public performances have been with The Blood? Fletcher remains quiet on the subject.

Vince Clarke: "All of these bands could have lasted just two days. They're just names. Rob and I always wanted to be in a band together, but we both had such egos. And we had quite different musical tastes. The reason why he and I connected was that we hated each other's music so much! We'd spend evenings just slagging each other's records off while playing them! So any kind of musical connection I had with Rob was always short-lived."

Bassist Perry Bamonte, a Sixth Form college friend of Rob Allen's, was introduced into The Plan's fold. Bamonte eventually went on to greater things as The Cure's keyboard player – an ironic move in light of No Romance In China's Cure-type aspirations. In 1980, seemingly on a whim, Rob Allen decided to go grape picking in France: [I was] "going to go away and be poetic or something, but I never actually went". The ever-determined Vince Martin decided the time was right to venture out in a solo capacity. Quite out of character, the insular Essex lad recorded a demo of some of his early Cure-inspired compositions at a four-track garage studio in London.

"I suppose I must have been totally committed – even then," Vince reflects. "It was quite scary – going up to London, sitting on the train and stuff, late at night, as was being in a studio, because I knew nothing about studios back then. I think I got the studio for £5 an hour, so I did three hours. I brought my guitar and drum box along, plus the studio guy had a string synthesiser – a Solina, or something – on which I just played root notes on these three or four songs.

"My next step was to go to college, simply because I knew I had to get some exams to get a better job – and with a better job, I could buy better equipment. That was how I thought you succeeded in the music business."

Somewhat predictably, Vince did not enjoy his "year or so" stint study-ing history at Basildon College of Further Education. Music was where his aspirations lay, but, in Catch-22 fashion, better equipment obviously required money. Another – quite literally – crappy job beckoned.

Robert Marlow: "Vince had this terrible job – Fletcher's dad got it for him, working for CS & S at the airport over in Southend, basically shovelling shit! Aeroplanes landed, and he drove out to the plane, took the 'portaloos' [toilets] out and put them in the back of this old Ford Console estate. It really was a *terrible* job, but he'd come home and put the money down on the kitchen table and not spend a penny of it. That's how he bought his first synth. There was no hire purchase involved, because they weren't in a particularly good financial situation at that time. His mum had just split up from his stepfather."

Vince Clarke: "What motivated me to actually buy a synthesiser was, again, probably Orchestral Manoeuvres In The Dark's 'Almost', which was their B-side to 'Electricity'. I realised that you could buy a synthesiser for a certain amount of money, and just by hitting one or two keys you could do things that sounded fantastic and contemporary – and sound like Gary Numan or Orchestral Manoeuvres."

Numan, himself, attested to the attraction of the synth, telling biographer Steve Malins, "They [synthesisers] provided an opportunity for people without any great musical training or ability to make pop music. You could rent them fairly cheaply, record them in little studios and they would sound incredibly powerful."

Vince Clarke: "I wasn't listening particularly to Gary Numan – not that I don't like Gary Numan; don't get me wrong, I was blown away by him on *Top Of The Pops* – but OMD sounded more home-made, and I suddenly thought, 'I can do that!' There was this sudden connection."

Rob Allen's venture into the world of subtractive analogue synthesis had clearly not been lost on his forward-thinking friend, who was still dreaming of his own musical pursuits – particularly when emptying those aircraft chemical toilets. "That was a *great* job," Vince Clarke states sarcastically. "At the time I worked totally just to make money. I had no idea about a career or anything; I had no plans for the future. It was all just about making a wage."

Andy Fletcher was evidently not one for shying away from a hard day's graft either. According to Rob Andrews, "Fletch delivered the *Evening Echo* newspaper and then went on to clean aircraft at Southend Airport for extra cash." This extra cash was presumably used to fund the bass guitar that he promptly put to good use with No Romance In China, and Composition Of Sound.

Unlike Vince, Andy, who had left Nicholas Comprehensive in 1979 with eight O levels and one A level, had been making vocational plans: "I took politics A level and wanted to go to university," he told *No 1*, in 1985. Had he taken the education path, Fletcher's part in the unfolding Depeche Mode story might well have been relegated to that of a bit part. Instead, he took to "being a regular commuter", working as an insurance clerk for Sun Life in Borough, South London. "It was well paid, but only qualified as an existence."

By night, Fletcher joined Vince Martin in Composition Of Sound. "The earliest [Composition Of Sound/Depeche Mode] songs like 'Photographic' were written then," he revealed in *No 1*. However, potential numbers like 'Photographic' required the added ingredient of synthesisers. What to do? While still scrimping and saving for a synth of his own, Vince set about finding someone else who already owned such an instrument.

In spite of any reservations he might have had about leaving high school, and an assertion that he'd "hardly ever been to London, which was half an hour away from Basildon by train," Martin Gore followed his Nicholas Comprehensive classmate Andy Fletcher into the City. His workplace was the NatWest bank on Fenchurch Street, just around the corner from Sun Life insurers.

Gore worked there for a year and a half at Grade One level. "It was mind-crushingly dull," he told *No 1*, "but my lack of imagination and confidence meant I couldn't see an alternative." With A levels in French and German, Gore had, in fact, wanted to utilise his foreign language skills, "but translation jobs were hard to find." So, for the time being, he stayed a clerk.

Working for the bank did have its advantages, however, which the 18-year-old was quick to exploit, by taking out a loan to purchase a Yamaha CS5 synthesiser* for £200 – not bad considering the instrument's original 1979 list price was approximately £349 ($485).

* In his *Keyfax Omnibus Edition* 'synth buyer's bible' of 1996, Julian Colbeck described this diminutive 37-note analogue monosynth thus: "Single-oscillator with clean, more than powerful, sounds. Good panel layout, multimode filtering. Safe bet."

"It was the first time I'd ever seen a synth and I knew nothing about them," Gore told *One..Two..Testing* in 1982. "I didn't find out how to change the sound for a month . . . actually I still don't know. Every sound I had was either a long one or a short one and I didn't even realise you could change the waveforms."*

In the aftermath of his UK chart-topping escapades, Gary Numan – who, according to Steve Malins, "had almost been alone in seeing the opportunity for a star of synth-based music" – arguably opened the floodgates for the wave of mostly British synthesiser-based acts that would trail in his wake. Groups like Sheffield's The Human League, who, in their original 1977 to 1980 incarnation, represented the country's first true synth pop group, enjoyed a modicum of success with their quirky electronic albums, *Reproduction* (1979) and *Travelogue* (1980).

While opportunist Numan had indeed stolen The Human League's thunder – albeit unintentionally so – several years would pass before he would drop the traditional rock instrumentation of drums, bass and guitars in favour of synth-only backing tracks. By which time, Numan was no longer leader of the synth-playing pack.

In November 1980, Ian Craig Marsh and Martyn Ware bailed out of The Human League; attaining some success as the driving force behind synth-funksters Heaven 17, a so-called 'business subsidiary' of their British Electric Foundation (BEF) production company. Ware made clear their new intentions: "Heaven 17 is a 100 per cent serious attempt to be incredibly popular, whereas BEF is no less serious but tends to be involved with more experimental projects."

The Human League borrowed heavily from Düsseldorf electronic pioneers, Kraftwerk (the German word for power plant). Originally an uncompromisingly experimental instrumental duo, Kraftwerk made an unexpected transition from obscurity to commerciality in 1974, courtesy of 'Autobahn', their hypnotic paean to the joys of motorway travel.

Martin Gore was a convert: "Obviously we were influenced by

---

* In brief, a Voltage-Controlled Oscillator (VCO) generates several selectable basic waveforms such as Sawtooth (an electronic signal containing odd and even harmonics), Sine (a signal containing no harmonics – a pure tone which is dull to listen to) and Square (a signal that contains only odd harmonics). Such noticeably different waveforms are then processed through a Voltage-Controlled Filter (VCF) that filters out certain frequencies – hence its name – resulting in a brighter or louder, or duller or quieter sound. Finally, a Voltage-Controlled Amplifier (VCA) 'shapes' the resultant sound.

Kraftwerk, but there was a bit of a scene going on then. There were quite a few bands like The Human League. I remember going to see The Human League; I was quite impressed with their show, and I quite liked their first couple of albums."

Andy Fletcher: "At the time (1979) punk had sort of ended and fizzled out, and new wave had come and gone, and there was this new scene with, I suppose, the early Human League and Kraftwerk – people were really getting into synthesisers. I think the main reason why it [synth-driven music] suddenly became popular at that time was because, previous to that, buying a synthesiser was a very, very expensive proposition – the Rick Wakeman style of synthesisers. But what happened in about 1980/81 was that you could buy a synthesiser – a monophonic synthesiser – for about 150 quid. And you didn't need an amplifier, because all you did was stick it into a PA system, so it was really easy.

"We [Composition Of Sound/Depeche Mode] came from the Seventies, when *everything* was guitar-based – first with all the progressive stuff, then on into punk, which was also guitar-based, but sounded great. Then along came these cheap monophonic synthesisers; it was like a continuation of the punk ethic: you could make new, weird sounds – without guitars."

Robert Marlow: "Synth pop, electropop – whatever you want to call it – was very exciting when it came out, because there were all these strange new sounds that you'd never heard before, but used with a pop sensibility. When we started listening to Fad Gadget, OMD and John Foxx, it was brilliant, ground-breaking and really exciting. They were almost writing the soundtrack to our lives in a new town – [John Foxx] tracks like 'Plaza' and 'Underpass' painted a very clear sound picture of where we lived and what our lives were like."

'Plaza' and 'Underpass' featured on former Ultravox! founder John Foxx's 1980 début solo album *Metamatic*. In using a primitive Roland CR-78 drum machine, rhythm loops and almost totally synthetic instrumentation, *Metamatic* was quite removed from rock conventions of the day.

John Foxx: "Apart from the ARP Odyssey [synthesiser], I also used an Elka string machine, one of the few truly polyphonic electronic keyboards available at that time, an Electro Harmonix phaser and flanger, and a MiniMoog – there was also an ARP analogue sequencer. I was lucky that I managed to get it all working, but it did happen."

In light of these recent electronic developments, news of Martin Gore's Yamaha CS5 purchase made him a hot commodity within Basildon's localised music scene.

Numan-clone, Rob Allen, was the first to come calling.

Robert Marlow: "At the same time as Composition Of Sound was starting off, I formed French Look, which was originally just me and a guy called Paul Redmond, who I basically asked to join because he knew everybody. And he brought along this 'herbert' Dave Gahan, to mix the sound, because everyone had to have a job. So I played synthesiser and sang; Paul played synthesiser – he had a Korg MS10, a little upright thing that was a great source of sounds; and Martin had his Yamaha with its Sample and Hold, a completely useless effect where you'd press a key and it would just play random notes! It was a good way to start a set, though."

Gore's involvement with French Look didn't deter Vince Martin, who was also swayed by Martin's acquisition.

Vince Clarke: "That's why we got him in – because he had a synth, not for any other reason; certainly not for his outgoing personality! Fletch knew Martin, obviously, from school, so we started rehearsing together, and then we decided that we'd play live."

Vince Martin had finally bought his own synthesiser: "It was about £125, I think; maybe even £200 – God knows where I got the money from! I saved hard."

Japanese electronics giant Kawai's obscure K100FS model constituted the object of Vince's desire, though there was a method to his apparent madness. "I was always impressed by the wrong things; I never actually did the proper research, so I chose it because it had so many knobs on it. Back then I had no real idea about synthesisers at all. But I could afford it."

Vince's synth was given its début public airing at a party thrown by his soon-to-be-girlfriend, Deb Danahay, at Paddocks community centre, Laindon, on May 30, 1980. Composition Of Sound's line-up that night featured Vince Martin on synth/lead vocals, Martin Gore on synth/ backing vocals, Andy Fletcher on bass, and none other than Rob Andrews on drum machine.

Vince Clarke: "Rob was on-stage, but he wasn't actually leaping about. He was just sitting there tapping in the right numbers or whatever."

Martin Gore summed up the band's *modus operandi*: "After punk, we felt that music shouldn't return to a rock band format – it had to be pushed; it had to go somewhere. And electronic music was, for us, the way forward; it really made sense for us to be a synthesiser band, doing something new, as opposed to being a [traditional] drums, bass and guitar band."

Deb Mann (née Danahay) explained how she came to organise Composition Of Sound's first-ever gig: "Vince, I knew, because a big crowd of us used to hang around together at a pub called The Highway, as it was then, at the top of the escalators in Basildon town centre. They wanted somewhere to play, and I was having this party. I was going away to work at Butlins, so it was a going away party. It was a great party with loads of people."

Quite how those revellers responded to Vince, Martin and Andy's début performance together is difficult to judge, over 20 years on, especially when the hostess admitted to being "a bit worse for wear on the drink front".

Fortunately, local Basildon fanzine *Strange Stories* was on hand to immortalise the event. 'Totally Hip-Flip' began by setting the changing music scene of the time: "The British scene of electronic music ranges from the chart-topping Bowie-clone Numan, artful Foxx, melodic OMITD [Orchestral Manoeuvres In The Dark] and Human League to the hard, dirty sound of Cabaret Voltaire. There is also a steady stream of new bands, such as Berlin Blondes, Fad Gadget, Silicon Teens and two more sampled here tonight.

"Two synthesisers and a bass are the structure of Composition Of Sound, as well as the inevitable drum machine. Their songs bounce along with a nice feel, but the comparison to The Cure I cannot see. Some of their numbers seemed good, but with new groups – in fact every group – they need improvement as I'm sure they know. I didn't like the version of [Phil] Spector's 'Then He Kissed Me' though."

Headlining the show was Rob Allen's French Look, featuring a moonlighting Martin Gore.

Strange Stories: "French Look opened with a tape of distorted voices straight into the force of three synthesisers. They played an hour-long set which included an old Ultravox number – twice played – and Sparks' 'Amateur Hour'. They could be better and vary their set, but I'm sure with a few gigs, their numbers will become familiar."

All in all, it was a promising start for both groups, though Martin Gore's loyalties would soon be tested, as would Vince Martin and Rob Allen's hitherto rock-solid friendship.

Composition Of Sound's next outing – with Rob Andrews still in tow – took them further afield; supporting Perry Bamonte's latest musical venture, The School Bullies, at Scamps nightclub, in the middle of

Southend's main shopping precinct. Dave Gahan is reputed to have been in the audience that night, as was Brian Denny: "Perry's band was basically an early tribute band that played a set of Damned covers, mostly from the *Machine Gun Etiquette* period, plus original songs such as 'I Don't Agree With You' and 'Third World War'. They also did a version of 'Ballroom Blitz' known as 'Great Big Tits'! The audience was made up of mainly hostile hippies who heckled or said nothing. When one hippy slagged off the Bullies for ruining a Sweet song, the band simply shouted, 'I don't agree,' and broke into 'I Don't Agree With You' – quite clever for some teenagers, don't you think?

"Composition Of Sound's song list included a version of 'Then I Kissed Her', and also a Roxy Music song – I think it was 'Virginia Plain'."

Unsurprisingly, newfangled synthesisers and drum machines did not fare too well in such an openly hostile environment, as Andy Fletcher recounted to *Smash Hits*: "The crowd didn't react so Vince lost his temper with them – plugs were kicked out."

Composition Of Sound played a third, as it turned out, final gig with the same line-up at a youth club at Woodlands School, Basildon, where their audience consisted of a bunch of nine-year-olds. "They loved the synths, which were a novelty then," remembers Fletcher. "The kids were onstage twiddling the knobs while we played!"

Unbeknownst to Composition Of Sound, this very location was to result in a major change of fortune.

Rob Andrews: "Dave Gahan was a face around Southend at that time and was friends with Paul Redmond who played keyboards with French Look. The two bands, Composition Of Sound and French Look, were rehearsing at Woodlands one Wednesday night. Dave came along to watch, mix sound and twiddle knobs for French Look, and during a break he came into another classroom to watch Composition Of Sound. A jam session ensued where Dave took the vocals for Bowie's 'Heroes', Vince liked what he heard, and the rest, as they say, is history."

3

A Fashionable Composition

"I always felt I was going to be a big star in my own right – right from the beginning, to be honest."

– Dave Gahan, 2001

David Gahan was born in Chigwell, Essex, on May 9, 1962. Like future bandmates Vince Martin and Martin Gore, Gahan came from a broken home. "My parents divorced when I was very young," he would tell interviewers, "so mum moved the family – my sister Sue and brothers Peter and Philip – to Basildon. She remarried and I always assumed my stepfather was my real dad. He died when I was seven."

Another shock was in store for Dave and his siblings when their biological father, Len Gahan, unexpectedly turned up at the door. "I'll never forget that day," Gahan recalled to *JoePie* in 1987. "I was 10, and when I came home from school, there was this stranger in my mum's house. My mother introduced him to me as my real dad. I remember I cried, saying that it was impossible because my father was dead. How was I supposed to know that this man lived with us until I was three? From that day on, Len often visited the house until one year later when he disappeared again – this time forever. All that my mother would say was that he moved out to Jersey to open a hotel."

Circumstance dictated that life wouldn't be easy for the Gahan family, but, as Dave later inferred, his mother, Sylvia, did her level best for her children: "I remember being at school, having free dinner tickets, and stuff like that – being in that line. I had pants that were so shiny in the arse that you could see my arse! They had hems that had been dropped down so many times that you had that line, but they were still too short. I think times were hard, but we never saw that, really. My mum was always protective."

30

By now Dave and his siblings were living in a typical Sixties three-bedroom, semi-detached abode at 54 Bonnygate, at the opposite end of Basildon. This virtually ensured that Dave would not cross childhood paths with Vince Martin, Andy Fletcher or Martin Gore.

Deb Mann: "Vince, Andy and Martin all went to Nicholas school – well, Vince went to Laindon, but it's still that side of Basildon – and they connected through church and the Boys' Brigade. They weren't in the trendy crowd. Then there was Dave, who was very, very trendy, just like me. So they came from one side of town, and Dave and me came from the other. Although Dave was a year younger than me, I knew him from school, nightclubbing and stuff. Me and my mates and Dave and his mates used to go down town to a [Basildon] bar called The Sherwood, because it was a trendy place, where all the trendy people used to go. But you wouldn't have got Andy and Martin going in there."

In common with his future bandmates, Gahan had a healthy interest in pop music. "I was buying 45s. I was listening to Slade, T. Rex – all that kind of [glam rock] stuff – and living for *Top Of The Pops* on Thursdays." His adolescent good looks attracted no shortage of female admirers, as former neighbour Mandy Morgan gushed: "The main thing I remember about him was his good looks – all the girls were in love with him, and I don't think anyone was surprised when he was a huge success. My friends and I used to sit on the grass outside his house, just waiting to see him come and go – very sad, but at 13 and 14, that's what we did!"

Dave's troublesome behaviour began to manifest itself in earnest when he attended Barstable School on Timberlog Close, near Bonnygate. "You get categorised into grades," Gahan explained to *No 1*, in 1985, "so I resented the clever kids, started bunking off, got into bother with the law. I was suspended and ended up in Juvenile Court three times for things like nicking motors, setting them alight and spraying walls. I was pretty wild. I loved the excitement of nicking a motor, screeching off and being chased by the police. Hiding behind a wall with your heart beating gives you a real kick – 'will they get you?'

"My mum did the best she could if the law would show up. I remember one time when this police car pulled up outside. She said, 'Is it for you?' and I said, 'Yes.' I distinctly remember her saying, 'David's been in all night.' But I'd written my name on a wall in paint!"

Dave's gratitude to his mother for standing by him, in spite of the fact that he "hung out with those sort of people", remains with him to this day: "I didn't know what kind of attention I wanted, but I wanted to be noticed; I put my mum through a rough time, to be honest – in and out of Juvenile Court and stuff; petty crap."

Schoolmates Nik Barnes and Mark Levey recollect the teenage terror's time at Barstaple.

Nik Barnes: "I remember an incident during a lunch break where we were in a sort of common room. I think Dave was winding everyone up so a few guys – possibly including Kevin King, Alan Hall, Gary Riddis and Gary 'Nobby' Hall – grabbed him by his ankles and dangled him upside down out of a second floor window in front of the teachers' staff room. I remember a teacher named Mr Ward looking up and asking him what he thought he was doing!"

Mark Levy: "He was loud, a bit of a lad with the girls. The only class we shared was Technical Drawing; he was almost as bad as me. He wasn't exactly a scholar! I remember the Technical Drawing teacher, Mr Vanner, giving him and his best mate Mark Longmuir a tough time when he caught them smoking in the toilets – normal teenage stuff."

Like Vince Martin before him, Dave couldn't wait to kiss his schooling goodbye. "I left at 16 – soon as possible," Gahan told *No 1*. "My qualifications [O levels] in Art and Technical Drawing didn't seem much use." And like Vince, his post-high school jobbing experience was chequered to say the least: "I went through loads of jobs. In eight months I had 20 occupations, from Yardley's perfume factory to labouring, and working at Sainsbury's.

"I was bringing home good money, giving mum some board, going down the pub, pulling, being a general wide boy. Finally, I realised I had no career, so I went for a job as an apprentice fitter with North Thames Gas. My probation officer told me to be honest at the interview – to say I had a criminal record, but I was a reformed character. Of course, I didn't get the job because of that. It cost me a lot of confidence, having been through so many IQ tests and been shortlisted."

Gahan's reaction? "I went back and trashed the probation office!"

Inevitably, such unacceptable behaviour eventually caught up with him, and he ended up in weekend custody for a year at a sub-Borstal "attendance centre" in nearby Romford. This experience was "a real pain in the arse," according to the one-time tearaway: "You had to work – I remember doing boxing, stuff like that. You had to have your hair cut. It was every weekend, so you were deprived of your weekend, and it seemed like forever. I was told very clearly that my next thing was a detention centre. To be honest, music saved me.

"I was very much a follower; I wasn't a dictator. I wasn't the one saying, 'Hey, let's nick a car' – that wasn't what it was all about. I was always following someone else, going along for the ride. But I did enjoy the thrill of it all."

As was the case with many of Gahan's peers, punk's revolutionary stance was a revelation: "I was drawn to it – probably because I was a bit of a troublemaker at the time. I hung around with kids who liked doing things that my mum [didn't like me doing]. It was this alienation thing – I didn't fit in. Seeing The Clash just made me think: 'I can do that.' I've always been a bit of an exhibitionist and when I was really young, the aunts would come round and I would entertain my mum by doing my best Mick Jagger or Gary Glitter impression across the room, making everyone laugh. I wasn't really good at anything else, but I saw that that really got a reaction. I was a bit of a prankster."

Soon, the teenager was toying with taking his musical ambitions further: "I rehearsed a couple of times with a few bands. There was one that my friend Tony Burgess played drums in. He didn't actually have a drum kit; he played biscuit tins – never played a gig, just rehearsed after school. They were called The Vermin. They were very famous in that one area of Basildon. In our own minds we were going to be the next Sex Pistols."

Before music actively entered his life, Dave Gahan undertook a Retail Display course at Southend College of Technology. Unlike Vince Martin, in returning to education, Gahan would find his niche – albeit temporarily.

Dave Gahan: "I liked art at school. The teacher was a nice geezer who let us smoke. After three years, I got the British Display Society award, which meant I could get a job doing display in a big store. That was around the punk period – 1977. Good times. I enjoyed college; I was designing clothes for mates, going off to see Generation X and The Damned. I had original Sex shop [the fetishist and rubber emporium on London's Kings Road, co-owned by punk clothing designer Vivienne Westwood and Sex Pistols manager Malcolm McLaren] gear. We used to stick labels on the outside and come down to the gritty London clubs like Studio 21."

Gahan's enthusiasm for The Damned ("I think the first album I ever bought was *Damned, Damned, Damned*") stirred him into joining their fan club, and regularly attending punk gigs at Chancellor Hall, Chelmsford. The Clash made an equally forceful impression: "It wasn't like I wanted to do what they were doing musically – it was never about that. But when I first went to see a band like The Clash, it was like, 'I can do that!' I'd been doing it in front of the mirror with a hairbrush for a long time anyway. I really had dreams of myself doing it, and it wasn't long after, that I found myself in that position."

Fellow dreamer, Robert Marlow confessed to having "never been into the punk thing." He had nonetheless bumped into Dave on occasion at Chancellor Hall: "We saw Ultravox!, X-Ray Spex and The Adverts, and he [Dave] was around then. So, briefly, there was a kind of link between that little crew – Debbie [Danahay], Dave and others – and me. Then I didn't see him for a while because of the punk thing."

Gahan later claimed Johnny Rotten came down to Southend College while he was there, as did the future Boy George: "George came to model and nick stuff. He got into trouble for that. They were flamboyant people, like [fashion designer] Steven Linnard, a big change after my rough and ready Basildon mates – rowdy, but artistic."

While Gahan may have been studying Retail Display, fashion was quick to catch his roving eye, as former Southend College Fashion Design student Karen Ashley confirms: "He used to spend a lot of time in the fashion department as he was good friends with a guy called Ivor Craig from Canvey Island. There was a bit of a scene going on in South-end at the time as Paul Webb from Talk Talk was also on the course and Boy George – just plain old George at the time – hung around occasion-ally; he was also friends with Ivor Craig, and even modelled in our fashion shows.

"I remember (Dave) being quite shy, and he would often blush when spoken to." This assessment differs from Gahan's rather bold assertion that he learned about sex "pretty fast" from female friends of his elder sister, Sue.

"I wasn't on the same course as Dave," says former student Dee Dye, "he was in the year above me at college – but our paths crossed on many occasions. His Display course was usually situated in another college build-ing called the Annexe. As part of my then-first year, we had four-week blocks of each aspect of art; this meant we had to study the display part in the Annexe, too. I can remember that Dave was always milling about, eating bags of Walkers, so we dubbed him 'Crisp' – this nickname was doubly apt as his hair at that time consisted of a *very* lacquered fringe that covered one eye! One day he came into college and his hair wasn't so stiff. When I asked him, 'Why the new look?' he replied that his sister wouldn't let him borrow her hairdryer!"

One individual who can vouch for the appeal of Dave Gahan's early image is his first wife, Jo Gahan (née Fox), whose diary dates their first meeting as January 12, 1979. "My best friend at the time was Fran Healy, who went to school with Dave," Jo recalls. "We were heading out to a party in Basildon, and as we were early we went to visit him at home first. I would have been 16, Dave the same. I thought he was OK. He was a good laugh. We went out in a foursome, as Fran started seeing Dave's mate, Paul Redmond, a few times, though it was nothing serious. We used to go to the Double Six [public house] in Basildon and The Music Machine in London.

"We started seeing each other on August 14, 1979. We would have both been 17 by then. I was attracted to his sense of humour. He also had a rapport with women – he could relate easily to girls, he was just easy to be with. He was also a bit different from other guys. He was a cool fashion icon, willing to push the boundaries of fashion. I remember him wearing tan leather trousers, which were *so* risqué for Basildon! He took care over his appearance and it didn't bother him if blokes thought he was slightly effeminate – especially with his hair. He would take forever to blow dry and lacquer it up into a peacock spike."

Before long, Dave and Jo had become inseparable. "I was living back home in Billericay with my parents. He lived with his mum in Bas, so we were on the telephone to each other constantly. He was my best friend and I adored him. We were each other's first serious relationship and often felt we were 'one' person. By November we had fallen in love; Dave asked me to marry him and on November 17, 1979 we got engaged, after just 12 weeks together."

Perhaps to make up for those days lost as a result of his misspent youth, trendy Dave and his new-found college contemporaries lived for the weekend. "A gang of us hung out together, saving up for a bag of Blues [amphetamines], going without dinner all week," Dave told *No 1*. "We'd go to London all night, end up at some party, then catch the milk train from Liverpool Street. It was a bloody long walk home! I got bored with that, but for a while it was exciting. I had a double life, mixing with the art school mob then going home to Bas. I'd go to the pub wearing make-up, but 'cos I knew the local beer boys, the spanners, I was OK."

Rob Allen had been something of a trailblazer himself, partly responsible for opening up Basildon's closed-shop mentality so that the likes of Dave Gahan could breeze into his local dolled up to the nines.

Deb Mann: "Rob Allen in particular was really into Gary Numan, and all the early electronic music. I remember going to the trendy electronic clubs to do our trendy electronic dancing to Fad Gadget and stuff. Rob was very trendy and used to get the mickey taken out of him because he was one of the first blokes in Basildon to wear thick black eyeliner." Indeed, some of those hurtful individuals responsible were actually friends of Dave Gahan!

Social attitudes in Basildon, *circa* 1979, weren't destined to change overnight. Dave Gahan took things in his stride, despite an omnipresent threat of violence which extended to non-individualists. Meeker mortals like Martin Gore shudder at the memory: "Even at the right places [in Basildon] you'd get into trouble, but if you strayed off the beaten track you were really likely to get attacked. When I was about 17 or 18, me and my friend were walking back from a party in Laindon, which is close to Basildon, and we heard this running behind us. We didn't think anything of it, but suddenly we were surrounded by six guys saying, 'Which one of you called my mate a fucking wanker?' One of those, you know?

"So then they started punching and kicking us. My mate ran off down a side street with a few of them following. He managed to get ahead of them, jump the wall, and hide in someone's garden, while I had this other massive guy punching and kicking me. So I went back towards this party and met some people coming out that I half-knew, and I told them what had happened. So they said, 'Don't worry about it, come back with us.' So we walk back and this guy's still waiting, saying, 'There he is – the fucking wanker!' So he comes at me again, and all these people just stood there doing nothing. And then one of them said, 'I think you'd better run.' Thanks a lot!

"They weren't fun times. Dave [Gahan] used to get beaten up all the time for dressing out of the norm." Small wonder that Martin Gore expressed a desire to escape from the town as soon as an opportunity presented itself.

Andy Fletcher: "To be honest, in Basildon there wasn't much else to do. You had to either steal cars or go to church."

Deb Mann: "Andy did an interview recently – I think it was in a local paper – where he said something along the lines of if he hadn't gone to church, he would have been a criminal. That caused a big furore 'round this way. I don't know what possessed him to say that, because it wasn't true at all."

For 17-year-old Dave Gahan, the real action lay beyond Basildon's claustrophobic confines. "I've been a soulboy, I've done it all, I've been everything," he once boasted. "I used to like soul and jazz-funk like The Crusaders. I used to go to soul weekends and hang around with the crew from Global Village [a disco held underneath the arches at Charing Cross, London] and I went to The Lyceum [on London's Strand] on a Friday night."

Gahan's fiancée, Jo Fox, was also regularly out and about: "My diary says it all – Killing Joke, Joy Division, Echo & The Bunnymen, Siouxsie & The Banshees, Spizz, Orchestral Manoeuvres, Magazine, Wasted Youth, Only Ones, Adam & The Ants, Cure, Human League, Teardrop Explodes, Clash, Classix Nouveaux, Martian Dance, Psychedelic Furs, Damned, Ultravox. Every week I was at the Music Machine or The Lyceum, or the Electric Ballroom.

"Dave wasn't doing the same gigs, although he liked and bought the music. He was more into The Goldmine scene. Wasted Youth at The Bridgehouse [in London's Canning Town] were big favourites of mine. Their singer's best mate was a family friend, and as I was born and brought up in the East End I knew the area well – Wasted Youth were the big local band. At this time I still had relatives who I would stay with when venturing up for concerts. Dave couldn't help but be drawn into this scene, and he soon became hooked. One big event Dave and I had to go to was the first Cabaret Futura weekender in Leeds, where Wasted Youth were on the bill, together with The Psychedelic Furs and Soft Cell."

Robert Marlow: "Dave started turning up at Barons nightclub in Leigh-on-Sea. By now he was hanging out with a whole different crowd; they were all into a famous club on Canvey Island called The Goldmine, where they played lots of northern soul. Dave was in with this guy called Paul Redmond, who was like the ace face – he'd been in the *Basildon Echo* for being a punk rocker. He was a few years older than us, so he was someone we looked up to a bit."

Dave Gahan: "I was hanging around with a bunch of guys who went to those [northern soul] nightclubs and listened to stuff like The Crusaders and Herbie Hancock – basically [being] Essex soul boys. And we'd go away on those soul weekends to [Great] Yarmouth and just have a riot. They were good fun, just getting drunk and sobering up a little bit, then getting drunk again, dancing and stuff. They were good times."

Robert Marlow: "I remember when I started hanging out in the South-end scene everyone was quite into the Futurist thing. On Friday nights we used to go to The Cliff, which was a gay pub in town, and buy French Sticky Blues – uppers; three for a pound from this bloke called 'Super-man', because he looked like Superman, all mild-mannered like Clark Kent. And that's when I started seeing a lot more of Dave. He was always dressed in black – with black leather trousers and his black, spiky hair, he did look good. He took his persona very seriously."

When exactly the 'Futurist' tag was first applied to electronic pop music is difficult to pinpoint, though Futurism itself is obviously well docu-mented.* With the likes of Kraftwerk's *Trans-Europe Express* winding its way across European dancefloors from 1977 onwards, modern electronic music's connection to its Italian ancestry is plain to see.

Former disc jockey Steve Brown was arguably Southend's main Futurist scenester: "I used to run clubs in Southend which were geared up to the alternative crowd – I was a greeter, so I chose who could come in and who couldn't. That's what I predominantly did, although I used to DJ at some clubs. In a way, we were really the first ever promoters; the only reason we did it was because the way we dressed and looked, plus the sort of music we were listening to, meant that we couldn't get access to normal places.

"One particular little club we used to do was above The Cliff pub in Westcliff, which was quite a well-known place back then. We used to have the upstairs and put on gigs – not so much gigs, but just a regular Friday night. Anyone who was a . . . I absolutely *abhor* the term 'New Romantic', but all the weirdos of the area used to come on up. That's when I got to know Dave [Gahan], though he was a relatively normal young chap at the time."

It emerged that Dave's college mate Ivor Craig formed the backbone of this mutual association. "Ivor would bring Dave, who's now Ivor's son's godfather, along to our clubs," says Steve Brown. "Not that it's something to be proud of, but I was the first person to sell him what were known at the time as Speckled Blues – just for kicks. So he used to come up to me

* Futurism: ". . . a far-reaching Italian movement that included poetry, literature, painting, graphics, typography, sculpture, product design, architecture, photography, cinema and the performing arts, and focused on the dynamic, energetic and violent character of changing twentieth-century life, especially city life," as defined by the website. www.futurism. org.uk.

and buy his few little pills, but he'd never really done anything up until then. Anyway, none of us really started taking any notice until he started telling everyone that he'd put some band together, or joined a band."

Dave had Rob Allen to thank for that. "Dave was hanging around with Paul Redmond, and that's how he came to be involved with myself as our [French Look's] sound mixer. He didn't have a clue, but then none of us did back then – there wasn't much to mix, to be honest! We used to rehearse in Woodlands youth club, which had actually been quite a seminal place in itself. They had The Who there in the Sixties – according to the bloke who ran it."

With Dave's swift musical transformation from passive observer to active participant, one of the final pieces in the Depeche Mode puzzle was about to slot into place.

Vince Clarke: "Dave Gahan was the local fashion accessory of Basildon; he was the New Romantic; he was rumoured to have attended Blitz [Visage vocalist Steve Strange and drumming sidekick Rusty Egan's] club in London, so it was all very glamorous. So we decided to get him in as a frontman, because he was kind of flamboyant and extrovert, and very confident. So we auditioned him."

By all accounts, Vince Martin was a reluctant frontman for Composition Of Sound. Deb Mann: "I know it sounds silly, but Vince didn't really like the limelight – he liked it but didn't, if you know what I mean."

Gary Smith backs up this observation: "Vince never wanted to be in the limelight – never, ever. Here's an interesting fact: we were walking back from Basildon town centre one day, and he said, 'Do you know what? I'd like to be like The Buggles.' I think he was trying to get across the fact that The Buggles were relatively successful as songwriters, but they didn't have a big fan following. I think what Vince wanted was success without fame."

Robert Marlow: "Vince had decided he needed a frontman and 'Gahan-y' had it all – he was from a different set. He was a lot more sort of worldly, in a way. He'd gone to clubs in London, whereas we'd just read about them and listened to all the music. He was a lot more street cred."

"Dave was just one of the crowd we used to go to the pub with," says Gary Smith, "and someone persuaded him to sing because his voice lent itself to their [Composition Of Sound's] kind of stuff. And he had a bit of an image as well, did Dave – a young, trendy sort. I think that was probably part of the reason why they got him in."

While remaining characteristically tight-lipped about his own supposed shortcomings, Vince Clarke recalls Dave Gahan's 'recruitment process' during that infamous Woodlands School rehearsal:

"Because no one came to our gigs, we decided that because Dave Gahan was very, very popular, we'd get him in the band. He really looked the part, so we decided to audition him to be the vocalist. I remember the interview we did with him, and I remember him singing. We gave him three songs – two that I'd written and one cover of a Bryan Ferry song . . . a Roxy Music song. He sang both of the original ones badly, I remember, but he sang the Bryan Ferry one quite well, because he was obviously quite familiar with it. So then we decided that he'd be alright for the job."

Somewhat inevitably, Dave Gahan has a different take on events, telling Stephen Dalton, in a 2001 interview:

"These guys were rehearsing – they were called Composition Of Sound, and Vince was in the band. I was humping gear for this band called French Look, and one night we were just messing around; we were doing some Bowie songs and we did a cover of 'Heroes'. Paul [Redmond], my friend, was trying to get me to sing in this band [French Look]. There was a guy in the band whose name was Rob Marlow – at the time, I think his name was Robert Allen; he was a singer/guitarist/keyboard player, and he was pretty good at it. But Paul, my mate, was like, 'Dave could sing, he looks good; he can sing – I've heard him!' But this guy [Rob Allen] wasn't having any of it. Anyway, on this particular evening I sang along to 'Heroes', and next door these guys were rehearsing. And so, about a week later, I got a phone call from Vince. He said, 'Was that you singing?' and I said, 'Yes' – it was actually a bunch of people singing, but I said it was me."

In an earlier account (for *No 1*, in 1985), Dave had an even more embroidered tale: "Vince Clarke, I met one day outside a pub in the centre [of Basildon]. He looked up to me because he was a bit scared of the skins."

Either way, with Basildon's very own fashion accessory – "a good Futurist/New Romantic clothes horse," as Robert Marlow deftly put it – onboard, Gahan became the band's missing jigsaw piece, as Stephen Dalton put it: "Although a mere mouthpiece for songwriters Clarke and Gore, his laddish charisma sent a jolt of punky rock'n'roll through their electropop machine."

"Futurist/New Romantic clothes horse" or otherwise, it appeared Vince Martin had made a sound choice in Dave Gahan, whose 'rent-a-crowd' tactics proved most useful in giving the Composition Of Sound band-wagon some much-needed momentum.

Dave Gahan: "We were lucky. Right in the beginning I had this bunch of friends who liked to dress up and go to gigs, friends that would sort of run various clubs – places in London, and places in Southend and Canvey Island; a little group of friends who were listening to music that was a little different to what everyone else was listening to: some electronic music, a lot of Bowie, Roxy Music, Kraftwerk, stuff like that – probably Iggy Pop. So we almost had this ready-made audience of about 30 people who were the cool people of Southend. Friday night people. The oddballs."

Oddballs like Steve Brown, who was quick to sing the new recruit's praises, offering an insight as to why having Dave Gahan fronting Composition Of Sound was a wise move: "Dave was a lovely bloke and had a bit of style about him, whereas the others, we regarded as complete squares. We could understand that Dave was in a band with them, but they weren't part of our scene. They were more like 'the Basildon casuals'. Then, all of a sudden, they got into it as part of being in a group. Dave was the real thing, they weren't."

4

What's In A Name?

"I just thought they [Composition Of Sound] looked dodgy – dodgy New Romantics. I didn't even hear the music at that point.

– Daniel Miller, 2001

Composition Of Sound's inauspicious stage début, with 18-year-old vocalist Dave Gahan, occurred on June 14, 1980. The location? Nicholas Comprehensive, Leinster Road, Basildon. The modest hand-drawn poster, designed by Vince Martin's brother, Rodney, billed their first performance thus: "Discotheque featuring French Look and Composition Of Sound at Nicholas School, June 14, 7.30 pm."

Vince Clarke: "Fletcher and me had the posters made up, and we went around town sticking them up in subways and stuff."

Reversing the bill from their earlier début performances at Deb Danahay's party, French Look supported Composition Of Sound. Both bands featured an all-synthesiser line-up with Andy Fletcher leaving his bass at home, instead using Rob Allen's beloved Korg 700 to play his parts, while Martin Gore again performed twice.

A year later, *Smash Hits'* writer Steve Taylor reported: "Gahan remembers [when] he stood outside the venue for their first performance as a four-piece, Nicholas School, where Fletcher and Gore had been pupils. 'You spent about half an hour outside trying to calm down,' says Fletcher. 'You had about ten cans of lager.' All Gahan can remember is repeatedly saying to himself, 'I don't want to do it, I don't want to do it.'"

As Gahan later conceded: "It's a lot scarier when you first stand up there in front of people than what you imagine. So it took me a good few years to actually move a step to one side or something during the gigs."

Vince Clarke remembered the Nicholas School performance as "being very good, actually, because that was the first gig we performed with Dave, and Dave had all his trendy mates there."

One such trendy mate was Steve Brown: "A few of us decided to go along, so there I was, driving around Basildon without a clue as to where this school was. I saw this bloke who looked like he might be going, so I stopped and asked him if he knew where the school was. He said, 'Yeah, I'm going down there now,' so he jumped in the car and I said, 'My mate Dave's playing.' Then, the next time I saw the guy he was up there, actually on the stage – it was Vince Clarke! He'd never said anything to me, but then he's such a quiet bloke."

Working the door was Nicholas pupil Robert Skinner, who, 22 years later, still remembers the gig well – if not the actual performances: "It was held in the upper school cloakroom. I didn't hear too much of the music as I was helping my sister's friend, Alison Jeffs, take the entrance money, which was 50p each!"

From an audience standpoint, Vince's assessment of what later became known within Depeche Mode circles as "the Nicholas School debacle" would appear to ring true, judging by this additional eyewitness account by attendee Mark Bargrove: "The school, although on one campus, had upper and lower school buildings. The upper school cloakroom was a large hall where coats were hung on moveable racks, which were moved to the side for parties, gigs and such like. As for the [Composition Of Sound] gig itself, I'm sure they played 'Ice Machine', which was the B-side of [Depeche Mode's 1981 début single] 'Dreaming Of Me'. They went down pretty well as they were local and the place was fairly full of the area's local New Romantic contingent."

However, with several fragile egos jockeying for pole position, tensions ran high.

Robert Marlow: "I cannot for the life of me remember what the argument was about, but there was definitely a big argument at the Nicholas School gig. They [Composition Of Sound] accused us of messing up their [synth] sounds."

Vince Clarke: "There was a bit of a falling out at the gig, because they [French Look] reckoned that we'd mucked about with their [synth] controls or hadn't plugged their equipment back in properly!"

Whether one band deliberately set out to sabotage the other's performance has never been conclusively proven, as neither the strong-minded Vince Martin nor his nemesis Rob Allen are prepared to stand down on the issue of the day. In actual fact, trouble had been brewing between the pair, prior to the school 'battle of the bands' clash.

Vince Clarke: "I think we had a bit of a falling out before that [gig]. In Basildon there were only a certain amount of players that could do certain things. There was only one drummer in Basildon, so every band had to have him! And it was the same with Martin Gore; Martin had the synthesiser, so it was all about us accusing each other of stealing him from each other's bands. And Martin, being so non-committal, just did whatever people told him to do."

Ever the gentleman, Robert Marlow agrees with the latter's assessment of the situation: "There was a kind of rivalry [between the two bands] – basically, it was over Martin. And Martin being Martin, there was split loyalties. Martin sort of floated between the two camps for a while, and Vince and I had a little spat where we didn't speak to each other, even though we'd see each other every day. I think it was about two weeks before we spoke again; I remember walking along the street, we saw each other, and we just burst into fits of laughter! In hindsight, they had a lot more going for them in that they had Vince actively seeking gigs and really putting his mind to it, so in the end Martin went with them, though he did make occasional guest appearances with me in another band I had, called Film Noir."

Gary Smith: "Robert Allen had a different band every week! Martin played in both bands [French Look and Composition Of Sound], but I think Vince was also playing in more than one band. There were an awful lot of bands around Basildon, and they were always trying to steal each other's talent."

Having made up, Vince Martin and Rob Allen moved out of their respective parental homes – into what the latter temporarily termed a Basildon "squat, although that sounds insulting to the guy whose place it was!"

Their new-found landlord was ex-No Romance In China drummer Pete Hobbs. Vince Clarke: "He had a council bedsit, so all three of us lived there."

No doubt such cramped conditions made Vince, who was by now signing on the dole, all the more determined to move onwards and upwards.

Robert Marlow: "Vince wasn't there a lot, because he was out every day. I'm not taking anything away from Martin as a musical force, but in those early days it was definitely Vince's personality and pragmatism that got them the gigs. He would be on the train every day up to London, looking for gigs. As for the rest of us in the flat, I wasn't really going to college much and sort of sat at home smoking dope, but Vince was up, washed and out – doing it."

With Martin Gore and Andy Fletcher still committed to their day jobs in the City, Vince Martin had the most time on his hands, and, by that same token, the least to lose. Nevertheless, landing gigs as a relatively unknown band was no easy task. Vince was quick to realise that having a demo tape to hawk around potential venues would be advantageous. Soon after Dave Gahan's recruitment, Vince set up the future Depeche Mode's first recording session at a small studio in Barking, Essex, with the unlikely name of the Lower Wapping Conker Company!

Some 22 years after the event, Vince Clarke's recollections of the session are fairly vague – all the more so since he no longer has a copy of the recording in question. "I was the experienced one, because I'd been in a studio once before. From what I remember, we did four songs in the demo studio. But none of us knew what reverb was, so we couldn't work out why it didn't sound as good as the demo I'd done before, which did have reverb on, making everything sound great."

Gary Smith accompanied the band to the recording session, and reputedly, retains the only existing copy of the demo: "They [Composition Of Sound] paid £50 for one tape at the studio and I was the only person with a tape-to-tape recording machine at home, so I made a copy for each of the band members, so there were originally five tapes in total. Talking to Fletch, he thinks they've all gone and seems to think mine is the last one. He hasn't heard it for years. Anyway, if you hear the demo, it's very . . . raw."

When quizzed by Stephen Dalton as to what the demo might sound like today, Andy Fletcher replied, "I suppose we'd be like a dodgy Cure or something! It's quite good." Is it? "Well, possibly." Clearly, the spectre of Robert Smith's contemporary gothic outfit was still hanging over Composition Of Sound.

Martin Gore's memory of the band's first collective studio visit focused on his ongoing naivety at navigating his perplexing Yamaha CS5 synthesiser: "You know that sound that goes – WAUGH? I was stuck on that for ages. And when we made our first demo all the tracks have the same sounds [on them]."

Whatever the outcome of this first session, at least Vince Martin now had something supposedly representative of Composition Of Sound that he could play to potential promoters; both on his increasingly regular London jaunts and on what Gary Smith termed "the local circuit" – in and around Southend. Another surviving Rodney Martin-designed poster – this time featuring a more futuristic typeface than the previous week's Nicholas School offering – advertised a Composition Of Sound show at the Top Alex on Saturday, June 21, 1980. Quite what a biplane and various bicycles signi-fied was open to interpretation, but the poster was duly photocopied (most likely by Andy Fletcher at work) and plastered across town.

According to Robert Marlow, "There wasn't a lot around Basildon in terms of places to play," a fact backed by Andy Fletcher. "Because there wasn't anywhere to play in Basildon, we played mostly in Southend. In Southend, there was a great tradition of R&B and also a soul scene – the Goldmine and all that sort of thing. Southend was a really great place – the Feelgoods, R&B mixed in with all the soul."

The temporary rift between Vince Martin and Rob Allen must have already healed by June 21, 1980, as the latter was indirectly involved in this early Composition Of Sound performance, as their lighting operator. "The Top Alex was in a Southend pub called The Alexandra," Marlow explained. "They had a room there at the top – Top Alex, see? I did the lights for that one – on or off! 'What do you want for this song? On or off?'"

Steve Taylor's *Smash Hits* report throws yet more light on this particular performance: "[Dave] Gahan remembers their four-piece début at the Top Alex, a Southend pub that's normally an R&B stronghold: 'We went down really well – they were banging their heads to our pop.'"

With only three eminently portable monosynths and a drum machine to their name, Composition Of Sound travelled light, putting into practice Andy Fletcher's assessment that "you didn't need an amplifier, because all you did was stick it [the synthesiser] into a PA system." With little or no money in the kitty, there were no posh keyboard stands for the fledgling Basildon boys.

Robert Marlow: "They didn't use those X-stands because, I suppose, they would have had to buy them. Chairs were what they used, I think – chairs, barstools, or beer crates, with a bit of cloth thrown over. There would have been some nod to some sort of sartorial elegance!"

Composition Of Sound might not have had a flash stageshow, but they were rapidly becoming a winning combination with an eye-catching frontman in Dave Gahan and, more importantly, a healthy selection of catchy, mainly Vince Martin-penned, songs.

Robert Marlow: "The good thing about them [Composition Of Sound] only using monophonic synths was that you had to have a tight arrangement if you wanted to have that sound. Vince was writing all the songs. When you look at them now, they're no great shakes, lyrically or whatever, but they were good songs; they *are* good songs. To me, they're just fantastic! The closing melody of 'Dreaming Of Me' fits in with the chord on which it's based. Vince would spend hours sitting there saying, 'Right, Martin, you do this.' "

Marlow also made allowances for Andy Fletcher's keyboard technique – or lack of it: "He did play, though a lot of it was just constantly repeating notes. In the general sound, you didn't really notice whether Fletcher was playing or not – that was another good thing about Vince's arrangements."

In self-defence mode Fletcher later claimed: "You didn't *have* to be a great musician at that time; you just needed to have decent ideas. We started off with just bass and guitar, trying to make new music. Everyone was young, and because of punk and new wave, everyone was just trying to make something that was different and interesting. Of course, by the time synthesisers came on the market very cheaply it was just really exciting, because you had the possibility of making really interesting sounds very cheaply."

When not performing or looking for gigs, Vince Martin busied himself honing his composing and arranging skills in readiness for the group's regular garage rehearsals, at the Martin family home in Mynchens.

Various acquaintances occasionally dropped in on proceedings, including Robert Marlow: "It was a three-storey place, with a garage at the bottom. Vince's mum obviously didn't like the noise. She was a very talented seamstress, and used to make up these raincoats for racing car drivers. So she'd be upstairs on the top floor, in her sort of sewing room, and all these various mates would call round so she'd have to keep running all the way down to let them in! We'd go into the garage and there'd be these four guys standing around with headphones on, because Vince's mum had put the mockers on them rehearsing in the day and disturbing the neighbours and disturbing her, because it could get quite loud.

"So all you could hear was their fingers clicking on their keyboards and Gahany's voice whispering *'Light switch, man switch . . .'* [opening lyric to 'Dreaming Of Me']. You'd sit there for a little while, then go, 'Right, Vince, see you later,' because you couldn't hear anything! At first it was quite good going along there – everyone used to hang out, but then it got a bit more serious. I do remember I added a bit to 'Photographic' – Vince was looking for a middle-eight, so I put in a little bit there."

Despite Robert Marlow's latter-day assertion that Vince Martin was responsible for penning all of Composition Of Sound's set, including a number of never-to-be-recorded titles like 'Reason Man' and

'Tomorrow's Dance', the band's increasingly popular shows were still peppered with a motley selection of cover versions – including The Everly Brothers' 'The Price Of Love', Gerry & The Pacemakers' 'I Like It', The Beach Boys' 'Then I Kissed Her' and Lieutenant Pigeon's 'Mouldy Old Dough', many of which harked back to the group's pre-Gahan outings.

Robert Marlow: "Martin's instrumental 'Big Muff' was in there, as was 'Ice Machine'. I think 'Dreaming Of Me' was performed differently to its eventual recorded version, because once they started adding sequencers to things it all became a lot more tidy. 'Photographic' was a very popular number of theirs; I remember everyone was originally just playing octaves for most of its duration, but it sounded really good – really fresh, and really exciting."

One Composition Of Sound anomaly was 'Television Set', of which, an early Depeche Mode Information Service song booklet reported: "'Television Set' is a popular song played by Depeche Mode, but it was not written by any of its members."

Robert Marlow partly solved the mystery: "There was another local band at school at the same time as Norman & The Worms that Martin also played in with two hippies. I can't remember their names, but one of them wrote 'Television Set'. The lyrics to that song were really good: '*Did you see them running to me, babe; did you see the light in their eyes; I'm just a mass of communication; I sell what everyone buys . . . I'm just a television set.*' Martin wrote a catchy synth riff for that, so it ended up in their set."

Regardless of its merits, Vince Clarke saw to its exclusion from the band's set list: "'Television Set' was written by a friend of Martin's; I don't know how or why we got it, but we used to perform it. I think we decided not to record it because we weren't getting any publishing for it, otherwise we would have probably recorded it for the first [Depeche Mode] album."

The band's collective £50 demo tape investment was paying off, and one fantastically named venue in particular proved lucrative for all concerned.

Robert Marlow: "They used to play very regularly down at Crocs in Rayleigh. It was so cool because they had a live crocodile there! It was a real old Seventies place, tailored to disco."

Vince Clarke recalls that Composition Of Sound played several shows, billed as being part of Crocs' so-called Futurist Night: "The building is still there; it's called The Pink Toothbrush now! It's a dive, but back then it was quite nice. They had a crocodile in a tank in a cage. I think the RSPCA got it in the end, but we used to play quite regularly on those Saturday nights. We played with Soft Cell there once."

Steve Brown was instrumental in organising these Futurist Nights; indeed, it's likely that his ongoing association with Dave Gahan played a part in landing Composition Of Sound their first spot at Crocs on August 16, 1980. "Back then it was called the Glamour Club, and Dave used to be quite a regular down there while I was on the door. Culture Club had their first ever gig there, as did Soft Cell. But Marc Almond didn't go down too well, and when he wrote his autobiography he said something like, 'They called it the Glamour Club, but there's more glamour in a fried egg!' We were all mortified!"

Perhaps Soft Cell's poor Essex reception was down to parochialism, or perhaps Composition Of Sound were simply the better of the two bands on the night. Certainly COS always went down a storm at Crocs, though Steve Brown remains at a loss to explain why: "They got a *fantastic* response, because it was as if one of your own had got a band together and done really well. Crocs was their testing ground, really – they *knew* they would get a good response there. The Southend crowd was *notoriously* difficult to please; everyone just used to stand around and say, 'Go on then, impress me.'

"When other bands supported them, no one would bother to watch, but when Dave walked on-stage, everyone would go over to the dancefloor and start singing along and joining in – all the girls used to know exactly what was coming next and dance accordingly, which was a *totally* alien response to anyone who was regularly down there, because that just didn't happen normally."

All told, COS played Crocs' Glamour Club five times. Steve Brown described a typical performance: "Dave always used to roll up at Crocs with his girlfriend [Jo Fox], and she used to stand at the front taking photographs. It was a bizarre spectacle: Dave used to do his little swaying dance upfront, hugging his microphone, but as time went on, he got himself a little bit of an image. Vince would just look studious and really involved, and the others just sort of stood there – in fact, you really got the impression that earlier on Vince had put little labels on the synths telling them what to press and when!"

Watching from the sidelines at Crocs one night was none other than Gary Numan, who was by now at the height of his all-too-brief synth-stardom: "They [COS] were on the edge of the dancefloor – no stage, no risers. I thought they were brilliant, but didn't talk to them at the time as something happened and I had to leave. I had an idea that Beggars Banquet might be interested in them, and thought it would be cool to try and get them a [record] deal. Unfortunately, I can't remember now if I ever mentioned it to Beggars, although I think I did."

Ironically, Beggars Banquet was one of several labels to give Vince and Dave the proverbial cold shoulder, on the sole occasion the pair hawked the band's demo around London in a valiant attempt to secure a recording contract.

Dave Gahan: "Me and Vince went everywhere, [we] visited about 12 companies in one day. Rough Trade was our last hope. We thought, 'Surely they'll like it; after all, they've got some pretty bad bands.' But even they turned us down. They were all tapping their feet, and we thought, 'This is the one.' And they went, 'Hey, that's pretty good. It's just not Rough Trade.' "

Vince Clarke: "It was quite exciting. We were all dressed up in our Futurist gear and stuff. The nicest people were at Rough Trade; they were prepared to sit and listen to the tape. Those were the days when you could still do that – you could go in with your tape and say, 'Will you play this?' So they'd listen to it in their office and say, 'No.' Even that would be nice now; I don't suppose people would even get through the door. Anyway, Rough Trade said, 'Look, we're not interested in this particularly, but maybe this guy [Daniel Miller] might be, because he's just started this new label [Mute Records].' And Daniel only listened for about five seconds and then said, 'No!' "

Daniel Miller remembers that initial, fleeting introduction: "I was at the Rough Trade shop [at 137 Blenheim Crescent, London W11] and the late Scott Piering – who became very well known in radio promotion, and a very important part of the independent music industry – said, 'Daniel, come over and meet these guys; you might be interested in these guys.' And there was these horrible, spotty, little New Romantics – and I hated New Romantics with a vengeance at the time. I had some technical problem with the printing of a Fad Gadget sleeve, and I just looked at them and thought, 'I don't need to listen to this stuff right now,' and went off to do whatever it was that I had to do."

Dave Gahan's response to Miller's snub was characteristically cutting: "We were at Rough Trade with our tape and at the end they went, 'Pretty good, but it's not Rough Trade, though I know someone who might like it.' And Daniel [Miller] walked in and he said, 'What do you think of this, Dan?' And he [Daniel] turned round, looked at us, slammed the door and walked out. And we thought: 'Bastard!' "

Alongside their regular performances at Crocs, Composition Of Sound inadvertently landed themselves another residency.

Gary Smith was present when this breakthrough occurred: "I had a friend whose mum and dad ran a pub in Deptford [South East London], and they used to regularly put bands on. So Vince and myself traipsed all the way to Deptford with this [demo] tape and played it to them. They listened to the music and said, 'That's not really what our clientele are interested in, but we have a friend who runs another pub who may be more interested; here's the number, give him a call.'

"When she wrote down The Bridgehouse name, which we already knew, we didn't believe it. But she was a fairly decent lady, so we rang this guy and he said, 'Yeah, by all means come along.' He only gave them a chance for one night, so we got as many people as we could to go down there, and they were a big success! This guy said, 'At least you filled the place out; you can come back next week!'"

The guy in question was Terry Murphy, a promoter at The Bridgehouse in London's Canning Town. In its time, this small, 350-capacity venue was one of the most popular live gigs on the London pub circuit, previously playing host to the likes of Generation X and The Buzzcocks. Composition Of Sound's lightweight synth pop went down well with Murphy's discerning punters, thanks, in no small part, to the continued success of Dave Gahan's 'rent-a-crowd' tactics.

A Bridgehouse performance – on September 24, 1980 – saw COS supporting The Comsat Angels, from Sheffield. "They were actually much better than us," Vince Clarke admits. "When you're that sort of age, you say you were better, but actually they were probably a lot better. They went on to do a couple of albums." A bootleg recording of a COS Bridgehouse performance from October 30, 1980, revealed a punky edge to songs like 'Television Set', not necessarily indicative of what was to come.

Radio DJ, Robert Elms, was witness to another early COS gig – in the strangest of locations: "This place was above a greengrocer's or a drycleaner's, or something; it really was a room only eight-foot by 10, with about 10 people in it, with silly haircuts and baggy trousers. I thought, 'There *can't* be a band playing here.' And then these four *frighteningly* young boys . . . I mean, I was only about 18 or 19, and these looked like my little brother! These were skinny school kids, basically, standing around some sort of Bontempi keyboards! I thought, 'God, this is really good; they're going to be terrible,' which is what you hoped, because it was like the sport of going to see the opposition football team.

And they started to play, and they weren't terrible."

Deb Mann: "They'd built up quite a little following by then. In the early days there was quite a few Goths in their audience – fashionable sort of people. And Dave was very fashionable."

Martin Mann recalls another vintage Bridgehouse show: "I was in the dressing room with them before they went on. There was a band on before them called Industrial News, and they were really heavy. I remember saying, 'They're a bit too industrial for me, this lot' – sort of like a punky, heavy-metal-type band. Then Composition [Of Sound] came on, which was totally different. They started the old drum machine up, but it was playing up and stopped at one point, and someone at the back shouted, 'Put another 50p in the machine!' But they were great; I can still remember some of the songs that they played that they never went on to record. In those early days they still had the full make-up job; I remember Dave [Gahan] with his spiky hair – that was the image they had before they became successful."

Robert Marlow: "Those early gigs were always fun-packed. A guy called Laurence Stewart used to drive them around in his big, white Transit van. I remember, after one of the gigs at The Bridgehouse, a load of people clambered into the back of the van because The Bridgehouse was in the middle of nowhere in East London somewhere. The band had played this rollicking set, so we were all cramped in the back in all our finery, and could just see Vince's suitcase with his synth edging towards the back of Laurence's van. Anyway, the fucking thing fell out on the road! We stopped the van, and you should have seen Vince – all the blood had drained from his face. We ran back down the road, expecting to find a case full of broken wires and keys, but it was fine!"

"It's more likely that *we* were falling out the back of the van," Vince Clarke chortled, while nonetheless confirming Marlow's anecdote. "He [Laurence Stewart] was a builder and had a Transit, so when we had all these London gigs, he used to take us up there."

Gary Smith: "I think Paul Redmond was involved as their manager for a while. One of his friends had a van, and *anybody* who had a van was a valued friend back then – for carting gear around!"

When questioned about Paul Redmond's supposed managerial role, Vince Clarke responds: "Ah, the infamous Paul Redmond! He was involved with Dave – he was a mate of Dave's, so he was more into managing Dave. Again, he was one of those guys who used to go to the Blitz – I think he probably introduced Dave to Blitz. Anyway, he was a brickie and back then, brickie's were quite well paid, so he could buy a lot of equipment – he had *two* synths when he used to play with Rob Allen's band!"

By now the seemingly easily manipulated Andy Fletcher had graduated to an instrument ideally suited to his supporting bass parts. "He'd bought a bass guitar, but we persuaded him to buy a proper synth," claims Vince Clarke. In Fletcher's case, what constituted a proper synth was the keenly priced – £295 in 1980 – Moog Prodigy, a beefy two-VCO, non-programmable monosynth.

Other changes were afoot within the ranks. For their October 29, 1980 appearance, upstairs at Ronnie Scott's jazz club, in London's Soho, as part of the venue's Rock Night, the clunky Composition Of Sound moniker was dropped in favour of a (literally) fashionable replacement: Depeche Mode.

Martin Gore: "The name Depeche Mode came from Dave. He was doing fashion design and window display, and used the magazine *Dépêche Mode* as a reference. It means hurried fashion or fashion dispatch – I like the sound of that."

Dee Dye: "Dave [Gahan] used to get rattled when people pronounced the band *Day-pech-ay* Mode – Essex twang a must – and insisted it was Depeche with a silent 'e'. He'd got the name from a [French] fashion magazine gracing the shelves of the college library."

Dee Dye attended that début Ronnie Scott's showcase: "We travelled to the gig in the back of the van with their equipment. The mood (at Ronnie Scott's) before the gig was quite tense – Dave getting anxious because he knew that there were record company people about; Vince being cool and more concerned with his 'electrickery' as he called it. There seemed to be plenty of pacing about, beers flowing. From what I remember, the gig itself was as good as it should have been. We danced our jerky dances, whooped and cheered at the songs, and encouraged a few others in the audience to sway and tap their feet. Looking moody was the order of the day. After they did their set, Dave was pretty hyped up – he had a good feeling about that night, he said."

Vince Clarke: "Things were *really* starting to happen now – one minute we were playing at Crocs, the next [minute] we were getting these London gigs. It all started taking off *very* quickly!"

Jo Gahan also sensed the tide was turning in Depeche Mode's favour: "I was with Dave when Depeche began to play their early gigs at Crocs and The Bridgehouse. They were amazing nights, packed full of admiring friends – a real good atmosphere. Depeche were so cool, so different. After a few shows word began to get 'round and then many new faces would appear in the audience. It was kind of a shame that their mates then couldn't get a look in. But people like Steve Hill still drove us around in his van, lugging the equipment from gig to gig."

While Dave Gahan was still studying at Southend College of Technology, Larry Moore, who was part of the Student Union, organised a night of live music there on November 14, 1980: "Top of the bill were The Leapers, of whom great things were expected and who were regularly featured in the [Basildon] *Evening Echo*'s music column. No. 6 was also on the bill somewhere . . .

"Depeche Mode was third from the top of the bill; they were by far the best. After the gig, I was handing out the curry takeaway riders in the sports changing room and I asked Dave Gahan if, as they were so good, they would like to come back and do another gig. Gahan glared at me and said that they would, but only if they were the headline act. 'Huh,' I snorted, as I turned away. 'You're not *that* good!' Hence, I became the guy who knocked them back as not good enough to headline Southend College. I think I had a point!"

That same month, Depeche Mode received their first ever press in the *Evening Echo*: "Posh clobber could clinch it for Mode – some of these per-fumed, ponced-up futuristic pop bands don't hold a candle to these four Basildon lads. They are Depeche Mode, who could go a long way if someone just pointed them in the direction of a decent tailor."

Robert Marlow felt the writer had a point: "The *Evening Echo*, which was the local rag, once ran a great headline: 'Posh clobber could clinch it for Mode.' These local rags always have hook lines like that – 'This bunch of fresh-faced chaps will go all the way with their snazzy dressing,' or whatever, but we all looked like complete dicks! We were ridiculous – all that make-up and hair. I remember a girlfriend of mine at the time saying, 'Men are terrible at putting make-up on, because they always look straight at the mirror; they never look one way or the other.'

"It always made me laugh that Martin and Fletch were still working. So when they were doing their early gigs as Depeche Mode, at The Bridgehouse, or whatever, they'd have to take their suits off and get into their Futurist garb. I remember going shopping one day with Fletch when the craze at the time was wearing sort of ballet pumps – I was quite lucky; I had to have them for my drama studies. Anyway, we couldn't find these in Basildon anywhere. You only have to look at Andy – he's got huge plates of meat [feet]! So I remember him having to go on-stage wearing his football socks and a pair of furry slippers!"

Dave Gahan was likewise quick to laugh at his bandmates' sartorial disasters: "Andy used to wear these plus-fours, slippers and football socks. It was *so* funny! And Martin had half his face painted white. And Vince looked like this Vietnam refugee – he'd tanned his face, had black hair and a headband!"

Vince Clarke: "Fletcher, Martin and myself didn't know anything about it at all. Dave was the man – the style-master! I can remember at the time people had this thing about wearing karate shoes – black, soft, strapless things. So we all had a pair of those, apart from Fletcher. He couldn't get any to fit him, so he went on-stage in a pair of slippers in the end!"

At this juncture, Vince Martin took it upon himself to change his surname. From now on he would be known to the world as Vince Clarke. It transpired this was an expedient measure to avoid a potentially sticky situation: "When we got our first review, I wrote to the paper, and sent a photograph from a session that Paul Crick did in my garage where we were all dressed up in these grey overcoats. We did the interview, and suddenly I realised that if my name appeared in print, there could be a problem, because I was still signing on. So I phoned up the people at the paper in a panic, saying, 'Please don't print my real name.'"

But why choose Clarke? "At the time, Dave Gahan's friend, Paul Valentine was into Fifties Americana, and there was a guy called Dick Clarke [*sic*] – a famous Fifties/Sixties DJ. I thought, 'Well, I can't call myself DickClarke [*sic*], because no one will believe that my name is Dick! So I just changed it to Vince Clarke."*

Quirky songs, an eye-catching frontman, and a distinctive name; all that the band needed now was a recording contract.

---

* Actually, the correct spelling for Vince's inspiration is Dick *Clark* – the host of top-rated US TV show, *American Bandstand* from 1956 onwards. In an understandable panic to avoid being detected, Vince had little time for fact checking.

5

Going U.P.

"Daniel Miller's been very, very instrumental in our success. I think if we'd have been on a major label we wouldn't be here now."

— Andy Fletcher, 2001

Although electropop rivals Soft Cell had fared badly on Depeche Mode's Essex home turf back in August 1980, the Leeds duo had taken an early lead, recording-wise, when synth player Dave Ball's mother funded their privately issued, limited-edition *Mutant Moments* EP début that same year. Despite failing to chart, the record's DIY charm didn't escape the entrepreneurial attention of Stevo (a.k.a. Steven Pearce), an illiterate school-leaver who, as a 17-year-old left-field London-based DJ, was making a name for himself compiling a weekly Futurist Chart for the British inky *Sounds*.

Soon after, Stevo formed his own bizarrely misspelt record label, Some Bizzare, with grand designs on releasing a compilation album of unsigned Futurist bands, including Soft Cell. Stevo also set his sights on Depeche Mode, possibly meeting them for the first time as a result of Soft Cell's unlucky support slot at Crocs. "Soft Cell were obviously managed by Stevo, so that's probably where we met him," reasons Vince Clarke.

On November 11, 1980, the still label-less Depeche Mode were gigging at The Bridgehouse, supporting Mute act Fad Gadget, the recording/ performance pseudonym of Frank Tovey, who's performance art had gained him a certain notoriety.

Vince Clarke: "We did the gig with Fad Gadget, and Stevo came backstage and said, 'Look, we're doing the Some Bizzare tour, are you interested in doing it? And are you interested in signing to Some Bizzare?' Then Daniel [Miller] came back as well; we kind of knew him because of 'T.V.O.D.' [the B-side of 'Warm Leatherette']. It was a case of [going

56

with] either. Stevo said, 'Look, if you sign with Some Bizzare, I can get you a support slot with Ultravox.' So it was a real heavy-duty decision, you know! But we decided, for some reason, that we'd go with Daniel. And then Daniel said, 'We'll just do a single.' "

"We would have signed any deal, we just wanted to put a record out," said Vince. "The band unanimously conceded that Daniel Miller was the first one that we could trust; he said that if either party didn't like the other, we'd call it a day."

Daniel Miller's recollection tallies with that of Clarke's: "I think it must have been within weeks, or a matter of months [of first seeing Clarke and Gahan at the Rough Trade shop]; Fad Gadget was playing down at The Bridgehouse in Canning Town, and Terry Murphy, the guy who booked The Bridgehouse, had booked Depeche Mode to support. The two things hadn't clicked in my mind at all. But, anyway, that's the connection with Fad Gadget, and that's when I first saw Depeche. I went backstage and said, 'Let's put out a single,' and they said, 'OK, then, alright.' And that was it. There was some kind of conversation, probably, where I said, 'You could be a really big pop band. I think what you're doing is fantastic; it's really new, but it's still pop. We've never had a pop hit, but I really believe in what you do. Let's put out a single and see how it goes. I don't want to tie you down to anything more than that, because I don't know what I can do.' So that was it, really; it was pretty much as simple as that."

When viewed from the perspective of today's hard-nosed corporate-driven music industry, Miller's *laissez-faire* attitude seems hard to believe.

Andy Fletcher: "He was offering nothing – no contracts, but, at the end of the day, we trusted him, liked him, and liked the music on his label. For some bizarre reasons, we didn't have any money; we were all still working – well, Vince was unemployed; Dave was still at college."

"I didn't see *why* we should have a contract," says Miller in hindsight. "I thought that if you're fair with an artist – if you pay them – and you give them freedom, [and] you do your best to promote their records, [then] why would you want a contract; [why] get lawyers involved? It just seemed impure, in a sense."

NME's Paul Morley concluded that "meeting Daniel Miller was the sort of lucky break that can be turned into legend" but Depeche Mode's label situation wasn't quite as "simple" as Miller maintained. Stevo was still sniffing around the band, and made them an offer too good to refuse. With his planned *Some Bizzare Album* about to happen, he desperately wanted Depeche Mode to contribute. The band were apparently only too happy to oblige.

Over two decades on, Vince Clarke's youthful excitement still shines through: "The next thing we know, it's like, 'Can you do a track for this compilation album?' which was *amazing*!"

Dave Gahan: "We had no recording activities going on at all. Stevo approached us and asked us if we'd like to put a track on this compilation so we thought it would be a good idea."

Meanwhile, Miller and Stevo supposedly struck an informal verbal agreement. Miller went on to produce 'Memorabilia', Soft Cell's first single on signing to Phonogram in 1981, and Depeche Mode's début recording, 'Photographic' for Stevo's *Some Bizzare Album* in November 1980.

Daniel Miller: "When I first worked with them [Depeche Mode], they'd never been in a studio before. To be honest, at that time *I'd* hardly worked in one either! I felt like I was a really experienced producer compared to them, but I wasn't really. I think I did help them get the sounds they needed with the very small range of technology at our disposal. I was trying to show them the possibilities open to them."

Vince Clarke: "I remember the studio [Tape One in London]; it was very impressive. I remember it being quite dark. Apparently, Stevo turned up to listen to it ['Photographic'] and was sick on the mixing desk! I don't remember actually seeing it, but it's so locked in my memory that it seems like it happened."

Stevo thinks that Vince could be confusing this incident with Miller's Soft Cell production: "I walked into this little East End studio at 10.30 am. I was drunk. It was Daniel Miller's birthday and he'd been up all night, so I said, 'Happy birthday, Daniel,' and he spewed [vomited] all over the floor. It stank. I reckon that's what gave the record its raw edge."

Stomach complaints aside, it was Miller's technological skill that impressed Vince Clarke. Miller consequently claimed that his recording protégé was smitten with his much-loved ARP 2600 synthesiser – a more complex, Seventies-vintage semi-modular affair, enabling individual sound modules to be externally patched together by the user for added flexibility – which he'd bought cheaply from Elton John, and its attendant analogue sequencer in particular.

Daniel Miller: "I had my ARP Sequencer synched to tape and Vince just couldn't believe it! It only had 16 steps ['notes'], but was a tremendously creative tool. I remember the first time I showed it to Vince; he was mesmerised by it, and so the ARP [sequencer] became crucial to the early development of Depeche Mode. They immediately got into it. In terms of structure and arrangement, I left their ideas alone, because I thought the songs were great and wanted them to go down [on tape] as faithfully as possible."

Vince Clarke: "We had the song ['Photographic'] off to a tee, obviously, because we'd been playing it live. I remember we used the sequencer, so Fletcher no longer had to play the bass. The sequencer could lock up with the drums, which was cool, and all the other sequences. Martin still played – he's a proper player who can play in time, whereas Fletcher and me used the sequencer to trigger the notes."

Chances are Vince Clarke was forced to sequence his parts using one of Miller's synthesisers, on account of his own Kawai K100FS resolutely refusing to co-operate when he attempted to hook it up to the ARP machinery, much to his horror.

Vince Clarke: "When we first met Daniel, he introduced us to sequencers, so I thought, 'That's good; I'll try and trigger the Kawai [K100FS].' But nothing happened! So I took the thing apart one day and [discovered that] none of the trigger input sockets were connected to anything! It was just a con."

In discussing Depeche Mode's contribution to the *Some Bizzare Album*, following its January 31, 1981 release, journalist Pete Silverton commented: "There seemed to be a lot of optimism in your track compared to the other stuff, which all seemed to be about gloom in Barnsley." Dave Gahan: "Well, it's not us, really. Vince doesn't write gloomy songs."

Certainly from the moment that Daniel Miller's faithful Korg KR55 – "a very cool drum machine with auto-fill on it," according to Vince Clarke – instantaneously kicked in, what became known as the 'Some Bizzare Version' of 'Photographic' was fast-paced, akin to how the group performed it live – only tighter, and with Dave Gahan being credited with electronic percussion. As fellow Basildon pop star wannabe Robert Marlow posited, "That's when it lifted off a level – when they got the bass lines and a lot of Daniel Miller's sequenced stuff onto tape. Before that, it was literally bum notes and all that, but they still sounded really good; I was jealous as hell!"

NME's Chris Bohn concluded that Depeche Mode's début recording was "very assured, neatly structured, with entwined synth melodies which are partially marred by the Thirties Futurist lyrics, but saved by the persistent quiver of a melody line."

In revealing his *modus operandi* to *The Face*, Vince Clarke admitted that his main lyrical interest was in the sound of words rather than their meaning: "I like the way words fit together and rhyme. For instance, when I write a phrase or something, I think about how easy it is to sing, to fit in with the melody. I think in the sort of stuff we're doing, it's good to use certain words. I think words are very fashionable. I'll give you an example, right? Words to use in a good electronic song – 'fade', 'switch', 'light' – anything like that. 'Room', 'door' – words like that. 'Fade' – that's an excellent word. It's the word for '81 – it's got to be!"

Despite appearing among a full line-up of allegedly Futurist acts on Stevo's album Dave Gahan was keen to distance Depeche Mode from the movement: "All the bands involved with it are in one bunch together and they'll never escape from it. Soft Cell are about the only ones with a good chance. I don't like to bitch, but Naked Lunch have been going for years. We write pop music – electric pop, so we couldn't get tagged by appearing on that album. Once people hear the single, they'll change their minds!"

Before the divisive *Some Bizzare Album* was released, Depeche Mode were back in the studio with Daniel Miller – recording the single that Gahan had mentioned in the band's first major *Sounds'* feature interview.

The venue this time was engineer Eric Radcliffe's Blackwing Studios, sited in the deconsecrated All Hallows Church at 1 Pepper Street, South London – the scene of Daniel Miller's earlier recording excursions as The Silicon Teens. Miller had originally chosen this relatively low-cost facility because of its sizeable control room being more suited to his unorthodox recording methodology; with no live instruments to speak of, he simply needed space to set up his collection of analogue synthesisers – which, at the time, included the same Korg 700S so admired by Robert Marlow – close to the mixing desk. Blackwing and Depeche Mode were a well-matched pairing, with the group's resultant single, 'Dreaming Of Me' and B-side, 'Ice Machine' being completed within a couple of days.

Vince Clarke: "It was an exciting situation because it was another *proper* recording studio – a 16-track, in fact, because when Daniel did his first record there it was still an eight-track. I remember in-between recordings we had a big party in Basildon, so when we arrived to do the B-side we were quite hungover!"*

Even the normally subdued Vince Clarke was not immune to the thrill of finally committing two of his compositions to vinyl: "I remember walking in London and being afraid of being run over in case I missed out on all of the excitement, thinking, 'Wouldn't it be a bummer if I got run over now.' I was extra careful crossing the road; it was *that* exciting!"

As to who was responsible for choosing the tracks that would make up Depeche Mode's début 7″, "that was down to Daniel," Vince Clarke clarified. "We were like, 'Whatever you say!'"

It has been theorised that Daniel Miller initially viewed Depeche Mode as a way of making his 'fictional' synth group, The Silicon Teens, reality. Understandably, this cuts no ice with Miller himself: "The Silicon Teens was kind of appropriate for what I hoped might happen – not that I wanted to *force* anything; I never tried to make them into The Silicon Teens. They already had their own sound when I first saw them – before I met them; they blew me away when I first saw them playing. I certainly didn't make them in my own image, but they fitted very much with what I was hoping for.

"I had this kind of vision of how things might go with electronic music at that time; I had this kind of hope that, because *I* was so into it, the synthesiser would be the first instrument [that new bands would turn to] – before guitar and drums. There were lots of possibilities that hadn't been explored, whereas rock – apart from a few exceptions – was going around in circles since the Sixties. There were *so* many more possibilities of moving things forward and doing interesting things with pop and more experimental areas. [We] had some kind of . . . what I was looking for in my dreams – an epiphany, I think it's called."

Stevo's temporary hold on Depeche Mode was about to play itself out with his Bizzare Evenings tour, promoting the *Some Bizzare Album*, taking them north to Leeds (Warehouse, February 2, 1981) and Sheffield (Limit Club, February 3, 1981). Vince Clarke doesn't remember the tour as

* The group's collective exhilaration during the December 1980 'Dreaming Of Me' recording session was inadvertently revealed on the CD reissue of Depeche Mode's long-playing début, *Speak & Spell*. Thanks, in all probability, to an error on the part of a hapless recording engineer, someone can clearly be heard whooping for joy during its extended fade-out – together with one or two of those troublesome "bum notes" to which Robert Marlow refers.

being particularly salubrious: "It was about four or five dates, though we'd moved on from travelling in the back of a Transit to the back of a box van with the PA, trying to get some sleep!"

Perhaps this sleep deprivation affected Andy Fletcher's outlook, telling *Look In*, shortly after the tour: "Up North it's such a struggle; they're so different to Southern audiences. They don't react because they don't know our stuff. They go wild at the end, though."

Dave Gahan: "I think it's just the way Northern people are. They listen to it more; take it in more. But in London they just go mad from the start!"

When later asked why Depeche Mode chose to go with Daniel Miller and Mute as opposed to Stevo and Some Bizzare, Vince Clarke replied: "Maybe we even felt that Stevo was a bit creepy, but bear in mind there wasn't a deal as such – there was nothing signed. It was just a case of an agreement: 'Do you want to do a single? Let's go into a studio.' He booked it, and we turned up and did the single."

Clarke's character assessment of Stevo was not far off the mark as the Some Bizzare supremo's plush London Mayfair offices were rumoured to feature a chapel and confessional box for future signings; unconventional behaviour that would hardly have sat well with the former churchgoers.

Still booking gigs, Clarke managed to secure Depeche Mode's first prestigious London show (which Daniel Miller believes to be the first major New Romantic concert), supporting the now Midge Ure-fronted Ultravox, at The Rainbow on February 14, 1981, as part of Steve Strange and Rusty Egan's fanciful 'People's Palace Saint Valentines Ball'. Other eclectic electronic acts performing at the event included the robotic dance troupe Shock and the unfashionable – and generally unheard of – Metro.

Depeche Mode held their own; the buzz of playing to bigger audiences overrode any intimidation that their chief songwriter might have felt at going up a level, as Vince Clarke confessed: "We were doing lots of speed as well, which made it even *more* exciting! It concentrated your nerves. You see, it wasn't just a case of doing the gig and then analysing it all afterwards, saying, 'Oh, didn't we play shit?' The whole thing was just *so exciting* – people liked you!"

Martin Gore: "I knew about drugs, but I used to be quite pious. I was quite anti-drugs; if I saw anyone doing them around me I would walk away. I just didn't want to be involved. It was kind of a moral thing at that time – I don't know why. Maybe it was fear, because I'd been quiet, sheltered and never done it. I just didn't want to get involved."

Other than stimulants, as far as Vince Clarke was concerned, the formula hadn't really changed: "We were still playing in the same way as we always had, [playing] along to a Boss Dr Rhythm drum machine – Fletcher was always on bass, because he used to play bass guitar with the band; Martin used to play all the lead riffs, because he could play keyboards; and I used to be the man in-between."

Reviews following the February 20, 1981 release of 'Dreaming Of Me' were generally encouraging. *Sounds'* Betty Page called it "Deep, meaningful, heavy and arty" whereas *NME*'s Chris Bohn countered with "Despite the narcissistic title, 'Dreaming Of Me' is as sweetly unassuming a slice of electronic whimsy as anything by Orchestral Manoeuvres In The Dark. Deadpan vocals, programmed rhythm rejoinders and a candyfloss melody make for a pleasant three minutes."

Over in the glossies, *Smash Hits* were equally supportive from the outset, favourably reviewing Depeche Mode's – "frozen" (according to *NME*'s Paul Morley) – London performance at Cabaret Futura on February 16, 1981, before lavishing praise on 'Dreaming Of Me': "On the fringes of the Blitz Kids scene by virtue of their electronic music and evident taste for makeup and flash clothes, Depeche Mode in fact far outshine many a better known name by virtue of their ability to write *great tunes* and treat them right – like a cross between the bright synthetic pop of The Silicon Teens and the more weighty personal song stories of Foxx/Numan, etc.

"Two of these gems have now been committed to vinyl and the simply wonderful 'Dreaming Of Me'/'Ice Machine' is unreservedly recommended to absolutely everybody. Tasteful and tuneful, danceable and intelligent, it deserves to be utterly huge. Buy it!"

The photographs accompanying the article – which describe Depeche Mode as "looking scarcely a day over 14 but claiming to be 18-plus" – reveal that, despite having 'signed' with Mute, the band were financially no better off than before. Vince and Martin are pictured standing side by side their respective Kawai K100FS and Yamaha CS5 monosynths, sharing what appears to be a sizeable removal chest.

'Dreaming Of Me' started picking up radio play, courtesy of BBC Radio One DJs Peter Powell and Richard Skinner, and several weeks after its release, the single peaked at number 57 on the UK Singles Chart – not bad going considering Mute Records lacked the financial clout and distribution of a major label. That said, 'Dreaming Of Me' did top *Sounds'* independent singles chart; moreover, it was still holding out at 27 as late as September 26, 1981 – enough to secure its rightful position as the number one independent single of the year.

When quizzed about his 'Proudest Achievement' for publication in an early 'Personal Facts' sheet produced for the Depeche Mode Information Service – effectively the group's first official fan club (run by Vince Clarke's then-girlfriend Deb Danahay from her parent's Basildon home with assistance from Jo Fox and Anne Swindell) – Dave Gahan's response was fitting: "Hearing 'Dreaming Of Me' on Radio One."

On the other hand, the replies of his bandmates under the same category make for revealing reading: "Passing driving test" (Vince Clarke); "Getting Gold in Junior Section of Boys' Brigade" (Andy Fletcher); and "Not much" (Martin Gore). Equally edifying are their apparent ambitions: "To be successful" (Dave Gahan); "None" (Vince Clarke); "To be a better keyboard player" (Andy Fletcher); and "To be a millionaire" (Martin Gore).

"When Depeche [Mode] started to break, it took on another dimension," Daniel Miller told *Sound On Sound* in 1998. "I had never had anything like a hit single, and this was the band being chased by every label in the country very soon after I started working with them. They were very young, and they had all these labels banging at their doors, so I felt a sense of responsibility to get it right for them. Also, all the majors said that Mute [Records] could never have hits, so I wanted to prove them wrong! It made me very focused."

Smash Hits' Steve Taylor reported, "The fact that the formerly indifferent majors have suddenly started finding Depeche Mode's demo tape and phone number is a great confidence booster for both the band and [Daniel] Miller."

Andy Fletcher: "In the first year we were taking these demos around – couldn't get anyone interested; and it went from that to every single A&R person chasing us, but, for some reason, we went with a guy that was offering us no money at all, and no contracts, but we liked the music on his label.

"It was funny, because when I was in New York I met Roger Ames, who was involved in Island [Records] – now he's the chairman of Warners worldwide, and 20 years ago he came down to have a pint with us in a pub in Basildon, to try and sign us with Chris Briggs and a guy called Martin Dean. Martin Dean later signed Wham! to the worst deal of all time, and *we* could have been signing that worst deal of all time!"

This meeting stuck in Martin Gore's memory for the same reason: "Some of the people after us were [from] Polydor; one of the people after us was Martin Dean, who went on to sign Wham! – that whole fiasco."

Vince Clarke: "That was after the *Some Bizzare Album*. They were suddenly interested when we had a release and the whole Futurist thing started taking off. People started knocking at our doors."

Martin Gore: "At the time we were being courted by quite a few major labels, and they were offering us ridiculous amounts of money – sums that we just couldn't have comprehended at the time. Vince was on the dole, Dave was at college, and me and Andy were working to survive to the next payday."

Vince Clarke: "All these people from London Records and stuff started coming to our gigs, and chatting to us. But we didn't have a lawyer; we didn't have a manager, so there was no one doing deals for us. At the time it *seemed* like silly money. It sounds terrible, but I remember having a conversation with a publisher, and they were offering me £10,000 for all of my work for the rest of my life – I thought that was amazing! I just couldn't *believe* that!"

Daniel Miller's tiny independent operation, which, only the previous year, had been run from the Golders Green flat that he shared with his mother, moved to a small, one-room office at 16 Decoy Avenue, North London, just in time for the release of 'Dreaming Of Me'.

"We just felt we wanted to make a record," said the songwriter, in rationalising Mute's appeal. "The excitement of actually *releasing* a record was enough. We didn't want to get involved with a big record company, and Mute Records, at the time, was incredibly credible; they had Fad Gadget, The Normal and The Silicon Teens – all the kinds of records that we were listening to, whereas all [of] London's records weren't particularly brilliant. Everything that Mute did – even if it wasn't successful – was really cred, so I suppose we were always conscious of that."

Martin Gore: "There was a lot of soul-searching going on; I think it was mainly Vince who decided we should go with Mute – I give him credit for that to this day. We went along with what he was saying, because we were fans of Mute as well. But I think he was the main person pushing for us to do that, and we were very lucky that we did."

Deb Mann: "It was Vince's choice to go with Mute. There were other record companies that were interested, but Vince chose Mute. As I remember it, Daniel was prepared to let Vince have a say in it all, rather than going with a major label, who would just tell them what single they had to have out or what songs to have on an album, or whatever. Vince didn't like that."

Vince Clarke was correspondingly complimentary about the Mute man in Depeche Mode's first ever *Sounds* interview (dated January 31, 1981): "We've got a better chance on Mute. Daniel's been good to us and we like the way he operates. We listened to a few other companies, seeing what they had to offer, but we decided to stick with him. He had a big success with The Silicon Teens, and we've got that same sort of lightweight feeling to us. Daniel's got a good nose for things like that. He's an underestimated man."

The enigma that was – and is – Daniel Miller was further elaborated upon by a non-credited band member, during an *NME* interview in August: "We emerged just as all the big labels were searching for their Futurist group. We came very close to signing with a major. But we can do anything we want with Daniel. We could, if we wanted, just do a record that's just a continual noise for three minutes and he'd release it as a single. The people he's got on his label, like Boyd Rice, really are out of order. He puts out a single even though he knows it'll only sell 1,000. He does it just because he likes it . . . I still don't understand Daniel Miller. I don't see how he's made any money until us."

To give Daniel Miller credit, the initial one-off deal he offered Depeche Mode was very fair indeed – all the more so since it was consummated with a simple handshake; no written details; no formal contracts. "It's basically a 50-50 deal, so Mute put up half the costs for the recording, manufacturing, and everything else," Vince Clarke openly clarified. "Then the record is put on sale, and, after paying off all the expenses, whatever's left – the profit – is split 50-50, which is the same as I still have it today. Daniel based it on Rough Trade – that's how their deals used to be."

Andy Fletcher [*Look In*, dated October 24, 1981]: "We have a 50-50 deal, so everything's shared equally between us and the record company. We share all the costs, but you end up with a lot more."

PART II

Just Can't Get Enough

"To be honest, we never really saw ourselves as being on Top Of The Pops. *We were enjoying playing gigs; it was just a bit of fun among friends. We never really saw ourselves as being hugely successful, and certainly didn't think we'd still be here 20 years later."*

– Andy Fletcher, 2001

6

"The Beatles Of The Indies"

"We didn't have to work at it, you know? It was really fast. I went round to mum's and said, 'Mum, I can't believe it; I'm on fucking Top Of The Pops *next week!' It was just unbelievable."*

– Vince Clarke, 2001

The fact that Depeche Mode and Daniel Miller waited until May 1981 – six months after their initial visit to Blackwing Studios – to record a follow-up to 'Dreaming Of Me', suggests band and producer were happy to ride on the success of their first independent chart run.

Andy Fletcher and Martin Gore were both reluctant to quit their regular City jobs in favour of committing themselves full-time, and were happy to continue living with their parents, as, apparently, was Dave Gahan.

"We didn't want to stay in garages, but we never thought it would happen. It just has!" Andy Fletcher told *Sounds* (November 7, 1981). "We've never struggled and we haven't been gigging for years and years. When we first took our plugger [Neil Ferris of Ferret Plugging] 'Dreaming Of Me', and he said it was amazing, we didn't really believe him."

Vince Clarke celebrated Depeche Mode's recording breakthrough by moving into a third-floor, one-bedroom local authority flat on Vange Hill Drive in Basildon. Yet he could hardly be accused of living the highlife. In a valiant effort to stretch his social security payments to their limit, Vince was thrifty out of necessity during this period, as Andy Fletcher confirms: "He was unemployed and he used to get thirty quid, and he used to save £29.86! He used to get one loaf of bread a week! Vince was always the ambitious one; he was the driving force behind the band initially."

Reading between the lines, those much-needed royalty cheques had yet to start arriving. Andy Fletcher: "We didn't get paid for 'Dreaming Of

Me' – you only got paid afterwards. There was no advance at all. I think Vince got a small publishing advance, and we got a hundred quid, so we didn't have any money; that's not to say we didn't have any money at all, because we were working. All we ever wanted was our beer money and to give our mums ten quid a week, and that was it."

Deb Mann: "Vince obviously was very channelled, and very ambitious – that was his dream, but for the others, it just sort of happened, really."

Robert Marlow: "Vince didn't have a lot to lose, whereas the other two just kind of floated along – I think Martin and Fletch were definitely best pals. Gahan-y was keen, but I can't say too much about him, because I've never really known him that well. He was always aloof."

Vince had been far from idle as Depeche Mode were still gigging consistently, playing some 15, mainly South Eastern, shows during the lead up to their next recording session. These shows included a headlining return to Southend College of Technology (from which Dave Gahan had by now been "politely urged to leave" because of a poor attendance record – due in no small part to Depeche Mode's swelling diary dates) on April 2, two triumphant nightclub performances on their Basildon home turf, at Sweeneys and Raquels, on April 28 and May 3, and a prominent slot supporting The Psychedelic Furs at Hammersmith Palais on June 2.

Reviewer Winston Smith waxed lukewarm: "Depeche Mode added some sparkle to the proceedings with a laudable display of futuramic dance music. Their drum machine patterns and keyboard catchphrases are repeated much too often for their own good, and one's attention inevitably tends to wander." Still, at least they fared considerably better than opening act Siam, whose singer's stage movements were harshly slated for being "akin to those of an epileptic stick-insect on angel-dust."

In May, Depeche Mode returned to Blackwing, with Daniel Miller and several new Vince Clarke compositions.

Daniel Miller: "Vince learned really fast about technology and was very keen. He was starting to lay down the tracks, and I was helping him with the sounds and stuff. Then Fletch and Martin Gore would come in with a takeaway from their City jobs, and Martin would go down and play on a [games] machine, and say, 'Do I have to go down into the studio? Oh, alright, then.' And he'd do a little riff or something.

"Martin was obviously very musical; you could get him in the studio for five minutes and he'd play something that would bring a track to life, even if it wasn't the lead line. It's such a classic [story]; I remember him with his Chinese takeaway in one hand, playing the synth with the other hand – just wanting to eat his meal, really; not wanting to do anything!"

Already the unconventional band dynamic that remains Depeche Mode was beginning to take shape. Vince Clarke: "I was in the studio most of the time with Daniel, I suppose. I'd written the songs, and they [Andy and Martin] both used to turn up after work. Everybody played on the record; although Fletcher was never a brilliant keyboard player – and probably still isn't, it wasn't a case of someone taking over and saying, 'I'll play the bass for you.' That was his role."

On this occasion, the songs in question were 'New Life' and 'Shout!' – the former destined to become Depeche Mode's second single. The latter track – musically, a simplistic, meandering bass drone and occasional harmonious chorus, set against a backdrop of clattering analogue percussive tones courtesy of Miller's sequenced synths – would make for its B-side. Music journalist Ian Cranna was present for part of the recording session, reporting in the June 1981 issue of *The Face*: "Depeche Mode like to laugh a lot. Tonight, in a small recording studio in South London, a good deal of laughing is being done – mostly at the expense of non-vocalist member Andrew Fletcher who is struggling to find and hold his note in the four-part harmony which the band are laying down for their latest single, 'New Life' . . . 'From the heart, Andy,' calls producer Daniel Miller helpfully over the studio intercom. 'I'm *trying* to do it from the lung,' replies the beleaguered Fletcher."

The troublesome four-part harmony that appears towards the end of 'New Life' is remarkably reminiscent of The Beatles' throat-shredding version of 'Twist And Shout'. As for any possible pre-meditated parallels with Liverpool's finest in this regard, Vince Clarke replied, "Probably. We were taking stuff from all sorts, you know? In the studio you can overdub and try these things." Indeed, when quizzed by early Mode champion Betty Page for *Sounds* about "that riveting little synth riff" peppering 'New Life', Vince simply said it was "just an old R&B riff".

Certainly the new single was more upbeat than its predecessor. In keeping with Daniel Miller's assessment of Vince Clarke's increasing technological prowess, the arrangement featured a complicated pattern of melodic, seemingly sequencer-driven synths lines vying for attention in the highly danceable mix. "I think Daniel knew his equipment a little better by then," stated Vince Clarke

Dave Gahan was typically succinct: "We learned a lot from 'Dreaming

Of Me', came in here [Blackwing Studios] and just did a better job on 'New Life'.

'New Life', featuring an effective black and white sleeve showing an obscured individual unzipping himself from an egg (designed by Vince's younger brother, Rodney, who was studying art at Southend College of Technology), was released on June 13, 1981.

Two days previously, a Depeche Mode session for the *Richard Skinner Evening Show* was broadcast on BBC Radio One. Bizarrely, considering it was their new single, 'New Life' was conspicuous by its absence. Instead, the band performed live versions of a Vince Clarke song, 'Boys Say Go', 'Photographic', plus two Martin Gore compositions, 'Tora! Tora! Tora!', and an instrumental, 'Big Muff' (possibly named in reference to a popular American-manufactured distortion effects pedal).

While Gore's contributions contained virtually the same melodic ingredients as Clarke's, he later expressed misgivings: "I don't really consider them to be songs of mine. What I was trying to do was fit in with what Vince was doing at the time."*

The music press reviews for 'New Life' were largely positive: "This is the way that honest synth pop should sound," raved Steve Rapid for *Hot Press*; *Sounds'* Edwin Pouncey was nearer the mark: "Tinkly bonk excursion groping in the dark for the switch that will hopefully turn on the torchlight of success."

Three weeks after its release, 'New Life' breached the UK Top 30; ironically being broadcast on BBC Radio One alongside 'Computer Love' by Teutonic electro pioneers, Kraftwerk. Dave Gahan was moved to rank this melodically moving song at third place in his *Smash Hits* 'All Time Top 10' of 1981: "The beauty of Kraftwerk's records is that they're so simple and still so great."

The first verse of 'New Life' was lauded by none other than John Foxx as "Young, fresh electronics; good fun". It was the *sound* of the words rather than their *meaning* again. "In fact, Clarke is just about the ultimate in constructionists," wrote Ian Cranna, in *The Face* (June 1981).

Dave Gahan winced when recounting an incident involving 'New Life' to *Smash Hits*: "I remember walking through the town in Basildon one

* That Depeche Mode have time and again denied the BBC an opportunity to officially release this much-requested archive session speaks volumes of Depeche Mode's fastidious quality control.

night and I saw these two girls following along behind me. I knew they'd recognised me. And they start singing, y'know, (high-pitched squeak) *'I stand still stepping on a shady street.'* And I start walking a bit faster, turns up me collar! And then . . . (wails) *'And I watch that man to a stranger.'* And I'm thinking: 'Oh no, this is embarrassing! Do they *understand* these lyrics?! Perhaps *they do* and *we don't!'* "

The ambiguity of Vince Clarke's primitive lyrics were unintentionally exposed when, in late-1981, *Smash Hits* published the rhyming couplet: *"Fused and saw a face before . . . Like association whore"* (from 'Dreaming Of Me') as *"Views that saw a face before . . . Like association hall"* – thereby dramatically altering their meaning – if indeed there was any to be had in the first place.

Martin Gore: "I never understood what Vince was writing about – often the grammar was a mystery to me, let alone the meaning!"

Vince Clarke: "There were no meanings in the songs *at all* – nothing! They were very stupid lyrics, you know?"

The chart placing for 'New Life' was enough to secure the group their television début on *Top Of The Pops* – the UK's most nationally monitored music show – on July 16, 1981. That same day, Basildon's *Evening Echo* proudly reported: "Way back in May [1981], the *Echo* reported that Depeche Mode, from Basildon, were being hailed as leaders of the latest cult movement, the New Romantics. This week, more than two months after we tipped them for fame, the foursome of synthesised music are in the charts – and rising fast. And this evening they are on TV's *Top Of The Pops.*"

While being interviewed for *Smash Hits* in The Highway public house (Basildon), on the afternoon before their first TV appearance, Dave Gahan asked, "When Simon Bates introduces us on *Top Of The Pops*, he makes a special point of saying we come from Basildon – why?"

Martin Gore: "Because nothing good ever comes out of here?"

With 'New Life' streaking up the independent charts long before 'Dreaming Of Me' had exited, in the same *Smash Hits* interview, Andy Fletcher couldn't help but crow, "We're going to be The Beatles of the indies!"

"I didn't sleep a wink the night before," Martin Gore admitted. "We were young – 18 or 19 – and *Top Of The Pops* was *the* programme at the time. I was absolutely nervous. I can't remember very much about the performance; I think I just kept my eyes down and prayed that it would soon be over – and that I didn't look like I was shaking too much!"

Dave Gahan: "We couldn't really believe that it was our record that was going up the charts. It was a pretty nerve-wracking experience watching it creep up every week. Even hearing it on the radio thrilled us! Every time we heard it and we weren't together, we'd phone each other up to make sure we were listening! But doing *Top Of The Pops* was the best. Once you've appeared on that you feel like you've [got] a hit on your hands. It's terrifying being in front of the cameras knowing that all those people are watching you."

Vince Clarke: "We rehearsed a few times, and we'd obviously never done that before, so I was making sure that when a note sounded on the speakers, my hand was hitting the key. That [to me] was important; I thought that people would notice that kind of shit – probably after watching *Top Of The Pops* myself *I'd* be looking at my fingers, but no one else cares!"

Andy Fletcher: "I felt a bit like a prune, pressing a keyboard and singing into a mike with a lead going nowhere – halfway through you think, 'God, what am I doing here, looking like a prat in front of millions of people?'"

While major label-funded, successful contemporaries like Duran Duran and Spandau Ballet were being chauffeured about – Depeche Mode and a small circle of close friends – arrived at the *Top Of The Pops* studio in London by public transport. Practising his self-imposed policy of separating business from pleasure, Vince Clarke forbade girlfriend Deb Danahay from attending, much to her dismay: "I wasn't allowed to go to *Top Of The Pops*, because Vince didn't want me getting in the way, because that was a business thing. Anne [Swindell] and Jo [Fox] went – can you imagine how gutted I was when I heard about that? But that's how Vince was – business first."

"We got up *really* early to get the early train," recalled Vince Clarke. "We took the synthesisers on the train; because when we lost our various drivers we had to get trains."

Andy Fletcher: "We were on *Top Of The Pops* with [former Deep Purple vocalist] Ian Gillan, and people like that – rocker pap. We travelled in on the tube with our synths and things. We used to get off at the tube station down Wood Lane, and they'd say, 'Well, who are you, then?' And we'd say, 'We're on *Top Of The Pops*,' and they didn't believe us! We'd have our fans waiting, saying. 'They *are* in the group!' Meanwhile, these limos are pulling up."

Deb Danahay relates an amusing account of someone joking with the Basildon boys on the train to *Top Of The Pops*: "Not long now until you do a greatest hits album and play at Wembley!"

Another apparent discrepancy was Depeche Mode's dress sense, with Dave Gahan admitting (to *Look In*) that he bought most of his clothes from junk shops: "I also shop at Kensington Market in London, and places like that. My girlfriend also gets some cast-off shirts for me . . . It's no good going on in a pair of jeans."

With this thought in mind, Depeche Mode toned down their earlier penchant for heavy make-up in favour of a leather biker's look for their first *Top Of The Pops* appearance. Dave Gahan was undoubtedly the driving force behind the move, yet, reading between the lines, it looked like he had turned to an old associate for inspiration.

In habitually tuning in to the show, trendy Southender Steve Brown couldn't believe his eyes that particular Thursday night: "We were a pretty extreme and very high-profile group of people – I'm talking about white faces and full make-up here, and then we took to wearing all-leather gear, because no one else was. We all dressed up like leather queens; even though we liked to think we were very macho, it was all body harnesses and leather caps, and what have you. No sooner had we adopted that look, then, lo and behold, they did as well.

"Dave sort of said, 'I hope you don't mind, lads, but where did you get your leather hats and stuff, because we're going to get some.' We used to get this stuff from some little sex shop down in King's Road, and the next thing we knew, there was Depeche Mode on *Top Of The Pops* wearing all-leather gear! I didn't fall out [with Dave Gahan] over it because he asked our permission, and he didn't actually need our permission, but then we felt we couldn't go out wearing that kind of thing anymore, because, all of a sudden, people would say, 'Who do you think you are? Depeche Mode?'"

Such are the vagaries of fashion. And fashion – at least a lack of a coherent look – would soon become a thorn in the side, not that this immediately troubled either Andy Fletcher or his bandmates: "After we did *Top Of The Pops* I had to go into work the next day – everyone gave me a standing ovation!"

Dave's former Southend College tutors were likewise suitably impressed. "They sent me a note the other day, saying congratulations on the success," he gloated to the *NME*, soon after leaving.

The time also arrived for Andy and Martin to leave the comparative security of their day jobs to give Depeche Mode the attention it now warranted. According to Fletcher they were faced with a "very peculiar" scenario: "We had to give a month's notice! I think that was when we started to get our first [royalty] money, and gigs were getting a little bit of money in. It was good fun – great days."

News of Depeche Mode's *Top Of The Pops* appearance had an instant effect on their Basildon hometown in more ways than one; Robert Marlow professed to having mixed feelings about his best pal's runaway success: "It's really hard to put your finger on the pulse, because while I was really pleased that someone I knew was doing so well, I couldn't help thinking, 'Why isn't it me?' But then all of us have our moments of self-loathing; I was thinking that I hadn't tried hard enough."

Martin Mann: "None of us knew that it was going to take off as it did; it was amazing when 'Dreaming Of Me' charted, but then came 'New Life' and that was it – they were away!"

Depeche Mode were indeed on the road to somewhere, for the latest single's sales were being bolstered by the release of an accompanying 12″ version; though this wasn't intended as a specific marketing ploy that would become particularly prevalent in the Eighties and beyond, when endless extended remix permutations flooded the marketplace.

Vince Clarke: "We recorded 7″, and Daniel [Miller] made them into 12″. 12″ in those days weren't about joining tape together – extended mixes weren't even in our vocabulary at that point; 12″ were about making the record louder, because on a single you could only cut the groove so deep. But the deeper the groove is, the louder the record is, so [at first] we made 12″ to be played in the clubs. What we used to do was mix stuff in and out – drop the bass drum out for a couple of bars, or whatever."

A typical gig from this time would often open with Martin Gore's 'Big Muff' instrumental, then continue with 'Ice Machine', 'The Price Of Love', 'Dreaming Of Me', 'New Life', 'Television Set', 'Reason Man', 'Photographic', 'Tomorrow's Dance' and 'Addiction', before closing with Gerry & The Pacemakers' 'I Like It'.

With Daniel Miller tagging along, it was fitting that Depeche Mode's first live show after recording 'New Life' was at Rayleigh's Crocs Glamour Club on June 27, 1981 in what proved to be their farewell appearance at the Essex venue that had nurtured them. "We must have played at Crocs 15 times," Andy Fletcher told *Smash Hits*, "and that gave us a lot of encouragement; we weren't really nervous anymore."

Rob Allen relates another side to the normally reserved Daniel Miller from that night. Robert Marlow: "I've never been very impressed by the fact that Daniel Miller, who was The Normal, wasn't a pop star – he's a completely normal fellow, I suppose! He struck me as being painfully shy – it was bad enough with Vince, but here was somebody I didn't know being painfully shy. But the bloke who ran Crocs, who was a bit of a ducker and diver, wouldn't pay Depeche Mode. They'd pulled a lot of people in there, so Daniel apparently pulled him over the bar! I just can't imagine it, because Dave was always the one ready to give someone a dig, but Vince swears it's true!"

Following a spectacular 15-week chart run, 'New Life' peaked at number 12 on August 1, 1981, having shifted over 500,000 copies. Dave Gahan was quick to praise his producer: "All the majors [record labels] told him [Daniel Miller] that he wasn't going to make it and he's proved them wrong. And as for us, so far things have just happened – and at this rate we're happy to just let them keep happening.

"We would much rather have points [higher royalties] than big advances, and we've got that with Daniel. He's proved he can get us what we want; there's nothing he can't do!"

Depeche Mode's first low-key European show was a solitary outdoor appearance at the 'Parkpop Festival', held in the Hague's Zuiderpark on July 25, 1981, with the hands-on Daniel Miller presiding over the soundcheck.

Besides Miller, a select group of individuals were working hard in breaking Depeche Mode outside Britain.

Rod Buckle of London-based publishing company Sonet had signed up Vince Clarke from the outset – hence the songwriter's "small publishing advance", of which Andy Fletcher had made mention.

Vince Clarke: "When Daniel formed Mute Records he got his advice on how to set companies up and do deals abroad via Rod Buckle; Rod [had] sort of sorted out The Silicon Teens' licensing. Then he obviously signed myself and Martin [Gore] individually as writers; he did publishing deals with us."

In assisting Miller in setting up various overseas licensing deals, Buckle was indirectly responsible for extending the longevity of 'New Life' well beyond the summer of 1981.

Another influential catalyst who would become crucial to Depeche Mode's American success was New York-based music industry figure, Seymour Stein, the founder of Sire Records. In 1981 Seymour had begun taking business trips to the UK in the hope of making his next big discovery.* On one visit, Stein befriended Daniel Miller whom he often used as a sounding board. Inevitably, Stein got to hear about Depeche Mode; making the journey out to Basildon to catch their Sweeneys club show of April 28, 1981 – later regaling all with outrageous music industry tales from a seemingly different world over a slap-up meal.

Vince Clarke: "When Daniel was sorting out different deals for us in Europe, Mute wanted to get an American deal, so Seymour flew over to a gig in Basildon. He said, 'By the way I like that song 'The Price Of Love' that you do – it's *really* good!' Again, it was all so fast and so exciting. Everything was positive, you know? There were no negatives at all."

Stein was impressed enough to strike a deal with Daniel Miller there and then. Vince Clarke: "Who's the guy who plays the director in *Young Frankenstein*? That's who Seymour Stein looks like – Mel Brooks!"

Having branched out solo in December 1979 after working for various record companies for nine years – including a stint in EMI's promotions department – by 1981, 27-year-old Neil Ferris was successful in his field, with UB40, The Human League, and Heaven 17 among his charges. By taking on Mute Records act, Fad Gadget, Ferris regularly received calls at his Regent's Park office (or on his in-car phone) from Daniel Miller, a move which invariably led to Depeche Mode joining Ferret Plugging's roster.

As a synth-based pop act, Depeche Mode were in good hands, for it was Ferris who had transformed The Human League into a successful singles chart proposition. "It is really great to see [The] Human League doing so well now," Ferris told *Record Mirror* in 1981. "When I first started work on them about the time that 'Boys And Girls' [their first single after the departure of founder members Ian Craig Marsh and Martyn Ware] was released it was very difficult to get anyone's interest going. With each single it became progressively easier."

In such a moderate musical climate, the way was clear for Ferris to convince radio programmers that Depeche Mode were to be the next synth pop sensation.

On August 22, 1981, Depeche Mode featured in a documentary focusing on Essex's past and present music scene, broadcast as part of London

---

* That same year, Stein discovered and signed an unknown female singer called Madonna to Sire Records.

Weekend Television's weekly magazine show *Twentieth Century Box*.

During an advance meeting with one of the film-makers, Dave Gahan joked, "You can film my usual Saturday morning routine: have a sauna, go to a brothel, then a commando course . . . Nah, it'll be Andy waking up at 6 am, having his toast and going down the newsagents for his paper round – boys next door!"

That Gahan had already picked up on the band's press image is worthy of note. "If you pick up the write-ups from the time, it was always 'the nice boys from Basildon'," pointed out Deb Mann. "But that's really how they were. They were innocent, as we all were. None of them had groupies, because they all had steady girlfriends; Fletcher was *very* quiet – he didn't have a girlfriend at all. He was very shy, actually; Fletch just used to bring along Rob Andrews as his partner, sort of thing. Martin was very subdued. The loudest would be Dave, but even he wasn't loud!"

Depeche Mode's segment in the resultant half-hour documentary began with a close-up of a *Space Invaders* arcade game being played by a grey track-suited Dave Gahan, before moving on to shots of all four casually dressed band members playing Ten Pin bowling, overlaid by the opening narration: "Depeche Mode show just how much Futurism has changed now it's hit Essex. They don't fit into the London Futurist pattern. Andrew Fletcher worked for an insurance company; Martin Gore had a job in a London bank; Vince Clarke did a series of casual jobs; and Dave Gahan was in technical college in Southend."

Of most interest from a historical viewpoint is documentary footage of an early performance (June 27, 1981) at Crocs nightclub, set to a pounding 'New Life' soundtrack. Dave Gahan could be seen hugging his microphone stand for dear life, while the others did their level best to introduce whatever movement they could – not an easy proposition when riveted to the same spot behind their individual keyboards.

Also readily apparent is the intimacy of this Crocs gig, with the band performing almost at eye level with an audience that couldn't have numbered more than a couple of hundred jubilant supporters.

In all probability, the Crocs show was booked in advance of 'New Life' climbing the charts, yet in the eyes of some, Depeche Mode were a letdown by virtue of failing to tailor their performances to suit their newfound celebrity.

Dave Gahan recounted one such encounter with an air of disbelief: "There was this bloke come to see us the other day and he said to me after the show, 'I think it's really bad the way you have all your friends in the audience talking to you and that, and then we're over here and you don't react to us.' I said, 'Well, what do you mean?' He said, 'I think it's really bad that you have, like, all of your friends in the changing room.' I said, 'Well, what do you want me to do? Say, "C'mon all the audience into the changing room!"' He thought that we should be like Gary Numan and have the distant lonely look and image. Because we play synthesisers and that, we're supposed to look strange at people, and not smile. The bloke didn't like the way I smiled at people!"

Like Vince Clarke, Dave Gahan remained an admirer of Numan – if not necessarily his musical attitude. "I think he's very good, but like so many other synthesiser groups, he has a morbid sound. Vince calls it 'B&I', standing for 'Bleak and Industrial'. We're 'U.P.', standing for 'Ultrapop!' – bright, melodic and cheerful."

Vince Clarke: "I think the word 'pop' is really good, because it's light and happy. I think it's a nice word."

This early assessment is echoed by outside commentators.

Steve Malins: "[Depeche Mode] were the first teenage electronic band; they were kind of a synthesiser boy band, really."

Paul Morley: "They looked about 14, but it was *so* modern. They made the most intensely *sweet* pop music, and they were just *so* cuddly."

Still lacking professional management to guide them, Depeche Mode were learning the game as they went along. "We've got no transport costs really, all our gear goes in the car [an old Renault belonging to Daniel Miller, who often drove the band to their shows]" Dave Gahan told *Smash Hits*. "We don't employ any roadies. So if we get paid £250 for a gig and £50 goes on hiring the PA, we can come out of it with a reasonable amount each. Everything about us is independent, even the promotion of the new record ['New Life'] we hired ourselves."

Smash Hits' Mark Ellen wrote: "Rocketed from virtual obscurity to fair-sized hit singles in a matter of months, they [Depeche Mode] readily admit that they hadn't the time to adjust the live act accordingly. One minute, Crocs in Basildon; next, the Lyceum Ballroom in London – six times as big and no way to fill up the vast empty space behind them. No film, no slides, no backdrops. It speaks volumes about their music that they still set the whole place on its feet."

Melody Maker contributor Robert Colbert, shared Ellen's views when reviewing one of Depeche Mode's first headlining performances at The

Venue, in Victoria (July 23, 1981): "They haven't adjusted to staring down intruding *Top Of The Pops* cameras because their single is scrambling up the charts. They haven't learnt how to end songs, only reining them to a clatter-hoofed halt when the taped drums run out . . . But at least after Thursday they must have a clue about dealing with two tiers of The Venue dancing itself stupid on tables, chairs and any clear space. And they sure know how to put out sheer pulsing pop and slap a pretty face on."

Although 'New Life' had been a fair-sized hit, only Vince Clarke had invested in better equipment, shelling out around £1,800 for a Roland Jupiter-4 [JP-4], a rather cumbersome, programmable polyphonic analogue affair, capable of sounding four notes simultaneously – not that this mattered much to Vince, who resolutely remained a player of the one-fingered variety.

Although not necessarily the best synthesiser around, the 1978-vintage JP-4* was nonetheless a step forward from the diminutive Kawai K100SF monosynth that Vince had struggled so hard to finance a year earlier. Compare this change of fortune with that of Duran Duran's keyboard player, Nick Rhodes, who was by now readily flaunting Roland's latest and greatest flagship analogue polysynth, the mighty eight-voice Jupiter-8, boasting 16 oscillators, 64 memories, and a hefty £4,000 price tag to boot.

The group were also aware of the need to improve their simple stage setting, but, as Martin Gore stated, implementing change was easier said than done: "We used to have this idea of having rails on-stage and we would be on platforms so that we could be moved backwards and forwards on-stage although we didn't have to actually move! We really want to make our show good but we haven't had a chance to sit down and think about it . . .

"We've had loads of ideas since then, but ended up using none of them. One idea was to have these drum majorettes on-stage. Another was to have someone up top operating these life-sized puppets. The thing is, you *can't* have films and slides and things like that because it's all been done before and people'll say: 'Oh, it's not as good as The Human League,' or whoever!"

---

* "Pretty much of a preset synth on the cusp of organ synthesiser. Single-oscillator design makes for thin tones, but good filtering, arpeggiator [an electronic musical feature that replays the individual notes of a chord in a predetermined sequence – often up, down or up/down] and the chance to store [sound] modifications in eight memory locations. Four-voice polyphony. Hip at the time." Julian Colbeck, *Keyfax Omnibus Edition*.

Whoever might well have included Kraftwerk, who, that very same year, tackled the perennial problem faced by motionless synthesiser bands by incorporating both showroom dummies *and* synchronised slide films – courtesy of four large, expensive video screens custom-built in Japan by Sony – into their latest state-of-the-art technological *tour de force*.

Vince Clarke was evidently also already thinking ahead in this regard: "We don't want to get like Kraftwerk; we don't want to use tapes live anymore," adding, not without a hint of sarcasm, "We've got a rhythm unit [drum machine] with a TV screen that plays *Space Invaders* as well!"

Back in Basildon, Deb Danahay was keeping a diary in which she chronicled Depeche Mode's increasingly event-packed schedule. With the assistance of Jo Fox, Deb formed the Depeche Mode Information Service from her parental home at 521 Long Riding.

Deb Mann: "The band just started getting letters. If anyone had written in to Vince then I took the letter and answered it from home, and Jo took Dave's. That's how it worked. It was all very basic."

That it was. An early information sheet, typed by Jo Fox, was sent out to all contactees précising Depeche Mode's brief history which read, literally, as follows: "Depeche Mode were originally a three piece band playing guitars and one synthesiser under another name until June 1980 when Dave joined, the name was changed to Depeche Mode and they switched to three synthesisers. A demo tape was made with the new line-up and taken to various record companies and venues without much success except a gig at The Bridgehouse in London in September supporting The Comsat Angels.

"Meanwhile, back home in S.E. Essex a club called 'Crocs' was opened and Depeche Mode were asked to play there on the opening night and subsequently played there six times until Christmas. On the 12th of November a gig was arranged at The Bridgehouse supporting Fad Gadget, it was here that they met Daniel Miller of Mute Records and this is where things really started happening for Depeche Mode.

"A track was made – 'Photographic' – with the help of Daniel for the *Some Bizzare Album* which didn't meet with much success, and so in February 1981 'Dreaming Of Me'/'Ice Machine' was released on Mute Records, this reached number one in the independent chart and number 54 in the BBC UK Chart. The band were now becoming so much in demand that Andy and Martin began to contemplate giving up their full-time jobs.

"With the taste of success not far from their grasp they went back into the studio to record 'New Life'/'Shout' on both 7″ and 12″. It was released at the beginning of June and got to number 11 in the BBC UK Chart and stayed at number one in the independent chart for many weeks."

Pete Swindell designed the first official Depeche Mode T-shirts, available in small, medium or large sizes, priced at £3.50, including package and postage, and available by applying in writing to: P. Swindell, 10 Hawksway, Basildon, Essex SS16 5YQ. "It was all very incestuous – first with friends in Basildon, then with Daniel [Miller], Eric [Radcliffe] and Rod [Buckle] when it all began to take off a bit," Deb smiles, more than two decades after the event.

The Danahay Diary dates the band's first photo session, arranged especially for the fan club, as being June 21. Deb Mann recalls the photographer, who worked for a local photographic shop, as being called Tim: "He was Depeche's first ever 'number one' fan. He was really excited to be involved with it all, and he took some pretty good photos as well."

The location of this début photo session was outside Vince's flat on Vange Hill Drive, with the four posed in front of Deb Danahay's father's beloved Morris Marina. Tellingly, in one of the photos, Vince Clarke is seen to be standing back from his three colleagues – nor was he looking the camera in the eye.

7

The Summer Of Discontent

"The whole [fame] thing went right to my head. Suddenly everybody – me included – assumed why things were going so well was because of our own great talent."

– Vince Clarke, 2001

The summer of 1981 saw a succession of synth-based acts assault the UK Singles Chart. In August, The Human League were finally enjoying some serious chart action when – thanks in no small part to the ceaseless resolve of Depeche Mode plugger Neil Ferris – 'Love Action (I Believe In Love)' peaked at number three.

Depeche Mode's one-time Essex stagemates Soft Cell went one stage – and two all-important chart placings – further. By fortuitously choosing to record and release an electronic cover version of Gloria Jones' mid-Sixties Northern Soul stomper 'Tainted Love', the synthesised duo took pole position in the UK Singles Chart throughout August.

Martin Gore: "At the very beginning [of our career] there was a kind of movement going on. There were bands around like Soft Cell, The Human League and Orchestral Manoeuvres – I didn't really like a lot of that. A lot of stuff that was supposed to be our bag didn't really do much for me. A lot of the bands that were starting out at the same time used synthesisers, but some of them only had *a* synthesiser. People like Duran Duran and Spandau Ballet were put in the same basket; we only ever used to bump into them occasionally at TV shows. It was never a big deal."

Mute maestro Daniel Miller was in a better position to disentangle the confusion surrounding the New Romantic/Futurist synth-orientated scene: "Most New Romantic bands were basically rock bands with a synth player – they [Depeche Mode] considered themselves as a Futurist band, not a New Romantic band; [there's] subtle differences, you know? But then there was another group of bands – Human League, Soft Cell and OMD – that were proper electronic bands."

"As recently as a year ago it wasn't fashionable to say that you played pop music," Dave Gahan explained to *Jackie*, "but now lots of groups are actually admitting it, there's no fuss. Basically, we're just a group who write good, catchy tunes. We're a pop band; it's as simple as that."

Andy McCluskey, of Orchestral Manoeuvres In The Dark – themselves no strangers to the UK Singles Chart with two Top Five entries ('Souvenir' and 'Joan Of Arc') – told *Smash Hits*, with faint sarcasm: "I think we could leave the synth pop tunes to Depeche Mode – they're better at it than us these days."

According to Deb Danahay's diary, work on what was to become the *Speak & Spell* album commenced on June 14, 1981 at Blackwing Studios. Accompanied by photographer Jill Furmanovsky, journalist Pete Silverton observed the album's uneasy first phase in *New Sounds, New Styles*: "Depeche Mode are rehearsing in a deconsecrated church on the south side of London's dockland. Vince Clarke is using a Roland [Jupiter-4] synthesiser and operating the drum [machine] in a maroon shirt. Andrew Fletcher is on a Moog [Prodigy] in a green shirt. Martin Gore plays a Yamaha [CS5] and wears a chunky-knit white sweater over a black T-shirt. And in front stands Dave Gahan, singing in a baggy peach shirt with white cuffs, tan cord trousers and mid-brown, heavily belted boots. The band play very quietly, working on a new song – probably to be called 'Let's Get Together'. They're having trouble with the harmonies."

Andy Fletcher: "That sounds too much like the Beverly Sisters." Vince Clarke: "Everything sounds like something."*

"In the early Depeche days I didn't go up to the studio because Vince just wanted to think about himself," Deb Mann states. "But because Martin and Dave wanted them there, Anne and Jo were always at the studio. You can't imagine it today – girlfriends wouldn't be allowed in the studio 12 hours a day!"

---

* When quizzed as to whether the song-in-question could possibly have been an in-progress version of their next single, Vince Clarke claimed: "No. 'Let's Get Together' was from my Christian days." The mystery deepens when one unofficial on-line resource claimed that 'Let's Get Together' was an early Vince Clarke-penned Depeche Mode song, once aired on a "BBC show" alongside Dave Gahan reminiscing about the band's formative years.

Unsurprisingly this state of affairs caused some dissension within the group's seemingly closed ranks.

Vince Clarke: "Not that I didn't get on with Dave, exactly, but he had a girlfriend, and he always seemed to be in moods and stuff, dealing with all this personal relationship shit. That, it seemed to me, got in the way of the band, you know? In retrospect, it was probably more important that he did that – I've really come to realise that now. But, at the time, I just had a driving ambition for the band to do well."

Vince later relented enough to allow Deb to visit Blackwing: "It was a big church, so it was very cold and sort of crypt-like."

As far as Vince remembers it, Daniel Miller was still in the guiding seat at this delicate point in the proceedings: "Daniel said, 'Right, let's do an album!' That's probably how it happened, I imagine. We had enough for a set – 10 songs, which was enough for an album."

Daniel Miller: "When I first saw them [Depeche Mode] play, they kind of very much set the sound picture and format for the first album."

Martin Gore's 'Tora! Tora! Tora!' and 'Big Muff' – premièred during the BBC Radio One *Richard Skinner Evening Show* broadcast – were also laid down during the album's start-stop recording sessions. In retrospect, Gore has mixed feelings about both the album and his contributions. "Of course, I've got fond memories of it, because it was the first thing we ever did. We actually recorded 'Photographic' for the *Some Bizzare Album* just before that. We were playing those songs live for a year or so before that. I have all those memories, but I still see it as Vince's album, because he wrote nine of the 11 songs on it."

While the band had been perfecting the majority of the songs as a result of regular gigging, the recordings sounded noticeably different, thanks to Miller's creative and technical input. In its original incarnation, 'Photographic' was fast-paced, with a simple yet effective arrangement. When re-recorded at Blackwing, it took on a sparse, almost haunting character, arguably more in keeping with the nonsensical lyrics.

Vince Clarke: "That was Daniel Miller's influence. I remember being really frustrated because it seemed to me that he'd spend all day doing a bass drum sound, and I couldn't work out why that would be."

"We'll explain to Danny what we'd like and he says 'just a moment' and it's there," Dave Gahan told *One..Two..Testing* in 1982. "We could be playing around for five hours and still not get it . . . so we read the papers instead."

Andy Fletcher: "Danny would read a synthesiser manual; he reads them at home – probably on the toilet or something! That's his hobby."

The band would come to thank Daniel Miller for his meticulousness. While admittedly time-consuming, Miller's mastery of the subtractive (analogue) synthesis system employed on a vintage ARP 2600 synthesiser – still the mainstay of the early Depeche Mode sound – gave the band an edge over their rivals. The bass drum sound and other percussive tones Miller achieved were unique; more importantly, they are able to stand the test of time – unlike commercially available drum machines such as Linn Electronics' LM1, the first to feature digitally sampled sounds to simulate real drums.

Depeche Mode's as-yet-untitled début album was preceded by their second single – 'Just Can't Get Enough' – on September 7, 1981. Perfectly crafted and quite possibly the most infectious slice of synth pop to be committed to vinyl, early Mode champion Betty Page reported on its creation at Eric Radcliffe's Blackwing Studios for *Sounds*: "One look at Vince Clarke sitting confidently at the mixing desk and shorts-wearing Martin Gore's welcoming smile and I knew things would by hunky-dory."

'Just Can't Get Enough' was not entirely a problem-free affair, however, with Dave Gahan divulging that "we just couldn't concentrate on recording and the first time we did 'Just Can't Get Enough' it was terrible. We got rid of most of what we had done, and recorded more tracks," adding elsewhere that the song "took an age to record, because we still had 'New Life' on the boil."

Interviews too were eating into the band's time, but Vince Clarke was by now refusing to play ball. Speaking to the *NME*'s Paul Morley, an (uncredited) band member recounted: "There was this guy who interviewed us for the *Daily Star* – Ricky Sky – and he was desperately looking for a headline, an angle, and he was saying to us, 'Haven't you done anything really exciting? What's been happening?' We said, 'Well, nothing, really, although when we played at Ronnie Scott's once all the lights went out!' He was excited by this, then he started to talk about looks, and he said, 'Do you think it's an advantage to be good-looking and be in a band?' Vince said, 'Yeah, obviously, it's an advantage in life to be good-looking.' Rick Sky made it out that Vince had said, 'Ugly bands never make it. If you're good-looking then you're number one.' Since then, Vince has never ventured out of his flat! He is so upset. It really hit him hard. He hasn't been out for six weeks and he had a real bad depression."

Sky's verbatim report went as follows: "Depeche Mode are one of the best-looking bands around. And they reckon that gives them an edge over the competition. Vince Clark [*sic*], 21, says: 'Ugly bands really don't get anywhere in this business. But let's face it, being good-looking gives you a real advantage in life. It opens a lot of doors.' "

Two decades on, Robert Marlow claims those twisted words from the sensationalist side of the journalistic spectrum were "the clincher" when it came to pinpointing his friend's media distrust: "When he was asked, 'So, do you think you're pretty?' there was an element of irony in his reply, because Vince has an ironical sort of jaundiced view on life. When it was printed, Vince was absolutely beside himself. He's quite a sensitive bloke, and he's not vain – there's no way he's ever considered himself as being a good-looking guy, you know?"

If Depeche Mode had been signed to a major label with professional management securely in place, it's possible that Clarke would have been advised to demand a retraction. As it was, while the other three were pre-pared to meet the increasing demands of being in the public eye head on, Clarke increasingly retreated.

When taking time out from the studio to talk to teenage girls' magazine *Heartbeat*, Clarke's absence was again duly noted. Dave Gahan's cover-up was telling: "He [Vince Clarke] talks about clever stuff, while we giggle and gossip on the 'dumb table'. He likes to get really involved in the studio and when he's concentrating, he blanks himself off from everything. He's going through a stage right now where we can't get anywhere near him, so we just leave him alone till he comes out of it."

In a more light-hearted moment, Dave Gahan jested with *Look In* that his mother had the final say in the band's releases! "Daniel Miller, who runs Mute, takes her quite seriously. She listens to our records and tells us what she thinks. She listened to 'Just Can't Get Enough' and said it was too choppy. If it's choppy then it's not good so we remix it. Then she sits and listens and says, 'It's got a good beat – more dance-y than the other one.' That means it's alright!"

"By popular request and especially for their mums and dads, here are resi-dent Basildon chart sensations, Depeche Mode, who are now so wealthy they can afford to pay full fare on the buses. After the Top 10 success of 'New Life', they've got a new single, 'Just Can't Get Enough'. It's on the small, independent Mute label, whose guidance they've repaid with loyalty when other groups might have sold their souls to major record firms." (from a local Basildon paper)

Vince Clarke: "There was always that thing of selling out – even in the early days, because independents were so important then. It was exciting, you know? It was like being trendy, from what I remember. And I liked trendy."

Dave Gahan: "The people round here [Basildon] sort of think that if you've got a single in the charts you're going to be driving around in a Rolls-Royce, but we still use buses. They see you in the chip shop or the Wimpy and they think it's really odd . . .

"There's no glamour [in Depeche Mode]. We drive around in Dan's Renault . . . we don't now because it's broken, so we get trains. Nothing's really changed. We might have a few more pennies in our pockets, and when I say pennies I do mean pennies, but same friends, same places to go. You always think, 'Wouldn't it be great to have a hit single,' but when it actually happens nothing really changes."

Gahan's comment coincided with the *NME* putting Depeche Mode on their August 22, 1981 cover. Although framed in the foreground, rising photographer Anton Corbijn blurred the hapless Gahan, focusing instead on the other three members.

Dave Gahan: "I was really disappointed. I was on the front but . . . I wasn't. It was quite cheeky of him [Anton Corbijn]. It went completely over my head, the whole photograph. I remember thinking, 'What a bastard! He's got me completely out of focus.'"

News and reviews in the music weeklies were upbeat, albeit more to the point. "Top new synthesiser band Depeche Mode release their third single this week, following up their 'New Life' hit. It is titled 'Just Can't Get Enough' and backed by an instrumental song called 'Any Second Now'." But could the fact that Vince Clarke evidently no longer required singer Dave Gahan's services on this flipside recording be read as a sign of things to come? Maybe.

"As 'New Life' [drops] out of the charts after four months, the new Depeche Mode single, 'Just Can't Get Enough', [comes] charging in looking like it'll be the biggest example of the Basildon sound yet, although it has to be said that the lyrics are a trifle on the repetitive side. Maybe that's the sort of thing that happens in Basildon, but having never been there we wouldn't know. One rock critic recently called them 'The Bay City Rollers of the electronic age', or something like that, so if they're really going to be big, we'd better soon memorise all their names. Here we go – Vince Clarke writes the songs, while Dave Gahan sings them,

Andrew Fletcher and Martin Gore play (you guessed it) synthesisers, and there's a drum machine in there somewhere . . ."

Record Mirror awarded 'Just Can't Get Enough' their coveted 'Single Of The Week' status on September 12, 1981: "Bubblegum is back! OK, the title's embarrassingly banal, and its repetition throughout the song gets very wearing, but the thing as a whole is hugely enjoyable, bouncy and boppy and very close to irritating. The latter quality is essential in bubble-gum; it's got to get on your nerves a bit, to be *annoyingly* catchy, and this record is. A hit of generous proportions – these baby faces will be back on *TOTP* before you can say 'The Archies'."

Before long, those baby faces were, once again, beaming forth from *Top Of The Pops*, premièring 'Just Can't Get Enough'. This time they were sporting clothes tailor made by Rose Martin; out went the leathers, in came high-waisted trousers, braces and a neat line in shirts – all that is except Martin Gore, who, by opting out of wearing his shirt during the show's actual performance, revealed the beginnings of what would later become something of an obsession: displaying varying degrees of flesh, both on- and off-stage.

Fully or part-clothed, those "sartorial nightmares" to which Robert Marlow had earlier alluded were to plague Depeche Mode for some time to come. "They definitely had an image problem," Daniel Miller agreed. "Dave had a sense of what he thought they should look like – he was the fashion student. A lot of his mates were fashion designers – part of the London scene. They did have this early New Romantic look, but they didn't believe it or live it; it was just a passing fad more than anything else."

As the most image-conscious among the band, Gahan was keen to keep the style-fixated Futurist/New Romantic scene at a distance: "We have moved away from it; we don't want to become over-identified with a posing movement. We toned down and changed our earlier look. We're going for a stylish and smart Fifties image with drape trousers, high waist-coats and bow ties – a sort of spiv 'Flash Harry' look."

Daniel Miller: "Everybody regrets what they wore when they were 18. There was this other [Depeche Mode] look around that time which was this real leather, S&M camp look, which was very much to do with the region. There was a whole gang of people from Southend [who dressed up like that]. I remember going to Crocs, which was their local venue in Rayleigh in Essex, up the road from Basildon. Before I met Depeche

Mode, Fad Gadget played there, and I couldn't believe it: there were all these suburban kids completely dressed up, and mixed in was a whole gang of Southend lads – not horrible lads – all dressed in leather. Only after I met Depeche Mode did it all fit together . . . I certainly wouldn't dream of telling anyone what to wear."

Depeche Mode resurrected this decidedly dodgy leather look when filming the promotional video to accompany 'Just Can't Get Enough'. For Vince Clarke, this was a disconcerting process: "For a start, in those days you didn't make a video until the song was in the charts – at least Top 10, because it wasn't worth the money. And there wasn't that many places to play a video, anyway; there weren't that many shows."

Shot on a comparative shoestring by director Clive Richardson, the promo remains charmingly simplistic in its execution. The freshly coiffured, Aviator shades-wearing Dave Gahan is seen to pull off a perfect rendition of his self-dubbed "daft dance", the effect of which he had revealed to *NME*'s Paul Morley: "Did you see [British morning TV show] *Razmatazz* yesterday? We were on it and all these little girls in the background were trying to imitate me – copying me, weren't they? I didn't know when we were doing it, but they were there doing exactly the same dance – like you go through loads of times before the real performance, and the girls must have perfected it towards the end."

The leather, biker-capped Vince Clarke and Andy Fletcher were caught "hipping and hopping" around their synthesisers "like puppets with broken strings," to quote Morley.

Andy Fletcher: "It used to be the main criticism of us, that we didn't move enough. We've relaxed a bit now, and we dance, but we used to be really young."

Martin Gore: "We used to be really young?! It was only six months ago!"

Depeche Mode's varied fan base pushed 'Just Can't Get Enough' to number eight in the UK Singles Chart before September's end. Accompanying the single was an extended 'Schizo Mix' 12″ version weighing in at almost seven minutes, complete with rhythmic interludes and a drawn-out, hypnotic instrumental outro.

The lyrics to 'Just Can't Get Enough' were on the repetitive side, yet this time Vince's words apparently had a meaning, albeit a hidden one. According to Deb Mann, the song is about Vince's infatuation from afar with a particularly striking young lady who was often seen around

Basildon at the time – not that the reserved songwriter ever made his feelings known to the girl in question.

By way of a taster for the forthcoming album, in September 1981, *Flexipop!* magazine featured an "exclusive" Depeche Mode track – a contagious upbeat synth pop number paradoxically titled 'Sometimes I Wish I Was Dead' – on its cover-mounted flexidisc. The song's nursery rhyme lyrics make no mention of the title, whose morbidity may have been down to the fact that Vince Clarke had to complete the recording virtually solo?*

With the album ready for release, more live work beckoned throughout the summer of 1981 and beyond. Before setting off on a short, four-date European jaunt – respectively taking in Hamburg's Markthalle, Amsterdam's Paradiso, Disco Rouge in Brussels and Bains Douche in Paris on September 25, 26, 28 and 29 – Depeche Mode played two free UK shows.

The first was at Christ's School in Richmond, Surrey, the only occasion since their four-piece Basildon début that the band had played an educational establishment. The music weeklies picked up on this unlikely choice of venue: "Do you want Depeche Mode to play at your next school concert?" wrote Brian Harrigan. "All you've got to do is emulate the example of Paul Warburton, teacher at Christ's School in Richmond, whose sister knows one of the band. The Mode played at the school's last charity function for nothing, to raise money for the school fund: £500 in all."

Even more admirable was the second show – a return visit to The Venue, performing what was billed as "A special benefit for Amnesty International" on September 19. Entrance to this 5 pm, soft-drinks-only show for under-18s was a mere £2, as was its over-18s follow-up, scheduled for an 8 pm kick-off.

Andy Fletcher: "We face a dilemma because a lot of our audience are under 18 and the places we play, only older kids are allowed in. So a lot of people can't come and see us. We tried early evening shows, but it's really tiring playing twice a night."

Given the distinct lack of venues catering to their audience's swelling teenage ranks, this Venue gig ended up being the band's most widely reported outing to date. *Smash Hits* were predictably supportive. "By the

---

* While Dave Gahan made a token vocal contribution, Martin Gore and Andy Fletcher were apparently on holiday abroad.

time Depeche Mode had covered 'New Life', 'Dreaming Of Me' and the pleasing new single, 'Just Can't Get Enough', they were into their second well-deserved encore and had won over just about everybody in earshot," gushed Mark Ellen – including, it would appear on paper, one Mick Nicholls who was moved to remark, "Behind David, the synths and drum machines boil up a cauldron of rhythms, and there's not an anchored ankle in the house. This goes on for some time, through a lot of new material. Most of the songs stick to an unswervingly high standard, as strong as the hits and then some. Three encores including a class Everly's 'Price Of Love' and the crowd still feel short-changed. Depeche Mode have arrived and without the hype. Their eventual album will shoot straight into the Top 10. Meanwhile, they'll grow bigger and better, even if those freshly scrubbed faces do acquire a few lines in the process. Just can't get enough? You said it, boy."

Contrast and compare with the following venomous offering from *Sounds'* Dave McCullough, headlined *Depressed Mode*: "Depeche Mode are terribly self-conscious. Individually because they look like nanas and musically because the synths and the attempted pop-swing don't ever gell. 'New Life' probably comes closest. They gyrate and draw attention to each other's defects. It's a very cold partnership for a very frosted proposition . . . all must be crushed, sooner or later. Probably in Dep Mode's case, sooner."

Barney Hoskyns, meanwhile, attempted to rationalise Depeche Mode's appeal: "At The Venue, the group came across very professionally as a kind of English working-pop Kraftwerk, and were received with nothing short of rapture. A companion made the observation that one doesn't so much dance to Depeche Mode as respond/flinch to the stimulus of their machines."

Printed opinions apart, on the surface, all was apparently going well in Depeche Mode's continuing ascension. Or was it? Tellingly, when Fletcher, Gahan and Gore, plus the intimate Depeche Mode entourage, headed back to Britain following the band's Parisian show of September 29, Vince Clarke and girlfriend Deb Danahay stayed behind. With the picturesque French capital putting some much-needed distance between Vince and the realities of fame back home, the songwriter confronted his demons and came to a momentous decision: he was going to cut off what he saw as the source of his discomfort by leaving Depeche Mode.

"That was when I was pissed off," Clarke confirmed. "I was just being miserable and didn't want to be in the group anymore."

93

Deb Mann: "He's a very complex character, is Vince – a very complex man. He was like that with me as well – we were always on, then off. He's just that sort of person. I don't know whether he starts feeling a bit claustrophobic with people – people make him claustrophobic and he feels he's got to have a break for a while. He was very impulsive."

Clarke's timing was impeccable. The release date of Depeche Mode's eagerly awaited début album was looming, and numerous venues had been booked in anticipation of the band's first proper UK tour.

Upon returning to the UK, Clarke commendably took it upon himself to visit the respective homes of each member to individually inform them of his intention to leave Depeche Mode. Also admirable was his decision not to totally leave them in the lurch, agreeing to first complete the all-important tour to promote the album (or, as his colleagues would unkindly speculate following his eventual departure, to increase his *own* publishing royalties).

Clarke later put his actions into context. "Everybody was down by then – everybody was kind of depressed. I had been thinking about it [leaving Depeche Mode] for a long time. I had been sulky, like I always used to be as a child, because that was the way I always used to handle things – by sulking, if I didn't get my own way. It was generally not very pleasant, you know?"

It was sensibly decided that any formal press announcement should be postponed until after the tour's planned completion date of November 16, 1981, by which time copies of *Speak & Spell* would be in the shops.

Back in January 1981 *Sounds'* Betty Page had voiced concern about Depeche Mode being criticised for using drum machines as opposed to a live drummer. Dave Gahan had promptly countered: "I don't think it'll happen now. The tapes we've got now sound like real drums anyway. I know Orchestral Manoeuvres were put down for using a drum machine on-stage, but the worst thing they ever did was to get a drummer. It was really bad after that. We don't need one anyway – it's just another person to pay!"

But relying on tapes had its downside. "I remember one show we did where the tape broke midway through the set," Gahan recalled. "I was frantically trying to mend the tape so we could start the next song. Luckily I managed it in the nick of time and although I must have looked a bit hot and bothered, nobody in the audience seemed to notice."

In a 1982 interview with *One..Two..Testing*, Andy Fletcher confirmed what was on that notorious backing tape: "A hard sequencer line to play, some percussion or something you can only get the sound for in the studio, not live. A lot of people think everything is on the tape, [and] we're just singing or miming, but that's not true. Ever since we started as a band our aim wasn't to come across as good musicians."

According to Fletcher, it was the noise restrictions set by Vince Clarke's mother that had shaped the group's drum machine-driven, three-way synth line-up: "When we started rehearsing, using a drummer was impractical because of the noise and lack of room. So we used various drum machines, which were all bad! The first one was like one of those they put on organs. It had rumba and samba, and rock/waltz. All the drum machines we tried have [had] their limitations, but now we pre-record all the drum rhythms and play them at gigs. We don't use any machines at all now."

Dave Gahan: "We tried computerising them [the drum sounds] but that didn't work. So now we use our own tapes."

If the main photograph – possibly taken during one of the group's several *Top Of The Pops* performances throughout 1981 – accompanying *Sounds'* two-page Depeche Mode spread is anything to go by, Gahan could well have been referring to the Movement drum computer (partly visible in the background).*

Later, when talking to *One..Two..Testing*, it became apparent that the subject of Gahan's valiant attempt at techno-talk was indeed the Movement drum computer. "The bloke who was doing the [Movement drum computer] programming for us took the ARP [2600 synthesiser] bass drum sound and said he could get the Movement to sound exactly like it. But when it came back it wasn't like it at all. We stick to the 'famous [Daniel] Miller fat bass drum'. It's got real thump to it, a real bottom end, much better than all the drum machines."

The subject of drums remained something of a thorny issue with Depeche Mode.

Andy Fletcher: "We are still trying to find a drum machine to connect

---

* The Movement was an early, German-built, digital drum machine, along the lines of Linn's more popular LM-1 – which featured digitised recordings of real drum sounds – but with the added benefit of an accompanying VDU (Visual Display Unit) to ease the tedious programming process. This could well have been the same device to which Vince Clarke made his tongue-in-cheek *Space Invaders* comment re: Kraftwerk's *Computer World* stage setting.

up with, and Vince is into it as well. He's making a collection of synths. It's an expensive hobby." Perhaps Andy was subliminally letting slip that the errant Clarke was already making plans for some kind of musical life beyond Depeche Mode?

Whatever the future might or might not have had in store for Depeche Mode, the clear implication of Martin Gore's November '81 conversation with *Sounds* was that synthesisers were to continue to feature prominently. At one point Gore quoted Daniel Miller as saying, "If you have really good ideas in your head, you have to be a good musician to get them out. But a synthesiser helps a lot! Rock musicians say you can't express yourself with a synthesiser. Soulless is the word. But what is there in whacking a guitar? Every heavy metal riff is near the same anyway."

Andy Fletcher: "We've got nothing against guitars, and we have played them in the past. We may experiment with guitars one day, but it's so much easier with a synthesiser. There is a lot of good guitar music around but you have to be pretty good to use the guitar."

In *Jackie*, Dave Gahan was eager to talk about the forthcoming album: "That's the test of a new band. If the first album sells, you're on your way. We think it will, though, because nowadays people want music to dance to, and that's what we aim to give them."

Yet later, when quizzed by *Sounds* as to whether 'Just Can't Get Enough' was wholly representative of what to expect, the singer adjusted his answer accordingly: "It's much more varied, as you can hear on the album. If they played a track on the radio, you wouldn't be able to say, 'Oh, that's Depeche Mode.'"

As predicted, when *Speak & Spell* (possibly titled in an unknowing nod to Kraftwerk's *Computer World* album) was finally released on October 29, 1981, not a guitar was to be heard. That same week, Paul Morley chose to simultaneously review OMD's latest long-player, *Architecture & Morality*. The Liverpudlians' album failed to impress with what Morley termed "guiltless hymns to dying glory, yearnings for order, rock steady studies of immensity and the sense of sacredness and in time and space."

He was far more charitable towards *Speak & Spell*: "Where Orchestral Manoeuvres are sanctimonious and ultimately insubstantial, Depeche Mode are quaint, obtrusive and uplifting . . . Depeche Mode's guitarless bubbly-fun pop is cohesive and supple: insinuating, well highlighted, untainted by any serious thoughts of historical conditions or examinations of charisma . . . I have enough trust in the wit and wile of the group to suggest that they will go the ways of Fad Gadget, mentor [Daniel] Miller, [ex-Tangerine Dream] Peter Baumann – ironists, absurdists, parodists – rather than transform into religious maniacs."

On the face of it, some of Vince Clarke's songs – 'New Life' included – could be described as meaningless, never mind lightweight.

On the other hand, according to Deb Mann, at least two of Clarke's contributions to *Speak & Spell* had some significance. 'Puppets' supposedly stemmed from Vince's drug dabbling. Similarly, with its infectiously repetitive, heavily harmonised Fifties-style chorus, 'What's Your Name?' could be construed as a dig at Rick Sky's *Daily Mirror* distortion. Beneath those beautifully crafted vocal arrangements, Vince Clarke was still smarting . . .

Andy Fletcher: "That was supposed to be taking the mickey out of the worshipping routine – a real poppy tune, one of the last Vince [Clarke] wrote for the band. By then he was very disillusioned with the [pop] routine and being public property."

Adding to the album's positive press reaction, one 'Sunie' gave *Speak & Spell* a maximum 'five-star' rating: "A good listen to their first LP reveals smartness beneath the simplicity. The whole thing opens with 'New Life' and closes with 'Just Can't Get Enough', a very tidy device. In between are eight sparkling songs and one instrumental, much to admire and little to disappoint . . . 'What's Your Name?' fairly jumps off the vinyl to proclaim itself 'The Next Single'. Cheeky bubblegum backing vocals give added zest to the insanely catchy chorus: it's a sure-fire monster hit . . . 'Photographic' – like Numan at his best, but better; all the sinister phrases, both lyrical and musical, but with a rapid, danceable beat instead of the solemnity that Gazza always laid on with a sequinned trowel."

With a clutch of positive reviews ensuring album sales, the band were about to embark on a nationwide tour in the company of a resolutely unhappy songwriter about to jump ship.

8

See You, Vince!

"It's not real, is it? It's an illusion. How can you miss an illusion? It was all a bit of a joke, really – just a joke. It is funny, if you think about it."

– Vince Clarke, 1982

"I did feel guilty for a while, but then they wrote 'See You', and that did well. So they were off and running without me, so it wasn't a problem."

– Vince Clarke, 2001

Blissfully unaware of Vince Clarke's impending departure, *Sounds* caught up with the band during rehearsals for their so-called Speak & Spell Tour in November 1981. As might have been expected by those few in the know, Clarke was absent during the interview, though, ironically the article opened with a reminiscence of Rose Martin calling the shots: " 'Stop that clacking!' Depeche Mode couldn't win. Even when they plugged headphones into their synthesisers, Vince Clarke's mum complained about the noise – of clacking keys. But those eerie, silent rehearsals in a draughty Essex garage have brought them exciting rewards."

The 14-date Speak & Spell Tour was set to take the band the length and breadth of the country, from Edinburgh's Coasters nightclub to Brighton's Top Rank. For Dave Gahan, the prospect of leaving behind small club and pub venues once and for all was a welcome one. "When we used to support, we got treated so bad. Especially at certain places in London, which I won't mention, by groups I won't mention. They tread all over you, and to the PA blokes, you're nothing. It's always 'Where's the support?' They won't even mention your name. Now we are the headliners – they love us. We're playing two nights at the Lyceum – so *we* are the big band now!"

Vince Clarke personally picked the support act – Blancmange – on

Depeche Mode's behalf. The synth duo had been featured on the *Some Bizzare Album* earlier in 1981, and, accompanied by Deb Danahay, Clarke went to see Neil Arthur and Stephen Luscombe in action, possibly at The Venue on September 21. Also performing on that particular bill was Naked Lunch, themselves previously part of Stevo's Futurist compilation. It's possible that the departing Depeche man had an ulterior motive for picking Blancmange; being keen to see how a streamlined synth partnership would hold up. With this in mind, one could speculate that Vince could have been plotting, or at least pondering, his options?

Meanwhile, Dave Gahan was still chewing over Depeche Mode's lacking of a stage show. "I'd like to sit down and design a show," he told *Sounds* a week or so before the tour began, "but none of us have had time to think about it. Maybe we'd like to have a lightshow . . ."

This was hardly the time to implement any such costly changes, with Vince Clarke further distancing himself from his erstwhile bandmates. Within months of completing the tour, Gahan remarked that Clarke "just sat in the front of the van and didn't talk; he only spoke when he was spoken to."

Yet Clarke remains adamant that this road moodiness affected all the group: "Everything happened for us very, very quickly. We *all* had *massive* egos by that time, and sitting in the van was intolerable, really – for all of us. We were all intolerable to each other – no patience. I mean, we were pretty young, and it just went to our heads."

When Depeche Mode took to the stage at Newcastle University on October 31, 1981, their performance setting was familiarly minimalist. Photographs from the tour show Vince Clarke and Martin Gore assuming their standard side by side standing positions, with keyboards and backing vocal microphones prominent. While Clarke brought along his recently acquired Roland Jupiter-4 polysynth, now ably supported on an adaptable X-stand, Gore stuck with his trusted £200 Yamaha CS5 monosynth.*

Andy Fletcher plumped for The Source, an expensive £945 dual-VCO programmable analogue monosynth with 16 memories, and the distinction of being the first to feature digital parameter access control instead of

---

* According to one source, Gore had blown a sizeable chunk of his band money on an open-topped beach buggy car, but was kind enough to treat his grateful parents to a new washing machine.

the usual knobs and sliders. The specialist musical equipment press soon picked up on the instrument's distinctive colour scheme of brushed chrome into which was set various coloured dayglo membrane touch switches – one went as far as to unkindly compare The Source to a ceramic hob! When asked about the Moog's supposed saving grace, the normally obliging bass synth player seemed at a loss for words: "Er . . . the colours. No, I do like the sounds. Moogs are great for bass lines. I used to use a Prodigy and I still carry that around as a back-up."

During the Speak & Spell Tour, there was an aesthetic reason behind the close proximity of Clarke and Gore on-stage – namely their similar respective heights of 5′ 6″ and 5′ 8″. Whereas, at 6′ 3″, the comparatively lofty Fletcher stood off to stage left.

Behind the three synthesiser players and the group's backing tape machine placed centre stage, the sparsely filled stages were usually complemented by the non-intrusive presence of a plain, dark curtained backdrop. Thanks to a six-Kilowatt (6,000W) PA system hired from Showtec, the band were able to hear themselves over their enthusiastic audiences.

Depeche Mode received a hero's welcome upon their return to their hometown; playing to an 850-strong capacity crowd at Raquel's nightclub on November 10, 1981. Basildon's *Evening Echo* saw fit to devote an entire page to the exciting homecoming spectacle and the accompanying photos show beefy bodyguards bracing the crash barrier protecting the band from fanatical fans. As local reporter Don Stewart described: "It is around 10 o'clock at night when the support bands have done their bit and Depeche Mode make their appearance. There is a release of restrained hysteria as the audience of mainly young girls shriek a welcome. A few years ago their shrieks would have drowned the musicians – but not anymore. Those amps are too powerful. They crush screams and the beat hits the body like powerful punches. Hundreds crush against the barriers and the strongmen attendants of the disco make themselves [into] human props to hold back the barriers from the stage. Six months ago Depeche Mode were good. Now they are very good, their professionalism is complete."

In addition to Blancmange, special guests Film Noir – fronted by none other than Rob Allen – shared Raquel's cramped stage with Depeche Mode that night.

Robert Marlow: "It was quite funny, because Vince said to just ring up this promoter, who was a real cowboy of a fellow, and he said, 'They've already got Blancmange supporting them.' I said, 'But Vince said we can play,' and he said, 'Well, you can play, but you won't get any money for it.' In the end, Vince gave me the money – 50 quid, it was. But that wasn't important; he'd asked us to play, so we went on before Blancmange, and then it was Depeche Mode.

"It was nice for me. I really enjoyed supporting them. I played guitar and we had a synthesiser player; Perry [Bamonte] was playing bass, and we had a tiny [Boss DR-55] 'Dr Rhythm' drum machine – one of the programmable ones. It was good; we went down well. Blancmange were excellent – I'd never seen them before; they were really, really good, and they were nice guys as well. The Modes were themselves, but Vince was quite withdrawn and not very happy."

Keeping up appearances of all being well within Depeche Mode for 10 consecutive shows was obviously taking its toll on Vince Clarke's increasingly fragile state of mind. Marlow attests that Clarke wasn't feeling particularly well that night, an unfortunate fact that only served to heighten his sense of discomfort. "It was quite funny. Vince had a dose of diarrhoea! They'd been on tour up and down the country for a while, and so I think he was happy to be home. But I remember going around to his flat during the day for a chat and he said, 'It's alright; I've been dosing myself up with syrup of figs.' Silly arse."

While back in Basildon, Clarke temporarily suspended his policy of not talking to the press. However, his few comments to the *Evening Echo* were far from uplifting in their limited scope. Don Stewart wrote: "Vince, 20 [*sic*], said that as far as he was concerned success meant that they [Depeche Mode] worked harder and he smoked more cigarettes. How was life, pop star-style, with a wardrobe full of expensive clothes, cars, high living? 'I bought myself a new pair of leather boots in Edinburgh,' he said. 'They cost me £10.'"

Stewart conveyed some sense of the logistics of taking Depeche Mode's first headlining tour to the British masses: "The Depeche Mode circus moves around the country in three vehicles carrying a tour crew and 15 musicians. Instruments and amplifiers are packed into an HGV [Heavy Goods Vehicle]; a car with five technicians follows it. Then comes the minibus with the Basildon four, two musicians of the support band, Blancmange, the tour manager [Don Botting] and the fiancées of Dave and Martin, respectively Jo Fox, 19, and Anne Swindell, 18, of Basildon. The girls work on the promotional side of the tour, dealing with requests from fans and selling T-shirts."

Dave Gahan: "It's pretty hard for them. They see girls coming up to us all the time after gigs. Jo used to feel very uncomfortable with the rest of the band too – as if she was in the way. We thought it might split us up and we decided we had to do something about it."*

For that local touch, the *Evening Echo* pictured Martin Gore drinking tea with his proud mum, Pamela, at their Shepeshall home. "Fame and fortune, what's that?" he said. "We're not famous . . . not really famous. And we have not made a lot of money."

Bearing in mind that *Speak & Spell* purportedly had advance orders totalling 80,000, Gore's financial standing was set to alter significantly.

Melody Maker's Paul Colbert spent three days on the road with Depeche Mode throughout November 1981. An initial observation focused on the tour minibus, crammed with suitcases and stage clothes designed by a Kensington acquaintance – probably of Dave Gahan's.

Reference was made to Vince Clarke's polite refusal to talk shop: with an hour to kill before sound-checking at the Birmingham Locarno on November 4, 1981, ". . . the band and hack settle down for an interview – or at least three-quarters of the band do. Vince feels he got a rough deal at the pen of a Fleet Street journalist and is presently off the press."

Vince Clarke: "I'm not sure why I stopped doing interviews. I think I got fed up with what everyone else was saying. Everybody had the right to put their oar in, but I suppose I got jealous of everybody else putting their oar in."

It's just as well that Clarke wasn't in the line of fire for Colbert's question – was it still fun touring the UK circuit?

Dave Gahan: "We still have a laugh, but it's not as much fun. It used to be a thrill just to play; you were so nervous before a gig you were nearly sick. Perhaps it's because you get used to it and it seems easier, or maybe it's that when we started we were all doing something else during the daytime and worrying about the weekend gig. It's not that it's becoming a job – I wouldn't put it that far – but on tour you're doing the same things every day."

Colbert described the ensuing pandemonium when an erratic power supply played havoc with Clarke's Roland Jupiter-4, ultimately paying

* Jo gave up her job as a nurse to assist Deb Danahay with running the fan club and helping Anne Swindell – who had just left school – with the merchandising on tour. Predictably, Deb stayed at home for the tour's duration.

tribute to the disillusioned songwriter's professionalism: "His newest synthesiser has the electrical equivalent of a nervous breakdown – every fourth note is going haywire. 'Hmm . . . different,' is the sternest curse he can conjure before borrowing one of Blancmange's instruments and unpacking an unfamiliar reserve keyboard of his own. All that and he still succeeds in getting through the set without dropping a duffer. That takes some doing."

By now Depeche Mode had finely honed their live set. Out went the majority of obscure early compositions in favour of mainly *Speak & Spell* tracks, plus the obligatory hit singles: 'Any Second Now', 'Photographic', 'Nodisco', 'New Life', 'Puppets', 'Ice Machine', 'Big Muff', 'I Sometimes Wish I Was Dead', 'Tora! Tora! Tora!', 'Just Can't Get Enough', 'Boys Say Go!' and 'What's Your Name?' Encores included 'Television Set', 'Dreaming Of Me', and either The Everly Brothers' 'The Price Of Love' or Vince Clarke's long since forgotten 'Addiction'.

Andy Fletcher: "I think we've become more professional. We used to be stilted in front of an audience, now if there's a mistake you look at the person who made it and laugh." The irony of this sentiment is that Fletcher himself was, by and large, still the butt of his colleagues' jokes. When once asked why 'Fletch' was so often picked on, Dave Gahan replied, between bouts of laughter: "He just can't help it! He always does everything wrong. He damages things. We don't banish him to another room or anything, but if anything goes wrong – it's always Andy."

Of more consequence was Gahan's throwaway remark that "Vince has written a lot of material in the past, but we're all starting to write now." Given that neither Gahan or Fletcher had contributed any songs to *Speak & Spell*, *Melody Maker*'s readership had no way of verifying the veracity of Gahan's words. But perhaps this was a public hint that contingency plans were already being made in the face of Clarke's imminent departure . . .

The official announcement that Vince Clarke was quitting Depeche Mode broke on November 30, 1981 – a fortnight after the 'Speak & Spell Tour' concluded with two performances at London's Lyceum on November 15 and 16. In light of the tour's success – all but two of its 14 shows sold out – it's possible that Clarke was given some breathing space, if not necessarily an opportunity to reconsider his decision. However, his mind was made up. The line initially fed to the UK's music press was that of an amicable split; not ruling out the possibility of future collaborations with his former colleagues.

"*Au revoir*, Vince," lamented *Smash Hits*. "Vince Clark [*sic*] has left Depeche Mode. No hard feelings or anything; he's now just 'not a permanent member'. He's off so he can 'concentrate on songwriting' and intends to offer the results to anyone who wants them, including Depeche Mode."

Basildon's *Evening Echo* was quicker off the mark: "Vince Clarke, songwriter and keyboard player with chart-topping Basildon band Depeche Mode, has left the group. A spokesman for the band's record company, Mute Records, confirmed that the 21-year-old synthesiser player had left the band to concentrate on his songwriting. 'It was an amicable split and Vince is going to continue to write some material for the band, which is carrying on without him.' The band had no plans to replace Vince with a new full-time member, but would probably take on an extra player for live work. In the past year Vince's songs helped Depeche Mode to rise from obscurity to the Top 10 with two hit singles, 'New Life' and 'Just Can't Get Enough', both written by the former Laindon Comprehensive pupil."

Another locally printed source strongly denied rumours that Andy Fletcher was also quitting Depeche Mode, claiming reports of a "split-up of the New Town band will break hearts among the group's thousands of fans who gave them a heroes' welcome when they appeared at Raquel's the other week."

Although unfounded, Robert Marlow, for one, was not entirely taken aback by such a rumour: "If I think back to those days, Fletch really had his future mapped out: he would go and progress through the bank or insurance company, or wherever it was he worked, get married and settle down."

Melody Maker's Paul Colbert, fresh from being on tour with the band, had marginally more insight: "Depeche Mode are now a three-piece – keyboard player and main songwriter Vince Clarke has left. He'll continue providing material for the band, but won't be touring or recording. Tensions have been building in Depeche Mode for some months. Vince was reportedly unhappy about the touring aspect of their work and has quit to concentrate on songwriting. The three remaining members, David Gahan, Andy Fletcher and Martin Gore, are looking for a replacement – not necessarily a permanent one – and recording a new single for release in January."

All things considered it was difficult to predict with any degree of certainty just how things would pan out for Depeche Mode *sans* Vince Clarke. Like

Pink Floyd and Genesis before them, the group had lost their key song-writer at a crucial juncture, and like those rock behemoths, their future initially didn't look promising. At the same time, even though Clarke's talent had unquestionably blossomed during those successful, albeit uncomfortable, months spent with Depeche Mode, commercial and critical reaction to his future endeavours was far from assured.

Robert Marlow: "I had to say to Vince, 'Fucking hell; you're really brave! This is not the sort of rational thing that most people would do right now.' Having that kind of confidence in your own ability to say, 'Bollocks! This is not what I want' – I mean, who would do that? To have two or three Top 10 hit records, or whatever, then say, 'Right, I'm going; I don't want this anymore,' was really brave."

December 3, 1981 marked Clarke's final commitment with Depeche Mode – a one-off gig in Chichester filmed for broadcast by TVS. "I did loads of speed and then I drove home" was Clarke's pithy recollection.

When questioned about the immediate aftermath of leaving the band he'd founded barely two years previously, Clarke admitted: "I felt guilty. I remember I said to Depeche that if they were interested I would write for them. I knew I'd left them in the lurch. I think Fletcher felt it worse than anyone else. He was afraid, because I'd been writing the songs. But then they slagged me off immediately afterwards anyway. They were quite bitter, but justifiably so."

An oddly contrasting view came from Andy Fletcher: "I've known Vince since the age of five; I mean, he's been one of my best friends. It was like, 'I'm leaving.' 'Oh, OK; fair enough.' It wasn't a big thing. And Vince said, 'I'm going to leave, but I'm going to do the tour and everything.' It was very amicable – 'I'm going to continue to write songs for you,' and things like that. It was all very nice. We should have theoretically been really worried, but we weren't." He told a similar story to *Look In*: "It put us out on a limb really, but luckily we thought Vince was going to leave a few months before he did so we'd been planning, sort of thing."

So *why* did Vince Clarke choose to walk from the band he'd worked so hard at making a success, at the precise moment it looked like they were about to break on a major scale?

"There's a bit of a block between us . . . It's a Him and Us situation," the three remaining Depeche Mode members told *Smash Hits'* Mark Ellen. Clarke was interviewed separately for the same feature: "I never expected the band to become this successful. I didn't feel happy, or contented, or fulfilled. All the things that had come with success had suddenly become more important than the music. We used to get letters from fans saying: 'I really like your songs'; then we got letters saying: 'Where do you buy your trousers from?' Where do you go from there? There was never enough time to do *anything* – not with all the interviews and photo sessions."

Ellen was obviously not swayed by Clarke's train of thought: "The obvious reaction to all this would seem to be: what did he expect?" Clarke countered that he wanted "more control" and wanted to "keep playing smaller venues – the kind of things The Police were always rabbiting on about till they found they could fill Wembley Arena three nights in a row."

"It lost its enthusiasm," Clarke told Paul Colbert. "It was turning into a factory production line and that was worrying me. The techniques were improving to an extent – the way we were playing, but even then I found there were things in the way, preventing us from experimenting. We were so busy; there was something going on every day and no time to play around."

In a more candid conversation, Clarke admitted: "Overall, I could say it was just the fact that probably I felt I was the person doing most of the work, and was the most committed. And I probably felt I could do it all on my own, so it was total ego on my part. That's an honest answer."

A contemporary statement from Andy Fletcher lent some credence to this: "Vince always wanted to do a lot in the studio and the rest of us would feel restricted. If we had an idea, we'd be frightened to say anything."

Colbert assessed both sides of the coin: "Painting Vince as a victim of success is not only daubing him with a cliché, but hammering a cruel spike into the hearts of thousands of unemployed fans who'd give a year's benefit to be able to suffer so badly. No, he's hardly tortured – and he's the first to admit it. But for someone who's heart lies in tinkering with synthesisers and writing songs, the spaceless diary of Depeche Mode pulled him out of an ambition and into a job."

Vince Clarke: "Looking back at it, it's nothing; it's no real loss. It's given them a chance to develop their own ideas and let me do what I want. Martin now has a good opportunity to explore his own songs and put them into practice – they're better than mine anyway. It's just that before he never bothered to do it . . . he's always had the ability . . ."

By early 1982, the two parties would not be on quite so friendly terms.

In the March issue of *New Sounds, New Styles* magazine, Martin Gore sniped: "We don't have any contact with him now except through other people. He may be writing for us; we don't know. We have to treat him as 'another songwriter' now."

"I'm sad because our relationship has suffered – that's the thing I'm most sad about," Clarke lamented to Colbert. "Our split has been amiable . . . up to a point. I've only seen them briefly since the Christmas *Top Of The Pops*. I just hope the whole incident will be forgotten. No one's lost anything, but I suppose that's hard to understand when it's actually happening.

Midway through 1982, Dave Gahan was still trying to make sense of Clarke's actions. "He didn't like touring or the way Depeche Mode were becoming public property. He just wanted to do things on his own, but he could have done that anyway, that's what I don't understand. He could have done something and still been in Depeche Mode."

As it turned out, contrary to what had previously been mooted, Vince Clarke would *not* be contributing songs to Depeche Mode – at all. "But when would he [Vince] have had the time?" Martin Gore reasoned from a sympathetic standpoint. "He wouldn't have had any time this year (1982) to do anything."

Twenty years on, the Vince Clarke scenario is still a touchy subject within Depeche Mode circles. When asked in 2001 whether Clarke's exit was a blessing in disguise or a setback, Daniel Miller diplomatically answered: "I don't think it was either, really. Martin was always a strong songwriter – he wrote two songs on the first album, but it was very much Vince's group, in a sense. He wrote the majority of the songs; he organised most things – it was his vision, I think. He was more driven; the others were kind of 'Well, you know, let's have a go.' Fletch and Martin were in day jobs; Dave was at college – Dave was quite driven, but didn't really have a direction, particularly. Vince was *very* driven, and he pushed things along a lot. But then, for whatever reasons, he decided he wanted to move on."

Gary Smith: "He definitely didn't want fame. It frightened him, I think. It's not what he's about. For example, he'd never had a car in all the years we were growing up – he never had money to waste on anything, and, when he actually had the opportunity to go out and buy a car, he said he'd really like to go and buy a convertible Rolls-Royce or something, but people would look at him. So then I think he said he'd rather have something ordinary, like a Ford Escort. I think he wanted success; I think he wanted to be known in the industry, but not just be known for being a pop star."

Robert Marlow: "Vince is a very private person. And at that particular time he was still living in Basildon. But I knew things were wrong when we [Film Noir] played that gig with them at Raquel's on the Speak & Spell Tour – he wasn't happy. Part of the reason was that he didn't like playing gigs. I said to him, 'Well, you've chosen the wrong profession, then, haven't you?' Because if you're a pop star, you have to record the product, then go out and play it. And he said, 'Yeah, but I don't like doing that.'

"Little things gypped him – like when he would take them up to London in his car, because he was the only one who drove, and no one would give him any petrol money. Now, to you and I, that probably seems trivial, but in those days they weren't banking any major money or anything. For a while, the other guys still had their jobs, and he was probably thinking, 'Hold on, I haven't got a job.' I also think that he felt they weren't interested in reinvesting in the group – he was the one who went out and bought the new [Roland] MC-4 MicroComposer, for example.* We're not talking about huge amounts of money, because they didn't have huge amounts of money back then – they had an independent deal, so obviously they didn't get an advance; it was all royalty-based, though they were doing fairly well out of it. And Vince just thought, 'Well, surely you could give me a fiver for petrol!'

"I think he felt strongly about the others being happy to sort of drift along, which I can perfectly understand, whereas he was more like, 'Come on! Let's build on this. We can't just rest on our laurels here.' He was learning things all the time – he became firm friends with Eric Radcliffe back then, and Eric was teaching him a hell of a lot about recording."

But, however close he might have felt to Vince Clarke, even Marlow was forced to admit that those apparently insightful observations were pure speculation on his part: "Vince never actually took me under his wing and said, 'Right, this is what's happening.' And still to this day, his left hand doesn't know what his right hand is doing! He's very . . . secretive is the only word I can think of."

Secretive indeed . . . "The impression he likes to give is that no one knows him," Andy Fletcher told *New Sounds, New Styles*, to which Dave Gahan added: "We thought we knew him, but we discovered we didn't."

Not long after his Depeche departure, Clarke claimed: "I've never been

* A then state-of-the-art, 11,500 note-capacity, microprocessor-controlled four-channel step-sequencer capable of simultaneously controlling four synthesisers.

as friendly with the others as they were with each other – apart from Fletcher, who I grew up with."

Like Gary Smith and Robert Marlow, Fletcher's latter-day assessment of Clarke, tallies to a certain extent: "He was really ambitious, and we weren't particularly ambitious; it was more like a hobby for us – [we were] just enjoying what we were doing. In the end, I think Vince didn't really like the fact that when the pressure started to bite, we had voices – we started to raise our voices and say that we didn't particularly like some of the songs that he was writing. Also, I think Vince thought he could do it all by himself. He was always a bit of a loner, anyway – even growing up."

Martin Gore remains equally perplexed by his former colleague's complexities: "I don't really understand why [Vince Clarke left Depeche Mode]. I think he felt that he could do everything on his own and the band wasn't necessary; I think it was something like that. Maybe it was personal; maybe there were frictions – minor frictions compared to what we've put up with for the last 20 years!

"One thing that might have been a turning point was that he came along to a rehearsal with two new songs; he was teaching us how they went, and when he went out to the toilet we just looked at each other and said, 'We can't sing these; they're terrible!' And when he came back we said, 'Vince, we really don't like these.' He never said at that point, 'OK, I'm leaving'; he went, 'OK.' And then a few weeks or months later he said, 'I'm leaving.' But it must have been a big thing when you come along to your band with two new songs and they say, 'We can't sing them – they're terrible!'

"For me, Vince left at a very dodgy point. He actually told us he was leaving before the first album was even released. I think it was a sad time for us, of course; he was our mate. I think we were shell-shocked! I don't know what would have happened if he'd stayed around longer, but I think everyone's a lot happier now. For me, it was a godsend, because it brought me to the forefront as a songwriter. Had he stayed, I wouldn't have been able to write the sort of songs I've written, because it wouldn't have fitted in with Vince's style. I would have got lost somewhere in the mists of history."

9

Friend Or Foe?

"It was difficult to integrate myself, because we came from different backgrounds. I sensed there was also quite a tension there, given that Vince [Clarke] had just left at such a crucial time for the group – nobody thought that the group would be able to carry on having lost their chief songwriter."

– Alan Wilder, 2001

"When [Vince] left, the [other] three in the band and me felt very strongly about moving forward," Daniel Miller asserted. "I was kind of co-producer/collaborator; and we knew that Martin was a really strong song-writer. The rest of the band grew up because of that quite quickly; they suddenly had to take responsibility, whereas Vince had done quite a bit of that. I wouldn't call it [Vince's leaving] a blessing, but what came out of it was very strong. It certainly changed the direction of the band, musically, because Martin's songs are very different to Vince's, but, musically, we still had this very hardcore, purist electronic approach, which the band were very, very keen to keep going. We set ourselves parameters, because we didn't want to challenge ourselves with the sound a lot."

Martin Gore was forced into the songwriting hot seat, almost by default. "My style of writing has changed since I started writing more seriously," he told *Look In*. "In a way it's less poppy."

Gore imparted a little more information about his developing technique to *New Sounds, New Styles*: "Vince was more interested in the flow of the words and rhymes than in the meaning. I care a lot about what I'm saying. If I had a good tune and I didn't like the lyrics, I'd drop the song. The middle-eight [of 'See You'] goes: 'Well I know five years is a long time and that times change/ But I think that you'll find people are basically the same.' It's good – serious, but funny. I like it because those words aren't used much in songs. It's just the things people say. I can't tell the story behind it. I wrote it when I was 18."

Having seemingly survived the potentially disastrous departure of Clarke, Andy Fletcher couldn't resist a dig: "Words were never Vince's strongpoint. As a matter of fact, we were sometimes quite *embarrassed* by his stuff! We didn't understand a lot of his songs. He'd never tell us what they were about!"

The unlikely forum of *Look In* exposed the flimsy nature of Fletcher's catty comments. When asked why the songwriting responsibility now seemed to fall solely on Gore, Fletcher responded defensively. "I always try. It's hard for me; I've never really written before and I'd have to come up with a song that's possibly going to go in the English Top 10 or something. It might take me years to get up to that writing ability."

In November 1981, the three-man Depeche Mode re-entered Blackwing Studios with Daniel Miller to record what would become their fourth single, Martin Gore's 'See You' – a song paradoxically dating back to his guitar-fixated Norman & The Worms days. Gore had finally purchased an expensive (approx. £3,000) new synthesiser – Wave 2 from German synth specialists Palm Productions GmbH (PPG), a pioneering eight-voice polyphonic affair on account of its wavetable-based digital/analogue hybrid design.*

Needless to say, the Wave 2 formed the backbone of the arrangement and Gore was quick to sing its praises. "It's unique," he gushed to *One.. Two.. Testing*. "There's nothing else that seems to be able to make sounds like it. They're very clean and bell-like, though it can also do good brass and choir sounds. And I find it easy to use. You get a sound using the keypad and then modify it with the other analogue controls. It can play up to eight notes at once and there's a sequencer built in . . .

"You might not believe this, but Daniel 'Anti-Rock' Miller has been encouraging me to play chords. Sometimes we go out of the studio for a while and come back into the room to find him playing chords on the PPG [Wave 2]!"

An interview with *Smash Hits* emphasised the trio's keenness to move forward. "Before we used to rely on Vince," Andy Fletcher admitted,

---

* Fellow techno pop architect Thomas Dolby described its innovative operation to *One.. Two.. Testing* in 1982: "It uses digital oscillators to generate complex waveforms, but familiar analogue filters to treat them. This is a joy to keyboard players who miss the ease and speed of their old MiniMoog or ARP when it comes to tailoring sounds. It also gives the PPG a character quite unlike any other synth I've played: crystal clear, easy to slot into the perspective of guitars and drums, and full of surprises."

"now we've got to try a lot harder. And it'll be different. Martin writes music around his words, whereas Vince used to write the tunes first and then fit the lyrics to them. After 'New Life' a lot of people thought Depeche Mode were sweet and cute and everything, and we wanted to show them we could be a lot of other things as well. On the new B-side, 'Reason To Be', we tried to sound really *mean*! Didn't work, though."*

Martin Gore: "I think everybody was better off – after we'd gone into the studio and carried on. Because obviously that was a big decision: 'The main songwriter's just left the band – what are we going to do?' To just go into the studio and make a record was a big thing, but because we were so young we didn't think we were doing anything really important or big."

'See You' – released on January 29, 1982 – featured a catchy bell-like motif, unusual clangorous tones underpinning the melodious middle-eight and Depeche Mode's then-characteristic vocal harmonies.

Vince Clarke: "I thought it was fantastic! Martin had bought a PPG [Wave 2], and there were all these sounds that you'd never heard before – I'd never heard them, anyway. They were really unique, and I thought it was fantastic. I knew the song, because it was a Norman & The Worms song."

Clarke commendably sent his former colleagues a congratulatory message, telling the press he thought 'See You' was "the best they've ever done. They've proved themselves to themselves." *NME* and *Melody Maker*'s opinions were predictably poles apart with the former's Danny Baker sniping: "Their last single was trying and now this is insipid," while the latter's Lynden Barber countered with, "Vince splits, the world gasps, Depeche fade. No? No!"

Smash Hits' Mark Ellen was, as always, supportive: "Light years ahead of the rest. Listening to this you can hardly believe that – even a year back – the mention of 'synthesised pop' conjured up images of doomy one-dimensional treks to the space-lab in even the most light-hearted of listener. 'See You' sounds warm, colourful and surprisingly durable and even has a few Beach Boys harmonies thrown in. If it doesn't make number one, I'll write and complain."

---

* In actuality, this interview must have substantially pre-dated the single's release on account of the fact that the B-side, to which Fletcher was referring, ended up as 'Now, This Is Fun' – a perfectly functional, yet workmanlike slice of synthesised pop.

While 'See You' didn't quite make that coveted top spot, it nonetheless peaked in the UK Singles Chart at number six – Depeche Mode's highest chart placing to date. The threesome were justifiably proud of this not inconsiderable achievement, not least that they had proved they could still cut it without Clarke's melodic Midas touch – with assistance from Daniel Miller, of course.

But even with their highest hit single to date, they weren't quite out of the woods yet.

Andy Fletcher: "We realise 1982's the most important year for us. We either establish ourselves or go to pot. What do I hope to achieve? A couple more hit singles in the bag and a copy of the album that doesn't jump!"

The success of the single necessitated the swift production of another promo clip to accompany its journey up the charts. In contrast to predecessor Clive Richardson's similarly rushed effort for 'Just Can't Get Enough', director Julian Temple chose a more storyboarded approach to 'See You'. In an atmospheric opening shot, the casually dressed Dave Gahan is seen on a railway platform at night, clearly looking for someone. Thereafter, the video rapidly reaches embarrassingly awkward depths of parody with Dave singing in a photo booth, holding a photo of his lost girl, later looking around a supermarket while bandmates Martin Gore and Andy Fletcher are glimpsed 'performing' keyboard parts on cash registers! As the story unfolds, Dave eventually finds his mystery girl – played by Gore's girlfriend, Anne Swindell – when purchasing a copy of 'See You' at the supermarket checkout. It was hardly eye-catching stuff.

Having reached number 10 in the UK Albums Chart soon after its release, *Speak & Spell* was still effortlessly topping its independent counterpart at the turn of the year. Farther afield, the album's sales were boosted further when, on the strength of the favourable response to its preceding singles, through Seymour Stein, Depeche Mode signed a potentially lucrative five-album deal (commencing with *Speak & Spell*) with Warners subsidiary, Sire in the United States. By signing with a major, it could be argued that, even at this early juncture, Depeche Mode were betraying their 'indie' roots.

This new arrangement undoubtedly confused matters, as evidenced during an interview with *New Sounds, New Styles*. Dave Gahan: "We still haven't signed any formal contract with Mute." "I think we did when we accepted the deal with Sire through Mute," Martin Gore reasoned, forcing Gahan to counter with: "No, we didn't. Did we?" They hadn't . . .

Ironically, that "spaceless diary" which writer Paul Colbert had pin-pointed as pulling Vince Clarke "out of an ambition and into a job" was now staring his former bandmates in the face. "Last summer, we could sort things out week to week," Martin Gore griped to *New Sounds, New Styles*. "It's horrible now to look in your diary and see that every day for the next six months is planned!"

During the summer of 1982, the group undertook numerous European television appearances to promote 'See You'. As previously predicted, Vince had been replaced, though not necessarily permanently so.

Andy Fletcher: "We put an advert in *Melody Maker* – something like 'Electronic group needs new keyboard player' – and Daniel [Miller] sort of vetted them. And the funny thing was, they had to be under 21!"

Smash Hits were among the first to file a press report of the successful applicant, together with an accompanying photograph: "Depeche Mode are a four-piece on-stage and a three-piece in the studio. That's the odd piece . . . Alan Wilder. The 22-year-old synth-player first cut his teeth with The Hitmen before being plucked from Hampstead to brave the surging throng at Crocs, Rayleigh, in the New Year. He may join up yet, say the threesome: it's just a 'trial period'."

The 'DIY' Depeche Mode Information Service was a little late in officially confirming Vince's departure and Alan Wilder's appointment because Deb Danahay had moved on after Vince made his fateful decision. Thereafter, Anne Swindell stepped in; dealing with communications from her parent's Basildon home at 10 Hawksway. Those sending a stamped, self-addressed envelope each month would receive typed sheets of the latest Depeche Mode news, plus information about exclusive merchandising.

In January 1982, Anne's first newsletter opened with the following statement: "Vince Clarke has left Depeche Mode, leaving Dave, Martin and Andy to continue as a three-piece. The reason for leaving is that he wishes to concentrate on being simply a songwriter. However, he will be replaced for live appearances." Coincidentally, the same newsletter made mention of 'See You' – if not by name: "There will be a new single out around January 16. The song, although it has been recorded, does not have a title yet. It was written by Martin and recorded by Dave, Martin and Andy."

A month later came the news of Vince's replacement: "We are pleased to announce that the fourth member of Depeche Mode has been found. The position as a keyboard player/vocalist, which was made vacant after

Vince's departure before Christmas, has been filled by 22-year-old Alan Wilder from London. Alan has played with many bands and is an experienced synthesiser player. Although his position isn't yet permanent, he will be playing with Depeche Mode during their British and European tours."

Other than being blessed with chiselled good looks tailor-made for pop stardom, further information about the new recruit was non-forthcoming for the time being. The little that Andy Fletcher could be coaxed into revealing didn't amount to much – no more, in fact, than the few words printed by the likes of *Smash Hits* based on whatever guarded press release Mute chose to issue: "At the moment he's a live session man. He just plays live for us, not in the studio, but that might change."

For Dave Gahan, evidently also unwilling to mention Wilder by name, the thinking behind this hesitant approach was simple: "I don't think it's right, really – not yet; it's just like someone jumping in after you've been together for two years. And if he came in the studio now it would be hard for him to fit in."

Alan Wilder subsequently confirmed those fears: "They were a very tight unit, somewhat self-deprecating and lacking in confidence. All the musicians I had been involved with prior to this had exuded self-belief, while enjoying little or no success. I'd never met a group like this one, and it made me wonder how they had come so far in such a short time. Then I realised how much of an influence Daniel Miller had over them. As I got to know them, it became clear that it was actually Vince Clarke and Daniel who had been the driving forces up to that point. Daniel was extremely protective of the group, and I found him a difficult person to get to know. With the others, they were friendly enough, but I must admit to feeling like an outsider. Differences in our backgrounds were never far from the surface . . ."

Wilder was referring to these class differences several years after being adopted by Depeche Mode: "Unlike the others who are from Basildon – or Bas, as they call it, I'm from Acton, West London, and was brought up in a fairly normal, middle-class environment."

Daniel Miller: "They were very Bas; they were close-knit, shall we say. All their friends were from Basildon, and Alan came from a slightly different – slightly posher, in their eyes – background. He was technically and musically very adept, and, at the beginning, slightly snobbish about the fact that everything they played was one-finger monophonic stuff. He could play everything they requested with one hand tied behind his back."

Long after Wilder's initiation into Depeche Mode, working-class Basildon roots influenced the outlook of at least one member. "I think it shapes the feelings within the group," Andy Fletcher declared with self-congratulatory overtones. "Still nearly 90 per cent of our friends are from the same background – we've kept the same friends. Lots of them – not just me – have done well in their careers. When people ask, 'Why are you still going?' it's because we came out of Basildon at 18 or 19 and didn't have anything – we grasped something, we worked at it, and we don't want to let it go!"

Differing backgrounds apart, there was more to Depeche Mode's talented newcomer than first met the eye.

Alan Charles Wilder, the youngest of Albert and Kathleen's three sons, was born in Hammersmith, West London, on June 1, 1959. By all accounts, the Wilder household was a musical one, so it was inevitable that young Alan would follow in the footsteps of brothers Stephen and Andrew in taking up the piano.

"My two elder brothers are both classically trained," says Alan. "One is an accompanist who works with singers – he's excellent; the other is teaching in Finland. They are five and seven years older, respectively, so they teased me a bit when they were bored, but I think I was too young to be really bothered."

At 11, the academically minded youngster was already ahead of his music classmates at St Clement Dane's Grammar School on Du Cane Road in London's Shepherd's Bush. Though it was but a few minutes walk from Wormwood Scrubs prison, it was light years removed from Laindon High Road and Nicholas Comprehensive in Basildon. Alan Wilder was soon learning the flute as well as the piano, becoming an enthusiastic member of his school's orchestra and brass band. He would eventually make top Grade Eight on the piano, an achievement that would profoundly affect his post-educational outlook.

Despite having passed the 11+ examination necessary to enter the long since disbanded Grammar School system, Alan didn't see himself as being scholarly in the traditional sense. "I went to St Clement Dane's Grammar in Hammersmith, a good school, but I wasn't interested in being a student," he declared. "I got three O levels in arty subjects. I liked music and languages, and I was forced to have piano lessons and do grades."

Other outside obligations were also expected of the youngest member of the Wilder family, with one in particular going some way towards

Depeche Mode's original 1981 line-up (Martin Gore, Andy Fletcher, Dave Gahan and Vince Clarke) - caught halfway between Dave Gahan's "spiv 'Flash Harry' look" and leather-clad 'bikers'. (*Peter Anderson*)

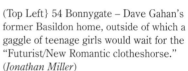

(Top Left} 54 Bonnygate – Dave Gahan's former Basildon home, outside of which a gaggle of teenage girls would wait for the "Futurist/New Romantic clotheshorse." (*Jonathan Miller*)

(Top Right}59 Mynchens – Vince Martin's (a.k.a. Clarke) former Basildon home, scene of the first Composition Of Sound garage rehearsals. Vince's mother told them to "Stop that clacking!" (*Jonathan Miller*)

(Left}101 Woolmer Green – Andy Fletcher's former home in Basildon. (*Jonathan Miller*)

Woodlands School, Takely Drive, Basildon – scene of an early Composition Of Sound rehearsal that led to Dave Gahan joining the group that would become Depeche Mode. (*Jonathan Miller*)

5th Basildon Boy's Brigade (circa-1969), whose junior section met at Janet Duke Primary School in Markhams Chase, Laindon – Vince Clarke (third row, third from right), Andy Fletcher (first row, third from left). (*Chris Sheppard*)

Nicholas Comprehensive, Leinster Road, Basildon – attended by Andy Fletcher and Martin Gore – scene of the first four-piece Composition Of Sound performance with Dave Gahan (June 14, 1980). (*Jonathan Miller*)

Self-confessed 'Numanoid' Rob 'Tube' Allen (a.k.a. Robert Marlow) and Deb Mann (née Danahay). (*Deb Mann*)

Dave Gahan and future first wife Jo Fox, 1981. "He was my best friend," said Jo, "and I adored him."(*Deb Mann*)

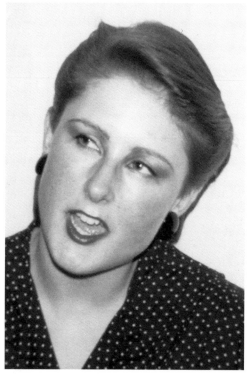

The former Deb Danahay, 1981 – one-time girlfriend of Vince Clarke, and co-founder of Depeche Mode's first fan club. (*Deb Mann*)

Norman & The Worms, circa-1979 – Martin Gore (left) and Phil Burdett (right). (*Uncredited*)

Poster created by Vince Clarke's brother, Rodney, advertising Composition Of Sound's second Gahan-fronted performance – at the Top Alex, Southend, June 21, 1980. (*Rob Andrews*)

Hot off the press, Andy 'Fletch' Fletcher and Vince Clarke display Depeche Mode's second single, 'New Life', June 1981. The record went on to sell over 500,000 copies. (*Deb Mann*)

Vince 'Harold Wilson' Clarke, 1981. (*Deb Mann*)

'Amiable' Andy Fletcher backstage at Flicks nightclub, Dartford, May 25, 1981 (*Deb Mann*)

Martin Gore displaying an early penchant for apparel removal – backstage at *Top Of The Pops,* 1981. (*Deb Mann*)

Dave Gahan backstage at Flicks nightclub, Dartford, May 25, 1981. (*Deb Mann*)

Daniel Miller, circa-1981, at the time of signing Depeche Mode to his Mute label. (*Mute*)

Eric Radcliffe, circa-1982 – one-time owner of the now-defunct Blackwing Studios where Depeche Mode recorded their first two albums and early singles. (*Deb Mann*)

Backstage at *Top Of The Pops*, 1981. Vince Clarke departed from the group at the end of the year. (*Harry Goodwin*)

As a three-piece, early 1982 (l-r: Gahan, Gore and Fletcher) (*Eric Watson*)

explaining his aversion to organised religion: "I was required to go to Baptist church every Sunday by my father until I was 16 – the perfect way to turn a teenager away from church for the rest of his life."

School soon became something of a bind, too. "During my teens I couldn't take schooling seriously – it wasn't what I needed at the time. My mind would wander. The only thing I excelled at was music, which obviously worked on a much more subconscious level, although both my brothers were – [and] are – much better musicians."

Aware of where his talents lay, from a relatively early age, Wilder claimed to have an almost serene sense of where he wanted life to take him: "Arrogant as it may sound, I always had total conviction that I would get somewhere in the music business. It's all I ever wanted to do."

His interest in highbrow classical music – a prerequisite for his ongoing piano studies – eventually wore thin. Out went Bach and Beethoven; in came a reckless rush of rock and pop – principally David Bowie and Marc Bolan, though when pressed to name the best concert he ever attended, Alan cited The Who's 1974 show at Charlton football ground.

Alan Wilder: "The reason I got involved [in music] was really because it was in the family. I was encouraged by my parents to learn the piano, which I did as a young lad, and that just evolved into an interest in popular music, as opposed to classical music which, presumably, they expected me to be interested in, or follow my brothers – my two brothers are both pianists, and I was sort of expected to follow suit. But for some reason I got interested in blues music and rock'n'roll."

In 1975, aged 16, Alan returned to St Clement Dane's to study A levels, but dropped out after attending only one term: "I left school during the sixth form and went on the dole until my parents pushed me into writing off to recording studios, the only thing I'd expressed any interest in. After being turned down 40 times, I got a job at DJM Studios in New Oxford Street."

Alan's job was as a Tape Operator, more commonly abbreviated as Tape Op, the first rung on the ladder for all recording studio employees. "I was a tea boy, really – an overworked gofer," he later told *No. 1*. Be that as it may, Wilder later recommended this same route into the recording industry. "I would get your training from real experience in a commercial studio, rather than trying to learn in a classroom. Working in the area of music entails so much more than simply twiddling knobs and knowing how to mike up a band. You'll have to start at the bottom – making the tea and being abused by producers, but you'll learn so much more than you would at any school."

Although this lowly job at DJM Studios only lasted a year, it had its advantages. Wilder was soon working on the organisation's in-house productions as well as outside artists. He even met The Rubettes! "I was great at the more musical aspects of studio work, such as tape editing, drop-ins, etc., but useless when it came to the patch bay or routing the mike lines through to the tape sends" – the more technical stuff, in other words.

All the hours spent religiously practicsing the piano to Grade Eight standard were not wasted, as the studio apprentice was often called upon to put his keyboard skills to work on various sessions. "The good thing about DJM was that when bands finished recording they'd often leave their instruments behind, so I could muck about on a keyboard or bash some drums," he reflected. "It was an ambition to be a musician, but not one I thought would come true until a band called The Dragons came in. We became friendly; I ended up joining them and moved to Bristol."

Wilder lived in Chandos Road in the Bristol suburb of Redlands, close to Dragons colleagues Huw Gower, George Smith, Nick Howell and Jo Burt. The group recorded a solitary single – 'Misbehavin'' – for DJM Records, which sank without trace. A surviving publicity shot shows the five-piece standing in a churchyard with shoulder-length hair and flared trousers – the order of the day. Wilder grimaces at the distant memory: "That was a pre-punk, soft-rock group – nothing special, but I did gigs and we made a single."

The lack of success was testing, and The Dragons inevitably went their separate ways when DJM's deal and its associated financial fringe benefits ran dry. Wilder and Dragons bassist Jo Burt headed back to London.

Alan Wilder: "After two years in Bristol, life got too lethargic, so I was glad when a friend dragged me home to join a band called Daphne & The Tenderspots. That was a restaurant-type group, playing jazz blues until it was decided that New Wave was happening. We had these terrible clothes made and wore skinny ties. We were awful, but, again, we had a deal and made a single, 'Disco Hell'."

Wilder assumed the pseudonym of 'Alan Normal' – "a necessity in the anarchic days of punk" – just in time to strike a deal with Gordon Mills' MAM label. The single bombed, and Wilder's dress sense evidently hadn't improved much either, judging by a contemporary live review: "There are all sorts of influences at work in the music, and lyrically they [Daphne & The Tenderspots] have the same cynical/lyrical outlook on modern times as Joe Jackson or mid-period Kinks. 'To Be A Star' featured an insistent keyboard riff from Zebra-crossing-jacketed Alan Normal – one of the nucleus of the band."

Other reviews made for equally disheartening reading: "Sometimes this city depresses me intensely. It certainly did last week, when Tuesday night saw Daphne & The Tenderspots playing circles to a crowd which could have fitted comfortably into the group's van."

Realising he was on another road to nowhere, Wilder jumped ship and joined Real To Real, a group he would later describe as being "white man reggae". Having signed to Red Shadow Records, Real To Real released several singles, the first, in March 1980, entitled . . . 'White Man Reggae'. *Sounds* were impressed: "It's precisely what the title suggests and very effectively executed, too. A band and record label to watch out for."

The *Huddersfield Daily Examiner* similarly saw Real To Real as being a band with a promising future when reviewing 'Mr And Mrs' a year later: "This is tight, urgent, modern rock'n'roll with lyrics that slam suburban sell-out. It comes from the LP *Tightrope Walker* and while as a single it may not find a lot of success, it bodes well for the album and for the future of a very pro band."

It was a definite case of close but no cigar. Still hungry for success, Wilder and his keyboards – which by now, as a discernible result of several record deals, included a MiniMoog monosynth and a Wurlitzer electronic piano – moved on to their next disaster: a Bowie-esque rock outfit optimistically called The Hitmen. Despite cash injections from CBS, they failed to live up to their name.

One particularly scathing review slated their single 'Ouija': "Rubbish! I'm running out of patience with this sort of well-crafted, terribly professional pop. Pop? It's not even worthy of the name. Only this job could ever induce me to listen to it. The winning thing about the Depeche Mode single ['Just Can't Get Enough'] is its simple enthusiasm, its complete lack of cynicism. The Hitmen are so calculating – even down to the clever, clever name. It's unbelievable; the only remotely comforting thing about all this is that they haven't a dog's chance of ever getting a hit."

It was fortunate for Wilder that he understood how to operate a synthesiser: "After various bands, like The Hitmen, I was in my customary state – broke, bored and leafing through the classifieds in the *Maker*. I saw an ad which said, 'Known band seeks synth player. Must be under 21.' I applied for the audition, but I had to lie because I was 22."

Closer to home, Robert Marlow was another luckless musician who could have tried auditioning for Depeche Mode, perhaps by virtue of the French Look connection. It was not to be.

Robert Marlow: "That's something people have asked me before . . . Obviously, in hindsight, I would have loved it, but I don't think there was enough room [in Depeche Mode] for so many egos. At the time, I would have sold my mother to become famous! In fact, out of all of us, I think I was the one who wanted that career more than anybody. Loads of people have said to me, 'You must be really upset,' and I always say, 'No, that's just the way the cookie crumbled.' If life hadn't gone that way, I wouldn't be here now, and I really enjoy my life as it is today."

Deb Danahay vaguely recalls a close friend of Andy Fletcher's new girl-friend, Grainne Mullen, as being a possible contender for filling the vacancy: "I think when Vince left they were actually thinking about having Leia in the band at one point, because she could play the flute and piano."

Alan Wilder was rather underwhelmed on discovering Depeche Mode were the 'known band' he was trying out for. "I wasn't too keen on the simplistic poppyness of the sound," he admitted, "but I could see that there was something about the approach and the use of electronics – plus I needed the cash!"

Andy Fletcher recalled the auditioning process: "Daniel [Miller] met the people first, and then we had an audition – at Blackwing. It was down to about five people. Heaven knows what the ones were like that Daniel booted out! But the funny thing is that Alan lied about his age – he was over 21. But he was easily the best. There were some real Depeche Mode fans there, but Alan's a really great classically trained musician, and we sort of went: 'Now, what you have to do is play this little thing here, but the hardest thing is that you have to sing this as well!' So he did. We were like, 'That's amazing – in two seconds he's done that!' It was really funny."

For someone with aspirations of joining the Rick Wakeman school of mountainous keyboard rigs, auditioning for Depeche Mode was an eye-opening experience for Wilder, both in terms of technology and technique: "Pre-Depeche Mode, my ideal set-up would have been a Hammond C3 [organ] with Leslie Cabinet, a MiniMoog and a full-size Fender Rhodes piano. It was quite a shock because at the time they were using three of the smallest synths you could find. At my audition, Martin had a little Yamaha CS5 – which was only about a foot wide, Fletch was on a Moog Source, and I was given a Moog Prodigy. We all played one-note riffs, and I have to admit I felt a bit naked without more keyboards around me.

"I went to two auditions before landing the job. Most of the people they'd auditioned were either no-hopers or fans who'd learnt the hits off by heart, which they didn't want. Actually, I had mixed feelings about Depeche. I was aware of 'Just Can't Get Enough' and 'New Life', the two hits before Vince left, but I thought they were a bit wimpy – understandable at the time. On the other hand, they were charming and friendly, and the music was simple. I could appreciate that. When I listen to Vince's songs now I realise he based them on blues and classic heavy metal riffs. I did think it would be better if they had more bollocks but I was careful not to tell them that! I just said, 'I think you're OK.'"

After confessing to his real age, Wilder's honesty was rewarded with being given the Depeche Mode gig on a trial basis. "They initially employed me as a kind of part-time member, really; someone who could appear on the TV shows, who could go on tour, play the parts live – all that sort of thing," he recalls. "But they didn't really want to be seen to be bringing in some musician to take over and take control, so I didn't actually partake in any studio sessions for a while – for another nine months after that, in fact."

Andy Fletcher: "I think we put him on about £50 a week, plus expenses. And he came to New York. I remember it was so funny – he had a little jacket on and a woolly scarf, only New York must have been minus 40 degrees!"

Alan's first Depeche Mode commitment was a low-key, 'warm-up' performance at Crocs, their old testing ground in Rayleigh. One source reported that Wilder seemed somewhat shaken by the mayhem surrounding the group when kids were lifted to safety from the front row as the crowd surged forward.

Wilder sardonically recalled the early, unrecorded songs that peppered the live set at the time: "I have had the dubious pleasure of actually performing 'Television Set' which was part of the Mode live set when I first joined the group. I'm also familiar with 'Tomorrow's Dance', although I've never played or heard an actual performance of the song. Dave's rendition/impersonation of the embryonic Depeche Mode performances were enough to have left an indelible imprint on my musical memory!"

As *New Sounds, New Styles* observed: "Of course, Alan will only experience the second phase of Depeche Mode's fame. For the others the helter-skelter force of change can't be overlooked and mostly they don't like what they see."

In keeping with that downbeat observation, Andy Fletcher was reported by the same publication as bemoaning the changing expectations of Depeche Mode's audience. "Even when you make a lot of mistakes and think you've been terrible, they don't seem to care," he complained. "They don't come up and say, 'Great gig,' any more either. The music aspect has gone. At Crocs they didn't even clap for us to come back; [they] just stood and waited. All they want to do is *watch* you. We've become an event."

Indeed, it appeared that Vince Clarke's concern at Depeche Mode becoming public property was manifesting itself in the seen-it-all-before antics of those first generation fans at Crocs. A crudely produced, local fanzine with the bizarre title of *Bionic 'Barney's' Bumper Fun-Book* – possibly aimed at hospitals on account of an opening interview with a Basildon Hospital physiotherapist – was witness to Alan Wilder's début performance.

Their observations matched those of Andy Fletcher: "Eventually Crocs was absolutely packed with people wanting to see Depeche Mode with their new member. The audience was surprisingly varied, ranging from the very normal to the very punk to the near naked! By the time that Depeche Mode came on at 11.30 everybody had almost forgotten they had come to see a band, and so they were given a lukewarm reception. The songs were played as well as ever, but the band did not look too happy or enthusiastic. The music had everybody dancing, but nobody seemed very bothered about an encore. All in all, the music was very good, but the atmosphere wasn't. The Basildon concert at Raquel's [November 10, 1981] was far better."

According to Fletcher, Depeche Mode's début American performance wasn't much better, either: "We played The Ritz club in New York (January 22 and 23, 1982), one of the first gigs that Alan played. We'd done *Top Of The Pops* the night before – why we agreed to, I don't know. But Mute decided to send us over on Concorde. Unfortunately, it was probably the most disastrous gig of our lives. None of the equipment worked; we didn't go on-stage until 2.30 in the morning. A guy outside said to me afterwards, 'What happened to you lot? You used to be good.' That was also the time when Dave had his tattoos removed. We did five or six gigs with his arm in a sling, which, for a frontman, is not what you want. It was one of those bodge jobs."

Fletcher did appreciate the chance to experience life outside his home-town. "We haven't travelled much outside of Basildon. It's weird meeting these people in the business who are much older than us and have all these stories to tell. I'm just starting to live now, through being in a band."

Conversely, Alan Wilder had hardly been *inside* Basildon's boundaries, though what little he saw of his bandmates' New Town home left a lasting impression, though not a particularly positive one. "I'm pleased to say that my knowledge of Basildon is extremely limited due to the fact that I've only been there about three times. All my visits were early on in my career with Depeche Mode, and at a time when I was really into photography and I used to routinely carry around a shoulder bag containing my camera equipment. My overriding memory of Basildon is sitting in a disgusting pub and being told by Daryl Bamonte [who by then had left school and was virtually working for Depeche Mode full-time, initially as a roadie] to uncross my legs and hide the shoulder bag or I was likely to get the shit kicked out of me for being a poof. Nice, eh? I hate it when journalists refer to me as a 'Basildon Boy'."

10

Pop Rival

"I think maybe Vince Clarke was actually saying, 'Forget trying to be cool, forget wearing all the latest designer clothes, forget all the art; it just comes down to making records, and I just keep having hit after hit after hit.' This bloke could make your secretary number one! That bunch of barbers [Flying Pickets] covered his song ['Only You'] and had a hit."

— Rusty Egan, 2001

Away from the spotlight, Vince Clarke had been far from idle. "I didn't have any particular plans, other than staying at home to think about things," he told *Sounds*' Chris Bohn, a few months after leaving Depeche Mode. "But after a week I got fed up of doing nothing, and so I decided I'd like to do 'Only You' . . ."

Vince first began work on the tender synth ballad almost immediately after finishing touring with Depeche Mode in November 1981. "I'd bought an MC-4 and it'd just been gathering dust for months in my bedroom. I thought I'd like to muck about with one of these things and I never got the chance to do anything like that. I just wanted the chance to muck about with the equipment I'd got at home, basically!"

Roland's MC-4 MicroComposer wasn't the only piece of technological wizardry Vince had bought from his Depeche Mode earnings. He'd also splashed out around £500 on yet another synthesiser, Sequential Circuits Inc's newly launched Pro-One – a flexible, twin-oscillator analogue monosynth – with the express intention of playing it from the MC-4, to form an *ad hoc* one-man electronic band. Always keen to talk technology, Vince simplified his *modus operandi* thus: "I program the sequencer, and it triggers the synth; I use a sequencer called a Roland MC-4. The MC stands for MicroComposer, and the number four indicates that it can be used to control up to four synthesisers at one time – it all sounds terribly complicated, but it's not, really. Starting from scratch, I work out the basics of a new song on the guitar. When I've got that straight, I go to the MC-4 and program in the various parts. When connected to a bank of synthesisers, the sequencer will have one of them playing bass, one playing melody and so on. Working from one small console, I can control the notes played by the synths, the step-tones, which are the gaps between the notes, filter changes and note shapes."

The irony of this breakthrough was far from lost on Vince, who self-deprecatingly confessed: "I can't play for the life of me. I got voted 19th Best Keyboard Player of the year in *Sounds*, and I never actually touched the keyboard! It was all programmed!"

With so much musical control at his disposal, is it any wonder Andy Fletcher consequently remarked, "I think Vince thought he could do it all by himself, and he proved it – he *could* do it by himself."

When interviewer Ian Cranna asked Clarke if he'd thought of going solo when leaving Depeche Mode, Vince was adamant in his reply: "I'd never go solo! I haven't got it in me! I haven't got the confidence, I suppose."

It was this distinct lack of self-confidence that led the likes of *Smash Hits* to announce that Clarke initially intended offering his songwriting efforts "to anyone who wants them, including Depeche Mode." With the assistance of some studio trickery and the promotional talents of Depeche Mode plugger Neil Ferris, British a cappella group Flying Pickets took Clarke's song 'Only You' to number one in November 1983.

Neil Ferris: "I went with 'Only You' because it was one of Vince Clarke's songs and I'd worked with him since the start of Depeche Mode because their manager Daniel Miller is my best friend. No disrespect to them as a group, but the [Flying] Pickets aren't really my sort."

Clarke had, in fact, originally offered 'Only You' to Depeche Mode.

Andy Fletcher: "He [Vince] did a small tour with us, and he was supposed to be continuing to write songs. The story was that after he'd left he came to us with this song, and he sang it to us, and me and Martin went, 'That sounds like something else; we don't like that' – it was 'Only You'! It's a mistake anyone could make – great song."

Martin Gore's recollection of the event differed slightly from that of his colleague, but the outcome was nevertheless the same: "I think he played 'Only You' to Andy and Dave – he never played it to me, and they thought it really sounded like something else."

Having been knocked back by his former bandmates, Vince Clarke was forced to turn elsewhere – a *Melody Maker* advert, as it happened. The ad was placed by Alison Moyet, a fellow Basildon native who coincidentally had attended the same Laindon High Road music classes – not that they knew each other.

Vince Clarke: "I had this song written ['Only You'], and I wanted someone to sing it for me. Alf's number was in the *Melody Maker* looking for 'a rootsy R&B band'."

While 'Only You' could hardly be described as rootsy R&B, Vince made the call. "I advertised for a rootsy blues band and Vincent answered," Alison Moyet confirms.

Vince Clarke: "I knew Alison anyway, because she'd played with Rob [Allen in The Vandals]. I didn't really know her that well. Everyone was scared of her because she was in a punk band! I'd never spoken to her, but she'd advertised for a blues band, and I knew it was her advert. I knew she was a brilliant singer, so I responded to her advert, saying, 'I've done an album [*Speak & Spell*], but I'm not a blues band. But I've got this song, so would you come round and demo it? So she did – it was *fantastic!*"

Such was Clarke's enthusiasm for the results of this home recording session that he was soon seriously toying with extending his collaboration with Alison – an album was begging to be made. But before being given the chance, Clarke's musical rejuvenation was very nearly nipped in the bud.

Recording and releasing 'Only You' proved more difficult than anticipated. "The initial reaction was very negative," he revealed. "I went into Seymour Place, where Mute had their office at that point, and played the song to Daniel, who was farting about with his ARP 2600. He seemed more interested in that. But that same evening, it just so happened that Sonet, the publishing company, came in with their Swedish big guys – Sonet were Swedish-owned – and they said, 'That's a really, really good song.' They responded to it very positively, but I remember coming away from that meeting thinking, 'That's it.'"

That's it? "All that I can remember is that when I started Yazoo, and played the demo of 'Only You' to Daniel, and he didn't respond, I thought, 'Well, that's it, then. I'm back to working again. I'll have to get myself a proper job now. It's over. That's the end of my music career.' And it almost could have really ended for me there, I suppose."

At least Vince Clarke still had an ally in *Sounds'* Betty Page who had been a fan of his work from the outset. Early on, she supported his latest musical endeavour by mentioning Yazoo's demo tape in her publication's playlist quite some time before any of the duo's recordings commercially saw the light of day. That said, Clarke needn't necessarily have worried, as Daniel Miller soon changed his tune.

Yazoo's 'Only You' – backed by the equally enjoyable electro-funk workout, 'Situation' – became Mute Record's 20th single on March 15, 1982, following not too long after Depeche Mode's 'See You'. Unfortunately for Vince and Alison, its chart progress wasn't nearly as swift as that of their more established Basildon rivals.

Vince Clarke: " 'Only You' was released very soon after their song. It's just that our song took much longer to chart; it took *ages* – that was the amazing thing. 'See You' did really well, really quickly, and I was really jealous, obviously. Then, week-by-week, 'Only You' just went up and up and up. It was just *amazing*!"

Linette Dunbar, who knew Andy Fletcher from Markhams Close, had spent a summer working alongside Alison Moyet at the same Yardley's cosmetics factory that had briefly played host to Vince Clarke and Dave Gahan. Linette was delighted at her old workmate's success: "Alison was fabulous – warm and funny. She kept me going in the haze of the airless powder section. It was awful! Alison had us all singing 'Shout' at the top of our lungs, while packing and repacking talc for Marks & Spencer. I remember hearing 'Only You' for the first time, soon after we rubbed shoulders on the factory floor. It was played on *Roundtable* on Radio One one night; it gave me goosebumps. I was *so* excited for Alison. She had finally made it!"

When 'Only You' finally peaked at number two in the UK Singles Chart on April 17, rivalries with his former bandmates intensified to such an extent that Clarke claimed: "We'd completely fallen out. It was terrible, really. When 'Only You' did better than 'See You' I was like: '*Yes!* Up yours!' It was like that – a real kiddy thing."

Relations deteriorated further still when 'Situation', the B-side of 'Only You', topped the US disco charts later in the year while bubbling under the all-important *Billboard* Top 100 national chart. "They [Yazoo] took the master over there and Americanised it by adding bongos and an awful jazz-synth break in the middle," cringed Andy Fletcher.

Martin Gore: "We were surprised [that] Vince agreed to that, because Daniel was against it."

Looking back, Vince Clarke holds no grudges: "I don't regret anything. At the end of the day, it's kind of worked out for everyone concerned. I don't take time to think, 'Oh, what would have happened if . . .?' Because life doesn't work out like that, does it?"

Andy Fletcher: "Alison didn't help – you had to be careful with her because she'd just beat you up! She was in our class at school and she was the best fighter in the year. There was one time when we were in this small Mute office: she thought we were laughing at her, and she came up and said, 'Fletch, if you laugh at me once again, I'll kick you in the bollocks!' Never laugh at Alison Moyet; she would kill you on the spot."

As the music press were quick to pick up on, Alison and Vince were certainly an unusual pairing. "At the time, Depeche Mode never impressed me," she told Chris Bohn. "I never listened to chart music at all – I wasn't even exposed to it before I was with Vince, let alone impressed! I can't accept the fact of blues with synthesisers at all – you can't bend the strings of a synthesiser, can you?"

Undeterred, Clarke further fuelled his growing reputation as a synth boffin by cultivating an exaggerated foppish fringe and granting *One..Two.. Testing* permission to graphically reproduce the control panel plans for the synth sounds he'd used on 'Only You'. Taking a leaf out of Daniel Miller's DIY percussive manual, one such patch constituted the hit song's bass drum. "They're drawn up to match the synthesiser he used, the Sequential Circuits Pro-One," the publication explained. "But you can convert his ideas and patches to your own machine to follow the Yazoo route."

In fact, Clarke was so smitten with this particular synthesiser that he agreed to review it for *One..Two..Testing* in their inaugural issue. He glowingly concluded: "In the studio I've used it for nearly everything. I've very rarely found a sound it can't get."

At the very least, blues purist Alison Moyet could appreciate the synth-meister's maturing lyrics: "Towards the end of being in the band (Depeche Mode), I started writing more straightforward lyrics; just more sensible, rather than nonsensical! I think they're more serious – not just to be serious, but not just words for the sake of words like they were before."

Back from their underwhelming Big Apple début,* the recently expanded Depeche Mode undertook a 14-date UK sojourn in support of 'See You'.

---

* Coincidentally, Yazoo's initial American foray was similarly disastrous. According to a Basildon *Evening Echo* report (October 13, 1982): "Hit band Yazoo have been clobbered by an incredible £3.5 million law-suit threat – in a row over their unusual name." Although Alison Moyet originally named the duo after an obscure American blues label, unbeknownst to her, a little-known American rock band were also already calling themselves Yazoo; rather than risk being dragged through the law courts Vince and Alison agreed to be billed as Yaz in readiness for their forthcoming first – and last – US performances.

Starting at Cardiff's Top Rank on February 12, and ending on February 28 at London's Hammersmith Odeon, on the penultimate night, the band played an unexpected gig at The Bridgehouse in Canning Town. Original promoter, Terry Murphy purportedly attempted to pay them the princely sum of £1,000 for filling the place to the rafters, but the band were adamant that the fee should instead be used to renovate their old haunt.

New Sounds, New Styles reported that Depeche Mode "were guaranteed £22,000 for their British tour – more now that the Hammersmith Odeon has sold out, giving them £5,000 for one show." It was a far cry from the £250 per gig (minus £50 for PA hire) that they'd survived on only a year earlier, though the majority of that handsome five-figure sum had been spent on equipment, lights, travel and hotels before band and entourage even set foot on the tour bus.

Quite apart from the financial realities of competing in the music business, success in itself continued to bring its fair share of problems. When being interviewed by Johnny Black, an unidentified Mode member recalled: "We were signing autographs in the dressing room after the Hammersmith [Odeon] show. Outside the window was all these blokes trying to crash in, shouting, 'We put you there and now you just ignore us.' That kind of thing really hurts us, because we try to sign as many as we can."

At the time, the Depeche Mode Information Service was still practising its policy of arranging to have anything sent in by subscribers personally autographed by the band. Within a year this would be amended to a polite request that fans only send in *one* item each, which was still generous under the circumstances.

For Alan Wilder, landing the Depeche gig brought with it a new synthesiser – a Roland Promars, probably chosen as it was effectively a cut-down monophonic version of the same company's Jupiter-4, previously used by Vince Clarke. Compared to Martin Gore's PPG Wave 2, it wasn't particularly a flashy affair, but it was programmable; a breakthrough in itself now that *all* of Depeche Mode's onstage instruments were built that way. Such progress pleased Martin Gore no end: "Programmable synths help. You don't hear the 'urt, urt' before each song to make sure you've got the sound right. I don't know how we got away with what we did. We used to come on-stage and tune up, then go off again and come back five minutes later to play the gig. We thought of wearing masks! Now we've got silent electronic tuners."

Wilder's main memory of those February performances focuses on the travelling escapades of his three bandmates: "They wore plus-fours,

Haircut 100 [woolly] jumpers, were very shy and sat at the back of the bus eating crisps with their girlfriends. I suppose, in some ways, they seemed naïve on first impression."

Further evidence of Fletcher and Gore's naivety was supplied by a former Nicholas Comprehensive School colleague who recalled the famous Basildon pair attending a sixth form disco at the school in 1982, only to walk out in disgust when the DJ refused to play a Depeche Mode record!

With their triumvirate synthesiser line-up, Depeche Mode, complete with trusty TEAC 3340 four-track reel-to-reel backing tape, were still far from being a conventional pop group onstage – or, for that matter, television; miming 'See You' on *Top Of The Pops* for the first time remains stuck in Alan Wilder's memory:

"It was an all-day affair, mainly spent hanging around our dressing room while the union-led BBC staff took their various tea, lunch and back-strain breaks. The audience consisted of about 15 people being goaded with cattle-prods to move them swiftly around the studio from stage to stage. We had the dubious honour of appearing on the same show as one-hit wonder Adrian Gurvitz. If your memory isn't capable of resurrecting his unforgettable tune, the lyrics were as follows: *'Gonna write a classic, gonna write it in an attic . . .'* – he's still up there, apparently!"

After finishing their second headlining UK tour, plus a host of obligatory television slots, Depeche Mode were bound for Europe. Starting with two nights at Rock Ola in Madrid, Spain, on March 4 and 5, their touring itinerary took them to Denmark, Germany, Holland, Luxembourg, France and Belgium, before ending at Guernsey on April 12 with Blancmange once again supporting. No doubt benefiting from the exposure of playing to Depeche Mode's audience, by October 1982, the Lancashire duo finally scored a UK Top 10 hit single with the Eastern-influenced 'Living On The Ceiling.'

News of Depeche Mode's most recent touring escapades, courtesy of the Depeche Mode Information Service, was both good and bad: "The band have just returned from their European concerts with a tale of woe! Apparently all three synthesisers packed up at one time or another, the tape machine just stopped in the middle of 'New Life' at four gigs and the coach broke down in a village in the wilds of Luxembourg. However, all of the venues were packed and everyone seemed to enjoy themselves."

On April 26, 1982 Depeche Mode unleashed another Martin Gore-penned single, 'The Meaning Of Love'. Credited as being produced by

Depeche Mode and Daniel Miller, and engineered by Eric Radcliffe and John Fryer, the track had been recorded together with several other possible candidates for a second album back in early February 1982 at Blackwing (without the participation of Alan Wilder).

The strangely titled 'Oberkorn (It's A Small Town)' – named in recognition of a nondescript Belgian hamlet – was its unassuming instrumental B-side.

Martin Gore: "We rarely bother to look at our [touring] schedules and so naturally thought we'd be playing Brussels. But instead we found ourselves pulling into a tiny village called Oberkorn. It was a curious kind of village with a population that would hardly fill the first few rows of any ordinary theatre, so it was quite a fascination for us to find out just what would happen.

"Instead of our gig being [to] a handful of people, the place was packed as the audience came from all around and even from across the borders. But there was an interesting twist to this concert. When we got back to our hotel our record company told us that whilst the A-side of our single was all set, they needed a title rapidly for the B-side. We're never all that good with names and the first thing that sprang to mind was the name of this village, Oberkorn. So that's the title we used!"

The, by now, obligatory 12″ version of the song was titled 'The Meaning Of Love (Fairly Odd Mix)' – a fairly apt description given that the group augmented the song's straightforward arrangement "with a 'Stars On 45'* chord change that spins out of nowhere," according to one observer. "It was a good laugh," Dave Gahan told *One.. Two.. Testing* magazine, "but some of our fans wrote in saying what was wrong with our new records. They were going a bit strange."

While 'The Meaning Of Love' was not necessarily as strong as 'See You' in its lyrical content, or arrangement, *Sounds'* Valac Van Den Veen's critical assessment of the new song's "lead melody line" as being "identical to their last hit" is rather harsh, not to mention being totally inaccurate!

Alan Wilder: "The British press – music and otherwise – love to build people up just to enjoy knocking them down the next week. Music journalists in particular love this sense of power, because most of them are failed – and consequently bitter – musicians themselves!"

* Starsound (a.k.a. Dutch record producer Jaap Eggermont) scored three UK Top 20 hit singles under the 'Stars On 45' banner by getting session singers to perform excerpts from popular golden oldies over a monotonous drum machine beat.

Dave Gahan: "What really upsets me more than anything in Britain is the kind of criticism we receive. We're never averse to constructive criticism, and can take flak from the music press. In fact, we prefer criticism, because we often learn from that, but we are totally angered by comments that are directed at us rather than the music. That seems quite irrelevant!"

The success of the band's recent UK tour virtually guaranteed another swift chart entry for 'The Meaning Of Love'. While breathlessly informing fans that Andy Fletcher and Martin Gore had been advised to wear glasses because of their poor eyesight, the May 1982 Depeche Mode Information Service newsletter advised: "With the latest single having only just been released, there isn't a lot to say except 'Make it a hit'!" Disappointingly, the record stalled outside the Top 10 at number 12 on May 8, a mere two weeks after its April 26 release.

Consequently, in June, the DMIS announced: "After the disappointing drop in the charts from 12 to 17 on the May 18, 'The Meaning Of Love' is not likely to be followed up by a new release for a few months." Having played 40 'traditional' shows in 11 countries over four months, the first two weeks of July were declared an "Official Mode Holiday". Martin Gore and Anne Swindell headed off for sunny Portugal; Andy Fletcher went on a canal boat trip, while Dave Gahan and fiancée Jo Fox flew to the Greek island of Kos on June 29. Anyone wanting to wave the latter couple off were told they would be "flying from Gatwick Airport at about 11.00 am."

To make matters worse, the single's performance paled in comparison to the 14-week chart run for the very song Depeche Mode had previously turned down. No sooner had 'Only You' dropped out of the charts than another Vince Clarke song was ready to replace it. A classy combination of catchy synth hooks, Alison Moyet's rip-roaring vocal and a pounding bass line capable of setting dancefloors alight, Yazoo's 'Don't Go' couldn't fail to impress. On July 17, it reached number three in the UK Singles Chart. So much for Clarke's fears that his career was washed up.

Writing for *The Face*, Lesley White summarised Yazoo's winning formula, and even managed to drop in a thinly disguised dig at Depeche Mode: "While Vince masterminds the Yazoo operation and flicks the switches, Alf generates the emotion with an astonishingly strong and subtle vocal style, humanising (the feminine touch?) and proving that *à la mode* music doesn't need syrup-sweet voices and pretty boys in bow ties for commercial viability."

Even if it appeared that the tide might be turning against Depeche

Mode on their home turf, the fact remained: Mute Records now had two happening chart acts on their expanding artist roster. "There's no skill in it," Daniel Miller would modestly proffer. "I didn't get Vince out of Depeche Mode and put him to work with Alison Moyet saying, 'Hey, you could be stars!' "

Depeche Mode returned to New York's The Ritz on May 7 to begin an eight-date, coast-to-coast North American tour, playing to intrigued and occasionally enthusiastic audiences in Philadelphia, Toronto, Chicago, Vancouver, San Francisco and Pasadena, before winding up at The Roxy in Los Angeles nine days later. In coming to terms with the cultural differences involved, the Stateside reaction to Depeche Mode left Dave Gahan bewildered: "In America, we seem to attract musical aficionados or the intellectual side of the music business, which is really strange. In Britain we're very well known and have a huge following of the usual type – lots of young girls, naturally. But in the States we don't receive that kind of reaction at all. People who come backstage or to our gigs tend to be much more upmarket. It's quite weird and we don't know how to react."

Although again plagued by troublesome technical hitches throughout the tour, the band were able to laugh it off, thanks to Daniel Miller's indispensable troubleshooting skills.

Andy Fletcher: "The Roland, the Moog, the PPG – they were all causing trouble. We had to hire another Source and Danny programmed it in 45 minutes before the show started! And then when we went on, there was a big crash and we thought the PPG had blown up. It was the PA – even that had gone wrong! In Pasadena we had all the needles pinned – it was really loud, like a punk gig. We couldn't hear a thing we were doing. In Philadelphia we went off after the set and they were all shouting for more, and suddenly the [Moog] Source started up on its own going 'eep, urp, oop, oop' and making noises. The crowd thought it was the encore!"

"We're not really technicians," Fletcher told *Sounds*. "We couldn't mend anything. If it didn't work after giving it a kick, we would have to throw it away." On the strength of this admission, Depeche Mode didn't readily fit the half-musician, half-scientist boffin image being projected by a new generation of synth-based acts like Thomas Dolby, who even went as far as naming his 1982 début album *The Golden Age Of Wireless*. Dolby certainly presented EMI with a marketing dilemma; one early press release read: "His one-man stageshow is a bizarre hybrid of computer-generated music, video, slide and film projections, perhaps closer to fringe theatre or performance art than rock'n'roll."

When Depeche Mode re-entered Blackwing Studios in July 1982 to begin work on their all-important second album, Alan Wilder was in for a shock: "When the second LP came to be made, I'd done my bit and I thought I warranted involvement. I had something to contribute. Still they [Depeche Mode and Daniel Miller] said no. The problem was that they had something to prove to themselves. The three of them didn't want the press to say they'd just roped in a musician to make things easier after Vince left. I was pretty upset and there was ill-feeling from me about that."

From a more detached perspective, Wilder was able to offer a different perspective: "There was a degree of caution from the others – mostly Daniel – about my musicality; I was often referred to as the 'muso', which, in a post-punk atmosphere, was undoubtedly something to be suspicious of."

In July 1982, Alan Wilder was far from being in any kind of bargaining position: "I would have liked to have been involved in the studio for that [second] album, but was told by Daniel Miller – the band would never have spoken to me about it – that I wouldn't be needed."

Ignoring the obvious option to quit, for now, Wilder could only bide his time.

PART III

Pop Games Without Frontiers

"We were all very keen on pushing technology – the electronic music side of it, the technological side, the sounds – as far as we could, and trying to be original and create our own sound for Depeche Mode, rather than just sounding like lots of other groups."

– Daniel Miller, 2001

11

When Three Became Four

"I stopped being an employee and became a full-time member [of Depeche Mode] during 1982, but it was a gradual process integrating myself fully into what was – and still is – a very tight unit."

– Alan Wilder, 2001

While Alan Wilder nursed his wounded pride on the sidelines, British music recording magazine *One..Two..Testing* was invited into the now fully fledged 24-track Blackwing Studios to witness the three founder members of Depeche Mode ostensibly hard at work on their second album, *A Broken Frame*. One staged photograph accompanying the published feature shows Martin Gore in the foreground playing his PPG Wave 2 synthesiser. Behind him Dave Gahan and Andy Fletcher are turning knobs on the studio's expansive mixing console.

It's unlikely that Gahan and Fletcher were directly involved in the actual mixing – that technical task was more than likely taken care of by Daniel Miller, assisted by Eric Radcliffe and John Fryer. Yet the band could have been roped in to help with any complicated mixes. In such cases, standard practice was to line up in front of the console, assign each a bunch of faders, knobs and buttons, then pray for a perfect take when mixing the multi-track recording down to stereo – a delicate balancing act of concentration and co-ordination. There was an alternative to this hit-and-miss technique, but in 1982, automated mixing consoles had only just been introduced into top-end commercial recording complexes.

Martin Gore: "We don't make elaborate preparations with music and lyrics, before going into the studio. Usually we have a loose framework to build upon, although there might be a few songs we've completed, worked and rehearsed. With studio time being so expensive you can't be in there too long."

As was evident from the *One.. Two.. Testing* photographs, alongside Miller's old and battered ARP 2600 synth, all manner of weird and wonderful equipment was shown strewn around Blackwing Studios. For Martin Gore, the Roland MC-4 MicroComposer favoured by Vince Clarke also represented the greatest technological advance for Depeche Mode. "We used it in the studio to run sequences," he explained. "Danny has an old Roland SH-1 synth where every key has a number written on it in red. That's the number you put into the MC-4 to get that note. It's also useful because I can take it home and work on a song, then bring it back into the studio and play it back. Even if you don't use any of the riffs or sequences you've still got the length of the song programmed in. The only problem is that it won't run the PPG [Wave 2]."

Gore had highlighted a perennial problem facing most early-Eighties electronic musicians: synthesisers from different manufacturers didn't always adhere to the same interfacing standards and so weren't guaranteed to link together. In Germany, electronic trailblazers Tangerine Dream and Kraftwerk had partly resolved the issue by employing third-party technicians to modify offending instruments. It's unlikely that Miller and Depeche Mode were prepared to go down that costly route.

Modified or not, in 1982, getting synthesisers compatible to one another was a tricky business as *One.. Two.. Testing* explained: "Each note on the keyboard has an identifying voltage and this can be sent to another synth from an output on the rear panel to tell it what pitch to play. The second synth also needs instructions on when to start this note and when to stop – a trigger, carried by the Gate output that carries a signalling voltage for as long as the key is held down. Different synths have different systems so not all of them can be patched together."

Consequently, Depeche Mode's one-volt-per-octave MC-4 could only communicate with instruments working to the same system of a one-volt increase in the control voltage, producing an octave increase in pitch – unlike Gore's Wave 2, for which PPG were in the midst of developing a proprietary interfacing system in readiness for a forthcoming digital sequencer of their own. And yet some musicians had the audacity to say that sequencer-based synth groups had it easy!

Andy Fletcher: "It's annoying that different synthesiser makers won't put the right clocks and gates so you can use their equipment with someone else's. They all want you to carry on buying their gear, but every firm is good at some things and not at others, so you'll always want to swap around."

Eager to progress from the simplistic sounds of their début album, Depeche Mode turned to more obscure electronic instrumentation like the French-made RSF Kobol, a rack-mountable keyboard-less mono-synth, similar in some respects to the MiniMoog. Fortunately, the Kobol *could* be linked to the MC-4. "It's sort of . . . lumpy," Fletcher explained at the time, adding that the band had been using it since 'See You'.

Daniel Miller: "The first two Depeche Mode albums were all done with analogue gear, although by the time we got to *A Broken Frame* we did have a [Roland] TR-808 drum machine. We used it for a few things, but not for the whole [drum] kit, because we were really into using drum sounds we made on synths. We'd make our own bass drums and snares, because we didn't want to sound like everybody else. We also didn't use things like the LinnDrum [digital drum machine] for the same reason – it was full of good quality sounds, but it robbed you of your identity. I suppose we were working to our own ideology."

Dave Gahan was convinced that, once released, the new album would show a progression in the band's use of synthesisers: "Some of it is quite atmospheric, and at the moment there are no two tracks that sound the same."

Oddly enough, Sylvia Gahan was being consulted during the recording process. "My mum still listens to our work," Dave freely admitted at the time. "We recorded a slow track, more like 'See You'. I played it to my mum and she said, 'I like it, love, but I don't think you should have it as the next single. It's a bit too slow.'"

Sylvia Gahan wasn't the only musical mothering act. According to Martin Gore, Andy Fletcher's mother, Joy, had also taken to offering an opinion on her son's work: "What was it she said? She liked it [the slow track], but that it was like an Egyptian death march!"

It could well be that Joy had been privy to a song destined to make an appearance on *A Broken Frame*. Lyrically, Gore's 'Shouldn't Have Done That' chronicled the life of an unnamed character, from early childhood to adulthood. Musically, the track is a veritable mixed bag, even breaking into a music box-like dream sequence at one point and ending with the synchronised sound of marching soldiers. There's no denying the song differs considerably in scope and sentiment to the likes of 'See You' and 'The Meaning Of Love' (both of which resurfaced on *A Broken Frame*).

Martin Gore slowed things down a little for Depeche Mode's next single. Recorded during the July 1982 sessions for *A Broken Frame*, and released on August 16, 'Leave In Silence' was a less melodious and more moody sounding affair than its predecessors. Together with another instrumental B-side – 'Excerpt From: My Secret Garden', set to feature in vocal form on *A Broken Frame* – it offered fans a glimpse of what to expect with the new album. More importantly, 'Leave In Silence' would come to be regarded as a significant turning point in Depeche Mode's history; the crossroads which led them towards darker, yet somehow uplifting song-scapes that eventually became the band's trademark.

Writing for *Melody Maker*, Karen Swayne sensed that changes were afoot: "'Leave In Silence', the current single, does mark a change in style for Dep Mode. It shows the way their sound is maturing. The rather harsh, brittle edge of their early 45s is gradually being smoothed out and there's more obvious emotion and feeling evident. It's an important time for the band – they've just completed their second album *A Broken Frame*, and they're determined to prove that they can do just as well without Vince Clarke, if not better."

Dave Gahan talked confidently about Depeche Mode's new-found approach, well aware of the risks involved in releasing a less commercial song. "The new single is a lot different to the others we have done, and the new album has the same sort of weight, really," he claimed. "We did have other things we could have released which we think would have got into the charts and would have probably been successful, but it didn't seem right. You can't carry on releasing stuff every few months and having a hit with something catchy. We thought this was more of a risk to release because it is not so instant. You've got to hear it at least five times before you can really begin to listen to it."

In the eyes of a major record label this move might have constituted commercial suicide. Not so Mute, who were clearly committed to backing their most established act all the way. The freedom of this fact was not lost on Gahan: "I think we've got a much better deal than most bands; we're far more in control of things. We manage ourselves, too. We have to budget more carefully all the time, but we can release anything we like. We have no firm contract with Daniel, but it's good to be able to deal direct with one man all the time."

"I think Depeche were reasonably financially aware from the beginning," Daniel Miller told *MasterBag* magazine in September 1982. "I've always tried to explain to them in detail the way our finances work, the cost of pressing, or why we can't pay royalties every week because we only get them once a month. They seem to appreciate that."

With its catalogue number of BONG1, 'Leave In Silence' also marked Depeche Mode's departure from Mute Record's self-explanatory standard single cataloguing prefix of MUTE.

Alan Wilder: "The only 'Bong' I'm aware of is a term used for a hash smoking device, which is not something you would really associate with DM."

Guest reviewing for the August 21 issue of *Melody Maker*, The Jam's Paul Weller was unmoved by the band's subtle stylistic shift. "I've heard more melody coming out [Jam roadie] Kenny Wheeler's arsehole."

At the opposite end of the appreciation scale, *Record Mirror*'s Daniela Soave was full of praise: "A tower of glory! This pounds with atmosphere, creating a dramatic soundtrack for a film which is created in your mind's eye."

Speaking of film, another nondescript promotional video, again directed by Julian Temple, was made to accompany 'Leave In Silence'. The strange sight of four band members rhythmically smashing a seemingly endless supply of everyday household objects being carted in front of them on a conveyor belt was limited in its appeal – arty it was not. In years to come, Depeche Mode would not be thanking Temple for an off-the-wall scene in which they are dressed in white, in a white room, each with different coloured faces, bouncing around on space hoppers!

Yet Dave Gahan was clearly excited by such concepts at the time: "In our new one [video] we're all painted different colours – I'm blue, Martin's red, Andy's yellow and Al's green. We're not really known as a video band, which could be something to do with the first one we made ['Just Can't Get Enough'] – it wasn't that bad, just a general cheapo. I enjoyed doing this one, though. It was good being painted, 'cos it's like you're hidden behind a mask and you can do anything you want."

Alan Wilder: "You can pretty much lump all the Julian Temple videos – 'See You', 'The Meaning Of Love' and 'Leave In Silence' – into one collective disaster. In those days, we were very naïve. Also, video was a very new and experimental genre at that time, so we weren't the only ones to suffer at the hands of spotty students fresh out of film school."

Despite the band's shaky entry into the video age, regular television appearances were still deemed an important part in determining a single's chart trajectory. Depeche Mode had still to reach a comfortable plateau where they could afford to be more selective about their onscreen appearances – hence their agreeing to perform 'Leave In Silence' outdoors at Alton Towers theme park, much to Wilder's consternation. "It was possibly the most embarrassing TV show ever," he grimaced.

But more small screen discomfort was to come, courtesy of an appearance on *Jim'll Fix It*. Wilder once again supplied the gory details: "For those of you who aren't familiar with the British institution that is *Jim'll Fix It*, it's a show hosted by an ex-DJ called Jimmy Savile, and it involves kids writing to him with their ultimate dreams – in our case: 'Dear Jim, please fix it for me to meet my fave pop group, Depeche Mode. I've always liked them, especially that Dave Ga-han – he's *gorgeous*.'

"Anyway, this girl's dream came true in the form of performing a song with us. For some reason I was nominated by the others to give her this prize of some cacky little keyboard and the all-important 'Jim'll Fix It' badge. After the song, Jim called me over, saying in his own inimitable style, 'Now then, now then, Mr Producer-man, sir, do you or do you not have something for this 'ere young lady what performed so well tonight there?' Anyway, I gave her the badge and she looked a bit pissed off that she got a snog from me, not Dave."

Dave Gahan: "When we first started, it wasn't like we were misguided. We just basically did whatever was put in front of us and were very happy to do it. We couldn't *believe* it happened so fast, and all these magazines were interested, and all these TV programmes – your *Swap Shops* and *Smash Hits*. But we were making this music that didn't quite fit in; it wasn't quite right – the first album, yes, but after that we had some weird sense that we were getting away with doing this weird music on programmes like *Swap Shop*, when we played 'Monument' from *A Broken Frame*."

Regardless of Depeche Mode's lengths in promoting the single, the British record-buying public's response was muted, and 'Leave In Silence' disappointingly stalled at number 18 on August 28. Yet all was not lost as thanks to Depeche Mode and Yazoo, Mute Records had bagged themselves a 2.7 per cent share of UK singles sales during the previous six months of 1982 – not bad going considering the company only had three full-time staff working with seven acts at the time! That corporate bigwigs CBS could only muster 5.3 per cent during that same period made this not inconsiderable achievement all the more remarkable.

Little wonder that Daniel Miller was toying with employing a full-time bookkeeper and moving office again before the end of the year, despite originally asserting that he had no intention of becoming a successful record company. "We've had a good year," he concluded. "Maybe next year won't be so good, but I still want to be in business. It would be easy to get a flash office and lots of staff, but I want to keep it under control. If everybody left and we had no more hits I'd still want to keep releasing the music I enjoy, even if I knew it wouldn't make a lot of money."

While Depeche Mode had clearly played a considerable part in keeping Miller in business, perhaps they were expecting too much of their teenage fan base with 'Leave In Silence'. Although slicker-sounding than anything they'd released before, it lacked the kind of memorable chorus that had punctuated past Depeche Mode offerings. Regrettably, the happy-go-lucky image conveyed by the band was also at odds with the introspective words. Taken at face value, it trod a well-worn lyrical pathway – that of doomed relationships.

When released on September 27, 1982, *A Broken Frame* faced a barrage of criticism. Writing for *Record Mirror*, Jim Reid was typical of the band's dissenters: "On the evidence of *A Broken Frame*, Depeche Mode face an uphill battle if they are to maintain the instant charm of their earlier work. Simply, Depeche are becoming predictable, safe and a trifle trying. Depeche do make attempts to broaden their music, but too often their pleasant synth patchwork can do nothing but *indicate* a mood, rather than *realise* it. Perhaps they should stop being so consistently nice. Depeche are never less than pleasant, well scrubbed suburban boys. Nothing on this album touches on raw feeling; Depeche make you smile, they'll never make you laugh or cry. Perhaps we should expect no more from the Basildon boys, yet whilst Alf 'n' Vince are brewing up such a powerful soulful sound this LP can be nothing more than a pleasant distraction."

Sounds' Chris Burkham was similarly scathing: "The main problem for Depeche Mode is that the use of synthesised sounds, to the exclusion of almost everything else, within a pop song is rather limited. The reason that Yazoo – to pick a rather obvious comparison – manage to make their songs succeed on more than the perfunctory 'nice tune' level is the way the hard synthesised beat is juggled against Alison's vibrant vocal style. David Gahan's voice serves the instrument – barely intruding, always obeying, never giving any orders – instead of playing off against the flat sheen on the Moog."

Frustratingly, for Depeche Mode, the spectre of Vince Clarke seemed to taunt them. Ironically, Yazoo had also chosen to record their début album at Blackwing, even going so far as to name it *Upstairs At Eric's* in acknowledgement of owner Eric Radcliffe's input while Daniel Miller concentrated on Depeche Mode.

Vince Clarke: "That's why things were initially a bit negative from Mute — because Daniel *wasn't* that involved. I didn't know of any other studios, so I just assumed that Blackwing was the only studio I could record at. It was always busy with other Mute projects."

With Blackwing booked for fellow Mute artist Fad Gadget, Yazoo were left to their own devices; resorting to using studio downtime in order to make *Upstairs At Eric's*. This entailed recording early in the morning at a reduced rate when the studio would otherwise have stood empty. "We'd record at *ridiculous* hours," Clarke concurred. However, working those ungodly hours paid off as *Upstairs At Eric's* effortlessly sailed up to number two on the UK Album Chart, not long after its August 1982 release.

While admittedly not selling as well as its predecessor, *A Broken Frame* actually beat *Speak & Spell*'s highest chart placing by two positions when settling at number eight — not a bad result considering Martin Gore was still finding his songwriting feet. When asked if he'd found it easy to come up with an album's worth of songs, Gore replied: "It was a question of trying to write them in the little time that we had. I was trying to fit in doing them in-between all the other things, and in the end half of them were written in the studio. I'd obviously rather not do it [that way], but I think they came out alright."

Dave Gahan was quick to leap to his colleague's defence: "We wanted to get into Martin's songs, because he had a couple of songs ['Big Muff' and 'Tora! Tora! Tora!'] on *Speak & Spell* and just from the reactions of fans writing in, it was clear that they were a lot of people's favourite tracks. When Vince was with us, we were happy to let him write because I think a lot of songwriters in a band can be a bad thing. If a band has, say, three songwriters all wanting to do singles and things, it can get too much.

"Things were happening so fast around the time of 'Just Can't Get Enough'; Vince was writing hit records and we were happy — we didn't question it. There was no time to think about exploring more, so when Vince left it did us a lot of good, because it gave us a kick up the arse. We went out and made 'See You' and it was our biggest selling record."

A cursory listen to up-tempo tracks like 'A Photograph Of You', and Andy Fletcher might want to reassess his original assessment of *A Broken Frame* as being "a lot weightier, not so lightweight and poppy."

One thing *A Broken Frame* did have in its favour was the striking sleeve design by Martyn Atkins, whom Alan Wilder later affectionately described as being a "northern, motorbike lad". Depicting an old woman hard at work under a darkening sky, single-handedly harvesting a cornfield armed only with a sickle, the cover is certainly eye-catching.

Despite being photographed in the county of Hertfordshire, any apparent Soviet social symbolism was never picked up on – not in the context of Depeche Mode's music, anyway. In January 1989, the striking image made the prestigious front cover of *Life* magazine as part of a feature on the best photographs of the Eighties. Alan Wilder was obviously impressed for a framed print of the *A Broken Frame* sleeve adorns a wall of his Sussex studio.

It was a far cry from the best-forgotten arty image of a swan in a plastic bag that served as the sleeve of *Speak & Spell*! When talking to *Sounds* in 1982 Dave Gahan was already embarrassed by it: "The guy who did it, Brian Griffin, also does the Echo & The Bunnymen sleeves. When he was explaining it, he was going, 'I imagine a swan floating in the air.' And we're going, 'Yeah, right!' Then he was talking about it floating on this sea of glass and it sounded really great. It turned out to be a stuffed swan in a plastic bag! It was meant to be nice and romantic, but it was just comical."

Depeche Mode stayed clear of being photographed for any of their record sleeves from the outset – unlike most of their contemporaries. "We don't have any pictures of us on our record covers," Dave Gahan explained. 'We don't like photos because they date so quickly – like the [first] Duran Duran cover, [where] they were all dressed up."

From a musical standpoint, Martin Gore was able to put *A Broken Frame* into its rightful place: "After Vince left the band we were still having to carry on in the way that had been started for us. So with *A Broken Frame* there was a real cross-section of songs – a lot of the really poppy stuff I felt we had to do, because that's what we were doing on the last record. There were a few other tracks that were more experimental, but I think we were still suffering from '*Speak & Spell* Syndrome'."

Andy Fletcher agreed: "I remember Dave having a serious cold and having to do most of the vocals [for *A Broken Frame*] sitting down. It's a weird album, with lots of odd bits on it – halfway between the old Depeche and the new Depeche, very much an interim album. It consisted of songs that Martin had written in his youth, before Depeche, and some newer songs. Those newer songs tended to be a bit darker and the older songs were more innocent and poppy. I suppose it was an album of getting to grips with Vince not being there, but it has some good tunes on it."

Dave Gahan was not nearly so forgiving of what he perceived to be a seriously flawed recording: "We all feel that it was our weakest album by far," he said in 1990. "It's very patchy – very badly produced. That's when we got labelled as a doomy band. It was very naïve. Basically, we were just learning at that point. It was Martin's first album as a songwriter. He was thrown in at the deep end, to be honest. In many ways we weren't ready to release an album so soon after the first. We rushed into it. It embarrasses us now to look back on [it]."

At least from a 1982 stance, Gore was satisfied Depeche Mode had made their point: "After Vince left and went [on] to form Yazoo, we were getting ready to record a new album. Alan started playing with us, but we wanted to make certain that any change in direction in our music wasn't attributable to Alan joining. We needed to show we were capable of musical alteration by ourselves. So we recorded *A Broken Frame* with that in mind, although Alan will be playing on our tours when we perform songs from the album. Now we feel free for him to become a full-time member of the group now the change in pattern has been established!"

Daniel Miller: "There were two stages of him [Alan Wilder] joining the group. First of all, he joined just for live stuff – a session musician, hired to play live. He wasn't part of the recording of *A Broken Frame*. But at the end of that [album] they got on with him – everybody was getting on very well – and they asked him to join the band full-time."

The Depeche Mode Information Service broke the news to fans in their October 1982 newsletter: "Alan Wilder is now a permanent member of Depeche Mode. He joined the band at the beginning of this year as a keyboard player/vocalist when Vince Clarke left to form Yazoo. Alan has toured Great Britain, Europe and the United States with Depeche Mode, and although he didn't play on the last three hit singles or *A Broken Frame* he will be joining Dave, Martin and Andy in the studio from now on."

Having been officially welcomed into the Depeche Mode fold, road work in support of *A Broken Frame* prevented Wilder from making his presence felt in the studio for quite some time. The so-called 'A Broken Frame Tour' would, in effect, last from October 1982 to March 1983, by far the longest performance stretch undertaken by the foursome to date. Starting the UK leg of the tour in Chippenham on October 4, Depeche Mode played 22 dates over 26 days, including two consecutive nights apiece at Birmingham's Odeon Theatre and London's Hammersmith Odeon. Mute Records sent along a camera crew to capture the second, October 25 Hammersmith Odeon gig for posterity with a view to releasing a concert video in the not too distant future.

146

The group performed for the first time in Dublin, Cork and Galway, and also returned to Edinburgh and Glasgow, before winding up at the St Austell Coliseum, Cornwall on October 29.

While commenting on the Vince Clarke-penned numbers still in the set, *Smash Hits'* Josephine Hocking was nevertheless impressed: "Depeche Mode have grown up. They perform their bright, slight pop with a newly found sophistication which belies their old wimpish style. Dave Gahan still looks like a member of the Lower Sixth, but as the only member of the group who is not synth-bound, his confident dancing is the main visual point on the stage. The slightly tame crowd are continually urged to dance and enjoy! And so they do! Soft and seductive material from the new [*A*] *Broken Frame* album – songs like 'My Secret Garden' and 'A Photograph Of You' – impress and show the more thoughtful, mature side to Depeche Mode. This, the last date in a sell-out tour, illustrates there is far more to them than pretty tunes."

Alan Wilder refused to be swayed by another *Smash Hits* jibe at Dave Gahan's "gimpy" dancing. "It's not gimpy,' Alan retorted, aware of Dave's value as a frontman. "I like it. I certainly couldn't do it."

Martin Gore: "It's alright for Dave as he can move around, but we're stuck behind the keyboards like robots."

Interestingly, the photograph accompanying the *Smash Hits* review showed Depeche Mode's TEAC 3340 recorder still positioned centre-stage. Also visible is an unidentified cheap, white keyboard – possibly a Casio toy electronic organ – perched atop Martin Gore's PPG Wave 2 synth. Scrawled in thick black ink on the back panel is the word 'Fairlite' – most likely a dig at Vince Clarke, who'd recently blown an unbelievable £23,000 on a multi-purpose Fairlight CMI (Computer Musical Instrument) in readiness for Yazoo's own UK tour.

Vince Clarke remembered the purchase well: "It was *very* expensive! The [London-based] company that sold them, Syco, was very posh, and I was young and impressionable – and I had a few quid. It wasn't a music shop, as such; it was a showroom, with leather couches and coffee. I think I was a bit of a mug, really, but we used the Fairlight a lot."

Clarke intended running the entire Yazoo live set, including slideshow, from the Fairlight CMI: "I've ordered this computer that's similar to the MC-4 but rather than operate four synthesisers like the MC-4 does – like a multi-sequencer – its actually got eight voices in it already. The whole computer is the synth and the programmer. What I want to do is program the whole set into the computer so that rather than use tapes for backing tracks, all the music will come out of the computer. On top of that, we're getting into slide projectors which are also programmable via computers and can be synched off the main computer, so the whole show will be electronic in the true sense of the word."

Having succeeded in putting his forward-thinking plan into action, Depeche Mode couldn't help but enthuse about Clarke's 'multimedia' show when checking the competition out for themselves. "We all think Yazoo are really good," Dave Gahan told *Smash Hits'* Peter Martin. "We went to see them at the Dominion [Theatre] in London and were really impressed – especially with the slideshow."

For the time being, Depeche Mode were effectively touring with the same stage set-up as they'd used earlier in 1982, and although they briefly discussed the idea of using their Roland MC-4 for live work, either alongside or possibly in place of their backing tape, any plans were shelved through fear of road failure.

"We have to be our own roadies at the airports," Dave Gahan revealed, again highlighting the group's independence. "And we see how the stuff comes down the chute: *Crash!* I don't think the MC-4 would stand it. If it went wrong on-stage, you've had it. At least with a tape you can rewind and start again."

As might be expected, following the release of *A Broken Frame*, the contents of the backing tape had been substantially altered since previous live outings. By way of an atmospheric introduction, it now opened with 'Oberkorn (It's A Small Town)' before proceeding to run through a varied 17-song set list which included all of the new album, interspersed with several old favourites like 'New Life', 'Boys Say Go!', 'Tora! Tora! Tora!', 'Just Can't Get Enough', 'Shout!' and 'Photographic'. That same set was resurrected on November 25, when Depeche Mode returned to Stockholm to begin the 14-date European leg of the tour, ending at Amsterdam's Paradiso on December 14.

Notable in their absence were any concert dates in France. "We don't go down very well in France," Gahan observed. "There doesn't seem to be any reason for it, but we didn't feel at ease on our last tour there."

Could it be that the French took exception to an English band naming themselves after a popular French fashion magazine?

Dave Gahan: "I'm sure it's something to do with our name. Mind you, I wouldn't like to be in a band called *Woman's Own* over here [in the UK] that much!"

Alan Wilder: "They [the magazine] weren't too happy in the early days, but obviously, as the band became more successful, they quickly changed their tune. I don't think it was a copyright issue."

Apart from eligible bachelor Alan Wilder, the band members' respective girlfriends joined them on the road. "For us, that really is a luxury," said Andy Fletcher. "We don't feel they get in the way, although there are quite a lot of bands who feel girls on tour are an unnecessary burden. With us, it's like taking your best friend along, although when we first took the girls [on tour] they took a while to adjust to the fan reaction.

"That was funny really, because our girls also run our Information Service and so you'd figure them knowing what to expect. But the reality of hundreds of girls trying to rush us and kiss us was a bit too much! It seems to be Alan the girls are attracted to – we don't mind him shouldering that responsibility."

Touring is a mind-numbing experience with too much time to kill, be it in hotel rooms or travelling between shows. Having been an avid student during his schooldays, Martin Gore's favourite early road pastime was reading. "It occupies a lot of my travelling time," he confessed in 1982. "None of us are really film freaks, so we rarely go out to the cinema or anything like that. Our film-going is usually done on the coach on the video. Alan occasionally nips down the pub for a drink, but that's about the limit of our raving it up!"

Still on friendly terms with Depeche Mode at the time, Robert Marlow can vouch for Gore's rabid reading habits. "Part of the charm of Depeche Mode is that they are a gang – it's like old school friends. I remember going 'round to Martin's one summer when they were going on tour and he had this whole flightcase devoted to all his old schoolbooks. There was me thinking he had all his stage clothes and everything in it, but he was going to take them to read on tour! Then again, Martin has always been completely and utterly potty!"

Andy Fletcher: "I'll never forget those first tours. We were crammed into a van along with our equipment and driving for what seemed like years along motorways. Now we've got a luxury coach and can do it in some style. There are video recorders and a stereo onboard, and you can't beat a bit of comfort to put you in a good mood when you arrive in a foreign city and have to go straight to do soundchecks before you can rest."

Returning to British soil, Depeche Mode were back in Blackwing Studios, laying down a new single, 'Get The Balance Right!', with the usual crew of Daniel Miller, Eric Radcliffe and John Fryer. This time Alan Wilder *was* included in the December 1982 recording session – with noticeable results.

"Interestingly, this was the first time we had concentrated on producing a dance 12″," he recalled. "Although remixes had been made for previous releases, this one was very much geared towards the clubs. At that time, Mode tracks were always recorded with the LP version in mind. From there, we would either edit down for a 7″ version or expand for a 12″. To make a 12″ involved running off differently mixed sections [of a song] onto two-track [stereo] tape until we had enough pieces to edit the new version together. The tape editing process was much more limiting and took longer than current digital methods. The mere fact that it was much harder work to create a totally different and new version of a song probably contributed to the style of those early mixes and accounts for a lot of their charm. They were usually thrown together fairly quickly with time running out at the end of a mixing session."

Andy Fletcher: "We could be a conventional band if we wanted to. Mart is an excellent guitarist, Alan can play the drums and I can play the bass. David has even been known to sing! But, really, we're not interested in the instruments, just the sounds they make. We still think synthesisers produce far more interesting sounds than traditional instruments, so we'll carry on using them. For instance, Mart plays guitar on 'Get The Balance Right!', but to make it sound more interesting we put it through a synth and phased it out of time."

Despite its straightforward title, Gore's lyrics were becoming even more introspective and open to interpretation. At the time, he appeared to have his feet firmly planted on the ground: "We're not the kind [of people] who enjoy partying it up every other night or going travelling to clubs. Most of the time when we're not working we tend to stay at our parent's places in our hometown, which is a fair way from London. We all feel that it's essential to have this firm home base, because otherwise you tend to find yourselves leading a rather insular existence, only mixing with people in the music business, and that isn't really good for your lifestyle. You need outside stimuli – even if other people think it's trivial. We only travel into the capital when we need clothes or have to go into business meetings."

Andy Fletcher: "People expect us to live in some kind of penthouse flat, but living at home suits my needs. I can't really afford to buy somewhere, anyway. I used to think, 'One hit single and you get your Rolls-Royce,' but I think it takes about 10 albums to be comfortably off so you don't have to work."

Elsewhere, Dave Gahan set about deciphering 'Get The Balance Right!' to *Smash Hits*: "It's about telling people to go their own way. It also takes a dig at people who like to be different just for the sake of it. You've just got to reach the right balance between normality and insanity."

Despite being over two years into their professional recording career, Depeche Mode's innocence, a result of their continuing self-sufficiency, showed no signs of abating. This was apparent in Alan Wilder's comment concerning another unremarkable promotional video – this time directed by Kevin Hewitt – to accompany 'Get The Balance Right!': "The video, confusingly, features myself lip-synching Dave's voice over the first verse. This was because the director didn't actually know who the singer of the band was, and, for some reason, made the assumption that it was me. As an indication of our naivety, we were too embarrassed to point out this mistake. Consequently, the final cut of the promo remains this way today."

The classical music leanings of the instrumental B-side, 'The Great Outdoors' – co-written by Gore and Wilder – led fanatical fans to speculate that Wilder had forced the issue, threatening to leave the group if he wasn't allowed to contribute in a writing capacity. Understandably, Wilder hotly contested such conjecture. "'The Great Outdoors' was the only track that Martin and I actually sat down and knocked together in the studio. It was all done very quickly."

When 'Get The Balance Right!' was released on January 31, 1983, *Time Out*'s John Gill asked: "I often wonder why God bothered with Depeche Mode." Johnny Waller's *Sounds* review astutely noted that "Depeche seem to have fallen from grace with the critical cognoscenti, but this is the sort of single they do better than anyone else."

Loyal fans agreed with him, propelling 'Get The Balance Right!' as far as number 13 by February 12. Whether the band would ever return to the Top 10 remained to be seen, but after the disappointing performance of 'Leave In Silence', the chart position was encouraging. As Andy Fletcher would later reflect: "I think we were searching for a direction."

His words were borne out in that 'Get The Balance Right!' would not feature on their next album. However, as reported in the March 1983 edition of the Depeche Mode Official Information Service newsletter, an individually numbered, limited edition "extra 12"" of 'Get The Balance Right!' helped prolong interest in the song. Tastefully packaged in a blue

151

'mock leather' sleeve with embossed gold lettering, the A-side was the same 'Get The Balance Right! (Combination Mix)' as featured on the standard 12″ while the B-side comprised four tracks – 'My Secret Garden', 'See You', 'Satellite' and 'Tora! Tora! Tora!' – recorded live at the Hammersmith Odeon on October 25, 1982.

Other information deemed newsworthy at the time included Dave Gahan having a tattoo on one of his forearms removed by laser surgery at a London clinic. Having boasted a tattoo on each forearm since he was 14, Dave had apparently "become very self-conscious about them." This presumably explained why he was forced to subsequently perform several concert commitments with his arm in a sling, as previously recalled by Andy Fletcher.

Martin Gore unveiled Depeche Mode's 1983 masterplan to *Smash Hits*: "We want to get into the more album-orientated market, but it's still important for us to have hits. Bands like Echo & The Bunnymen and Simple Minds do well in both [album and singles] charts. We just want to produce a really fine album that will hopefully establish us as a major act. Another year like the last two should seal our success and enable us to stick around for quite a while."

A one-off gig at Frankfurt's Messehalle on February 7 was timed to coincide with that year's Musikmesse, Europe's leading musical instrument trade fair, with the express intention of checking out the latest music technology on display; March 24 saw the band back at New York's Ritz before heading on to larger venues in Toronto, Chicago, Vancouver, San Francisco and Los Angeles.

For an independent British synthesiser band like Depeche Mode, cracking the American market was to be an uphill battle.

Andy Fletcher: "This is where we really miss out by being on a small label; we just don't get the same publicity or promotion. We played The Ritz recently in New York – 300 people were turned away. We had a good reception everywhere we played, but none of it got back to Britain."

Depeche Mode then ventured East for the first time, arriving in Tokyo on April 2 to play three shows over two days, followed by shows in Hong Kong, concluding with two consecutive shows at Bangkok's Napalai Hall on the 9th and 10th.

In a later tour programme Depeche Mode described their Far Eastern sojourn: "We spent seven days in Tokyo doing lots of interviews, TV shows and three concerts, all of which were sold out in advance. It was our first visit and we were surprised how well known we'd become. Then it was off to Hong Kong; we wandered out into the airport pushing our bags on trolleys when suddenly we were surrounded by hundreds of people who had come out to the airport to meet us. It was very frightening, but also very flattering. They had to call the police to clear the airport and we finally made it safely to the hotel.

"After two more sold-out shows it was [off] to Bangkok where we played two gigs and spent several days wandering around the temples and generally soaking up the atmosphere. Then we drove seventy miles south to lie on the beach for five days in a place called Pattya. It was like paradise – pure white sandy beaches and clear blue seas, with the temperature in the nineties, day and night . . . enough said! Then it was back home and straight into the dark of the studio for two months to record our new album . . ."

If travel broadens the mind, the Far Eastern visit was to prove an eye-opener for Martin Gore, who was playing around with ideas for the third Depeche Mode album – slated for an August release. "The new songs are less personal, so people will be able to relate to them more easily," he told *Smash Hits*. "They'll deal with the problems of the world and things like that."

12

From Basildon To Berlin

"We were seen as a sort of throwaway pop act, and the transition from trying to change people's minds that we were something else was difficult in England."

– Andy Fletcher, 2001

In April 1983, the Depeche Mode Official Information Service made the following announcement: "The follow-up album to *A Broken Frame* will be recorded in May/June/July; all of the songs have been written by both Martin and Alan and the provisional title for the LP is *Construction Time Again*. A new single will be released in July from the album which is due for release in August."

When Depeche Mode regrouped with Daniel Miller in May, a collective decision was made to move to a different recording location with a new production team to attempt freshening up their sound. The new venue chosen was The Garden Studios at 1 Hollywell Lane, in the rundown industrial environs of East London's Shoreditch.

The Garden was owned at the time by John Foxx, being named after his critically acclaimed 1981 album, *The Garden*, for which the artist had temporarily set up his recording gear in a rented country house, even recording in its gardens to capture the dawn chorus on the title track.

While still actively recording and releasing records, Foxx's pop visibility was waning by 1983. The initial flurry of public interest surrounding *Metamatic*, his 1980 solo début, had since dissipated with the arrival of what were perceived as more upbeat synth-acts – including, of course, Depeche Mode. Nonetheless, Foxx had fared well enough to set up The Garden. At the time of Depeche Mode's arrival the studio was well stocked with a 36-channel Amek mixing console; MCI 24-track recorder; a useful selection of outboard processing equipment, (including a Lexicon digital reverb and Eventide Harmonizer), and an impressive 800-watt Eastlake monitoring system.

Foxx's memory of his one-time communal studio's inception is vivid: "A lot of my friends have always been artists, so we just happened to be looking for a workspace at the same time. That was a very interesting period, because the area is now tremendously fashionable, but back then our building actually had trees growing out [of] the roof! In 1982, that area [Shoreditch] was empty; hardly anyone was there, and the street was totally deserted. It had this wonderful atmosphere – like we almost had London to ourselves! Actually, now it has the greatest community of artists in Europe."

The former Ultravox! frontman denied claims that he was forced into opening The Garden to other artists on account of spiralling costs in light of his fading career. "I could afford to build somewhere of my own, because my records had been selling quite well," Foxx declared. "But it *was* a case of trying to get the best gear in when it opened, because that studio was one of the better ones in Central London. I wanted to make a musician's studio where conditions were comfortable. After I'd had it for a few years, I found *I* couldn't get in there anymore, because it had made quite a name for itself when bands like Siouxsie & The Banshees, The Cure and Depeche Mode came to record there – all bands I liked, actually."

The feeling was mutual as far as Alan Wilder was concerned: "It's fairly nondescript all around; John Foxx, who owned it, seemed like a nice bloke, though."

The individual responsible for guiding Depeche Mode and Daniel Miller through The Garden's technical labyrinth was a reluctant freelance engineer Gareth Jones, "a hippy, Freudian BBC drop-out," according to Foxx. Jones had cemented his professional partnership with Foxx when the latter had chosen to record *Metamatic* at Pathway – a low-budget recording studio in Islington, North London, where Jones had landed an engineering position.

Gareth Jones experienced an early awakening to the possibilities of synthesisers back in 1969 when first hearing Walter (later Wendy) Carlos' ground-breaking *Switched-On Bach*, an American album comprising painstaking recreations of Johann Sebastian Bach keyboard pieces using only a primitive Moog modular system.

When John Foxx arrived at Pathway to record *Metamatic* armed with his own "cool electronic gear", Jones was in for some experimentation: "John had a clear artistic vision and a wealth of experience, having already recorded three LPs, most recently *Systems Of Romance* with German [record producing] guru Conny Plank. These facts helped provide a supportive atmosphere for us to experiment and develop, as did the budget John had arranged!

"John wanted to make a minimal record, and he went for minimal resources to do it. This meant we were pushing the envelope with all the equipment – that was a great thing, creatively. And, of course, we were listening to Kraftwerk and Neu! My first contact with Mute Records was when John and I listened in awe to the fantastic sound of The Normal's 'Warm Leatherette'."

As the unassuming personage behind The Normal, Daniel Miller had gorged himself on a similar 'Krautrock' diet before establishing Mute. As the founder of what was, by now, considered to be Britain's leading electronic label, Miller was well aware of Foxx's musical pedigree, which probably had some influence on the decision to record the third Depeche Mode album at The Garden.

Gareth Jones: "John encouraged me to meet Daniel and Depeche at a time when they were looking for something new. I was invited over to Mute, which I believe was at Kensington Gardens Square at that time, where I met everyone for a chat. It was a fairly short meeting – just so they could get a look at me, I think. At that time I was wearing black nail varnish and a jacket I had bought in Morocco somewhere!

"I was initially reluctant, because of their teenage bubblegum synth pop reputation, but it turned out that we had compatible approaches in the studio; we all wanted to discover new sound worlds, and give a sense of depth, scale and edge to the songs and music. Basically, they were looking for a change of scene – John Foxx's new studio, built to satisfy his own electro needs, was obviously an attractive option: new and vibey with a Futurist influence, and not too expensive."

Before the sessions commenced, Daniel Miller followed Vince Clarke's lead, sinking an undisclosed five-figure sum into purchasing New England Digital's Synclavier II, an American-built music computer system, similar in concept to Clarke's Fairlight CMI.* For Miller, the main attraction of the Synclavier was its sampling ability – to make short digital recordings of

* As Thomas Dolby described it in 1982: "The Synclavier system has a potential which far outweighs anything else on the market. The digital sampling is at 50kHz and can sample up to 54 minutes of sound if the maximum memory is employed. New England Digital claim their machine will never be outdated. This may well be the case, but I feel that their prices are a little too prohibitive for mere mortals. They seem to be aiming at colleges, universities, film score writers and very rich American rock stars."

real–world sounds that could then be manipulated within a musical context.

Strictly speaking, this was not an entirely new concept; back in the late-Forties, Parisian radio broadcaster Pierre Schaeffer had pioneered *musique concrète*, an early form of electronic music based upon editing together tape-recorded fragments of natural and industrial sounds. His initial 'compositions' such as *'Etude Aux Chemins De Fer'* ('Study With Trains') and *'Etude Aux Casseroles'* ('Study With Baking Pots') involved splicing, speeding up, looping and reversing recordings of sound sources like trains and rattling cookware.

German electronic trailblazers Kraftwerk attempted to bring the idea into a more accessible genre when dangling microphones out of a speeding vintage Volkswagen Beetle with intentions of capturing an appropriately authentic backdrop for their 1974 album, *Autobahn*. Unfortunately, excessive winds rendered those field recordings unusable and they were forced to sculpt approximations of whooshing cars and hooting horns from analogue synthesisers. But as former 'Kraftwerker' Karl Bartos points out: "Sampling's been around since The Beatles – they did it all.* There's really no difference between using tapes and digital machinery."

Daniel Miller's Synclavier eased the burden of such musical experimentation enormously, if not necessarily financially. "Because we'd started working with sampling around that time, and because they [Depeche Mode] had started listening to bands like Einstürzende Neubauten and Test Dept – more experimental things – we kind of pulled all those elements together and tried to keep it very much in a pop format, but using interesting kinds of concept sounds, textures, and things like that."

By pressing pile drivers and drills into their unique sonic service, pioneering German industrial noise band Einstürzende Neubauten were certainly not fit for easy listening back in 1983! Daniel Miller was impressed, however, subsequently signing the influential quintet that had filled his head with radical sampling ideas to the expanding Mute roster. "I don't want to produce musical notes," declared founder member Blixa Bargeld at the time. "There are enough of them already. I want something to happen. I leave music-making to the musicians – the lackeys, in other words. I want to cause events to happen. Einstürzende Neubauten is a positive noise or the most positive noise of all."

---

* Bartos' comment undoubtedly refers to 'Tomorrow Never Knows' – with its 'flying seagulls' tape effects – from The Beatles' 1966 *Revolver* album.

Self-confessed record-collecting fanatic Martin Gore soon pricked up his ears at the metal-bashing antics of Bargeld and his Berlin-based noise-makers. "Metal music people like [Einstürzende] Neubauten have good ideas, some of which we may nick," Martin confessed, "but I can't listen to them. Kraftwerk – yes, they have instant melody. Sixties pop is good – The Beach Boys, even doo-wop. Simple harmony vocal stuff."

Gareth Jones: "I had started to work with [Einstürzende] Neubauten, too, of course, so there was a lot of cross-fertilisation going on. But because I was only just getting to know the band [Depeche Mode] at this stage, I couldn't say what everyone's influences were. I was keen to bring my influences to the table – young and pushy, I was!"

Nowadays sampling forms the backbone of many styles of pop music, but back in the early-Eighties such was the exorbitant cost of this ground-breaking technology that it was virtually unheard of. When later asked whether the Fairlight and Synclavier were worth the tens of thousands of pounds that they cost at the time, Daniel Miller replied, "In a sense they were. The Synclavier itself was slightly erratic and difficult to use, but it opened up a door to a world of sound that nothing else came close to – and we were able to make big hit records which we couldn't have made without it."

Alan Wilder: "The Synclavier was a state-of-the-art sampler/synthesiser that sounded great. It was an overpriced beast that took four grown men to assemble because of all its additional boxes, and it was a bit of a bastard to use. It was so expensive that nobody could afford one, apart from one or two top producers – Dan Miller, for example, and Trevor Horn, who produced Frankie Goes To Hollywood. We used it initially on *Construction Time Again* and subsequently on the next two Mode albums."

Gareth Jones' memories of The Garden sessions focused on "battling to keep things in sync as we made the transition to digital." Again, it was the recurring problem of trying to get different manufacturer's equipment to work in harmony – at least by working alongside Gareth Jones and Daniel Miller, Depeche Mode were in good hands in that regard.

As an inside observer, John Foxx is on record as stating that Gareth Jones "helped Depeche Mode move effortlessly from analogue synthesisers to the world of sampling and digital technology."

While flattered, Jones saw things differently: "I feel my major contribution was more to do with the acoustic space around the sounds, beats and riffs. Having moved out of the Pathway [Studios] cupboard I was now in a reverberant basement with interesting different acoustic spaces – mainly bright with short reverb times. I had a bunch of different amps hooked up in different rooms with mics near and far, so we were able to experiment with distortions and acoustic spaces easily.

"We continued this practice when we sampled ambient sounds on my stereo Stellavox SP7 – one track for a close sound and one for distant perspective. This sense of place was very important for helping to enhance and create moods and atmospheres. We were clearly making machine music, but on *Construction Time Again* we put the machines in an acoustic space."

Another instrument that was to prove invaluable in shaping Depeche Mode's new sound philosophy was the Emulator, a lower cost sampling keyboard from a small Californian company called E-mu Systems, Inc. When introduced in 1981, at $7,995, the Emulator was still far from inexpensive, but understandably, it was more limited in its scope than the Synclavier. The band were equally eager to break new ground with their latest purchase.

Gareth Jones: "I didn't have too much to do with the Emulator, but we all had a love/hate relationship with the Synclavier. On the one hand, it was a great quality sampler and an amazing additive FM [Frequency Modulation] synth, but on the other hand the sequencer was not very friendly – the usual bleeding edge sync and reliability issues!

"Another very important piece of new technology on this album was the E-mu [Systems, Inc.] Drumulator, programmed by Alan [Wilder]. This was a radical change for the group as they had not used this kind of machine before. The Drumulator was also getting the amp and room treatment, and was used on almost all the songs, although there is a [Roland] TR-808 on one song."

With its myriad building sites, run-down Shoreditch, *circa* 1983, proved to be the perfect surroundings for Depeche Mode in their newfound guise as first-generation 'samplists'. "With Gareth Jones and Daniel Miller it was like a pioneering expedition," recalled Alan Wilder. "All of us would go off to derelict areas armed with a hammer and tape recorder."

Gareth Jones: "There was a huge derelict railway yard nearby. I had purchased a Stellavox SP7 reel-to-reel as a high-quality recording unit; for one track in particular – 'Pipeline' – we decided to construct it from 'found' sounds, and that's how it turned out. We recorded close and distant sounds on the two tracks of the SP7 and mixed these – without EQ, incidentally – into the Synclavier to play all the parts of that tune.

Then we took the field recording idea a bit further: after we'd constructed the backing track, we recorded it onto an early Sony Pro Walkman I owned and then went back to the railway yard to record the vocals on the Stellavox – including a passing train! This was a time of great experimentation, indeed."

According to one online resource, Depeche Mode's new music "was given a hardened, more industrial treatment, thanks to the new sampling craze and use of discarded junk from any source at hand, including the building sites of Shoreditch in East London."

Yet, as Alan Wilder revealed, Depeche Mode hadn't entirely forsaken conventional synthesisers in favour of sampling technology: "We used a PPG Wave [2], which was our first digital synth, although we also had the Synclavier and E-mu Emulator by this point. What people forget about the Synclavier is that it's also a very powerful synthesiser. A lot of the synth sounds on *Construction Time Again* were actually generated from the Synclavier. Once the samplers appeared, though, our set-up didn't change very much."

Gareth Jones: "We were starting to use sampling a great deal – generally creating our own samples, of course, but I guess samplers generally played about 15–20 per cent of the parts. On 'Pipeline' it was all sampler."

As Depeche Mode's unconventional recording methods became increasingly complex, the musical roles between the various group members became all the more blurred.

Gareth Jones: "It was very much part of the philosophy at that time that it didn't really matter who played what – after all, it was all being played by a sequencer. Of course, Dave was the main singer, Martin wrote most of the songs and Daniel was designing most of the synth sounds, but what mattered was the end result, and we got there, by and large, together. We believed very much in the songwriters' four-track portastudio demos as the repository of the original inspiration, so we referred to them carefully. Of course, the finished production sounded very different, but it had the spirit of the demo, although the melodies and structure were sometimes changed in the studio."

When it came to the mixing of *Construction Time Again*, such was the complexity of the album that The Garden's 36-channel manual mixing console couldn't cut it. An automated console was the logical solution to the problem, as Alan Wilder explained: "In the earlier days we would record to 24-track with two – sometimes three – non-conflicting [musical] parts on each track. When mixing, one could rely on automation to separate out each individual sound to its own channel, with dedicated effects and so on."

In the case of *Construction Time Again*, the band, co-producer Daniel Miller and engineer Gareth Jones decamped to West Berlin to complete work on the album at Hansa Tonstudios, a state-of-the-art recording complex whose mix room featured a 64-input SSL (Solid State Logic) SL 4000 G-Series automated mixing console with 56-channels of Total Recall.

This ultra-modern facility proved an absolute godsend for handling the increasingly technically demanding requirements outlined by Alan Wilder, since all movements of the console's numerous knobs and faders were recorded for instant replay by an onboard computer, thereby easing the mixing process considerably.

Before long, Wilder would be praising the four-storey block of studios that, prior to Depeche Mode's arrival, had often remained unused: "Everything is computerised, which is what we've come to rely on. It's become more popular since we've been there."

British pseudo-progressive rockers Marillion were likewise impressed when recording their *Misplaced Childhood* album there soon after; for vocalist Fish, the attraction of the studio was more than just technical: "The main floor of Studio 2 at Hansa was impressive, as would be expected of a ballroom which at one time had hosted decadent parties – the building had once been an SS officers' club. The control room over-looked the [Berlin] Wall, which was only 100 metres or so away.

"This is where the inspiration for David Bowie's 'Heroes' came from as he watched a liaison between a couple in a dark alleyway that we trudged day and night between our digs at a nearby hotel and the studio. The *Heroes* album had put the studio on the international map, and the cheap rates appealed."

Hansa Tonstudios' historical locale was not lost on Alan Wilder: "Some of the most important albums of my generation were recorded there, such as the major Bowie LPs, *Low* and *Heroes*. It's all changed now, of course, because that whole part of Berlin has been completely rebuilt [following the fall of the Berlin Wall on November 9, 1989]."

The cost equation also conspired to make Hansa the perfect choice for Depeche Mode, as Gareth Jones confirmed: "I had already mixed there for WEA Germany and others, and was impressed at its then-state-of-the-art facilities. I was working in there on another project and Daniel was visiting

Nick Cave, who was working at the famous Studio 2 at Hansa. So I made sure I invited him [Daniel Miller] up to show him the mix room. He loved Berlin, as did we all, and at that time the studio was priced very well for UK users – the pound was strong."

As such, Gareth Jones could be credited with setting the Berlin ball rolling, although as he modestly volunteered, "Everyone just flowed easily into the idea."

Daniel Miller: "In those days in Berlin, when it was walled off, there was no incentive for anybody to start businesses there, because it was so cut off from the rest of Germany. Anybody who did start a business got amazing tax breaks, so studios were really cheap compared to London. And the DM [Deutschmark] was quite weak compared to the pound.

"Anyway, it turned out that to work in that technical level of studio [it] was actually cheaper to fly to Berlin, put them [Depeche Mode and Gareth Jones] up in hotels and work in the studio. Plus, we all fancied the idea of going to Berlin. So we ended up mixing that record [*Construction Time Again*] in Hansa. We all loved being there a lot, because London was pretty gloomy at the time. If you worked in a studio in London in those days, and you finished at one in the morning, there was nothing to do. You couldn't go out and have a drink or anything; you just had to go home. But Berlin was great, because you could go out and have a drink."

Martin Gore agreed: "Even in London you can work until two [am] and just about go out and get a drink, but I suppose in Berlin you could go out later – you could even go out to cafés at two in the morning. It probably didn't do Daniel's weight much good. I remember during one of the recording sessions he was on a strict diet, then during another he was going out and having deep-fried camembert."

Dave Gahan: "It was still back in the days where we were recording and then we'd all go out together to a club or a bar and get shit-faced, and start the process all over again the next day. We were young enough for our systems to handle it without taking a week off."

Luxuriously ensconced in the Hotel InterContinental on Budapester Straße, Depeche Mode were not immune to Berlin's decadent charms. Alan Wilder was most revealing regarding the band's recreational haunts. "There's plenty to do in Berlin," he told *No. 1* magazine. "When you finish work at 4.00 am you never feel like going to bed, and so you end up in a bar or a club. DNC is a favourite. There's a couple of good gay clubs – Corelles is alright . . . The Jungle."

When a fan later expressed undisguised concern at Wilder's revelations, he responded, "No, I'm not gay, but I've got no problem with going to gay bars or clubs. We probably went [to Corelles and Dschungel] because they had the best vibe and music."

Asked what he considered to be the most common, annoying or hilarious clichés about Depeche Mode, Wilder responded: "We're all gay; we're all from Basildon; we're big in Germany; we used to be big in the Eighties; we're miserable; our music is depressing."

Going to Berlin for the first time was like entering another world, as far as Andy Fletcher was concerned. "We used to have a few beers after being in the studio, but I think it was an eye-opener in terms of seeing how other people lived. There was certainly a very dark scene in Berlin, but we were still young."

Gareth Jones: "The band was pretty young when I started working with them – and so was I, so we were all developing rapidly, exploring and enjoying new environments."

Martin Gore wasted little time in falling in love with the city and its charms – including one of its residents, a Berliner by the name of Christina Friederich: "It was a significant time for me, personally, because before that I'd been going out with a girl [Anne Swindell] who was a devout Christian who really had me on reins. She was ridiculous – *anything* was perverted! If I watched something on TV, and there was somebody naked, I was a pervert.

"So when I finally decided that was a bad idea and left her, and started going out with a girl in Berlin, I suddenly discovered all this freedom, so personally it was a big turning point for me."

Dave Gahan's fiancée, Jo Fox, paid a brief visit: "I only went to Hansa once during the mixing of *Construction Time Again*. We stayed in the Inter-Continental Hotel [*sic*] in 1983. My memories are of the vastness of the [Berlin] Wall, the eeriness of the place along the Wall, and of Checkpoint Charlie. Hansa was right on the Wall."

As Andy Fletcher was an avid reader of political history at the time – particularly books about Germany between the world wars and the rise of Hitler's Third Reich – his youthful enthusiasm for mixing *Construction Time Again* in Berlin was understandably strong. "The studios were actually overlooking the Berlin wall. I'd only been outside of Basildon and London a few times. The first time I ever went outside of England was with the band. So, all of a sudden, to be put in this situation with guards looking at you with binoculars was amazing!

"We used to play the mixes on the top of the studio; we had speakers outside. It was a glorious summer. I have really strong, fond memories of it all – lots and lots of weird people around. We were only kids and Daniel would have Blixa [Bargeld] and [Einstürzende] Neubauten all coming up [to the studio]."

Miller later quashed rumours that Bargeld looked down upon Depeche Mode as being some kind of lightweight version of his own Einstürzende Neubauten. "I've heard that," he admitted, "but that definitely wasn't the way it came across with him [Blixa Bargeld] when he was around. I think there was a moment when maybe he thought we'd maybe stolen his thunder or something, but he was always very friendly – especially with Martin, and he used to come and visit the studio occasionally. I knew him because of the [Berlin] band scene.

"They [Depeche Mode] were obviously a lot poppier than most of the musicians they hung out with in Berlin, but people still admired them, because I think they understood what they were doing. They were doing experimental pop music, which is what they are – they're an experimental pop band. Some people were snobbish, but generally people accepted them as being part of the Berlin crowd."

Depeche Mode briefly left the mixing sessions to play a one-off open-air West German concert as part of the Shuttdorf Euro Festival on May 28, with Rod Stewart topping the bill. The pressure was on to perform similar shows, but the band refused to be baited.

Andy Fletcher: "Our agent [Dan Silver] is always telling us we have to play more, and he wanted us to do a few festivals this summer, so he booked 15! But we don't want to do those sorts of things, so we cut it back a bit – down to one, in fact. And that's enjoyable, it was good, and we didn't have time to do any more."

Alan Wilder: "Our lifestyle is so busy that it revolves almost totally around the group. Studio work interests me more than live appearances, which are basically louder reproductions of records."

The Berlin sessions also saw the conception of Andy Fletcher's ill-fated, intriguingly titled solo album, *Toast Hawaii*. "It's cheese and pineapple on toast," he explained. "I used to eat it everyday in Berlin – in the studio restaurant downstairs. I did this album of cover versions with everyone playing on it. It was never released. Daniel wanted to release it, but actually it was pretty awful! There's only one cassette copy that I haven't seen for many years, and hopefully it will never resurrect itself."

Although Alan Wilder's recollection of Fletcher's sideline project differed slightly from that of its instigator, they nevertheless highlight the harmony that existed between the two band members at the time. "An album called *Toast Hawaii* – Fletch's favourite dish from Hansa studios' café – which featured Fletch singing cover versions of his favourite tunes such as 'When The Saints Go Marching In' – accompanied by myself and/or Martin on piano – does exist somewhere. It was recorded in Berlin on a cassette machine in about 1983, and I took the photo for the album cover – a shot of Fletch; think Plug from *The Bash Street Kids*! We did, however, have problems convincing Dan Miller that it was worth releasing."

Gareth Jones summed up his first Berlin visit with Depeche Mode: "We had a ball. I remember the crazy Italian chef in the restaurant on the ground floor of the [Hansa] building; Andy Fletcher ordering Toast Hawaii; nights at Dschungel; baked camembert and weizenbier after the sessions; many multiple patch tape tracks – we were still using 24-track; Martin and Andy falling out and making up; visits from Matador, Einstürzende Neubauten and Chrislo Haas. We all knew we were making something important and influential, and the [*Construction Time Again*] album came together really nicely."

13

Trials And Tribulations

"One good thing about our career is that it was all very gradual. We hit big in this country, but it wasn't until Construction Time Again *that Europe started to get more into us."*

– Martin Gore, 2001

The first fruit of Depeche Mode's "experimental pop music" came to light with the release of a new single – the band's eighth – in anticipation of unleashing *Construction Time Again*. The Depeche Mode Official Information Service were quick off the mark with their June 1983 announcement: "Depeche Mode will be releasing a new single, written by Martin, in July which will be followed by a new album entitled *Construction Time Again*. The 45, which is yet to be named, although it has been recorded, will be available in both 7″ and 12″ in the middle of July." Evidently, Martin Gore's professed difficulty in coming up with song titles was still a problem.

'Everything Counts' opened with a heavily processed, powerful bass and snare drum pattern – courtesy of E-mu Systems, Inc.'s Drumulator 'low-cost' $995 digital drum machine – set perfectly in time against a panned scraping sound. "It's a sample, reproduced via the original Emulator," Alan Wilder explained. The keyboard player couldn't remember the exact source of this unique sound, speculating: "It was probably a result of our various trips around the building sites of Shoreditch in East London."

The record's production value glowed with an audio sheen befitting the upmarket equipment and recording facilities at the band's disposal. But there's *using* technology and knowing *when* to use technology. 'Everything Counts' unquestionably fell into the latter category – thanks in no small part to the contributions of Daniel Miller and Gareth Jones. More importantly, Martin Gore's ability to knock out a good pop tune shone through the impressive musical mixture with a memorable chorus. Gore chose to sing the chorus with Wilder ably handling its harmony vocal refrain. The result contrasted well against Dave Gahan's trademark baritone that carried the rest of the track.

Five days after the single's June 11 release, Garry Bushell turned in a scathing review for *Sounds*: "And the band played on . . . whether the members of Depeche Mode are actually dead or alive is a question that's baffled the medical profession for years." "He's an arsehole," spat Dave Gahan in *Sounds* a week later when reminded of Bushell's constructive criticism.

No.1's Mark Cooper was more charitable. "This is their strongest melody in a long while and a compelling picture of business Britain." Meanwhile, Cooper's *No.1* colleague Paul Bursche dug deeper into the song's sentiments when interviewing the group: "It focuses on the two-faced attitudes that abound in industry – and not only the music biz, but anywhere where money is involved. Gore states that behind all the ideals and motives lies pure selfishness."

"I'm not personally bitter," Gore told Bursche. "I lead a good enough life; it's just things that I've noticed."

For the record-buying public at large, sampled sounds and savage sentiments probably played second fiddle to the melodious song's catchy chorus. "A lot of people will just hum the tune and never think about it, just 'cos it's a good beat – that's exactly what my mum does," Dave Gahan admitted. On July 23, 'Everything Counts' peaked at number six, consequently representing Depeche Mode's highest chart placing since 'See You' although its 11-week chart run actually exceeded that single by a week. Far from alleviating any fears of waning popularity that the group might have been silently harbouring (in light of their previous two singles failing to crack the Top 10), Gahan was well aware of new pretenders like Tears For Fears infringing on their territory: "Every single for me is a real worry, because I wonder if those people still want to know us. There are ten bands I could name who have become really successful in the last year, and we've hardly had anything out."

Nevertheless, not only did 'Everything Counts' represent a quantum leap in the developing Depeche Mode sound, but also in the way in which the band were portrayed on screen. Thanks to a capable director (Clive Richardson) the accompanying promo video was watchable at last. "It was felt that after the Julian Temple years we needed to harden up not only our sound, but also our image," Alan Wilder reflected. "Clive had lots of new ideas which didn't involve storyboards where we were required to act."

That said, the promo did necessitate a certain degree of role acting as Depeche Mode's three keyboard players were portrayed as playing more visually exciting instruments. Andy Fletcher performed an infectious three-note motif on a shawm, the forerunner of the modern oboe – effectively extinct in European music since the seventeenth century; Alan Wilder took care of a more rhythmically challenging pattern on a wooden xylophone; and Martin Gore was seen to play the middle-eight's 16-bar instrumental break by blowing into a Melodica – a mutant toy keyboard-cum-wind instrument popular in Jamaican reggae. The reality was that all such sounds were sampled for the single, but their video counterparts looked intriguing when set against various Berlin backdrops.

"The video for 'Everything Counts' was done in Berlin – really bright stars," enthused Andy Fletcher. "I wouldn't say that I'm proud of the early videos. I think we were used as an experiment for some dodgy ideas in some of those. But that was really at the start of videos, anyway. They were all storyboard-type videos, and we had to do a lot of acting. We just weren't very good at that. We realised we weren't going to be the new Beatles."

On the subject of videos, such was Depeche Mode's heavy workload in terms of composing and completing *Construction Time Again*, it was looking increasingly unlikely that the previously planned concert video recorded at the group's Hammersmith Odeon show (October 25, 1982) would see the light of day. According to the Depeche Mode Official Information Service, "The work needed to finish off the [video] cassette has had to be shelved at least until August [1983] by which time the film will be almost a year old and Depeche Mode feel they would rather release new material then."

Instead, more of these vintage live recordings – namely, 'New Life', 'Boys Say Go!', 'Nothing To Fear' and 'The Meaning Of Love' – were paired up with 'Everything Counts' on August 1, to form another limited-edition 12″ single, complementing the already released standard 12″ comprising 'Everything Counts (In Larger Amounts)' backed by 'Work Hard (East End Mix)'. Another jointly penned composition from Martin Gore and Alan Wilder, the latter's mantra-like chorus was hardly memorable and it subsequently proved to be the last collaboration between the two, not that Wilder was troubled by the decision: "At one point I did try and persuade Martin to co-write because I thought as a team we might be able to write some good songs together, but he completely blanked that idea. He wasn't into it at all. That was fine."

168

"As soon as people hear the name [Depeche Mode] they start to think that here's another sweet pop single," Andy Fletcher groaned during another obligatory round of promotional interviews prior to the release of *Construction Time Again*. "I hope that people will give the new album a proper listen. They might be surprised!"

Dave Gahan was evidently thinking along similar lines in conversation with *Sounds*: "We feel a lot more confident now – and I think it shows in the new album; it comes across more. I feel a lot more confident about doing my vocals now; we've moved on so far from our first album. I just hope people give us a chance. What we can give them is what we think is a 100 per cent album."

Although 'Everything Counts' was rather sweet in terms of its melodic content, when released on August 22, 1983 *Construction Time Again* featured a stunning sleeve design by Brian Griffin in which a shirtless industrial worker wielded a sledgehammer on a mountainside – Mont Blanc in the Swiss Alps – with another mountain peak visible in the distance. This time the music press picked up on the visual statement, with *Sounds*' Johnny Waller commenting, "Although they deny any overt sympathies with communism or even a democratic kind of socialism . . . the new LP sleeve depicts a man wielding a hammer. The previous one [*A Broken Frame*] showed a woman with a sickle. The connection can be made."

So had Depeche Mode suddenly become political overnight? And if so, what was their agenda? That the socialist worker depicted on the sleeve was swinging his sledgehammer from right to left supposedly spoke volumes. SWP (Socialist Worker Party) card-carrying *NME* contributor 'X Moore' (a.k.a. Chris Moore) was determined to get to the bottom of Depeche Mode's apparent about-turn. Picking up on the construction theme, when finally catching up with his comrades at their Belfast Ulster Hall performance (September 10, 1983), X Moore demanded to know, "What needs to be built, then?" Alan Wilder was at a loss for words, and could only proffer, "Whole new ways of thinking" by way of a somewhat lame reply.

Wilder had in fact contributed two of the more thought-provoking songs to the album. "It wasn't until the third album, *Construction Time Again*, that things relaxed enough for me to introduce one or two songs, and, along with Gareth Jones, a few more radical ideas," he later revealed. Given that the end of the Cold War was still some way off, 'Two Minute Warning' focused on the threat of nuclear war that was terrifyingly real in Thatcher's Britain. "I really like the idea of people humming 'Two

Minute Warning' without realising what it's about," Wilder told *Sounds'* Johnny Waller. "It's almost surreal – the possibility of a nuclear holocaust is so terrifying, but to actually turn it round and try and make it beautiful – and the tune is very light and bouncy – is more of a challenge than making it doomy."

'The Landscape Is Changing' was equally downbeat in its subject matter. "I saw a TV documentary about acid rain which gave me the idea for 'The Landscape'," Wilder admitted.

Heavy subjects for what many still considered to be a lightweight synth act.

Alan Wilder: "I think the politically conscious aspects of Depeche Mode's early songs were more to do with age than any great desire to make a statement – we were hardly Billy Bragg! We never had a collective political view. We all had different ideas on most things – despite our backgrounds – and apart from the tracks on *Construction Time Again* I think you'd be hard pressed to find anything else that was directly politically motivated."

Andy Fletcher betrayed a swing to the right when airing his own political beliefs. "I'm not totally socialist, I'm very patriotic, very pro-British. I know some people think that's wrong, but I can't help it. I don't believe we should give up our side of the nuclear deterrent. If we surrendered our nuclear weapons, Britain's stature would disappear. I'm a bit of a soldier at heart."

NME's Mat Snow astutely noted that *Construction Time Again* was a departure. "You'll find no 'Meaning Of Love', 'See You' or even 'Leave In Silence' here," he wrote. "*Construction Time Again* avoids the personal. It's on its own soapbox, thinking aloud about the world and its woes with a voice in equal measure acute, uncertain, naïve and gauche. But there's an honesty, almost a shyness, that convinces you that Depeche Mode aren't just another bunch of two-bit pop stars sounding off the party-line to garner some intellectual credibility. They have made a bold and lovely pop record. Simple as that."

Martin Gore: "X Moore claims the [*Construction Time Again*] album was virtually a rewrite of the *Communist Manifesto*. I mean, that's just silly. The songs aren't so much political as songs of common sense."

As for the sensible socialist album's content, 'Pipeline' was a near perfect example of Depeche Mode's attempt at pushing the envelope with fledgling sampling technology.

Andy Fletcher: "When we actually made the album we did go on a sound-hunting expedition. We went down Brick Lane and just hit every-thing and then recorded it, and then took it back to the studio and then put it into the keyboard [sampler]. That's how we made the track 'Pipe-line' – smashing corrugated iron and old cars. The vocals were recorded in a railway arch in Shoreditch – you've got the train three quarters of the way through, and the aeroplane up above. It's really interesting doing that."

Dave Gahan: " 'Pipeline' was very experimental in that every sound on there has been made from us just out on the street hitting things, recording it and playing it back in different ways – even the vocal was recorded in a tunnel!"

He later revised his opinion slightly: "Despite its flaws, I still think of that [*Construction Time Again*] as one of our purer albums. Musically, I guess some of it was forced. Maybe we were trying too hard at the time. It was a massive changing point for us, both musically and lyrically. We were attempting to sample too much and trying to give a message without thinking so much of the structure of the song. We were missing the point, really. We'd go out everywhere and spend days sampling the sounds of building sites, like kids with a new toy. We'd spend too much time and energy *researching* the album, without really concentrating on the songs."

Alan Wilder: "I like *Construction Time Again*, because of its freshness and ambition to move forward. You can hear everything that's good about that LP in 'Everything Counts', for example. Not only did Martin break away from his very poppy style of writing – venturing towards more diverse subjects – but the sampler appeared on the scene for the first time. To me, there's a positive integrity about the LP."

Gareth Jones: "[*Construction Time Again*] was a great step forward for the band, for me, and for electropop."

From a 1983 standpoint, principal propagandist Andy Fletcher thought the band had done themselves proud: "We've got a really unique sound now; no one else sounds like us – especially our latest stuff – and we're vastly improving. This album should be the one, really; it'll be one of the albums of the year, I think."

Dave Gahan was equally buoyant in his outlook at the time: "It's just a different mood – the second album was quite depressive because that's the mood we were in at the time . . . but the mood in the studio this time was definitely up! So it's an up album."

Fletcher and Gahan partly had Alan Wilder to thank for that positive vibe. "I had no problem getting involved – the others weren't particularly precious about the studio," said Wilder. "The most protective person was actually Daniel Miller, who very much controlled the studio direction at that time."

Daniel Miller: "Alan is an extremely talented – and technically talented – musician, and also he can really play keyboards. He has a very good sense of arrangement and he loves working in the studio, which none of the others really do. When he joined, he kind of partly took Vince Clarke's place – he did write a couple of songs, but wasn't the songwriter. Martin was always very good melodically – and [at] arranging, but Alan added to that as well. He was more serious than they were; he'd been a pro musician before and I think it was an opportunity to make things work. I felt really comfortable with him, and he was trying to portray us in a good light. It wasn't like it was a job; he was definitely in it for the long term."

Vince Clarke, who later worked closely with Gareth Jones himself, was privy to some interesting inside information regarding his former band's working practices: "I hadn't realised it, but when Gareth worked with them, Alan was doing all the work, so to speak – all the studio stuff. So I suppose he kind of took over my role. Martin apparently got a bit lazy because Alan was more interested in the technical aspects of the studio."

Wilder's commitment to the task in hand shone through when talking about *Construction Time Again* to *Sounds'* Johnny Waller: "We've been making this album – including writing the songs and doing demos – since the beginning of the year, so that's eight months of our lives. You've got to have confidence that what you release is actually what you heard in your head when you first thought of the song."

Gareth Jones: "Alan and I were very interested in studios and recording technology, and exploring as wide a range as possible. Daniel was, of course, totally into experimentation as well. *Construction Time Again* really was a voyage of discovery for all of us."

Alan Wilder: "Songwriting didn't really come naturally to me. But I felt I should participate in the process. However, it became clear that my strengths were more to do with placement of sounds and the structuring of the music, and I suppose my classical upbringing was a factor in this. What I really added was an enthusiasm and desire to experiment more. I was also desperate for us to be taken more seriously, which meant producing a darker, more weighty sound."

Before going back on the road to promote *Construction Time Again,* Alan Wilder holidayed with Dave Gahan and Jo Fox on Lanzarote in the Canary Islands, Andy Fletcher stayed put in Basildon (apart from a day-trip to Clacton for a day) while Martin Gore headed out to Berlin to spend time with girlfriend Christina Friederich. In August 1983, Jo Fox announced that she would be taking over running the Depeche Mode Official Information Service from her parental home at 42 Hillway, Billericay, Essex, following Anne Swindell's understandable departure due to "personal problems". (In a twist of affairs, Anne later stepped out with Vince Clarke for a time.)

Jo saw fit to mention that Dave Gahan had failed to pass his driving test on July 27: "He had a very old and grumpy test instructor who failed him on two silly little points and just generally 'had it in for him.' Not to be deterred, Dave's applied for a second test."

When Depeche Mode's Construction Tour 83 took to the road on September 6, playing two nights at Hitchin's The Regal, Len Wright Travel and Eurotrux transported the band and a stage crew of 12 – including Daryl Bamonte, now promoted to stage managerial status. Stage set designer Dave Allen elevated the three instrumentalists and their keyboards on risers while lighting designer and board operator Jane Spiers, "the most amusing girl of the entourage," according to Andy Fletcher, brought the show to life visually.

The latest set list was heavily weighted towards *Construction Time Again* with almost total disregard for its predecessors, opening with 'Everything Counts' before proceeding to run: 'Now, This Is Fun', 'Two Minute Warning', 'Shame', 'See You', 'Get The Balance Right!', 'Love, In Itself', 'Pipeline', 'The Landscape Is Changing', 'And Then . . .', 'Photographic', 'Told You So', 'New Life' and 'More Than A Party' with 'The Meaning Of Love', 'Just Can't Get Enough' and 'Boys Say Go!' or 'Work Hard' reserved for encores.

Reproducing the more complex nature of the new songs live dictated a varied selection of state-of-the-art onstage instruments – a streamlined Yamaha DX7 digital polysynth and the Emulator sampler in Martin Gore's case, while Alan Wilder and Andy Fletcher remained resolutely analogue, with their respective Roland Jupiter-8 and Oberheim OB-8 programmable polysynth flagships weighing in at a cool £3,999 and £4,418 apiece. It's interesting to note that baffling foreign exchange rates dictated that Oberheim purchasers in the UK were charged roughly double that paid by American customers – not that Andy Fletcher would be troubled by this in light of Depeche Mode's financial gains.

By now Fletcher, Gore and Wilder had comfortably settled into onstage positions that would remain practically unchanged. "Being short with a bizarre appearance, Martin always seemed to look better in the middle," Wilder commented. "I always chose the position nearest the monitor desk for communication with the sound engineer [Andy Franks, in the case of Construction Tour 83]."

NME's Mat Snow was impressed with the result: "Their show is a careful mixture of spectacle and intimacy. Alan Wilder and Martin Gore appear first on-stage, being gradually enveloped in smoke as they brew up a swirling instrumental overture. Then Andy Fletcher walks on, as amiable and unstuffy as they come. Belying his backstage nerves, he casually switches on the backing-tape machine sitting centre stage as he strolls over to his synthesisers. Just by that casual press of a button, he sums up Depeche Mode's appeal; the technology of their music-making is instantly demythologised. You don't have to be a genius or rich or good-looking to stand a chance. Just like that other quartet of boys next-door 20 years ago, Depeche Mode bridge the gap between performer and the audience by showing the potential for magic in the most familiar, accessible things."

Heading across the Irish Sea, Belfast welcomed the slicker-than-ever touring machine to the Ulster Hall on September 9. "That was interesting – more so since the latest album hadn't been released there at that time," noted Gore. "But the new songs went down really well. Mind you, I think the crowds over there are a bit madder anyway."

Now charged with wardrobe and makeup while on the road with her fiancé, Jo Fox's enthusiasm for the legendary Irish hospitality spilled over into the October instalment of the Depeche Mode Official Information Service newsletter: "One of the best gigs had to be the Ulster Hall in Belfast; everyone was a bit wary of going there for obvious reasons, but it was well worth it as they played to a packed house of very appreciative Irish who hardly ever get to see live bands because of the troubles. The Depeche Mode show went down extremely well on the whole tour, with excellent lights by a young New Zealand girl [Jane Spiers]; it was, on the whole, a highly entertaining series of concerts for the band and the audience, too."

Markedly contrasting with previous tours, Daryl Bamonte has since implied that this was the year that "full-on hedonism" entered the Depeche Mode camp; exactly what went on behind the scenes in the name of entertainment goes unrecorded. "I'm not saying that we *don't* get up to these things," Dave Gahan coyly admitted. "It's just that if we do, they don't get out. I mean, most groups work for really large companies and there's always someone who will tell the press. Our company is so small that we know it wouldn't leak out."

The former Jo Fox discreetly sheds further light on these shenanigans: "I was aware of a scene which I was uncomfortable with, but it's hard to go all out for full-on hedonism when the girls were around! I think Dave was restricted; maybe not so the others."

Triumphantly winding up the 24-date UK opening leg of the Construction Tour 83 tour with three sold-out nights at the Hammersmith Odeon on October 6, 7 and 8, Depeche Mode could briefly kick back before continuing around mainland Europe throughout December. With *Construction Time Again* at number six, their current single, 'Love, In Itself' had a comparatively sub-standard seven-week run on the Singles Chart.

Alan Wilder: " 'Love, In Itself' certainly wasn't our strongest single, yet it still somehow managed to spawn a multitude of different remixes. I can't really remember how most of them, like the 'swing version', came about – probably a spin-off from the middle-eight of the original. All I can say is that listening to and actually liking some of them is sure to separate the men from the mice in terms of being a real devotee.

"Actually, it was a weird track all 'round, not least because from the moment we first heard it, a standing joke was born that the verses sounded just like a particular nursery rhyme – I can't quite put my finger on which one, but I'm pretty sure it's 'Ugly Duckling'. When pushed, Martin admitted that he had, in fact, based the tune around the rhyme and I'm afraid I could never quite listen to the song seriously again."

Before a remixed version of 'Love, In Itself' was released as the 'Love, In Itself 2' 7″ single on September 19, 1983, *Sounds'* Johnny Waller was already extolling the virtues of the original: "More recent songs like 'Get The Balance Right!', 'Everything Counts' and one superb new track 'Love, In Itself' hint at a new wistful softness at the centre of the recently discovered toughness."

Johnny Waller immediately picked up on the closing chorus line when asking its writer what was meant by *"Love's not enough in itself."* Gore reticently replied, "It's true – it's not," leaving Gahan to elaborate: "I think there's a lot of personal things in that song that maybe you wouldn't want to talk about in an interview – maybe Martin's trying to find out what else there is to life."

That Gore chose to harmonise three-quarters of the second verse an octave higher than Gahan's lead vocal in itself suggested a need to emphasise whatever sentiment lay therein. Barely 22 years old, the song-writer was clearly coming out of his shell in song, if not on paper.

"A sober tune [that] marks their continuing willingness to puncture any preconceptions you might have about them," wrote *NME*'s Chris Bohn on September 24. Wilder's jazzy piano break in the middle of 'Love, In Itself 2' was punctuated by a few seconds of acoustic guitar fretwork from Gore, later highlighted on Clive Richardson's promo video (filmed in some Welsh caves, together with a short clip taken from the group's per-formance at Bristol's Colston Hall on September 12).

Andy Fletcher: "Even to this day I still think [that] was a bit weird, because he's [Gore] actually a really good guitarist, and he still isn't a good keyboard player."

Sounds' Geoff Barton was convinced of the new single's future success: "Another big hit, and nothing short of driving a meathook through David Gahan's malformed cranium will prevent it." Backed by Alan Wilder's non-album 'Fools', by October 1, 'Love, In Itself 2' had stalled at number 21, representing Depeche Mode's lowest chart placing in their home country since 'Dreaming Of Me' peaked at number 57 over two years previously.

Meanwhile, having notched up yet another UK Top Five hit single – 'Nobody's Diary' – in May 1983, Vince Clarke was about to begin an extended sabbatical from the charts when winding up Yazoo after only four singles, two albums, one UK tour and a smattering of US club perfor-mances, barely two years since first recording with Alison Moyet. Here was history repeating itself, and loyal pal Robert Marlow was hardly sur-prised: "I think there were similar problems there – personality problems. I don't think Alison was particularly interested in what he did; she saw it as a way of getting her songs and herself known." That she did, signing a six-figure deal with CBS soon after and returning to the UK Top 10 as a successful solo artist within a year . . .

Subscribers to the Depeche Mode Official Information Service were informed the band intended to record "a completely new single in the New Year." In the meantime, two extra 12″ versions were available for those Depeche devotees wishing to prolong their fix: the first featured further variations on the 'Love, In Itself' theme ('Love, In Itself 3' and

'Love, In Itself 4'), plus 'Fools (Bigger)'; the second constituted the third –
and last – in the band's recent series of limited-edition releases with 'Love,
In Itself 2' being backed by four more live recordings culled from the
Hammersmith Odeon show – namely, 'Just Can't Get Enough', 'Shout!',
'Photograph Of You' and 'Photographic'.

Alan Wilder: "I think we toyed with the idea of 'And Then . . .' and
one or two other tracks, but for some reason the third single [from *Construction Time Again*] never materialised."

More uplifting news came from Germany, where *Construction Time
Again* reached number seven in the charts. According to the Depeche
Mode Official Information Service, the album was also doing good business in Belgium, Sweden, Switzerland and, surprisingly, France, "by far
outselling *A Broken Frame* in all countries." In fact, such was the album's
success in Germany – selling 250,000 copies, double what it shifted in the
UK, despite the fact that Depeche Mode had yet to muster a German Top
20 single – that ticket sales for the forthcoming European leg were to be
reviewed in mid-November with a view to possibly upgrading certain
venues. In the event, demand was such that the planned gig at Berlin's
Metropol for December 8 was moved to the larger Deutschland Halle,
where Depeche Mode performed to a capacity crowd of 10,000! "It's very
odd," observed a pleasantly surprised Dave Gahan. "When we play
German cities, the word gets around that we're some big hip band. I'm
pleased. It shows that our music does have wider appeal."

Andy Fletcher agreed: "It's pleasing that we've finally had a hit somewhere apart from England. But it's hard to understand why. After the
album had done really well here [in the UK], we put out 'Love, In Itself'
as a single and it bombed. We can't work that out. It may be that the
success is just a freak thing; maybe it'll never happen again."

The band rounded off their 18-date European trek with three consecutive nights at Hamburg's Musikhalle on December 21, 22 and 23, just in
time to head home for Christmas. The smell of Teutonic success must have
been all the more sweet for Martin Gore who, in addition to now having a
German girlfriend, had remained in close contact with the Frenzen family
with whom he had stayed in the Schleswig-Holstein state town of Erfden as
an enthusiastic foreign exchange student back in 1976-78. It was also to
Germany that Depeche Mode were to divert their recording energies.

14

Lasting Long-players?

"The attitude of a lot of British bands has been, 'We're British!' We started out big in Britain, then Scandinavia, then Germany, then France, then Spain and Italy, then America. It all went in stages."

– Andy Fletcher, 2001

Construction Time Again had proven to be the "fine album" that Martin Gore had been hankering for a year earlier – particularly in Germany where the band had made an unexpected jump into indoor arenas, much to Andy Fletcher's amazement: "We never saw ourselves as having vaguely Germanic overtones to the music. If you've heard German pop music . . . I don't see the connection."

Indeed, if '99 Red Balloons', the throwaway UK chart-topper in February 1984, from German pop sensation Nena, was anything to go by, then Fletcher had a point: Nena and her ilk were hardly in the same league, musically or lyrically, when singing in English – or German, for that matter.

Across the Atlantic, Sire dutifully released *Construction Time Again* on September 7, 1984, but to little avail. Raised on traditional rock'n'roll, America wasn't quite ready to embrace Depeche Mode's radical European found-sound sampling antics. As Andy Fletcher came to view it, "America had missed punk; of course, it had reached New York, but, generally, American radio and American youth had missed punk. So, basically, in 1981, '82 and '83 they were still listening to REO Speedwagon, Chicago – that sort of progressive yuck!"

Back in October 1983, the Depeche Mode Official Information Service had announced that the band were planning a series of US and Canadian shows throughout October and November of that year. By November, it was announced that the tour was to be postponed until the New Year. Yet come December, it looked like Depeche Mode would not be entering America for quite some time: "The proposed USA and Canada Tour will not be taking place in the New Year. There are no further plans for it."

Given the difference between the three-figure American audiences who turned out to see Depeche Mode in March 1983 and their five-figure European counterparts several months down the line in Germany, it's not surprising. In an interview with *Smash Hits* at the time, Dave Gahan offered an explanation of this sudden change in touring tactics. "We just had a meeting about America, and we decided not to worry about it," he confessed. "If we really wanted to be incredibly wealthy, we'd be over there trying to cash in on the British Invasion, but we don't see the point. Our sound is too English for American radio, and we're not prepared to change it to have hits over there."

Martin Gore echoed his bandmate's sentiments: "The Americans tell us to write dance records, but we're not prepared to do that just to get a hit."

However, that elusive Stateside single would soon be forthcoming – without Depeche Mode compromising their increasingly distinctive sound . . .

Alan Wilder: " 'People Are People' was the first track to benefit from a period of pre-programming to save studio time – even if it was done in a dodgy rehearsal room in Dollis Hill, North London. We would have finished it sooner except that some of the work had to be redone after the 'infamous incident' when a particular member of the band turned up, only to trip over the main power cable and pull the plug."

Wilder would not be drawn into naming names, but given that one of Martin Gore's favourite studio pastimes at that time involved hiding hapless Andy Fletcher's spectacles, perhaps the short-sighted synth player was the guilty party. "It's not always a bad thing – especially in Germany where we get some right nutters headbanging in front of the stage, but if friends come to see us and they're waving like mad, I never see them so they think I'm ignoring them."

When it came to recording and mixing 'People Are People' in January 1984, Depeche Mode and Daniel Miller knew when they were on to a good thing and regrouped with Gareth Jones at Hansa in West Berlin. This arrangement undoubtedly suited the freelance engineer who was, by now, living in the divided city on Potsdamer Straße, a move he described as being "part and parcel of the Berlin rush." Prior to starting work on 'People Are People', Jones had further familiarised himself with Hansa when working there with Fad Gadget, and German experimental act Palais Schaumburg, whose Thomas Fehlmann would eventually lend his outlandish talents to British ambient outfit, The Orb.

Jones remembered the Berlin-based 'People Are People' recording sessions as being even more radical than his previous work with Depeche Mode: "We went even more extreme in our practice of sending instruments out into different rooms and amps. We rented two studios at Hansa – the huge hall, Studio 2, as well as the mix room. In Studio 2 we put a huge PA system and an array of mics going down the hall; many of the beats went out into this. We also had another system in the bright reverb-y recording room upstairs by the mix room. Lots of these effects were running live in the mix."

Alan Wilder concurred: "The vocals were recorded in a big room – that is, the vocals were sent down through a PA into a big, live room so we could not only get a great, big sound, but so we could put effects like echo on the vocal while it was being recorded and mixed afterwards on the desk."

Before Depeche Mode, Daniel Miller and Gareth Jones could begin dealing with the complicated task of mixing 'People Are People' using Hansa's SSL SL 4000 G-series computerised console, a wide palette of original sampled sounds was required for the band and its production team to play with – in fact, the lead vocals were pretty much the only sounds that *weren't* sampled for the song. Thanks to the sales of their Drumulator digital drum machine, E-mu Systems, Inc. launched their new improved Emulator II sampling keyboard for £5,600; bristling with numerous accessories over and above those offered by its predecessor, the Emulator, which had served Depeche Mode so well (alongside Daniel Miller's Synclavier) on *Construction Time Again*. Despite Dave Gahan's assertion that *Construction Time Again* had suffered from *too* much sampling, the Emulator II soon made its way into the band's growing instrumental arsenal, helping to create 'People Are People'.

Gareth Jones: "There was a crucial chorus sound on 'People Are People' that was laughter and chatter that Martin had recorded on a plane, and after some discussion about possibly recreating the sound we, of course, simply used the original as it would have been impossible to recreate anyway."

Martin Gore remembered it well: "I took a stereo [Sony] Walkman when I was going on a plane from England to somewhere. I originally brought it along to tape the takeoff, but while the air hostess was telling everyone to 'Check the instruction cards under your seat,' the door flew open and all this wind rushed in which made a real noise and everyone laughed. Anyway, I looped the end of what she was saying and the laughter, so it goes, ' . . .tion cards, ha, ha, ha, ha . . .tion cards, ha, ha, ha, ha,' which sounds funny, but I used it in conjunction with a choir sound and it added a really nice texture to the bridge on 'People Are People'."

Alan Wilder explained the three throaty clunks dominating the end of each chorus: "First of all we sampled Martin going 'Unk, Unk, Unk,' with his throat, then we added a bell sound and a timpani to give it depth."

Having fully immersed himself in the technical world of sound, Gore was keen to take readers of *International Musician And Recording World* through his latest hit in the making; in the process illustrating just how far Depeche Mode were prepared to go in improving their electronic art: "The bass drum at the beginning [of 'People Are People'] was just an acoustic bass drum sampled into the Synclavier, then we added a piece of metal to that – just a sampled anvil-type sound – to give it a slight click and make it sound a bit different. That's the beauty of the Synclavier – you can edit sounds together to make what we call combination sounds. The main synth sound is the actual synth sound on the Synclavier – that's the one that plays the bass riff. But the bass sound is a combination sound, too, with part of it being an acoustic guitar plucked with a coin, which sounds very interesting when the two sounds are sequenced together."

On the subject of sequencing, by now the universal Musical Instrument Digital Interface, better known as MIDI, was making its presence felt in recording studios around the world, finally allowing the latest electronic instruments from different manufacturers to talk the same language, as it were. Because Depeche Mode's Emulator II featured MIDI – as did the Yamaha DX7 digital polysynth used by Martin Gore – and that, according to Gareth Jones, everyone felt that Daniel Miller's Synclavier's internal sequencer was not "friendly enough", sequencing duties were instead handed down to a lowly BBC B Micro (computer) – more readily used as a teaching tool in British schools – running an early specialised music software package called UMI. "The UMI is very good for programming song structures, because it's so flexible," Gore explained. "The Synclavier is OK, but isn't very practical because once you've programmed a song, it's very hard to change the structure."

Once again, 'People Are People' wasn't about individual performances, but the end result. "There's very little playing going on in 'People Are People'," Alan Wilder confirmed. "Virtually everything was sampled into the Synclavier. With the guitar sounds we altered them slightly once they were in the Synclavier because you sample in one note and then you can alter the length and dynamic of every note in the sequence for the guitar part so it will give expression, but it will still be completely in time.

"You can't help, after you've been involved with sequencing for a while, noticing three millisecond or five millisecond discrepancies, so you end up time-shifting every sequence until its perfect," Wilder admitted to *International Musician And Recording World*'s Adrian Deevoy in 1984. "Then we got into consciously putting things slightly out of time – like, for example, the choir sound on 'People Are People', we used a combination sound of different choir sounds on different synths and then put them slightly out of time with each other. We took one sound from the Synclavier, one from the PPG [Wave 2] and one was on the Emulator [II]."

Martin Gore: "Even though Alan has Grade Eight piano, his playing is still incredibly out of time compared to the Synclavier sequencer – and even that's out!" If Gore's tongue-in-cheek comment from the same interview is to be believed, it's unlikely that Depeche Mode ever considered becoming serious techno architects.

On February 3, 1984, Depeche Mode played an abbreviated 40-minute show at the Birmingham Odeon for simultaneous BBC2 television broadcast on Radio One DJ Peter Powell's *Oxford Road Show*. In spite of its enforced brevity, the gig quickly sold out. According to *Melody Maker*'s Simon Scott: "In spite of (because of?) the extra lights, and burly cameramen following their every move, the Modes turned in a far more lively and physical performance than usual. David Gahan had obviously spent some time studying Michael Jackson videos, and has adapted at least one of his dance steps. In contrast, Andy Fletcher and Alan Wilder stood still and concentrated hard, while Martin Gore stared moodily through made-up eyes under his punky barnet. It's sad to report that Depeche Mode remain firmly rooted in the stagecraft they've used since their inception. A couple of robot lighting towers, a hip swivel here and a handclap there do not a decent live gig make. They really can't rely on chestnuts like 'New Life' and 'See You' to maintain the excitement level forever."

The Depeche Mode Official Information Service listed the songs performed as being 'Everything Counts', 'Two Minute Warning', 'The Landscape Is Changing', 'See You', 'Shame', 'Told You So', 'More Than

A Party' and 'Just Can't Get Enough'. No sign of 'New Life'. Perhaps Scott wasn't at the gig.

Also notable in its absence was 'People Are People', although admittedly its release date – and indeed its title – had yet to be formally announced. Perhaps the band weren't ready to risk performing a new song for the first time when dealing with the added pressure of a televised concert. A more plausible scenario is that they hadn't the time to prepare a backing tape from the original multitrack recording for a one-off performance – hence simply resurrecting the backing tape used on the European leg of the Construction Tour 83, albeit in cut-down form. The full-length version of that backing tape was finally laid to rest following five further mainland European performances in Spain and Italy between March 5 and 10, after which the Depeche Mode Official Information Service announced that ". . . all plans for touring have been shelved so that the band can concentrate fully on the new single and writing the next album."

As had become common practice, 7″ and 12″ versions of 'People Are People' were simultaneously released in the UK on March 12, 1984, with Alan Wilder's 'In Your Memory' on the B-side. When the songs were extended in both content and name for the standard 12″ offering, 'In Your Memory' became 'In Your Memory (Slick)'. The bracketed addendum possibly referred to the band's nickname for Wilder on account of his slicked back hairstyle. When one obsessive online devotee later asked, "Is it slik or slick or silk?" his reply was suitably terse: "It's whatever you want, but I don't like it and nobody has used it for years."

But when it came to offering a recipe for creating 'Hot Hair (*circa* 1983/4)' Wilder was more obliging: "You will need: stupid prat (preferably aged about 22); large mirror (doctored to look as flattering as possible); head of straggly, unkempt hair (do *not* wash thoroughly); full hold hair gel (two tubes); Hovis bread (one loaf); 'Elnette Turbo-Nutter-Bastard Strength Hairspray' (three cans); blinkered attitude; one 'poofy' Eighties pop band; gaggle of teenage girls; and one packet of condoms.

"Take stupid prat and stand for half-an-hour in front of large mirror. Start by coating straggly hair thoroughly with both tubes of full hold hair gel, being careful to ensure sideburns are not missed. Using comb, scoop upwards to resemble loaf of bread and immediately cover *liberally* with hairspray (remembering to save some for the garnish). *Do not move until set!* Next, ignore the fact that everyone's saying 'Look at that stupid prat who looks like he's got a loaf of bread on his head' and place firmly in an equally badly dressed and follically disastrous Eighties pop band. Finally, add one more spray of 'Elnette' and serve immediately to gaggle of teenage girls who'll tell him he looks great . . ."

Although the Depeche Mode Official Information Service announced on two occasions that 'People Are People' would *not* be accompanied by another limited-edition 12″ single, in April 1984 the band enlisted the services of pioneering remixer Adrian Sherwood to tailor the song specifically for the dancefloor. Remixing has since become an everyday – some would argue unfortunate – fact of life in today's music industry whereby a happening record producer or DJ effectively deconstructs and rebuilds a track for a particular market. This practice was far less commonplace back in 1984, and British producer Adrian Sherwood, co-founder of the infamous ON-U Sound label, was one of its first sought-after practitioners, often wildly experimental with studio techniques in his quest to add the ON-U Sound stamp to a record.

Alan Wilder: "Adrian used to capture sounds in an AMS [digital] delay unit to create many of his effects, which was quite unusual for the time. I suspect this was how he created the additional voices [on 'People Are People']. To be honest, I find Adrian's stuff a bit hit or miss. There tends to be some inspired moments, but also some disasters – all within the same mix. I remember when he came to Hansa to do the ['People Are People'] mixes and due to his mind-altered state he required a large box of fuses because he'd blow the speakers every five minutes!"

Martin Gore's stance on the subject of multiple mixes was firm: "When we do a remix of a single we make sure that it *is* something really different that gives value for money, but we've been lucky that the real fans have always bought the singles."

Dave Gahan: "We *had* to do these 12″ records, so we made sure they were interesting all the way through. We spent a lot of time putting them together so that people would want to listen to them from end to end."

Culture Club's Roy Hay, guest reviewing for *Record Mirror*, was one of the first to pass judgement on 'People Are People' a week before its UK release: "I really laughed the first time it came on." Such churlish comments didn't deter the British record-buying public pushing the single to number four by March 24 in the UK Singles Chart, the band's highest chart placing to date on their home turf.

Alan Wilder: "Not bad for a song whose rhyming hook – *'People are people so why should it be/ You and I should get along so awfully'* – is a candidate for worst lyric ever written, almost on a par with Culture Club's *'War is naughty/ Really, really naughty/ And people who start them should go to bed early . . .'"*

Joking aside, 'People Are People' represented a serious condemnation of mankind's capacity for cruelty. Having previously been assaulted as a teenage Basildon partygoer, and later as a fully fledged pop star while walking near London's Portobello Road with a journalist in broad daylight, mindless violence was obviously a subject close to Martin Gore's heart, so much so that he chose to sing the song's moving, melodic refrain. The inspiration behind the second verse was, in all likelihood, equally autobiographical.

Unfortunately for Depeche Mode, a scheduled *Top Of The Pops* performance was cancelled due to BBC industrial action; had this not happened, 'People Are People' would almost certainly have reached number one.

Martin Gore: "If I'd been writing reviews at the time, I'd have given us a bad review – not for all the stuff, but at least the first couple of albums. We didn't do ourselves any favours because of the music on the first couple of albums – that was always like an albatross we were trying to get rid of. Once people hate something and get a bee in their bonnet about it, you have to really work to gain their trust back. It took a while before people said, 'Actually, that record's not too bad!'

"We also suffered because of our image – we happened to come along at a time when image was going through a really wild phase. I [recently] found a bunch of pictures from the Eighties and *everyone* looked terrible in the pictures – not just the band, but also all of my friends. And we happened to be in the spotlight at that point with dodgy haircuts, wearing dodgy clothes."

Germany's wholesale adoption of Depeche Mode continued unabated, with 'People Are People' topping the German charts for three weeks. The song, possibly Depeche Mode's most melodious offering since 'Just Can't Get Enough', and its unique production values helped set it apart from the increasingly run-of-the-mill, sample-infested pop fodder of the time. As Vince Clarke stated: "I got sick of hearing samples on records. I think some people do it really well. I really admire the stuff Daniel [Miller] does with Depeche because he never repeats himself."

Even the least technically inclined member of Depeche Mode was far from inspired by what he heard outside of his own group's musical endeavours. "I look at other people that use sampled sounds in disappointment nowadays," Dave Gahan told *NME*'s Don Watson in 1984. "They just seem to hire a Fairlight [CMI], sample a few orchestral sounds, and that's it. It all seems really boring. If you're going to spend that amount of money hiring a piece of equipment, then why not explore it? We still haven't explored it to the full – not in the slightest."

Depeche Mode turned again to the optical talents of director Clive Richardson for the 'People Are People' promo. Shot on HMS Belfast, a retired British naval cruiser permanently moored on the River Thames as a floating museum, Richardson effectively cut images of Fletcher, Gore and Wilder bashing various eye-catching components in the 1938-vintage warship's massive boiler and engine rooms, to coincide with the song's pounding mechanical-sounding soundtrack. These were subtly interspersed with stock footage that fooled some fans into thinking that Depeche Mode had ventured behind the Iron Curtain to film.

Martin Gore: "We've been happier doing videos since 'Everything Counts'. We have been able to find a director we like in Clive Richardson. We work well with him and now put a lot more time and energy into them."

When Sire dutifully released 'People Are People' in the US on May 16, with a 12" version appearing on July 11, it's highly unlikely that either record company or band had any great expectations for its success. After all, Depeche Mode's four previous Stateside single releases had failed to crack the all-important *Billboard* Hot 100 Singles Chart. While *A Broken Frame* had followed in the promising footsteps of its predecessor, *Speak & Spell* – mustering eight weeks on the *Billboard* Top 200 Albums Chart, reaching 177 at the beginning of 1983 – *Construction Time Again* failed to chart. Perhaps the latter's supposed socialist sympathies didn't sit too comfortably at the height of the Reagan Administration, whose political agenda included a massive military build-up to put the superpower on a stronger footing internationally.

Yet Depeche Mode had influential Stateside supporters, not least British expatriate DJ Richard Blade, champion of all things New Wave (and electronic) on Burbank-based KROQ 97.6, Southern California's most popular radio station throughout the early Eighties and beyond. "From their second album onwards, people began to wake up to them," recalled Richard Blade. "And then with their third album, it was just all over; suddenly the phones at KROQ were going absolutely nuts! People were saying, 'We love this band!' And unlike Duran Duran – who were happening at the same time – and Spandau Ballet, it wasn't, 'Oh my God; I love Martin Kemp!' or, 'Oh my God; I love John Taylor!' This was, 'Oh my God! I *love* the music of Depeche Mode!' "

Andy Fletcher: "What happened is that the kids started desperately looking around for something, and – a bit like in Essex, where we used to buy loads of American soul imports when we were young – they were starting to buy millions of UK imports, of which we were one of the bands. Then these radio stations that were college stations went on to start their own shows, playing all this new stuff, and we were considered alternative, because we *were* alternative to what they were listening to – or what they were being *forced* to listen to."

In Depeche Mode's case, the effect of this unexpected Stateside support made 'People Are People' début on the American *Billboard* Hot 100 Singles Chart on May 25. Peaking at number 13, the song remained on the chart for 18 weeks, during which time an executive decision was taken to release an American-only Depeche Mode retrospective album, also titled *People Are People* on July 2. As well as the single, the album featured a bizarre mixture of the band's relatively recent output, including 'Told You So' and 'Pipeline' from *Construction Time Again*; B-sides 'Now, This Is Fun' and 'Work Hard'; plus the flop singles, 'Leave In Silence', 'Everything Counts' and 'Love, In Itself'.

"It was done out of necessity, without any real continuity," confessed Alan Wilder. However, the feebly disguised marketing ploy paid off handsomely; the album clocking up 30 weeks on the *Billboard* Top 200 Albums Chart.

Ironically, Depeche Mode were too busy preparing their next album to capitalise immediately on this new-found Stateside success. Micky Senate hinted at the band's plans for the immediate future when rounding off his March *Melody Maker* feature interview: "Depeche Mode are currently on route for Spain and Italy. They'll be back in May to record the follow-up album to *Construction Time Again*, which should, all things being equal, be out in September. In October, they'll tour Britain and in November revisit Germany, after which they'll probably have another stab at the States."

The Depeche Mode Official Information Service's April 1984 newsletter reported: "During April the group plan to decide on the studio they'll use to record the new album from mid-May onwards, probably mixing it at Hansa in Berlin again. All or at least most of the songs have been written and indications are that in August the LP will be released with touring to begin in September – no dates, venues nor towns are settled yet." In the event, the band chose to record their fourth album, *Some Great Reward*, at Music Works, located off London's Holloway Road.

Given that no expense had been spared when recording and mixing 'People Are People' in Hansa's plush, hi-tech surroundings, *Melody Maker*'s Mark Jenkins speculated that cost was "an increasing preoccupation in the band's considerations" when it came to recording at the considerably less luxurious Music Works.

Certainly there had been times in the past when Depeche Mode's independent operation had necessarily restricted them financially – *Speak & Spell* reportedly weighed in with a comparatively lightweight studio bill of £8,000 – but quite why that should still be so in 1984, when the band had recently benefited from their highest grossing hit single on both sides of the Atlantic, is somewhat baffling. Gareth Jones later set the record straight. "Cost has never been a real issue on Depeche records. A more likely explanation was that members of the band and Daniel needed to be in the UK for some of this period."

By the time that *Some Great Reward* was released in September 1984, Gareth Jones would be rewarded with a co-production credit of equal standing to Depeche Mode and Daniel Miller. "Basically, I felt that my contribution was worth a production credit and when I asked Daniel and the band, they agreed – luckily for me! My role didn't change that much, however; we were all pulling together in the service of the songs and our quest for new sonic panoramas."

A month was spent recording songs for *Some Great Reward* at Music Works, during which time Daniel Miller's sampler/sequencer took centre stage. The opening vocal to Martin Gore's lyrically ambiguous 'Master And Servant' was yet more sampling fodder for the NED Synclavier, as Alan Wilder explained: "Firstly we got a lot of people singing the high, 'It's a lot,' and sampled that. Then we all sang the low, 'It's a lot,' and then a low, 'Like life.' You don't have to play one [sample] slower or faster than the other to get the octave either, because you make a patch on the Synclavier keyboard for each part and then you play the parts in their natural pitches and both at the same speed, which is very handy."

Unlike cheaper sampling devices like E-mu's original Emulator, a single sample would not increase in pitch as it was replayed up the NED Synclavier's keyboard, producing what became known as 'munch-kinnisation' on account of its similarities to those squeaky-voiced midgets from *The Wizard Of Oz*.

Further fuelling speculation about Martin Gore's possible S&M tendencies, 'Master And Servant' featured the vocal talents of Daniel Miller standing in the studio, hissing and spitting to simulate the sound of a cracking whip.

Taking up where *Construction Time Again* left off, the band continued with their outdoor sampling sojourns, even frequenting Hamleys, the world famous toyshop on London's Regent Street, in their quest for new sounds.

Martin Gore: "One morning me and Andy went down to Hamleys and bought as many toy instruments as we could find – pianos, saxophones, xylophones, and we took them all back to the studio and sampled them. One we used a lot was a marimba – a toy one, very strange – but after we'd sampled it, it was great. It sounded pretty terrible as a toy, but when we took it down a couple of octaves it sounded really good."

Gareth Jones: "I feel that Depeche Mode have always tried – and succeeded – to do something different on each album. At that time, a sampler for us was a way of creating whole new musical instruments. We were, of course, *not* using the sampler to create already existing instruments."

Elsewhere, the metal-bashing antics gave rise to more earthly pursuits as Depeche Mode took the *musique concrète* concept to a logical and literal conclusion. "On one of the tracks on the album, 'Blasphemous Rumours', we sampled some concrete being hit for what turned out to be the snare drum," Alan Wilder imparted at the time. Keen to get away from what he termed the "Howard Jones factory preset and Drumulator syndrome" of "really boring synth sounds," Wilder recalled the convoluted process of creating another strange effect for the same song, involving processing speech through a modular synthesiser, and possibly some additional outboard effects, before giving the unrecognisable result a final sampling makeover from the Emulator or Synclavier.

Having themselves previously experimented with E-mu's Drumulator, Wilder explained to *International Musician And Recording World* that Depeche Mode were now sampling all of their own drum sounds: "We always record the initial sound in an ambient space. We like to vary the snare sounds a lot so we record all different acoustic snares and close mike them or mike them from a distance, depending on the width of the sound that we require."

Not that their sampling exploits were entirely trouble-free in execution.

Martin Gore: "There were all these builders in next door at Music Works. We'd have the track running with us hitting skips and concrete, and they'd be next door tearing a wall down and we couldn't tell which was which! It was very confusing at times."

It was only a matter of time before the Musicians' Union started taking an interest in Depeche Mode's modern machinery.

Alan Wilder: "We got this percussionist in for the afternoon to sample his drums and the different techniques of playing them. We didn't try to hide the fact that we were sampling him. We said, 'We hope you don't feel raped,' and he agreed to be sampled literally just hitting one drum, once at a time. Anyway, we sampled all his drums once, maybe twice. Now [in 1984], the Musicians' Union [hadn't] really caught up with sampling; this bloke had obviously contacted them when he got home, because he gave us this bill for about 50 different sessions, plus a consultation fee. It was enormous, and the stupid thing was that most of the sounds weren't [any] good; we only used about two for maybe two seconds each on a couple of songs."

Sampling conundrums notwithstanding, in August the six-man Depeche Mode production collective relocated to West Berlin to continue working on *Some Great Reward* at Hansa, a move that no doubt delighted Martin Gore who had taken to renting an apartment on Heerstraße, conveniently located near the studio complex. On one occasion, he oddly insisted on being interviewed by *Record Mirror*'s Nancy Culp while lying down in the street at midnight. "I moved to Berlin because the 24-hours aspect of city life suits me," he told *No. 1*. "I'm happy to stay out all night – is that decadent? I haven't been able to spend much time in my Berlin flat yet, but it's close enough so that I can be back in Basildon in two hours."

Having lost his best mate and drinking partner to seedy Berlin, Andy Fletcher opted for a less adventurous, Essex-based lifestyle, moving in with biology student girlfriend Grainne Mullen and her mother in the Noaks Hill area between Basildon and Billericay. Dave Gahan and Jo Fox further cemented their partnership by buying their first home together in Laindon.

Basildon was now a very different – even difficult – proposition for the changeling Martin Gore, who told *No. 1*: "Sexual barriers are silly. My girlfriend and I swap clothes, makeup – anything. So what? It's a shock, though, to read in a magazine like [German teen publication] *Bravo* that I walk around dressed as a woman. They'll invent anything!"

Yet at its most extreme, Gore's self-confessed leather fetish extended to a bout of skirt wearing. "Dressing in skirts is not a gay thing, particularly," he argued. "Most transvestites or cross-dressers are heterosexual. I never went through a phase of thinking I was gay. It was never a gay thing at all; I never equated it with being gay. Over the years I've met so many people that have naturally assumed I'm gay – I don't have a problem with that."

Be that as it may, Gore's unusual choice of attire momentarily proved to be a cause for concern for his bandmates. "I was never comfortable with Martin dressing up in girl's clothing," confessed Alan Wilder. "And the rest of the group often used to comment and try to dissuade him. But I think the more we might do that, the more belligerent he'd become about it, so he had his mind made up.

"The interesting point, however, is that Martin is not gay and it annoys him when people make the assumption that he is. Strangely, he seems oblivious to the fact that many people still associate transvestism with homosexuality. Ironically, he now gets irritated when people bring up the 'dress' period – what did he expect?"

Martin Gore: "I started dressing like that *after* I moved out of Basildon. There were times when I forgot that you couldn't go back to Basildon dressed like that. I remember going back one Christmas and going down to The Bullseye, which was the pub in the centre of town, and I'd forgotten that I was wearing black nail varnish. So this guy said to me, 'What the *fuck* is that on your nails?' My hands were shaking!

"I honestly don't know what was going through my head when I was doing that. There was some kind of sexuality to it that I liked and enjoyed, but I look back now and see a lot of the pictures and I'm embarrassed."

At the time, however, *NME*'s Danny Kelly described the effect of Gore's relocation to Berlin as being "pure Road To Damascus". Andy Fletcher, "in his role of Best Mate," was reported as implying it was Martin's lucky escape from childhood sweetheart Anne Swindell that had so dramatically liberated the songwriter, "rather than where that escape propelled him to."

Dave Gahan sympathised to a degree: "Mart missed out on his teens; just generally going out, seeing different girls every night and getting drunk all the time – y'know, not caring. Everybody should go through that phase. Personally, I think he's doing all the things I did when I was 16. I went to clubs with people much older than myself. I wore tons of make-up, and dresses too! I look at a lot of things Martin does now and just laugh."

In the same interview, Wilder made light of the situation when stating, "He [Martin Gore] does enjoy it when we go through customs and they ask him if he wants to go into the men's or the women's cubicles to be searched."

Martin Gore: "At the moment they're most worried about the way I dress – about my *dresses*, in fact. Maybe I'll get them all wearing one."

In the summer of 1984, inside the relative safety of Hansa, it was business as usual for Depeche Mode – or so they thought.

Alan Wilder: "It's difficult to say how much being in Berlin actually affected the *sound* of the records, but we certainly saw Martin come out of his shell during this time. It seemed as though he had some catching up to do, having been a quiet and reserved teenager by all accounts. Frequenting clubs and bars became more routine and we all saw a very different side to Martin as he was let loose, so-to-speak – heavy drinking followed by apparel removal being top of his list of favourite activities."

It would appear that this particular "favourite activity" spilled over into recording 'Somebody' – an unusually simplistic track in that it featured a rare piano performance from Wilder. "It's performed all together – it just needed three takes, mainly to get the sound OK – and really uses the bare essentials," the mischievous Gore told *Melody Maker*. "In fact, I sang it completely naked in the cellar of the studio which we use for ambience, and the others sent the female tape op [Stefi Marcus] downstairs while I was doing it to 'check the connections'."

Gareth Jones: "Martin sang that downstairs in Studio 2, I believe, when we were at Hansa. He was allegedly naked, though we only have his word for it, since there was no visual contact with that room."

Having made their first – and possibly last – concession to the formulaic piano ballad, "based on a sort of Jonathan Richman back-to-basics theory," according to Gore, the arduous task of mixing the album commenced in time for the planned September 1984 release date – arduous for those band members easily tired of studio work. For a while it looked like the finely tuned Depeche Mode machine might run off the rails.

Alan Wilder: "After the initial recording at Music Works, we returned to Hansa to mix the album, but ended up getting horribly behind schedule. As a result, myself, Dan and Gareth completed the album alone because the other three band members had all booked their summer holidays and didn't want to cancel them. I foresaw the fact that we were going to go over deadline and held off arranging one myself because I didn't want to miss out on the whole mixing process.

"I remember that Killing Joke were also at Hansa at the same time, working on their *Night Time* LP. When they arrived, they let off a metal dust fire extinguisher all over Studio 2's Neve console, much to Gareth's annoyance. When he voiced his concerns, his name was entered into Jaz Coleman's 'little black book'."

While Gareth Jones retained no such memories of any little black books, that three-quarters of Depeche Mode were absent from mixing the majority of their latest album hardly made his job easier: "It's always nice to get the band's input to mixing, and I prefer it that way."

Gareth needn't have worried; within two weeks of its *en masse* arrival in European record stores *Some Great Reward* had already shifted around 85,000 copies in the UK and some 200,000 in Germany. In spite of their detractors – of which there were still many – it was looking like Depeche Mode were going to be around for awhile yet . . .

15

Risky Business

"There's never been a time when I've felt like winding the band up, but I always felt after each project that it was 50-50 whether the band members would actually get back together and feel the enthusiasm and passion to start another project."

– Martin Gore, 2001

Discussing the controversial content of 'Master And Servant' (released August 20, 1984), Dave Gahan told *Melody Maker*, "You have to take risks. You can't be safe all of the time, even if the kind of people you might offend are just the sort to kick up a fuss and start petitions and that sort of thing. They're still a minority."

When mixing 'Master And Servant', Depeche Mode's stated aim was to improve the "fat, round bass sound" that had dominated such contemporary recordings as Frankie Goes To Hollywood's 'Relax'. According to Alan Wilder, "We went completely up our arses and ended up with exactly the opposite, topping it all off at the end of a seven-day mix by leaving out a small detail – the snare drum! The cost of this crucial omission was realised when Gareth [Jones] and Dan [Miller] hot-footed it down to a local Berlin club one night, armed with a test pressing and fully expecting to blow the locals' minds. By the law of sod, the track came on straight after 'Relax'. Not surprisingly, it cleared the dancefloor, leaving both of them standing, red-faced in their raincoats, clutching their briefcases."

Depeche Mode did regain some face, by subsequently drinking the Frankie mob under the table in Dortmund. "There was a lot of tequila involved, and we won," crowed Alan Wilder. "I remember we played football, and won convincingly, against the German record company in about 1985, and, to top off our victory, someone from our camp succeeded in breaking one of their player's legs! By way of apology we

194

couldn't resist sending a 'Get Well Soon' card that simply read: '1945 . . . 1966 . . . 1985.' "

Apart from Frankie, Depeche Mode had little contact with their other rivals. "We used to bump into Spandau [Ballet] and Duran Duran all the time in the early Eighties," Alan Wilder revealed. "I think there was probably some rivalry."

Andy Fletcher: "We used to hate people like Spandau Ballet and The Human League – not so much Spandau, but definitely Duran Duran, because on *Top Of The Pops* [Duran vocalist] Simon Le Bon was like, 'I really like some of the stuff you're doing, yah.' They saw themselves as top of the premier [football league], and we were struggling third from the bottom, or first division or something. They had 24 bodyguards, 64 cars! Many years went by when we used to bump into them."

'Master And Servant' took a staggering seven days to mix. "It was quite a laugh recording it," said Alan Wilder. "If you listen very carefully, as well as the whip sounds, you can hear two Basildon girls singing, 'Treat me like a dog.' "

With words like that, Depeche Mode only narrowly escaped a BBC ban. As Dave Gahan recalled, "We had problems with 'Master And Servant' when the BBC called for a copy of the lyrics, but only one guy thought they were obscene, and he was away on holiday when the final decision was taken! The girl who took the decision agreed with us that it's about love and life, which of course it is."

Having navigated a safe passage past the censors, 'Master And Servant' reached number six in September 1984, despite dissenting reviewers – like *Time Out*'s Dave Walters, who crudely asked, "What do you expect from this bunch of lame dickheads?" – and another Clive Richardson-directed promo filmed in Berlin, featuring what Alan Wilder remembered as "the most embarrassing video moment ever – and, believe me, there were many." That "moment" in question was the so-called 'eetsa lot, eetsa lot' dance routine, courtesy of a hired French choreographer.

Alan Wilder: "More worrying, however, was the cancellation of a day's filming after fisticuffs ensued between two band members. Brought about when one party berated the other for excessive drinking, the Depeche Mode camp was decidedly uncomfortable for an entire week thereafter until the status quo was eventually restored, a peace agreement reached, and the happy couple reconciled over Hansa studios' Space Invaders machine – not that I'm mentioning any names, of course, except to say

195

that when Dave [Gahan] tried to attract my attention to witness this amusing spectacle, I was preoccupied with something else and missed it."

NME's Adrian Thrills was another writer none too thrilled by 'Master And Servant': "Their concern here is the game of sexual humiliation and whether they are serious (doubtful) or merely making an ironic observation on the leather 'n' dominatrix market (pointless), it is the listener who ultimately suffers for their art."

As far as Martin Gore was concerned, critics were way off the mark: "There's always been a certain amount of humour about our music that people have never seen – we never even get asked about it. On the current LP [*Some Great Reward*] there's a verse [from 'Something To Do'] that starts, 'You're feeling the boredom too . . .', and everyone just accepts it without a thought."

"So many of the songs are really funny; there's lots of Bas phrasings," Andy Fletcher told the *NME*'s Don Watson. "Things that you'd hear people saying in Basildon, but not so much elsewhere. Most of them are quite humorous in themselves, but most people don't get them – particularly if they're not Basos; things like, *'The world we live in and life in general'* [from 'Somebody']. I mean, people really seem to think we're serious when we write things like that."

Indeed, the band went as far as incorporating that exact 'Basildonian' saying into the album's outer sleeve artwork – which juxtaposed a bride and groom against a dimly lit metallic factory backdrop. "That cover was actually inspired by what we felt to be the lyrical content of the record: a romantic couple facing the real world," Wilder explained.

Yet, as Fletcher told *Melody Maker*, the band didn't always get an easy ride: "In Basildon, I get a lot of abuse. A lot of people still think we're like teeny wimps – wimps on synths. It's very like what we call a 'Span Town' – spanners, beer boys. I suppose it's because we've always lived there – they've seen so much of us that they've turned against us. Elsewhere, we actually get praised by some people. I think it's a good contrast, because we don't like the pop star thing. It's good to get a bit of abuse; it brings you down to earth."

In America, response to the latest single – cracking whips and all – was somewhat subdued in comparison to 'People Are People'. Making its *Billboard* début on September 7 (following simultaneous 7″ and 12″ releases on August 14), 'Master And Servant' peaked at number 87 before disappointingly dropping out after only three weeks. Not even more 12″

tamperings by radical remixer Adrian Sherwood – including a virtually unrecognisable version of 'People Are People' (appropriately re-titled 'Are People People?') – could reverse its fortunes.

While 'Master And Servant' would be Depeche Mode's last Stateside single for some time, interest was sustained on the *Billboard* album chart, with *Some Great Reward* notching up an impressive 42 weeks, peaking at number 52 – not bad going for supposed 'one-hit wonders'.

Andy Fletcher: "That was our first big album in America. There was a strategy in the sense that we wanted to get out of Berlin and, secondly, we wanted to show people abroad that we were doing very well – that we weren't a typical British band; that we considered ourselves to be a European-sounding band."

The main question was whether Depeche Mode felt confident enough to build on that success by touring America in 1984. Certainly Dave Gahan made no mention of any impending US concerts when informing *Melody Maker* that the band was "about to embark on a huge tour – more dates than we wanted to do, really, ending towards Christmas and taking in Germany, Sweden, Holland, Belgium, Italy and Switzerland.

"After this lot most of us will be wanting a holiday. The last German tour finished right before Christmas and by that time it had got very difficult to do something different every night. My mind used to drift sometimes and I'd forget the words. It's even worse for the others, because they're going to be stuck behind two Emulators, and there's no way you can move *them* around. But a lot of the audience don't seem to notice that we don't move too much. I like moving around on-stage now – at one time I used to just keep still and clutch the mike stand, but now I go to different parts of the audience and play up to them."

By now, the pattern of the band's touring schedule was taking on a familiar form; despite admitting to getting a nightly kick from commanding audiences of several thousand enthusiastic fans, Gahan was aware of the potential pitfalls of such lengthy road trips. "There are a few days off, but the gigs are mostly back to back. When we do get a day off it's always a Sunday in Hanley. Have you ever been in Hanley on a Sunday? You look at a couple of antique shops, wander about thinking, 'What the hell can I do?', you go back to the hotel and watch a couple of videos. It's awful."

The backing tape put in an appearance – albeit now off-stage – throughout the 'Some Great Reward Tour'. "We're aware of the limitations of using a backing tape – it takes away a lot of the spontaneity, but we can't see ourselves playing with a live drummer at this stage," the band told *Melody Maker*. "Nobody could play precisely enough or give us all the sounds we've used in the studio, but we've found other ways to make things a bit more visual. We've got a moving set with lots of scaffolding, slide screens and so on to match the [*Some Great Reward*] album sleeve. Jane [Spiers], who worked with us last time, wanted to take some of the ideas a bit further."

Certainly Jane Spiers' inventive lightshow was more impressive than before, particularly during 'Blasphemous Rumours' – another controversial song destined for release as Depeche Mode's next single – when large triangles of brightly lit neon tubes rose majestically around the three keyboard players, effectively contrasting with mock church stained glass windows projected onto overhead screens.

In addition to the usual onstage mix of synthesisers and samplers, the percussive set-ups now featured corrugated iron and bicycle wheel spokes, as Alan Wilder's future wife, Hepzibah 'Hep' Sessa, delighted in merrily mocking: "When I was sorting and categorising a huge trunk of DM memorabilia, I came across a very detailed diagram – drawn by Alan – to illustrate an elaborate percussion set-up, which included bits of scaffolding, a hammer and various other building site paraphernalia. Silly bugger!"

In fact, *Melody Maker* reported Depeche Mode as being one of the first groups to take E-mu's latest sampling dream machine on the road: "Emulator 2s [*sic*] were rapidly picked up by Depeche Mode and other discerning musos – the Basildon boys actually took the thing on-stage while it was still steaming from the attentions of Syco's service department, but had few problems with the machine's software."

Alan Wilder: "It was a logistical exercise. The live versions were structured in such a way that everybody could load their sounds in time to be ready for their first keyboard part. Sometimes extended intros were programmed to cover this problem. Since it took about 30 seconds for each bank of sounds to load, it was often touch and go whether everyone would make it on time. The later Emulators had internal hard disks, so we were able to store the whole set of sounds onto them without the need for floppies [floppy disks]."

At the Liverpool Empire on September 29 – three shows into the 29-date UK leg – *Melody Maker*'s Penny Kiley was less than impressed: "The music starts and so do the screams, the whole theatre bouncing by the time the curtain rises on four ramps, three lots of keyboards, a tape recorder and one leather-clad hip-swiveller. The stage set, an impressive design in

198

fashionable grey, combines hi-tech metallics with occasional projections and clearly wants to say something about the music. But, if there's any metal in the sound, it's molten. There are no edges. Whether the music's bubblegum, metal-bashing or ballads, the event is simply pop and the strongest messages are visual."

The UK tour finished up with four consecutive performances at the Hammersmith Odeon on November 4, before heading over to Scandinavia to begin a punishing mainland European touring schedule that would see the band performing 30 mainly arena-sized shows with only two days off. At the same time, Depeche Mode had another single, 'Blasphemous Rumours' in the UK charts.

Andy Fletcher: "When Martin first played me 'Blasphemous Rumours', I was quite offended. I can see why people would dislike it. It certainly verges on the offensive. The song stems from our experiences [at Boys' Brigade]. There was a prayer list of people who were sick in some way and you'd pray for the person on the top of that list until they died.

"I turned away from religion because I found I was leading a really boring life. I wanted to live life to the full, but I was trapped, and I thought, 'If I die tomorrow that'll be it.' It's a shame that Christianity is perverted and hyped so much, because it does have something to offer."

Despite Dave Gahan's insistence that 'Blasphemous Rumours' was not an anti-religious song, but rather "a personal statement on Martin's part," Depeche Mode must have known that certain people would be annoyed by Gore's observations. With a possible ban in mind, 'Blasphemous Rumours' was partnered up with the considerably less controversial 'Somebody' as a double A–side when released on October 29.

Martin Gore: " 'Somebody' is pretty much a straightforward 'I love you' song if you like, certainly not an anti–love song."

Andy Fletcher: "[It's] not just a love song, it's a real moon-in-June lovey-dovey [song] . . . Martin's in love again, see?" ('Somebody' was, no doubt, inspired by Gore's girlfriend, Christina Friederich.)

Martin Gore: "A love song can be completely throwaway or it can ring true. Some people tend to think that love songs shouldn't be treated seriously, that it's only if you're writing about social problems that a song becomes serious."

However, by 1990, Gore had a different view: "I simply can't write your conventional pop fare. A pleasant song to me is unfinished; it isn't telling the complete story, which is why I introduced the twist at the end of 'Somebody' because the song was just too nice.

"You [can] say I'm cynical about love in my songs, and perhaps I am, but I think that's an interesting angle. Otherwise you become mundane like most chart music. Relationships do have their darker side, and I like to write about it."

The serious side to 'Somebody' was underscored by the subtle sound of a heartbeat beneath Alan Wilder's piano accompaniment. As one observer put it, "The song became a live favourite, pulling the heart strings of every girl in the audience who couldn't help but feel it was directed solely at them, and who marked their appreciation with screams every time Martin paused for breath."

Unsurprisingly, it was 'Blasphemous Rumours' that garnered the majority of attention. *Smash Hits'* assistant editor Neil Tennant viewed it as "a routine slab of gloom in which God is given a severe ticking off."* Far from sounding gloomy, the chorus was both upbeat and uplifting, though, admittedly, the same could not be said of the doom-laden verses – where Gahan, usually backed by Gore, sang of various characters, including the grieving mother of a 16-year-old who had attempted suicide and the death of an 18-year-old hit-and-run victim who had found God – set to a backdrop of chilling sound effects and mournful reversed oboes. The band skilfully resurrected the music box-like dream sequence idea, first explored on 'Shouldn't Have Done That' for the *A Broken Frame* album, only now it took on a more nightmarish quality, further enhanced with a cunningly disguised 16-bar instrumental rendition of the children's hymn 'Jesus' Love Is Very Wonderful'.

Clive Richardson's newly launched company, Clive Richardson Films Ltd, were once again called upon to script and film promotional videos in October 1984. The simplistic 'Somebody' featured a close-up of a fully clothed Gore miming his lead vocal throughout most of its duration, interspersed with profile shots of Wilder performing on a Bösendorfer grand piano, sporting his then-trademark 'Hovis' quiff. Mock home cine-film footage of the remaining members frolicking on a beach completed the scene – functionary rather than award-winning stuff. 'Blasphemous Rumours' was filmed on the Some Great Reward Tour UK tour, giving a first-hand impression of what a current Depeche Mode concert was like – bicycle spokes and all.

---

* Within three years Neil Tennant would ironically be doing much the same thing when his own synth-driven duo, Pet Shop Boys, topped the UK Singles Chart with 'It's A Sin'.

Voices were raised in concern over the song's supposed blasphemy. Having taken Martin Gore's hook line at face value, one local Southend clergyman said, "If we can say God so loved the world that he sent his only son – if he did that, he cannot have a sick sense of humour."

'Somebody'/'Blasphemous Rumours' evaded a BBC ban and clawed its way up to number 16. Considering that both songs were readily available on *Some Great Reward* (although 'Somebody' had been remixed while 'Blasphemous Rumours' was slightly edited), this was a reasonable chart showing. A full six-minute, 12″ version of 'Blasphemous Rumours' was soon made available, coupled with four live tracks recorded at the Liverpool Empire show of September 29 – namely, 'Somebody', 'Two Minute Warning', 'Ice Machine' and 'Everything Counts'. Additionally, a four-track 7″ EP comprising the two songs from the standard single, plus live versions of 'Everything Counts' and 'Told You So', was issued to tug at the purse strings of fanatical Mode fans.

Following the conclusion of the European leg of the Some Great Reward Tour in Deinze, Belgium on December 18, Dave Gahan got his reward – a long holiday. Almost three months, in fact. Having worked without respite for the last year or so, Depeche Mode had certainly earned the right to take time out.

Suitably refreshed, in March 1985, the band regrouped once again with co-producers Daniel Miller and Gareth Jones at Hansa in West Berlin. A new single, 'Shake The Disease', was released on April 29, reaching number 18 in May. *Sounds'* Carol Linfield was impressed: "Flexible rhythms, Classic Mode stuff . . . thoroughly infectious." The obligatory, extra limited-edition 12″ featured a live recording of 'Master And Servant' (from the Liverpool Empire show of the previous year), alongside the so-called 'Metal Mix' of 'Something To Do' from *Some Great Reward*.

Ever the studio perfectionist, Alan Wilder had mixed feelings about 'Shake The Disease': "This is still one of my favourite Martin songs, but I don't think we really got the best out of it. I suspect everybody was trying too hard to make it sound extra special, not least Daniel [Miller]. I think there was a time when Daniel got too involved in the technology: I can remember one particular sound we created for 'Shake The Disease'. The part itself was virtually moronic – a two-note riff. And we ended up using 24 sounds layered on top of each other – every sound in the orchestra! These, of course, all then cancelled each other out, and the end result sounded like a sine wave! That epitomised how far up your arse you could go."

Although unquestionably a polished recording, 'Shake The Disease' was not a worthy successor to 'People Are People', 'Blasphemous Rumours' or even 'Everything Counts', being let down by a lacklustre synth bass line and a labouring drum machine accompaniment. According to Gareth Jones, "the ['Shake The Disease'] session didn't gel perhaps as well as our other sessions together."

Still, Dave Gahan turned in a creditable performance, having recently taken singing lessons with renowned London-based voice coach Tona deBrett – "scales and things, and I didn't see much application to singing pop songs, but I wanted to do more for [my] breathing control," Gahan told *Melody Maker* in September, 1984. Indeed, the song's harmony vocal arrangements were as good, if not better, than on any Depeche Mode song to date.

A new director Peter Care, was drafted in for the single's video, shot in and around London's then-derelict Docklands area. Alan Wilder, an amateur photographer in his spare time, described the filming process: "The promo uses free fall sequences that make for a fairly simple optical illusion. The subject is strapped to a motorised pole that runs through the back of his jacket. As the pole rotates, taking you with it, the camera follows at the same angle giving the impression that the subject is remaining still and everything in the background is actually moving. Peter also used another similar trick where the camera is attached to you on a kind of stiff harness – no cameraman [is involved]. As you move around with the camera, you again appear still while the background moves around."

"Understand me," pleads a heavily made up Martin Gore, miming to the song's memorable refrain. One glance at Gore's unusual choice of black attire, dramatically offset by an explosion of frizzy bleached blond hair erupting from the top of his shaved scalp, and it's likely that many tried to!

Depeche Mode's latest recording and filming ventures were bookended by a 16-date, coast-to-coast North American tour (their first since 1983), taking in Washington DC, New York City, Boston, Montreal, Toronto, Detroit, Chicago, and Rock Island before a one-off at Carbondale, Pennsylvania, followed by Texas, culminating in California's West Coast, at San Franscisco's Fox Warfield Theater on April 3, 1985.

The 3,500-capacity Hollywood Palladium show of March 30 reportedly sold out within 15-minutes of tickets going on sale, while massive oversubscription for the follow-on Southern California show forced the promoters to chance booking the huge 10,000-seat Irvine Meadows outdoor amphitheatre, Laguna Hills in its place. Unbelievably, the gamble paid off as the band notched up another sell-out, all the more remarkable considering that their one US hit single, 'People Are People' was almost a year before.

Unremitting radio support from the likes of KROQ 97.6 was obviously paying dividends, as Alan Wilder subsequently confirmed: "They were very supportive of DM for a long time, which helped our career in the US."

Martin Gore: "The first two times that we'd gone there we'd got a really bad response from the press. We seemed to be defending ourselves wherever we went, and we almost gave up on America. We decided not to play there. Someone talked us into going back, and the whole thing had just changed so much."

The American viewing public got their first small screen taste of Depeche Mode in May 1985, courtesy of I.R.S. Records' *The Cutting Edge*, shown on the MTV network. Superimposed over a live performance of 'Blasphemous Rumours' (filmed at Hamburg's Alsterdorf Sporthalle on December 9, 1984), all four members mulled over their working practices – practices that must have appeared alien to the current American rock climate.

Having recently reached for the peroxide bottle, a blindingly blond Dave Gahan spoke first: "When you're using electronics, you don't have to be technically an excellent musician; you don't have to be able to technically play a guitar and be a great guitar player. With a lot of groups it's about who's the best with the musicians, but with electronics you can have good ideas."

Next up was Alan Wilder: "I've never understood the attitude that synthesisers don't produce real music, because with any instrument it's the people that produce the music anyway. It's not the instrument; it's how you use the instrument, so that's what's important."

Andy Fletcher – also showcasing a bleached barnet – unwisely attempted to take a more technical route when stating, not entirely truthfully: "We don't use many synths anymore, really. We use quite a lot of computers, which are different. Because with computers you actually make your own sounds, but synths are really just electronically formulated sounds."

Martin Gore reticently rounded off proceedings: "I'd still go with the songs as being the most important thing. Even though we use this thing called the Synclavier, and are very interested in doing things in a very modern way, on our last album, for instance, one of the tracks ['Somebody'] was just an acoustic piano and vocal, because we felt that that song needed that sort of treatment. We wouldn't like to restrict ourselves and say, 'We've got to record this song in this way.' We're just interested in interpreting the songs in the best way possible."

Depeche Mode were back on MTV screens, being interviewed by mainstay VJ Mark Goodman on July 3. Goodman began by getting an uncomfortable-looking Gahan and Gore to define the band's unusual moniker before talk moved predictably to the use of synthesisers and computers at the expense of guitars. "We actually always have a lot of trouble trying to describe this process," stated a flummoxed Gore. "We do a lot of sampling," he began tentatively. "People have probably heard of things like the Fairlight. Well, we use an instrument called the Synclavier, which is very similar to the Fairlight, and you can just sample natural sounds or instruments – anything you like – into the computer. Then [when] you've got them in the keyboard, you can just sequence those sounds and do anything you like with them."

Feigning mock amazement, Goodman was clearly none the wiser. Temporarily putting the interview on hold after a couple of minutes to accommodate several minutes' worth of brash commercials, he jokingly reintroduced Gahan and Gore as "close personal friends" of REO Speedwagon, following the AOR act's latest video yawnfest, perfectly highlighting Andy Fletcher's earlier comment concerning Depeche Mode often being sandwiched between such "progressive yuck" when first breaking through in America.

A brief series of Japanese performances in Tokyo and Osaka, were followed by another European jaunt. The band's appearance as part of an outdoor rock festival at Athens' Panathinaiko Stadium on July 30 was particularly memorable.

Alan Wilder: "Culture Club got bottled off-stage, and there was a full-scale riot out on the streets – I don't know why. I have it all on video, though. Luckily, we went down really well, but it was a strange day. If I remember rightly, Dave also got punched in the face the next day while out shopping. Aggressive bastards, aren't they?"

In spite of Depeche Mode's mushrooming US profile, 'Shake The Disease' failed to crack the *Billboard* Singles Chart upon its October 30, 1985 release, some six months after its success in Europe. The vast North American continent was proving to be a tough nut to crack in some regards, after all.

Furthermore, the band were noticeably absent from Live Aid – the televised musical marathon staged on either side of the Atlantic that gripped the Western world on July 13, 1985. Alan Wilder was sceptical about some of those who responded to the rallying call of Bob Geldof, the charismatic Boomtown Rats frontman: "I doubt very much that we would have accepted the invitation, had we been asked. My personal view is that giving to 'chariddy' should be a totally private gesture, out of which no personal gain should be made. Inevitably, nearly all the artists who took part in Live Aid achieved a considerable rise in record sales and, being the cynic I am, I wonder just how much of the profit gained from those sales actually ended up going to Ethiopia."

Since becoming successful, Depeche Mode had traditionally spent much of the summer ensconced in a recording studio somewhere, working on an album in readiness for touring throughout the autumn and winter. 1985 looked to be no exception as July saw the band (and Daniel Miller) booked into former Human League producer, Martin Rushent's Genetic Studios in the wooded countryside village of Goring, Berkshire. Genetic was truly state-of-the-art, counting both a Fairlight CMI and one of only two NED Synclaviers in the country (the other, ironically, belonging to Miller) amongst its impressive equipment inventory, with recreational facilities of a swimming pool and tennis court. On paper at least, Rushent and Depeche Mode seemed a match made in heaven, but a crucial ingredient in the distinctive Mode sound – the otherwise engaged Gareth Jones – would be sorely missed. The first fruits of the sessions, 'It's Called A Heart' (mixed at Livingstone Studios in London's Wood Green), caused dissension in the ranks.

Alan Wilder: " 'It's Called A Heart' has to be my least favourite, dare I say most hated, DM single ever, and I was anti even recording it, let alone releasing it. In fact, I fought tooth-and-nail on behalf of the B-side, 'Fly On The Windscreen', which was far superior. To me, the whole thing was a serious backward step. I felt we'd worked diligently to build up recognition for a harder sound, with more depth and maturity, and here was this ultra-poppy number that did nothing for our reputation.

"Sadly, I was out-voted by the others, although they recognised that 'Fly . . .' was wasted as an additional track and agreed it should be promoted to the next album, *Black Celebration*. Even now, I have trouble listening to 'It's Called A Heart' and in the case of the [limited edition 12″] 'Slow Mix' which was reduced to half-speed, making the experience twice as long and twice the agony, you need to be particularly devout to endure it."

The song's accompanying video – intended to depict a burning Indonesian jungle, by all accounts – fared no better in Wilder's scornful view: "You'll have to ask the director, Peter Care, quite how he equated 'calling something a heart' with twirling cameras around on the end of a string in an exotic Reading cornfield, dressed in a skirt. But then the track *was* asking for it! What's it all about, eh?"

Whatever Wilder's feelings, 'It's Called A Heart' was released on September 16. "If we were ever going to split up the band, it was at the end of 1985," Dave Gahan told *Melody Maker* in 1990. "We were really in a state of turmoil – constant arguing, very intense. We weren't really sure where to go after *Some Great Reward* so we decided to slow things down."

Perhaps that slowing down process was reflected in the fact that the single coincided with the release of *The Singles 81>85*, effectively Depeche Mode's first compilation. Other than serving to document just how far the band had come, *The Singles 81>85* was notable as the first Depeche Mode release to feature the band on its sleeve, albeit a tinted black and white photo in which Martin Gore appeared to be wearing a slinky, black off-the-shoulder number.

"It used to be great waiting for your reviews to come in," said Gore, "because at least 75 per cent of them would be so awful! That's why on our first singles album we actually printed one good [review] and one bad one – just for a laugh, and also to say that we don't really care."

Alan Wilder: "The idea behind the quotes, which are actually about 50 per cent good and 50 per cent bad, was to show that we didn't take ourselves too seriously and how unreliable journalists are with their comments.

"I suppose it was a pretty brave thing to do at the time. A good point was made, though – by placing a good and bad review of each single on the cover notes, it became obvious how little notice one should take of one's own press."

Although the divisive 'It's Called A Heart' was included on *The Singles 81>85*, it was omitted from the album's artwork on account of its sudden release. As well as the media clippings, a spread of snapshots chronicling the band's development over the last four years graced the inside of the gatefold, including vintage shots of the band's self-sufficient portable set-up at The Bridgehouse, back in 1980.

It was a far cry from the hi-tech trickery deployed on the 'Some Great Reward Tour', finally released on video as *The World We Live In And Live*

In Hamburg by the newly launched Mute Films imprint. The opening shots convey the band's backstage nervous excitement as the introductory strains of 'Master And Servant' fill Hamburg's vast 10,000-capacity Alsterdorf Sporthalle.

Andy Fletcher looks especially edgy when shown jogging on the spot, boxing-style, before heading off for the stage – rather remarkable considering the onstage cameras very rarely capture him playing anything on his synthesiser throughout the performance. Instead, Fletcher is occasionally seen clapping along or enthusiastically punching the air, leaving the keyboard work to Wilder and, to a lesser extent, Gore.

When witnessing a different show, *Keyboard* magazine's Bob Doerschuk automatically assumed that Fletcher was responsible for mostly playing bass lines. "Well, not really," was Wilder's telling response. "It's difficult to explain what everyone does, because we all swap over and do different things at different times." Doerschuk went on to describe Depeche Mode as "masters of pure European techno-punk." *Techno-punk?*

Accompanying *The World We Live In And Live In Hamburg* was *Some Great Videos 81>85* – the visual counterpart to *The Singles 81>85* compilation. That the forgettable promos for 'See You', 'The Meaning Of Love', 'Leave In Silence' and 'Get The Balance Right!' were omitted speaks volumes. (The collection skips straight from 1981's 'Just Can't Get Enough' to 1983's 'Everything Counts'.)

Away from the spotlight, Dave Gahan married long-term fiancée Jo Fox on August 4, 1985, opting for a low-key ceremony at Brentwood Registry Office, Essex. Afterwards, a huge party was held where a number of musical friends were in attendance, including Alison Moyet and Blancmange's Neil Arthur and Stephen Luscombe.

Although she was no longer going out with Vince Clarke by this time, the former Deb Danahay was in attendance: "I did go to the evening do at Jo and Dave's wedding and the memory that comes back to me was that it really was just like anyone's wedding – lots of relatives and friends – not at all showbiz or over the top like a lot of celebs seem to do now. I'm pretty sure that a Basildon mob got a minibus there, the party being in a marquee."

And what of the bride and groom? "I've been together with Jo for six years now," a delighted Dave Gahan told Belgian pop magazine *Joepie* in 1985. "But now we're married we want to have children as soon as possible, and as many as possible!"

Jo Gahan: "It was a small family affair in the morning, then a reception in a hotel – basically, the usual meal, followed by a load of mates having a party. It was a fab day."

Meanwhile, Andy Fletcher and girlfriend Grainne Mullen moved into a new flat in North London's Maida Vale area. Robert Marlow remembers Fletcher as remaining remarkably unaffected by Depeche Mode's mounting worldwide success: "I look back with real nostalgia to when Andy was living in Warrington Road, because he had a little flat there. Grainne and Andy didn't have any kids, so we'd go down and have pub grub in his local, The Warrington, plus we'd go to the betting shop and have a bet."

While Martin Gore remained Berlin-bound, Alan Wilder led a secretive – and almost reclusive – London-based life with his new girlfriend, Jeri Young, first moving into her Kilburn flat, then 'adopting' her son, Jason. "She isn't only the mother of my child," he revealed at the time, "but also a great hairdresser. Every morning she spends 20 minutes fixing my hair. It takes a whole bottle of hairspray!"

On November 11, Depeche Mode's growing American fanbase belatedly received *The Singles* compilation – albeit under the not-so-subtle title of *Catching Up With Depeche Mode*. Despite spending 18 weeks on the *Billboard* Top 200 following its December 7 entry, the album only peaked at number 113. Along with the *People Are People* compilation concocted in 1984, it would not be the last time that Depeche Mode suffered at the hands of Sire's marketing executives.*

At the same time, Martin Gore was writing songs destined for the next album.

Alan Wilder: "Martin [Gore] and I compose in totally different ways. Martin works on guitar and I on keyboards. Yet we present our songs to the band in a similar form. We work on our songs on a four-track machine, and basically get a demo to the point where there's a bass line, a rough rhythm track, most of the melodies and all the lyrics. That's what the band gets to hear. Then we all sit down with Daniel, pick the songs we want to put on the album, and talk over the good and bad points – whether we need to change the structure or add or take out bits here and there."

Ironically, while unrepresented song-wise on their next effort, Wilder was instrumental in fashioning the sound of what would be a radically different Depeche Mode album.

---

* 'Shake The Disease' sank without trace following its October 30 release, and a similar fate awaited 'It's Called A Heart', issued as a 12″ on January 22, 1986.

16

Back In Black

"We had Some Great Reward *out, with 'People Are People' and 'Master And Servant'. It was quite a commercial album, and it had commercially done very well. Perhaps we were expected to follow it with more of the same, but we didn't; we followed it with a darker album."*

– Andy Fletcher, 2001

Before the close of 1985, Depeche Mode spent a month at Worldwide International, Daniel Miller's small pre-production facility sited in the Rough Trade building in West London's Talbot Road, "just programming the [new] album," Martin Gore recalled. "We were able to work more on song structures and arrangements, whereas before we just programmed as we went [along]. With *Some Great Reward*, for instance, the recording had already started while we were still programming the songs."

Although Gareth Jones was not directly involved in the new album's pre-production proceedings, he remembered "really enjoying Martin's demos – we were out to capture a special atmosphere again and the demos already seemed to set the tone. Alan was working very hard at that stage transferring the demos into MIDI and preparing some sounds, I guess."

Unfortunately for Gore, reactions to his latest embryonic offerings were not so well received outside of the Depeche Mode inner sanctum: "Daniel had played my demos to our plugger [Neil Ferris] and some industry people in England, and they were saying that they didn't feel we had a single – I wasn't up to standard. I just freaked out! I thought something was going really wrong if we were starting to rely on pluggers and marketing people to tell us what we should be doing."

Such interference was an affront to Gore's artistry, and the songwriter went AWOL for a week, reportedly ending up in Hamburg. "At the time I just felt I needed a break," he explained. "It wasn't Hamburg, it was

[just] outside there. I stayed with a friend from my old school [exchange] days. They lived on a farm in the middle of nowhere."

While reacquainting himself with the Frenzen family in the Schleswig-Holstein state town of Erfden, Gore took time to visit his old German school where he was promptly met by a gaggle of gobsmacked small-town teenagers who got wind of the famous British pop star in their midst. "He was friendly and told us the whole story of how Depeche Mode was formed," a student told German *Popcorn* magazine. "Unfortunately, time slipped by too fast, but Martin promised to give us autographs and answer our questions when he visits Erfden again."

Gore's break evidently had the desired effect and, in November 1985, he turned his attention back to the new Depeche Mode album. The band, with Daniel Miller and Gareth Jones, settled into Westside Studios – close to the Shepherd's Bush roundabout – described by Jones as being "a much more sophisticated recording studio than The Garden or Music Works, owned at that time by Clive Langer and Alan Winstanley." Fortunately, in-house engineer Richard Sullivan was there to offer guidance.

Black Celebration, as the work-in-progress would become known, was the first 48-track recording made by the band – hence the need for a more upmarket studio. "It made developing the tracks easier – not because we had more musical parts, but because we were able to have each part on its own track," Jones justified. "In the past we had squeezed many different parts onto the same tracks, and this was problematic in monitor mixing. At the final mix, of course, we routed these tracks to different channels and used the [console's] mix computer to mute the channels in and out as necessary."

Gore touched on the same theme when describing Depeche Mode's developing working methodology to *MT*'s Paul Tingen: "We might start off a song with a single sound on a sequencer and as it progresses, bring in more sounds just to make it richer. We did that a lot on this album – making layers of sounds all play the same part to get a full and warm effect. We could do that because we went 48-track for the first time. Before, we used 24-track which meant we sometimes had to put three or four sounds on one track. This time we could minimise that, which made things a lot easier when it came to mixing."

As had been the case with its immediate predecessors, technology – and sampling in particular – was intrinsic to *Black Celebration*.

Alan Wilder: "One thing I might point out is on 'It Doesn't Matter Two'. There are lots of choir samples on that. It would have been easy to take just one sample and play it back polyphonically. But instead, we took a different sample for each choir note, so each note is slightly out from the others. It gives you a very realistic feel. We spent a long time getting that to work, so that it sounded human. That goes for all the stuff that we do, not just that one track."

At the time, Martin Gore confessed to making much use of Akai's not-so-illustrious sampling début, the six-voice, 12-bit, rackmounted S612 MIDI Digital Sampler: "They're very easy to use and the quality isn't bad."

In time, the likes of the genuinely low-cost Akai S612 would start a sampling revolution. With a hitherto unheard of £799 price tag upon its 1985 release, this undemanding machine was a mere drop in the ocean compared to the pocket-emptying £60,000 that Daniel Miller was prepared to part with for his treasured Synclavier.

Martin Gore: "The Synclavier is now mainly used for drums, because you *do* get a good, powerful sound from it. Most of the drum sounds on the album are Synclavier."

Gore revealed a few of the band's current music-making secrets. "Usually we spend two or three days before recording just sampling sounds," he told *MT*'s Paul Tingen. "Then we sample as we go. If somebody has a good idea, we just stop recording and do some sampling. Even David is joining in with that now, which is good, because he used to be just 'the singer'."

Perhaps more so than any other Depeche Mode album, on *Black Celebration*, the group were effectively a band without roles, to paraphrase Martin Gore, who took lead vocal on an unprecedented four – 'A Question Of Lust', 'Sometimes', 'It Doesn't Matter Two' and 'World Full Of Nothing' – of the album's 11 tracks. It could have been that Gore was still harbouring a degree of resentment at having his demos unfavourably dissected by outsiders, hence choosing to sing the songs himself.

A more conservative, yet plausible, explanation was that offered by Gore to *MT* in 1986: "We've noticed over the years that my voice is more suited to the slower and softer songs than Dave's."

Determining whether musical parts would be played by synthesisers or samplers within Depeche Mode's unconventional instrumental set-up was fairly straightforward for Alan Wilder: "When we want something that sounds definitely non-acoustic, something that doesn't really reflect or imitate a known instrument, we usually go for an analogue synth – often the ARP 2600. If we want something that *does* sound like another instrument, we turn to the digital or sampling machines."

Gore explained where the album's samples emanated: "Sometimes we use old favourites – like one sample that we first used on 'People Are People'. It's a Hank Marvin-type guitar sound, an acoustic guitar plucked with a German 50-pfennig piece. We've used that three or four times now. Then there's the mandolin-like part on 'Here Is The House'. That was an acoustic guitar sampled twice – once on a down-stroke and once on an up-stroke. We used them on alternate notes, so every other note was a down-stroke and all the in-between notes were up-strokes. It sounded very funny – almost like a real player . . .

"There's a Black & Decker drill in the opening of 'Fly On The Windscreen', and the rhythm of 'Stripped' was made up of an idling motorbike played half-an-octave down from its original pitch."

During 'Fly On The Windscreen – Final', Daniel Miller can be heard saying, "Over and done with." Stranger still, the producer was also sampled repeatedly saying, "Horse" on the same track.

Gareth Jones: "Again, we went as deep as possible into our sampling adventure. We sampled a lot of stuff – everything around us! Famous sampling events included setting up an array of mics in the car park and recording fireworks, Dave's Porsche starting up, lids rolling down stairs, aerosols going off in the gents' loo – you name it!"

In his conversation with *MT*'s Paul Tingen, Gore paid tribute to Jones, dubbing him the man who "puts it all together" in the studio. Bemused by this observation, Jones agrees that this was "one of the aspects of my job, perhaps. I was not doing it alone, of course. Alan played a major part in 'putting it all together', as did Daniel."

Daniel Miller: "We were recording it [*Black Celebration*] in the winter of '85, and on November 5, which is Guy Fawkes Day, we decided that we'd go and sample some fireworks. So Gareth arranged a very elaborate microphone set-up in the car park with about four or five microphones going down a 30- or 40-yard length of tarmac. And then we got a couple of bottles with firework rockets, and we fired them so that they [flew] over the microphones. So we were able to record different sounds of the fireworks at different times of their paths over the microphones, and then we sampled bits of it. That was probably the most dangerous bit of sampling we've ever done!"

Andy Fletcher: "We had this theory at the time that every sound must be different, and you must never use the same sound twice; so, of course, sampling was great for us."

Martin Gore preferred to take a "back seat" when it came to the complicated process involved in completing *Black Celebration*: "If Daniel or Alan and the others are doing something that I really don't like, I'll obviously say something. But I'm prepared to step back, because if I were to take over completely, there'd be no point in us being a band. It's good to have new enthusiasm for the songs, because I've already worked on them for maybe a month or two, while the rest of the band are really fresh, and more likely to come up with new ideas."

Although Gore praised Miller as being a "technical wizard when it comes to synths" with "a lot of good production ideas concerning song structures, especially on a commercial level," by the time the team moved over to Hansa, in Berlin, relations between band and mentor were becoming increasingly strained. "There were a lot of arguments going on around that time," the increasingly volatile songwriter later reflected. "I think we'd overdone the working relationship between us, Daniel and Gareth Jones. [*Black Celebration*] was the third album we'd done together and I think everybody started becoming very lazy, relying on formulas. So there was tension in the studio; we weren't getting on as well as we had in the past."

Although Daniel Miller allows that there was "a bit of tension" during the making of *Black Celebration*, his different take on matters is more enlightening: "We were trying to figure out the balance of how we were going to work in the studio, really. Alan, who's first of all a very good musician but also loved working in the studio and loved experimenting with sounds, was taking quite a big part in the recording of the record, and how the record was sounding. The way it worked, really, was Martin would do a demo, which would suggest a lot of ideas – sometimes very specific, sometimes more abstract – and then Alan, and everybody else, once we got in the studio, would develop those ideas. And, as time went on, Alan was becoming more and more influential in how those ideas were developed. Certainly, of all the albums I worked with them on, that was the most difficult."

Alan Wilder: "I can't remember who did exactly what on each track, but in the case of *Black Celebration* some melodies came from the original demo, some came about in the studio. Actually, Dan and I often felt that there were too many counter-melodies and not enough space in the music."

As Wilder took a tighter hold of the musical reins, Andy Fletcher took on a more managerial function within Depeche Mode. "We didn't think we needed a manager," he clarified. "Daniel Miller was very important to us, but [eventually] I did most of that management role."

With the dominance of Wilder, Miller and Jones in shaping Depeche Mode's distinctive sound, it became increasingly difficult to pin down exactly what Fletcher contributed on a musical level. Jones kindly cited him as being "important for the vibe".

When rock commentator Paul Gambaccini later brought up the subject of the band's complex vocal harmony arrangements, Fletcher admitted that his colleagues had dissuaded him from joining in. "Martin and Alan are so very red hot with their harmonies, and I get criticised a lot," he confessed. "My voice isn't up to it really, but I think it's better than they think it is."

In attempting to clarify Fletcher's position, Gambaccini asked whether Fletcher had tried to write songs. "I've tried writing, but, again, I've been in a band with two of the best modern-day songwriters, really. It doesn't do much for your confidence, you know – you present a song, and it's not up to scratch. So I basically gave up and concentrated on what I thought I was good at."

The likelihood of Depeche Mode producing another songwriter of Vince Clarke or Martin Gore's pedigree was extremely remote. Whether his colleagues were prepared to admit it at this stage, Fletcher's buffering role within the band would become increasingly valuable.

Alan Wilder: "It [*Black Celebration*] *was* a difficult record to make. Things were strained – too much time spent in close proximity to the same people, as well as overstaying our welcome in Berlin. And it signalled the end of a co-production relationship between the group, Dan Miller and Gareth Jones – although, I should add, not a falling out. Things did get silly, though. Band members would disappear while Dan spent up to three days getting a bass drum sound – which still sounded shit!

"Dan and I had grown as friends and musical associates, as well as developing a mutual understanding of the territory we felt Depeche Mode should be exploring. For example, our affiliation had been enhanced by spending long hours finishing off the previous LP, *Some Great Reward*, when everyone else had cleared off on their holidays. With *Black Celebration* we also ran well over our deadline, but it was perhaps when too many voices were brought into the equation that problems seemed to arise.

"Early indications of Dave's vulnerability started to become apparent at this time, too. In the studio, he was nicknamed 'caj' – as in *casualty* – since he would readily descend into mock 'Keef' Richards drawl in far too convincing style."

Gareth Jones sympathised with Wilder to a degree: "Mixing *Black Cele-bration* was not easy. Daniel and I were obsessing about the mixes – we would get a mix up, work on it, everyone would be fairly happy, then we would tear it down again because we felt we weren't hitting the spot, and this became very frustrating for the band. I remember Alan had to have a word with us, and pull us into line! Even at the end of the mixing we were playing the mixes out into Hansa's huge Studio 2 through my Yamaha 1000Ms [speakers] and recording them in search of that special vibe. Hopefully, we finally caught a vibe. It's a very special record, in my opinion."

Black Celebration remains Wilder's favourite Depeche Mode album from the Eighties: "The mixes sound very odd – too much reverb, not enough bottom end, and so on – but despite [its] many flaws, the LP is dark and complex, and that's why I like it."

Similarly, the album remained high in Andy Fletcher's estimation: "I think it's got one of the best collections of songs that Martin's ever written. All the way through, they're classic, but none of them are really commercial – just lovely songs, great lyrics. I think the traditional or big Depeche Mode fans would say that was their favourite album."

Martin Gore: "For me, one of the most dramatic changes [in Depeche Mode] came with *Black Celebration*. I pretty much like everything we've put out since then."

Gareth Jones: "The important thing to realise about *Black Celebration* is that Daniel had a [film director, Werner] Herzog-inspired idea of 'living the album' and that's what we did. We didn't take a single day off, except to fly to Berlin. This made for a very intense, creative, focused session. Of course on some days we didn't get that much material recorded to tape, but we maintained an atmosphere. Also, there was a kind of dark, neurotic, obsessive claustrophobia that fitted the mood of the LP."

Likewise, Daniel Miller felt that *Black Celebration* was "flawed", but conceded that "it's got [good] bits and pieces of experimental music, but that's a personal thing because I was involved, and I feel very close to it."

The shifting balance of power within Depeche Mode's self-sufficient set-up inevitably took its toll. "By the end of *Black Celebration* I felt that I'd done my job," Miller admitted. "I wanted to concentrate more on the label. They were taking a lot longer in the studio; it was taking its toll on me – trying to do both things at once."

Martin Gore: "Up until that point, we didn't have a contract [with Mute]. It was a handshake and honour kind of thing. But we started

215

thinking, 'Daniel's getting on now, and he's also overweight. So what would happen if anything happened to Daniel? What would our position have been?' That's when we thought we should get a very simple contract drawn up to clarify what the position would be if anything did happen. I think he understood our worries."

Perhaps Miller had good reason to worry himself. As he saw it, his label had continued to flourish, by and large, on the strength of always having had two winning bands on its roster by default: "We found Depeche Mode, who, of course, went on to be very successful, and then when Vince Clarke left them, he formed Yazoo, who were instantly commercially successful. Then, when Yazoo split up, Vince started Erasure."

Vince Clarke's first post-Yazoo studio project, involving old sparring partner, Eric Radcliffe was The Assembly, whose November, 1983 Top Five hit, 'Never, Never', featured ex-Undertones vocalist, Feargal Sharkey.

"When we did The Assembly it was meant to be an album full of different singers," Clarke told *MT*'s Tim Goodyer. "We started doing the album after the first single ['Never, Never'], but there were problems finding singers. People imagine if you're a musician it's like one big family, but really you don't know anybody else. I contacted a few people and they didn't want to do it or they weren't available, and when they were, there were contractual problems with other record companies.

"The result was [that] we spent a year in the studio, hanging around, writing songs, preparing for an album which never materialised. In the end, I was just sick of the studio. We started to do the next single, but we couldn't get the right singer, so myself and Eric took our synths and went home. It was a really bad time; it was a year wasted."*

Clarke then set up Splendid Studios within the same South London church that housed Radcliffe's Blackwing Studios. Following in Daniel Miller's footsteps, Clarke launched his own independent label, Reset Records, with a familiar Basildon face – if not name – fronting its first release.

Robert Marlow: "I went through a whole host of really terrible names, like Robert Garbo. But I'd been reading a lot of Raymond Chandler stuff, so that's how I came up with Marlow – by taking the 'e' off the end. I needed a name like Bowie, so I could record by my second name."

* This perhaps explains why *Melody Maker* reported Martin Gore as saying that Clarke was thinking of returning to Basildon during this time.

Like Clarke before him, the freshly christened Robert 'Marlow' – formerly Rob Allen – took to using this new name on account of the fact that he was signing on the dole when attempting to launch his own recording career – through sheer belligerence: "I would go around to Vince's house and pester him: 'Give me a day in the studio; I've got this song I'd really like to record.' And eventually I got my day, and that day turned into three weeks. At the end of it we had a single and two B-sides. So, after that, Vince said, 'Well, let's try and find a deal for it. We've done all this work for it.'

"Actually, *he'd* done all the work, really – and Eric [Radcliffe]. First of all, we looked at distributors. We went to Rough Trade and a group called The Cartel, who were working with them. Eventually, we ended up at RCA, and I think that RCA thought they were getting Vince! Now, if you've got Bowie and Elvis at the top of the RCA pile, then Robert Marlow and Vince Clarke were right at the very bottom, so, publicity-wise, we didn't do very well."

The Clarke connection ensured *Smash Hits* reviewed Marlow's first single, 'The Face Of Dorian Gray', although their opinion was lukewarm, to say the least: "This is the sort of stuff I expected to hear from Vince Clarke after he left Depeche Mode, rather than the gems he produced with Alf [Alison Moyet]. Pretentious words, clever, clever sounds and a catchy tune make up the first release on Vince's new label, and it sounds as though he played all the instruments as well (he did co-produce it!). RM has got a bland voice and the song is probably a Yazoo reject."

After four failed singles for Reset Records and an aborted album, Marlow summed up his 15 minutes: "There were two egos at work there, both wanting things done the way *they* wanted them, but one was saying, 'Look, I've already proven that this works this way.' Vince is not an easy person to work with – and nor am I, I guess. One of the criticisms of the records we were doing was that they sounded similar to what Vince was doing, but he worked hard at it. Still, I must say, my relationship with Vince was probably at its worst ebb when we were working together . . . My friendship with Vince is extremely valuable to me."

During this time, *The Sun* ran a not entirely inaccurate story reporting that Clarke was quitting the pop scene to earn "at least £100,000 a year" writing jingles for radio and television commercials.

Vince Clarke: "I did actually sign up to a jingle company to write jingles for TV adverts, because I suddenly thought, 'God, unless something happens, I'm not going to be able to pay the mortgage!' " Thankfully, he had, by now, learnt to take what he read in the tabloids with a pinch of salt: "In *The Sun* it mentioned these three products I'd never done ads for, and they said my agent was Jeff Lynne whom I've never met. I've never even bought an ELO record!" *

Clarke's latest duo project (with Andy Bell), Erasure, was currently enduring a barren 18-month period. Having recently moved into a lavish new house in Walton-on-Thames, Erasure's initial lack of success was understandably a cause for concern.

Andy Bell: "I think Mute were hoping we'd pack it in because the first album [*Wonderland*] had cost them around £250,000. Yet Vince was adamant that we should stick together, tour and do the next album on a budget."

Working with Bell had a positive effect on Clarke's legendary paranoia. "I think I'm easier to work with than I ever was before," he told *Melody Maker*'s Kris Kirk in May 1986. "Before I've always got to a certain stage and found I couldn't handle working with the people I was working with, or them me. The success thing happened very quickly with Depeche and the break was painful – you get wound up when there's slagging off, but I think I've softened down now. Andy and I were thrown together, really, and it's like an equal relationship [that] we've built up through working together."

In October 1986, the joint Clarke-Bell composition, 'Sometimes' climbed to number two, being held off the top spot by the dreaded Scandinavian pomp rock of Europe's 'The Final Countdown'. Thereafter, it was virtually plain sailing, as Vince Clarke was again able to match – and often eclipse – his former Depeche Mode colleagues on their home turf, hit for hit. But for a while there, it was touch and go.

From its opening seconds, 'Stripped' represented the first indication of the darkening Depeche Mode musical palate. A sampled acoustic guitar chord superimposed over a piano-based thump leads into a strange, disconcerting clanking sound – Martin Gore's slowed-down motorbike sample – joined by Dave Gahan's Porsche sample starting a menacing, heavily processed synth drone.

This was no ordinary single, and *Smash Hits* were quick to state as much soon after its February 10, 1986 release: "Depeche Mode were becoming

* The agent in question was actually Jeff Wayne – songwriter/producer for David Essex and the man behind *The War Of The Worlds* concept album.

very predictable, but this is the best thing they've done in ages. 'Let me see you stripped,' sings Dave Gahan, and bang goes their appearance on [British Saturday morning kids' TV show] *Saturday Superstore*. Actually, I think it's all about going back to nature and 'discovering yourself'. Slow and atmospheric, even though you can't work out what he's going on about."

But it was the *music* that *NME*'s Cath Carroll found difficult to get off on. " 'Stripped'," she concluded, "is a morose, tidal wearing away at the eardrum, perversely soothing – but try getting up after listening to it." *Melody Maker*'s Caroline Sullivan, who admitted to normally approaching a Depeche Mode release "with the avidity of a school kid going to sit an Applied Physics A level" was forced to concede that "the song manages to surmount the gloom-ridden vocal, being a delicately melodic oasis in the midst of a week strewn with mostly dreary disco songs; a real crackerette, it must be acknowledged."

While mystifying the music press, 'Stripped' struck a chord with the band's loyal fan base who propelled it to number 15 during its relatively brief, five-week chart stay. By now, a familiar pattern was beginning to emerge.

Martin Gore: "Most of our fans are crazy – they're *so* dedicated. They'll go out on day one and buy the records, and we've often suffered because of that – because we have got such a huge fan base obviously the record just drops after that."

'Stripped' followed another established pattern in that it acted as a precursor to the forthcoming album. Its accompanying promo video – the last to be shot by Peter Care – was filmed in Berlin just around the corner from Hansa Tonstudios where *Black Celebration* was being mixed. On the subject of mixing – or remixing – the 12″ version of 'Stripped' included no fewer than five tracks – namely, extended versions of the title track and its throwaway B-side, 'But Not Tonight', 'Breathing In Fumes' (effectively a more radical remix of 'Stripped'), yet another version of 'Fly On The Windscreen', and 'Black Day' (a peculiar, almost Aboriginal-sounding version of the as-yet-unreleased 'Black Celebration', surprisingly credited to Gore, Wilder *and* Daniel Miller).

Alan Wilder: "['Black Day'] was one of those rare tracks that just came together spontaneously in the studio while Martin was warming up in the vocal booth and Dan, Gareth and myself were fiddling about in the control room. It was all recorded live – an offshoot from 'Black Celebration' – and we decided that the fairest way to credit it was equally between those people that were in the room contributing at the time."

Depeche Mode further experimented with the concept by commissioning an 'external' extended remix of 'Stripped', which became known as 'Stripped (Highland Mix)'. Mark Ellis – better known as 'Flood' – was given the job, the start of his association with the band.

Alan Wilder: "Apparently, when plain old Mark Ellis served his apprenticeship as tape op at his first studio, he acquired the nickname due to his over-eager tea-producing skills. As the producer took his last slurp, Flood would provide a fresh cup within seconds. His aptly named colleague, 'Drought', never saw the importance of this career-breaking move and hasn't been heard of since."

Depeche Mode's fifth album, *Black Celebration* was released on March 17, 1986 to mixed reviews. "Opening with the title song, 'Black Celebration', which has nothing to do with the recently established Martin Luther King Day and a lot to do with being stoical in the face of life's sheer mundanity, the album establishes a mood that is dark yet faintly ridiculous," mocked *NME*'s Sean O'Hagan.

Steve Sutherland concluded his review for *Melody Maker* on an aggressive note: "*Black Celebration* is Depeche fucking with their formula and the real shock is the insight it provides into the troubled psyche of Martin Gore, a lad struggling to grow in public and, for all his opportunities, finding only sleaze and filth to feed off."

Fortunately, *Smash Hits*' Chris Heath was astute in his judgement: "*Black Celebration* doesn't only see them go a bit weirder with lots of dark, mysterious percussive episodes (sung by Dave Gahan) snuggling up against sweet, fragile and rather sinister ballads (sung by Martin Gore) but it's also the first time that they haven't had to throw in any second-rate stodge – their best album yet (apart from the very brilliant *Singles [81>85]* LP, that is)."

The diversity of the album is reflected in standout tracks like 'New Dress', Gore's world-weary study of the media's obsession with trivia over more important global matters. The lyrics possibly refer to the downing of Korean Airlines flight KAL 007 on September 1, 1983 by a Soviet interceptor, famine in Ethiopia, and a devastating earthquake in Mexico City on September 19, 1985, all overshadowed by the song's memorable hookline about Princess Diana's new dress.*

* This took on a greater irony following the Princess of Wales' tragic death on August 31, 1997.

Even back in 1986 that fateful line stood out on account of a studio trick to make it sound like a radio broadcast. Musically too, the song sustains interest as several sounds, spiced up with a basic five-note synth riff, lift the song towards its equally simplistic, yet stirring middle-eight.

Martin Gore: "Apart from the middle-eight, all the drum sounds on 'New Dress' are analogue ones from an old ARP 2600 synth."

On 'Sometimes', another haunting piano-based ballad somewhat akin to 1984's 'Somebody', Gore sounded remarkably like Art Garfunkel in 'Bright Eyes' mode. The blatant use of extreme studio effects made his vocal appear to be issuing forth from some cavernous cathedral, echoing his every sentiment.

MT's Paul Tingen drew attention to "the industrial sounds and treated vocals" of 'It Doesn't Matter Two'. "Musically, the piece is painfully reminiscent of [American minimalist composer] Philip Glass, almost to the point of plagiarism."

"Probably we were remotely inspired by Glass," Gore responded, "though I hardly ever listen to that kind of music. But it wasn't a parody or something. It was serious."

Black Celebration peaked at number three in the UK, continuing a Top 10 tradition that remained unbroken since *Speak & Spell*. Despite the poor performances of their recent singles, five years into their recording career, Depeche Mode had transformed into an album-dependent band *à la* rock dinosaurs like Pink Floyd. Their next tour would confirm that hallowed position.

PART IV

World Domination

"We never set out to conquer the world; we never had any great domination plan, so I think that helps. We've always looked at things with a real negative outlook, so maybe that helps as well."

– Martin Gore, 2001

17

Entertainment USA

"Imagine the Americans seeing us lot play live; they'd never seen anything like it before. They were used to seeing rock band after rock band after rock band. To see us on-stage – it was something new, wasn't it?"

– Andy Fletcher, 1998

A cursory glance at Depeche Mode's 13-date UK touring itinerary throughout the tail end of March into April 1986 confirmed their pre-eminent status. Booking the likes of Glasgow's 10,000-capacity SECC (Scottish Exhibition & Conference Centre) and playing two consecutive nights each at Birmingham's 12,000-seat NEC (National Exhibition Centre) and Wembley Arena not only embodied the band's growing confidence on their home turf but also spoke volumes about their rising popularity as a large-scale live act.

Because Depeche Mode were still rigidly tied to a backing tape – in the case of the 'Black Celebration Tour', two Tascam 38 eight-track reel-to-reel recorders – more than one interviewer pondered whether the band got bored reproducing the same parts, night after night. Martin Gore nodded his affirmation: "It *is* quite boring, but we owe it to the fans to play live because the concerts always go down well."

Dave Gahan had assumed an archetypical rock star reaction to tour boredom by claiming he often downed a bottle of brandy before *and* after each show. "Bands who say they *need* drugs to get through the boredom of a tour are talking crap," he told *Melody Maker* in 1984. "I think a lot of that went on in the Seventies; at that time that was what bands were expected to be like – totally out of it all of the time."

Remaining *compos mentis* didn't appear to rate particularly highly on Gore's list of priorities either, judging from a lively conversation with *Melody Maker*'s Danny Kelly: "When we're on tour, which is generally

225

very boring, we, or some of us, tend to go out every night, have a lot to drink and generally have a good time. I know it's expected of rock bands, but going out *is* enjoyable, drinking *is* enjoyable and collapsing *is* enjoyable."

The apparently level-headed Alan Wilder's duties now extended to preparing the backing tapes. "I give a challenge to those in the band who want it," he told *Keyboard*'s Bob Doerschuk. "In other words, if I want to challenge myself on-stage, I'll give myself the most difficult parts. I'll often play a sequencer type of part rather than something easier, so that I don't get totally bored in concert."

As far as Wilder was concerned, the pros of backing tapes still outweighed the cons. "You know it's going to sound pretty good. It's a very controllable way of doing things. On the other hand it is very difficult to change the set around; we can't suddenly decide one night to change something on the tape – well, I suppose we could, but it would be quite difficult."

However, Depeche Mode did just that when mixed audience reaction during the early shows of the 'Black Celebration Tour' led them to drop 'Here Is The House' – with Gahan bravely tackling Gore's studio vocal – in favour of 'New Dress' for the remainder of the tour.

Alan Wilder: "Live playing is only about reproducing our music in a very tight and good way. We *do* put on a good live performance. We're one of the most exciting bands around. First, we always get a good sound, because everything always goes into the PA system. Second, we have a lot of vocal harmonies, which make a very big vocal sound. And third, we take a lot of trouble over the stage set and a good light show."

When one interviewer dared to suggest that the stage effects for the 'Black Celebration Tour' were the same as their last, Wilder begged to differ: "We've been working with Jane Spiers, who also designed our last two sets. These particular [keyboard] risers that we're placed upon are hollow, so that the leads and plug boards and all the rubbish you don't want to see can be hidden inside. A person can also be in there; in fact, people *are* hidden in several places within the set.

"Also, the flooring is designed for Dave to be able to dance around without flipping over – we had problems with that on previous tours where we'd play on different stages with different floor surfaces. Actually, a lot of this set is [made from a] plastic inflatable material that is filled with helium and blown up. We couldn't see how it could possibly work without looking a bit stupid, but it worked in the end. With all of these things taken into account, it's a very practical set."

Even the best-laid plans occasionally backfire. "We've also got a curtain that drops at a specific time in the show," said Wilder. "It's a very dramatic effect, but when it goes wrong – when it only half drops or something – it's very funny."

Melody Maker's Paul Mather turned in a favourable review of one of the triumphant Wembley Arena outings: "From the moment the black curtains drifted to the floor like a chiffon scarf and the boy in front of me went bonkers, to the resonant blip of the second encore [either 'Just Can't Get Enough' or 'More Than A Party'] an hour-and-a-bit later, Depeche Mode skimmed electropop of the highest order somewhere between brain and groin."

Dave Gahan "now had a very snappy line in dance bum sculpture", according to Adrian Maddox, when reviewing the Mayfield Leisure Centre, Belfast show on April 4, also for *Melody Maker*. For the benefit of those further back, those leather-clad hips were often projected onto a giant video screen suspended above the stage. Maddox immediately picked up on Gore's unusual stage attire: "His [Gahan] mate Bubbles [Gore], the only other Depecher to come down off his pedestal, is a little kinkier, in his designer handcuffs, SS boots and the remnants of his girl-friend's lingerie torn around his tits."

Mather even went as far as picking out Gore as being the "real star of the show" on account of his conveying "an air somewhere between bewildered virgin and experienced dungeon master."

Surprisingly, BBC Radio One DJ John Peel, irrepressible bastion of all things alternative, needed no convincing of the band's merits at Wembley. "If we are to have bands filling the world's stadiums," he wrote, "then let them be like Depeche Mode."

Depeche Mode's apparent new-found success in Britain was all the more remarkable given their defiant, keyboard-driven approach, which Alan Wilder readily acknowledged in conversation with *Keyboard*'s Bob Doerschuk: "When we're on-stage we prefer to keep it to just keyboards and drum machines because there aren't too many bands around that do that anymore. Even some of the electronic bands that started around the time that we began have moved away from that. I suppose in that respect we like to stick to the look of electronics and keyboards, simply because it makes us a bit different."

Looking back, Andy Fletcher agreed: "We kept on playing electronic music, and by the mid-Eighties, with U2, rock music was very much in. It [electronic music] was considered a dirty word. All these so-called electronic bands like The Human League became normal bands, but we stuck to our electronic roots."

By the time the 'Black Celebration Tour' reached Bournemouth's International Centre on April 14, 'A Question Of Lust', the first single to be lifted off *Black Celebration*, was in the shops and *Smash Hits'* verdict was out: "With a provocative word in the title and a couple snogging on the cover, one would expect this record to be at least slightly 'steamesque' and pervy. But no. They don't take any of their clothes off at all! Once the black electro-clanks of the intro have settled down, we are presented with a floating, melancholic tune and a wheezing, breathy voice that's singing about love not lust (a word employed solely to rhyme with trust and dust). Moody and pretty, but entirely sauce-free. What a swindle!"

One fanatical female German fan was so enraged by another girl having the audacity to kiss Alan Wilder for the single's sleeve shot that she poured her heart out to *Bravo*.* The teen 'zine's responded sympathetically: "Calm down. We asked the photographers, Ashworth in England, and we can assure you it's not Alan on the sleeve. Because they had to hurriedly finish the photo, they just took a guy (Gary) and a girl (Nikki) from their neighbourhood. But we must admit that Gary looks like Alan – from the side, anyway."

The maturing Mode were by now becoming more media savvy, and far less reliant on such lightweight teenage-orientated titles.

Alan Wilder: "There came a particular time when DM wouldn't appear in *Smash Hits* magazine or *Bravo* because the band had moved on and was trying to shake the teeny-bopper image."

The "wheezing, breathy voice" that *Smash Hits'* complained about on 'A Question Of Lust' belonged to Martin Gore. "It was usually fairly easy to predict whose voice would suit particular songs," stated Alan Wilder. "Generally speaking, Martin's voice tended to suit ballads and Dave's tended to suit more raucous tracks."

A fact that more than one reviewer failed to notice. " 'Lust' is a fairly

* *Melody Maker*'s Steve Lake beautifully summed up *Bravo* in all its teen glory: "Apparently designed for gormless pubescents deranged by sudden hormonal shifts, *Bravo* juxtaposes glossy pin-ups with instructions on how to insert a tampon (and other similar teen brow-furlers) and laughs all the way to the bank with what must be the largest circulation of any pop periodical worldwide."

serious affair – well, as serious as a song written by a man in a leather skirt can get," began *NME*'s David Quantick, awarding it 'Single Of The Week' status. "Dave Gahan proves that his voice can travel, while the Dep Mode sound is as wonderful as ever – this group knows more than any other how to *use* sound."

Melody Maker's Caroline Sullivan similarly followed suit: "Each successive release convinces me afresh that the only factor impeding this group's ascent to ultra-stardom is the unrelenting glumness of singer Dave Gahan. A less oafish reviewer would recognise his juiceless tones for the affirmation of his sensitivity they obviously are; *I* hear a pretty good song, which incorporates the swelling grandiosity of Godley & Creme's 'Cry', rendered stultifying by Gahan's pallid murmur."

'A Question Of Lust' fitted the typical Eighties love ballad bill in all ways but one – the distinctive Depeche Mode production technique.

Alan Wilder: "With it's main focus of a big Phil Spector beat, the current spirit of improvisation manifested itself clearly in this track and included a castanet sound created by dropping a ping-pong ball onto a table and a string 'twang' that originated from a traditional Hungarian instrument somewhat akin to a zither – a favourite source sound used on several songs around this time, including 'Master And Servant' and 'People Are People'. No one knew its real name, but it became known as the 'Hung'!

"When 'Flood' eventually delivered his remix of 'A Question Of Lust', the band were surprised to hear that half of the sounds had been omitted. [We] were understandably annoyed, therefore, when it emerged that Mute Records hadn't actually sent him both the multi-track tapes!"

Rumour has it that George Michael was a fan of 'A Question Of Lust', so much so that at one point he was apparently planning a cover version. Ironically, Gore made disparaging mention of the former Wham! popster when broaching the subject of Depeche Mode's slumping singles sales: "A lot of our singles don't get played on the radio. 'Blasphemous Rumours'. . . even songs like 'Shake The Disease', because of the titles, didn't get any airplay. What people don't seem to realise is that it isn't easy to make a single.

"Take George Michael, for instance. He has a big name. But would 'Careless Whisper' have been a massive hit if you had given that to some unknown Italian singer? Even if *we* had released it, it wouldn't have been a huge hit. They would have said it was boring. It's so successful because it's George Michael. When we released 'A Question Of Lust' they said it was dreary, but that was a great ballad."

When it came to filming the obligatory promo for 'A Question Of Lust', Clive Richardson caught a reasonably dressed Martin Gore on-stage at Dublin's RDS Stadium (April 2). No titillating, torn up lingerie was to be seen, although Alan Wilder confirmed that Gore could almost be glimpsed naked at the beginning of the clip: "We were in a club somewhere, and, as usual, Martin managed to take all his clothes off. The director, Clive Richardson, decided to bring his camera along, and that's what he got."

Had it not been for preventative measures taken by shaven-headed security man Andre Arhle, also caught on Richardson's candid camera, then far more of Gore may have been revealed!

'A Question Of Lust', backed by the atmospheric 'Christmas Island' – used as intro music on the current Black Celebration Tour – shared a similar fate to its predecessors. Despite both tracks being predictably extended for a 12″ single (featuring a self-explanatory 'minimal' mix of 'A Question Of Lust', alongside an instrumental of 'It Doesn't Matter Two' and 'People Are People', live from the Liverpool Empire on September 29, 1984), the single stopped short just inside the Top 30 before dropping out of the chart after only five weeks. Not even a novel booklet- and badge-endowed limited-edition cassette featuring Flood's aforementioned troublesome 'Flood Mix' of the title track together with three more live recordings could do anything to further boost its sales.

Even worse, the US single again failed to make any kind of chart-worthy impression upon its May 28 release, perhaps because it had already been included on *Black Celebration*.

Yet, Americans flocked in their droves to see the Black Celebration Tour. "It sold out in a second," recalled an incredulous Andy Fletcher. "So then we had this bizarre situation: we'd never had a Top 40 album [in America] and we were playing to 30,000 people!"

Martin Gore: "Although we were doing well around *Black Celebration*, we were still playing to more people than we were selling records [to] in the States. We could go there and sell out everywhere we played – a very unusual situation!"

It was a bizarre *and* unusual state of affairs; a European-sounding synth band whose latest album had stalled on the *Billboard* Top 200 at number 90, yet whose 29-date US tour sold out New York City's prestigious 5,900-seat Radio City Music Hall three nights in a row, the 9,000-capacity Red Rocks Amphitheater in Denver, Colorado, for two nights, rounding off with two consecutive outdoor Californian performances at Irvine Meadows Amphitheater in Laguna Hills on July 14 and 15.

Alan Wilder summed up this unexpected breakthrough: "We went on a tour that just seemed to take off – particularly in America [where] it seemed we stepped up a gear from playing smallish club venues to quite big arenas. So things moved very rapidly from that point onwards."

Andy Fletcher: "Modern rock radio was just starting over there and they took us on board. It was the first time that Americans were starting to listen to music that wasn't Journey, Aerosmith, and that ilk. We thought we didn't stand a chance, but they took us on board. And from that, modern rock radio format bands like Nirvana and Pearl Jam came about – although they didn't sound like us, they cited us as being a reason for them to make alternative music."

Alan Wilder: "It seemed that we fitted in perfectly with what the all-American, white, middle-class kids seemed to be searching for – a band that was clean-cut enough to cross over, but subversive enough to push a few boundaries at the same time. I think we felt good about that, and enjoyed sticking two fingers up to England with its provincial attitude."

Daniel Miller echoes Wilder's view: "If anything, I think it's a kind of geographical snobbery – regional snobbery. They didn't come from London, or Manchester, or Liverpool, or Edinburgh; they came from Basildon, which is almost like Neasden or somewhere in its role as an Essex thing. That [Depeche Mode came from Basildon] was always mentioned in all the interviews in a slightly snidey way – [at least] in the early days. I don't know if that had an impact or not on how [British] people saw them. Maybe if they'd come from London or Liverpool they would have maybe been taken a bit more seriously."

Five open-air French and Italian shows in searing heat formed the closing leg of the Black Celebration Tour in early August 1986. Having played to over 300,000 people in four months, a "sickeningly tanned" Dave Gahan spent his first wedding anniversary apart from his wife, playing the large Roman-built Arena Des Frejus, between Nice and Cannes. "I had to celebrate it alone, because Jo has gone away with her mates to Ibiza," the glum singer told journalist Rob Newton, who tagged along for the ride.

"Jo's great," devoted Dave continued. "She does everything for me. She's so organised it's unbelievable. She doesn't like me being away, though. Towards the end of the (first) European leg of the tour, I was heavily depressed. I just wanted to go home. I did a lot of sulking because, even though this is an ideal job which I love, it's also physically and mentally exhausting."

The singer surprisingly perked up when talk turned to babies. "We've been thinking about having a baby during the last year. We even considered it before we got married, but it was hardly practical then."

Newton witnessed first-hand how exhausting staging a Depeche Mode show could be, not least for several crew members struggling to man-handle an unfeasibly large flightcase housing Gahan's extensive wardrobe.

Because his then-trademark leather gear was constantly being replaced – "I get soaking wet every night on-stage and the leather goes all hard – five gigs and they're ruined!" – Gahan was consequently forced to wear unhip white cotton 'stand-ins' for the Frejus show. Support act Eyeless In Gaza failed to show, prompting an unscheduled warm-up from the Blah Brothers, a duo comprised of Depeche Mode's stage manager, Daryl Bamonte, and a crew member going by the name of 'Nobby'. Rob Newton was not impressed: "Unfortunately, they sound like a weedy version of Blancmange, with every song having the same drumbeat and squealing saxophone (not to mention a singer who sounds like he's got a ton of cement lodged at the back of his throat)."

As if on cue, Eyeless In Gaza turned up 15 minutes after the Blahs took to the stage, having driven all the way from the Midlands with only one day's notice of their impending support slot. Naturally, they were not too impressed.

Gahan had enough to contend with – including prankish crew members plastering one of the stage ramps with pornography in an attempt to throw him off his stride – thanks to a post-performance injury after several celebratory drinks too many: "I got really drunk and didn't get back to the hotel until four in the morning. There I was, lying on the bed, and suddenly I wanted to go pee. I went back into the bathroom and fell asleep on the loo. After about an hour I tried to stand up, but I slipped on a towel and went flying through the shower – flat on my backside. I cried out for Jo, who got me back to the bed. I sneaked a look down at my ankle and nearly died when I saw the size of it. It was like an elephant's foot – huge!"

Thankfully, the tour was almost over, and the athletic frontman could rest his weary head – and foot. But first there was more drinking to be done, on the tour bus back to Cannes where Newton reported an obviously worse for wear Gore hysterically hollering, "You want a scoop for *Smash Hits*? Well, get a load of this! Everyone thinks I'm gay because of what I wear, but it's not me! There's only one member of Depeche Mode that's gay . . . and we all know who it is!" An accusatory digit was pointed at a rapidly reddening Fletcher, who slid sheepishly down his seat.

Depeche Mode's luxury coach wound its way around the French coast – to a scenic backdrop of exclusive beach resorts which failed to make much of an impression on the jaded passengers – into Italy for their Pietre Ligure performance. Newton added to his list of tour antics by being shown some of Alan Wilder's private home movie footage; its progressively more saucy contents including "a very horrible dressing room in Berlin, electricity failure in Washington, a party at Alison Moyet's house in Los Angeles and Martin cavorting around in a black, see-through body stocking . . . without the stocking."

No doubt a copy of the incriminating evidence is still stored under lock and key in self-confessed hoarder Alan Wilder's strong room, within "a huge trunk containing thousands of press shots and press clippings dating from 1978, fanzines, sales discs, early DM home video tapes, thousands of early DM photos, a huge case of fan goodies, plus various other little gems like my stage gear over the years – always good for a laugh."

Within days of winding up the tour at the French lakeside resort of Annecy on August 11, Depeche Mode released 'A Question Of Time', with the driving rhythm track remodelled from *Black Celebration* by 'Mix Master' Phil Harding. Alan Wilder explained the song's sampling procedure: "The chugging guitar part was generated by hitting a spring, and part of the bass sound was produced by hitting the end of a Hoover tube by hand. These sounds would invariably be processed through guitar amps to add character and weight."

As the last Depeche Mode record to have the Hansa signature, 'A Question Of Time' effectively closed another chapter in the band's recording history. Dave Gahan paid tribute to Gareth Jones' tenacity: "Until we first started working with Gareth, we had never experienced anything like that – running around, putting mic leads everywhere. We'd never have come up with that idea ourselves – that we could possibly play something and put it through an amp or distort it through a PA system. We did a lot of that in Berlin. We'd set up a big 2K PA, and we'd run a lot of stuff [through it] – like 'A Question Of Time', for instance; [we ran] the *whole* track through there."

The sheer volume of the session stuck in Wilder's mind – and quite possibly, his digestive system: "Even though we were predominantly working at the very top of the [Hansa] building in Studio 4, we hired out the main recording room of Studio 2 and set up a 2K PA system to send individual sounds through – effectively to beef them up and get the atmosphere of the room. This was done much to the annoyance of the Hansa café owner, I might add, who had to endure 'fours-on-the-floor' pounding directly above his head for three days on the trot – something akin to a road drill placed six inches from your ear. God knows what he used to put in our food as retribution!"

'A Question Of Time' eventually reached number 17 – having lost a verse from the album version along the way. Alan Wilder offered a plausible explanation for the omission: "The most likely reason was to bring it down to a more 'radio friendly' length, hopefully ensuring that dear old Radio One would be more inclined to play it – such is the wrath of the BBC that they can scare one into butchering one's own song because they cannot tolerate more than two minutes and 43 seconds of any given record before [DJ Simon] Batesy's *Our Tune* is due!"

Although it was still a long way off a Top 10 placing last enjoyed by Depeche Mode two years previously with 'Master And Servant', it was a substantially better showing than 'A Question Of Lust'. In the *NME* (August 16, 1986), Chris Long awarded rivals The Human League 'Single Of The Week': "Produced by Jimmy Jam and Terry Lewis, 'Human' is the League's attempt at world domination, and it's difficult to think of a chart that this single won't zoom into." He barely found space on the same page to acknowledge Depeche Mode's latest effort: "Depeche Mode's fans seem to crave for a diet of rigid, thrashing beats. That being so, 'A Question Of Time' is neither here nor there. It's just another Depeche Mode single."

Melody Maker simultaneously saw fit to bestow 'Comeback Of The Year' honours on The Human League's 'Human', but were observant enough to highlight the provincial attitude held towards Depeche Mode: "Any other band, preferably German, who hits big sheets of corrugated iron, wears leather miniskirts and wraps it all up in an acute pop sensibility would surely have the sassy youth wetting their pants, but just because it happens to be done by four Walters from Basildon, it tends to get locked away in the cupboard."

But even then the paper couldn't resist a final dig when asking, "Whatever happened to the wee lad who used to write all the songs?"[*]

---

[*] There's no pleasing some critics. When Erasure's half-million-selling *The Circus*, including no fewer than four hit singles was released in 1987, the same paper's David Stubbs lamented: "I yearn for Depeche Mode; the tinny translucent vocals, the sliding and the mischief, the snowballs, the slight narcissism."

Alongside its standard counterpart, Depeche Mode again resorted to a limited-edition 12″ of 'A Question Of Time' in August 1986, featuring new remixes 'A Question Of Time (Newtown)', 'Black Celebration (Black Tulip Mix)', and live recordings made during the recent tour.

In spite of Depeche Mode's rapturous reception from US audiences, Stateside singles success proved elusive as 'A Question Of Time' crashed and burned following its September 3 release. To the band's dismay, their US label then took the unpredictable action of making a B-side, 'But Not Tonight' into an A-side (with 'Stripped' as the flip), on October 22.

Alan Wilder was understandably appalled at having the track, in which the band had audibly invested so much time, relegated to backing a song that they had literally knocked together in an afternoon: "An incredible decision considering the chalk and cheese nature of the two tracks."

Yet there was a method to Sire's apparent madness as 'But Not Tonight' was tied in with Jerry Kramer's forgettable teen screen comedy *Modern Girls*. Sire even went as far as sanctioning a *Miami Vice*-style, Tamra Davis-directed video in which Depeche Mode were occasionally seen super-imposed against footage from the movie. The single predictably bombed.

To add insult to injury, Alan Wilder was none too thrilled when the extended version of 'But Not Tonight' (that had appeared on the UK 'Stripped' 12″) was later included as a bonus track on the *Black Celebration* CD: "It's rightful position was as the B-side to 'Stripped' and I always felt that including extra tracks at the end of an album CD disrupted the flow of the LP. The reasoning was to give value for money, but they should have remained on their intended formats only."*

Vince Clarke was also experiencing the vagaries of the mainstream American music business head on with Erasure: "We played LA and there were about 1,200 really enthusiastic people at the gig. LA is where Warner Brothers have their offices, so a lot of the Warner Brothers people were there. Backstage afterwards they were all there laying into the drink and Andy [Bell] came into the dressing room. The first thing anyone said to him was, 'Where's the corkscrew?' The second thing was, 'What do you do?' And this was *after* the gig."

"America was a real revelation to me," Clarke told *Melody Maker*. "It

---

* Although a similar underhand marketing manoeuvre was pulled off for Depeche Mode's next studio album, *Music For The Masses* and 1988's CD re-release of *Speak & Spell*, Wilder's protestations were heeded thereafter.

came back to us via 'Flood' [Mark Ellis], our engineer, that people in the company [Warner Bros.] in New York were saying they thought it was really bad that Andy was making it plain he was gay, because they were worried it would affect our sales. And yet when we were in San Francisco, Warner Bros was encouraging us to talk to the biggest US gay paper, *The Advocate*. There's a lot of hypocrisy."

'A Question Of Time' or, more specifically, its intriguing promo video, marked a turning point for Depeche Mode, anchoring their sound with a recognisable image, thanks to Anton Corbijn (who had shot the band's first *NME* cover). Using black and white Super 8 cinefilm, the surreal plot centres on a strange, goggled individual riding around an American desert on a sidecar-endowed vintage motorcycle. The biker finds a baby, which he ultimately places in Alan Wilder's outstretched arms.

As far as Wilder was concerned, the adage 'never work with children' certainly rang true on this shoot: "We had to work with the little baskets – sorry, babies – for hours before they would do what was required. There were mothers, nappies, bottles, toys . . . all kinds of chaos."

Although all four members eventually cradle the acting infant – with Martin Gore laughing as the baby girl pulls his hair in the final frame, Wilder unquestionably grabbed the most screen seconds, leading to the assumption that he was the only one to show up on time while his colleagues slept on.

"It is possible that I was the only one prepared to get up early enough," the keyboardist speculated. "The location was two hours outside LA, and I think the shoot was on a day after a gig. Directors always get you to the shoot at 5 am, just out of spite!"

Anton Corbijn: "They [Depeche Mode] offered me a video for 'A Question Of Time', and I had this idea of a road movie. And they just let me take over in that sense; they were quite happy, I think, not to have to take responsibility."

Depeche Mode were certainly united on the visual relief front. "Video was not an area where we'd ever felt comfortable," Dave Gahan confessed. "We kind of stood in the background, and then afterwards went, 'Oh, that looks really bad, doesn't it?'"

Alan Wilder: "As unbelievable as it may seem, all our respective image changes over the years have been of our own choosing, and – until Anton became involved – there was no continuity to the DM image. In fact, some of the earlier promos are embarrassing to the extreme. We allowed ourselves to be walked over by a series of not very good directors practising their trade – Julian Temple springs to mind. Anton's arrival was certainly a relief, although our acting abilities hardly improved with all the experience [we'd] had!"

Martin Gore: "We had a lot of bad experiences in the early days of our videos. I think a lot of the time when directors came in they just saw how young and naive we were, and they were just taking the piss, really: 'Let's see how stupid we can make them look – see how far they'll go.'"

Dave Gahan: "We were really searching for somebody that we could be comfortable with, and really from the moment that we sat down with Anton and started talking about ideas it was pretty obvious that he was going to be part of the team."

Corbijn wasn't backward in coming forward concerning his new-found role: "I don't think there was such a thing as a Depeche Mode package before I sort of got involved; there was nothing to really grab on to. Of course, the music was there, but if you're talking about a package, I think that wasn't really there. So I think the music and the visuals became one when I got involved."

Dave Gahan: "When we made the first video with Anton for 'A Question Of Time', and saw it, we realised that we could do OK with something like that, and someone visually could bring something to what we were doing. Anton, ever since then, seemed to get what we were doing, and was able to bring a shadowy image to what we were doing so that it wasn't so much . . . so that we didn't look like such misfits, basically. It was the right colour and right picture for the music."

Anton Corbijn: "Their music is quite filmic, and therefore I could make it quite epic. So I like to think that I definitely gave them a strength in the imagery, and also connected it to their music."

Andy Fletcher: "Look at our whole career: [if] you start from the beginning and start to move through it, it all starts to come together round about *Black Celebration*. During *Black Celebration* is when we first started to work with Anton Corbijn. Before that – as you can see from all our early videos, and all our early photos – we didn't really have control, or have much on the visual side; we weren't really happy. It was our fault. But from when Anton sort of came in and took hold of all our visuals, and also with our music also getting better as well, it all seemed to come together."

Interspersed within the 'A Question Of Time' video's vague narrative was split-second Stateside footage from the 'Black Celebration Tour'; serving to highlight the spectacle that was Jane Spiers' highly inventive stage set, including some bizarre percussive devices.

Alan Wilder explained these to *Keyboard*'s Bob Doerschuk: "We've had some things built which look like abstract objects standing on the back of our [keyboard] risers. We mic them with contact mics, and treat the sound as samples. In other words, we can produce all kinds of different sampled sounds by hitting these objects. Most people think we must be miming as we hit these things on–stage, because they can't understand how all these sounds could be coming out of one piece of metal. In fact, we're not miming; we're triggering the sounds."

This rather long–winded technical process involved feeding the microphones into an offstage Roland Octapad electronic drum kit, which in turn triggered two Akai S612 samplers (as used in the *Black Celebration* recording sessions) via the now widely adopted MIDI (Musical Instrument Digital Interface), thereby 'playing' the sampled sounds as heard by Depeche Mode's audiences. For Wilder, the end result was simple: "You can actually see us working on–stage, rather than just standing there."

In so doing, Depeche Mode single-handedly succeeded in adopting elements of Kraftwerk's blueprint by transporting it to amphitheatres, and eventually, stadiums . . .

18

Massive Attack

"Music For The Masses? A lot of our fans thought we'd gone for it. Martin saw an album called Music For The Millions*, and we thought it was quite funny, so* Music For The Masses *[it was]. But then again, it did become, in the end, music for the masses because we did this big gig at the Rose Bowl [Pasadena, California], which was the real highlight of our career."*

– Andy Fletcher, 1998

When quizzed by *Record Mirror*'s Francesco Adinolfi as to what had been happening with Depeche Mode during the first part of 1987, Andy Fletcher lackadaisically replied, "We've been taking it easy." As it was, life within the Depeche camp hadn't entirely ground to a casual halt following the lengthy Black Celebration Tour.

Martin Gore traded his decadent love affair with Berlin's nightlife – and his relationship with Christina Friederich – for a flat in London's Maida Vale, not far from Andy Fletcher and girlfriend, Grainne Mullen. Gore's short-term plans included penning the next album, and by the time the band were approaching recording again, Dave and Jo Gahan were well on the way towards expecting their first child.

Alan Wilder – who moved to a Hampstead home to accommodate his surrogate family (Jeri and Jason Young) – was harbouring a few musical plans of his own, as he disclosed to *Keyboard*'s Bob Doerschuk: "I like the idea of being totally self-contained, without having to answer to anybody, which means doing my own engineering, producing, playing, and everything. I'd only do it in my spare time, though."

Wilder had put some of the band's electronic instrumentation through its paces at his 16-track home studio. "I always had things like my MiniMoog, and I'd just bring [sampling] keyboards like the Emulators home. In fact, I was working with the internal sequencer in the Emulator

239

[II] for a while, which wasn't very good, but it was all I had around. In terms of recording, everything was going onto a four-track reel-to-reel, so it was a very basic set-up to begin with."

Basic it may have been, but the creative results of that early set-up inadvertently signalled the start of Wilder's low-key solo *alter ego*, Recoil, with the late-1986 release of the *1+2* mini-album on Mute. Comprising a bunch of skilfully manipulated Depeche Mode samples and other material using an Emulator sampler, Roland Jupiter-8 and PPG Wave 2 synthesisers, this offbeat experimental recording was never intended for commercial release.

As Wilder explained: "*1+2* was really just me mucking around at home. It was a cassette demo on a four-track Fostex or Tascam [recorder], and only ended up being released after I played it to Daniel [Miller]. He said, 'Could you re-do this?' I didn't really have time to do it properly, so we just decided to release it inconspicuously, as it was, and not pay too much attention to it."

Be that as it may, response from some quarters of the music press was surprisingly encouraging, as highlighted by the following review from *Dance Music Report*: "*1+2* is completely synthesiser based, yet bares no resemblance to the pretty pop ponderings of the group [Depeche Mode]. Mostly of an instrumental nature, some of it pulsates in the traditional sense, but serves mainly as ambience. It is nice to see D. Mode's members branch out into serious musical ventures, rather than take the easy route of producing merely bubblegum pabulum."

Looking back, Wilder was not entirely happy with his minimalist doodlings, claiming, "I didn't have time to do anything about it. We felt it was good to get anything out there and perhaps I didn't feel that precious about it because it was only a side project at the time."

Depeche Mode's next album involved a substantial period of pre-production at Wilder's home studio, where Gore's demos were worked upon. This time, Daniel Miller stepped down from co-production duties, citing the uncomfortable tensions that had arisen during the making of *Black Celebration*.

Fresh from recording Peter Gabriel's multi-million-selling, international breakthrough *So* (and attendant mega-hits 'Sledgehammer' and 'Don't Give Up') at Gabriel's Real World Studios, engineer/producer Dave Bascombe was employed (with Miller's blessing) to polish up Depeche Mode's sound. Gareth Jones was also absent; mixing and producing Mute artists, Holger Hiller (ex-Can), Nitzer Ebb and Wire, at Hansa, in Berlin, throughout 1987.

Born in Chester, England, Dave Bascombe grew up in London as an avid record buyer and radio listener, picking out melodies on the family piano. Interestingly, his teenage experience mirrored that of Alan Wilder: landing a tape op-cum-tea boy position at a recording studio where he proceeded to hone his recording skills during downtime. Bascombe's reputation landed him various freelance engineering jobs before securing a more full-time position at Marcus Studios, in Fulham.

In 1983, he part-engineered Echo & The Bunnymen's critically acclaimed *Porcupine* album at the facility, but his career shifted up a gear after engineering Tears For Fears' four-million-unit-shifting *Songs From The Big Chair* which topped the *Billboard* chart in the spring of 1985. The album spawned two US chart-topping singles in 'Everybody Wants To Rule The World' (which also won the 1986 Brit Award for Best Single) and 'Shout', both Top Five entries in the UK. ABC's Martin Fry once praised Dave Bascombe thus: "For us he's the quintessential engineer and producer, happy to spend 13 days working non-stop on a sound."

On paper at least, it seemed Bascombe would gel perfectly with Depeche Mode – the "group [who] knows more than any other how to *use* sound," according to *NME*'s David Quantick. The reality of the partnership told a different story, as Alan Wilder comically explained: "Of all the DM albums, *Music For The Masses* was probably the most self-produced record. With all due respect, Dave Bascombe's role was more as a good engineer rather than producer.

"A music producer is roughly the equivalent of the film director – someone who retains the overall vision of a record, who attempts to draw the very best from the raw material given to him by the artist, and someone who usually has the final say about how the finished product sounds. They come in different shapes and sizes: those that are very hands-on – even playing some instruments – through to those who are completely unmusical, but somehow have a great perspective.

"The role of an engineer is to realise the producer [and] artists' ideas from a technical point of view . . .

"Producer: 'I want the Peruvian nose flute sound to disappear into the distance and then explode.'

"Engineer: 'I know, I'll try sending it through delay unit 163457B and then gate it to the bass drum, distorted through a Leslie cabinet using three D72 mics at varying distances.'

"Producer: 'Don't get clever with me, sonny; if it sounds shit, I'll dump it!'

"Engineer: 'Whatever you say, sir.'

"Producer: 'That's right. *Boy*! Make me a cup of tea, and go out and buy me a can of tartan paint . . . Hoover the ceiling, while you're at it!' "

Displaying the band's typically humorous outlook of the time, Andy Fletcher explained the new album's title: "The title's *Music For The Masses*. It's a bit tongue-in-cheek, really. Everyone is telling us we should make more commercial music, so that's the reason we chose that title."*

The single that preceded the album, 'Strangelove', was recorded at The Kinks' Konk studios in Hornsey, North London. The song was reputedly very difficult to piece together, and, with the benefit of hindsight, Alan Wilder felt that the original version of the track, released on April 13, was "too cluttered".

Press response to Gore's latest bleak celebration of love, as depicted in the song's rousing chorus, was generally muted – with the predictable exception of *Smash Hits*, whose enthusiasm was no doubt bolstered by the single's lavish launch party, held in the Edwardian Suite of London's Kenilworth Hotel. Organised by publicist Chris Carr, appointed in 1982 by Daniel Miller as Depeche Mode's publicity officer, the no-expense-spared gathering, replete with a large, fluorescent orange megaphone with the word 'BONG' printed in its inside acting as an unsubtle centrepiece, was attended by the band and an entourage of Mute employees.

Smash Hits reported the subsequent alcohol-fuelled carnage: "Andy Fletcher is having a spook-conversation with a *Smash Hits* journalist, saying things like, 'It's not all like this, you know – sometimes doing this job is really boring, because it is a job, you know; it's a job, and when we're in the studio it's the most boring thing in the world; quite honestly I only do this for the money; for the money and the memories . . .' before going all wistful for a minute and then disappearing under the table to chew people's kneecaps (or something) where he's eventually joined by some record company foxtresses, and no one seems to know what's going on anymore."

Meanwhile, "bonkers bloke" Martin Gore topped his bandmate's

* Having been berated for the non-commerciality of his demos for the previous album, *Black Celebration*, the title may well have been a sarcastic in-joke on the part of Martin Gore.

behaviour by indulging in a spot of characteristic apparel removal while "best bitter" quaffing "Alan 'Wild'er" complained: "I think this is a complete farce. A set-up like this is nothing but a fiasco. I suppose you think that we all get on really well together, and it's like this all the time – well, it isn't! We argue constantly, and that's the real us. Yeah, I know I'm cynical, but I'm also realistic."

The uninvited *NME* waited three weeks after the UK release of 'Strangelove' to bemoan the lack of "the clumsy naivety that was so much a part of their charm before" and "the experimental edge to their sound" so evident in "the metal-pop of the lyrically inane 'People Are People'." The verdict was damning: " 'Strangelove' is another sortie into Soft Cell-type territory, but Martin Gore will never know as much as Marc Almond about the darker side of love, and Dave Gahan lacks the corruption necessary in the voice of an electronic torch singer."

Melody Maker's Sorrel Downer sounded like she was on a downer: "Of course it's beautifully produced with perfectly proportioned instrumentation and rich, distinctive vocals, but where have all those invigorating, off-the-wall ideas gone? The last one they had was all leather and lace, and I think it's about time they all got their heads together and had another one."

Martin Gore: "A lot of my songs are about relationships and love, and sex is a facet of that whole package. There's only about one or two songs that ever touched upon S&M. That was a time when I used to go out to a lot of those clubs, just out of interest. I was never heavily into it, but it was a fascinating scene."

Like its predecessor 'A Question Of Time', 'Strangelove' reached number 17, followed by a three-week tumble out of the UK Singles Chart.

Alan Wilder: "It was actually quite predictable – the pattern for DM releases has been the same for many years. The fans are so dedicated that they rush out and buy the records in the first week of release, resulting in a very high chart position, usually higher if it's a single pre-release of the album.

"This position is difficult to maintain or improve upon in the second and third weeks, and the record usually doesn't have time to cross over – if it's going to – before it is dropping down the chart. As soon as the single starts to drop, the radio stops playing it and the cycle is complete. Everything is over in three to four weeks – not necessarily a reflection of the music, just a syndrome that has become almost impossible to break away from. By contrast, 'Just Can't Get Enough' was in the charts for something like 18 weeks."

A brace of remixes were available on two separate 12″ versions to appease those fanatical followers desperate for a new Depeche Mode album, including a creditable turn from Daniel Miller – 'Strangelove (Blind Mix)' – and the 'MIDI Mix', which owed its moniker – and its very existence – to an unforeseen chain of events.

Alan Wilder: "The mix [got] its name from the fact that, at one point during the recording session, the MIDI configuration went haywire and all the [sequenced] instruments started playing the wrong parts. Someone thought it sounded rather good, so we tarted it up a bit and slapped it on the [limited-edition 12″] as a remix. I have my doubts as to the wisdom of this now, though."

There was no doubting the wisdom of having Anton Corbijn direct the accompanying promo. 'Strangelove' was another grainy, black and white effort, shot in Paris to coincide with *Music For The Masses* sessions at the Studio Guillaume Tell complex on Avenue de la Belle Gabrielle.

Alan Wilder: "Anton shot the video in Paris using his girlfriend, Nassim, as an extra. It marked the first inclusion of a characteristic Anton ingredient – the female of the species (in the form of models and actresses)!"

Again, the video took on somewhat surreal form as all the band were intermittently seen holding large megaphones imprinted with BONG 13 – the single's catalogue number – while the "extra" cavorted in and around a bedroom in varying states of undress. In editing the video, Corbijn created an element of continuity with its predecessor, 'A Question Of Time', for the closing shot had the band collectively collapsing in a giggling fit, having overdone the solemn method of acting.

Dave Gahan's experience of working within Studio Guillaume Tell was coloured by the "unbelievable" gall of their French fans: "They just sit outside the recording studio, and if any of us come out, they all barge up going, 'Was that eet? Was that the seengle we just heard? Was eet the seengle?' And there was one bloke, a complete weirdo, who used to sit outside our hotel for literally days and nights. And he never said anything – just took photos of us all the time. And he had on this combat jacket all the time and we thought he was going to blow us up or something, and we'd be going, 'Well, I'm not going out the door first!' He was well weird."

Likewise, beautiful Paree was anything but as far as temporary resident

Depeche Mode's second line-up, circa-1985 – Martin Gore, Alan Wilder, Andy Fletcher and Dave Gahan. (*LFI*)

Depeche Mode, circa-1983 – Alan Wilder (left) models his trademark 'Hovis' hairdo. (*LFI*)

Yazoo, circa-1982 – Alison 'Alf' Moyet (left) and Vince Clarke (right). (*LFI*)

Alan 'Slick' Wilder (*LFI*)

Andy Fletcher – with freshly-bleached barnet. (*LFI*)

Martin Gore – leather fetish in full-flow. (*LFI*)

Dave Gahan – sporting trademark Eighties flat-top. (*LFI*)

Martin Gore – underrated guitarist, and Depeche
Mode's chief songwriter following Vince Clarke's
departure. (*LFI*)

Depeche Mode were already commanding five-figure
audiences in mainland Europe – particularly Germany
– by the close of 1983. (*Rex*)

The innovative Black Celebration Tour 1986 stage set by designer Jane Spiers featured inflatable materials and
custom-built devices for triggering electronic percussion. (*Rex*)

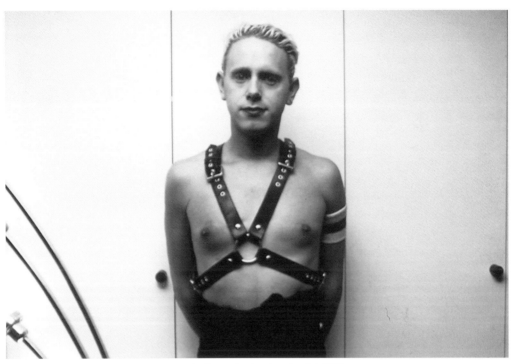

Martin Gore – let bondage begin! (*SIN*)

Depeche Mode, with Albert Einstein, in the mid-Eighties. "I was never comfortable with Martin dressing up in girl's clothing," said Alan Wilder. (*Eric Watson*)

The Assembly, 1983 – Vince Clarke, Feargal Sharkey and a sleepy Eric Radcliffe managed just one hit single, 'Never, Never'. (*LFI*)

Erasure, circa-1985 – Vince Clarke's synth pop duo with vocalist Andy Bell. (*LFI*)

Depeche Mode recorded three albums at Hansa Tonstudios overlooking the Berlin Wall between 1983 and 1986. (*Redferns*)

Music For The Masses. By the close of the Eighties, Depeche Mode had conquered the United States. (*Rex*)

Depeche Mode, circa-1988, at the time of D.A. Pennebaker's *101* 'rockumentary'. (*LFI*)

Andy Fletcher was concerned: "We stayed in this place in Paris that was christened 'Turd City', 'cos everyone there had a dog and there were turds all the way around it – turd city was an understatement, I'm telling you!"

By the time that the 'Strangelove' video was doing the rounds of European television, Depeche Mode and Dave Bascombe had left the magnificent sights, sounds and, if Fletcher is to be believed, smells of Paris, behind for Scandinavia's largest recording complex – PUK Studios, set deep in the wilds of Denmark – where Daniel Miller joined them for the mixing. With two exceptionally well-equipped, day-lit recording studios – four apartments, a large heated indoor swimming pool, a sizeable Jacuzzi, sunbed, Sauna, multi-gym, and snooker/pool table on site – completing *Music For The Masses* was a pleasurable experience.

Looking back, Alan Wilder ranked PUK right up there with Berlin's Hansa as the best recording facility he had the pleasure of working in. No doubt aware of the previous album mix sessions running over their allotted time, he appeared determinedly disciplined. "PUK's facilities included a swimming pool, gym and sauna which I used regularly, usually before starting work," Wilder recalled. "We also hired a car and I sometimes went off for long drives in the Danish countryside when I needed to get away from everybody. Nightlife was fairly limited, although on occasion we'd go into the nearest happening town, which was about an hour away."

The tranquillity of a peaceful fishing interlude near the studio was rudely interrupted by an uninvited guest – a wild bull: "We ran for our lives, and didn't see that the field was surrounded by an electric fence," Fletcher told *Joepie*. "We got quite a shock when we ran into it!"

If only the mixing sessions could be as electrifying, but for now the final outcome was still far from certain. "It's hard to speak about the style of the record, but the songs are really good," Andy Fletcher told *Record Mirror*'s Francesco Adinolfi. "It contains various moods. We've recorded 15 songs of which nine or 10 will end up on the album."

But, as was often the case with Depeche Mode, all was not necessarily as straightforward as it appeared . . .

According to some, Dave Bascombe was hasty in exposing the album's supposed shortcomings, but by rejoining Depeche Mode in Denmark, Daniel Miller demonstrated that the close production relationship previously forged with the band remained unbroken – in spite of the troublesome mixing sessions a year earlier. The team started by yet again remixing 'Strangelove' for inclusion on *Music For The Masses*. Miller had already created the 'Blind Mix' and the general consensus was that elements of this should be incorporated into the album version. The result was therefore an amalgam of the original 7″, released before the final mixing began, and Miller's remix for the subsequent limited-edition 12″.

'Strangelove' was not alone in the tampering stakes. An extra mix of 'To Have And To Hold' ended up featuring on the CD version of *Music For The Masses* as 'To Have And To Hold (Spanish Taster)'.* But why the need for *two* versions of the same song on the same CD?

Alan Wilder highlighted the musical flexibility that existed within Depeche Mode to a degree: "It's really very simple. Martin submitted his demo in the usual way, and although I liked the song, his original idea was too lightweight for my taste – and, I felt, the mood of the album – so I pushed it in a darker, more atmospheric direction. This was the primary version of the song that was always intended to be on the album. Martin, however, was very attached to his more poppy demo and said that he wanted to record it, too – hence the 'Spanish Taster' [version]. It wasn't a question of fighting with one another over this; it's just that Martin saw the song in a different way to me. He just wanted to include his demo on the album. I don't think there is a more perfect example of the musical differences between myself and Martin."

Elsewhere on the album, songwriter and arranger were in agreement as Wilder sought to improve upon Gore's original demos for their overall benefit. Nowhere was this more apparent than the song destined to become Depeche Mode's next single. Primarily programmed at Wilder's Hampstead home, 'Never Let Me Down Again' was initially restructured to emphasise its chorus, and in that sense, the song was no different to any other they'd worked on. Yet, according to Alan, "It stood out as an obvious single, and suggested a 'Stripped'-like feel."

'Never Let Me Down Again' was set to become a standout track in Depeche Mode's live set, thanks in no small part to the introduction of genuinely live parts, including a distinctive guitar riff from Martin Gore, subsequently processed through several effects. Elsewhere real orchestral

---

* The other bonus tracks were 'Agent Orange', the instrumental that had shown up on the limited-edition 12″ of 'Strangelove', with two other tracks set to make an appearance on Depeche Mode's next 12″ single – 'Never Let Me Down Again (Aggro Mix)' and 'Pleasure, Little Treasure (Glitter Mix)'.

sounds and beefy Led Zeppelin drum samples were employed to further flesh out the backing track with anthemic results.

Within days of the song's August 24 release date, one *NME* hack was already straining at the leash: "'Never Let Me Down Again' is oddly conventional and I wouldn't be surprised if it had something to do with drugs, man: 'I'm taking a ride with my best friend/ I hope he never lets me down again.' . . . Sarge, the sniffer dogs . . .'"

Alan Wilder wisely refused to be drawn into the ensuing debate amongst Depeche Mode's quizzical fanbase, but his speak-no-evil stance spoke volumes about his bandmate's behaviour. "I can't speak for Martin's songs – I know as much about what they mean as [the next person]. I also can't speak for Martin's lifestyle; you'll have to ask him personally if you want the answer to that one."

Smash Hits: "So often the Mode thump out the same old synthesised ploddings, but this one's definitely more memorable because it's . . . well, it's creepy. Shiver your spinal column to the hollow, jaggy and sinister toots; shake in your sandals at the eerie 'n' horrible choir sound searing over the top of it all . . . The B-side ['Pleasure, Little Treasure'] is quite a good disco belter, too."

Germany's *Bravo* spouted: "The 'Split Mix' of 'Never Let Me Down Again' goes on for a whopping 9:30 minutes on the 12″ maxi-single. To these ears it's the most exciting piece of music DM has ever released! The new Depeche sound is unbeatable, as is the melody."

Ironically, 'Never Let Me Down Again (Split Mix)' was to be the last time that the band had any direct hand in extended remix duties.

Alan Wilder: "It became the thing to do, to farm remixes out to other people who might have a fresher approach to the job in hand. We were always very drained by the end of a record, so it suited us. However, having witnessed the attempts of some of the remixers over the last 10 years, I'm now of the opinion that we were right the first time, and it's probably better to do it yourself."

Meanwhile, *Melody Maker*'s Paul Mathur concluded: "Not as pervy as their greatest moment ('A Question Of Lust'), but still possessing that uncanny ability to peel back the first couple of layers of contempt without shouting too loud."

Accompanied by another memorable monochrome Anton Corbijn video, centring on an unorthodox, three-wheel bubble car (prompting an incredulous American viewer to comment on its 'missing' rear wheel!) driving through fields of rape seed, it seemed that Depeche Mode were on the receiving end of a majority thumbs up. However, 'Never Let Me Down Again' failed, in paraphrasing Alan Wilder, to "cross over"; disappointingly peaking at 22 on September 5 during a by-now familiar four-week residency.

Alan Wilder: "I don't think we ever really could foresee what was happening with any of our records. We didn't really know what would come from them. I mean, Martin and Fletch in particular were always very pessimistic about what we were doing – 'Oh, we're not going to be able to do this; we're doomed,' kind-of-thing. We would just put [an album] out there and see what happened, go on tour, and hope it would do well."

On September 28, while Depeche Mode were in rehearsals at Nomis Studios in Shepherd's Bush, for their longest world tour to date, *Music For The Masses* arrived in British record stores. The album's stunning sleeve photography (from long-time Mode collaborator, Martyn Atkins) featured three of the bright red megaphones first seen as part of the 'Strangelove' single artwork and accompanying video, set beautifully against a cloudy sunset.

Alan Wilder: "[The] idea just came from our graphic designer, Martyn Atkins – [who came] up with this idea of a speaker, but, to give the kind of ironic element which the title has, to put this speaker in a setting which wasn't really to do with the masses at all. It was, in fact, the opposite. So you end up with this kind of eerie thing where you get these speakers or megaphones in the middle of a setting that doesn't suit it at all, like a desert or whatever."*

As well as the tongue-in-cheek title, further irony was had in that the megaphone was put to devastating use in Nazi Germany, spreading Adolf Hitler's disturbing dictatorial message. In a knowing nod to his reformed country's past, Kraftwerk's chief propagandist Ralf Hütter had once claimed that his pioneering electronic quartet created "loudspeaker music".

Archrivals *NME* and *Melody Maker* posted their all-important critiques on October 3. The former's Jane Solanas came to praise rather than bury: "What I want to know is, are Depeche Mode perves? Their minds are

---

* In the video to Erasure's October 1988 UK Top Five hit 'A Little Respect', former bandmate Vince Clarke sprayed paint all over a symbol that looked remarkably like the loudspeaker logo adorning the *Music For The Masses* album sleeve. "I think it was just a bit of fun from Vince, nothing more than that," commented Alan Wilder.

veritable sewers. Leastways songwriter Martin Gore's is, and the rest of the Modes appear to encourage him, happily singing and playing his bizarre songs. Martin Gore is the Depeche Mode with the fluffy blond hair and the penchant for wearing leather mini-skirts. Nothing wrong with that. Depeche Mode are unashamed pop entertainers, and this has been the key to their long success and the reason why Martin Gore has been able to develop his strange carnal visions and keep the Depeche Mode audience happy . . .

"I'm pleased to see that on *Music For The Masses*, Gore is at his obsessive best. Every single track is steeped in sin of one sort or another. For me, the recent single 'Never Let Me Down Again' is still an intriguing master-piece, combining homoeroticism with drug euphoria. Other high points are the closing track, 'Pimpf', which sounds suspiciously like the sound-track to the camp vampire film, *Daughters Of Darkness*; and the two tracks where Gore takes the lead vocal, 'The Things You Said' and 'I Want You Now'. His angelic tones fair send shivers up a female spine."

Melody Maker's Paul Mathur also picked up on the album's East European-tinged instrumental closer, but for the wrong reasons. " 'Pimpf' is a silly, sassy thing, rounding off a record that's seamless, fluid, and, once the lights are out, particularly dull," rounding off with an equally damning, if confused, parting shot: "It's not what I waited for, and it's never going to be the best of ammunition for barroom arguments over Pop's Grubby Tapestry, but I'll keep it around a bit."

Record Mirror's Eleanor Levy tipped the scales in Depeche Mode's favour when awarding *Music For The Masses* four out of five. "With the relative failure of 'Never Let Me Down Again' in the singles chart, some may be ready to bury the last nail in the Depeche Mode coffin. Yet common con-sensus among all, bar the record-buying public, would have it that this latest D Mode 45 is perhaps the best thing they have ever done. The fact is, this dark, sensual track is possibly far too disturbing for the Rick Astley fans among us and though it points to a more mature Depeche Mode, it may well be the beginning of the end of the common misconception that they are a 'girly synthesiser' band. Only stark chart failure will finally secure one of the most consistent bands of the last few years a place in the hall of credible chart fame . . .

"*Music For Masses* is, therefore, a contradictory title. It is far from that at this moment in time, for it contains an overall feeling of dissatisfaction, paranoia and vulnerability, far too warm and intelligent for that yardstick of what the masses want (i.e. the charts). Instead, you once again find yourself entering into the Martin Gore vulnerability landscape, none more so than the poignant 'The Things You Said' or 'I Want You Now'. Martin Gore's presence seems even more to the fore on this album; his voice becoming richer and more forceful, while Dave Gahan's vocals descend ever downward and butchward into Iggy Pop territory – one reason why *Music For The Masses* is possibly the most accomplished and sexy Mode album to date."

Ever the perfectionist, Alan Wilder felt there was room for improvement: "It's only natural to think, with the benefit of hindsight, that you could have done your previous work so much better. In fact, I'd be worried if I didn't think that about every single record I've been involved in. It's what drives you forward. *Black Celebration* has some good stuff on it, but the mixes do sound odd. *Music For The Masses* actually sounds better, but is not such an interesting record . . . I think we had used up our quota of metallic sounds by that stage. There are only so many ways you can hit a pipe with a hammer."

Yet Depeche Mode were still concerned with "pushing the frontiers of sampled sound," as Gareth Jones once put it. The strangely sexual 'breathing' sound introducing 'I Want You Now' was the product of sampling an inflating/deflating accordion without playing a note on it. Elsewhere, the spoken word still proved evocative, as highlighted by the Russian speech sampled at the intro to 'To Have And To Hold', which translated as: "The evolution of nuclear arsenals and socially psychological aspects of the arms race was considered in these reports." An apt contemporary passage in fitting the dark musical mood that Wilder was striving for.

More importantly, those involuntarily well-chosen words had added poignancy behind the 'Iron Curtain' where radio presenter Yegor Shishkovsky was one of the first Soviet DJs to risk playing Western rock music: "I will risk it and say that Depeche Mode is the biggest band in Russia since The Beatles. Obviously, it's a different music from different times, but they are the biggest artists since The Beatles. I can't think of anyone bigger than they are out there [in Russia] – not only bands, but I can't think of any performers at all . . . any artists."

Both band and record label obviously had high hopes for *Music For The Masses*; in an unprecedented move they took out full-page ads in *Melody Maker* and *Record Mirror*, coinciding with those publications' reviews, positive or otherwise. The *Melody Maker* advert listed January 1988 UK dates – 11 in total, including two consecutive nights at London's Wembley Arena and a return to Whitley Bay Ice Rink – for the forthcoming 'Music For

The Masses Tour'. *Record Mirror*'s readership was informed that limited quantities of the *Music For The Masses* album were being paired with a free 12″ single of remixed versions of 'Never Let Me Down Again' and 'Strangelove' with every album bought at HMV stores throughout the UK.

Depeche Mode's advertising gamble paid dividends as *Music For The Masses* reached number 10 on the UK Albums Chart. Mute applied a similar strategy to *Hydrology*, Alan Wilder's second solo album as Recoil, when a strategically placed ad appeared in the February 27, 1988 issue of *Record Mirror* informing readers that the CD of *Hydrology* also included *1+2*. That publication's review of the Recoil album was favourable, albeit grudgingly: "I'd say he's been listening to too much avant-garde arty composer Philip Glass, because this is very much like the *Koyannisqatsi* soundtrack, with lots of swirling, repetitive pianos which whisk you off onto another dimension; no singing here either, just the odd vocal effect thrown in, and, if you forget about the Glass comparisons, it's actually rather good, relaxing listening."

Martyn Atkins was drafted in to provide some suitably minimalist artwork for *Hydrology*. "The choice of images [including a 'dead' man] was down to his interpretation of the music," Alan Wilder explained. "I thought they fitted well."

Although *Hydrology* bore little resemblance to Depeche Mode's output, it did share one ingredient with *Music For The Masses* – foreign sampled speech.

Alan Wilder: "During the second track, 'Stone', there is a sample of a French train station announcer. Elsewhere, Polish can clearly be heard. It was the first thing that came on when I was fiddling around with the radio dial. I had no idea what it meant; I just liked the sound of the language, along with other Eastern European languages which sound like music to my ears."

In spite of its quirkiness, *Hydrology* couldn't hope to match *Music For The Masses*, sales-wise – nor, as a non-pop recording, was it really expected to do so.

Alan Wilder: "*Hydrology* was a step up from *1+2*. It was done on a half-inch 16-track Fostex machine. So there were limitations, but it was much more versatile than the first thing I'd done [*1+2*]. Recoil was still very much an aside to Depeche Mode, with no pressure on expectations placed upon it. In other words, it wasn't my main concern, and was always going to be an antidote to Depeche Mode in some ways; a way to alleviate the frustrations of always working within a pop format. I have nothing against the pop format, but if I was going to do something on my own, there was no point in repeating what I was already doing in the group. It was intended to be different and experimental. It didn't matter if it was too left-field or too weird for people, because I was still doing the pop thing on the other side."

In Europe, *Music For The Masses* put in a more impressive appearance, sales-wise – especially in Germany where it peaked at number two, prompting two Depeche Mode tours there in 1987 and 1988. Yet it was down to an exhausting but ultimately rewarding summer slog around the lucrative American touring circuit that saw the album climb all the way to 35 as part of an impressive 59-week stay on the *Billboard* chart following its October 6 release.

Interestingly, in spite of their bewildering release schedules, 'Strangelove' and 'Never Let Me Down Again' had recently represented Depeche Mode's best Stateside chart showings since 'Master And Servant' with respective *Billboard* placings of 76 and 63. A 12″ version of 'Strangelove' arrived on May 20, with a 7″ following a week later, and – as the record gained momentum – a cassette-based maxi-single on July 28. 'Never Let Me Down Again' was again given the 12″ treatment first (on September 29) followed by its smaller counterpart on October 20.

If Sire's actions in making 'But Not Tonight' an A-side had perplexed the band, the company's re-release of 'Strangelove' on August 23, 1988, in no less than four formats – 7″ and 12″ vinyl, cassette single, and 3-inch CD single – was equally mystifying. Surprisingly, the record went on to beat its original highest chart position by 26 places. Alan Wilder: "The exact reason why a second version of 'Strangelove' was made is lost somewhere in the mists of time, but an educated guess would lead me to conclude that, as usual, it was probably something to do with the American record company and/or MTV not being happy with Anton's original [video]. The second video was directed by Martyn Atkins."

Depeche Mode could hardly complain at an 'old' record notching up nine weeks on the *Billboard* Hot 100 Singles Chart.

On October 22, a European tour commenced, taking Depeche Mode through Spain, Germany, Italy and Switzerland, and France for three consecutive nights at the Palais Omnisports de Paris-Bercy. Nineteen-thousand French fans repeatedly held their cigarette lighters aloft while a constantly gyrating Dave Gahan was dressed from head to toe in dazzling white.

In her aptly titled 'Emotional Blackmail' review of November 28, *NME*'s Helen Mead painted a persuasive picture of the large-scale *event* that Depeche Mode's stageshow had become: "Moving round to catch the stunning lightshow, I glimpse an aerial view of the Parisian audience, a moving picture of the 'O'-level Biology slides of trillions of sperm struggling to invade the ovum; tails thrashing in time to the music and trying to penetrate the techno-wizardry produced by three banks of stacked synthesisers. The imagery seemed a pun: the idea of a humane relationship with so much *cold* machinery about. Then as I listen I realise the thought is counter-productive and a drip of salt-water makes a break on my cheek and I have to admit to being emotionally blackmailed by a bunch of Basildon Bonds . . . Music for the masses."

American and Canadian masses turned out to see Depeche Mode when they played 12 indoor dates stretching from San Francisco's Cow Palace to New York's colossal 20,000-seat Madison Square Garden – a substantial step up from the group's previous three night stint at the 5,900-capacity Radio City Music Hall.

Los Angeles-based KABC 7's Francesca Cappucci filed the following report for *Eyewitness News*, hailing the band's arrival in Los Angeles for two sold-out Forum performances on December 4 and 5: "Depeche Mode formed nearly a decade ago when synthesizer bands were popping up everywhere. Many of those groups dissipated while Depeche Mode continued to grow. Today they are one of music's best-kept secrets; they are a *tremendous* box-office draw. Depeche Mode has achieved success with very little radio airplay, but a lot of word-of-mouth."

Alan Wilder was delegated to speak: "It's more than a cult following in actual numbers, but in terms of live verses record sales . . . we can play to as many people, if not more people, live than we sell records to, which is strange. We've certainly got a hardcore following everywhere we go – the kind of people who buy our records in the first week without hearing it, every time they're released. And that's very healthy for us – especially in Europe, because it means you *don't* have to rely on the media to play your records, necessarily."

When Cappucci said that "much of Depeche Mode's appeal comes from Martin Gore's powerful lyrics," Wilder responded favourably: "He's able to be very honest within his songs – almost *embarrassingly* honest, sometimes. I mean, there's this whole business of soul, and what is soul?

People accuse us of not having any soul because we use electronics, but really all soul is is being honest, and there's a lot of that in our music. What we try and do with the music is just enhance those words, but we've always had a healthy interest in exploring the technology and seeing what we can do with sound."

The interviewer concluded by calling *Music For The Masses* "sophisticated and elegant in its instrumentation . . . The band is very unconventional, and their strength comes from the fact that they have *complete* creative control over *everything* that they do. They even *manage* themselves!"

In the lead up to Christmas, Dave Gahan was able to snatch some time to spend with wife Jo and their firstborn, Jack, who was barely a week old when the European tour forced the proud dad back on the road.

But there was no letting up; ten days after triumphing in the Big Apple on December 18, Depeche Mode sounded the release of their next single (from *Music For The Masses*) with the stereophonic clatter of a rolling hubcap (in reality, a sampled spinning saucepan lid, but just as effective).

As was often the case with Depeche Mode records, 'Behind The Wheel' was not as sonically straightforward as it might have first appeared. Take, for example, the composite nature of its prominent bass line, as orally deconstructed by the man responsible for its construction. Alan Wilder: "It was a combination of three different sounds: a hand striking the end of a Hoover tube and then sampled, a guitar-pluck sampled and pitched down, and a MiniMoog for added bottom end."

Despite such extraordinary lengths, it's unfortunate that gun for hire, American remixer Shep Pettibone (who later worked with Madonna), failed to do it justice on his 12″ remix of 'Behind The Wheel', much to Wilder's dismay. "I don't know who suggested him – probably Sire. He seems to be missing a huge selection of mid-frequencies on his mixing console, the ones with 'bollocks' written on the knobs."

Gore's absorbing lyrics featured some exemplary vocals, with the writer doubling Gahan's every line to create an added sense of urgency for a song with no chorus. The Mode faithful responded by pushing the record to number 21 on the UK Singles Chart.

Alan Wilder: "I'm not saying that commercial is a dirty word, but Depeche Mode has always obviously been a commercial venture, amongst other things. I think there's always an underlying pressure felt by DM to come up with hits, but, luckily, Martin's a natural pop songwriter so you couldn't say it was forced. Having hit records was important to the group.

Martin's songs clearly work within the confines of a pop format – verse/
bridge/chorus/middle-eight, et cetera."

The B-side to 'Behind The Wheel' was, surprisingly, a rock standard,
chosen not because of its appropriate vehicular connotations, but because
Gore's store of songs had apparently run dry. 'Route 66'* appeared to
garner more attention, as typified by *NME*'s Bob Stanley's review of
January 2, 1988: " 'Behind The Wheel' is standard Mode fare, Dave
Gahan's voice a virtual monotone while he drones on about rumpy
pumpy on the back seat – the B-side's another ball game *entirely*. 'Route
66'! This has been completely Mode-ified with twinkling keyboard noises,
but there's still a chugging guitar line in there trying to break loose.
Startling stuff."

What Stanley failed to notice in his excitement was that Depeche
Mode's cover cunningly incorporated the middle-eight from 'Behind The
Wheel'. 'Route 66' was also subjected to some under-the-bonnet tinkering for the 'Behind The Wheel' 12″, although this time Wilder actually
approved of the result: "The Beatmasters' version [of 'Route 66'] is the
most fun and suits the song well. It also grooves better than the original
[mix]."†

Continuity was further maintained in Anton Corbijn's latest black &
white screen caper: Italy, moped, girls . . . and more megaphones.

---

* Originally recorded by jazzer Bobby Troup in 1946, this classic paean to America's most
famous highway, has been recorded by countless artists, most notably Chuck Berry, and The
Rolling Stones on their eponymous 1964 début album.
† No doubt it also suited Daniel Miller, for The Beatmasters were the first of Mute Records'
affiliate, Rhythm King's trio of chart-busting dance acts. Their so-called house music anthem,
'Rok Da House', made number five on January 9, 1988 – ironically the same day that Depeche
Mode's 'Behind The Wheel' dropped out of the charts.

19

Electronic Music For The Masses

"All of a sudden, out of nowhere, it just exploded. From nothing, we'd suddenly become a stadium act."

– Andy Fletcher, 2001

On January 9, 1988, Depeche Mode's latest bid for world domination commenced at Newport's Centre followed by two sell-out shows at London's Wembley Arena, to a combined audience of 24,000.

Record Mirror's Nancy Culp was at Wembley on January 11: "With a stage set resembling a cross between a scene from [Fritz Lang's] *Metropolis* and a Nuremberg rally – all fake plinths and platforms with coloured flags hanging coyly from the lighting gantry – you're left to wonder if the band really are taking the piss out of their Germanic fetishes. The opening strains of 'Behind The Wheel' waft out from what one can only describe as Mrs Jumbo's old black net curtains. The lads are hidden from view as dry ice belches out, only to be revealed when the funeral net shudders sharply heavenwards in a gesture that verges on camp.

"Now here's the crux: Depeche Mode are awful and unintentionally hysterical. From Dave's manic pelvic thrusting and bum-wiggling; to Martin's fetching black leather joddies, motorcycle boots and black bondage harness which all make him look like Hooky's* little brother; to Fletch's curious knee-jerks and arm-waggling mid-song, Dep Mode are even funnier than Spinal Tap in their New Romantic period, and it's all totally unselfconscious to boot . . . [Depeche Mode] have matured immeasurably into a fine, but still criminally underrated, all-round group . . . My feet barely stopped moving for more than half a second all evening and the grin on my face will have to be surgically removed . . ."

---

* Joy Division/New Order bass player, Peter Hook.

NME's Danny Kelly performed a character assassination on each member, with only Alan Wilder escaping unscathed: "Dave Gahan treats us to his fabby new Essex Sex God act; we marvel at his *totally* convincing pelvic thrusts (complete with authentic, permanently erect, radio-mic accessory); we gape at his mastery of the Freddie-Mercury-'Ain't-Piles-Murder?' stance; and we stare gobsmacked as (combining the contortions of an arthritic battery hen, a B-movie stripper and Mick Jagger's grandma) he unveils the second worst dance routine on earth. The worst, of course, belongs to his colleague Fletch, who idles his evening away in bouts of sheepish amazement at the mayhem unfolding before him, and effortless demonstrations of his patented Crimes Against Choreography . . ."

Gore was described as a "nightmare of knees, nipples and nonsense." Apart from that, Kelly was impressed with one part of the show. " 'Black Celebration' is *breathtaking*, impacting like [an Arthur] Scargill rant in an episode of *Antiques Roadshow*, hammering even the most fundamentalist screamers into slack-jawed dumb *awe* . . ."

Melody Maker's Andy Darling: "I came not to praise Depeche Mode as Artists-now-Mature, nor as Golden Shit; more like something between the two," he wrote in the January 23 edition. "A bit like the suburbs, in fact. A bit of them eager to crash the parameters (usually signalled by Mark [*sic* – Martin Gore] coming to the front and singing), a bit of them eager to just have a laugh (when Fletch moves forward and claps his hands above his head), a bit of sex appeal (when Dave thrusts his groin), a bit of prudery (when the others positively don't). Suburban lads, not afraid to expose their feminine side every now and then. But not too much. The most fun you can have with your feet on the ground. You only sing when you're winning."

The first half of 1988 was taken up with a 33-date European tour, and four shows in Japan. On May 16, 'Little 15' was lifted from *Music For The Masses* as an unexpected French-only single.* This Martin Gore-penned ballad was not part of the tour set-list, and had it not been for Daniel Miller's encouragement, it might never have been recorded in the first place. French fans had an extra bonus in the form of an otherwise-unavailable instrumental B-side ('Stjarna'), as well as Alan Wilder's rendition of Beethoven's 'Sonata No. 14 In C#' – more commonly known as 'Moonlight Sonata' – at Gore's instigation for inclusion on the

---

* With its own unique catalogue number of 7 LITTLE 15.

accompanying 12″. In spite of his keyboard virtuosity, Alan Wilder later admitted to slightly messing up the end of the piece.

'Little 15' was based around a simplistic opening (sampled) string arrangement that tipped its hat towards the minimalist classical compositions of Michael Nyman.*

Depeche Mode's dedicated UK fanbase turned the record into a popular import; enough to make the single chart at number 60 on May 28, despite never officially being released in the band's home country.

Anton Corbijn's creative run was temporarily suspended as 'Little 15' saw Martyn Atkins resume directorial duties. Alan Wilder: "[It] seemed like a good opportunity to try a different director [as] it was only released in France."

On the subject of directors, the band's 30-show North American Music For The Masses Tour, was to be immortalised on celluloid by Don Allen (D.A.) Pennebaker, a renowned music documentary film-maker with *Don't Look Back* (1967), a behind-the-scenes look at Bob Dylan's 1965 UK tour, and *Monterey Pop* (1969), a visual record of the 1967 Monterey Rock Festival, to his considerable credit.

To most American cinemagoers, the resultant film, *101*,† must have seemed an alien concept; starring as it did a foreign, drummer-less electronic group from across the Atlantic. According to Pennebaker's notes for the video release, *101* was: "A film about music, about those who sell it and those who buy it. Those who direct it and those who write and perform it. But which is which?

"The new music: four young Englishmen. Friends who have grown up together. They began with keyboards and a tape recorder because drums made too much noise around the house. No manager (they do that themselves) and no contract with their record company (Mute – just a handshake).

"The concert tour: surrounded by a buccaneer crew of British and Anzac technicians, three forty-foot semis and equipment that belongs on a launch pad, they range across the landscape, setting up and striking, week

---

* Nyman first applied the word 'minimalism' to music in his earlier life as a musicologist, before becoming better known as a critically acclaimed film scorer.
† A Mute Film, co-directed by Pennebaker Associates Inc.'s David Hawkins, D.A. Pennebaker's long-time creative partner Chris Hedges, and Pennebaker himself.

after week, city after city. Up by afternoon and out before dawn. Not even time for a soundcheck.

"Engulfed by seas of fans, who slip through cracks in the walls and haunt them backstage, youthful Americans will soon inherit this landscape. And close behind, a special bus-full of fans, winners in a be-in-a-Depeche-Mode-movie-contest, trying to catch up with their idols. At the tour's end (the hundred and first concert) nearly 70,000 fill the Rose Bowl in Pasadena, California to watch a spectacle of lights and music performed by four friends, on three keyboards and a vocal mic . . . and a tape recorder.

"For me, it remains a dream memory, gone and over now, but still visible like a fly in amber for all time."

The opening moments of the movie feature empty blackness over which Depeche Mode's Production Director, Andy Franks intones, "Okay, start the tape."

"The machines would be started by the keyboard tech, Wob Roberts, at the beginning of the set, and were only stopped and restarted in-between encores," Alan Wilder explained. "There were two identical [multi-track] machines, which ran in sync – one was purely a backup to the other in case of breakdown."

Thereafter, *101* follows a pattern established by U2's *Rattle And Hum* – concert and backstage footage similarly shot during an American tour – as Depeche Mode prepare for the climactic (101st) concert of their world tour at the Rose Bowl, Pasadena.

D.A. Pennebaker: "Depeche Mode seemed such an un-do-able film, [but] these four guys, they couldn't have been nicer. They hadn't an idea in the world between 'em, but they'd figured out how to make a lot of money with a tape recorder off-stage. They had one guy, Alan, who's not even with them anymore, who's a really good musician. Then they had this incredible genius-from-outer-space, who could write these songs; then they had David! And the other guy. You had to love 'em, but what kind of film would *that* make? So we cooked up this funny idea of getting these fans to get on a bus, and . . . it worked. We couldn't believe it!"

Indeed, that "funny idea" first arises when Long Island-based Anglo-phile station WDRE's 'Malibu Sue' announces to around 350,000 listeners that, "Depeche Mode are making a movie, and they'd like some of their fans to appear with them."

A motley crew with assorted bad Eighties haircuts board the bus – including one sensational ozone-depleting effort comprising two razor-like rows of dyed grey spikes and a ponytail. Bus driver Dave Charest colourfully exclaims, "What! Are you shitting me? I'm taking a bunch of 12- to 15-year-olds across the country!"

Depeche Mode's interpretation of 'Route 66' had just topped WDRE's holiday weekend poll – much to the onscreen delight of hired American Press officer, Teresa Conroy: "Depeche Mode have more songs in the top 200 songs than any other band."

WDRE producer Denis McNamara appeared to have the band's appeal sussed: "They're a mixture. There's the dance fan, the young female fan who is probably now an Erasure fan also. Depeche Mode fans will be anxiously awaiting the new Cure album, and will have bought *Rattle And Hum*, but it won't be their favourite U2 album. They're not just teen-based; though more female than male, they have a tremendous support among young people between 18 and 28.

"Part of that came from the spectacular success in the dance clubs of 'Just Can't Get Enough', so they're people who've grown up with the band. Then there are the kids who dress in black and also like Einsturzende Neubauten and Nitzer Ebb, the industrial bands. And a lot of our station's listeners are young urban professionals. You'll find stockbrokers standing next to a Siouxsie look-alike at a Depeche Mode show . . ."

Andy Fletcher: "People take music in the States a lot more seriously than here [in the UK]. Because it's such an industry, geared towards making money, there is also an anti-Top 40 feeling. When we meet people backstage, the thing they ram through to us is, 'Don't go Top 40!' But if the radio starts playing it and it goes Top 40, what can you do?"

According to Martin Gore, "One of the working titles for the *101* film was *Mass*, because we thought it was a good sort of tie-in with *Music For The Masses* as well – just because of this sort of adoration and faith thing."

So how did Depeche Mode and the-then 62-year-old veteran connect? "The whole thing was presented in such a marvellously imaginative way, far beyond anything I'd imagined or witnessed at concerts in the Sixties and Seventies when you just saw amplifiers and people in their old clothes. Their show was as spectacular as anything you'll see on Broadway. I figured that anybody who put this much out for an audience would have something between them, [or] else they wouldn't have done it. I thought it was worth looking into.

"I liked their independence; they didn't depend on a heavy overhead.

The process of making successful popular music is about as subject to corruption as making films, so whenever I see people operating independently I'm always impressed. It didn't mean you were dealing with heavy intellectual forces, like Bob Dylan and whoever else has that strong hold on people's imaginations, but I think that the way Depeche Mode live their lives and make their music is interesting because so few people do it that way."

Alan Wilder: "He wasn't interested in the music – didn't pretend to understand it, and, in turn, we never knew what story he was going to tell, or how he was intending to edit it all together. His attitude was: 'Well, let's just film some stuff and see what happens.' "

Dave Gahan: "The words staging and script don't come into Pennebaker's brain at all. He films what's happening and what's real. The fit is honest. That's why we approached Don; we saw what he had done with Dylan and *Monterey Pop*, and the Kennedy documentary [*Primary*] – they're very factual. Too many bands make totally scripted, clichéd films, as glossy as possible."

An early scene set on Depeche Mode's privately chartered plane – a customised turboprop airliner complete with *Music For The Masses* megaphone logo – was a clear indication of the band's ascension to rock aristocracy.

Andy Franks is speaking on a state-of-the-art, housebrick-sized mobile phone regarding concerns over the forthcoming (May 27) show at Philadelphia's 18,000-capacity CoreStates Spectrum: "Because I believe it's a holiday weekend, we're just a bit worried that the place doesn't look too empty. Is it possible to move the stage forward in the arena in any way? The band are really worried that it doesn't look empty; 10,000 is still a pretty good crowd, I think."

On May 20, Depeche Mode were in Chicago at the Poplar Creek Music Theater. Peter Bracke, one of roughly 10,000 attendees, relates how much things had changed for the band since they last played the same venue (on June 6, 1986): "Although Chicago has always been a big Mode town, the number of fans and overall feel of the crowd did change considerably since the last time I saw the band on the 'Black Celebration Tour' two years previously, or even the previous *Music For The Masses* gigs in the fall of '87. The crowd was becoming more mainstream, and suddenly it didn't feel so much like DM was a secret anymore."

Orchestral Manoeuvres In The Dark – the Liverpudlian outfit largely responsible for spurring Vince Clarke into forming Depeche Mode –

were drafted in as the opening act for the tour's second leg. The irony was not lost on Andy McCluskey: "They had built themselves up into this huge, monstrous touring machine, particularly in America with this massive – what they called – *alternative* following. You can sell millions and still be classed as alternative in America. And here we were being paid $5,000 a night to support them, which didn't even cover our costs, playing sold-out arenas and stadiums with a band that had started because they had heard our first single! So we had to swallow our pride a bit on that one. But, in hindsight, I look at it and say [that] they stuck to their guns and delivered to an American audience something that an American audience wanted."

Which was exactly what Alan Wilder had been saying all along: "[Depeche Mode] had toured constantly in America and battled against a radio-play brick wall for many years until things started to happen. We hadn't forgotten about Europe – we played many concerts there, it's just that it was an important and exciting time for us in the US and we wanted to concentrate on [that] territory.

"McCluskey rates himself a bit too highly for my liking, which is always a bit dangerous if you're languishing in the 'Where are they now?' file. We bowled them all out for 10 runs in the DM vs. OMD cricket match – and I got McCluskey's wicket!"

Meanwhile, on the bus, the kids preen, dance and generally drink themselves stupid while travelling through visually evocative scenery – from derelict downtown cityscapes to baking hot deserts – eventually catching up with Depeche Mode at the A.J. Palumbo Center in Pittsburgh, Pennsylvania (June 11). There they witness their heroes soundchecking 'The Things You Said', which, thanks to some judicious editing from Pennebaker, segues into the evening's performance, providing a striking visual contrast between the empty venue's stark house lights and Jane Spiers' inventive lighting accompaniment to a full house.

Dave Gahan: "It's not about the *amount* of lights; it's the *way* it's done – the moods that are set for each song; that's what's really important with lighting. You get a lot of these bands who just have thousands of lamps blasting on at the same time, and after you've seen it once, that's it. But with the show that we're going around with now, every song has got something different happening on-stage – things move around and different backdrops come down. In every song there's a new change; the stage looks different. It's pretty complex, really."

Back to the afternoon soundcheck, and Alan Wilder provides an impromptu demonstration of one of his two Emax sampling keyboards by isolating the three sounds normally heard on 'Black Celebration' – one of the tracks making up the show's 19-song set list: "The keyboard has a total of 36 different banks, so each song has its own set of sounds. And on 'Black Celebration', I've got several sounds allocated to specific parts of the keyboard.

"So really you're only limited by what you can manage with your hands. You've got to remember where you put it [the sound], but that comes after a while. It gets to be automatic, really; your hands just sort of go there."

Explanation over, the keyboard virtuoso then proceeds to make a hash of the song's simplistic melody line.

It was expatriate English KROQ jock Richard Blade, who became the Mode's chief champion in California: "Their breakthrough was in '84, when they played the Palladium.* And they did a great show and got such good word-of-mouth that when they came back, they sold out two nights at The Forum [on December 4 and 5, 1987] with a capacity of 17,000, which even Duran couldn't sell out. So six months later we [KROQ] suggested we put them in the Rose Bowl with a 72,000 capacity."

Blade is heard in *101*, commentating on Depeche Mode's entry into the Pasadena Rose Bowl, riding a Fifties classic open-top Cadillac to announce their forthcoming show there. Introduced by the tanned, blond-highlighted Blade, a comparatively pale, self-conscious Wilder steps up to the mic: "We want to say 'good morning' to all our fans listening and watching this morning, and we'd like to announce that as a special final concert to our world tour, on Saturday, June 18, we'll be playing a concert for the masses here at the Rose Bowl, Pasadena."

Dave Gahan: "When you play a show like [the Rose Bowl], there is something that is very religious about the whole thing. And it's not just from the fans to the band; it's the other way as well. You definitely feel a mass of energy – well, I certainly do – from all the people that are out there, doing the things that you're doing and singing with you. I wouldn't go as far as to say it's like *worship* or anything like that, but there is an incredible energy that I don't think any of us understand."

* The correct date was March 30, 1985.

Not that D.A. Pennebaker understood it either: "When they [Depeche Mode] decided to go into the Rose Bowl, they stuck their heads out a little, and like any entrepreneur or anybody who hunts for treasure, they take a chance. I applaud if they win; I don't look on that as the process of a foul capitalist machine. I'm not looking to propose an answer – just showing what I see, which is complex and contradictory. What we're hoping to do with this film is show a simultaneity of views so that people can see the whole thing and make of it what they will."

On the day of the show, having just witnessed the colossal crowd, numbering nearly 70,000 people, Gahan experiences a moment of backstage panic: "I'm not sure about this at all. I dunno; what do you think? Oh, let's go back to the hotel. They've had a good time. OMD have played . . . Wire . . . Thomas Dolby. They don't mind." This is effectively underscored by Pennebaker's images of the crowd's 'Mexican waves' as Tangerine Dream's 'White Eagle' echoes around the vast venue.

His dilemma deepens, as he broods over his introduction: "I don't think I should say Pasadena. I've been thinking about this for days. It's been playing on my mind."

Alan Wilder: "Dave, I wouldn't let it play on your mind."

Dave Gahan: "I think I should say, 'Good evening, everybody.' "

Andy Franks: "Why not just say, 'Good evening, everyone. Welcome to a concert for the masses.' "

Dave Gahan: "Who do you think I am? Fucking Wordsworth?! I'm serious. What do you think I should say? Pasadena or Rose Bowl?"

In the event, Gahan opts for a perfunctory "Good evening, Pasadena!" As the curtain drops, the singer steps forward to face the thunderous applause greeting 'Behind The Wheel'. During 'Blasphemous Rumours', God became the band's uninvited choreographer when a freak rainstorm coincided exactly with the line "*. . . then came the rain . . .*"

Alan Wilder: "We had a word with 'im upstairs."

Richard Blade recalled that strange sight: "They were doing 'Blasphemous Rumours' when suddenly it began to thunder and rain. Do you know how rare that is in the middle of LA in July [*sic*]? And then the band followed that up with 'Sacred' and the rain stopped. It was really weird."

Wilder later admitted to sharing Gahan's pre-show nerves: "I remember being very apprehensive about it, worrying about all the different aspects of the show – the fact that for the entire tour we used one PA system and for this one special gig we were going to use something completely different; and that we had to hire in all kinds of extra lights and different people

264

to do this, that and the other; and that it was just a logistical exercise that we weren't really prepared for."

When later asked if there was one image that encapsulated his time with Depeche Mode, Gahan's response was instantaneous: "For me, that image of the Rose Bowl. There was one point during the song 'Never Let Me Down [Again]' where I jumped up on to one of the risers and I noticed a couple of people in the audience were sort of waving their arms around, so I joined in and then there was suddenly 70,000 people doing that! I was just overwhelmed; I kind of felt the tears in me, and sweat rolling down my face, but it was joy! It was like, 'It doesn't get better than this.' It was amazing – Basildon boy makes good."

Alan Wilder: "I'm sure Dave encouraged it [the waving], and I suppose it became something of a live trademark after the *101* film."

During the concert's climax, 70,000 fans joined Gahan and his cohorts for an emotionally charged, extended singalong to the chorus of 'Everything Counts'.

Dave Gahan: "Everybody that was in that concert, and part of it, felt that moment. And you know, I just kind of started blubbing on-stage. I tried to cover it up and still look very macho and do my thing, but I just stood there for a minute and stood on this big riser, and I looked. And at that moment everybody's arms were waving in the air. I looked out, and it sounds cheesy, but it looked like this big field of corn, or whatever, swaying. I just stopped. It didn't matter that I wasn't singing; it was just *happening*."

Pennebaker's cameras cleverly caught tour accountant Jonathan 'Baron' Kessler – an American who would forge even closer ties with Depeche Mode – and his team totting up the Rose Bowl's merchandise takings as the memorable *"Everything counts in large amounts"* mantra is being sung with such gusto outside their caravan. The figures speak for themselves, as Kessler exclaims: "$1,360,192.50. Paid attendance was 60,453 people, tonight at the Rose Bowl, Pasadena, June 18, 1988. We're getting a load of money. A lot of money; a load of money – *tons* of money!"

Dave Gahan: "It was a dig at America, the way money corrupts . . . When you tour America, suddenly things like merchandising are far more important than ticket sales. Merchandise finances tours. People talk about multi-million-dollar deals with merchandisers. Before you know it, you may as well be running a chain of T-shirt shops! To tour America, you need to sell T-shirts."

This is confirmed by an incredulous fan: "That's the question: how much money they've made. You figure. $23 [T-]shirts and $32 sweat-shirts, and how much were the programmes – five or 10 bucks or so? God, I'd *love* to be their accountant!"

By the time the Music For The Masses Tour wrapped up at the Rose Bowl, Depeche Mode had played to precisely 443,012 people. That's a lot of T-shirts.

Dave Gahan: "We like the idea of being quite open about these things, and we hope that people take it the right way. It's something that's always taboo with bands, though everybody knows that bands make lots and lots of money, sometimes far too much for what they do. But you must never talk about that because it detaches you from your audience who are supposed to be on the same level as you."

But Depeche Mode *was* a commercial venture, in spite of Martin Gore pleading otherwise: "We've always wanted to make what is *alternative music.*"

Dave Gahan: "When we made the *101* movie and we performed at the Rose Bowl in California, that was kind of like defying all the odds. People were whispering, 'They're never going to fill this place,' and that kind of stuff. You could feel it, but, at the same time, I had a real confidence that it was going to be just fine. And it turned out really well."

Andy Fletcher: "No one believed an alternative band could play to so many people, so that set the ball rolling for a lot of bands after us, but a lot of this period is a bit of a haze!"

The overpowering nature of the show was borne out, during some brief post-show dialogue with Wilder and the sound mixer who reveals that the vocals "were extremely hard work", to which an attentive Wilder replies, "I hope you put lots of reverb on them." Tour Director J.D. Fanger turns to a dazed-looking Gore, saying, "This is the sort of place where the vocals always come over extra dry; you can wet 'em, wet 'em, and wet 'em, but they still sound clear, don't they?"

Pennebaker then cuts to a backstage shot of a clearly overwhelmed Gahan, hiding his face in a towel, being consoled by a woman with her back to the camera – possibly Jo Gahan, who attended the show with baby Jack; seen earlier in the film being bottle-fed by his doting dad.

Martin Gore: "The Rose Bowl concert, of course, was a really special event, but I think because we were all so nervous that night, due to the filming and recording of the thing – plus the 75,000 [*sic*] people – I don't think we enjoyed it as much as we should have done."

Alan Wilder: "We weren't able to be in the moment – enjoy the moment – because we were just worrying about it too much. So, really, nobody enjoyed the gig. We didn't play particularly well that night. It's only when you go back, and it's been captured on the film, and the sound's been tarted up a bit, that you realise what a big, special moment it was for us as a group, and that we should have actually taken time to enjoy it a bit more."

Daniel Miller: "First of all, the sheer scale of it was magnificent – just the physical scale of the thing with 70,000 people; I'd never been to any concert with 70,000 people. Secondly, it wasn't just 70,000 people watching the concert; it was 70,000 people *participating* in the concert – really responding. Everybody there was a fan; it wasn't like a few people thinking, 'Well, let's go and have a look at this and see what it's like.' It seemed like there was 70,000 fans there – Depeche Mode fans . . .

"*101* was a record of an event that was remarkable in its size, to be honest. And nobody can quite believe it in England – or anywhere in the rest of the world – that we sold 78,000 [*sic*] tickets at the Rose Bowl stadium. That's an amazing response, and we wanted to record that, really."

Alan Wilder: "The Rose Bowl performance wasn't actually one of our best, due to monitoring problems, but it certainly gave us a credibility back in Europe where nobody could quite believe our popularity in the States."

Incredibly, nearly a month after the event in question, *Melody Maker*'s Paul Mathur reported Depeche Mode's American triumph in a scant five paragraphs; three of which dealt severely with the support acts: "Thomas Dolby should, by rights, be locked up. The next best solution is obviously to keep him holed up in LA where loud suits, inept rapping, songs about airheads and sets that last for ever and a day are common coinage."

Next on the literary chopping block, OMD – particularly their over-confident frontman: "Andy McCluskey is really going to have to stop that daft dance soon, or the men with the big nets will be round for a second opinion." Only Wire came out relatively unscathed: "It might have been 'Silk Skin Paws' that turned the event upside down, sounded like a dyslexic Springsteen, touched. There. Awesome or something." Mathur's indifferent conclusion: "The performance was longer than the summer's day it soundtracked, but there was still enough there to suggest that DM are girding their loins for something spikier than we might expect. The sun went down, we all went home and forgot it ever happened. Life's a beach sometimes, as the Mexican fellow under the seat remarked."

Daniel Miller: "It's stadium rock, yes, in terms of its context, but not in terms of the music – stadium experimental pop, really. They [Depeche Mode] didn't change the music to fit it. Stadium rock is a specific kind of music that's almost [tailor]-made [for stadiums] – Simple Minds; people like that."

Nonetheless, the fact remained. Depeche Mode – a British four piece featuring a singer, three keyboardists (with widely varying degrees of ability) and a backing tape had somehow managed to fill a gargantuan American sports stadium!

Depeche Mode's staggering Stateside popularity hit hard with Basildon bystander Robert Marlow, who by now had reluctantly laid his own pop star plans to rest: "I remember going to the première of *101*, the Depeche movie, which was mad in itself. I remember Dave coming through with Jack, his little boy, and he had to physically throw his little boy to his then-wife, Jo, because people were all over him! I hadn't seen that [kind of behaviour around Depeche Mode] before. All of a sudden, seeing that film *101* just blew me away – the whole Rose Bowl concert thing, that whole thing about flying on their own customised plane, and all that stuff. All of a sudden they seemed to have gone from playing a toilet at The Bridge-house with graffiti on the walls to having their own backstage green room area with *huge* riders – the whole thing!"

"It was all pretty embarrassing, actually," Alan Wilder sheepishly confessed. "Especially the première in London, with my parents and friends sitting there watching us make fools of ourselves in massive cinemascope."

Unsurprisingly, the American première of the movie on April 28, 1989 was just as manic – if not more so – with KROQ's increasingly visible Richard Blade filing the following 'Rock Report' for *Movietime*: "It was a scene like the early days of Beatlemania – hundreds of screaming fans showed up to greet British band Depeche Mode at the Los Angeles première of their new film. Here in LA, and certain cities in America, they have the same effect on their legions of adoring young fans as did Frank Sinatra, Elvis Presley, The Beatles and Duran in their day."

As if the excitable DJ-cum-television presenter's words needed backing up, several "adoring young fans" waiting outside the theatre for their idols' arrival offered up their own opinions. "They're original; their music is unique," said one fashionably dressed male, while a young woman modelling the same wide-brimmed black hat as worn by Martin Gore agreed. "Martin's lyrics are just too much; they're really deep, and they mean something."

Upon his arrival, Gore dodged the inevitable 'What next?' line of questioning. "I've really no idea. We plan a year ahead, and if we're still enjoying it, I suppose we'll be in the old routine: we'll be making records and we'll be touring – if we're still enjoying it. But if we stop enjoying it, we may not be around."

In comparing *101* to *Rattle And Hum*, a financial factor separated the two in that U2's rather pretentious affair reputedly weighed in at a heavy $5,300,000 production cost whereas the arguably more revealing Depeche doc was brought in for a comparatively lightweight $600,000; actually showing a considerable profit (netting approximately $50,000 within two weeks of its US theatrical release).

So what were Depeche Mode's true thoughts on the American roadtrip that was *101*?

Andy Fletcher: "I think we made one of the most honest videos about the music industry. We didn't really have an album that was high in the American charts, but we were playing to just ridiculous amounts of people! We'd already done a live video in Hamburg, so this time we didn't want a normal live video and we didn't want a rockumentary. So we came up with this idea of these kids winning a competition and following us around. And it works."

Alan Wilder: "From my personal perspective, I don't find the film to be a great eye-opener; it didn't attempt to examine the internal dynamics of the band and so I didn't really learn anything about myself. And we never really allowed Don Pennebaker to see the darker side of being on the road.

"I could have lived without the 'fans on the bus' angle, although I suppose without them it might have been just like any other tour film. Observing this almost religious ritual between band and audience was really the only perspective [that] Pennebaker was interested in – that's what he tried to explore, and, given the circumstances, I think he was right to do so."

20

Godfathers Of Techno?

"Over the years, we [Depeche Mode] just carried on producing music in our usual way and the band has moved in and out of fashion, depending on what's trendy at the time. It's always preferable to remain true to your ideals and maintain your integrity, rather than jump on the latest bandwagon."

— Alan Wilder, 2001

With Depeche Mode engrossed in cracking America, the path was clear for Vince Clarke to make a clean sweep of the UK with Erasure. Their third album, *The Innocents*, topped the lists in May 1988, selling over 100,000 copies within days of its release and spawning two Top 10 hit singles (with a third falling one place short).

Record Mirror's David Giles caught the ascendant duo in action at Birmingham's NEC: "The fans love it, and what they love the most is Andy's *campness*. The overstated body language and gaudy attire are enough, though. What's remarkable is that the arena is full of butch Brummies who would normally give an Andy Bell-like character a good kicking if they met him on the street. But up there on the stage he's a star, so it doesn't matter that he's a complete Jessie. He's a star, and Erasure are slowly, quietly, becoming massive."

Indeed, Erasure *did* go on to become massive, performing to 60,000 people at the Milton Keynes Bowl, on September 1, 1989. Clearly, the touring circus that Vince Clarke had despised during his brief Depeche Mode tenure had paid off.

In October 1988, four months after the mammoth Music For The Masses Tour, Martin Gore booked himself and one-time-Berlin-based producer, Rico Conning into Sam Therapy Studios on West London's Kensal Road, to record what would effectively become his first solo album, released as the *Counterfeit e.p* on Mute in summer 1989.

Conning was previously a member of Torch Song – a group that also boasted one William Orbit (né William Wainwright) in their ranks, who first crossed paths with Gore (or at least Daniel Miller) when creating the 'Black Celebration (Black Tulip)' and 'A Question Of Time (New Town Mix)' remixes back in 1986. "We employ people whose artistic judgement we accept 100 per cent," Miller stated, "and so we allow them to do what they want."

Conning also garnered a 'Thanks' credit on *Music For The Masses*, most likely for assisting Miller on his 'Strangelove (Blind Mix)' that became the basis for the track as featured on the album. Listening to the *Counterfeit e.p* (credited to 'Martin L. Gore') it's likely that Conning's credited co-production role was similar to that enjoyed by Dave Bascombe on *Music For The Masses* – more engineer than producer.

Reflected in its title, *Counterfeit e.p* was, quite simply, an Extended Play featuring six songs showcasing the songwriter's eclectic record-collecting tastes – from 'In A Manner Of Speaking' (originally recorded by the San Francisco, avant-garde collective, Tuxedomoon) to the traditional African-American gospel, 'Motherless Child' (with its haunting refrain, *"Sometimes I feel like a motherless child/ A long way from home . . ."*).

One selection should have come as no surprise – namely, 'Never Turn Your Back On Mother Earth', the third consecutive 1974 UK hit single for Sparks, the distinctive duo of Californian-born Russell and Ron Mael, who found success in Europe after relocating to the UK in 1973 (and to whom the likes of Vince Clarke's Erasure and Pet Shop Boys owed some artistic debt).

Gore had been a fan of Sparks as a teenager, and even paid tribute to the brothers Mael during several shows on the Music For The Masses Tour by performing 'Never Turn Your Back On Mother Earth' during his vocal spot.

Gore's vocal abilities shone throughout the *Counterfeit e.p*, illuminating the strength of his vocal contributions to Depeche Mode. "I think that the covers make perfect sense," he explained at the time. "When you're in a Phil Collins/Genesis situation, you only write a certain number of songs. And obviously I'd want to use the best ones for my solo record and the band would want to use the best ones for the band, and there can be conflicts. I didn't want to end up neglecting the band."

So what did Gore's bandmates make of his first solo outing? Alan

Wilder: "I quite liked his choice of songs – especially the Comsat Angels song ['Gone'] – but I didn't think he developed his versions much beyond the demo stage."

Record Mirror reviewer Phil Cheeseman went as far as awarding *Counter-feit e.p* a respectable four out of five on June 17, 1989: "Tracks as diverse as Vinni Reilly's 'Smile In The Crowd' and Sparks' 'Never Turn Your Back On Mother Earth' are all given the same Martin-tinkering-about-in-his-bedroom-with-his-machines approach, an approach surprisingly successful, despite the maudlin tendencies ever-present. And if it does sound a little like Depeche Mode, that's understandable. If you'd spent the best part of the last decade in Depeche Mode, you'd sound a bit like them too . . .

"Martin Gore (seeing as Martin isn't American we'll drop the 'L') has not only followed the second part of the covers rule (do it better or do it differently) he's also had the guile to call his 'here's me doing a few of my favourite songs' LP *Counterfeit*, though he might as well have called it 'Songs You've Never Heard Before', so little known are its contents."

While *Counterfeit e.p* wasn't designed to be commercially viable, Martin L. Gore had reason to regard it as a successful experiment.

As well as Gore's solo outing, *Strange* – a video compilation of Anton Corbijn's Depeche Mode promos to date – was released; described in suitably pretentious style as being "based on love or life or lust or maybe nothing in particular."

Record Mirror were effusive about the clips "shot entirely on that dark and grainy black and white Super 8 type film that's been so overused recently in tacky American videos. In the hands of Corbijn and the Depeche lads, though, it takes on a stunning, gritty, dream-like quality that transports you into a nightmarish, rather mesmerising world, travelling to places as far apart as Los Angeles, Denmark and France. Basildon, however, is strangely absent."

Despite having previously stayed clear of music industry-related gatherings, September 9, 1988 saw Depeche Mode perform 'Strangelove' at the MTV Music Awards in America. Alan Wilder explained their apparent change of heart: "We were encouraged by our record company and independent marketing man, Bruce Kirkland. It was good exposure for us. We were probably just trying to look cool. I think we met Aerosmith and Guns n' Roses, but I was drunk and don't remember all that much about it. I do remember upsetting Cyndi Lauper; MTV gave each band a video camera, but when I stuck it in Cyndi's face, she threw a wobbler!"

"It took a lot of persuading us to do it," Dave Gahan told MTV's Kurt Loder backstage. "Everyone just said it was a good idea to do it. We weren't going to be coming back [to the US] for a long time, so it's a good idea just to come over. We've only ever done one other TV [show] in America. We like to keep a low profile, really. We don't like to publicise ourselves too much."

Alan Wilder: "It would take a lot to get me to go to one of those award ceremonies – I really hate them and I don't want to be any part of them. They are always surrounded by hypocrisy – this media 'let's all pat each other on the back' [thing] is meaningless and doesn't do anything for the vast majority of music [that] never gets any airtime on MTV. How can people vote for music if they've never been exposed to it?"

When Loder expressed concern over the band's abandonment of America, Gahan revealed Depeche Mode's plans for the immediate future: "We've just been in the studio. When we finished the tour we went back and mixed a live album, which we recorded at the Rose Bowl. And we filmed it and everything as well, so that's what we're working on now. That's coming out in January [1989]. And then we start working on a new album – hopefully that will be out later on in the year."

The Rose Bowl show had been recorded by Randy Ezratty using the Westwood One Mobile, and the finishing touches to a double document of the event, *101*, were applied at Swanyard Studios in Islington, North London with engineer Alan Moulder, whose presence implied that there were overdubs involved. Skirting around the issue, Alan Wilder reasoned, "Put it this way, I doubt there's ever been a live album in the history of pop music that hasn't been touched up here and there."

Two days before its March 13, 1989 release date, *Record Mirror*'s Eleanor Levy had her suspicions about the authenticity of *101* but still awarded it four stars: "Now that the capturing of the live experience has become as techno as the studio variety, and as Depeche Mode have proved them-selves at the forefront of that environment, so they've come up with a double LP celebrating their last US tour that's as clean as [self-appointed British moral watchdog] Mary Whitehouse's diary, but with rather more going on between the lines – so clean, in fact, that on many of the 17 tracks here, there's little difference from the original records, with even Dave Gahan's famed live gutteral yobbo yells being mixed down to give added emphasis to his remarkably strong vocals . . .

"*101* is not so much a better than average live album; it sits as a timely reminder of Depeche Mode's position as one of the few truly subversive pop groups around at the moment."

Depeche Mode's legion of British fans were in unanimous agreement with that sentiment, for *101* effortlessly sailed up to number seven in the UK Albums Chart, continuing the group's hitherto unbroken run of Top 10 albums. *101* also performed well across the Atlantic, entering the *Billboard* Chart on April 1, reaching number 45 during a reasonably respectable 19-week chart run. Alan Wilder: "People don't generally like live albums – they feel they're being ripped off."

At least *101* was lavishly packaged with Anton Corbijn's monochrome imagery, including a mass of lucrative Depeche Mode merchandising which the live recording served to further profit from. "It totally sums up a big band in the Eighties," Corbijn told *Q*'s Mat Snow. "I got to know them and started liking them as people, and realised that my vision of them as a teenybop band was wrong; they're very crafty and very down-to-earth. They're like New Order – they do things their way and don't care what the trend is. Of all the people I've worked with, they're the bravest."

Alan Wilder: "The comparison to New Order really only relates to us both being on independent labels, both coming across as slightly miserable and perhaps remaining as fairly aloof. Musically, I don't think there was much similarity."

Andy Fletcher: "New Order have done it the opposite way, starting off really gloomy with Joy Division and then getting more and more poppy! It's just the way Martin writes songs. On the second album [*A Broken Frame*], after Vince Clarke left, there was pressure on Martin to write commercial tunes and it was a bit of a mish-mash. We consider *Construction Time Again* [to be] our first real album when we got our act together, and Martin was right into his gloom and doom by then!

"It comes from him, totally, but we would say that he's just being realistic and the other stuff is too optimistic. We don't consider ourselves gloomy; there's lots of melody. Perhaps some of the vocal lines are a bit on the depressing side, but on the whole I find it very uplifting and the fans do, too."

Simultaneously released on sell-through video, the *101* movie was subject to equally enthusiastic (re)viewing by *Record Mirror*'s Tim Nicholson: "Like U2's *Rattle And Hum*, the DM film starts and stops, cutting from live performance to backstage philosophy to embarrassing interviews with American journalists to Nashville shopping sprees."

Nicholson was referring to an onscreen moment when Andy Fletcher and Martin Gore exit a taxi in downtown Nashville. Fletcher, dressed in a black and grey striped pullover and blue denim jeans, is fairly inconspicuous but Gore, with bleached blond barnet and what could feasibly be described as openly gay clothing – skin-tight white vest under a black leather biker's jacket – is sensibly shadowed by a beefy security man.

Inside a music store, Gore promptly demonstrates his guitar prowess, performing an impromptu instrumental rendition of 'Route 66' in country music fashion. When an elderly female record store assistant asks Gore if he liked bluegrass, the axe hero replies, "Don't know enough about it. I'm just getting into it."

As far as Nicholson was concerned, "The highlights of the film for DM followers are bound to be the live performances, of which there are plenty. For that alone, *101* is a good account of their increasing popularity in the States. But for aficionados of pop stars in films, the off-guard footage of Dave Gahan waxing lyrical about his halcyon days as a supermarket shelf-stacker before the awful pressure of all that money came along has to be one of the great moments.

"Add to that Dave Gahan gladly retelling a tale of how he beat up a cab driver to a journalist, and Dave Gahan standing in a gruesome pair of black undies telling the cameraman about the steroids he had to take for his throat, not to mention Dave Gahan sobbing when it's all over, and you'll get the idea of who's the star of the show."

Gahan was the singing star of the single chosen to trailer the *101* album and video on February 13. "I can't remember who really pushed for 'Everything Counts' – I think it was fairly unanimous," Alan Wilder recalled. "It had been a very popular live track for a number of years."

Record Mirror: "This appetiser from their forthcoming live LP would sink the way of most tracks if the amusing spectacle of Dave's leather-clad wiggle etched so vividly on your brain didn't leap to mind. Basildon's synth brigade go rock'n'roll . . . almost."

Depeche Mode's 21st single was remarkable in that it was released in the UK on no fewer than *seven* formats – 7" and 12" vinyl, limited-edition 12" vinyl, 10" vinyl; cassette-single; CD single and limited-edition CD single – sharing four live recordings culled from *101* ('Everything Counts', 'Nothing', 'Sacred' and 'A Question Of Time') and seven remixes – 'Everything Counts (Remix By Bomb The Bass)', 'Nothing (Remix By Justin Straus)', 'Strangelove (Remix By Bomb The Bass)', 'Everything

Counts (Absolut Mix)', 'Everything Counts (1983 12″ Mix)', 'Nothing (US 7″ Mix)' and 'Everything Counts (Reprise)' between them.

"Being in this business, people are *constantly* trying to milk you and make their little bit out of your name," Alan Wilder told KROQ's Richard Blade. "But we've been very lucky; with having been on an independent label, we've been allowed to kind of just go along at our own pace and build gradually, and keep control over what we're doing artistically. We've basically been involved with some very good people over the years, which has kept us going. But you do become very cynical about the music business and people that are involved in it in general, because most of them aren't that interested in it."

In *Record Mirror*'s estimation, Tim Simenon's beat-laden 'Bomb The Bass' efforts were the best of the bunch – even better than the Depeche originals: "Those Depeche Mode boys aren't half lucky having their record company next door to the Rhythm King offices. All they have to do when they're stuck for an idea or two is pop along the corridor, drag Tim Simenon away from his sonic playpen, and plonk some Depeche hits on his lap. The results? 'Everything Counts' and 'Strangelove' have been bashed into a shape that fits the dancefloor very nicely. Of course, there's not a lot left of Martin Gore, or any of the other lads for that matter, but there's some good, hard stomping beats that give Nitzer Ebb a run for their money. Forget the live versions you hear on the radio. Get down to your record store and demand a copy of these remixes."

More than a few Depeche devotees heeded the advice, for 'Everything Counts (Live)' had worked its way up to number 22 on the UK Singles Chart by February 25 – not bad going for a basic in-concert version of a song that had already charted in July 1983. The band's American fanbase were not offered the same diversity of choice – just a single 12″ of 'Everything Counts (Live)' on March 21, was followed by 7″ and cassette singles four days later.

An online fan complained to Alan Wilder, "England always gets more singles, more mixes, more B-sides and other rare recordings while Americans have to pay ridiculous prices to import the stuff; who makes these idiotic decisions?"

Alan Wilder: "Certainly, radio in the US is a strange animal which dictates how the companies promote their product . . . The US market is completely different to Europe and the rest of the world. I don't pretend to fully understand it, but whenever we deliver product, they always want to do things differently to suit their market. Their argument is that 'we know our own market better than you do, so let us decide' – perhaps they are right."

Aside from these gripes, 'Everything Counts (Live)' fared well in America, peaking at number 13 on the recently formed Modern Rock Tracks Chart.* Unfortunately, this showing meant comparatively little on the *Billboard* listing where 'Everything Counts (Live)' failed to chart.

The accompanying promo video, opening with the familiar shot of tour accountant Jonathan 'Baron' Kessler exclaiming, "We're getting a load of money . . ." was a montage of *101* footage (and several out-takes), including a memorable parting shot of an airborne, heavy-lidded Alan Wilder sticking two fingers up to the camera. When a clearly confused viewer queried the gesture, Wilder replied: "Where I come from it means 'Fuck off' as opposed to 'Fuck you' which we English never say. As insults go, I am of the opinion that, despite the multitude of variables, you just can't beat a simple 'Fuck off' – especially when delivered by a tight-lipped, braces, Ben Sherman, and Dr Martens-wearing British skinhead. In this case, it was just a friendly 'Fuck off' to the invasive cameraperson who was trying to sneak a shot of my private sleepy moment."

Depeche Mode had undoubtedly got much mileage out of what could feasibly be termed their 'music for the masses' phase.

Martin Gore: "When we called an album *Music For The Masses*, we were accused of being patronising and arrogant. In fact, it was a joke on the uncommerciality of it. It was anything but music for the masses!"

Dave Gahan: "We had become aware of highs and lows. We were more conscious of building up atmospheres, heightening the songs to an absolutely massive feeling and then bringing them down again. We had discovered dynamics. It [*Music For The Masses*] was our first truly arranged album. At the same time, we had reached a point where we couldn't go any further in that direction. We knew we had to change our way of working. We had to go away and rethink everything."

In an increasingly rare conversation with *NME*, Martin Gore unveiled the brief for a 'new' Depeche Mode: "Over the last five years I think we'd perfected a formula; my demos, a month in a programming studio, etc, etc. We decided that our first record of the Nineties ought to be different."

---

* This was based on monitored airplay reports from modern rock format radio stations such as KROQ in Los Angeles.

Alan Wilder: "Usually we begin the making of a record by having extensive pre-production meetings where we decide what the record will actually sound like, then go into a programming studio. This time we decided to keep all pre-production to a minimum. We were beginning to have a problem with boredom in that we felt we'd reached a certain level of achievement in doing things in a certain way."

Ironically, Andy Fletcher implied that the root cause of that boredom may have been the more intricate nature of Gore's demos: "Over the years Martin's studio at home [had] got progressively better and better so the demos he was producing and giving to us were very good quality. If you listen to a song – say, 'Strangelove', which was a very full demo – after about 20 plays, the direction in which you're going to go is pretty much fixed. We were basically re-recording Martin's demos with better sounds, better production and Dave's vocals. For this album we said to Martin, 'Just present the demos on an acoustic guitar and organ – only lyrics and chords,' so we could decide [on] the direction of the songs as a group."

Rather than Wilder ironing out Gore's demos into a more flexible electronic musical framework at his home studio, Depeche Mode went straight to Logic Studios, sited on the Via Quintilliano, Milan, Italy, where a seven-week recording session had initially been booked.

The as-yet-untitled album represented the first time that the group used a producer, rather than an engineer/producer. The man chosen for the task was the upcoming studio hotshot Flood, whose previous association with Depeche Mode – if not Mute Records – had extended to one solitary remix in 'Stripped (Highland Mix)'.

Flood: "When I was an engineer, I was asked to work on [U2's] *Joshua Tree*, and I did that working with [Brian] Eno and [Daniel] Lanois. It was just, like, 'Here's the rule book – throw it away!' Everything you thought before was wrong. I [then] went to do the second Erasure album [*The Circus*], and that was coming from premier rock to premier pop and realising the cross-fertilisation that *can* be accomplished between the two. It doesn't mean that you have to play the second verse riff sound on a synth – why can't you have that concept in a rock song, and vice versa? So that opened my eyes."

Daniel Miller subsequently suggested a meeting with the prospective producer at Martin Gore's recently purchased country house in Harpenden, Hertfordshire. Alan Wilder remembered the occasion well: "This scruffy, bespectacled, rather unlikely looking bloke rolled up, raided the fridge a couple of times, slouched down on the sofa, pontificated for a bit and thus – a new production team was born."

Flood's affection for Depeche Mode was absolute. "I'd always loved them as a band; they had a very unique style of pop, which I didn't think anybody else was touching. At the time I was working with a lot of bands like Nitzer Ebb and Nine Inch Nails, and I was very much into the idea that a pop band could have a bit more edge to them.

"On *Violator*, they wanted to push into new territory; so I think that by me being new to the fold, some of the distance was made."

Dave Gahan: "We wanted somebody who could basically give us a kick now and again, and be able to pull us together and make the best of the songs without necessarily just [having] our perspective on it."

Martin Gore: "He really got us to push barriers and just do things that were totally unlike what we'd done before. He got us sort of performing a lot more, as opposed to just programming everything."

Progress during the initial Milan sessions was slow as Flood and Wilder laboured over the convoluted new sequences and sounds. "Our styles complemented each other," said the latter, "my musical angle coupled with his technical prowess."

Andy Fletcher: "It was definitely more enjoyable making this album because we went to Milan right at the beginning. We just went out, partied, and didn't get any recording done, but we had a good time and it cemented the spirit of the whole album."

Alan Wilder: "In the earlier years, everybody would be there [in the studio] with the result often being lots of chat and mucking around with little actual work being achieved. As time went on, we all realised that less people in the control room equalled more work done."

In turn, this soon-to-be-established Depeche Mode behavioural pattern led some to accuse the defensive Wilder of being boring. "The simple fact is that most people just don't understand or appreciate that producing a record properly requires an enormous amount of energy and concentration.

"Anyone can go into a studio for a couple of hours a day, take loads of drugs, twiddle a few knobs, whack it all onto a CD and call it a finished album, but invariably the end result sounds like what it is – lazy and ill-judged. I can't just roll into the studio at five o'clock in the afternoon with a raging hangover and expect to be able to work effectively. This doesn't mean that I never take a break during a session, but, as a rule, I like to keep work time and playtime separate so I can give my absolute best to whatever project I'm involved in. If this makes me boring, then fine – I'd rather be boring but have a really good record . . .

"Studios can be incredibly claustrophobic places – even more so for those who perhaps don't play a big part in the nuts and bolts of the process. Boredom is an especially powerful and destructive force. For example, one of the most annoying things is if I'm working on a complicated sample – which I want to cut up into many pieces and reconfigure into something new – the process is inevitably complex and, until the procedure is complete, things will usually sound chaotic and meaningless to anyone listening in. If someone who doesn't fully understand this procedure interjects negatively at an unfinished stage, it can be really irritating."

Although Wilder was not directing his comments at anyone in particular, Daniel Miller noticed the cracks that were beginning to open in what was generally perceived to be a close-knit working unit: "I think there were problems because Alan was from a very traditional musical background. I think he found it difficult while he was sitting in the studio for 12, 13, 14 hours a day and Fletch would wander in and make a pragmatic comment and wander out again."

Contrary to what Andy Fletcher had told *Record Mirror*'s Lisa Tilston, Depeche Mode achieved one worthwhile result during the initial Logic Studios sessions.

Andy Fletcher: "Martin wrote this song, 'Personal Jesus', and we loved it. We thought it was a *great* song – great sound; we recorded it; François Kervorkian remixed it in Milan with us, and we thought, 'This record is not going to get played at all.'"

Alan Wilder: "The main stomp was a recording of two or three people jumping up and down on flightcases, working alongside Martin's John Lee Hooker guitar riff and the Kraftwerk-style synth parts.*

"François was quite loud and opinionated, as well as being prone to mood swings for no apparent reason. I liked him, though, and his methods. We never took him or his stroppiness too seriously, and a healthy amount of piss taking would usually force a smile to his face. He looks something like the [Olympic javelin-throwing] British athlete Fatima Whitbread, so her poster ended up on the studio wall – much to his disgust. He liked to work long hours and is something of a perfectionist

* Because of Kervorkian's remix work on Kraftwerk's 1986 album, *Electric Café*, it was inevitable that 'Personal Jesus' inherited some of that feel.

— again, something I admired. For him, it must have been as strange an experience to work with us as it was for us to work with him. I hope he looks back on it fondly."

Reading between the lines, recording 'Personal Jesus' hadn't been a trouble-free ride, yet the finished product was undeniably a resounding success — 'electro-blues' tinged with what, at first glance, appeared to be potentially blasphemous overtones.

Andy Fletcher: "We had these great songs, but the single we wanted to release was 'Personal Jesus'. What we always do is to try and think, 'What is the best track?' — not 'What's the most commercial?' Then we thought, 'Why are we releasing this track? It's going to be a complete disaster! We're going to get into real trouble with the Americans' — even with 'Blasphemous Rumours' we got loads of trouble over there!"

Martin Gore: "We thought that, especially in America, it might struggle for airplay, and we were totally proven wrong."

For the promo video shot in Spain, Anton Corbijn perfectly parodied the long-established spaghetti Western genre. "We had the whole stuff on — the [Stetson] hats, the leather chaps and everything, and there [were] horses," Dave Gahan recalled with delight.

Andy Fletcher: " 'Personal Jesus' could have been my worst experience, because we were actually in this desert town in Spain — one of [those] cowboy towns, where they make all the Westerns and stuff. And all day they'd been telling me, 'Well Fletcher, you know you've got a horse to ride later.' And I was thinking, 'I can't ride a horse; I *can't ride* a horse!' And they said, 'Don't worry; he's nice, he's calm — he's *big*, but he's OK.'

"It came to this bit, and everyone was with me to watch me ride this horse, because I'd only ridden a pony once when I went trekking, and that ran away. It turned out it was a rocking horse! There's a bit on the video where I'm like [rocking back and forth]. It was one of those nice wind-ups, but it *did* spoil my whole day, thinking about [having to do] that."

An equine close-up was deemed offensive enough to be subsequently edited out to appease the censors. Martin Gore: "It was after it got sent out to video stations. I think MTV objected to it — the shot of the horse's arse comes when there's all this heavy breathing on the track! I don't know if Anton was consciously trying to be perverted, but I think it was more coincidental that it happened at that point. Obviously these video people see things very strangely!"

Alan Wilder: "Arses are a no-no for American TV — it's OK if you're blowing someone's brains out, though. I couldn't begin to explain what goes on in the censors' minds. The irony of censorship is that, in most cases, it simply highlights the very thing it's trying to suppress. Just look at the notoriety of films such as *A Clockwork Orange* and *The Exorcist* which are now considered tame by comparison to current box office films."

There was further discomfort for Wilder when being photographed (fully clothed) with a naked woman by Corbijn for the single's black and white back sleeve: "It was all a bit embarrassing, really. The girl was 17 and very shy."

Soon after its August 29, 1989 UK release date, both fans and critics alike showed their appreciation of 'Personal Jesus'. "The Glitter beat is back," began *Record Mirror's* Iestyn George when awarding it 'Single Of The Week' on September 2, 1989. "Basildon's finest plunder the past, dress it up in leather trousers and add a Duane Eddy guitar lick for good measure. I never thought the day would come when I'd say something nice about Depeche Mode, so this is something of a personal landmark."

Martin Gore: "We always underestimate our fanbase. In England, with 'Personal Jesus' we had this plan to go in the charts really low, so that it had time to build. So we just released the 12″ [for the] first week, and we were totally shocked – it went in at number 25, just on 12″, which totally ruined our plan! We got *Top Of The Pops* [in the] first week."

Partly on the strength of that crucial primetime British television appearance, 'Personal Jesus' peaked at number 13 by September 9, representing Depeche Mode's best British chart showing since 'Master And Servant' exactly five years earlier. It remained on the singles chart for eight weeks, thanks to the staggered availability of three remixes* by François Kervorkian and two by Flood (plus three distinct versions of its B-side, 'Dangerous', by Flood and Daniel Miller).

In Detroit – the home of techno – the musical movers and shakers in the city's club land were citing Basildon's finest as the genre's godfathers (alongside Kraftwerk and, to a lesser extent, The Human League and New Order).

Martin Gore: "I heard someone [Kevin Saunderson of Inner City] saying that 'Get The Balance Right!' was the first house record, which was nice and funny."

Ironic would perhaps have been a more appropriate word, for Depeche

---

* Again these were spread over seven different formats – standard and gatefold 7″ vinyl, 12″ and limited-edition 12″ vinyl; cassette-single; CD single and limited-edition CD single.

Mode's 1983 single wasn't even deemed fit for release in the United States, yet, according to *The Face*'s John McCready, imported copies ended up changing hands as "a $25 'Disco Classic' in Manhattan's hip Downstairs Records."

During a brief break from recording, Depeche Mode accepted an invitation from *The Face* – Britain's self-styled "The World's Best Dressed Magazine" – to meet Detroit techno guru Derrick May for a guided tour of the Motor City's dance clubs like The Music Institute – a move that surprised accompanying journalist John McCready: "Here, in the interests of providing another view of a group whose name is always accompanied in British magazines by an italicised cynicism from an unidentified 'Ed', Depeche Mode are taking a Techno holiday, their curiosity stirred after hearing some of the city's innovative new dance music; the trip also provides a way of approaching a group who are now in a position to refuse the standard tape-recorder-on-the-table trial."

As a band known for being "fond of a drink or three," in the words of McCready, Depeche Mode were reported as being collectively amazed by The Institute's "dance-till-dawn concept of the [alcohol-free] juice bar." "They have dance in their blood," May told McCready. However, Gore was perplexed: "We can't create dance music, and I don't think we've ever really tried. We honestly wouldn't know where to start."

Andy Fletcher: "It mystified us that we're told there's all these people saying we did connect. I remember doing *The Face* article when we went to see Derrick May in Detroit; we got mobbed by all these pretty young black kids. We weren't getting much attention at home [in the UK], so to be mobbed by black kids in Detroit really was something! We thought we must be doing something right . . ."

McCready implied that Depeche Mode were struggling to find a connection with their musical admirer when wanting to know "why almost every house track utilises the very specific sound of the Roland [TR-] 808 drum machine?"

Looking back, the falseness of that meeting left a somewhat sour aftertaste.

Alan Wilder: "We all went to May's flat and pretended we were part of this [techno] scene. Derrick May was horrible; I hated him. He was the most arrogant fucker I've ever met. He took us into his backroom where he had a studio and played us this track, and it was fucking horrible."

Andy Fletcher: "He was a really nice bloke, but it was a bit [of an] odd situation. In those days, that scene was all orange juice and no drugs. We went to The [Music] Institute and they were all on [orange] juice. We just wanted a beer; it was frustrating on that point."

As something of a 'techno godfather' himself, Daniel Miller addressed the possible bond between Depeche Mode and the dance-orientated music cultures that repeatedly namechecked them as pioneers: "When techno started, and rave culture – but more techno than rave – a lot of techno musicians cited them as being a big influence. But they didn't quite understand that . . . initially; I understood it completely. They don't really like it very much – [they're] partiers, yes, but not ravers."

In an age where synthesisers and electronics have become prevalent – from TV commercials to a dazzling array of guises (techno, house, hip-hop, trip-hop, *et al*) – electronic music has inadvertently become something of a generic term. "I feel part of it in some ways," Gore claimed, "but alienated in others. A lot of it is *so* simplistic, but I love electronic music. It's one of my passions."

Quite how the underground techno scene related to Chicago house music – and, indeed, *its* derivative, acid house – could be confusing to non-aficionados as MTV's Kurt Loder found out when asking three-quarters of Depeche Mode to explain the term acid house.

Alan Wilder: "I've no idea. What does it mean?"

Martin Gore: "Acid's acid, innit!"

Dave Gahan: "If you've done acid, you'd know what acid house is."

Alan Wilder: "What's with the house, then?"

Dave Gahan: "The house comes from [the fact that] you take the acid in the house."

Needless to say, their exchange went unaired.

21

Bigger Than Jesus?

"Violator was [Depeche Mode's] biggest-selling album to date; it did over six million around the world."

— Daniel Miller, 1998

When Depeche Mode reconvened in the summer of 1989 to resume recording *Violator*, it was in the familiar environs of PUK Studios in Denmark. According to the band's personal assistant, Daryl Bamonte, the sessions "took on a frenetic pace and by the end of August [1989], *Violator* had taken shape."

Alan Wilder: "The PUK period was much more prolific, and although some of the tracks like 'Clean' and 'Policy Of Truth' went through many guises before the final versions were settled upon – with 'Clean', we never had the delayed bass line until the very end; with 'Policy [Of Truth]' it took forever to find a lead riff sound which worked – we had the most productive and enjoyable time."

But not everyone enjoyed themselves at PUK this time around. Andy Fletcher in particular became alienated in the remote Danish countryside, as Martin Gore explained: "There are many reasons that aggravate Andy's problems, and you can guess at some of them! I think it was 12 years ago that he had his first depression, and it's still dragging on to this day. It was absolutely hopeless; it didn't matter what you said.

"I think it was during the recording of *Violator* that it first came out; he would sit in the studio, moaning – he had the longest face on, then he would get up and kind of shuffle to the door like an old man. There was one day after he walked out, the rest of us looked at each other and burst out laughing because it just looked like an act! We were thinking, 'He can't be serious!' But he was. That was the first week of it happening."

Fletcher's colleagues' amusement at his bizarre behaviour soon turned to genuine bafflement. "We had no idea he was going through depression," said Gore. "It just looked like [he was] putting on some misery act. He started thinking all kinds of things – that he had cancer. We'd tell him, 'You haven't got cancer! Go and see a doctor.' And he'd go and get two doctor's opinions, because he didn't trust the first one, and they both told him he was absolutely A1. And he still didn't believe it, because there's some kind of misfiring going on in his brain!"

Alan Wilder: "He sort of developed this depression, which the rest of us became aware of gradually during some of that recording period. So we sent him home to get some advice and health or whatever. And that kind of helped things, in a way, because we didn't have this distraction of someone who was somewhere else having a problem."

Fletcher headed back to the UK and promptly booked himself into The Priory, a private Roehampton (South London) hospital specialising in the management of psychiatric illnesses, including depression and anxiety, in what was to be the first of many visits. Looking at the brighter side, Fletcher recalled, "It's quite funny, because when I went there [a] geezer from The Cure was in there – we were both in the same situation, which was quite humorous. It was quite a normal place, but now, of course, celebs check in there as a career move, or to say, 'Hey, I'm doing something about it,' which certainly wasn't the case with me. The day I went in there for the first time I thought I was going into a mental institution!"

For the troubled keyboardist, the hospital provided much-needed sanctuary, but not a solution to whatever was responsible for triggering his depression: "The Priory didn't teach me *anything*! It was quite a while after when I got in touch with some good people who helped me out. The Priory was a place to go because I couldn't handle being at home. I was only in there for four weeks; after that I was left to my own devices."

Vince Clarke, who had briefly re-established a relationship with Fletcher after his old friend came along to one of Erasure's first London gigs, was just as perplexed as the rest of Depeche Mode: "I did kind of hook up with Fletcher again, I suppose. We had quite a good time; we went skiing together and used to take the piss out of each other on holiday, but that was nothing to do with the band or music, before he became ill – I don't know what that's all about. There was a bit of history with his father – I know that, and with his sister dying; that was something he had to go through."

Tragically, Fletcher had lost his sister Karen to cancer several years previously, an unthinkably painful event worsened further still by her leaving behind a child and a husband. "That was part of it, definitely," he admitted later. "I wasn't allowed to deal with that initially because I was away [with the group] all the time."

Robert Marlow agreed: "That was very hard for him. Fletch had always been 'Mr Affable' down the pub, but suddenly things weren't quite the same anymore. I remember I went on a skiing trip once with him – there was me, Vince . . . quite a few of us. Anyway, we were all in the bar in the evening and we were having an argument – I think Fletch had one of the early mobile phones, and he was going to the hotel reception every morning to pick up his faxes. We thought he was being a bit poncey about it all, so we ended up having this big argument about modern technology, I guess.

"Fletcher was saying that this was going to be the way ahead, and we were going, 'What do you need a phone for when you're on the bog, or whatever?' And he said, 'Oh, you don't understand. I wish I had my *yes-men* with me!' That always sticks in my mind. I mean, he was joking, but there was also an element of truth in that. And that's how things changed over the years."

Andy Fletcher: "All these factors go together – the spiralling out of control within the group. I don't want to say that the job I do is more stressful that any person in the street – this sort of thing happens all the time and people's families know about it. I was brought up as a working-class kid, basically designed to work nine to five: dinner on the table, video, bottle of wine, go to bed.

"In a band it's 24 hours a day, but in your late-teens/early twenties it's that whole thing of hangovers – you get absolutely paralytic and just wake up the next morning. But as you get older with more responsibilities those hangovers get worse; it takes two days – three days – to recover . . .

"I think part of my problem is in my genes – my dad suffers from ODC [Obsessive-Compulsive Disorder] and I get a side of that from him – and part of it is related to my lifestyle; the job of being in a band basically became all too much. But I'm glad that it happened, because I learned a lot about myself very quickly and learned how to deal with problems that arise. But I think it would have happened whether or not I was in the band."

Without the "distraction" of Andy Fletcher, as Wilder so delicately put it, the other three members of Depeche Mode, together with Flood, were able to make haste during the remainder of the Danish lap of the *Violator* production at PUK. By September, when the team relocated to The Church studios in North London's Crouch End – owned by Dave Stewart of Eurythmics fame – they had eight songs in the bag. Making up for lost time in Milan, François Kervorkian began mixing while the band continued recording upstairs, assisted by the initially reluctant engineer Steve Lyon who soon got fell into line upon hearing 'Personal Jesus'. Lyon would, in time, become a trusted associate in Depeche Mode's ever-expanding musical entourage.

Alan Wilder: "François had mixed 'Personal Jesus' with us in Milan, and brought with him an excitable and, at times, 'quite-difficult-to-work-with' personality. However, the tension that resulted from this was good for the record and provided the individual tracks with some extra touches, as well as a much-needed new angle. *Violator*'s a lot more electronic than I remember it being; François brought an electro influence, too. Obviously, that kind of sound was what felt right at the time, even though we were also introducing more drum loops* and guitars as well.

"Part of the reason drum machines sound [machine-like] is because of the lack of human feel. No two snare beats sound the same when played by a drummer – I like that. Most of the drum sounds on *Violator* were sampled, apart from the obvious electro sounds [like the Kraftwerk-esque 'pewt' noise – courtesy of François Kervorkian, no doubt], but the rhythms were still programmed. Some hi-hat patterns – 'Policy [Of Truth]', for example – were played and sampled as loops, and in the case of 'Halo' and 'Clean' it's all loops. Again, I prefer the looped parts because of the performance element."

Depeche Mode's vocalist made his recorded instrumental début on *Violator*. "Dave plays a unique form of guitar; he has his own special style," Wilder declared. "We used some of his playing as sound effects in one of the crossfade sections on *Violator* [linking 'Enjoy The Silence' and 'Policy Of Truth']."

It seemed Fletcher's absence wasn't missed musically.

Alan Wilder: "He says he used to play bass guitar in the very early incarnation of DM, but I've never actually heard it put to the test."

Having reaped the financial rewards of Depeche Mode's continuing success, Fletcher's problems may have been aggravated by the fact that he was no longer contributing musically to a band now possibly poised to become one of the world's biggest.

---

* Short digital (sampled) recordings of actual drum performances.

288

Vince Clarke: "Fletcher's always been nervous of his position. In my day, he was aware of the fact that he's not necessarily the most important musical person in the band – he's always been aware of that. And that's probably made him a little unbalanced, although I don't think he really appreciates the full value of his worth in the Depeche situation as it stands, and nor, probably, does anybody else."

Dave Gahan: "It definitely had an effect on the band, not musically or creatively – Fletch would be the first to tell you that, but, definitely, we were all worried about him. It seemed like a long time until Fletch was doing well."

Martin Gore: "In the Sixties, people were just musicians, and a lot of people got ripped off. People didn't really take care of the business side of things. Now you don't need four really brilliant musicians in a band – you've got technology there to help you. One good musician, really, is enough for a band, and then the others can do their various roles."

Dave Gahan: "Alan's involvement's a lot heavier – right down to arrangements and things like that. Fletch's involvement is heavy as well, but he goes off in other areas. He gets involved in all sorts of things that *bore* the rest of us, basically – the more sort of management side of things."

A presumably (partially) recovered Fletcher said much the same thing in conversation with *Record Mirror*'s Lisa Tilston when embarking on the *Violator* promotional trail two days before the album's eventual March 19, 1990 UK release: "Not having a manager helps, because you have to learn the business side yourself. We're in control, because I take care of that side of things. There's no pressure on Martin when he's writing, or Alan when he's putting together the music, or Dave . . . in fact, *I* get all the pressure!

"It's something I'm quite interested in anyway, because I studied economics at school. I think a modern band has to be interested in that side of things; we remember stories of Gary Glitter going bankrupt, and we're always very conscious of that. We have total control over what we do, because we're not in a major label conglomerate situation; *we* make the decisions."

According to Depeche Mode's "one good musician" – Alan Wilder – there were no hard and fast rules when working in The Church: "Sometimes the songs drastically changed from the demo and sometimes they were pretty similar. Martin didn't like to explain his songs to anyone and, knowing that, the other group members would rarely ask him what they were about. It's clear to me that the ambiguity of his words and the subversive quality of some of them (with their possible dark meanings) is what makes them interesting."

Andy Fletcher: "Martin doesn't get around the table and say, 'Listen lads, this is what this one's about.' He never explains the lyrics at all. In the old days, when we used to make videos with storylines like 'See You', he hated it because they interpreted his songs too literally.

"I've heard about 10 different interpretations of 'Personal Jesus' and that's what Martin really likes. 'Personal Jesus' was on a general theme, that's the important thing. The lyrics are very ambiguous, so although it could have been controversial, in fact it turned out not to be at all. Most people thought it was a pro-Christian anthem, which wasn't intended. If you release a song with the word 'Jesus' in it, you've got to expect trouble, but we wanted to release it because we thought it was a good song."

Martin Gore: "Religion's one of the themes that crops up a lot in my songs. I think I *have* got this fascination with religion, and I think that's inherent in everything – from the feel of the music to touching on things in lyrics."

Despite Fletcher once claiming that he only turned to born-again Christianity as a "source of making friends", admitting that it was important in "building our personalities – certainly my personality," being in a group featuring a songwriter so preoccupied with religion could well have been a contributory factor in Fletcher's depressive episodes.

Andy Fletcher: "I've still got two friends who are ministers and I always say this to one of them: 'You know what the Bible says – I'm going to be spewed out of God's mouth when I die!' I'm worse than a non-believer, because a person who believes and then doesn't is supposedly going to be spewed out of God's mouth. Then I'll go down to the boilers and stoke coal. But if you're not a believer, you're just going to go straight down to the boilers; you don't get spewed out of God's mouth. Allegedly, you can repent."

Interestingly, 'Personal Jesus' was one of the few Depeche Mode songs where Gore actually agreed to talk about its inspiration – *Elvis & Me*, Priscilla Beaulieu Presley's candid autobiography of her time with 'the King'. "It's a song about being a Jesus for somebody else, someone to give you hope and care," explained Martin Gore. "It's about how Elvis was her man and mentor, and how often that happens in love relationships – how everybody's heart is like a god in some way, and that's not a very balanced view of someone, is it?"

With the religious right holding some (considerable) sway in America,

neither Depeche Mode nor, in all probability, Sire had any great expectations for 'Personal Jesus' following its simultaneous Stateside release on 12"
vinyl, cassette maxi-single and CD maxi-single on September 19 – until
the controversial 'Telephone this number for your own Personal Jesus'
adverts came into play, whereby any misguided soul calling the number(s)
was treated to a taster of Depeche Mode's new single – at an exorbitant
rate per minute, of course! (Oddly enough, many papers that obligingly
printed soft-porn phone lines refused Depeche Mode's advertisement on
the grounds of religious offence.)

When quizzed as to whether the band themselves were responsible for
this spot of ingenuity – in view of the song's *"Lift up the receiver"* hookline –
Alan Wilder admitted, "[It] must have been some wag in the marketing
department."

'Personal Jesus' made its presence known on the *Billboard* Singles Chart
as of December 9, peaking at number 28 in a 20-week chart run –
Depeche Mode's best Stateside single performance since 'People Are
People' back in mid-1985. It fared even better on the alternative Modern
Rock Tracks Chart where it climbed to number three. "It sold half-a-
million records before it started being played on the big radio stations," an
incredulous Gahan told *Melody Maker*'s Jon Wilde. "It just built up in the
clubs for five months and the radio ignored it. They just [didn't] get it."

Andy Fletcher: "We put it ['Personal Jesus'] out six months before the
album [*Violator*], and it was still in the American charts when we released
the next single! It's the biggest-selling 12" in Warner Bros. history – that's
more than Madonna, or anyone like that; it's phenomenal!"

Musically, *Violator* had its highs – the repetitive, one-note delayed bass line
opening 'Clean' sounded remarkably like that of 'One Of These Days',
from Pink Floyd's 1971 classic, *Meddle*. "I recognise the similarity,"
Wilder conceded, "but it's not a Floyd sample. It was programmed using a
combination of analogue synth and sampled bass guitar."

On a similar note, the inventive, trance-like sequencing underpinning
'Waiting For The Night' also paid homage to past influences, this time
Tangerine Dream's Seventies Moog doodlings.

Alan Wilder: "Flood and I had been listening to Tangerine Dream and
decided to try and create a similar atmosphere for this track. The main
sequence was put together using his ARP and the Sequencer that accom-
panies [that] synth. Due to its many velocity and filtering possibilities, this
unit has a unique quality that is difficult to replicate using a modern-day

sequencer triggered by MIDI. Once it has been set up, in order for the sequence to be transposed to follow the chord structure of the song, I needed to play in each chord from an external keyboard.

"A similar principle was applied to the 'bubbling' bass part, which, together with the main sequence, forms the backbone of the track. The charm of the ARP Sequencer stems from the slight tuning and timing variations that occur each time the part is played. This gives a sense of fluidity and continual change which seems to suit the song."

Coincidentally, together with fellow producer (and synth enthusiast) Ed Buller, engineering sidekick Gary Stout and musical accomplice Dave Bessell, Flood went on to record a virtual Tangerine Dream pastiche in 1995's *Node*, released on the obscure London-based Deviant label.

Alan Wilder: "I think it was just a one-off LP, produced by Flood, Ed Buller and someone else whose name I can't remember – sort of ambient/ electronic, more in the style of, say, Tangerine Dream rather than Aphex Twin. They did a gig in the concourse of Paddington Station [excerpts of which were subsequently released on Deviant in 1995 as the single 'Terminus'], which worked quite well, actually – especially when the station announcer started speaking."

Thanks to the imminent success of *Violator*, the syncopated sequencer sound pioneered by Tangerine Dream was about to crossover thanks to Depeche Mode's popular appeal.

"*Violator*, I think, was a breakthrough in the States, because it *really* had a pop feel," rationalised KROQ's Richard Blade. "And it wasn't because Depeche Mode sold out; I think it was because everybody else bought in. Depeche Mode didn't change; they were always evolving. You listen to every Depeche Mode album, and each one is a step ahead of the next. And, I think, with *Violator* what happened was that America was ready for Depeche Mode; they were ready for 'Policy Of Truth' and 'Enjoy The Silence' – absolutely brilliantly, brilliantly crafted songs."

The much-anticipated album was preceded by another single.

Daniel Miller: " 'Enjoy The Silence' – the story behind that is quite interesting. It actually started out as a ballad, and I think Alan Wilder had the idea of kind of speeding it up and turning it into more of a beat-orientated track. And he did that, and that worked really well, and then Martin added the kind of guitar riff to it."

Alan Wilder: "We asked Martin to give us demos in their most basic form, and 'Enjoy The Silence' was very basic. Strangely, the thing that immediately came to mind was that I could hear [Pet Shop Boys' vocalist] Neil Tennant singing it in my head – something about the line *'All I ever wanted'* sounded very hamster . . . er, Pet Shop to me! And it occurred to me that it could work brilliantly as a sort of up-tempo dance track. I felt that to have taken the simple ballad approach for this song ['Enjoy The Silence'] would have been to criminally pass on it's massive commercial potential. It was a great tune, crying out for the kind of treatment it eventually got.

"I think the others were a little dubious, but after a little bit of persuasion they said, 'Well, why don't you and Flood put together something that you think will be appropriate for this track, and we'll go away and come back when you're ready to play it to us.' And that's what we did with several tracks on that album [*Violator*].

"Flood and I worked on the backing track before calling Martin in to play the guitar riff. As the track came together, I think it dawned upon everyone – even Martin, who had been the most reluctant about taking the up-tempo route – that we had a hit on our hands."

Fletcher soon changed his tune upon hearing the result. "That's one of the most magical moments I've ever had with Depeche Mode," he gushed. "We were in PUK Studios in Denmark, and we had this ballad called 'Enjoy The Silence', and we just decided to speed it up; then Martin got the guitar out and put this riff in, and within an hour we knew we had a massive hit record!"

Dave Gahan recalled a somewhat less direct journey to glory: "I remember him [Gore] sitting there, playing the guitar, and then coming up with this riff, and then I sang the song, and everyone was surprised that I sang it so well – including myself! And *then*, we spent a week trying to make it into something, saying, 'Wow! I think this could be a single. Why don't we try and do this and that? And maybe we can redo the drum pattern. And Martin, maybe you could play the guitar a bit better.' And in the end, of course, we came right round, full circle, and it was like, 'Well, it sounded really good the first day that we recorded it.' Everything about it was in place, and it wasn't because we had tried that hard; it just happened – by far, they're the most special moments."

Recording the single might not have been particularly trying, but mixing it certainly was, as Wilder recalled: "We mixed the LP [*Violator*] with François; personally, I [didn't] think there was much wrong with our mix of 'Enjoy The Silence'. The guitar [sounded] fine and the overall sound [had] a bit more sparkle. [But] Daniel [Miller] had a bee in his bonnet about the mix and felt very strongly that he could do better. We let him have a go, and after two or three attempts, as you can see from the credits, decided that his mix was acceptable for the 7″ version. Had he not pushed for it, I think we would have happily gone with the original mix. Funnily enough, our most successful single ever was one of the flattest, dullest-sounding mixes, with a snare drum that sounds like a sticky toffee pudding!"

At the time, Fletcher had a more positive approach to the release. "'Enjoy The Silence' is probably our most commercial song for quite a while," he argued. "It's got a good tune and a housey beat, but it still seems gloomy compared to the bouncy dance music like Black Box and Technotronic. In some ways, perhaps, we're in our own little world; we don't aim to be subversive, but if we are, it's very natural."

'Enjoy The Silence' was awarded 'Single Of The Week' by the *NME*: "These are naughty boys who get to talk to the little girls *and* their big brothers; they also get to rhyme 'silence' with 'violence' and to put out introspective gloom songs which everybody can dance to when they get their leather-clad loins on *Top Of The Pops*, and it matters sod-all that this brooding, tender piece sounds like New Order."

Guest reviewer Jon Marsh of The Beloved, who had just enjoyed a UK Top 20 hit of their own ('Hello') added his ten cents worth: "Well, having always been a sucker for a good New Order song I thought that ['Enjoy The Silence'] was brilliant. It starts off a bit dodgy, but with most Depeche Mode songs I tend to not really like them until I've heard them about half-a-dozen times. But I thought that was their best for a very long time and I'd definitely invest my hard-earned pennies in that. But then I like cold, European, melodic tunes."

Melody Maker's Simon Reynolds wasn't entirely convinced by what he heard: "Depeche studiously keep their finger on the pulse of contemporaniety [*sic*] (the choral synths nod to the New Age thang [*sic*], the guitars to New Order), but somehow the glum, earnest vibrato in the singer's gullet makes this feel very dated: New Romanticism infected with C86* miserablism [*sic*]."

Reynolds' "New Romanticism" and "C86 miserablism" tags wore somewhat thin when applied to Depeche Mode's new sound for the Nineties. Frustratingly, in the same issue, the reviewer awarded 'Single Of

---

* C86 being the name of a tape issued by *Melody Maker* in 1986 showcasing new talent along the lines of Jesus & Mary Chain and other groups with similar indie and/or Goth leanings.

The Week' to new Mute act A.C. Marias for 'One Of Our Girls Has Gone Missing', calling the song "at once sumptuous and austere, the kind of rarerified [*sic*] and confounding experience we'd ceased hoping for from pop these days."

For 'Enjoy The Silence' no less than seven* different remixed musical versions were made available to the British record-buying public as of February 5, 1990. In addition, the releases featured two distinct Gore-penned instrumental B-sides: 'Memphisto' on both the 7″ and limited-edition 12″ as well as the cassette-single, and 'Sibling' on the 12″ and CD single. 'Enjoy The Silence (Harmonium)' – as featured on the limited-edition 12″ and CD singles – constituted Gore's "very basic" demo with the songwriter singing against a sparse, organ-based chordal accompaniment.

Alan Wilder: "Most DM songs changed tempo to some degree from the original demo, although none I can think of have been that extreme."

If Depeche Mode's loyal fans were confused by the numerous configurations, it didn't show in the single's sales, for 'Enjoy The Silence' turned out to be the crossover record that had eluded Depeche Mode for so long. Not only did it reach number six on the UK chart by February 17, but more remarkably, it scooped the charitable BRIT (British Recording Industry Trust) Award for 'Single Of The Year', as voted by BBC Radio 1 listeners, "a bizarre achievement in itself considering DM's 'see-saw' relationship with the radio audiences in their own country," noted one observer. The band voted with their feet by boycotting the event.

Alan Wilder: "We were all pretty like-minded about avoiding industry-based ceremonies – best left to Sting and Elton."

No doubt the single's success was helped by Anton Corbijn's accompanying promo video – shot, for a change, in colour.

Dave Gahan: " 'Enjoy The Silence' was Anton at his best."

Andy Fletcher: "We went into a studio and Anton said, 'This is only going to take a while,' and we said, 'Yeah, yeah . . . this is going to take all day.' And after half-an-hour he said, 'Right, you can go home now,' so we thought, 'Great!' Then poor old Dave had six days of filming in freezing conditions!"

---

* Consisting 7″, 12″, limited-edition 12″, 'extra' limited-edition 12″ sharing the same four remixes of the title track as the CD single, limited-edition CD single and 'extra' limited-edition CD single.

Those "freezing conditions" left a lasting impression on Gahan: "We spent about a week filming that [video]. It was quite hard work, but it was a lot of fun. And I got to dress up as a king, with a crown and everything. We went to Portugal; we went to Scotland – Balmoral; we went to the French Alps. It was basically myself and Anton, and the producer – Richard Bell – travelling all over Europe.

"It was the right colour and the right picture to the music. He's worked well with Bono and U2, and I've always felt really comfortable with Anton. He gets me to do stuff in videos that no one else could do. Anton always says – and it's very flattering – that I'm the best actor he's ever worked with; I don't know how many actors he's actually worked with, but I don't want to make Bono jealous!

"There are shots in that video that weren't actually me. Towards the end of filming there was this one shot where I'd really had it – I just wanted to go back to the hotel. We had taken this helicopter, which we had on standby at the top of this mountain, and Anton wanted me to do this shot where I was, like, *way*, way, away. There was this beautiful scene; it was just all snow, and I'm, like, [tiny]. And so I just thought, 'You know what, Richard?' I took the crown off, and put it on his head; I took the robe off and put it on him, and said, 'You fucking do it!' I got in the helicopter and went down and had a cup of hot chocolate in the hotel!"

On February 27, 'Enjoy The Silence' was made available on 12″ vinyl, cassette maxi-single, plus jewel and slip cased CD singles. Once the likes of MTV put the video on strict rotation, the single breached the Hot 100 on April 14, 1990[*]; climbing to eight (the group's highest *Billboard* placing) in a staggering 24-week run. Better still, the single topped the Modern Rock Tracks Chart in a 12-week residency beginning on March 10. By then, Depeche Mode's Stateside standing was such that 'Dangerous', the B-side to 'Personal Jesus', enjoyed so much airplay in its own right on the same alternative chart, that it had peaked at number 13 two months previously.

Depeche Mode were now officially 'Big In America'; with the un-precedented publicity surrounding the March 1990 launch of *Violator*, they were about to get bigger . . .

---

[*] By which time Sire additionally issued a 7″ and cassette single.

22

Stadium Synth Stars

"There's still this cult feeling. No matter how big we [seemed] to get, I always felt –
even when we played stadium shows – that there was a kind of intimacy."

– Martin Gore, 2001

"Yesterday in Los Angeles, British band Depeche Mode broke all previous records when they made an appearance at one of the biggest record stores in the world. Some 5,000 fans had camped outside the store for four days with the queue extending for nearly two miles. By the time the band arrived, there were more than 17,000 screaming fans outside, with The Beverly Center opposite invaded by fans trying to get a better view. The LAPD closed down the event after 90 minutes because they felt the band's lives were in danger. 200 police units, including helicopters and mounted officers in full riot gear, tried to calm the fans down. Eventually, the police moved the band out of their hotel under escort. The police chief told us, 'This is our biggest police operation since the Presidential visit.' "

The band's ill-fated signing at the Wherehouse record store on La Cienega Boulevard, Los Angeles, resulted in several fans being hospitalised with minor injuries. The following day on KROQ, Richard Blade announced that Daniel Miller would be pressing up 25,000 copies of an exclusive recording of rare interviews and previously unreleased material for all the fans who were not able to get into the Wherehouse. "They'll go to anyone who sends in a stamped self-addressed envelope to KROQ from the LA area," the ever-supportive DJ stated. "That shows how devoted the band is to their fans, and that's why their fans stick with them. They always go that extra mile for them."

Of course, the feeling was reciprocated, as *Spin* magazine highlighted the lengths that some of Depeche Mode's fanatical followers were prepared to go to. Take, for instance, "typical Valley girl" Kelly, who, with

325 Depeche Mode albums to her (then–15-year-old) name, was cited as being "one of their biggest collectors in the US, possibly the world," and was purportedly prepared to consider sacrificing her life for the group!

At the time of *Spin*'s 'Pop a la Mode' feature, 20-year-old DJ Danny (a.k.a. 'The Brat') had just crafted a 56-minute danceable "mega–mix" of Mode faves: "I first got into them when 'Master And Servant' came out – not so much for the sexually provocative tone of the song, but for its ahead–of–its–time techno dance groove. I'm not a big house [music] fan, but I do like industrial dance music, and, to me, they really lead the way." (Ultimately, 'The Brat' would become Webmaster of the official Depeche Mode website.)

Spin sought Blade's professional view on the band's US upsurge. "Their music just hits kids right between the eyes. They can relate to Martin's songs because he doesn't write about love in the way, say, [schmaltzy American singer/songwriter] Richard Marx does, who comes up with 'I love you, I lost you, I'm sad.' Martin is about angst, about teenage love when it feels like the end of the world; [when] you're so self-conscious that when somebody looks at you the wrong way, it can be devastating."

Like *Music For The Masses* before it, *Violator* entered the *Billboard* Top 100 Albums Chart a mere 18 days after its March 20, 1990 release; unlike *Music For The Masses*, it retained its residency for an overwhelming 74 weeks by which time Depeche Mode had completed the 88-date World Violation Tour, by far their most successful to date.

Nashville would be strangely absent from the opening 44-date US leg of the touring itinerary, however.

Alan Wilder: "The one and only Nashville concert we ever played [at the Ryman Auditorium on May 24, 1988] was well received, but had the lowest turnout of any show on the whole [Music For The Masses] tour; I suppose this was the reason why it wasn't high on our agenda to return. It's not the local DM fans' fault; it's just that Nashville seems to have such a one-dimensional music scene."

Fortunately, that wasn't the case elsewhere in America . . .

While some earlier Depeche Mode tours featured recycled backing tracks, they were reworked from scratch for the World Violation Tour – for example, 'Behind The Wheel' segued into 'Route 66' in what Alan Wilder jokingly termed "true cabaret style". "The World Violation Tour [16-track backing] tapes were prepared at Worldwide International – Mute's studio – mainly by myself, with [*Violator* engineer] Steve Lyon," Wilder explained.

Thereafter, the band, their road crew (including a wardrobe person for *each* band member), and a vast stage set – designed by newly appointed 'visual director' Anton Corbijn (featuring, for the first time, video screens to project the Dutchman's films) – was shipped out to sunny Florida to begin rehearsals.

Alan Wilder: "We were always aware that three blokes stuck primarily behind keyboards would never really make for a dynamic show, and, to this day, much of the performance rests upon Dave's shoulders. Even in the early days, with a very simple line-up of keyboards and tape machine (which used to sit in the middle of the stage), we tried to incorporate background changes and unusual lighting. Inevitably, the production became more elaborate as the venue sizes increased and it was obvious that we needed to supplement the show with extra interest to really come across – hence the more elaborate stage sets and, later, the film shows. The films enhanced the production to such an extent that it was impossible to remove the use of them once established. By the time of the World Violation Tour we were taking 11 articulated lorries and a crew close to 100."

The World Violation Tour kicked off at Pensacola's 10,000-seat Civic Center on May 28; the first time Depeche Mode had performed in the Sunshine State with three 15,000-plus-sized Florida shows following. Atlanta, Georgia, was followed by the *pièce de résistance* of two consecutive sell-out shows at the 80,000-capacity Giants Stadium in East Rutherford, New Jersey, home to the New York Giants American football team. 42,000 tickets had reportedly sold within four hours of going on sale!

Violator producer Flood was blown away at the sheer scale of the spectacle: "I remember going to see them in Giants Stadium, and they broke the merchandising record; of Bon Jovi, U2 – all these bands – Depeche Mode were the biggest!"

It was the same story on the opposite coast as KABC 7's *Eyewitness News* presenter Francesca Cappucci reported when covering the Brit sensation's August 1 return to the station's broadcasting base: "It's difficult for Depeche Mode to do anything subtle because of the passion their fans have for them. The last time that the band was in town to launch the release of their new record, *Violator*, 15,000 [*sic*] fans showed up and the scene became dangerous because so many turned out. Well, Depeche Mode is back, this time for a series of concerts. Two Dodgers Stadium shows were instant sell-outs."

48,000 tickets were sold within half-an-hour for what was originally the final US date of the World Violation Tour at the 56,000-capacity Dodgers Stadium, home of the LA Dodgers baseball team, on August 4 – and this occurred two months *before* the gig! Within 72 hours, a second perform-ance was scheduled for the following day, which also promptly sold out, news of which was reported – albeit in an aside – by British broadsheet, *The Guardian*: "The highpoint of their current tour, a relatively short jaunt of six months, were two LA gigs in front of a total audience of 110,000."

A confident Depeche Mode held a televised press conference in Los Angeles following three consecutive sold-out shows at the 13,000-seat San Diego Sports Arena. When asked why they decided to play in the more intimate surroundings of the 6,300-seat Universal Amphitheater immedi-ately prior to the colossal Dodgers Stadium outings, a tanned Dave Gahan, sporting America's trademark Aviator sunglasses and a black vest exposing increasingly tattooed arms, replied: "We did the same in New York when we played Giants Stadium; we played Radio City [Music Hall] as well, just to do a gig in a smaller place just for a completely different atmosphere. In fact, I found it a lot more nervy doing that than doing the stadium gigs, because you're right on top of everyone – you can see everyone's face."

A more casually attired Alan Wilder added: "It was actually quite diffi-cult to try and distribute tickets fairly, because there is a scalping problem that I'm sure a lot of people are aware of – people buy them in bulk and then a lot of people miss out. So we had to try and figure out a way to dis-tribute tickets fairly."

Talk then shifted to Depeche Mode's self-managerial status and associ-ated insistence on having complete artistic control over all aspects of their career. Alan Wilder: "It *is* complicated, but luckily we are able to allocate roles, and they've sort of emerged, really, rather than being designated to each other. It's just [so] we don't tread on each other's toes too much when we're making music, and when we're doing the manager's job."

Dave Gahan: "Fletch [Andy Fletcher] takes on a lot of that sort of stuff . . ."

Cutting off his colleague, mid-flow, a bespectacled Fletcher joked: "Luckily, I'm not creative one bit!"

Alan Wilder: "There are times when it can be a bit of a pressure, partic-ularly when you're on the road and you have to make 20 different decisions about some really stupid things and some really important finan-cial things, and all that kind of thing. That pressure mounts up, and it can cause tension and stress, and all that stuff."

Dave Gahan: "I don't think we'd like it any other way."

Wilder recounted a typical day on the road with Depeche Mode, *circa*-1990: "For a band member in the US, for example: check out of hotel at 1 or 2 pm, travel to local airfield. Fly by private jet with immediate entourage (about 12 people) to next city. Arrive 4 pm, approx. Go straight to the gig for soundcheck. Back to hotel at 6 pm, quick sauna/workout, if there was time, leave for gig at 7.45 pm. Onstage 8.30/9 pm; off-stage 11 pm, followed by hospitality and night on the town until the early hours." . . . repeat 44 times!

The World Violation Tour took a three-week break before (re) packing its innumerable flightcases in readiness for the band's first Australian appearance at Sydney's Horden Pavilion on August 31.

Andy Fletcher: "That was a great trip east, but you get into a Catch-22 situation with your production and stuff, [because] they really haven't got the equipment there."

The production next set down in Japan for several dates, followed by a string of European shows, starting in Brussels on September 28. A month later, *NME*'s James Brown was agape during three consecutive performances at the Palais Omnisport De Bercy sports stadium in Paris where Depeche Mode played to a grand total of 50,000 people – three times the average First Division football crowd. Brown was granted an audience with Andy Fletcher inside "a hotel so expensive it didn't even look like a hotel!", but by now the excitement was waning for the keyboardist: "The irritating thing about this European [tour] is that we've played a lot of these halls six or seven times and it's always the same faces; there's not that sense of excitement we still get in America of playing somewhere new."

Then again, the tour was 64 dates into a slick show that remained virtually unchanged night after night, bar possibly Martin Gore's solo acoustic spot. "Even when Martin takes up a guitar and serenades us solo," observed Brown, "the fans accept it as pure Depeche and roar appreciatively as he gets as sensitive as a man who makes pop music from production line sound effects can be; in truth, the relentless shiny throb of Depeche's synthesisers gets a bit monotonous after a while, but they weren't playing it for me, they were playing it for the fans.

"When the band come on, the masses quit being merely excited and hit hysteria full on the jaw. The screaming audience are louder than the band. The combined effect of the screaming – and this isn't teen-screaming of the New Kids [On The Block] type, it's adult – the lighters, and the ridiculously hyped-up fans isn't just shocking, it's awesome. They don't need to be told 'Depeche Mode are big all over' – they saw it years ago. They're not hard up for attention, but it wouldn't be amiss for a band so successful worldwide to be given more consideration back home."

Fletcher summed up the group's uneasy relationship with Britain when asked whether Depeche Mode would go down in history: "In other countries we certainly will – especially Germany and the Eastern Bloc; in England we're more hated than liked. [That] is the only country we've got a history in, you see, because in the first two or three years we produced our worst records; we were at our most famous and at our sickliest. We smiled in every photo, we were in *Smash Hits* every week, and people still remember that. They also think we went from that to doom and gloom, so there's these two extreme views of Depeche Mode in England – we're either pop, or doom and gloom, but we're actually both!"

Fletcher went on to explain the origin of the album's title: "We called it *Violator* because we wanted a very heavy metal title. The last album, *Music For The Masses*, was another sarcastic title which no one understood; it doesn't really matter because we know we're being sarcastic. The Germans especially didn't get *Music For The Masses* at all, because over there we really *are* music for the masses, and they don't understand sarcasm – they were saying, 'Oh, so what is this? You are making commercial music?' I think people miss the humour in the band, because unless you're a real devotee you don't look that seriously at groups, you just glance at a video on *Top Of The Pops* and make a snap decision about whether you like it or not."

"With the current musical climate settling so far into electronically produced music," began Helen Mead, writing for *NME* two days before the March 19, 1990 UK release of *Violator*, "it's very hard to think of anything in this genre as being other than House music or clanging Front 242 New Beat bastards, but that, of course, is forgetting Depeche Mode, who – in terms of new product – have been off the scene since '87's *Music For The Masses*, a lush, dense escapade into the world of grandiose pop songs.

"So *Violator* – a preposterous title for a Heavy Metal album or a hardcore porn comic – either way Radio 1 won't ban it – just titter wryly, 'cos Depeche Mode are nice boys and thankfully don't seem to have anything to do with drugs – *or* the Acid House scene! The nearest Depeche Mode ever get to being trippy is on their version of Tangerine Dream's [*sic*] 'Clean'."*

---

* Actually, that closing comment was not as strange as it might first have read, for the menacing, mid-paced, pounding drum pattern of 'Clean' bore more than a passing resemblance to 'Darkness', performed by the German synthmeisters on the 1985 soundtrack to Ridley Scott's *Legend*.

Melody Maker's Paul Lester's review of March 10 hardly started promisingly: "Depeche Mode have always been the poor relation of New Order and Kraftwerk, offering pedestrian, sometimes inconsequential variations on the electro-pop theme . . . *Violator*, their seventh studio album, contains Depeche Mode's most arresting work to date. Surprisingly, they are presently judged by Detroit and Chicago's House cognoscenti as prime movers in the new dance culture – not that Depeche Mode have made an Acid [house] record.

"Whereas House is notoriously anonymous music, the identity of this unit is patently obvious from the opening synthetic rush of 'World In My Eyes'. In a recent interview, Dave Gahan described the sound the band [was] aiming for on *Violator* as future blues, to establish a modernist setting for traditional, hard-edged blues chord progressions. 'Sweetest Perfection' and 'Clean' are the standout examples of this experiment here, the gadgetry and fuss of early Mode clatter such as 'Just Can't Get Enough' pared down to the barest essentials, Gahan's voice brutally upfront in the mix . . .* *Violator* is black and dark and not a little vicious."

Describing 'World In My Eyes', Gore revealed more of his inner self by proclaiming, "It's a very positive song; it's saying that love and sex and pleasure are positive things . . . I'm probably as influenced by [Albert] Camus, [Franz] Kafka and [Bertolt] Brecht as I am pop music. I *do* write this stuff for a reason."

Whether the average Depeche Mode fan shared Gore's fascination with existentialism was academic; on account of the success of 'Enjoy The Silence', Depeche Mode only just missed out on chart-topping territory as *Violator* ascended to number 2 on the UK Albums Chart.

The album's Anton Corbijn-designed cover featured a vast swathe of darkness offset by a bright red rose motif, variations of which were also featured in the 'Enjoy The Silence' artwork and video. *Record Mirror*'s Tim Nicholson was impressed: "With *Violator*, they have fashioned a veritable dungeon of songs for you to jangle your manacles to. 'World In My Eyes' is at the cellar door and is the perfect introduction to this compromise between pop music and something a little more sinister. There are no noises out of place in this perfectly formed void; the songs are like bright stars in a black sky, or silver studs on a soft black leather jacket. The wonder is that the more they strip it down, the bigger they get."

---

* It was Martin Gore who sang lead on 'Sweetest Perfection' and also on the self-proclaimed "pervy song", 'Blue Dress'.

In America, this was definitely the case, but on the British front, it seemed like Depeche Mode had arrived at the indoor arena plateau in 1986.

Before completing the opening US leg of the World Violation Tour, a third single was extracted from *Violator*. 'Policy Of Truth', with its many hidden layers of interweaving sonic imagery, could hardly be described as having a stripped down sound; indeed, it had gone through numerous recorded revisions before being included on the album.

Alan Wilder: "Usually this would signify problems with a song, although in this case we knew it was a strong track – not least a potential single. The main riff of the song proved such a problem to get a sound for, and we must have tried 100 different variations before settling on what had become perhaps the sound of the album – slide guitar." (In a first for Depeche Mode, Nils Tuxen, an outside session musician was employed, playing pedal steel guitar on 'Clean'.)

'Policy Of Truth' was first released in the UK on May 7.* The stripped back, trance-like 'Policy Of Truth (Trancentral Mix)' by the KLF – the 1991 chart-topping ambient/techno duo of Bill Drummond and Jimmy Cauty – was particularly notable as displaced snippets of Gahan's vocal vied for attention alongside birdsong, sheep, ringing telephones and a raving, Cockney accent intoning, *"I'm not a politician; I'm a businessman!"*

By May 19, 'Policy Of Truth' had peaked in the UK at number 16; perhaps due to its familiarity from the *Violator* album. Invariably, the limited releases catered only to Depeche completionists for whom the various remixes proved irresistible, as did Gore's instrumental B-side, 'Kaleid' (pronounced *collide*), recorded at Mute's Worldwide International studio in London, and mixed at Konk studios by Daniel Miller and one George Holt.

The single fared marginally better Stateside following its May 22 release on 12", maxi-cassette and CD maxi-singles†. 'Policy Of Truth' débuted on the *Billboard* chart on August 11, reaching 15 during a 16-week run.

Anton Corbijn returned to his monochrome filming habit to produce a suitably provocative promo in which a lascivious lass is seen cavorting with

* This time with five different mixes spread over six formats (7", 12" and limited-edition 12" vinyl; cassette single; and CD and limited-edition CD singles.
† Accompanied by additional 7" and cassette single releases as of July 24.

each band member in and around various New York City locations.

Melody Maker reviewer Jon Wilde wrote in the May 5 edition: "The runt of the litter from *Violator*, this lardy, lugubrious marathon of mixing-desk tics has been remixed by François Kervorkian; well, François, old pal, you're a tosser in anyone's language."

Between finishing up at Tokyo's Budokan on September 12, and starting a run of 38 European dates at Brussels' Forest National on the 28th of that month, a fourth single was taken from *Violator*.

Alan Wilder: " 'World In My Eyes' had, in fact, been recorded very early on during the Milan sessions [at Logic Studios] and, perhaps, for this reason, displayed familiar Depeche elements linking it with previous albums. It was completed in London, and, with its 'drop' third verse and use of vocal double-tracking to fill out and build the later choruses, was probably the most electro sounding track on the LP – something of a homage to Kraftwerk, in a rhythmical sense at least."

This time, *NME* were quick to pick up on the Düsseldorf connection: "One of the true pluses of Depeche Mode's rise and rise is that their urge to experiment has not dissolved as they stare ever-deeper into the great black hole of the American mainstream. Taking many soundcues from Kraftwerk, they and their posse of appointed master-mixers are surpassing themselves. No sign here of a shift to black dance patterns, but, then again, no need."

A similar chart fate awaited 'World In My Eyes'[*] following its September 17 tactical release on the usual six formats. As well as six remixes of the title track, two previously unreleased Martin Gore songs, 'Happiest Girl' and 'Sea Of Sin' were controlled by Kervorkian's heavy remixing hand at New York City's Axis Studios.

Alan Wilder: " 'Happiest Girl' was recorded during the making of the LP and was subsequently relegated to a B-side having originally been earmarked for inclusion on the album; 'Sea Of Sin' was always a B-side and recorded afterwards. I'm not mad on either track, to be honest."

'World In My Eyes' was bolstered by a Corbijn promo video, using slowed down colour footage of various performance excerpts from the ongoing World Violation Tour. Gone were the on-stage metal-bashing

---

[*] 'World In My Eyes' reached 17 on the UK Singles Chart on September 29. By contrast, it stalled at 52 on *Billboard* and 17 on the Modern Rock Tracks Chart, for a four-week duration.

antics of yesteryear; visual interest was maintained courtesy of Gore's more regular guitar-playing and the monstrous modular system positioned behind Wilder with its intriguing set of red LEDs blinking sequentially, Tangerine Dream-style. (Without any obvious patchwork of protruding cables, the vintage synth's presence was purely for show.)

A video *Strange Too* (released in November) purported to be about "Depeche Mode, life, love and lust, and getting closer to all four."

According to *Melody Maker*'s Caroline Sullivan, that translated "as six arty clips featuring deckchairs ['Enjoy The Silence'], adobe huts ['Halo'], *Mean Streets* cityscapes ['Policy Of Truth'], and the Depeches looking grim and preoccupied [throughout]. The incessant flow of colours and images in each vid – the songs are DM's last four singles ['Personal Jesus', 'Enjoy The Silence', 'Policy Of Truth' and 'World In My Eyes'], plus two tracks ['Clean' and 'Halo'] from the *Violator* album – seem to have been chosen for their visual impact rather than for any relation to a song, so watching is a pleasantly surreal experience. This Anton Corbijn-directed collection is a nice demonstration of what you can accomplish with a Super 8 camera."

Also in November, 'Halo' made it to number 21 on America's Modern Rock Tracks Chart. Although an album-only track, at one point, as Alan Wilder recalled, the song was considered for release in its own right: "As for [*Violator*-era] singles, 'Halo' was on a shortlist, but was never really a contender. We ended up using it in a roundabout way by making a video – as well as one for 'Clean' – to fill out the *Strange Too* compilation."

'Halo' saw Depeche Mode returning to the baking heat of a Californian desert, much to Andy Fletcher's initial dismay: "That was the least fun to shoot, because it was the last one, and by then it was during the tour and we were totally wacked out. Anton said, 'We'll need you for two days' – the usual thing, but actually we were really pleased with that video in the end. It seemed to suit [the song]."

Martin Gore preferred his screen role in 'Clean'; perfectly understandable, given it's 'difficult' storyboarding: "Basically, I just had to spend an afternoon kissing some girl in her underwear. That's just about the best video I've ever made!"

Depeche Mode arrived back on their home turf in November 1990 to perform six sold-out shows shared equally between Birmingham's NEC and London's Wembley Arena – with a total of 70,000 attendees bringing in takings approaching seven figures.

Alan Wilder: "With a touring business as large as ours, it can take anything up to two years to tie up all the accounts, pay taxes and make a proper financial distribution of profits to the directors – just like any other business, in fact."

Melody Maker's Paul Lester reviewed the latest live spectacle: "When Fast Fashion shoot down to Wembley Arena from the planet Basildon, it's like Madonna and Janet Jackson never happened – like maybe Depeche Mode are about to become the biggest Revenge Of The Normals mega-platinum attraction since that bunch from Merseyside a few years back. When Depeche Mode materialise, with quartz-precision, at nine o'clock on this testicle-refrigerating Monday night, and 12,000 believers wail, stomp, clap, squeal and generally tear clumps out of their eyeballs, it occurs that – for one teeny, weeny, reason – their cult of the diamond geezer is several trillion light years removed from the likes of Ocean Flowered Turtles. *Depeche Mode are enormous* . . .

" 'Personal Jesus' inspires an astonishing display of audience participation, wherein every single last person in the Arena holds their arms aloft and chants *'Reach out and touch faith!'* The anti-religious icon point of the song is lost so massively on the crowd it almost scores on the rebound, and their dunderhead will-to-power, glassy-eyed submission takes on a fascistic beauty that only those who are present can appreciate."

The British dailies turned out in force to investigate the Basildon phenomenon. In reviewing the November 19 Wembley show, *The Independent*'s Giles Smith dryly picked up on Corbijn's unsubtle visual contribution: "Halfway through, they throw down the gauntlet by including a film sequence, beamed onto screens at the rear of the stage, in which a hand was seen painting the word 'clean' on a wall. The camera held steady while the graffiti dripped: at which point the audience was, quite literally, being asked to entertain itself by watching paint dry.*

"In front of some more film footage – this time featuring a slowly blossoming rose-bud – [Martin Gore] ran through two ballads on the

---

* U2 later effectively incorporated Corbijn's film footage into their own increasingly elaborate stage setting, prompting a flurry of accusations from Depeche Mode's ardent fanbase that the Irish stadium stars had copied the workings of Depeche Mode's World Violation stage set. Alan Wilder: "Correct me if I'm wrong, but I don't think Anton was involved in any of U2's stage designs, whereas he was very closely linked to ours."

theme of burning up inside and worrying about the emptiness of every-thing in 'a world full of nothing'; the overall plangency was somewhat tempered by the kind of delivery which you would be hard pushed to forgive, even coming from a busker: his voice wandered away into alter-native keys during the high bits, while his hands mashed away at the strings as if he was wearing a pair of Pyrex gloves – it made you long for the musical warmth which only machines can generate."

Adam Sweeting (*The Guardian*): "The final section of the show was akin to a celebration, if 'Clean' or the lugubrious 'Never Let Me Down Again' could be thus described; 'Personal Jesus' certainly could, as Gore thrashed at his guitar to bring the Mode as close as they've ever come to Status Quo; busty cowgirls adorned the back-projection as the Mode swaggered moodily by in cowboy hats – electropop with jokes? Revolutionary, my dear Watson."

Jasper Rees (*The Times*): "Depeche Mode reconstruct a thin slice of the past with machine precision, mainly because they have the machines to help them; if it were not that he was evidently a ghost inside one of said machines, the drummer would have to be marked down as a hard worker in the band . . .

"A genuine instrument, it should be reported, was sighted during song-writer Martin Gore's acoustic interlude. One sensed that he made too much of the moment as if to let the audience know that it really was him pulling the strings. He stepped forward again in 'Enjoy The Silence', one of a clutch of lugubrious songs the band performed from the new album *Violator*. Tantalising us with the hitherto remote possibility of a bona fide solo, he opted instead to treat his curvaceous instrument as a dance partner. To most members of a full house high on the excitement improb-ably whipped up by Depeche Mode's identikit brand of electropop, the symbolism of the moment would not have counted for much."

In an article published in *The Guardian* (November 15), Bruce Dessau conceded the synthesiser "may not ooze the glamour of flesh-and-blood instruments" on-stage, but its "creative potential is greater."

Martin Gore: "We've always placed quite a lot of importance on playing live, and I think we really helped to make people realise that elec-tronic music was powerful and did work in a live environment," the savvy songwriter reflected in 1998. "And now it's accepted that bands like The Prodigy have great live shows."

Dave Gahan: "We probably in some way helped people to get over the idea that it [electronic music] wasn't 'real' music. That kind of label was stuck to us for a while – it's not *real* music, which is silly."

When Dessau persuaded him to list his 'Top 10' lyrical themes of the moment, Gore self-consciously replied, "Relationships, domination, lust, love, good, evil, incest, sin, religion, immorality."

The 88-date World Violation Tour finished up at the Birmingham NEC on November 27. Alan Wilder's summary put paid to *NME*'s earlier observation about those "nice [Depeche Mode] boys": "I wouldn't say the tour was any more intense than at many other times. We were on a high, because of the success – particularly in the US; tickets were selling like hotcakes, and we were enjoying ourselves.

"There was a lot of ecstasy around, but [I] couldn't say that anybody was adversely affected by that. Apparently, Dave was using heroin, but this wasn't obvious in his performances, and there was the usual amount of drinking and frivolity. It was a long tour, and maybe there was a delayed reaction with the cracks appearing later – perhaps when it dawned on us that expectations had risen, and we would have to try and follow *Violator*."

Just prior to heading off on the World Violation Tour Dave Gahan was holed up for a day in a luxurious suite at the Kensington Hilton International, to face a long line of European journalists.

"I'm a family man now," Gahan told *Melody Maker*'s Jon Wilde. "I like to go back home and be with my wife and little boy, going about everyday things like everyone else. That may seem pretty boring, but a lot of people have this idea that pop stars lead this life of Riley where they're out on the razz every night – that just ain't the fucking case!"

Robert Marlow: "Martin used to ring up from wherever he was – often pissed, because he's always had a problem with the old suds – saying something like, 'We're in the back of a limo; we're in Detroit!' This would usually be in the middle of the night, and I'd say, 'Oh yeah? Right. Are you having fun? What's happening?' And he'd say, 'You wouldn't *believe* what's going on!' And there I was, lying there, due at work in a couple of hours!"

Fame evidently had its bonuses, but for the 29-year-old Gahan, a married father, it was weighing heavily on his shoulders. By the time the tour ended, he had changed from the home-loving individual (as he'd described himself) to one who had walked away from his wife and child in search of a different life, effectively mirroring his own father's destructive behaviour, some 25 painful years earlier.

"Moving away opens your mind," he told *Melody Maker*'s Jennifer Nine. "I needed to get out. I felt trapped by everything that was around me. The last go round [tour] was great, we had a lot of success and *Violator* was huge round the world – and I should have been on top of the world, and I wasn't. I had everything I could possibly want, but I was really lost. I didn't even feel like I knew myself anymore. And I felt like shit, 'cos I constantly cheated on my wife, and went back home and lied, and my soul needed cleansing. I had to figure out why."

It wasn't only his soul that needed cleansing. "After the [World Violation . . .] tour ended, I spent a few months in London and that's where my habit got completely out of hand," Gahan told *Q*'s Phil Sutcliffe in 1999.

"I just packed a bag and split; went off and rented a place in Los Angeles," he confessed to Nine. "During the *Violator* tour I split with my wife. My [next] year was really spent doing a lot of soul-searching and trying to find out what had gone wrong with my life, and thinking, to be quite honest, about whether I wanted to come back and do the whole thing – records, tours, fame, Depeche Mode – again. Just tearing myself away from everything that I had really grown up with and known, including my wife at the time, and my young son, Jack, as well . . . all that stuff was quite painful to me."

Looking back, the more mature and world-wise 39-year-old of 2001 was able to reassess that heartbreaking experience with a greater sense of clarity: "[Leaving Jack] was something that I greatly regret. [At the time] that was always tormenting me; it was like I was walking away from something that really was a part of me, and I really wanted to nurture [him] in my life. I guess I felt fucked up over that for a while – trying to drown the feelings [of guilt]. But I spent more time drowning [those] feelings than actively getting off my ass and doing something, which would have been the right thing to do at the time, instead of just whinging."

Having positioned himself over 5,000 miles away from his five-year-old son and heir, Dave cementing the move by taking up with the vivacious Teresa Conroy who, according to the Internet Movie Database, had appeared in several hardcore pornographic films under the name of 'Terri' before accompanying the band across America as Press Liaison officer on the 1988 and 1990 treks. Looking back at his rash American move, Gahan admitted, "I fell in love with a girl during what was the *Violator* tour, [so] there was that, and I always wanted to [live there] – I brought up the idea of moving to California and trying something different."

"I was really bored and really safe," Gahan told *The Times*' Paul

Connolly, in 2001. "I felt really safe in my life in England in lots of ways, and I didn't like it. There I was with a loving, caring wife, a new baby, a big house in the country, a couple of cars in the drive, and it just didn't feel right. I wanted to move to California, but Joanne didn't want to."

Gahan's anguish was further compounded by his estranged father's untimely death. "My dad died in 1990, and after that I got a bit curious about him and asked my mum about him. I think he liked a drink. She only had a couple of pictures of him, but one of them was of him in a pub. I thought, 'Yeah, that's my old man alright.'

"I think what happened there was [that] I was very distrusting of myself, and my own abilities to judge what was good for me or not. I've always had trust issues, and I didn't realise that stemmed from the fact that I probably didn't trust myself. I wouldn't say that was to do with the family; it was just inherently in me from when I was a little kid.

"I never really felt comfortable when I lived in England – a nice house in the country, a couple of cars in the drive; it didn't feel like it was me. So I think a lot of that [move to California] was to do with me really soul-searching – kind of searching for some kind of relevance to myself: why I'm here; what I'm doing . . . what are we *all* doing?

"I wouldn't say I was 100 per cent comfortable in either [situation] – I definitely needed family and stability, but I was always itching to get out and play. Somewhere along the line – especially after all my antics during the late-Eighties and early-Nineties, I found a way to keep both and do both."

PART V

Synths, Drugs & Rock'n'Roll!

"The whole kind of rock 'n' roll lifestyle . . . what we think that is . . . when you actually live it, and you try to live it – everyday, it's really fucking tiring!"

– Dave Gahan, 2001

23

Hopelessly Devoted

"Dave went off to live in LA after the [World Violation . . .] tour, and by the time we reconvened after a significant break to begin working on Songs Of Faith And Devotion*, things had certainly changed."*

– Alan Wilder, 2001

Way out west, Dave Gahan got swept up in the 'American dream': a large house in the Hollywood hills; the quintessential 'dream machine' – a powerful Harley-Davidson motorcycle . . . the whole enchilada. "It definitely was [more comfortable] for me in Los Angeles," he stated. "I fell quickly into that lifestyle, and, for a while, it was great fun."

Free to lead what he later termed as a "very selfish lifestyle", Gahan partied harder than ever; partly thanks to new partner Teresa Conroy's music biz connections, he was welcomed with open arms into LA's established rock fraternity, a select group for whom drug taking, if not necessarily heroin addiction, was almost *de rigueur* – a dangerous place for a wealthy individual in a highly strung emotional state to inhabit. As the singer said, "I could be falling over myself, but I'd still get in anywhere I wanted to go: 'It's David, it's David! Come on in, David; here's a booth – can we get you any special requirements?' 'Well, yeah, actually!' "

In April 1992, following what was reported by the British tabloid press as being a "messy, year-long divorce", Gahan finally tied the knot with Teresa Conroy. Like Gahan, Conroy was also a heroin user, someone he later termed as being ". . . a partner I could play with, in all sorts of ways, without being judged, because she was joining in. In fact, she didn't *make* me take heroin; [but] she gave me the opportunity to try it again. We made a pact early on that I'd never use intravenously; but, of course, [with me] being a junkie and a liar, it didn't take long."

The nuptials took place in the somewhat tawdry surroundings of the

Graceland Chapel at 619 Las Vegas Boulevard, South Las Vegas, with an obligatory Elvis Presley impersonator acting as guest of honour.*

"Of course, everything was plastic – false," Dave confirmed to Jennifer Nine. "They wouldn't even light the candles in the chapel, 'cos they were just there for show. We were a little upset! And they had a fake Elvis who we *thought* was just going to sing one song, but ended up doing about a half-hour set. In the end, I had to say, 'Will someone get him the fuck out of here? I want to get married!' And so Teresa's mum, Diane, sort of politely said, 'Um, excuse, Mr Elvis, do you think you could stop, 'cos I think they want to get married.' And so *he* says, 'We-ell, I've just got one more song, darlin'.' And he leans over to me and asks, 'Have I offended you in some way?' And I say, 'No, just carry on with it, mate; get it done and get out!' "

None of Gahan's bandmates were present for the inauspicious occasion – even if they had been, chances are they would barely have recognised the rake thin physical parody of an archetypal American rockstar pushing 30, standing at the altar. Unsurprisingly, neither was his ex-wife or son. *Daily Mirror* columnist Rick Sky, the man who had helped turn Vince Clarke into a recluse a decade earlier, quoted the remarried Gahan as saying: "My dad left me and my young sister when we were very young and I've done the same to Jack. I was with Joanne for a long time, and we're great friends, but what happened was 90 per cent my fault. But I'm determined to see Jack as much as I can. Thankfully, Joanne understands."

While Gahan divided time (and money) between his Tinseltown playground and his riverside flat in Wapping, shared with Daryl Bamonte, Gore, Fletcher, and Wilder heard little – and saw even less – of their errant vocalist. Meanwhile, Daniel Miller provided a sympathetic shoulder for the confused Gahan to lean on when, during the infrequent London visits, the singer toyed with throwing in the towel. "Several times when I'd hit London, mostly to see Jack, my son, I'd go out to dinner with him, and he'd say, 'Look, I know you're going through a lot of stuff at the moment, but you've got to keep going and you've got to keep pushing.' "

* At the time of writing, a so-called 'King's Package' was listed at $495 (including chapel, witness and music, bridal cascade bouquet and *boutonniere* for groom, floral spray or corsage for brides-maid, *boutonniere* for best man, 24 colour photographs, videotape of wedding ceremony, garter for bride, two T-shirts, two champagne glasses with complimentary champagne, and certificate holder; not forgetting, of course, the crowning *pièce de résistance* . . . an entertaining Elvis. If it was good enough for Jon Bon Jovi, it was good enough for Dave Gahan.

It was during one of those meetings that Miller recognised the extent of Gahan's drug use: "I hadn't seen him for a while – he was living in the States; it had been a break period – then he came over to England for some reason and came into my office to say hello, and he looked terrible. He'd lost stones in weight. He used to do this great impersonation of a rock casualty – really funny, but he fell into the character, and that was when I first realised."

When later probed by *Q*'s Phil Sutcliffe as to *why* he had started taking heroin, Gahan said: "Well, it's no secret [that] I've been drinking and using drugs for a long time – probably since I was about 12; popping a couple of my mum's phenobarbitones every now and then; hash; amphetamines; coke came along. Alcohol was always there, hand in hand with drugs. Then all of a sudden I discovered heroin, and I'd be lying if I said it didn't make me feel like I've never felt before. I'd actually played around with it [heroin] back in Basildon, but from the moment I first injected I wanted to feel like that all the time and you can't. After a few months I was always chasing that high and I never found it again. I was just maintaining a very sad existence. On schedule, I'd start shaking – in the morning, in the afternoon, in the evening; I needed my fix."

Miller confirmed that drug-taking was not new to the Essex contingent: "I think people have the right to do whatever they want – up to a point, but I just think that creatively more often than not it has a negative attitude. It affects so many people in so many different ways that you can't really have a general philosophy about it. But, especially when they [Depeche Mode] were much younger, I felt kind of protective towards them a little bit – I'd met their parents and everything; I felt like I was their chaperone, in a sense. But they were using drugs before I met them, as kids in Essex are [prone to doing], so it wasn't something that happened when they started becoming famous.

"The thing is, they knew my attitude towards drugs, so they were always careful about doing anything in front of me. It wasn't much [a part] of their life in the studio, to be honest, but on the road, it became increasingly evident that it was. I felt that it had become a real problem when I saw Dave at that moment."

The World Violation Tour had garnered a reputation as having been a hedonistic, substance-fuelled affair.

Martin Gore: "There were different levels of debauchery for all the different members of the band. I think I was worse on the World

Violation Tour – there was a lot of ecstasy still lying around. We used to go out all the time and take quite a lot."

Andy Fletcher: "Ecstasy has never been my choice of drug – most people under the age of 40 have tried it. But, you never know, I could be Prime Minister one day; I just tasted it and spat it out again!"

It was an exhausted Gore who holed up at his Harpenden home at the conclusion of the World Violation Tour with his pregnant Texan girlfriend, Suzanne Boizvert, whom he had met in Paris.

Around this time, Gore was understandably shocked at the revelation that the man he had always thought was his father was, in fact, his stepfather. "Martin rang me up one day in a fair old lava," an old school friend revealed, "but with Martin you have to wait until you get to a point where you can say, 'So, what's happened?' And he said Suzanne was carrying their first child, Viva Lee. And then he said, 'You're not going to believe this, but my old man's a black man!' Basically, Martin's mum went out with this guy – they weren't married – and Martin was the offshoot of it all.

"But the strange thing about it was that his nickname at school was 'Curly' – because of his curly locks . . . and he's got a big, long, brown nob. We used to go swimming at school, and getting changed you'd think, 'Fucking hell! That ain't the same colour as mine!' Anyway, the only reason Martin's mum told him [about his biological father] was that Suzanne, who's a white Texan, was having his baby, and she didn't want them to have a little black baby and not know about it."

While Gore remained ostensibly Caucasian in appearance, there was the possibility of his parent's mixed race union having a profound physical effect on his own offspring. Viva Lee Gore was born on June 6, 1991; in the event, such concerns proved unfounded.

Gore's biological father had been an American GI stationed in the UK when he met Martin's mother with unplanned consequences. The same unnamed source reveals that although Martin did eventually meet his father, reading between the lines, it was not under pleasant circumstances: "He lived in a shotgun shack, somewhere in the Deep South. He still lived with his own father – 'Grand-pappy' – and I think there was an element of this guy having found his long-lost son, who was famous and very, very rich. I remember the last drunken conversation we had, and I said, 'Did you ever get in touch with your dad again?' and Martin said, 'No, it didn't work out in the end.'"

Gore's view on the matter was understandably curt: "It brings up family traumas; I can't believe that came out — it's one of those things I'd rather not talk about."

On a more positive note, Gore had commissioned the construction of a private recording studio, sited in a double garage attached to his seventeenth century Herefordshire home. Designed and built by Electric Eel Studio Design's Kevin van Green, it featured a custom cabinet housing three ARP 2600 synthesisers. Gareth Jones later visited the workspace, which he described as being "a pleasant, spacious room, with lots of daylight and a view of trees and countryside."

Meanwhile, Andy Fletcher and long-term girlfriend, Grainne Mullen, celebrated the birth of their first child, Megan, on August 25, 1991. Gore and Fletcher — once jokingly described as Tweedle-Dum and Tweedle-Dee by Robert Marlow with "their own sense of humour" — took advantage of their first serious break to adjust to a more family-orientated lifestyle.

Fletcher also opened a restaurant, Gascoigne's at 12 Latimer Terrace in North West London, a venture he later described as being: "A very small community restaurant; I don't publicise it at all. There's 15 or 16 staff, and 80 per cent of our customers are local people — as I only cook scrambled eggs, it's very difficult! It's not a big earner — it would be nice if it *was* a little earner! I eat there about six times a week as I only live 70 yards [away]."

Despite its owner's self-effacing attitude, many pleasantly surprised food critics stumbled across its culinary delights, including one who feigned surprise at their host being a pop star, having been under the misapprehension that the establishment belonged to Geordie soccer ace, Paul Gascoigne! Not that Gascoigne's proprietor wasn't adverse to an ale or three — or holding gatherings to attract the rich and famous.

Robert Marlow: "Vince is not as much of a socialite as Fletch or Martin, but he's always asked me about my life. He's very involved in my life, whereas every time I was invited up to Fletch's restaurant, off Abbey Road, I thought, 'Why am I here?'

"There was one point where Andy's missus was quite good friends with Patsy Kensit, so Patsy and [Oasis vocalist] Liam [Gallagher] were sometimes there — and also people like [England footballer] Gary Lineker, so I suddenly thought, 'This is not how it used to be.' It just got to the stage where I was going up to all these parties and I didn't know anybody anymore, and — although all the old faces were still there — I didn't have anything in common with these people; I've had my 15 minutes of fame.

"For the first 10 years [of Depeche Mode's success], I'd say everything was cool; everything was normal. Nowadays it's all about [Andy and Grainne] having somebody come around and walk their dog for them! I never thought the starry thing would appeal, but that's how much things changed . . .

"There's a great line in Hanif Kureishi's book, *The Buddha Of Suburbia*, where the central character/narrator's friend from school becomes a big popstar – a bit like David Bowie in the Seventies, and he flies his friend over to New York. I can't quote it verbatim, but it did stick in my mind that this character wanted him there as a mirror to his old life. All of us, if we have something fantastic happen to us, want our old mates to see it – not to rub their noses in it, but if you're hanging around with people who are at the same level, and have done the same things, then it's normal. So I kind of resented fulfilling that role. I think it's a bit of a shame, and I'm really grateful to still be good friends with my old best mate, Vince, who's not like that at all.

"But Depeche Mode were playing in front of *70,000* people, and selling so many millions of discs – units – worldwide, so I defy anybody in that privileged position to keep in touch with reality, in a way."

Despite being at pains to point out that he holds no grudges against Depeche Mode, Marlow had made a valid point: fame almost always has an attendant downside, as Gahan had become painfully aware.

By maintaining a low-key profile, Alan Wilder's feet remained grounded as he married long-term girlfriend Jeri Young in August 1991. The couple abandoned London for a large country estate set deep in the Sussex countryside near Horsham.

Alan Wilder: "I've never really made any rash purchases. I've invested a lot back into music via my studio and all its equipment, and also into my house and estate. I try to keep a perspective on wealth, because it all could have been so different – one should always remember how lucky one is."

The house had another, smaller property set in the grounds. Dating back to the mid-nineteenth century, it had suffered from badly executed alterations in the interim, but, over a six month period, an expert team of builders, electricians and steel workers converted the building into a home recording studio. Wilder desired "a living, breathing space, designed not necessarily for controlled sound, but with the feel of a workshop, with plenty of light."

During the conversion of the cellar, the chance discovery of a disused underground water tank resulted in a unique drum booth, accessed by a sliding trapdoor in the floor. On the upper floor, a spiral staircase lead up to a mezzanine bedroom area, together with a fully equipped stainless steel kitchen and bathroom. The individual charged with running all the necessary cabling for the recording equipment – including a sizeable 36-channel Soundtracs L3632 mixing console and Dynaudio monitors, suspended, somewhat unusually, by chains from the overhead steel structure – was Electric Eel Studio Design's Kevin van Green, who had recently designed Martin Gore's (less striking) home studio. "Alan Wilder's studio [was] originally a three-storey house, stripped of its interior walls and floors to create a vast space," van Green commented.

Having developed a keen interest in interior design and architecture, The Thin Line, as Wilder named his workspace, further reflected its owner's character with the inclusion of a three-piece suite created from the seats of his first car, a 1974-vintage Citroen DS. "It was always my intention to design the studio so you could simply remove all the [recording] gear and be left with a really interesting open-plan building. I particularly like the way the bedroom gallery overlooks the whole room; and the floor-to-ceiling shuttered windows provide fantastic views. The only problem I have is that in the winter the place is so bloody cold!"

As it was, the expansive rural property was not the first time that Wilder had settled outside of London, having previously owned a picturesque moat house in Suffolk: "It was in Felsham, near Bury St Edmunds, but I didn't use it much so I sold it. I originally left London because I wanted more space and a nicer environment to live in. I don't miss living in the City at all, although there are drawbacks to living in the country – namely, a lack of good restaurants, cultural events, bars and convenient shopping."

Using the advantage of what he once termed "the first real break the band had taken in 10 years," in January 1991, Wilder began – "recording digitally using my Akai DR1200 machines" – the third Recoil album at his Cricklewood home, and produced Nitzer Ebb's fourth album.

Fresh from a lengthy pre-production (mainly programming) session at London's Sync City, in June 1991, MTV's Dave Kendall caught up with Nitzer Ebb and Wilder at Konk studios, where Nitzer Ebb member, Bon Harris revealed that there had been "a few staff problems at the start of the studio time." His partner, Douglas McCarthy narrowed this down to being "studio ownership problems". (Apparently, all was not well within The Kinks camp.)

Bon Harris: "We're getting more interested in putting more melodic elements in the music, and Alan seemed like quite a good person to pick for the direction, because we could so easily get lost with melody and so on. Alan seemed like a good person for the job, we approached him and he wanted to do it."

Alan Wilder: "They *insisted*, rather than approached! They've toured with us quite a lot, so we get along very well. That problem had already been overcome before we started, so we knew we'd be able to get along. The way we approach making music is quite similar – once we get into the studio with electronics, and what have you. But really, I think, there's quite a big gap between the two groups, because the songs dictate the direction of the group in the end. The way they write songs, and the subject matter, is very different to the way in which we, in Depeche Mode, write songs."

Despite a shaky start as The Kinks ironed out their differences, and an assertion duly broadcast by MTV that the album was "on schedule", Wilder later let slip that completing Nitzer Ebb's *Ebbhead* (released October 1991) proved troublesome, particularly when using sub-standard session musicians on 'I Give To You' and 'Come Alive': "The strings, brass and marimbas were all recorded live – arranged and conducted by Andrew Poppy. Some of the performances – mainly the brass – were so sloppy that we had to put them into samplers afterwards in order to re-tune them and put them in time. [That] is not uncommon when hiring classical musicians.

"We started [*Ebbhead*] without Flood, in a programming room. Bon and Doug already had some very loose sketches of some tracks but apart from this, the programming and recording of the album was one and the same. Flood joined us towards the end of the programming period and left again to work on the U2 record [*Achtung Baby*] shortly before the end of the recording period. I finished the recording and mixed the album with Steve Lyon at Konk studios. Doug is a dream to work with – very open-minded and willing to be flexible on all matters. Bon is more protective and subject to overdoing a good idea. I would point out that despite this, I still got on very well with Bon. Generally, I found their attitude to be something I respect – they were both very conscientious and hard working, and wanted to get the absolute best out of the record."

In the event, *Ebbhead* didn't fare well, following its September 30 UK release. Wilder wasn't overly concerned by the disappointing outcome, simply stating, "I didn't have any great expectations that the Ebb would suddenly become incredibly popular."

Nevertheless, Nitzer Ebb received some spoils when the 'Godhead' and 'Ascend' singles both scraped into the Top 50 in 1992.

Alan Wilder: "I'm glad I did it, but it got a bit tense towards the end. I wasn't sorry to see the project finished and I must admit, it's made me very hesitant about taking on other production jobs – I'm a musician first and foremost, and I found the role of producing someone else's music energy-sapping and ultimately, perhaps, a little unfulfilling. This doesn't mean I didn't enjoy it, I just prefer to concentrate on doing my own thing."

Workaholic Wilder had barely called time on the draining Nitzer Ebb experience at Konk before returning to that very same studio in October to spend two months mixing his own Recoil album, *Bloodline*. Returning the favour, Douglas McCarthy sang lead vocal capacity on a cover of Alex Harvey's 'Faith Healer' which was issued as the first Recoil single.*

While the previous two Recoil albums were resolutely experimental instrumental efforts, Wilder was looking to make *Bloodline* a more commercial affair by the recruitment of outside vocalists and lyricists to supplement his soundscapes.

"I certainly didn't feel a pressure to make it more conventional, but I did feel that I couldn't just keep producing experimental instrumental music all the time," Wilder told *Sound On Sound*'s Bill Bruce, in 1998. "I'd often get to a stage where I thought the music lacked something, and reasoned that if I was to progress with it in any way, I would have to bring something else in – be it vocals or whatever – to enhance what were basically backing tracks. I brought the vocals in, but I didn't really see it through in the way I should have done; I think I lacked the energy. By the end of that year [1991] – while also producing a Nitzer Ebb album – I'd just run out of energy. I think the album suffers because of it – especially the vocals. They're there as almost last-minute atmospherics, rather than to make real songs."

Fortunately, Wilder's critics didn't agree when casting their votes, *Vox* being especially complimentary: "*Bloodline* indicates that Alan Wilder has been a key figure in Depeche Mode's development, from their early pop nursery rhymes to the darker, heavily textured style they adopted in the

---

* 'Faith Healer' represented Alan Wilder's only solo UK chart entry when peaking at 60 on March 21, 1992.

mid-Eighties. Wilder concocts the filmic soundscapes, slow-burning things that slip into a melodramatic grandeur through a side door; Douglas McCarthy blisters Alex Harvey's 'Faith Healer'; Curve's Toni Halliday drenches 'Edge To Life' and 'Bloodline' in drowsy paranoia; 'Electro Blues For Bukka White' has long-gone disembodied bluesman White muttering and wailing under an Eastern drone that both eulogises and ignores him . . . the effect is disconcerting, but ultimately very moving."

Select displayed equal enthusiasm: "Delving deep into the world of technology, *Bloodline* pitches his electronic symphonies against the disparate individual styles of the guest vocalists. The result is an often brilliant concoction that swings the chilling [Toni] Halliday-led title track (harsh, unfriendly, ominous) to the daft, but inspired 'Electro Blues For Bukka White' (warm, weird, wonderful) – a glorious case of 'We have the technology!' "

Alan Wilder explained how he put that technology into action, by resurrecting the deceased bluesman, as it were: "The original Bukka [White] recording is virtually a cappella – he is actually singing to an acoustic guitar, but the guitar is just about inaudible. It therefore seemed to be a very interesting source of material to try and do something unusual with. I also loved the sound of his voice – particularly when he talks in his own unique language/babble. Certain lines were sampled, restructured and then filtered to eliminate most of the hiss."

Notable for his omission from the reviews was a young American by the name of Moby (né Richard Hall) who, in October 1991, had just scored an unexpected British Top 10 hit with 'Go', a danceable slice of techno, based around a sample excerpted from the theme to David Lynch's surreal TV series, *Twin Peaks*. Back in 1992, reviewers couldn't have predicted that the chameleon-like musician would develop into a highly regarded singer/songwriter, who would, ironically, sign to Mute Records and ultimately outsell Depeche Mode.

The scheduled break turned out to be incredibly busy for Wilder, who somehow found time to assist in compiling two lavishly packaged box sets produced to a limited run of 5,000 by (the now-defunct) Alfa Records of Japan (in conjunction with Mute) released in April 1991.

Alan Wilder: "I was involved in the compiling and mastering of the music, and Martyn Atkins was responsible for the artwork. The Japanese originally requested them, as their particular market seems to desire this kind of compilation with extensive artwork – something that traditionally doesn't do so well in Europe and the US. They were expensive to produce, necessitating a high retail price – again, something not suitable for other markets."

As *Music Collector*'s Graham Needham noted in July 1991: "The first set (*X1*) has three discs of 12″ mixes and one of so-called 'Strange Mixes'. The second set (*X2*) has a disc of instrumentals, one of B-sides and two discs with live tracks on. It's nice to see that the eight discs have been split into two boxes and made available separately, and also that the boxes have been split well, offering differing music in each.

"The first set bodes well for club/dance-oriented music fans and the second set lends itself to those with an interest in Mode's live and more unorthodox tracks. The number of the tracks on the eight CDs total 79, and as box sets go that's quite a good figure. At around £40 per box it works out at roughly one pound per track. Simply on that basis, both sets are not a bad investment."

Time proved Needham right, for a commited Depeche devotee would have to pay, at the very least, three times that figure – that's if a copy came up for sale.

"After that last [World Violation . . .] tour we decided to take a break for about a year," Martin Gore told MTV's Dave Kendall in June 1991. "But we were teased out of retirement by being asked to do a track for a new Wim Wenders film [*Bis ans Ender der Welt* – released in edited form in America as *Until The End Of The World*], so we did that over about three or four days, and now we're back resting [with a view to] possibly going back into the studio sometime next year."

Alan Wilder: "Martin obviously wrote the song, but the backing track to 'Death's Door' was mostly my work. The guitar parts were sampled, but not from the demo. I reworked Martin's previously recorded guitar from 'Blue Dress' and also used some pedal steel out-takes played by Nils Tuxen, which were recorded direct to DAT when we hired him to perform on 'Clean'. Whenever we finished an album, we always made a point of recording each individual sound onto DAT.

"Dave didn't want to come to England just to do this [one] track, so I worked on it myself at my home studio and called Martin in to do the vocals later on. It was mixed with Steve Lyon at Konk."

And the film itself? "I had seen *Wings Of Desire* [Wender's previous film], as well as *The Goalkeeper's Fear Of The Penalty* (not a classic) and a few others. *Until The End Of The World* was his most anticipated release, but it fell a little bit flat. It was good in parts, but was definitely too long – boredom set in after about two hours.

"We didn't pay any attention to the concept; nor did anyone else by the sound of it, although there is a track about space and 'humans from earth', I think!"

Depeche Mode's contribution, 'Death's Door' was released on the accompanying Warner Brothers album, *Until The End Of The World: Original Motion Picture Soundtrack*, alongside U2 (who supplied the title track), Talking Heads, and REM, among others. As one online reviewer commented: "Simply put, the soundtrack gathered the cream of the music scene: opening and closing tracks in charge of Graeme Revell/David Darling; mood swings in charge of Talking Heads, Depeche Mode, Elvis Costello, Lou Reed, REM, Nick Cave, Patti Smith, Daniel Lanois and U2, among others; and one of the most beautiful songs of all time, 'Calling All Angels' by Canadian Jane Siberry, topping it all."

Alan Wilder: "We never consciously tailored our music towards what we thought people might like. It's better to stick to your principles and retain your integrity."

Meanwhile, on MTV, Andy Fletcher dodged the when-can-we-expect-a-new-album-from-Depeche-Mode question with a non-committal answer: "I don't think we're planning on going into the studio until January, at least – probably a bit later. It all depends on whether [Martin] comes up with the songs or not."

Fletcher *did* hint at a repackaging exercise: "Over here [in the UK] a lot of our early singles haven't been released on CD, so I think there's a plan to release them – with a box set as well, so that should be quite good."

In the event, three such box sets – 'CD Singles Box Set #1', '2' and '3' (each featuring six CD maxi singles) – were respectively released on November 19, 26 and December 3 in a limited-edition capacity by Sire/Reprise in the United States.

Alan Wilder: "I had quite a lot of input on the content. It wasn't supposed to be a complete set – just favourite/best-of tracks at the time."

Thereafter, all 22 of Depeche Mode's pre-CD singles – from 'Dreaming Of Me' through to 'Strangelove' (which was briefly previously available as a 3″ CD single) were consecutively released as individual CD maxi singles, starting with 'Strangelove', 'Never Let Me Down Again', 'Behind The Wheel' and 'Everything Counts (Live)' on June 9, 1992; ending with 'A Question Of Lust', 'A Question Of Time' and 'Little 15' on June 8, 1993.

Mute Records instigated a similar release schedule in the UK, and remarkably, all still remain in print.

In 1992, Vince Clarke's Midas touch was showing no signs of abating. Erasure enjoyed two top five UK Singles Chart entries ('Chorus' and 'Love To Hate You') that summer and autumn from their chart-topping album, *Chorus*, and their camp command of the stage was confirmed by *The Independent*'s Giles Smith: "For the pop duo Erasure, putting on an outstandingly ridiculous visual spectacle is largely a matter of exceeding standards set by themselves; last time they toured, a pterodactyl flew across the stage, an interstellar craft crashed into a mountain, giant mechanised flowers bopped, and everyone on the stage spent at least some portion of the show in a spacesuit."

Before the year was out, Erasure would finally top the UK Singles Chart with their tongue-in-cheek cover version of Abba's 'Take A Chance On Me' – the most played track from their *Abba-Esque* EP (which also included the Erasure take on 'Lay All Your Love On Me', 'SOS' and 'Voulez-Vous').*

Vince Clarke was still the reluctant popstar: "We did one show where we did a dance routine all together, and I found that very, very difficult; I didn't feel confident enough to do it."

Such reticence contrasted markedly with that of Clarke's former frontman, Dave Gahan.

Alan Wilder: "I try to encourage him, or at least let him know that I value what he does on-stage; because he really does take the brunt of the attention, and it's a very difficult thing to do. There's very few good frontmen around, and I think he does it well."

"My wife works in the music business," Gahan told *Melody Maker*'s Jennifer Nine. "At the beginning of [Depeche Mode's] year off, she was out working on the Lollapalooza tour, the first one with Jane's Addiction. I went out on the tour kind of as a fan, just hanging out. It was *different* just walking around in the crowd, really not [being] bothered by the fans at all. I noticed the audience was the same as the one we have, or The Cure – or a lot of other bands, for that matter. Americans really see it all as just new, alternative music. And Jane's [Addiction] were just the most incredible

---

* Clarke and Andy Bell appeared in drag as Abba vocalists Agnetha Falskog and Anni-Frid 'Frida' Lyngstad in the accompanying promo video.

thing I'd seen in a long while. Sometimes they were really shit, and some-times they were just so mountainous and fantastic."

In fact, so mountainous and fantastic that Gahan ". . . spent the year trying to find the sort of music I wanted to be involved with. There was so much really good new music coming out of the States at the time, much more so than where it usually comes from – Europe or London. It felt that what was happening back home – all that Techno stuff – was really boring."

Any doubts that Gahan may have harboured concerning Depeche Mode's future, or at least his role within the band were dispelled when, at the close of 1991, Martin Gore submitted the demos destined for the band's next album. "I have more rocky and bluesy influences than the others in the band," Gahan later claimed. "So when Martin started sending me bluesy demos for the new record, like 'I Feel You' and 'Condemnation', which was really gospely, I thought, 'Great!' And the lyrics were completely appropriate to the way I was feeling. It was almost like Mart was writing the stuff for me."

Gore's lyrics obliquely mirrored certain aspects of Gahan's lifestyle, something Gore vigorously denied on more than one occasion: "Well it's good Dave *thinks* the songs are hand-crafted for him; it enables him to give his all performing them. I suppose the illusion comes from our similar upbringings and all the years [we've been] together in the band. But I never try to write from Dave's perspective. I don't think it's possible to write truthfully from another person's point of view."

In truth, Gore had barely heard from or seen his errant bandmate since the conclusion of the World Violation Tour.

Paul Lester (*Melody Maker*): "If you look at him [Dave Gahan] in 1980/81, he looked like the kind of kid that you'd see in Dolcis [shoe store] on a Saturday, getting you the right size Hush Puppies."

Paul Morley: "And then when he came back [from LA] he was Jesus! He was tattooed from head to toe; he was skinny – all the puppy fat had gone; he was incredibly intense. It was such a long way from the little Beanie Baby he had been."

The transformation from the fashionable, fresh-faced, 18-year-old innocent who had first appeared on *Top Of The Pops* wearing a peach-coloured blouse, to "Satan-sponsored makeover" (quoting the *NME*'s Keith Cameron) was apparently triggered by *The Stones*, Philip Norman's biography on The Rolling Stones, and Keith Richards, in particular. "*Keef*, man," gushed Gahan in 1997, sounding suspiciously like the rock 'n'roll incarnate himself. "Keef was for real. And I look at him now, and I love him."

Aware of the disparity between the public perception of Depeche Mode and what he saw as the real deal, Gahan actively set out to change the band's focal point – himself: "We've always been a band that have gone out at night and ripped it up – gone out drinking together, and all that kind of stuff, but then our public image wasn't like that. It was all bollocks for a while, and I thought, 'Why hide it? Hundreds have gone before me and got away with it.' So I thought, 'I'll have a go.' And that's how it kind of started.

"We had some tremendous success in America, and we started [travelling] all over the world, playing these huge arenas with loads of people working for us, running around taking care of your every need – someone dressing you, doing this, doing that, getting you whatever you need at any time of night. So I went along for the ride, and got carried away with it, basically. The problem with that [was] the idea of it became bigger than a person; the character – me – that I'd had a big part in creating got out of control. Even when [we] weren't touring I sort of felt like I had some kind of image to live up to. I wasn't making any music – I might pick up a guitar now and then and have a pathetic attempt . . . a terrible jam when my mates were around – but other than that I was just going out, playing the part."

When Gahan's bandmates finally laid eyes on their long-haired, goateed, tattoo-covered singer – looking (and sounding) every bit the American grunge star he so desperately wanted to be, the shock finally sank in. As late as 1999, Gahan was still gobsmacked by his own self-mythologising recollection of the meeting: "I'd changed, but I didn't really understand it until I came face to face with Al, Mart and Fletch. The look on their faces . . . *battered* me."

Andy Fletcher: "During *Violator* he was absolutely fine. He had short hair. Then we didn't see him until after the World Violation Tour for about a year or something. When he came to Spain – this was at the beginning of *Songs Of Faith And Devotion* – he had long hair, he was saying that we should become a grunge band, and disappearing in his bedroom for about four days at a time. So it was a real massive change."

"He looked like he'd been living in LA for a year," Wilder pithily summed up.

Martin Gore: "I was a bit confused by it all at first, because we hadn't seen him for a while when we started recording *Songs Of Faith And*

Devotion. Suddenly his hair had grown drastically, and he was covered in loads of tattoos. But, after a while, you [got] used to the look; it seemed natural to me after a while. People have got all these preconceived notions about being in an electronic band – you shouldn't have long hair and tattoos. I think that's wrong; the way you make music shouldn't dictate the way you make music."

Be that as it may, but recording *Songs Of Faith And Devotion* was not going to be an easy ride . . .

24

Home Is Where The Art Is?

"It [Songs Of Faith And Devotion] was a very hard album to make. Dave was off at that point very much in his own world; Alan kind of felt that he wanted to make the album, and he really didn't need anybody else around to do it. The tension in the band was pretty bad; they weren't really talking to each other."

– Daniel Miller, 2001

When Depeche Mode regrouped in January 1992 to begin working on their eighth studio album, *Songs Of Faith And Devotion*, it was in Madrid – several kilometres outside of the Spanish capital, to be precise.

Daniel Miller: "They [Depeche Mode] had this thing where they wanted to work in a different city for each album, which is quite a good thing in theory – if you can find a studio which is appropriate for their needs. In Madrid, at the time, there wasn't, so what we did was rent quite a big house and built a studio in it. They lived in the house."

The concept of working *and* living together in close proximity might have been new to Depeche Mode, but the reality of maintaining harmony between four very distinctive band members – one of whom was now barely recognisable to the others who were dealing with problems of their own – was a difficult proposition, as producer Flood recalled: "They were always a very close-knit unit, and then, after the World Violation Tour, when we started to make *Songs Of Faith And Devotion*, I dunno . . . 'A lot of stuff had gone down,' I think is the phrase."

Dave Gahan: "I came back [to Depeche Mode] really inspired by a lot of other bands like Jane's [Addiction] – not so much for what they were doing, but for the passion that they had. The *danger* really appealed to me. I'd felt quite safe [musically] in the last few years, and maybe I wasn't trying as hard as I should've. So I think when I came back into the studio in January in Madrid, everyone was a little bit afraid of me somehow. I think I was giving off quite a vibe at the time. I was very aggressive about what I wanted and what I felt we should be doing, and how, once again, we should be a band of spirit!"

Andy Fletcher: "He may have wanted us to become more guitar-orientated and more traditional – drums, guitar and bass; that was the sort of music he was listening to. In some ways, the tension actually created something exciting and different – for us, anyway."

Several years later, Gahan was better equipped to offer some perspective: "I was determined that we should be something that we weren't – we should be trying to do new things with new instrumentation; if we didn't, we were just going to crawl up our own ass, and become the [kind of] stereotypical band who just put out the same stuff all the time. I was pushing to be heavier – to give us a rockier feel; I wanted to combine both things, and I didn't feel like that had been done properly yet. There were a few bands at the time doing that – like Nine Inch Nails and Nitzer Ebb . . . that had a kind of harder and bluesier edge to them. I felt like I wanted that at the time – I wanted to *rock*! And, to be honest, I kind of got my own way a little bit."

Alan Wilder: "We needed to push the boundaries a bit, and try and do something completely different to *Violator*. I'm sure, subconsciously, there was a big pressure there to repeat that success, and the obvious thing to do would have been to make a very similar record. None of us really wanted to do that, and I think particularly Flood, Dave and myself wanted to make it as different as we could, and surprise people with it."

Dave Gahan: "What we were aware of was that, after *Violator*, Martin was under pressure to come up with these songs, and subconsciously that made us go the other way – I don't think there was one song on that album that was under five minutes!"

Alan Wilder: "After some discussion between myself, Flood and the others, we agreed that our approach should be more towards performance whilst trying to push ourselves into areas we hadn't explored. Some of the songs like 'I Feel You', 'In Your Room' and 'Rush' suggested a looser, more 'live' feel and it's probably fair to say that myself, Flood and Dave were the main instigators of this open and fluid sound. This more performance-based style of working threw its own spanner in the works which some of us found hard to come to terms with."

This last comment was undoubtedly directed at Andy Fletcher who played a minor role in the recording process.

Alan Wilder: 'Condemnation'. "The idea of that track was to enhance the gospel feel that the song originally had without going into pastiche, and to try and create the effect of it being played in a room, in a space. So we began by getting all four members of the group to do one thing each in the same space. Fletcher was bashing a flightcase with a pole. Flood and Dave were clapping. I was playing a drum, and Martin was playing an organ. We listened back to it. It was embryonic, but it gave us an idea for a direction."

A similar approach was applied to developing 'Walking In My Shoes' – this time without any contribution from Fletcher: "It was constructed using an unusual method for us – i.e. jamming together. Martin played the guitar, I played bass and we ran a rhythm machine – this was just to get the basic feel of the track, and after much trial and error, the chorus bass line and guitar pattern fell into place.

"From that point onwards, Flood and I would begin the 'screwdriver' work – constructing drum loops, string arrangements, and all the other bits and pieces. Despite sounding cracked and raw, Dave's voice somehow mirrored the intensity of the music – it seemed to be full of emotion. Martin and I didn't always see eye-to-eye – on 'Judas', for example, we actually recorded the track in three or four different ways – and I think he was generally less enthusiastic about the style changes than, say, Dave was."

According to Wilder, the final version of 'Judas' wasn't completed until ". . . very late in the day, and Martin didn't say much about it, which is his way of indicating he doesn't like something."

Lyrically, of course, 'Judas' remained unchanged in its recorded variations, going as far as an AIDS-related reference, something that Gore later described as a "counterweight" to balance out all his "nice love songs".

Martin Gore: "Sometimes I think there are times when we think, 'Oh, maybe we made a mistake there.' I mean, in some ways we were maybe turning into the band that we were rebelling against when we started out being electronic. It's definitely the rockiest we ever got."

Dave Gahan: "[Martin] came up with a bunch of songs that were leaning towards the rockier side, and a lot more blues-based – more rock 'n'roll. 'I Feel You' has a classic, bluesy, rock'n'roll sort of riff."

Daniel Miller: "The thing is, they're not a rock band, because a rock band would have a lot of problems, I think, with 99 per cent of what they do, musically, because it's not pure [rock'n'roll]. There's this horrible kind of authenticity about rock music, and they're definitely *not* authentic in that sense."

Alan Wilder: "I suppose the emphasis is much more on performing on this record [*Songs Of Faith And Devotion*], but once that performance was created, we applied all the technology we've come to know and love over the years to put it together in a way that's still uniquely Depeche Mode."

For the recording, Wilder used Akai's latest model of stereo samplers, and a conventional (1990-vintage) S1100 series. "We've still got the same collection of samplers – Akais and Emulators," the main keys man told *Sound On Sound*. "And lots of rack-mounted and modular synths: a MiniMoog, Oberheims, the Roland 700, ARP 2600. The older synthesisers have an organic quality – a roundness and grittiness – that you just don't hear on digital things. But the flexibility is important, too. You've got so much flexibility of routing the sound on the older gear; you can create your own patches [sounds] without adapting somebody's factory sample. So [on *Songs Of Faith And Devotion*] there are fewer modern synthesizers than ever before – no DX7s, PPGs or things like that."*

A near-perfect example of that sonic "flexibility" can be heard on 'Higher Love'. Within seconds of its menacing opening (which momentarily includes an electronically created thunderstorm), Flood's Moog IIIC modular system contributes a distinctive, chugging bass sequence, again recalling Seventies-era Tangerine Dream by association.

Alan Wilder: "We still sequence quite a lot of the performance, but we're using the sequencer to restructure what we do. When we just go in and play together, we end up sounding like a pub rock band. That's the problem: we're not capable of going into a room, playing together, and coming up with some magical piece of music. We have to apply all that technology to make it sound more spontaneous and human. One of the things I felt before we started this record was that the last album [*Violator*] – good as it was – had a slight rigidity. We wanted to make this record much looser, less programmed."

With that in mind, Wilder stopped using drum machines to programme the drum tracks. "The last time I did that to any great extent was during the making of *Violator*, even though there are 'live' drum loops on that album as well. Since then, the majority of drums have come in the form of loops, although I still might programme certain percussion parts, hi-hats and cymbals.

---

* That said, on the *Songs Of Faith And Devotion* sleeve artwork, a PPG Wave 2.3 digital polysynth can be seen sitting below a keyboardless Oberheim Xpander in one of Anton Corbijn's black and white photos taken during one of several visits to the Madrid sessions, but perhaps it was surplus to requirements.

"It wasn't until *Songs Of Faith And Devotion* that we switched to Steinberg's Cubase [sequencing software], which was run [on] an Atari [ST computer], plus 21-inch monitor [screen]. We ran things live [from the sequencer] for a while until we were happy with the song structures. Then we recorded most parts to multitrack."*

However, even Wilder's seemingly boundless studio energy would be severely tested, as became apparent to Daniel Miller during an early visit to Madrid for a *Songs Of Faith And Devotion* 'progress report': "I let them get on with it for a few weeks, then I turned up and it was just such a bad vibe. Nothing was really happening; nothing *had* happened; nobody was really communicating with each other.

"Alan was off playing drums with headphones on and Fletch was reading the paper, Flood was trying to get some sound without anyone really helping him or giving him any kind of feedback, the engineer had his feet up on the desk and was half asleep. It was like: 'What the *fuck*! This is the *beginning* of the album, it *should* be a really exciting time.' The songs were there, but Dave was up in his room painting. I then knew that we had a bit of a task [ahead of us]."

The divisive nature at Depeche Mode's makeshift Madrid base was plainly evident when broadcaster Paul Gambaccini visited with a filmcrew to film an EPK for *Songs Of Faith And Devotion*. Welcoming 'operations manager' Andy Fletcher was seated in an expansive office – what he jokingly termed his "den of iniquity", replete with occupied goldfish bowl (calming) and black designer desk (imposing). Alan Wilder was rehearsing "a bit of 'One Caress' " on a grand piano, while Dave Gahan sat cross-legged in his room, with numerous church candles permeating its darkened, spooky interior.

"It's been a long time since I've seen you, and I think it *is* you, isn't it?" asked an incredulous Gambaccini, ruffling the singer's locks in a manner that didn't sit well with the singer, who was soon waxing lyrical about his tattoos: "They all tell a story . . . to me; they all mark some kind of personal change or something that went on in my life. Like the first one I had, I had [done] very young. I had another one removed, just because I didn't like it. At that time I thought about getting both of them removed. But there's been some other things done . . . they all kind of mark events, really.

---

* Two-inch analogue with Dolby SR noise reduction, in the case of *Songs Of Faith And Devotion*.

It's like my warpaint, really. I'm going to have some more done before we go on tour."

Gahan gave another guided tour of his "warpaint" to *NME* journalist Gavin Martin; claiming he first went "under the needle" of a tattooist called Clive on Southend seafront at the tender age of 14. "He had a tattoo round his neck – *'cut here'*, with all the dots," Gahan fondly recalled.

According to Gahan, Clive's work on the vocalist's skinny forearms was nonetheless admired by LA tattooist-to-the-stars Bob Roberts, who was responsible for the massive pair of wings etched across Gahan's back: "It was like my wings, really, for the tour; it was, like, my weapon for the tour – if you can do this, you can do anything. If you can sit under the needle for 10 hours, you can do anything, man! It really killed me, but I had to do it."

Looking like a pale shadow of his former self, Gahan struggled to answer a long-winded question from Gambaccini, who likened ". . . the kind of spiritual and mental relationship" Gahan shared with Gore to ". . . that of Roger Daltrey in The Who, who sang songs written by Pete Townshend."

"Over the last couple of years I think I've felt a lot closer to Martin," Gahan falteringly replied. "I've got to know him a lot better, and I've liked him a lot more. I'd like to think he felt the same about me. Martin's a really brilliant songwriter, and I'd like to think the rest of us – Alan, myself and Fletch – bring out the best of those songs."

Gore was filmed separately; being attended by a make-up artist while sprawled across a luxurious bed within London's Portobello Hotel, his beloved guitar under his arm. "I think at the moment everybody expects us to come out with a *techno* album – like a hard dance album, but I think there's so much of that music around at the moment, and the [art of] song's really getting lost.

"So I don't think I consciously sat down and tried to react against that, but I think it's just something that you do because you listen to the radio and you go to clubs, and you're immersed in this same sort of music every-where you go. So you go home and, for me, when I sit down and write a song I think it just comes out differently, because I want to hear something different."

So what caused the well-oiled Depeche Mode recording machine to go off the rails? Alan Wilder proffered an explanation: "In the earlier years, everybody would pile into the studio accompanied by varying levels of interest in the record-making process. The result would be lots of chat and mucking around with little actual work being achieved. Over the years we combated this problem by slimming down the production team to whoever was actually needed or really motivated at the time.

"We forgot all about this at the start of the Madrid sessions, and actually magnified the problem by not only constructing a home studio, but also living together in the same environment for 12 weeks. This was a disaster, and I hated it! You couldn't escape for one minute, and the vibe reached an all-time low. By this time, Dave had clearly deteriorated, and retreated to paint or play guitar in his room. He occasionally surfaced to sing a couple of takes or offer a few words of encouragement, and would then disappear again."

One such vocal take proved to be an unexpected standout from the troubled singer, prompting *Melody Maker*'s Jennifer Nine to comment, "Specifically, it's the soul-drenched atmosphere of 'Condemnation' that's the *real* key to the changes Depeche Mode have been through. Its heart-felt, 'I-stand-accused' dramatics would be a meaty delight to any torch singer; Gahan sings his heart out and calls it 'by far my best vocal performance'."

Dave Gahan: "Some of the lines like, *'I'm not asking for absolution/ Forgiveness for the things I do'* – there are a lot of words in there that were entirely apt to the way I was feeling. And I really felt, for the first time, the words flowing through me as if I had written them.

"It was done under the studio in Madrid, a low-ceilinged place – very concrete and metal, and echoey and cold, and it had a great sound and a great ambience. When I came out, everybody in the control room went all quiet and turned around, and suddenly Flood said, 'That was fucking *great!*' And Alan and everybody said, 'That's probably the best vocal you ever did' – and I thought, 'Yeah, it was.' It was completely breaking me up inside, and, at the same time, it was really optimistic and uplifting."

Curiously, optimistic and uplifting were the very words that Alan Wilder would later choose in describing the album: "I don't agree at all that *Songs Of Faith And Devotion* is a dark album – it's the only Depeche Mode album that leaves you feeling uplifted. 'I Feel You', for example, or 'Higher Love' [and] 'Rush' all have an overriding sense of optimism."

Martin Gore: "['Condemnation'] wasn't one of the tracks that we used other people on, or backing singers – gospel singers. But it is actually sung in an old gospel quartet style. We basically worked out the parts and sang them – we didn't sample vocals, we just sang the parts like a quartet. So it was very interesting to do that, and I think Dave has given his best vocal performance ever on that track."

Alan Wilder: "We did that particular vocal ['Condemnation'] in Madrid, and the house we'd set up the studio in had a very echoey, tiled room, down in the garage. And he [Dave Gahan] sang down there, and he enjoyed singing in that space – just the way the room set off the sound of his voice was pleasing to him and therefore he sang well."

Dave Gahan looked back on his 'Condemnation' performance with a combination of pride and honesty: "That was the song where I really sang my heart out – I really felt connected to something; it still really moves me. It was almost touching on what I wanted to do, but I didn't have the energy or I wasn't there enough to really follow it through. It was really Alan and Flood sitting there at the desk."

Occasional recording highlights notwithstanding, Gore was uncharacteristically more forthcoming regarding Gahan's deterioration: "Dave was taking a lot of heroin at the time, which took me a while to realise. I'm not a drug expert – I don't know all the symptoms, but he was disappearing into his room all the time. We wouldn't see him sometimes for three days.

"At the same time, I felt totally detached from the band; I really didn't want to be there [in Madrid]. Up until that point we always felt like a gang, and then suddenly we didn't see Dave for days. It really felt wrong for the first time. Alan refused to go out with us any time we went out . . . during the period we were recording in Madrid he was isolated in the villa we had – he *couldn't* come out with us."

Given the unpredictable nature of some of the band's recent outings, it's more likely that Wilder no longer felt the *urge* to socialise: "I have a very strong work ethic – when I'm working, I'm working, which is the only way I can complete a project and know I've given my absolute best. Flood and I found it increasingly difficult to concentrate with some of the distractions we encountered in the villa. There were some extremely difficult moments during the Madrid sessions."

Not least one member's increasingly erratic behaviour, as Wilder confirmed: "These things don't happen overnight, but I think Dave was increasingly living in his own world. The most unsettling thing was that his drug use adversely affected his personality, either through enhanced aggression or the loss of his greatest asset: his sense of humour. I think I [first] noticed it during the recording of *Violator* in Milan – the 'spanner' in him came to the fore. I remember, for no reason, he deliberately picked a fight with about 10 locals just walking down the street. I was petrified, expecting to be knifed at any point, but somehow he always got away with that sort of behaviour. He caused another incident, totally unprovoked, in a Madrid nightclub by insulting a group of Hell's Angels, which resulted in a street brawl.

"All this made normal communication more difficult, which was an added pressure in an already quite tense group relationship. A distance formed, which I found sad, considering what an enthusiastic and vital person he really is. Dave also has a very generous, open nature, but therein lies the problem, maybe. Everyone tried to help him in their own way, but I don't think that any of us had a clue how to go about it. Nobody else in DM has ever taken heroin as far as I know, so I imagine Dave felt alien to the rest of us at the time."

Wilder's assessment cut both ways if Gahan's contradictory statement to Paul Gambaccini in 1993 was to be taken at face value. "To be honest, I feel a little bit sad that I haven't become much closer with the three other people that I work with, and have worked with for a lot of years. I would like to have changed some of the things that we've done. Our relationship, to me, is really, really important . . . what we have. The whole atmosphere that Depeche Mode creates when they're in a room together – as much as sometimes I fucking hate it, I love it so much as well. And each person I love as well."

Admirably, Gahan later shouldered responsibility for the situation. "To be honest, I was so kind of 'out there' that I didn't notice *anything*. I wasn't communicating with anyone. I was painting in my room; I'd come down sporadically with bursts of creative emotion, then I'd go back to my room. The struggle on that album was – all of a sudden, after all of those years together – we were becoming very separate. Individually, our own lives were drifting apart – that's what was hard.

"The hardest job of all was probably for Flood, pulling it all together. I think that album almost destroyed him, too. He said to me afterwards that the hardest album he's ever worked on was *Songs Of Faith And Devotion*, but, at the time, I wasn't really aware of that! I was absent a lot, too – chemically absent and physically absent; even if I was there, I wasn't really 'there'."

Alan Wilder had said much the same thing to Gambaccini. "There's been big changes in each individual member of the group, which I couldn't sum up in a few sentences – particularly in the last few years, I think, since we've sort of got [into] our thirties, kind of thing. You can see within everybody that certain aspects of their lives have become much more important. With having had a significant break away from each other before we started making this record, when we came back together you could really see the changes with everybody."

Andy Fletcher: "I was going through a rocky patch myself; I had my own problems, which made it all 10 times worse!"

Frustrations were further compounded by the fact that Depeche Mode had just two tracks to show from two recording sessions spanning their 12-week Madrid stay. Something clearly had to give.

Alan Wilder: "Naturally, the complex atmosphere of an album reflects the state of the individuals involved at the time, and, in this case, Dave's drug use *was* a factor during the making of the record. It was obviously disappointing – not for any moral reasons, but because it adversely affected his personality; he wasn't really 'there' a lot of the time and I missed his wit. It's also true that he was out of it for much of the time, so his active role was somewhat limited. Martin got very introverted, and Fletch started complaining about feeling depressed.

"By the time we started the Hamburg sessions in an altogether more suitable commercial studio [Chateau Du Pape], we had remembered that less people around equalled more work done. Fletch went back to England and booked himself back into The Priory; Dave only really showed up to do his vocals, and that left myself, Flood and Martin – who perked up a bit – to get on and knock the album into shape. We recorded eight tracks in six weeks, compared to the two or three we'd scraped together in Madrid."

Gore hinted at Wilder's more upbeat disposition while working in Germany: "Alan didn't particularly get on with Andy, and Andy went home during the recording period in Hamburg; that's probably why Alan cheered up and started coming out – he was out with us every night! He's a Gemini; he's odd! There are always two sides to their moods."

Vince Clarke briefly crossed paths with his old bandmates when Erasure played two nights at Hamburg's Sporthalle on September 12 and 13, 1992 as part of Erasure's 103-date Chorus Tour – a.k.a. The Phantasmagorical Entertainment Tour.*

Vince Clarke: "We did go out, but Dave was a 'smackie' by then, so I

---

* The UK leg had seen the duo perform at Manchester's Apollo Theatre an incredible 12 times, followed by seven similar-sized 'intimate' shows at Edinburgh's Playhouse, and an unbelievable *15* consecutive appearances at London's Hammersmith Odeon, and then *another* 11 nights back at Manchester's Apollo – a British attendance total of 150,000; roughly doubling Depeche Mode's UK tours.

don't remember it being a great all-mates-together kind of thing. I never really knew Martin, and Dave I didn't really know either. At the end of the day, the person I was closest to was Fletcher, because of Boy's Brigade. I knew him for a long, long time, and then we've only kind of really not connected since he's been ill. He changed, but life's all about change."

And as far as Flood was concerned, the upheavals reflected on *Songs Of Faith And Devotion* – significantly, the last record he co-produced for Depeche Mode: "There was tension throughout the whole thing; it's a very dark record – very dark."

Still largely unaware of Gahan's drug addiction, the British public's first taste of those dark or – depending on one's viewpoint – optimistic and uplifting recordings came with the February 15, 1993 release of 'I Feel You', Depeche Mode's first single since 'World In My Eyes' in September 1990.

Anton Corbijn's accompanying black and white promo, shot at one of his favourite haunts in the desert outside LA, centres on a long-maned, tattooed Gahan, vocal chords rippling as he eventually strips in front of British actress Lysette Anthony. Fletcher 'played' keyboards, Gore struck some suitably aggressive headbanging poses, while Alan Wilder 'drummed'.

Alan Wilder: "With 'I Feel You', I went in and played drums along with the track in one particular style, then did it again in a funkier style, and so on. We recorded those drums in a villa we had rented in Madrid. We set up a studio in the basement. The two drum kits – the smaller and the larger one – were recorded in different spaces, which gave each a different kind of edge.

"Plus, they were played in very different ways. Most of them were sampled and then sequenced in the form of drum loops. That's not to say that they don't change as the song goes on. There's a series of loops, which are sequenced together, using [Steinberg] *Cubase*, in a different structure from how they were originally performed. At the beginning of 'I Feel You' the drum kit is played, sampled, put through a synth, distorted, and then reduced to half-level."

Gahan bragged to *Melody Maker*'s Jennifer Nine that *he'd* persuaded Wilder to pull up the drum stool: "I definitely won my battles, to be honest – 'cos when we began this record [*Songs Of Faith And Devotion*], I knew it would be good for us to get a drummer. We've done this for so long, I thought, 'Why not add another element to our sound?' So I kept pushing and pushing, and, in the end, Alan got on the drum kit and said, 'Well, *I'll* fucking do it, then!' "

That's not quite how Wilder himself remembered it. "I'd been considering it for a while and eventually mentioned it to Dave, who thought it was a good idea."

Gahan maintained it was his idea, telling the *NME*: "I bullied Alan into drumming, because I said, 'I want live drums.' Fletcher thought I'd gone crazy; he said, 'Dave's gone crazy, he wants drums; next thing he'll want backing singers.' And I did."

Depeche Mode couldn't have chosen a more powerful track with which to unveil their new sound in advance of returning to the performance arena – despite Gahan actively pushing for 'Condemnation'. "That's the song I would like everybody to hear first," he told Paul Gambaccini. "Because I just think we captured something really, really special."

Alan Wilder: "If I remember correctly, everyone else felt 'I Feel You' should be the first [single off *Songs Of Faith And Devotion*], including Daniel Miller. The main reason for the choice was that the track had attitude and was radically different to what we had done before. We hoped it would surprise people and make them curious about the rest of the album."

With such a dramatic return, the music press sat up and took notice. *Melody Maker*'s Jim Arundel: "Almost as deadly as they'd love to be, 'I Feel You' is an exercise in scaling the charts the hard way. They positively *pulp* a backing track while the newly grunged-up Dave Gahan has his nuts tattooed live in the studio. Synths fart, squelch and whine, amps howl, The London Symphony Dentists pop in for a few bars and the chorus goes either *'This is the dawning of Allah'* or *'This is the dawning of Alan'** – presumably a reference to 'new boy' Wilder now being allowed to stay out as long as he likes without being accompanied by an adult."

NME's Gina Morris jibed: " 'I Feel You' kicks off with a mighty elongated guitar screech before Mr Body Art starts turning the wheels of insipidness. Far more old-style white trousers and crew-cuts than his new hard-rock image would indicate; powerful enough, yet desperately forgettable. Depeche Modules everywhere will be dribbling in anticipation."

---

* Gahan actually sings, *"This is the dawning of our love."*

Judging from the song's eventual chart performance, Morris was correct. Assisted by the usual gamut of remixes – seven versions of the title track (including two remixes by ambient pioneer, Brian Eno) plus 'One Caress' (from *Songs Of Faith And Devotion*) spread over the usual mixture of cassette, vinyl and CD (limited-edition or otherwise) – by February 27, 'I Feel You' had risen to number 8 on the UK Singles Chart.

America's alternative youth lapped up its grunge overtones, propelling 'I Feel You' to the top of the Modern Rock Tracks Chart following its February 9 Stateside release; the first time that a Depeche Mode record had been issued prior to its UK date. It only managed 37 on *Billboard*, after entering on March 6, for a total of 12 weeks.

Songs Of Faith And Devotion finally saw the light of day on March 22, 1993 in the UK (the following day in America) – much to the delight of those "dribbling Depeche Modules everywhere".

David Fricke reviewed the album for *Melody Maker*: "Times have changed. Depeche Mode have adjusted. Never just a synthesiser group, they *are* synthesisers, expert magpies with a striking gift for genre digestion and mimicry. They have thus retooled themselves for the Nineties with a most admirable con here, an ingenious and defiantly transparent collision of U2's *Achtung Baby* and REM's *Automatic For The People* – industrial pop crackle with a grim, obsessive confessional twist."

Elsewhere, Fricke got unintentionally close to the mark when observing: "The sustained theme of hurt, possession and *faux*-forgiveness is just short of repellent. It's almost unrepentant-junkie-talk . . . At times, the relentless, ego-driven grimness – even when the Gahan/Gore persona dons the victim's hairshirt – makes you distrust the supposed irony of it all. In 'Get Right With Me', it's hard to tell if the singer is some kind of laconic self-help guru or just worships at the Church Of The Asshole."

The U2 comparison reared its head again with the *NME*'s David Quantick: "It's got some guitars on it, a string quartet and some excellent scraping noises, it's bloody loud and Dave Gahan, judging by Anton Corbijn's somewhat Anton Corbijn-esque liner photos, has lost about nine stone and grown a beard . . . Style fans will therefore note that Depeche Mode – nearly out-Depeche Moded by U2 on the Corbijn/Berlin/monochrome/Eno-styled *Achtung Baby* – have returned with an album which out-'Achtung Baby's *Achtung Baby*'. *Songs Of Faith* . . . is Depeche Mode in all-out moody Euro art stadium rock, um, mode, and it leaves all the competitors at the starting gate."

A Depeche devotee, desperate for information concerning the Mode's new recordings, later claimed he asked what the album's working title was during a chance meeting with tour/production manager Andy Franks, who apparently quipped: *Achtung Baby 2*.

"I think this was his famous West Country wit," is Wilder's response to the anecdote. "There are certainly parallels between DM and U2, but musically they are world's apart. The production teams weren't actually the same – I think *Achtung Baby* was produced by Eno and [Daniel] Lanois, with Flood's role being that of an engineer; in our case, Flood was a co-producer.

"With Anton taking photographs of both groups there were obviously going to be similarities there, because he has such a distinctive style. The cover of *Achtung Baby* is actually very similar to the cover of *101*, and whenever you see another of Anton's videos you notice all kinds of characteristics that are very particular to him."

The string quartet to which Quantick fleetingly referred was, in fact, a somewhat more extravagant gathering than a simple foursome, assembled to accompany Gore for the album's token ballad, 'One Caress'.

Alan Wilder: "Once we decided we wanted 'real' strings, there was really only one or two choices as to who should arrange them. Wil Malone arranged the strings for Massive Attack's 'Unfinished Sympathy', a particular favourite of both myself and Martin. The strings were recorded at Olympic Studios (in Barnes, South West London), using a 28-piece string section, to which Martin sang the vocal 'live' [alongside the performing string players] – thus equalling the fastest ever recording of any one DM track, the other being 'Somebody'."

Quantick also observed: "*Songs Of Faith And Devotion* follows the Mode tradition of having a portentous title, a vague linking theme between the songs and a sleeve that will look majorly dated in a year or so's time.

Alan Wilder: "I have to agree it wasn't one of the greats. But nobody wanted to hurt Anton's feelings having given him the job of artistic direction – one of his problems is that he is quite inflexible once he has an idea for something. When it comes to cover art, I always felt Anton should have really focused exclusively on his photography, which is what he does best, and let others take care of layout and graphics."

Notable in his absence from all but one of the sleeve's distinctive black and white snaps was Andy Fletcher who was, in all probability, still under care at The Priory.

"Anton turned up for a few weeks here and there, and all the photos were natural; Fletch wasn't in them because he wasn't around at the time," is Wilder's simple summation.

On April 10, in an unprecedented achievement for Depeche Mode, *Songs Of Faith And Devotion* entered the American *Billboard* Top 200 Albums Chart straight at number one, only the sixth British act to achieve such a distinction to date.* The album also entered the UK Albums Chart at pole position – all of which boded well for the band's next touring extravaganza, planned with former tour accountant, Jonathan 'Baron' Kessler.

Alan Wilder: "The tours were planned by ourselves, our agent and Jonathan. Between us all, taking into account many factors, we would decide which countries and cities to play and when. Once we had a general plan, the specific routing would be optimised, again depending on travel times, venue availability, local promoter advice, record release dates and other logistical considerations."

Alan Wilder charted Kessler's rise through the ranks to self-appointed 'spiritual adviser': "He became more and more involved in the co-ordination of the tours, and his skills go way beyond pure financial organisation. As his tour negotiations invariably involved talking to record companies and promoters, it was, for him, a natural progression towards management. He is the kind of manager who does not get involved in the musical or artistic aspects of the band, but rather excels at public relations and people management."

And as a public relations and people management exercise, the marathon 'Devotional Tour' was on the grandest of scales.

Alan Wilder barely had the time to absorb the success of *Songs Of Faith And Devotion* for he was holed up in his Thin Line studio, feverishly working up concert backing tracks with Steve Lyon, aided by an unspecified new hard-disk recording system from Japanese hi-tech musical instrument manufacturer Roland.

Alan Wilder: "Unfortunately, putting the Devotional live show together proved to be more of a handful than either myself or Steve had bargained for. We knew when we started that we didn't have a lot of time on our hands, and it didn't help that the Roland sequencer was giving us continual problems. However, we persevered and had nearly completed the work when disaster struck: the machine couldn't handle the sheer volume

---

* The others being The Beatles, Eric Clapton, Pink Floyd, Elton John and Def Leppard.

of traffic we were demanding from it and one day the whole system just crashed – we lost everything; three-and-a-half months of work! Luckily, we had had the foresight to back up all the music onto multitrack [tape], but the edits had gone.

"With the new single, 'Walking In My Shoes', due for release and rehearsals beckoning, we found ourselves with the mammoth task of re-editing everything in about two weeks. We worked night and day and then sued Roland. After a long battle, they refunded the purchase price of the two machines. I can't remember the exact price, but it was a lot (possibly £20,000). The problem was that we had also invested in loads of data-DAT backup equipment, which became redundant. Also, at the last minute, we had to acquire two [Sony] digital multitrack machines to take on the road instead, so we still lost out financially.

"Actually, that experience taught me a very valuable lesson about cutting-edge technology – don't touch it with a barge pole! It's not fun being the guinea pig for a piece of gear that hadn't been tested in the field by professionals, only to find it's full of design flaws."

The all-important digital multi-track tapes for the Devotional Tour were prepared by Wilder and Lyon at Olympic Studios, and completed at Thin Line.

Alan Wilder: "DM always used a certain amount of pre-recorded music during their live shows. From a personal viewpoint, I like to have something to do on-stage, although in the end I don't think it really matters as long as people go home having experienced a good time."

When quizzed as to what percentage of a typical Depeche Mode concert of the time could be considered to be a genuinely 'live' music experience, Alan Wilder replied, "About 50 per cent. Our policy was to always play as much as we could manage (without bringing in lots of extra musicians)."

No stranger to using backing tracks himself, Karl Bartos (ex-Kraftwerk) saw those Devotional Tour tapes being put through their paces on more than one occasion, both pre-recorded and live, and was impressed by what he heard. "Nowadays, every big so-called synthesiser group, like Depeche Mode, uses 32-track digital machines to play back studio recordings on-stage," he observed in 1997. "I mean, it's cool; they can play and they are really good, but I think that way of performing is too much fuss. You need a lot of people for maintenance and two 32-track machines in case one breaks down!"

Depeche Mode's tremendous touring budget meant that when it came

to presenting 'Condemnation' in a live setting, Wilder would be performing on an acoustic grand piano – with attendant piano tuner – rather than
using a sampled approximation, with Gore accompanied on backing
vocals by session singers Hildia Campbell and Samantha Smith (who were
also credited with "additional vocals" on 'Get Right With Me' on *Songs
Of Faith And Devotion*).

"It's easy to forget that putting together a live show is a complicated and
time-consuming activity," Alan Wilder continued. "It isn't just about
revamping the songs, which of course can be very exciting. There are a
million other jobs to be tackled, like deciding what will be on the backing
tapes and what will be [physically played] live, or who will play what parts
and how that will effect the way I program the keyboards – which is a
logistical nightmare in itself!

"There are also questions about the track running order and the different set lists themselves – this was to be a long haul and to play exactly the
same songs night after night for 15 months would have been agony. You
also have to consider each different country, because every audience reacts
differently, preferring different songs that have been particular to their
territory.

"Consequently, we had four set lists – red, green, yellow, blue. It was
standard practice to change the set if we were playing one venue over two
or more nights, or if we were revisiting an area [we had] already played on
the tour. We had eight separate tapes – basically four different set lists,
which were each split up into two halves and broken up by an acoustic
song somewhere in the middle, which allowed for the tape change. Effectively, therefore, we could mix and match any combination of first and
second half tapes. Along with a few different alternatives for Martin's
acoustic songs, this gave us the opportunity to perform many different
[song] running orders, although all of them had the same overall shape and
structure. So, for example, a quick chat beforehand might result in 'Let's
play the blue/red set tonight with 'Somebody' instead of 'I Want You
Now' in the middle.' We could also change tapes for the encores, if
necessary.

"Then there are incidentals such as the time you'll be going on-stage.
For example, with the European and first leg of the American tour, in
spring and autumn [1993] respectively, we knew it would be twilight
when the show kicked off, so it seemed a good idea to capitalise on this. I
think the resulting opening sequence of thunder and lightning preceding
'Higher Love' and accompanied by the huge curtains, appropriate

lightshow and the magic hour itself, was one of the most dramatic moments of the whole tour."

Wilder had already hinted at what preparations Depeche Mode were making in readiness for their next tour to Paul Gambaccini: "We always work in conjunction with other people when we're putting stage shows together – Anton's working on this particular stage set with us, and we'll be looking to him for some very strong ideas. Plus, we're trying to put as much thought into it as we can to try and do it in a very different way than we have before, which is generally how we approach most things."

25

Road Failure . . . Or Mode Failure?

"I kind of liked the idea [of becoming a rock band] – that we were that, but it still didn't quite fit. That's probably what Mart, Fletch and Alan were worried about: there was way too much focus on me. We went out on the Songs Of Faith And Devotion *tour [Devotional . . ./Exotic . . . tours] and played nearly 200 shows to sell-out audiences everywhere, so, again, I was getting a lot of attention, but it was the wrong kind of attention."*

– Dave Gahan, 2001

Bathing in the runaway success of *Songs Of Faith And Devotion*, Martin Gore invested nearly £1.2 million via the pension fund of one of his companies on a 12,300-square-foot building in London's Docklands, let to NatWest Bank* since 1987 for the not-so-insubstantial annual rent of £170,000.

The hush-hush nature of the sale led *The Daily Telegraph* to report: "The purchaser is not known. There is a rumour that it is The Rolling Stones." The game was up when investigative *Daily Telegraph* financial columnist Richard Northedge named the buyer as Grabbing Hands, Gore's music publishing company (named after a line from 'Everything Counts').

Andy Fletcher wed long-term partner Grainne Mullen on January 16, 1993 in a church ceremony in London's Lisson Grove, within walking distance of his Maida Vale restaurant and home. A lavish reception – "no expense spared" according to Rob Andrews – was held in the basement function suite of a Hyde Park Corner hotel. Deb Mann was also in attendance: "I think Pete Tong was DJ'ing, and I remember a lot of Mute people being there (including staff from abroad). I don't remember [any]

---

* Ironic considering that Gore was once employed by the same bank in his only pre-Depeche Mode employment.

celebs being there – like Dave and Jo's [wedding], it was lots of friends and relatives."

For the upcoming tour, Martin Gore contemplated being more animated on-stage with his guitar playing, helping to ease the visual problem of multiple static keyboards. "With every album I think we incorporate more guitar parts, just because it seems more natural, so I *have* to perform [them] live, and I actually enjoy it as well.

"I think we've managed to get a good balance between rock and electronics; I don't think the show's over-rocky, which is always our worry. I just think it adds a new dimension to the show when you come forward, instead of the three of us being stuck behind keyboards. I think we're going to try and do more of that sort of thing on the next tour with drums."

Alan Wilder fulfilled the drummer's role, telling Paul Gambaccini: "I've got quite a lot more practising to do if I'm going to play them live, which is what I'm going to attempt to do on the next tour – on certain songs, not all the songs."

On April 3, *NME* exclusively revealed that Depeche Mode were set to play their first UK date for two-and-a-half years at London's Crystal Palace National Sports Centre on July 31, with Goth-rockers The Sisters Of Mercy confirmed as the main support act for the 35,000-capacity show. The £18.50 tickets first went on sale through Channel 4's early morning *Big Breakfast* TV slot on an exclusive phone line before being made available through the usual ticket outlets the following day.

The *NME* also carried news of the band's forthcoming single, 'Walking In My Shoes', for UK release on April 26, with remixes from dance act Spirit Feel (*sic* – actually Spirit Wheel), Jonny Dollar (later better known for his work with Bristol trip-hoppers Portishead) and William Orbit.

When released, six remixes (with subtitles like 'Grungy Gonads Mix', 'Random Carpet Mix', 'Anandamidic Mix' and 'Ambient Whale Mix') shared space with two versions of 'My Joy', a track recorded at Chateau Du Pape and briefly earmarked for inclusion on the album. According to Wilder: "It was going to be on *Songs Of Faith And Devotion* at one point, but we didn't think it was strong enough in the end. It was mixed by Steve Lyon and myself; I reconfigured the track for the 12″ version, with Steve engineering."

Alan Wilder was more forthcoming regarding its A-side: "One of the first *Songs Of Faith And Devotion* tracks to be recorded, and one that went through many incarnations, 'Walking [In My Shoes]' is probably the best example of the new multi-layered DM sound. The more organic feel was created with the use of live bass and guitar, plus a dynamic string arrangement and a series of different drum loops, blended with both old and new Mode techniques.

"The e-bow guitar (playing the end melody) endowed the track with a haunting quality, which was also evident in Dave's voice mirroring the distorted piano and harpsichord riff. Electro elements were still present, but their role had shifted and they were used more in the form of bubbling synth parts to provide atmospherics, rather than to carry lead melodies. The result was a unique emotional experience."

Anton Corbijn's bizarre accompanying promo* made for a unique viewing experience, one which, as Wilder recalled, "It was certainly one of Anton's most surreal promos, and the actual filming was quite a different experience for us. I remember how odd it was being surrounded by all these people with every manner of deformity – especially at meal times. It brought a smile to my face standing next to a hunchback, dressed like a gothic nightmare, and hearing him ask the catering girls, 'Have you got any Ketchup, love?' "

NME and *Melody Maker* were divided in their respective views of 'Walking In My Shoes'.

NME: "Disguised as a small book, with gangs of silly pictures from some video, the new Depeche Mode single is best enjoyed as part of its overpoweringly moody LP *Songs Of Faith And Devotion*, rather than in this format, where it is not quite top enough to be a single. Eerie and powerful for all that, though."

Melody Maker: "Oh, come on guys! We all saw that 'Enjoy The Silence' video a couple of years back, where a clearly demented Dave Gahan cast himself as King Canute. So now, obviously, he's gone the rest of the way round the twist, and you've had to have him locked up. But did you honestly think we wouldn't notice when you got Zodiac Mindwarp in to replace him? Dave/Zod pleads that we should never judge him too harshly, because we can't possibly imagine how hard it can be being an international pop star and sex symbol for the young and tasteless. The hearts of the homeless haemorrhage, I'm sure."

The single's UK chart performance followed a familiar pattern; peaking

---

* MTV in America demanded a less gratuitous edit of the video, *sans* shots of semi-naked women sitting astride Fletcher, Gore and Wilder.

just outside the Top 10 at number 14 on May 8, after a brief four-week run. In the US, it performed a little better when simultaneously released on 7″ vinyl, cassette single and CD single on April 27, with 12″ vinyl and cassette maxi singles appearing one week later.*

Songs Of Faith And Devotion ultimately sold some five-million copies – a figure undoubtedly boosted by the band's latest global outing. Lille's Espace Foire was the venue chosen to unveil the ambitious production for the first time (May 19).

Alan Wilder: "[Lille] was a good venue for pre-production rehearsals, and wasn't so huge to be considered risky – given that first night performances are bound to be a bit nervous and problematic."

Spiritualized were the initial support act, but within a month *Melody Maker* reported that they'd been taken off the tour. A Depeche Mode spokesperson was duly quoted, "They'd been going down badly. It's a very partisan audience, and they couldn't hack it. Rather than see them suffer every night, Depeche decided to knock it on the head. The band told Spiritualized on Friday [May 28] in Gothenburg that they wouldn't be needed after the [May 29] Stockholm date. They refused to play the Stockholm date, so in the end Depeche got the hotel band to fill in for them. They went from playing a hotel bar to playing a 20,000-seater stadium!"

Thereafter, Mute labelmates Miranda Sex Garden stepped into the support slot at short notice, just in time for the Hanover show (May 31).

Alan Wilder: "Daniel always tried to encourage Mute bands for obvious reasons, but we would consider anyone who seemed to vaguely fit the bill. As always, everybody had different opinions as to who was most suitable. I must admit, it wasn't something I felt very strongly about, so Martin or Dave usually had final say." However, it's likely that Wilder tipped one Mute act in particular, Parallax, for a Devotional Tour support slot as Jason Young, Wilder's then-stepson was among their ranks.†

Miranda Sex Garden's vocalist-keyboardist-cum-violinist Hepzibah 'Hep' Sessa: "MSG originally consisted of three female vocalists who were discovered singing madrigals on [London's] Portobello Road by Barry

---

* 'Walking In My Shoes' topped the Modern Rock Tracks Chart, during a 16 week run; 69 on *Billboard* (for an eight week term).
† Parallax released several singles on Mute before changing their name to Hoodwink. Further releases followed but the band failed to complete an album, and were dropped from the label.

Adamson. They later expanded to include drums, bass, guitar, keyboard, violin and viola, which was the line-up when I joined the group. I find it very difficult to describe the music; in fact, it's easier to say what it wasn't, rather than what it was! It incorporated rock, classical, ambient [and] industrial elements, but wasn't 'groove-based' enough for me, and some of the ideas were somewhat naive . . .

"I remembered DM from my youth, but I'd never bought a record or knew anything about the band. In fact, in some ways I had a twisted prejudice against them when we first went out as support, because of my experiences working in a record shop in Southern California during 1989/ 90. We never seemed to sell anything but The Cure's *Disintegration* and that *101* thing.

"And when the Wherehouse riot occurred [in LA], the shop was besieged by fans, all clambering for [Depeche Mode] T-shirts. As an example of DM's obvious influence, when I heard the show for the first time, I found I was strangely familiar with the songs and lyrics. I first talked to Alan on the second night of our support leg, which was also his birthday [June 1] – I had no idea who he was, or what he did. We used to wind each other up a lot after the show, and he'd ask me to go out to clubs. It was about three days into the tour that I realised he was the bloke who played the drums! We became pretty inseparable from that point."

Hep's first impressions of the other Depeche Mode members were on a par with other outside observations. "Dave was very much like Alan – very funny and extremely charming. He used to call me Beelzebub! Martin was also very nice, but quite a Jekyll and Hyde character – he's a total extrovert when bombed out of his brains and completely the opposite when sober.

"The first show in Hanover was quite an eye-opener, to be honest. I remember thinking, 'How am I going to survive this for four weeks?' The crowd's dismissal of us before we'd even got on-stage was completely unexpected, because we were feeling pretty good after a really enjoyable tour with Einstürzende Neubauten and some excellent headline dates. When we got back to the dressing room afterwards, I remember [lead singer] Kat [Katharine Blake] laughing and saying it was the most invigorating performance she'd ever done. We all agreed that DM audiences were fiercely partisan and impossible to convert, so the best line of defence was to attack and really wind them up – after all, did they really think we were going to allow ourselves to be booed off-stage by a bunch of leather-clad nancy boys with loaves of bread on their heads?"

Those partisan audiences were enthralled from the moment that the same electronically generated thunderstorm effect used on the *Songs Of Faith And Devotion* album closer 'Higher Love' audibly signalled that it was showtime. The chest-crushing volume of the intro was (literally) moving; an exciting moment further enhanced by the synchronised blinding mock 'lightning' lighting. The gargantuan dark gauze curtains (which tantalisingly hinted at what was to be unveiled) eventually dropped at the end of 'Higher Love'; quite possibly the most visually stunning several minutes of synth-rock theatrics mounted by the foursome.

The masterstroke that was Anton Corbijn's stage design was evident. During 'Policy Of Truth', Fletcher, Gore and Wilder were positioned up on a high platform as a backline. The front of this dominant structure avoided the visual cliché of multiple Marshall stacks; on first impression, it appeared to feature five ($8' \times 8'$) squares of varying backlit colours, which transformed (during 'Walking In My Shoes'), into full-blown synchronised video screens, through which 'walked' several disturbing Corbijn-created characters. These included a 'bird-headed' woman lit blood-red, strutting in a slow-moving, strangely sexual predatory manner, set against a deep blue background. Down below, Gahan scurried around the vast stage in a mouse-like manner, the sole human focal point in the unfolding hi-tech spectacle.

Melody Maker's Paul Moody was witness to the slick Mode machinery in action at Hanover's 20,000-capacity Garsben Stadium: "The show is the stuff of Gary Numan's dreams. It's a masterpiece of subtlety; a stark Bauhaus reminder that stadium pomp, when stripped of the hoary trappings of MTV, can still hold you in awe at its sheer mind-blowing magnitude; likewise, the dreaded synths. Being regularly in the company of people for whom electric guitars are barely less essential to existence than life itself, it's amazing to discover that having them surge towards you from titanic speakers is a purely pleasurable experience."

Alan Wilder: "There were a series of concealed floor monitors at the front [of the stage], as well as two sets of side-fills [speakers] with separate mixes. The front pair were primarily for Dave's preferred balance [of the live music mix], and the back pair for the musicians."

The Devotional Tour also represented another first for Depeche Mode on the monitoring front.

Alan Wilder: "The Songs Of Faith And Devotion Tour was the first where I could actually hear what I was doing. This was down to 'in-ear' monitoring, which is the most controlled form of foldback [sound] available. The main advantage for me was the fact that it blocked Dave's side-fills, which [threw] out his vocals at ball-busting decibel levels. The volume of his voice used to be so loud that it could obliterate all the rhythm tracks as well as our keyboards and vocals.

"In my headphones, I would only listen to a mix of certain tape channels and my own keyboards, drums and vocals. I didn't need to hear anyone else's performance or any other vocals. I also had a floor monitor [speaker] for low bass frequencies. Even though it [took] a few gigs to get used to this enclosed listening environment, the headphone route is easily the most accurate monitoring set-up you can get."

As for those synths "surging out" as *Melody Maker*'s Paul Moody described it, technically there wasn't a synth among Depeche Mode's on-stage (and off-stage) armoury, but several hard-disk-endowed Emax IIs, in which all manner of sounds were stored.

Alan Wilder: "The sounds were spread across the keyboard, sometimes using several different presets for different song sections. The Emax hard-disk had enough memory to store all the banks of sounds for all the songs. Each preset, or new bank, was loaded using a footswitch."

Wilder's main keyboard was actually longer than his colleagues' – more out of necessity than ego, as he explained: "The Akai keyboard was used as a 'mother' keyboard, because it had more keys on its board than the Emax – and I needed as many keys as I could get. It was still, however, triggering [offstage] Emax sounds via MIDI. The Emax keyboard itself was for backup only, which, when needed, would still have been accessed through the mother keyboard."

As had been the case with past performances, there were no rules as to who played what keyboard parts on-stage. "It was a question of logistics," Alan Wilder claimed. "I would just spread the sounds over the keyboards as conveniently as possible."

"Conveniently as possible" usually meant Wilder giving himself the trickier parts to play: "None of the individual parts were tough, but I had many different bits to play in quick succession [on 'Walking In My Shoes'] that occasionally led [me] to having to cross hands to play a part (with my left hand) at the top of the keyboard, while also playing a part with my right hand, as well as changing a preset with a foot pedal."

Later in the show, more of Corbijn's films were projected onto two 24-foot-square film screens set side by side behind the keyboard rostrum.

Wilder explained the inner workings of the much-admired motion picture aspects of the changeable show: "Everything was linked. We provided a SMPTE* feed from the tape machines to the film production crew to sync the films to. In the case of a regular song like 'Judas', the film ran using the [SMPTE sync] code [from the multitrack tape]. When we played alternative songs, the same film 'free-ran'. The images of the burning candles for 'Judas' were so slow moving that it didn't matter. I loved the seven screens on the Devotional Tour, although I wasn't so keen on the four abstract shapes [suspended] at the back of the set."

When it came to performing 'I Feel You', Depeche Mode completed their apparent transformation into a rock act when both Wilder and Gore stepped down from their lofty keyboard positions to join Gahan on the main stage in their respective drumming and guitar-playing capacities.

Alan Wilder: "We couldn't reproduce the sound of the records faithfully – particularly *Songs Of Faith And Devotion* – without incorporating drums and guitars. We also thought it would add to the dynamics of the show, as well as giving Martin and myself an opportunity to move away from standing behind the keyboards all the time. As Depeche Mode's popularity increased, it was necessary for the music and shows to grow – it would have looked pretty ridiculous to have four blokes bleeping away on little synthesisers in a massive stadium. Visual dynamics and depth are important considerations, too."

Fletcher finally ascended to the lower stage for the closing encore; joining Wilder at another set of (temporarily positioned) keyboards for a rhythmically reworked (by Wilder) rendition of 'Everything Counts'.

Alan Wilder: "It was purely a visual consideration for the encores, to try to create less of a detached feeling and more of a group atmosphere."

Even so, keyboards and backing tape were an invaluable addition to Depeche Mode's adoption of the ultimate rock'n'roll symbol – the electric guitar – in a live setting, as Wilder explained: "For 'Walking In My Shoes' the double-track guitar sound was played on a keyboard – it had been processed through a synth for the original recording anyway, so perhaps that was appropriate. The second guitar on 'I Feel You' came from [the multi-track backing] tape."

In keeping with the *Songs Of Faith And Devotion* recording process, drumming along to the backing tapes was no easy task for Wilder: "I used to play to a 'headphone-only' sequencer part, which would feed one ear only. On the other side, I would have a floor monitor with the drums and

---

* Society of Motion Picture and Television Engineers – the technical group that develops standards for film and television post-production.

selected sounds from the rest of the balance (without vocals). The mix was provided by the monitor engineer [Anzac Wilson], although I could adjust the level of the headphones myself."

As his drumming technique improved as the tour progressed, Wilder extended his time on the drum stool beyond the four songs – 'I Feel You', 'Never Let Me Down Again', 'Rush' and 'In Your Room' – situated midway through the set, to include additional tracks such as 'Stripped' and 'Halo'.

Alan Wilder: "The main pleasure you get from drumming is the response you get from real drums, and at that time, a lot of the *Songs Of Faith And Devotion* songs were recorded with real drums. I did have a couple of electronic pads which were incorporated into the kit for triggering samples – 'Personal Jesus', for example, [but] to have played the older songs on an electronic drum kit would have been very difficult since many of the parts are unplayable – the fast hi-hats, et cetera. I also don't think it would have been as much fun."

Having since put some distance between his present-day lifestyle and Depeche Mode's gruelling rollercoaster touring schedule, fun was the point of the exercise.

Alan Wilder: "Personally, I had a lot of fun and found the touring far less stressful than making the record."

Having missed much of the album sessions due to depression, Andy Fletcher was typically more downbeat: "During the whole recording of that [*Songs Of Faith And Devotion*] album, all the early signs of the break-up that was going to come were starting to become apparent. And we agreed to do this year-and-a-half tour – straight from the album, straight on tour. It was probably the worst two years of our lives."

By 1993, as the writer of 'Judas', Martin Gore had taken to signing hotel registers as 'Mr Iscariot': "For me, it always seems that I'm stepping out of real life into a film. From the moment you start on the first day of the tour until you get back home it just seems you're living in a total fantasyland. Personally, I just try to accept it, try to have as much fun as I can and then come back down to earth at the end of it."

Alan Wilder: "At whatever level you tour – from a new band starting out to a big act like Depeche Mode – there are pressures. It's exciting to be able to visit so many different places and meet new people, but constant travelling and hotel life can get you down. Obviously, the social side of things is great – clubs and restaurants want you to frequent their establishments and will lay everything on for you.

"The downside of this kind of treatment is that it's very easy to get carried away and lose track of reality – it's very true that life on the road is like living in a bubble. As far as the shows go, it can get boring playing the same things night after night, which is why variation in the stage show can be so important. And as for having nothing to worry about, just because you're 8,000 miles from home doesn't mean that you don't have to pay your bills and keep a check on family life."

In what leaned more towards the sensationalistic side of journalism, *NME*'s Gavin Friday entered the inner sanctum to report on the touring Mode machine. It was not a pretty sight. "He doesn't look or sound like a well man," he wrote. "His skin is sickly grey in the half light, his eyes sunk into blueish sockets. Beneath his vest, tattoos embellish his biceps and torso, but the inside of his long skinny arms are all bruised and scratched. Later someone tells me they are scratch marks inflicted by rabid fans who tore their idol apart when he launched himself at them from a stage in Germany."*

The journalist was, of course, referring to Dave Gahan, who had just come off-stage on an adrenalin (and probably chemically enhanced) high after performing in front of 25,000 rabid East European fans at Budapest's MTK Stadium on August 27. Some 38 shows into the European leg of the Devotional Tour – seen by some 700,000 people – the singer's voice was already "worn away to a raw, husky rasp," according to Friday, who went on to describe his interviewee as having "all the trappings, and a few of the problems, of a Rock God. His 'problems' have become Depeche Mode's dirty little secret – everybody in the camp knows about them. Gahan talks about them in vague terms. He means to get things sorted out, he says. But everyone knows a rock'n'roll tour isn't really the place to start sorting things out."

However, steps were taken to help Gahan through those 'problems', for fear of road collapse. "We had a couple of meetings where the question of Dave's drug usage was addressed," admitted Wilder.

Gahan's "dirty little secret" was actually discovered by Wilder, who confronted the secretive singer: "He used to do quite a bit of snooping

* In the second part of his feature, Friday revealed that Depeche Mode had initially refused any dealings with the *NME* on account of its "taking the piss" by running a 1985-vintage Mode feature in their March 13, 1993 issue.

around and he found some 'works' in my room [during the Madrid recording sessions]."

Martin Gore: "Then we had our first ultimatum meeting with Dave. We said to him, 'You've got to sort yourself out; you're putting yourself in danger.'"

Coming from Gore, the advice didn't sit too well. "They were genuinely concerned about my health," Gahan later acknowledged. "Of course, I couldn't see that [at the time]. I said to Mart, 'Fuck off! Get off my back! You drink 15 pints of beer a night and take your clothes off and cause a scene. How can you be so hypocritical?'"

Dave Gahan, of course, had a point there, but the band persevered, nonetheless, as Alan Wilder revealed: "It was put to Dave that if he didn't clean up his act, we wouldn't make it through such a long tour. He agreed."

But agreeing to something was one thing; doing it was something else entirely. In Depeche Mode's case, drastic needs called for desperate measures.

Alan Wilder: "When I look back, it seems incredible that we paid an on-the-road psychiatrist $4,000 per week to listen to our ramblings – something I think I instigated. The idea was that he could provide some kind of support for those who wanted it, although the real reason was to try to persuade Dave to come off the smack, because we weren't confident that he was going to make it until the end of the tour. Ironically, I think everybody went to see the shrink at some point – apart from Dave, who was far too wise to the scheme!"

Gahan had his own gang tending to his personal 'needs' – purportedly including his dealer on the payroll. Friday's depiction of Gahan's comfort zone conformed to a hedonistic haven: "Gahan's own private dressing room has been transformed into a darkened coven. Candles burn on tabletops, on flightcases and other surfaces provided by his makeshift on the road furniture. Loud music blasts from his hi-fi. Jasmine incense sticks are burned to give the atmosphere he desires. Behind him there's a red carpet, the final touch in this full rock'n'roll Parnassian set-up. Such are the trappings of a man playing, or trying to play, the role of a Rock God . . .

"Gahan is treated with something bordering on mild contempt by at least one of his colleagues. 'Did he meet you in his harem, then?' sneers keyboard and business operative Andy Fletcher."

The parallels between Depeche Mode's touring antics and *This Is Spinal*

Tap★ was not lost on Daniel Miller. "Obviously, it was very sad in some ways – many ways. But if you saw the funny side – the ridiculous side, it was Spinal Tap, too. You look back on it and laugh, but Dave had become the character he used to take the piss out of, and it was very hard to communicate with him. He is one of the funniest people I know, and he completely lost his sense of humour and his ability to laugh at [Depeche Mode]. They always laugh at themselves; it's something that doesn't come across often."

Gahan agreed – albeit after the event: "Slowly but surely, it crept up on me; and I'd become that [clichéd 'rock casualty' character myself], so I could no longer poke fun at it, because I'd look in the mirror and that was me. I did lose my sense of humour. Drugs will do that to you; they're not very funny."

Friday was amazed that Gahan had revealed so much during their 20-minute après-show meeting – much more than Gore had done during an earlier hour long interview. "It's hard to believe that the chat has been so brief," he wrote. "It's also been such a sad charade; it's hard to believe it has been allowed to happen at all."

"Dress up as a female for a start; as a bloke, you've got no chance!" was Alan Wilder's response to a naive (or hopeful) male fan's enquiry on how to get backstage.

Gavin Friday confirmed the wisdom of this advice: "Somebody in the Depeche camp obviously does like young girls. After the show in Hungary there was a whole retinue of them; fresh-faced pubescents, some unable to speak more than a few words of English, clad in stockings and suspenders. Eagerly lined up to enter the hallowed portals behind the scenes at a rock 'n'roll event.

"There's something almost comical in its innocence, the girls dressed up like that, sitting round watching the band playing table football. It could be something unbearably sleazy, the beginning of a dive into debauchery."

Friday painted an unflattering picture of Alan Wilder "described by some as the Keith Richards of the band, meaning he sculpts the sound of their records with [co-]producer Flood and fills out the Depeche canvas, gives vital tension, drama and atmosphere to Martin Gore's potentially

★ Rob Reiner's 1984 spoof documentary comedy classic in which the 'legendary' British band, Spinal Tap attempt an early-Eighties American comeback tour with ridiculous results.

morbid ditties; these days, 10 years ahead of time, he is also taking on the appearance of the latter-day Sir Keef – Wilder by name, Wilder by nature, knocking back double tequila shots, and his face is becoming a well-worn road map of rock'n'roll excess."

When encountering a group of Hungarian fans gathered outside his hotel, "Wilder staggered up towards them. 'Go on, fuck off!' he said. 'Get away from the fucking window.'"

Unsurprisingly, Wilder told a different story: "I remember in particular being chased through the streets of Budapest with Hep once during the Devotional Tour. It started out with a few fans seeing us eating outside a restaurant and following us back to the hotel, asking for autographs. Then, as onlookers became more inquisitive, the crowd began to grow. My security man, Joel [Hopkins], started getting nervous, and said, 'One, two, three, *run!*' And we had to leg it back to the hotel with a crowd of excited Hungarians hot on our trail. When we eventually made it inside, they were all banging on the windows of the bar, so I went out to have a word. I explained that we weren't the only guests in the hotel and it may be slightly unsettling for the other people in the bar to feel like they were in *Night Of The Living Dead*, but that I'd sign a few autographs if they promised to leave us in peace.

"In the kind of situation I described, the whole thing becomes a bit like a hunt, where the chase is actually more of a thrill than the original point of getting an autograph out of someone. Hep and I laugh about it now, and at the time we never felt physically threatened; it was just alarming to witness the power and speed with which the event turned from a simple lunch to loads of people baying for blood, if you will. That said, the aspect that I did find rather hurtful was the fact that people reported that I'd told them to 'Fuck off', when I was only attempting to ease the situation for the comfort of other guests in the hotel."

Having staved off one of his "panic attacks" with a little help from some borrowed Nurofen [headache tablets], Martin Gore, known for his appreciation of a tipple or several, was depicted by Friday as indulging in "tequila slammer-fuelled" horseplay, piggyback fighting around the bar area until he, quite literally, dropped.

Friday also introduced the so-called Depeches. More religious cult than mere Depeche Mode fans, this group of fanatical Hungarian youth "took their style, slogans and rationale from [the] band." Such was the enduring appeal of Depeche Mode behind the former Iron Curtain that the Depeches were able to fill a monthly Mode convention in a Budapest civic hall with up to 2,000 fans in the six years leading up to their heroes' first performance in the city.

Not that the Hungarians were alone in organising such gatherings – by now the Depeche Mode convention was a worldwide phenomenon, as confirmed by Terry Coolridge, an American Erasure fan: "My brother attended a DM [Depeche Mode] convention in LA. Richard Blade of KROQ was in attendance and acted as MC for most of the activities. As my brother was heading out to leave, some DM fans asked him why he wasn't participating in the look-a-like competition that was coming up soon. I guess they felt my brother resembled Fletch, being tall and bespectacled.

"My brother thought it would be fun to meet Richard Blade, so he hopped up on-stage when they called for contestants. I think everyone else was either doing Dave or Martin, and my brother was the only 'Fletch'. Each contestant had to perform to a 10-second clip from some DM tune. The 'Daves' all did signature hip thrusts and spinning; the 'Martins' did bleach-blond mop flopping and pacing, but when it came to my brother's turn he just stood there, then took a step to the side and did a big off-the-beat clap, and then stepped back. He may have also pretended to hit a keyboard with one finger. He brought down the house and won the contest – all in good fun. We love Fletch!"

For his part, Fletcher felt it was important to meet and greet after a show, so more often than not it was the seemingly inseparable one-fingered keyboard player and Gore who would usually be spotted socialising backstage. A fanatical 'Depeches' – an English-speaking Hungarian by the name of Judith reported that Andy "was the nicest, the most approachable." Gore, meanwhile, was deemed as not "being his natural self [and] putting on a rock star tour-madness act, because it was what was expected of him."

"[Judith] was repelled by Alan Wilder," reported Gavin Friday. "He looked dreadful and she didn't think it was right the way he was messing round with the young girls at the bar."

Alan Wilder: "I was often around after the show, although I liked to spend a bit of time having a shower and relaxing with a greyhound [woman] – not in the biblical sense, of course – before going into the hospitality area. Dave tended to stay in his dressing room, but sometimes he'd be around."

"The [band] knew he [Gahan] had problems," continued Friday, "you didn't need to see him up close for too long to see that."

On July 31, Depeche Mode headlined at London's Crystal Palace National Sports Centre. Witnessing the curious contrast between people making up the 35,000-strong audience, much was made of the differing dress sense between rival supporters of the two main acts. Writing for *The Independent On Sunday*, Ben Thompson described the Mode masses as being "uniformly attired in newly purchased T-shirts."

Black was predictably the order of the day for those in favour of Leeds-spawned The Sisters Of Mercy. "Front Sister Andrew Eldritch, romantically moody or mildly silly in large sunglasses, prowled the stage aggressively," observed *The Guardian*'s Caroline Sullivan. "He's the personification of his music, which is a brooding blend of panoramic rock and quasi-classical with a Teutonic edge. Wagner would have related to it."

Unfortunately for The Sisters, due to the earlier hour of their scheduled performance, the moody effect of a darkened stage swathed in dry ice, occasionally punctuated by blinding white light, was lost. Perhaps this partly explained Eldritch's behaviour as he walked offstage at the end of The Sisters' set, sneering, "Enjoy the puppet show."

Alan Wilder had the last laugh: "Nothing went on backstage – we didn't see Eldritch or his band. Where's his puppet show now? 'The Dog And Duck', Luton?"

Caroline Sullivan drew attention to Depeche Mode's increased musical – and vocal – scope on-stage: "One minute they're ushering on a string quartet (which waved its bows and capered in startling fashion) for the pretty love song 'One Caress'; the next minute, Gahan is exhorting the audience to 'Make some fucking noise!' Which, of course, it does, Nuremberg-style."

Melody Maker's Chris Roberts: "Gahan (now as overwhelmingly narcissistic on-stage as they come) and Gore seem genuinely *freaky*. Gahan is a splendid showman – his much-improved dancing (and, for that matter, hair) are so unapologetic as to be very nearly sexy, and his repeated mic stand abuse is exemplary. Only an overt penchant for 'Hello Lon-dern!' and 'Awwwlraaat!' mar his football.

"I do lose patience with Dashing Dave when (during the finale of the exquisitely doleful 'In Your Room') he adopts crucifixion pose and mounts the heads of his parishioners, who of course try to feverishly take home slices of the contents of their personal Jesus' trousers."

Alan Wilder defended Gahan's stage-diving fixation of the time: "He never announced he was intending to do it, but you could see the idea brewing in his mind over the course of several gigs, so it was no surprise when he went for it. Looking back with the benefit of hindsight, there are good and bad points to any stage show, and we were all responsible for them. I think Dave had a very demanding job to go out there every night and engage the audience, so it would be unfair to criticise him for a particular move, no matter how much of a rock cliché it was."

According to *NME*'s Dele Fadele: "When 'World In My Eyes' mixes the personal with the trans-global; when 'Personal Jesus' critiques the Basildon Boys' position; when 'Enjoy The Silence' crystallises melancholy New Order; when you're stripped down to the bone you know that Depeche Mode give great stadium. The feeling is there and shared like euphoria, and even some sceptics are moved to obeying Gahan's on-stage exhortations."

Not everyone was converted. Writing for *The Independent On Sunday*, Ben Thompson observed, "Depeche Mode have rocked up the tone a lot, but Gahan's mid-Atlantic yowl does not convince, and there is something rather incongruous about a man shouting, 'Yeah! Alright! Let's see those muthafuggin' hands!' while standing in front of a pile of synthesisers."

Alan Wilder: "Dave's taken on a classic mid-Atlantic accent, although as the old adage goes, you can take the boy out of Basildon but you can't take Basildon out of the boy."

Asked if he was ever annoyed at spending so long "putting together a fantastic, almost subliminal swell to bring the drums in" only to have his work obscured "by some lout in a vest going 'Way-hayeeee!'", Wilder tactfully replied, "They weren't the most subtle of guttural enhancements, but perhaps they were apt for the occasion."

Daniel Miller: "I think the fact that Dave moved to America and absorbed that culture brought in certain ideas that weren't necessarily there before, but I think everything he did was balanced by what the others wanted. As a performer he is *amazing*! That's where he comes into his own, really, as a live performer."

For Gavin Friday the most exciting Depeche Mode performance took place *backstage* at Crystal Palace, in the early hours of August 1, when "The End Of The Depeche Mode European Tour Party" was in full swing. Up a spiral staircase, behind closed doors, was the VIP free tequila and champagne bar, a room that purportedly included live sex acts for the entertainment of the band and their special guests. Friday failed to gain entry (if you'll pardon the pun), but nevertheless reported that the band had taken steps to "protect their decadent image" by inviting "statuesque girls, suitably attired in conical bras, fishnet tights and no knickers" to 'perform'. One invitee apparently described the goings-on as being "very enjoyable".

There was more juicy gossip in store for Friday, such as Gahan being briefly reunited with ex-wife Jo and son Jack in his dressing room: "Seeing him with his relatives was really weird; seeing him with his son – there seemed to be an invisible wall between them."

Having completed the first leg of what was to become an 18-month tour, another unnamed "Mode insider" expressed his concern at Gahan's mental and physical condition. "It's a hard job fronting Depeche, but he must know that if it wasn't for Martin, there'd be no songs; if it wasn't for Alan, the records wouldn't sound the way they do; if it wasn't for Fletch, there probably wouldn't be any money. I think it's hard for David to accept that. I think he does a good job, but he has a lot of problems. I think he's looking for something, really. I really think what he needs is love – he needs to be loved."

26

Synth! Rock! (Till You Drop)

"With the targets, the deadlines, the party-load, even the back and forth between craziness and normality when you had a few days off, I just lost it. I displaced stress into worries about bodily symptoms. I couldn't sleep, I couldn't think, this headache wouldn't go away. I thought I had a brain tumour. But it wasn't; it was a breakdown."

– Andy Fletcher, 1997

With more than a month's gap scheduled between finishing off the European leg of the Devotional Tour in London on July 31 and the commencement of its North American counterpart in Canada's Quebec City on September 7, Andy Fletcher, Martin Gore and Dave Gahan took a much-needed break from the road. Not so Alan Wilder, who headed straight for Dublin and U2's Windmill Lane Recording Studios.

Together with Steve Lyon, Wilder set about mixing the live sound for a video of the Devotional Tour – simply titled *Devotional* – and a live version of the *Songs Of Faith And Devotion* album based on recordings made by Lyon in Copenhagen (May 27), Milan (June 4) and Liévin (July 27), assisted by Euromobile's Peter Brandt. Upon its eventual release on December 6, the live album featured exactly the same tracks (in the same running order) as *Songs Of Faith And Devotion* – hence the title *Songs Of Faith And Devotion Live* . . .

Understandably the music press were muted in their response to this thinly veiled marketing move. "What, you might ask, is the point?" asked *Melody Maker*'s Andrew Smith. "Well, live albums can sometimes, in theory, capture the spirit of a band, as expressed in those telling moments of madness, the spontaneity of which tend not to escape the studio. On the other hand, Depeche were never known for throwing caution to the wind and embarking on brave, bloody sojourns to the outer reaches of their

366

tunes. By all accounts, one night is pretty much [the same] as another. There's nothing wrong with it. It's fine. We just don't learn anything new."

So what *was* the point? Alan Wilder: "The *Songs Of Faith And Devotion Live* . . . CD, with its particular running order, was a marketing tool instigated by the record company as a deliberate – some might say cynical – attempt to prolong sales of the studio album of the same name. Having the identical running order meant that it could be given the same catalogue number – hence the elongated chart position. I also think the general consensus was that it was too soon after *101* to do another similar live album, and, anyway, we were putting together [the] *Devotional* video that would give an even greater feeling of a DM live show.

"As for the choice of performances, there are many considerations as to what can be used, the most obvious being the best vocal performance. We couldn't find a decent version of 'One Caress' using the various 'real' string quartets, which accounts for the sampled one. Most of the hired musicians played astonishingly poorly."

Wilder was quick to cover for Gahan's vocals: "I worked personally with Dave for many years to get the optimum performance out of him and I actually believe that some of his best vocals are on the *Songs Of Faith And Devotion* album. Dave's voice on tracks such as 'In Your Room', 'Condemnation', 'I Feel You' and 'Walking In My Shoes' absolutely mirrors the intensity of the music. Obviously, there is a degradation in his vocals during some of the live performances from [the] Devotional Tour, but this is partly down to the stresses and strains of extensive touring and perfectly understandable. That said, I would rather hear a cracked and rough sounding voice that is full of emotion [rather than] one that is technically perfect, but bland and lifeless."

Nevertheless, the live versions of 'I Feel You' and 'Condemnation' were lowered by a semitone. "They were pitched down to help Dave sing them live. The only way to do this successfully was to adjust each sound individually. The tempo remained the same, so any non-musical part didn't need to be changed."

Jonathan Kessler was now officially credited as Spiritual Adviser on *Songs Of Faith And Devotion Live* . . . with tour accountancy duties handed over to Derek Rauchenberger, credited as Band Advisor on the *Devotional* video. Predictably, punters failed to buy into the 'spiritually advised' live 'replica' album concept; a solitary week at number 193 in *Billboard* on Christmas Day 1993; ditto in the UK, where it became the only Depeche

Mode album to fail to crack the Top 10, reaching 46 following its December 6 release.

It would be some time before Dave Gahan was in a position to articulate any misgivings regarding his position within the established Depeche Mode set-up. When he did open up, his feelings were clear: "There were periods where I felt a bit outside [the loop] – like, 'I've got these ideas, but no one wants to hear them anyway, so why bother?' Which was stupid. I felt undervalued, but it wasn't like I was asking for more value or saying that I had more to contribute and that I wanted to be heard. I was going about it in the wrong way – again, I was trying to get attention and be noticed: 'I don't need you guys anyway.'"

Following a fruitless appearance at the 1993 MTV Video Music Awards at the Universal Amphitheater in his adopted Los Angeles, a swaggering Gahan, still dressed in his 'Devotional' stage clothing (figure-hugging white vest and skin-tight black jeans) talked with John North about playing "scaled down" indoor arena shows. "That's just the way it is now. It's a shame that there's a lot of people now [who] don't seem to go to so many concerts – maybe they're sitting at home watching TV! We're doing alright; it's been going really well. The tickets have gone on sale and we're selling out everywhere."

While New Jersey's Giants Stadium and LA's Dodger Stadium were absent from the band's touring itinerary, with 48 shows set to take them to the end of November 1993, Depeche Mode were indeed "doing alright".

No sooner had Depeche Mode landed in Canada to play Quebec City's Coliseum on September 7, than their vocalist was charged with assault after an altercation at the Fairmount Le Châteaux Frontenac. In a press statement issued by the band's PR, and subsequently published by *Melody Maker* under the headline 'Gahan-Land Attack', the incident centred around Gahan and a group of friends returning late after a meal only to find their hotel in total darkness with all power cut off while maintenance work was being carried out. Extra security was on hand to guide guests to their rooms by torchlight.

According to a spokesperson, "There was a brief scuffle after one of the security men failed to recognise Dave and refused him and his friends entry into the hotel. The staff were shocked, and there were four police cars there within 10 minutes. Dave and another guy, who wasn't one of the band, were taken to the police station and charged, and they had to go back the next morning to give statements. But the charges were dropped, and the tour is going ahead as planned."

There was more . . . Roving *Daily Mirror* journo Rick Sky later reported that "keyboard star" Martin Gore, having angered hotel workers in Denver, Colorado by refusing to turn down the loud music blaring out of his room at four in the morning, was charged with disorderly conduct and fined. The band allegedly confessed to Sky that this kind of thing occurred on a regular basis. " 'We just happened to get arrested this time,' Dave Gahan bragged."

While not up there with the standard rock'n'roll practice of jettisoning hotel furniture into swimming pools, such incidents were indicative of Depeche Mode's road antics, nonetheless. Sticking with his principle of having as much fun as possible on the road, Gore cited practical reasons for the band's extravagance: "Separate hotel floors just meant that if Dave was having a party, or I was having a party, we didn't disturb Andy or Alan. Dave and Alan [also] had their own separate limos; me and Andy always travelled in the same car."

Alan Wilder: "Martin and Fletch were always a definite faction; Fletcher would often act as a kind of interpreter/spokesperson for Martin, who tended to clam up whenever something important needed to be discussed. I wouldn't say Dave and I necessarily formed a counter-faction – we were more inclined to do our own thing."

As the travelling and accommodation arrangements suggest, relations within Depeche Mode were hardly harmonious as their gruelling touring schedule continued unabated. *Q* magazine's Phil Sutcliffe painted a dark picture: "They took to separate limos, separate dressing rooms – Gahan's was a fetid, candlelit lair whence, after the show, minions would cart his smack-blasted body back to the hotel."

Daniel Miller: "Dave was obviously heavily on drugs throughout all that tour. The band weren't talking to each other. You'd have Martin and Fletch go to the gig in one car, Alan would go in another car, and Dave would go in another car. Dave didn't really speak to the other three members of the band throughout the whole tour; the only time he really saw the other members of the band was when they were on-stage. Off-stage, he went into his dressing room with his candles and everything. Alan went into his dressing room. It was a very, very unhappy situation."

On June 29 and 30, Depeche Mode played two consecutive nights at the Palais Omnisport De Paris Bercy. With two free days before performing in

Brest, Alan Wilder, with Steve Lyon, went into Studio Guillaume Tell* to remix 'Condemnation' (from *Songs Of Faith And Devotion*) for release as 'Condemnation (Paris Mix)'.

According to one online source, "This remix was no mean task, incorporating extra hip-hop drum loops and, to further compliment this impressive sound, the use of additional female gospel vocals – provided by Hildia Campbell and Samantha Smith."

Alan Wilder later put the record straight regarding rumours that the use of the two backing vocalists (who had previously featured on 'Get Right With Me') met with resistance and only proceeded at co-producer Flood's insistence: "I'm not aware that there was any resistance to the use of gospel singers or any other additional musicians. At the time, everybody was into the idea, and there was certainly no 'Flood vs. Band' debate – I don't even think the gospel singers were Flood's suggestion."

All seven formats of the single were released in the UK on September 13, including limited-edition 12″ and CD singles featuring four tracks – 'Condemnation', 'Personal Jesus', 'Enjoy The Silence' and 'Halo' – recorded live on June 4 at Milan's Forum by Peter Brandt on Eurosound Mobile. US fans were treated to a 12″, cassette maxi and CD maxi singles featuring the same Parisian remix.

The single's reception contrasted in both territories. While 'Condemnation' made number nine on the UK Singles Chart by September 25, it failed to make any impact whatsoever on *Billboard*, the first time this had occurred since 'Everything Counts (Live)' in 1989. Even the usually receptive Modern Rock Tracks Chart proved disappointing, with 'Condemnation' crawling to number 23, dropping out of the chart within five weeks – the band's poorest showing since 'Halo' in 1990, and that track wasn't even released as a single!

Alan Wilder: "In typical fashion, the US record company wanted a different release to 'Condemnation', so they insisted that we [stood] outside all day in the freezing cold [just outside of Chicago] to make a video for 'One Caress', which, in the end, they decided not to release at all. The only amusing part of the whole event was when half of these creatures [featured in the video] escaped into the trees, and the crew had to spend the rest of the night coaxing them down – pretty hard when you're talking about a cockroach!"

---

* The name quite literally translates as William Tell, hence the use of an apple in the company logo.

With 'One Caress' and its accompanying Kevin Kerslake-directed video duly shelved, Americans were treated instead to 'Condemnation' and another Anton Corbijn video shot on July 28 in the Budapest countryside.

Alan Wilder was equally downbeat in his recollection: "In the cold and rain, Dave was dragged across a field in a messiah-like pose by Sam [Samantha Smith] and Hildia [Campbell], while Anton dressed the remaining band members as monks and . . . well, let's just say it wasn't the highpoint of the DM visual experience."

The less than overwhelming response to the single Stateside may have been due to a British band drawing their inspiration from the blues and black spirituals, selling coals to Newcastle. A less demanding explanation could be that American fans had owned *Songs Of Faith And Devotion*, and therefore the original version of the song, for several months.

John Harris reviewed the single for *NME*: "Perv-gospel, if you listen to this lift from *Songs Of Faith And Devotion* in the right way. *'Feel elation/ High/ To know I can trust this/ Fix of injustice,'* thunders Dave Gahan, as a newly-added choir draped in ecclesiastical robes do the backing vocals, Martin Gore hammers at a church piano and a vicar lurks in the vestry with a horse-whip."

The successful US leg of the Devotional Tour drew to a close on November 26, following five sold-out nights at the LA Forum, where Depeche Mode played to a total of 85,000 people. The *New York Times* reported that the band ranked at number nine in the Top 10 concert grosses for North America between mid-August and mid-September 1993 when they netted $327,375 for one performance in Landover, Maryland. Apart from Rod Stewart, who pocketed $417,057 for a show in Ottawa, they were the only British act to make the grade. Pole position went to The Grateful Dead for the $1,242,400 netted in Richmond, Ohio. Had this been 1988, Depeche Mode would have eclipsed that impressive figure with the $1,360,193 received for their June 18 performance at the Pasadena Rose Bowl.

Less than halfway through the North American leg, during the New Orleans Lakefront Arena show of October 8, Dave Gahan allegedly suffered a heart attack. "It was during the last song," the singer recalled. "I literally couldn't hear anything, so I went off. Something was going on – I couldn't breathe, and the other guys were like, 'We've gotta do an encore!' So Martin and Alan decided to go back on and do a song, and the only song they could do off-the-cuff was 'Death's Door', which was for a

Wim Wenders film [*Until The End Of The World*]. So while I was being wheeled off on a gurney on the way to hospital, I could hear that in the background!

"Everyone was crazy on that tour – it was crazy across the board. We were on the road for 15 months, and you're in this cocoon – it's like another world. So the reality of being taken out on a gurney after a gig and being told by the doctor in hospital that maybe I should continue the rest of the tour on a stool – I was actually told to do that, because my heart probably wouldn't be able to take it . . . I looked at my manager [Jonathan Kessler] and said, 'I can't do that!' So we cancelled the next show – I got one day off, and then I just carried on."

Next in line for tour trouble was Martin Gore, who suffered a seizure at the Sunset Marquis Hotel near West Hollywood's equally famous Sunset Boulevard. "I didn't eat anything. We were shooting a video a couple of days before that happened, and I went straight from the video shoot into a bar and started drinking. Then I went on to a club, met some guy who gave me some stuff; I was up all night with this guy until probably nine or 10 in the morning. We had a band meeting at 12 o'clock, and I managed to sleep for about an hour.

"Then I got up and I've never felt so dreadful in my life. I managed to literally crawl to this meeting; I then had to just lay down on the floor, just saying 'Yes' or 'No' – that was all I could muster. At some point, I tried to get up – I don't know why, because you lose your memory when you have a seizure – and went into convulsions caused by alcohol and drug withdrawal. Band meetings were particularly stressful, but after you've only had an hour's sleep they're a nightmare!"

Alan Wilder: "Nobody enjoyed business meetings very much. In fact, Martin would always do his best to avoid them – mainly because there would usually be an 'off' at any given point, typically over something trivial. The two members who were most prone to scrapping were the two that, luckily, never actually came to blows!"

While Wilder's professionalism prevented him from naming names, Gahan had no such qualms. "Fletch has had a fight with everyone [in Depeche Mode] but me," he told Gavin Friday. "He's never actually tried to hit me. But just lately I think he's potentially been thinking about it."

Shocked at seeing Gore's seizure, fighting was the last thing on the emotionally fragile Fletcher's mind: "Martin just collapsed. It was all very frightening; he had to be trundled off in an ambulance. We thought, 'That's it!' I was very upset – he's my best friend, but he was fine."

Depeche Mode, circa-1997: "I never wanted to be in a pop group *all* of my life – somehow it seems a bit juvenile to be caught up on the pop circuit at the age of nearly 40."(*LFI*)

L.A. press conference, April 17, 1989 – promoting the *101* album and video documenting Depeche Mode's triumphant performance at the Rose Bowl, Pasadena, on June 18, 1988. (*LFI*)

Another L.A. press conference, August 6, 1990 – the maturing Mode publicise two sold-out shows at the 56,000-capacity Dodgers Stadium which closed the US leg of the World Violation Tour. (*LFI*)

Dave Gahan gives good stadium, 1990. (*SIN*)

Martin Gore backstage in New York with The Cure, who covered 'World In My Eyes' for the Depeche Mode tribute album *For The Masses*. Keyboard player Perry Bamonte (far left) was an early Basildon associate of Depeche Mode's. (*WireImage*)

Dave Gahan, circa-1994 – the lengthy *Devotional*/*Exotic* tour takes its toll. (*Redferns*)

Dave Gahan being taken from the L.A. County Sheriff's Department's West Hollywood Station after almost dying from an overdose of heroin and cocaine at the Sunset Marquis Hotel, May 28, 1996. (*Splash*)

Martin Gore, Dave Gahan and Andy Fletcher announce *The Singles Tour*, Depeche Mode's first global outing as a three-piece, at Cologne's Hyatt Hotel, April 20, 1998. (*Rex*)

The Smashing Pumpkins' Billy Corgan guests with Depeche Mode at the K-ROQ Christmas Party, Los Angeles, December 12, 1998. (*LFI*)

Vince Clarke at 37B, the futuristic dome-shaped recording studio in the grounds of his Surrey home. (*Retna*)

Solo artist Martin Gore – on tour promoting the *Counterfeit2* album, 2003.

Dave Gahan finds his own voice – recording *Paper Monsters*, 2003. (*Retna*)

21 years on – Depeche Mode are awarded the inaugural 'Q Innovation Award' "which recognises creativity, invention and courage in the face of adversity" at the *Q* Awards, London, October 22, 2002. (*Rex*)

It transpired that Gore had suffered another seizure prior to the Sunset Marquis Hotel episode. "It happened two weeks previous to that, but I didn't know, because I was on my own. I suddenly woke up and couldn't remember where I was. So when it happened the second time I realised that [it] had happened a few weeks before. It was a real warning to me." Looking back, Gore added, "I'm convinced that stress played a big part in my seizures. Your brain overloads."

A handful of 'Devotional' dates lay ahead, starting with two nights at Mexico City's 21,000-seat indoor Palacio de los Deportes (Sports Palace) on December 3 and 4; ending with a final show 16 days later at London's Wembley Arena.

As far as *NME*'s Johnny Cigarettes was concerned, the lengthy touring stresses and strains were paraded for all to see on the Wembley stage: "The *Spinal Tap* ghosts are threatening to descend from the moment Dave Gahan bellows the first notes from behind a huge opaque curtain intended to show just his huge iconic shadow. The man once cruelly dubbed 'The Ugliest Man In Pop' by *Smash Hits* is now a stadium sex *fuhrer* of doom rock; he must be because he rubs his crotch, wiggles his bum and gropes his nipples a lot. Reservations of a different kind creep in when the other three are revealed, up on high podiums with cornflake-packet futurist silver trimmings, mooging away like your mates in a fifth-form talent contest . . .

"[There's] one thing you can't deny about Depeche Mode. They've never lost the ability to pen a brooding, stirring tune. 'Everything Counts' finishes off the evening, reminding us that they can also write a pithy lyric to accompany them occasionally. But it's a cruel world, and even those talents are not sufficient to override the misguided avant-garde pretensions, pomp, shabby cultural baggage, confusion, cliché and bullshit this band are wallowing in. An unholy mess, frankly."

Perhaps Christmas 1993 might have been a good time for Depeche Mode to call time on touring for a spell. Although the band took a needed break following the conclusion of the 95-date Devotional Tour, the road beckoned them back in the New Year.

Earmarking singles had never been a particularly clear-cut process given the diversity of Depeche Mode's musical make-up.

Alan Wilder: "We would usually reach a consensus of opinion to form a shortlist of potential singles. For example, 'Higher Love' was [originally] on this for the *Songs Of Faith And Devotion* singles, but never made it, and there were differences of opinion about in which order they should appear. Dave, for example, felt very strongly that 'Condemnation' should have been the first single, but he was outvoted. I wanted 'Walking In My Shoes' as a second single and got my way, but I really wanted the original version of 'In Your Room'. This is all a good example of the problems of democracy – somebody usually ends up disappointed."

As it was, on January 10, 1994, 'In Your Room' became the fourth song to be lifted from *Songs Of Faith And Devotion* – albeit in a remixed form.

Alan Wilder described its original album incarnation as being "another very difficult track to complete," being, as it was, an amalgam of three different versions of the song: "The track's particular strength lay in the subtle layering of instrumentation – a bubbling synth part, hypnotic groove and rousing strings – and from start to finish it was characterised by an ever-building tension that kept the listeners on the edge of their seats. This sense of anticipation is dynamically realised in the impassioned lyrics of the third verse and in perfect sync, the music steps up a gear, led by the intensity of the drums and spills over into the final chorus."

Despite Wilder "campaigning vigorously on behalf of the album version to the point where various different edits were tried," 'In Your Room (Zephyr Mix)' saw Depeche Mode quite literally being 'butched up', to paraphrase Dave Gahan.

Alan Wilder: "[I] was eventually outvoted in favour of a remix by Nirvana producer and current grunge darling of the press, Butch Vig. Unfortunately, as is often the case with outside remixers, Vig's interpretation did not relate to many aspects of the original, and the track lost much of its Depeche Mode character, falling short of its intended sensuality and intensity."

Vig's mix of 'In Your Room' climbed all the way up to number eight on the UK Singles Chart on January 22, dropping out of the chart three weeks short of the seven-week showing for 'I Feel You'. The usual array of remixes were offered up, including a lavishly packaged digipack CD single – including Vig's 'In Your Room (Zephyr Mix)' and 'In Your Room (Extended Zephyr Mix)' (recorded and mixed with additional guitars by Doug Erikson at Smart Studios, Madison, Wisconsin) alongside live recordings of 'Never Let Me Down Again' and 'Death's Door' (recorded at Liévin by Manor Mobile's Dave Porter and mixed by Wilder and Steve Lyon at Windmill Lane, Dublin).

The five-way folding cover in which purchasers were invited to buy a limited-edition CD single of four more live Liévin tracks ('In Your

Room', 'Policy Of Truth', 'World In My Eyes' and 'Fly On The Wind-screen') and an 'extra' limited-edition CD single of yet more 'In Your Room' remixes on sale the following week. After all that, 'In Your Room (Zephyr Mix)' failed to chart in America.

Anton Corbijn's camera incorporated monochrome pastiches of earlier Depeche Mode videos linked by an unfocused image of a lightbulb; the shots contrasting markedly with colour footage of the various band members strapped to a chair in a way that bore a passing resemblance to America's dreaded electric chair. Was Corbijn subtly symbolising the death of Depeche Mode or, particularly, Dave Gahan? Later on, Corbijn admitted as much.

For Wilder, at least, there was consolation in the transference of 'In Your Room' to the live arena with an arrangement that owed much to the original album version. As one online observer put it: "Its awesome power was enhanced by Alan's drumming, Dave's heartfelt live performance and Anton Corbijn's breathtaking film show ensuring it was also a high point of the tour."

While his former bandmates' prolonged touring was taking its toll – and having spent much of 1992 on the road himself with Erasure – Vince Clarke was taking his first serious sabbatical since the duo's initial success back in 1986. Since then he had racked up no fewer than 20 hit singles with songwriting partner Andy Bell – 13 of which had been Top 10 entries back home on the UK Singles Chart, an achievement which the duo com-memorated with their aptly titled *Pop! – The First 20 Hits* compilation.

Amsterdam was now home to Clarke who rented a workspace to house his growing collection of vintage analogue synthesisers temporarily while he awaited the completion of his new home studio back in the UK. Clarke's studio didn't follow a conventional structure – nor, for that matter, did the Chertsey home (in the southern English county of Surrey) where it was based.

Clarke was not the first musician to own the voluminous estate. The original property belonged to film director Peter Collinson (of *The Italian Job* fame), who, when refused planning permission to extend the property, promptly blew it up and constructed the outlandish Tara House – named after his son, Tara – on the site. Suitably impressed, the Who's Keith Moon bought Tara House in 1971, where it gained no little notoriety as the venue for Moon's many outlandish pranks. After relocating to America, Moon sold it to 10cc's Kevin Godley in 1975. Come 1990,

Godley was similarly seduced by the American dream, and sold it on to Clarke. Like Collinson before him (and unfortunately for Who fans), Clarke demolished the structure to build his own dome-shaped home and recording studio, having spent two years mulling over numerous futuristic architectural designs.

Electric Eel Studio Design's Kevin van Green – who had previously completed diverse workspaces for Martin Gore, Alan Wilder, and Daniel Miller – was employed to make Clarke's dream studio a reality. "Vince Clarke's home studio is housed in a copper-clad domed structure, looking more like the control room of a spaceship than a studio," its designer revealed.

According to Electric Eel's website, "Kevin van Green resolved the design challenge by installing an equally unconventional semi-circular, central mixing desk and workstation. Following the *Dr Who* feel, Vince's vast collection of synthesisers are positioned wall-to-wall, creating, in effect, one seriously big synthesiser."

One early visitor, impressed with the set-up, was former Human League member, Martyn Ware*, by now a major league record producer with a diversity of credits to his name, including Tina Turner and Terence Trent D'Arby.

"Vince has this amazing studio which is circular," Ware told *Sound On Sound* in 2000. "It has walkways with all the synths arranged around the walls, connected by CV [Control Voltage] and Gate patchbays. Almost every keyboard he has in the studio, he has a duplicate of in the basement, in case they break down. That's also where he keeps synths [that] have fallen out of favour or he hasn't got room for. It's like a National Gallery for synths – you can only show about 50 per cent of the stuff at any one time!"

Vince Clarke: "It was a challenge for everybody, but a lot of time was spent researching it all. Everyone did a brilliant job!"

The first material to be partly recorded at 37B, as Clarke christened his new workplace, was Erasure's next album, with Ware sitting in as producer. It proved to be an eye-opening experience for the electropop pioneer – who later described himself as "a bit of a jack of all trades" and Clarke as "very much the master of his" – on more than one level: "Vince [gave] me a couple of synths; he has people searching the world looking for stuff for him, and he gave me one of the original Roland System 100s –

---

* Ware claimed that Vince Clarke confided that Depeche Mode might not have started had it not been for The Human League's début example, 'Being Boiled'.

I couldn't believe it, I was so touched – and also the very first synth I ever owned, a Korg 700. He had two of those and he said, 'Oh, you can have one' – that's the kind of guy he is."

Reviews of the album, *I Say, I Say, I Say* were generally in Erasure's favour; *The Daily Telegraph*'s Tony Parsons wrote: "They are the Mills and Boon of vocal/synthesiser duos; I like them best when Bell is howling pitifully at the moon and Clarke is bleeping away in the background like a melancholy Dalek which is conclusive proof that only Andy Bell's stage clothes stop Erasure from being ranked as one of the great British songwriting partnerships."

Bell's homosexuality seemed destined to remain forever inextricably linked to his career. When pressed on the subject by *The Sunday Times'* James Lockhart, the singer responded, "I'm not a politician and I get letters using the gay guilt thing saying I should speak up even more about gay issues, but I make pop records, for goodness sake. Music is a separate thing from politics."

Despite failing to follow its five predecessors to the top of the UK Albums Chart, the Martyn Ware-produced *I Say, I Say, I Say* still spawned two Top 10 UK hit singles in 'Always' (number four in April 1994) and 'Run To The Sun' (number six in July). Clarke's musical Midas touch was still intact – or so it seemed in July 1994. Yet Erasure would not perform live again for quite some time – unlike Mute labelmates Depeche Mode . . .

Alan Wilder's Christmas/New Year break was considerably shorter than his colleagues, for on February 9, 1994, Depeche Mode recommenced touring for a 28-date so-called 'ROW' (rest of the world) jaunt, taking in South Africa, Australia, the Far East and South America, ending on April 16 in Monterrey, Mexico.

Because the concerts in those territories coincided with longer daylight hours, the Devotional show that Wilder had tirelessly arranged had to be restructured. The impressive introductory mock 'thunder and lighting' sequence preceding 'Higher Love' making use of natural twilight (during outdoor performances) was dropped in favour of a frenetic techno sequence leading into a more dynamic version of 'Rush', featuring live drums.

A radically reworked 'trip-hop' version of 'I Want You Now' (from *Music For The Masses*) also made it into the set list. "It was recorded in a Milan studio during a three-week session in January '94, just before the start of the ROW leg of the tour," Alan Wilder revealed. "The only people present were myself, Steve Lyon and Daryl Bamonte. This is also where the techno 'Rush' introduction and various other bits and pieces were done.

"The remaining members of the band didn't hear 'I Want You Now' or any of the other [additional] music until it was played on-stage."

The 'Exotic Tour' was plagued with problems. Depeche Mode's first visit to South Africa – performing seven times in Johannesburg and twice each in Capetown and Durban between February 9 and 26, 1994, was memorable for some.

Alan Wilder: "Whilst on the road, each member had a large flightcase wardrobe that would contain stage gear and usually the majority of one's personal clothing. During our stay in South Africa, my entire wardrobe was stolen overnight, and considering the building was securely locked and patrolled by guards, we concluded that it must have been an inside job. I lost about £10,000 worth of clothing, some very personal bits and pieces, and, of course, most of my stage outfits, which had to be remade. The only consolation was a nice, fat insurance cheque and the excuse to go out and spend, spend, spend!"

Getting over that calamity was a relatively painless experience, unlike the excruciating agony Wilder suffered which led to his hospitalisation in South Africa. The cause turned out to be kidney stones, no doubt a result of his excessive drinking throughout the tour. Co-Tour Manager Daryl Bamonte was especially amused at Wilder's treatment, and was later recorded asking him what it felt like to have a laser inserted into his "member" and whether "the South African nurse [had] a nice uniform."

Wilder replied, "Well, as you know, Mr Bamonte, I was asleep during the operation, although if you've ever thought about how it would feel to urinate pins and needles, then you can imagine what the after-effects felt like. One's member requires a couple of weeks recovery time before being fully functional again, so the attire of the South African nurse was largely irrelevant!"

Asked whether he stopped drinking as a result of this experience, Wilder responded: "No! I'd rather die of kidney stones than cabin fever! I just drank more water afterwards and took it a bit easy – for about three days."

The Exotic Tour headed East for a solitary show at Singapore's Indoor Stadium on March 1. When asked whether the band was given a hard time "regarding narcotic issues" by customs officials, Wilder joked, "No, they managed to get us all the drugs we requested!" When Singapore's strict death penalty for heroin possession was pointed out, Wilder stopped smiling: "I wasn't aware of that at all."

Australia's sunny delights were next on the schedule with well-received performances in almost all of that vast country's major cities (Perth, Adelaide, Melbourne, Brisbane and Sydney). Come March 16, Depeche Mode were back in Hong Kong, the first time that the group had played in the city, considered by many to be the gateway to the East, for several years.

Andy Fletcher: "Peter Gabriel played a week before, and he played to basically 80 per cent Europeans; we got a crowd that was three times as big, which was 98 per cent Chinese . . . Our records are selling well in India, and places like that – same with South Africa and South America – and, of course, Eastern Europe, we're absolutely huge. It is an achievement."

Despite such positivism Fletcher's recurring battle with depression forced him to bail out of the Exotic Tour after two performances at Honolulu's Blaisdell Arena (on March 25 and 26). With one man down, talk turned to extending the trek beyond its scheduled six South American dates for another 35 North American dates before the Exotic Tour would finally finish.

"I wasn't in favour of a second American leg," admitted Andy Fletcher. "After the *Violator* period we thought we were kings; we thought we could tackle anything!"

In March 1994, Fletcher wasn't in any fit state to tackle anything, to the point where Gahan and Wilder approached Gore to *demand* Andy's with-drawal. "It was very difficult," Gore reflected. "Andy's been my closest friend since we were 12, but, for the other two, he'd become unbearable. I justified it by thinking that it would be better for Andy if he went home and got professional advice."

Dave Gahan: "For a while there, he [Fletcher] was off trying to take care of himself, and I was off doing what I was doing. He was absent a lot of the time during the Devotional Tour, and he continued on. It's tough, this stuff, sometimes. To be honest, I was starting to get wrapped up in my own stuff."

Andy Fletcher: "I had had a nervous breakdown when we were record-ing the album [*Songs Of Faith And Devotion*]. And then I went straight on tour, and it was a very long tour, a very stressful tour. And it just went on and on and on, and then they decided to do another American tour, and I just didn't agree with doing it and thought it was a mistake, bad for our careers. I just needed a rest, so [I] decided not to do it. I regret they didn't make the same decision, but they were on a whole party-sort-of-wave."

For Daniel Miller, the scope of Depeche Mode's problems reached beyond Fletcher's depression: "Fletch was finding it very difficult; he was having personal problems – they were *all* having problems. I was extremely worried. When it came to a decision about doing a second American tour, that was kind of when I put my foot down – to no effect, I have to say, unfortunately. But I put my foot down and said, 'I don't really think you should do this. You absolutely should not do the second half of this tour. It's really dangerous for the individuals involved, and there's no point.'"

According to Wilder, however, there *was* a simple point: "I think if one is truthful, it would be financial . . . There weren't many other reasons that I can think of why you would want to do it – except that we did play a few territories that we wouldn't have normally got to, like South America. But, I think, if you weigh everything up, the sensible decision would have been to say, 'Well, we don't *need* to go to South America; let's just stop.'

"During the Devotional Tour, for internal flights in the USA and Europe, we hired a private plane, which held approximately 15 passengers. We took commercial flights for international or long-haul journeys – the band would generally fly Business Class (sometimes upgraded by the airline to First).

"For South America we charted a plane to carry band, entourage, crew and gear. The best thing about having a private plane for the majority of the flights – in the US, for example – was that your car could just drive straight up to the plane on the tarmac, and when you landed at the other end, there would again be a car waiting."

But booking entire hotel floors and chartering private planes was clearly costing the band dearly.

Alan Wilder: "Touring is big business. Merchandising alone can earn a small fortune, so the financial benefits of a long tour are very enticing – the longer you keep a production on the road, the easier it becomes to create a healthy profit margin. But, of course, we've all seen how lengthy touring can take its toll on individuals."

Added to this, Gahan's already tenuous grip on reality was tempered further still by his spiralling substance abuse.

Alan Wilder: "Of course, everybody was concerned about his welfare, but addicts are notoriously difficult to dissuade from their cause unless they themselves really want to change. At the time, Dave wasn't really in the that frame of mind, and therefore any advice given to him fell on deaf ears."

It's been claimed that Wilder was the main instigator behind extending the Exotic Tour beyond its original final South American shows. "Actually, Dave also wanted to do another leg, and the others didn't object at the time . . . It was just [the] USA [and Canada], because there are more areas to cover there and different types of shows – and audiences – depending on the time of year. For example, the first US ['Devotional Tour'] leg was done in the winter months in indoor arenas while the second ['Exotic Tour'] concentrated on outdoor summer venues, known as 'sheds'."

Andy Fletcher: "Alan particularly wanted to do it, which makes me very suspicious. It might have been a case of milking the band, because he knew he was going to leave. I don't know if he'll admit to that, but that's what I think now, looking back the way it was done. He saw this as the last tour; he thought it was going to be the end of the band."

Predictably, Wilder flatly denied the allegation: "I didn't think about it being the last time for me as I didn't decide to leave the band until 18 months later."

As late as June 1996, *The Sunday Times* was still reporting that Andy Fletcher ". . . left the [Exotic . . .] tour before it even finished, ostensibly to be with his wife when she gave birth, but really, claim insiders, because he had allegedly suffered a nervous breakdown, brought on, they suggest, by his increasing guilt and embarrassment about the fact that he'd never really had any significant musical role."

Although the Fletchers' second child, Joseph, was born on June 22, 1994, roughly midway through the US leg of the extended tour, Fletcher would eventually admit that he had indeed suffered a nervous breakdown, citing "the stress and tension of a 24-hour-a-day job, seven days a week" as being its primary cause.

Depeche Mode overcame the setback of Fletcher's departure, by an old friend valiantly stepping into the breach.

Alan Wilder: "While everyone was sunning themselves on the beach and enjoying a well-earned rest, Daryl [Bamonte] and I spent a week cooped up in a hotel room in Hawaii where I taught him the entire set. He subsequently played it perfectly for the rest of the tour – pretty good, considering he'd hardly ever played a keyboard before in his life."

Wilder's comments didn't exactly say much for Fletcher's keyboard technique, adding further credence to insider claims that his lack of musicality contributed to his nervous breakdown. The other members of Depeche Mode played and partied on regardless.

27

When Four Became Three

"My honest decision to leave the band came during the making of the Songs Of Faith And Devotion *album. I can remember one or two occasions that stick vividly in my mind where, during that recording – particularly those first sessions – I thought, 'This is not enjoyable; I don't want to be doing this; this is the last time I want to be in this situation.' "*

– Alan Wilder, 2001

Having got through South America without any reported mishaps, the press had a field day when it was announced that Primal Scream would be supporting Depeche Mode for 11 weeks on the North American leg of the Exotic Tour. Given the Scottish rockers' wild reputation, this could be seen as being a somewhat suicidal move on Depeche Mode's part given that Gahan showed no signs of curbing his substance abuse. So much for the $4,000 a week on-the-road shrink!

Martin Gore: "It didn't really work, because, although Fletch saw him occasionally, the rest of us never did. After six weeks, we knocked it on the head."

Alan Wilder: "Dave pushed very strongly to have 'Primal Tap' join the tour – I can't imagine why! I felt it was probably a recipe for disaster, but I didn't care enough to argue. By that stage, I was very much heads down, on the home strait, just trying to survive until the last gig."

Indeed, there was no arguing with the determined Gahan who was desperate to get the Primals on the Exotic Tour: "I *insisted* on it! I loved their attitude and the album they'd made at the time – *Give Out But Don't Give Up*. I wanted us to be able to swing like that, and be that loose. It was my idea, and Teresa was working for Steve Rennie, who was managing them at the time. I just hung out with them."

Q's Phil Sutcliffe summed up the scenario – and with it the general press

382

consensus: "For the final American tour, Gahan wangled a support spot for his presumed narcotic soulmates, Primal Scream. But, insiders allege, the Scream were so shaken by Depeche Mode's level of excess that, thenceforth, they fervently foreswore sin and their forthcoming album was recorded with zero input of powder, pill or spliff."

That observation was borne out to a degree by Andy Fletcher: "I was in hospital during the Primal Scream tour, but I think it was probably bad news for the Primals more than Depeche. I don't even think they realised the state everyone was in at that point. I think they were shocked! The length of the tour was a mistake."

Given that he was physically present, Wilder was better positioned to make a more objective judgement as to what Primal Scream were actually like. "Bit smelly – especially Bobby [Gillespie]," he joked. "To be honest, I didn't really spend any time with them, so I couldn't [talk] about their personalities. Dave and Daryl liked to party with them the most, but that generally meant hotel room gatherings. I preferred to get out and about after a show."

Martin Gore: "The bit [of the Exotic Tour] that was most written about was the leg that we did with Primal Scream; that only lasted for three months and the tour itself lasted for 15 months. When they weren't there I'm sure we weren't angels, but it really wasn't an orgy; it wasn't completely out of control all of the time. We wouldn't have survived if it had really taken on the epic proportions that everybody speaks about."

Select magazine's Andrew Perry travelled with Primal Scream, and witnessed potential trouble from the outset. "Gahan was obviously in awe of them, but the Scream were in complete disarray from the minute they joined the tour in California. They'd just completed three weeks in Britain, and they were cream-crackered. When they landed in San Francisco, they were immediately given a hard time by customs who assumed that they must be carrying drugs because they were a rock band. And that night [May 12] they had to play [the Cal Expo Amphitheater in] Sacramento."

Primal Scream lived up to Gahan's warped expectations, all the same: "We had a lot of fun, actually – a lot of good times. They were always in my dressing room."

No prizes for guessing why. "It was brilliant," Gahan maintained, adopting a passable Glaswegian accent. "There'd be a knock at the door before the show, and it's [Andrew] Innes, or 'Throb' [Andrew Young], or Bobby [Gillespie]: 'Have ye got a wee sniff, Mr G? I cannae make it tonight, I've been on the Jack [Daniel's] all day. I just need a wee sniff, Mr G.' And, of course, I'd supply them with whatever they needed. Bobby saw right through my little game, and I felt I saw through his. He gives off this great image of being a wasted fuck-up, but he's a real smart, clever guy. Bobby balanced it really well; he knew where to stop. I didn't. I didn't realise that nobody actually did play the game that hard. And the Scream proved that."

At the time, Gahan remarked, "The problem is, the more out of it you become in their company, the straighter they seem to be getting."

"It wasn't druggie," Bobby Gillespie told *The Guardian*. "It was the least amount of drugs I've done in my life! It was just really boring."

Be that as it may, within a fortnight of his arrival, guitarist Throb managed to land himself on the wrong side of the law when he narrowly avoided being charged with indecent exposure after swimming naked in the San Antonio River with three of his road crew. "They threatened me with indecent exposure, but just gave me a warning," he said at the time. "I regretted it all the next day. It must have been the drink." (Primal Scream's security man, Steve Malloy, wasn't quite so lucky; he was arrested for criminal mischief and released on bail.)

As reported by *Select* magazine in February 2000: "On the band's nightmarish US tour supporting Depeche Mode in '94, they were strung out and dispirited by the time of their own headline gig at Baltimore's tiny 8 By 6 Club. Duffy arrived at the soundcheck hopelessly drunk, sporting a couple of broken fingers and a sign round his neck that said, inexplicably, 'No Martial Arts'. Words were exchanged and Throb suddenly went at Duffy – trying to smash the keyboard player's head open with his guitar – and for an hour or two the band had officially split."

Indeed, life on the road with Depeche and the Primals sounded like it was anything *but* boring. Perry turned in the following report from backstage at the Jones Beach Amphitheater shows of June 16 and 17: "Gahan was in a right state by then, with ropey American rock chicks hanging around him, all ripped fishnets and stilettos, incapable even of putting their lipstick on straight. They had a roadie who would go out every night and pick out the 15 or 20 most beautiful girls in the crowd and take them backstage, evidently for the Mode's pleasure." No change there, then.

"[Primal] Scream always took boxes of records and had a couple of decks in the dressing room," Perry continued, "so there were all these people dancing, and Dave Gahan sitting in the middle of the room in an armchair, apparently shovelling cocaine up his nose at a frightening rate.

"Suddenly, he seemed to realise that I was a journalist, and he pointed at me and one of his big flunkeys came and got me. I had to kneel down beside the armchair to make it possible for him to talk to me. He started burbling on about how people didn't understand him, but then his mood changed suddenly and he said, 'I'm gonna curse you!' and the next thing I know he's bitten me on the neck! By now he was shouting and everybody was watching him until he stormed out of the room, still yelling about putting a curse on me. I assumed he was completely out of it, but then, on-stage, he was totally together and professional."

Alan Wilder: "On the whole, no one indulged in anything much, pre-show; I don't really know about Dave's exact pre-show condition on the Songs Of Faith And Devotion Tour, but he always seemed to me like he was going to be able to perform OK."

So what did 'Dracula Dave' have to say about Perry's impressions? "I thought we were having a good time – that was the Jones Beach [Amphitheater] show. I remember reading about it, but I don't really remember doing it. I think I had some fascination at the time with vampires, but I was really starting to move into this place where I really believed what I was creating. I definitely could have been a vampire, in my own head; I was fascinated by it at the time. Even the bed I slept in, in Los Angeles, was in the shape of a coffin – a huge double bed, shaped like a coffin! My whole life was *Spinal Tap* at that time, but I did still laugh at that. When it was good – when you hit that spot on tour, we had real good fun."

Alan Wilder: "The myth that has been building up around the Devotional Tour now seems to be fully out of control; in actual fact, it wasn't really any more 'rock'n'roll' than other Depeche Mode tours over the years. Everyone had their own little 'on tour' world that existed alongside a professionally run live show; it was just longer than the others and has subsequently been better documented.

"The well-oiled machine meant that, quite often, our paths would not even cross, apart from the two hours on-stage. Most of the stories have an element of truth about them; everyone was indulging in their own thing – sometimes with destructive results, but that's all part of the private way you deal with such a bizarre and unreal world. There were also other incidents like bad flights and fights, which caused tensions, but that's inevitable when you have that many people careening around the world for 18 [*sic*] months."

The bad flight Wilder mentioned occurred during a weekend tour break.

Alan Wilder: "Martin and I were on a flight from Dallas to the Caribbean when, after about 20 minutes or so, there was a loud bang and I think all the oxygen masks came down. It was some kind of pressurisation problem. There was a fair amount of panic, and the air hostesses, tearfully embracing one another, didn't exactly inspire confidence. The pilot had to turn around and we sat through a hair-raising 20 minutes as the plane tried to make it back to Dallas. Later on, we were reliably informed that had we been at our proper cruising altitude, this would have been a major accident! We ended up getting blind drunk in the airport, eventually hiring a private plane at great expense and woke up in the sunshine of the West Indies with a headache."

Having spent some 13 months on the road over a 15-month period during the draining Devotional and Exotic tours, Depeche Mode finally played their last performance thereof at the Deer Creek Music Center in Indianapolis on July 8; having been witnessed by nigh on two-million people in total.

Alan Wilder: "In spite of all these things, there were loads of good moments, too. Not only was it the most successful tour with some of the best shows we'd ever played, but, personally, I can't see what all the fuss [was] about – I had a great time!"

A great time was no doubt had by all at another extravagant end-of-tour party at St Andrews Hall, Detroit. According to Alan Wilder, "[It] was pretty much on a par with the reputation the band had acquired – at least all the standard Depeche Mode requirements were met: scantily clad girls, erotic dancers, Martin dressed as a woman."

Surprisingly absent from the festivities was Dave Gahan, who had taken his stage-diving antics to their extreme by taking a 12-foot jump off the stage at Indianapolis, landing shoulder first against some seats that were fixed to the concrete floor. Once again, he was stretchered off to hospital with two excruciatingly painful broken ribs haemorrhaging from the inside. Only the wasted singer didn't physically feel any pain for 24 hours as he had been so drunk at the time. Against medical advice, Gahan opted to recover on his own terms, discharging himself from St Vincent Hospital in favour of renting a small North Californian cabin in Lake Tahoe with wife Teresa, where he remained strapped up for three weeks.

Not that the Exotic Tour had been all bad, as Wilder recounted some traditional end of tour high jinks: "Jez Webb – the guitar tech – emerged, to my surprise, from the shell of the piano during 'Somebody', I think. This is a typical last-date-of-the-tour prank, as has become tradition amongst the rock'n'roll touring fraternity. We also experienced tour managers-turned-backing vocalists in drag (Andy Franks). Other favourites include talcum powder on the drum skins, 'Mrs Mop' coming on with a broom to sweep the stage during Dave's finest moment, and exposed arses at the side of the stage – oh, how we laughed."

Nevertheless, the touring rush had ended, and when that fact finally hit home with Dave Gahan, it hit home hard. "I really enjoyed the [Songs Of] Faith And Devotion tour; I enjoyed that whole two year [*sic*] experience. I was right in it: 'I'm going to fucking do it, goddam it! And no one's going to stop me!' It took me a few years to come down from it."

Meanwhile, across the Atlantic, an associate of Andy Fletcher's took him back to The Priory in Roehampton. Safely ensconced in a private room, Fletcher was apparently convinced that Dave Gahan was the Devil, out to get him! Said associate tried to calm him by opening the curtains to a darkened skyline as a solitary thunderclap crashed overhead, almost on cue. "It's him! It's Dave!" the bassist cried.

Understandably, Fletcher's own recollection of his hospitalisation was more guarded: "Back home, I went into hospital for four weeks. I've recovered ever since I took up yoga, relaxation. I think I'm much stronger now. Hopefully, there won't be a repeat."

While Fletcher was recovering from his latest bout of depression, Gore set about making extravagant arrangements to wed partner, Suzanne Boizvert at Brocken Hall in Hertfordshire on August 27. The ubiquitous Rick Sky reported one guest as saying, "No expense was spared, the champagne flowed all day."

Rob Andrews was in agreement: "Yes, it was very lavish, with coaches [laid on] from London. It went on until late – no expense spared is right."

Gahan reputedly staggered into the wedding reception in the early hours of the following morning, accompanied by various members of Primal Scream, with whom he had been jamming at the Reading rock festival. Set adrift from the comparative sanctuary of his touring highlife – however crazy that had clearly been – things were looking bleak for the singer. "Teresa decided that she wanted to have a baby," he told Q. "I said to her, 'Teresa, we're junkies!' 'Cos let's not kid ourselves, when you're a junkie, you can't shit, piss, come, nothing. All those bodily functions *go*. You're in this soulless body; you're in a shell. She didn't get it."

As if Andy Fletcher didn't already have enough on his plate, he suffered a financial upset as an unfortunate investor in the disastrous Lloyd's of London insurance market crash. Having been introduced to Lloyd's by Leon Nahon, a senior partner at London-based accountants and business advisers Levy Gee, Fletcher was understandably less than happy with the outcome of his involvement and instructed his solicitor to write to Nahon for an explanation. *The Times* reported the business adviser as saying: "We get correspondence from a lot of people. Everyone who was in Lloyd's and lost money is shooting at anyone he can." Fletcher subsequently fired a damaging legal broadside. "I did win most of it back when I sued my previous accountant," he declared. "It was a real con!"

Despite this financial setback, Andy and Grainne built a luxury weekend home on a wooded island, on the River Thames, near Marlow in Buckinghamshire. "We had looked at all sorts of properties, but it was only by chance that we decided to take a look at what the estate agents described as 'a Thames island property in need of extensive modernisation'.

"In truth, what we found was little more than a shack in need of demolition. The site, however, was perfect. We fell in love with it and decided to buy almost immediately. We have one of the best views of the Thames, and it is ideal for fishing, which is one of my hobbies."

Grainne Fletcher: "Our initial ideas were somewhat restricted by the planners. Unfortunately, they insisted that we [kept] to a single-storey design and wouldn't allow us to increase the size of the building we were replacing by more than 10 per cent."

With those restrictions in mind, the Fletcher's appointed architect, John Newton, designed their weekend retreat to a Swedish log construction system, instigating a cunning two-tier building scheme allowing for future expansion into the roof area: "The initial design had three bedrooms, open-plan kitchen/living and dining area, plus two bathrooms. The second stage added a master bedroom suite in the roof-space, with a gym and gallery."

Robert Marlow couldn't help but be impressed: "Fletch's summer house is very nice – a log cabin on an island called The Rock, in the Thames. I think he's still got his boat; we used to go out on his boat. We've had some lovely weekends. He used to throw these excellent parties there."

Meanwhile, Wilder opted to unwind, post-tour, by taking a leisurely drive around the Scottish Highlands with new partner Hep Sessa. What was planned as a pleasurable break descended into a nightmarish, near-death experience, just weeks after his Caribbean flight escape. A month later, *Melody Maker* picked up the story: "Depeche Mode's Alan Wilder narrowly escaped death when an RAF Tornado plane crashed into a hillside near Lochearhead, Perthshire, in Scotland on September 1, killing the two airmen [31-year-old Flight Lieutenant Peter Mosley and his navigator, Patrick Harrison, two years his senior]. Wilder was showered with debris which scattered across the A85 trunk road after the plane crashed some 200 yards away from his open-topped car."

Wilder issued a detailed statement giving a gruesome account of the tragedy, which the music paper printed in full: "As I approached a sharp bend in the road, the sound of the Tornado appeared behind me, and as I looked up, I saw the underside of the aircraft no more than 50 feet above me. Within a split second, to my complete astonishment, the plane had crashed beside the road into the glen about 200 yards ahead. Apparently, it had been travelling at nearly 400 miles per hour.

"As I swerved off the road into a farm track, I heard the sound of the impact and witnessed an enormous explosion from which the smoke and debris almost engulfed me.

"Another witness ran to call the police as I drove around the bend to the site. At the same time, particles of carbon, et cetera, began to rain down onto the open-top car.

"Beyond the bend, parts of the dead airmen's bodies were clearly visible in the road – parts of a seatbelt with guts attached, lumps of gore, et cetera; a parachute, burning shrapnel and a strong, sweet smell of fuel.

"After the police arrived, I decided to leave the scene to avoid delay as many other cars had arrived, and there was nothing further to do. It was only at this point that I realised what an incredible escape I'd had. I would surely have been killed or, worse, severely maimed, had I been 10 seconds further into my journey.

"The most incredible thing is the one in a billion chance of that happening and me being there at that particular time, given the circumstances."

Several years down the line Wilder was still audibly shaken by his brush with death at such close quarters. "I didn't find religion or have any life-transforming experience, but it left its mark. It was the surreal quality of the event that I remember most. The thing that struck me was that such an instantaneous tragedy is immediately followed by the banality of continuing life. As two dead airmen were splattered across the road, the sun shone, the birds sang, and no music played."

Irrespective of his dice with death, like Gahan before him, Alan Wilder was having serious doubts as to being a member of Depeche Mode and had been harbouring these thoughts for some time. By June 1, 1995 – Wilder's 36th birthday – his mind was made up. He wanted out.

Alan Wilder: "I called a meeting at our [London] office to tell Martin and Fletch, and then I sent a fax to Dave in LA, which, after having tried to contact him several times by phone, was the only way I could let him know. I didn't hear back directly from Dave, but he did send Hep [whom Alan married in 1995] and I a huge bunch of flowers when Paris [Wilder] was born [in 1996]. I'm sure he understands perfectly why I left, and he has been nothing but a perfect gentleman regarding the whole situation."

The reaction of the band members present at that fateful London meeting was more immediate. As Alan Wilder remembered it: "Martin shook my hand and looked a bit embarrassed, and Fletch got quite defensive and seemed to take it rather personally – I don't really understand why, since I wasn't casting aspersions against anyone."

According to Fletcher, "We just had a meeting – me, Martin and him – and he just announced it. We just sort of went, 'Oh, why's that?' There was no sort of trying to persuade him not to go."

That same day, Wilder issued a statement to the press regarding his decision to leave Depeche Mode: "Due to increasing dissatisfaction with the internal relations and working practices of the group, it is with some sadness that I have decided to part company from Depeche Mode. My decision to leave the group was not an easy one – particularly as our last few albums were an indication of the full potential that Depeche Mode was realising.

"Since joining in 1982, I have continually striven to give total energy, enthusiasm and commitment to the furthering of the group's success, and in spite of a consistent imbalance in the distribution of the workload, willingly offered this.

"Whilst I believe that the calibre of our musical output has improved, the quality of our association has deteriorated to the point where I no longer feel that the end justifies the means. I have no wish to cast aspersions on any individual – suffice to say that relations have become seriously strained, increasingly frustrating and, ultimately, in certain situations, intolerable.

"Given these circumstances, I have no option but to leave the group. It seems preferable, therefore, to leave on a relative high, and as I still retain a great enthusiasm and passion for music, I am excited by the prospect of pursuing new projects.

"The remaining band members have my support and best wishes for anything they may pursue in the future, be it collectively or individually."

In light of Depeche Mode's geographically fragmented status, Mute hurriedly issued a succinct statement of their own: "We are very sorry to have to inform you that Alan Wilder has decided to leave Depeche Mode after 13 years. The band have no plans to replace Alan, and Martin is currently writing new material. Martin, Dave and Fletch intend to continue as Depeche Mode."

In reflecting further on his Depeche departure, Wilder claimed: "I don't think any of [the other band members] were aware that it was coming, and even if they were, I don't think they thought actually I'd go through with it . . .

"The advantage of a statement is that it's a good way to close the lid on something. I have no wish to elaborate further on what was said in it; suffice to say that things are never as straightforward as they appear from the outside.

"It probably didn't go down well, but I wanted to try to summarise succinctly some of the reasons for my departure, rather than have the press speculate and inevitably draw the wrong conclusions."

Fletcher drew his own short-term conclusions: "I personally thought that he felt there wasn't going to be another Depeche Mode album, and I think he thought he'd get his bit in first. And, of course, the state that Dave was in at the time . . . at any point we could have got a phone call saying he was dead."

Wilder touched upon this when writing, "It is commonly thought that I left the band due to Dave's obvious problems, but [that] was not the case; I did think, however, that DM continuing was down to whether or not Dave could sort himself out, and, at that time, things were pretty bleak."

Andy Fletcher: "Reading between the lines, I think he thought I'd be the first one to get out. He also didn't say too many nice things about Martin and myself, but I can understand that. There's many people I've fallen out with over the years – you say things you don't really mean in years to come."

"When Alan left the band he was insistent on making a big press statement," Gore griped to the *NME*'s Keith Cameron in 1997. "One of his main points was that he felt the workload over the years had been unfairly distributed. And if that was the case, it was because he decided that was how it should be, because he was a control freak. If the work was unfairly distributed it was because he made it that way."

When asked in the same interview if Depeche Mode remained in touch with Wilder, Fletcher suggested that they hardly saw him when he was still in the group, only to be cut off midflow by Gore: "I don't think we should ever get into a slanging match with Alan, because he was an integral part of the band who had a lot of input and a lot of say in what the band were doing."

But any apparent softening on Gore's part was short-lived when he apparently accused Wilder of being a "misanthropist".

Alan Wilder: "Well, there's probably an element of truth in [that], but misanthropist is perhaps a little harsh. I don't have a huge army of so-called friends because I don't suffer fools gladly and I'm also not so insecure that I need an entourage of sycophants singing my praises all the time. I'm very selective about the people I socialise with.

"I suspect Martin meant that I was cynical and sarcastic, which is pretty much right. I recognise how easy it is to go with the flow in an interview and say things you perhaps don't really mean. I also understand how journalists can either misunderstand or deliberately twist people's words, so I don't take too much notice of everything that was said."

All the same, Fletcher was determined to have his say: "We haven't had one conversation with him since our meeting, which was now two years ago. There are a few little things where he's been a bit weird over instruments and guitars through our tour manager. Alan was never an original member of Depeche Mode. He became, through the grace of us, a full-time member of Depeche Mode after he was employed by us as a musician, and he chose to leave. If it had been Martin or myself or Dave leaving, it might have been more serious, because we are the original spirit in the band."

In a more sober state, Gahan passed comment as to Wilder's leaving: "This might be presumptuous of me, [but] I think that what happened was that Alan, during the making of *Songs Of Faith And Devotion*, had already made his decision. I think there was a lot of bad feeling, and Alan was very uncomfortable with the way things were for a long time."

As it happened, Gahan's presumption was partly correct.

Alan Wilder: "The Madrid *Songs Of Faith And Devotion* sessions brought home to me that I wasn't enjoying life in the group enough to warrant sticking with it, especially given that I didn't feel there was anything more

I could achieve within its boundaries. I simply needed change and wanted to do something different."

Martin Gore: "I can't say I was surprised, because there had been times during *Songs Of Faith And Devotion* [where] he obviously wasn't happy, and on the tour he wasn't really happy. One of his main problems was that he didn't really get on with Andy – I'm sure that wasn't the only reason, but that was one of the factors. That was difficult for him, because we've always been honest about the fact that Andy's not really musical. When we play live we give him parts to play, but [they're] not exactly taxing."

Gore's appraisal was partly accurate. "Yes, there were some difficulties and communication inadequacies," admitted Wilder. "Dave's state of mind obviously compounded everything to a degree, but I wouldn't say it was a major factor in my decision. Any tension between myself and Fletch – and it's true to say that there was some – was largely immaterial, since it made no impact on the important issues, like how the records were made or how they were performed."

Gore pointed to what brought about the "tension" between Fletcher and Wilder: "Alan, around that time, felt he was so involved in production and arrangement. I think he felt it was wrong that he was making the same money as Andy, who basically doesn't do anything in the studio. I think that became a stumbling block – he never said this to me, by the way. He never came out and told me that, but I can imagine that might have been one of the reasons that he didn't like Andy – apart from the fact that their personalities clash."

Given that all Depeche Mode's studio albums on which Wilder actively participated – from 1983's *Construction Time Again* to 1993's *Songs Of Faith And Devotion* – were credited as being produced by the band and the likes of Daniel Miller, Flood, *et al* on the latter, had Gore touched a nerve?

Alan Wilder: "I don't think the credits on [Depeche] Mode [records] really reflected the truth about who produced them, but, to be honest, at the time I just couldn't be bothered about getting into big discussions on the whole subject. I was happy to do the work because it was enjoyable and something I was good at."

The crux of the breakdown, according to Wilder, lay elsewhere. "The relationship that never really flourished was between myself and Martin. I felt that it was mainly he who didn't really value the effort that I put in, and that disappointed me, because generally we got on OK, and I respected his talent as a songwriter. I guess the introverted side of Martin's nature made it difficult for him to show appreciation or hand out praise."

Daniel Miller: "The way Depeche Mode have always worked is very unconventional in terms of who does what. The way it generally works is Mart writes the songs, and he'll be involved in the studio as well, but he doesn't really like being in the studio very much. Alan would do a lot of the legwork in the studio, and Fletch, who doesn't really play an instrument, would be the one to shake it up from time to time by asking difficult questions or making a comment, which would make them think – not quite a catalyst, [more] a referee or a man in the street kind of attitude; very pragmatic, a pragmatist: 'You're spending much too long on this track; come on, get a move on.' And that's worked, really, one way or another.

"While that was all part of the chemistry of Depeche Mode, Alan was becoming increasingly frustrated with things like that and felt that maybe his role was not being appreciated enough by everybody."

Dave Gahan: "It got to a point where it was like factory work. There's one picture that was taken of us during the *Songs Of Faith And Devotion* sessions when we were in the studio in Madrid; we're all just – not purposefully – sitting together and looking in totally different directions. It really summed it up, basically."

Daniel Miller: "I don't know if he was justified in his reason for leaving, but I think he was justified in feeling that his contribution was undervalued by the other members of the band. He put an awful lot of work in, and I don't know if they ever really appreciated what he did."

Alan Wilder: "I think Dan [Daniel Miller] felt my leaving was on the cards and was perhaps a little sad to see it happen, but very understanding and always totally supportive."

So has Wilder ever regretted his decision? "In the immortal words of a great woman, *'Je ne regrette rien'* ['I don't regret anything' – Edith Piaf]. My involvement with Depeche has been good to me; I consider myself privileged to have seen the world and gained so many rewards from my time with the group, something that only a few people are lucky enough to ever experience or achieve.

"Some of the things that have been said are disappointing, but I have no problems with the other members of the group. Life is too short to bear grudges, and my dignity would never allow me to resort to petty squabbling in public. The members of the group and I have resolved any outstanding legal matters . . .

"For the most part, I did [enjoy it]. There were obviously boring moments like waiting about in airports, which reminds me: when Charlie

Watts was asked how it felt to be a member of The Rolling Stones for such a long time, his reply was, 'I've only actually spent five years in The Rolling Stones, and 20 years hanging about.' That just about sums it up."

As it happened, Wilder wasn't the only one to leave the Depeche Mode fold. Having married the sister of Dave Gahan's ex-wife, Jo, long-term confidant Daryl Bamonte – who, over the years, had graduated from roadie to personal assistant and finally co-Tour Manager – jumped ship to join his keyboard-playing brother Perry in The Cure, as their Tour Manager. Apparently, Bamonte approached the newly solo Alan Wilder to join Robert Smith & co.

Alan Wilder: "It was more of an enquiry, rather than a direct question. I thought it was a joke at first, but I'm assured they were serious. Daryl Bamonte, who used to work for DM and now works within The Cure organisation, asked me. The last thing on my mind was to go and join another band. I never wanted to be in a pop group *all* of my life – somehow it seems a bit juvenile to be caught up on the pop circuit at the age of nearly 40. As you get older, you don't want to be tied to just one group of people or one activity."

In an even more bizarre twist, Vince Clarke apparently approached Martin Gore about reforming the original Depeche Mode line-up follow-ing Wilder's departure. "He actually suggested quite a few times that he wanted to replace Alan and get the original line-up back together, and we laughed about it for about the first 15 times," Gore claimed. "But every time we met he kept saying it, and [it] made us think: 'Maybe he's serious.'"

So *was* Vince Clarke serious? "I don't know," Gore continued. "I hadn't actually said to him, 'Do you fancy coming back for one record?' I don't know. Maybe he would have done it. But I think our [respective] music has gone in such different ways. I don't think it would have worked at all, anyway. I don't think we'd be compatible anymore."

When asked about approaching his former Depeche Mode bandmate, Clarke admitted as much, but didn't sound serious: "I may have joked about it – probably when I saw him on some drunken evening!"

Then again, at the time, Clarke may have been smarting from Erasure's first comparative album failure, 1995's *Erasure*, where the duo deviated from their three-minute catchy synthpop formula in favour of more extended pieces. As *Future Music* magazine observed in November 1995: "Where previous albums have seen little expansion of Clarke's box of sonic tricks, with tracks like 'Guess I'm Into Feeling' it's as though he's finally absorbed what's going on in the world of electronic music in the Nineties. This may, in part, be down to working with (amongst others) Orb collaborator Thomas Fehlmann, as might the journeys into near-ambient textures. These meandering moments initially make the album less cohesive, [but] ultimately they prove to be the most satisfying. The shiny pop days of 'Sometimes' and 'Blue Savannah' may be gone, but Erasure are handling their maturity well."

Unfortunately, Erasure's more conservative fanbase didn't respond favourably to such stylistic changes. "We were going to do kind of like a Pink Floyd *Dark Side Of The Moon – Bright Side Of The Sun*," teased Andy Bell. "I think there was one song from the *Erasure* album ['Stay With Me'] that was number 14 [*sic* – 15], or something."

When asked if he'd ever considered joining Erasure after leaving Depeche Mode, the bemused Alan Wilder cracked: "That's a bit like leaving the cast of *The Fast Show* to go and appear on *Cannon & Ball*!"

PART VI

A New Beginning?

"We all realise that we've created something special, and the elements just work. We had Vince leave very early on; and with Alan, I think we did create some kind of legacy, so when he decided to leave I don't think we really thought about ending it there. We thought, 'We've just got to carry on' . . . through all the thick and thin; through all the problems with Ultra."

– Martin Gore, 2001

28

The Beginning Of The End?

"It was a case of over-excess – in every way. There were times when if I'd got a phone call saying Dave had passed away, for instance, I wouldn't have been surprised. When you get [into] that situation when you're trying to work and concentrate on things, it's very difficult. We really were on the edge during those times."

– Andy Fletcher, 2001

Alan Wilder was now free to enjoy the lifestyle he had created for himself, and pursue the "new projects" he had hinted at in his press statement. "Recoil was going for a long time before I left Depeche Mode – as a side project. It was something I wanted to continue and expand upon after my departure. It's a very different, much more open-ended kind of project, which I do find more satisfying, creatively. That's not to say I didn't enjoy being in the band, but, as far as I was concerned, it had a shelf life."

Meanwhile, former colleague Dave Gahan's LA-based life was mapping out in a different, darker way. "I think Dave's easily influenced and I don't think living in Los Angeles has had a good effect on him," Wilder said with typically understated diplomacy.

Anton Corbijn: "I didn't realise how deep at some point Dave had got into the state he was in. I remember, at some point, getting a call from [REM's] Michael Stipe, saying, 'Well, I've seen Dave; I think he needs help, and you should just give him a call.' I think some other people were shocked by this thing, and we probably thought, 'Oh, it's just Dave going through another phase.'"

By now Gahan's latest phase was getting seriously out of hand as he ventured out of his Hollywood home to score. "I got myself in deep shit there, and I didn't know if I was going to be able to get myself out," he later confessed to Q magazine's Phil Sutcliffe. "I was so fucking paranoid, I carried a .38 around with me at all times. Going downtown to cop, those guys you hang out with, they're heavy people; they have guns sitting on the table in front of them. I was scared of everything and everyone. I'd wait [until] four in the morning to check the mailbox and then walk down to the gate with the gun tucked in the back of my pants. I thought they were coming to get me, whoever 'they' were."

Displaying all the classic symptoms of drug-induced paranoia, when the 'tooled up' Gahan wasn't dealing with gun-toting lowlife, he was holed up at home watching the weather channel for up to 12 hours at a time. "Yes," Gahan subsequently confirmed, "but with this illusion that I'm this big rock star; that's what I'm supposed to do – what's the problem? I couldn't kid myself anymore that it was fun in any way – it certainly wasn't!"

Faced with a (literal) dead end, Gahan began looking for a get-out clause, and came up with the following solution: "That was when I started toying with the idea of going out on a big one – just shoot the big speed-ball [cocaine and heroin mixture] to heaven. Disappear. Stop. I wanted to stop being myself; I wanted to stop living in this body. My skin was crawling; I hated myself that much – what I'd done to myself and everyone around me."

Despite plumbing the depths, Gahan still managed to "keep it together" for the sake of his visiting son, Jack, but that too backfired, as he recounted to Q's Phil Sutcliffe: "It came to a point where I was so sick [that] I rang my mother in England and said, 'Mum, Jack's due here in a couple of days and I've got a terrible flu. I can't cope on my own; can you come over?' She came over, and I tried to do the whole thing – get up in the morning, make him his little egg, tried to be the dad. But I was kidding myself, and I was cheating on my son; I was cheating on my mother, I knew it."

One night, after Gahan had put Jack to bed and with his mother asleep, Gahan fixed up in the living room, and blacked out. "When I woke up I was scrawled across the bed. It was daylight, and I heard voices from the kitchen. I thought, 'Shit, I left all my shit out!' "

In a panic, Gahan raced down to the living room to find all of his drug paraphernalia had vanished. Running into the kitchen, where his mother and son were sitting, he asked, 'What did you do with my stuff, mum?' She replied, 'I threw it in the rubbish outside.' He ran out the door, returning with six black bags (five of which were his neighbours) and emptied them out onto the kitchen floor, rummaging through other people's garbage until he found what he craved.

Shutting himself in the bathroom, the door burst open for Gahan to be confronted by his immediate family. "I'm lying on the floor with wounds open and everything. I say, 'It's not what it looks like, mum; I'm sick. I have to take steroids for my voice . . .' All this fucking trash comes out of my mouth. Then I look up at my mum, and she looks at me, and I say, 'Mum, I'm a junkie; I'm a heroin addict.' And she says, 'I know, love.'"

As if things couldn't get any lower, Gahan's seven-year-old son took his father's hand, led him into his bedroom and knelt him down on the floor. "'Daddy, I don't want you to be sick anymore.' I said, 'I don't wanna be sick anymore, either.' He said, 'You need to see a doctor.' I said, 'Yeah.'"

"I guess my mum must have rung Joanne. She came and picked Jack up and . . . that was the last I saw of them for a long while. My mum stayed on for a bit to settle me down. She'd say, 'We don't want you to die.' And that didn't stop me. That didn't do it."

For a brief moment, it looked as if the removal of his son shocked Gahan into trying to kick his habit on his own. "I lay on the couch for a week like a zombie," he told Sutcliffe. "Then one night, I turned to Teresa and said, 'I need help.' So I went into rehab for the first time."

Having made that all-important admission, Gahan voluntarily booked himself into Sierra Tucson, nestled in the foothills of the Santa Catalina Mountains near Tucson, Arizona, at 39580 Lago del Oro Parkway. Describing itself as a "national treatment center dedicated to the prevention, education, and treatment of addictions and behavioural disorders", the Depeche Mode singer was not the first – nor the last – rich and famous individual to visit the self-styled "place where pain is met with compassion, fear is met with reassurance, and anger is met with understanding."

Unfortunately for Gahan, when he checked out of the $500 per night facility, it sounded like he was still pretty angry with the world: "I was serious about it when I was there, but once I left it was like, 'Fuck this shit!'"

More than likely that anger was compounded by Teresa Gahan's reaction to her husband's 'recovery'. "When I came out, Teresa met me," Gahan recalled. "We went to get some lunch and she said, 'I'm not gonna stop drinking or using drugs just because you have to. I'll do whatever I want to do.' She didn't use like me – regularly. But in rehab they said that if one of us wasn't going to give up, it would be impossible for the other. At that point I knew our relationship would have to be over if I was gonna have any chance. I'd thought we loved each other. Now I think the love was pretty one-sided."

As it was, Teresa walked out on Dave soon afterwards, anyway, ". . . to get her life together, as she put it," he told Sutcliffe. "After she left, I stayed clean for a little while, but I slipped back into old habits and found myself going [back] to rehab."

When profiling Dave Gahan in 1996, *The Sunday Times'* Christopher Goodwin reported an unnamed Depeche Mode associate as saying, "The others were back in England, and Dave just took himself out of the loop. There was nobody around to tell him he was being a fool, as there would have been in England. He lost his hold on reality."

Later still, Gahan attributed his downward spiral to "the responsibility of living in a world that I didn't feel comfortable in. Of course, the more trouble I got myself in, the worse it got. I'd tried moving places, going somewhere else, being with different people, being in a different relationship, and still, at the end of the day, feeling like I wasn't around. The drugs helped me for a while with that, but then they did the opposite thing."

That "opposite thing" reared its ugly head on August 1, 1995 when Gahan was accused of headbutting one Roy Anderson, a Tucson-based art expert who claimed to have befriended the singer several months earlier (most likely as a result of Gahan's visit to the Arizona rehab clinic). The art dealer had been waiting for Dave outside a Hollywood hotel when ". . . he suddenly bashed me with his head, right about my left temple; blood was pouring out like a faucet."

The injured party, who required seven stitches to the wound, speculated that the altercation was the result of a joke he had made in poor taste; having met up with Teresa Gahan the previous day to talk about the couple's marriage problems, he told Dave the two had ended up sleeping together. "He was incensed," said Anderson, "but it was completely harmless." For the emotionally fragile singer, it was anything but harmless. Fortunately for Gahan, Anderson decided not to press ahead with the lawsuit.

Events took a turn for the worse when Gahan left Arizona's Sierra Tucson facility for the second time on August 9. Still feeling far from happy over his crumbling marriage – however much he felt Teresa let him down in the crucial early stages of staying clean – and with Depeche Mode being musically inactive for the past year, Gahan booked himself into the familiar surroundings of the Sunset Marquis Hotel. "I didn't want to live at home, because it was too big and too empty," he explained in 1999. "But when I went up to my house [on August 17] to get some clothes I found it had been completely looted: my two Harleys, the studio, tapes of a few songs I'd written, the stereo system – everything, down to the cutlery!"

Since his Hollywood Hills home featured electronically operated metal security gates and a coded alarm system, which the looters "even had the fucking cheek to reset," Gahan came to a depressing conclusion: "It must have been an inside job. Some of my so-called friends had gone in there, knowing that I was in rehab. I thought, 'I can't believe this; this is my fucking life! My little world – 'Daveworld' – was falling apart."

The turn of events hit Dave where it hurt. "I lost everything; I planned to slash my wrists that night," he told *Globe* in September 1995. "I was angry at how mean people can be. My home was an empty shell."

So, according to Andy Fletcher, was his life. "Various people had tried to speak to him, but it went past that. I think when he got to his lowest level, the only thing he had left was the band, which might seem a bit weird, but I don't necessarily think the band caused everything – it was one of the only things he had left in the world."

Possibly with that thought in mind, Gahan went back to the Sunset Marquis Hotel, hell-bent on self-destruction. "I quickly got loaded and drank a lot of wine, and took a handful of pills. I rang my mother and she said Teresa had told her that I hadn't been to any rehab; I wasn't even trying to get clean like I'd promised – and I *was* trying; I was doing the best I could. I was in the middle of that phone call to my mum, and I told her to hang on, I'd be back in a minute, went to the bathroom and cut my wrists, wrapped towels round them, and came back to the phone and said, 'Mum, I've got to go; I love you very much.' Then I sat down with my friend and acted like nothing was going on. I put my arms down by my sides and I could feel them bleeding away, but she had no clue what was happening until she noticed a pool of blood gathering on the floor."

Gahan subsequently passed out. His hotel room companion dialled 911, and paramedics were promptly dispatched to deal with the stricken singer. Richard Blade was quite possibly first to break the news on KROQ. "I had a phone call from a paramedic," he recalled. "He called me and said, 'You might want to know this; we've just admitted Dave Gahan to Cedars-Sinai hospital for multiple lacerations.' And I was recording his phone call. And then I asked what his name was, and he said that he wasn't allowed to give it, but he officially wasn't allowed to be making the call; as medical personnel, those records are privileged. So I never revealed his name, and I never played that call. But thank goodness I recorded it, because I went on the air and I announced it. I said, 'I think Dave Gahan has tried to commit suicide.'"

Over in London, on August 18, Mute Records speedily issued the following statement: "Dave Gahan, lead singer of Depeche Mode, was admitted to Cedars-Sinai Medical Center in Beverly Hills, California, USA, yesterday morning. He is resting comfortably and expects to be released soon."

When asked in 2001 for an opinion as to how Dave Gahan ended up in such a sorry state, Daniel Miller offered: "I think he bought the whole American lifestyle . . . over-bought it – invested too heavily in the lifestyle and the culture, and I think some of the people surrounding him at that time, who were further down the road than he was, kind of represented that lifestyle for him. When he wasn't on the road or in the studio, there was a period [when] he was living in LA, and I think he got involved with the wrong crowd, almost. But I think you have to be open to it [drug-taking] in the first place, so I wouldn't blame it just on that. It's complicated."

As it was, when Gahan finally came to, the complicated character found himself under lock and key at Cedars-Sinai Medical Center at 8700 Beverly Boulevard, Los Angeles. "I was in a psychiatric ward, this padded room," he remembered. "For a minute, I thought I might be in heaven – whatever heaven is. Then this psychiatrist informed me that I'd committed a crime under local law by trying to take my own life. Only in fucking LA, huh?"

West Hollywood Sheriff's Department Detective Joel Brown found a razor blade at the scene: "He sustained a 2-inch laceration to his wrist. It wasn't like he was dying or anything."

While Gahan (according to Detective Brown) was being "evaluated for mental competency" at Cedars-Sinai Medical Center, his New York-based publicist, Michael Pagnotta, fended off all calls regarding the singer's alleged suicide attempt, calling the incident a "private matter". The battle-hardened publicist later "pooh-poohed" rumours that a rift between Gahan and Martin Gore had contributed to the latter's depression and resultant "suicide attempt".

It didn't take long for the press to pick up the trail. In the UK, the *Daily Mirror* reported the bare facts on August 22, under the typically lurid headline of "Rock Star 'Death Bid' ". "I don't think I ever tried to kill myself," Gahan reasoned, moving onto a somewhat surreal explanation for reaching for the razor: "Again, I think I was just crying out for some kind of attention, and really going about it in an odd way. I wasn't sitting around going, 'My life's shit.' It was [about] feelings of wanting to disappear – still be here, but just be floating around.

"I want to make it clear: it had nothing to do with Teresa; I was very much in love with Teresa. It was to do with *myself* not being comfortable. I probably blamed other people for a long time, and I regret doing that, but [that's] the way I felt at the time."

Within a year or so of his first 'close-call' Gahan gave vent to those feelings of resentment: "I was really pissed off about it, because all that really seemed important to Mart and Fletch was if I was dead [then] there'd be no Depeche Mode anymore. I didn't get any support at all, verbally, from Fletch or Mart at any point."

Daniel Miller all but admitted as much. "He was literally physically too far away. Fortunately, Jonathan [Kessler], the manager, was there; he took Dave under his wing, very much – he always [did], really."

After being given the all-clear, Dave Gahan was duly discharged from Cedars-Sinai Hospital several days after admission; any criminal charges pending against him for attempting suicide were presumably dropped.

Dave Gahan: "As soon as I got out I was up to my old tricks. I'd clean up a bit, then use again, and every time I needed more, I wanted it quicker – there was never enough; I just [had] to keep fucking going until I [blacked] out, or whatever."

Back across the Atlantic, concerns were mounting at Mute over the obvious risks posed by Gahan's addiction. Yet Daniel Miller dismissed any talk of forced intervention, having had similar experiences with other artists on his label – reformed junkie Nick Cave, for example, later looked back on his addiction as "a huge chunk of life" claiming, "wonderful things happened there."

Daniel Miller: "We talked about it, and I didn't really feel that the time was right in his [Gahan's] head to do it. I'm not really experienced; I've had a few situations like that, but you have to pick the moment to say the word, and they've got to want it. You've got to pick the moment – whether they're feeling weak, somehow, or feeling self-doubt about their own problems, whereas at that time he was sort of feeling good about the whole thing. It was very difficult. But then if you try to force the issue, you can make it difficult later on; you just kind of skirt around the problem with all the other people involved."

Martin Gore and Andy Fletcher were now talking about recording again as Depeche Mode. It would seem Gahan was also up for the idea, as his publicist, Michael Pagnotta, made it known that Gore had been busy writing songs and apparently already had five completed at the time of his colleague's release from Cedars-Sinai. At the time, Pagnotta stated that the 'recovered' singer was set to fly to Britain in early October 1995 "to begin work on a new Depeche Mode album."

Yet Gore was not necessarily thinking that far ahead: "We said that when I had a few songs together, we'd think about getting back into a studio again and just testing the water, really – just to see if we were getting on OK and if things were still working, and we were still enjoying it. We didn't plan a whole album. We just said, 'We'll do a few tracks to start with, and, if we're lucky, we'll get a single out of it; if we're not enjoying it then we'll just stop.'"

That was easier said than done, however. Depeche Mode were now a trio, and Alan Wilder's considerable contributions would be sorely missed.

Dave Gahan: "To be honest, I felt like if anything was going to split up the band, that was what it was. A very valuable person had left. Suddenly, musically, for me, there was a big hole. That inspiration and musicality wasn't there. We were floundering."

Later, in conversation with *Q* magazine in June 2003, Gahan's lament for Wilder's departure from the Depeche Mode ranks ran deeper still. "I didn't respond to his leaving as much as I now realise I wanted to," the singer confessed. "I really miss Alan's input on everything we [now] do musically, but I miss him as a friend. He was probably the person I felt supported by the most in the band and I wish I'd fought harder for him to stay. What Alan really wanted was for Martin to turn around and say, 'You've really contributed something great,' but Martin's not someone who hands out compliments very often."

Alan Wilder: "Dave's always been willing to recognise the contribution of others – he has a very generous nature, and I believe he is sincere in his comments. I was possibly the closest to him in the group and I would imagine, DM having always been a very insular group, that it's been pretty strange working with all sorts of new people – perhaps this is part of what he means. In many ways, it would be easier for him to avoid the subject and say nothing, so the fact that he has gone out of his way to say such nice things about me makes me feel good. Although I'm very happy doing what I do now, I also miss having him around."

Andy Fletcher: "He [Gahan] could have felt a bit isolated with Alan leaving, because it used to be two and two – Dave and Alan, and Martin and me."

"It was both difficult and not difficult," said Fletcher, in looking back at those 1995 sessions as a trio. "Obviously, Dave's problems were still there; we were working without Alan for the first time in a long time. We had to find our feet – it was *A Broken Frame* again."

The *A Broken Frame* analogy was applicable in the sense that it followed the departure of then-principal songwriter Vince Clarke. But Depeche Mode *circa*-1995 was a different animal to the happy-go-lucky threesome barely out of their teens in 1982. As *The Times*' Paddy Rhodes put it: "Depeche Mode threw themselves into a life of Classic Rock Debauchery with such fervour that [the] Devotional Tour injury sheet looked like this: Martin Gore – seizures; Andrew Fletcher – nervous breakdown; Alan Wilder – left to pursue solo project; Dave Gahan – heroin addiction, culminating in suicide attempt."

A sympathetic presence was clearly needed, somebody who was capable of pulling their disparate personalities together and to somehow fill the considerable void left by Alan Wilder; an insurmountable problem, on the face of it, but one that Daniel Miller was able to solve.

Dave Gahan: "I think Daniel came up with the idea of Tim Simenon. He'd worked on a few things for us before; he'd remixed a few songs – 'Strangelove' and 'Everything Counts' [in 1989]."

At the time of writing, Tim Simenon is still a renowned dance DJ-cum-producer, running his own independent Electric Tones label out of Amsterdam. His keen interest in things of a turntable-based nature began as a 15-year-old back in 1983. "The DJ'ing came about because I had a vast collection of records," he told *Music Technology*. "My family are really into listening to Motown and funk, so I've been listening to a lot of black music since I was a kid. Then I branched off into listening into avant-garde stuff like Brian Eno and then on to Depeche, Fad Gadget and Robert Rental – I've always liked Daniel Miller's production work – and that branched into the electro scene with people like Bambaataa."

Parallel to his turntable exploits, Simenon's keen interest in electropop also saw him dabbling in creating music of his own: "I started saving up my pocket money from paper rounds and bought a [Yamaha] CS1 ['mini' analogue monosynth], [Roland] SH-101 [analogue monosynth], [Roland] MC-202 [MicroComposer dual-channel step-pattern-based sequencer] and [Boss] DR-55 Dr Rhythm [drum machine].

"I started doing simple melodies over electronic beats and typical Kraftwerk or Yello bass lines. My friend had a vocoder [a device that analyses the 'excitation' input – usually a human voice – and then super-imposes its characteristics over the top of a synth sound] and we discovered how to operate keyboards and structure very basic songs."

The blurring of these two disciplines led Simenon into taking affirmative action in September 1986, enrolling on a course at London's recently opened SAE (School of Audio Engineering), featuring a 16-track Fostex multitrack recorder and Soundmaster mixing console. The ambitious Simenon's studies were rudely interrupted within a month when he achieved an unexpected hit single under the guise of Bomb The Bass: "Around October [1986] a friend of mine booked some studio time in Hollywood Studios, so I worked on 'Beat Dis' then."

The friend in question happened to be James Horrocks, a managing director at Mute Records offshoot Rhythm King, who promptly signed Tim Simenon and pressed up 1,000 copies of the début Bomb The Bass single, which sold out within a week. "The word got 'round, and the pirates were playing it like mad. One minute I was at college and I'd got a job as a part-time waiter in a Japanese restaurant, and next I was at number five in the charts!"

Thereafter, Simenon abandoned his original gameplan for entering the recording industry as he scored three more successive UK Top 10 hit singles as Bomb The Bass, featuring various guest vocalists: "I planned to be a tape op at a good studio and, two or three years after that, produce. But I missed all that tea-boy business out. The whole idea of the [SAE] course was to produce a record, so I suppose I was exempted by 'Beat Dis'."

In October 1988, Simenon's strategy was conveyed to *Music Technology*: "Bomb The Bass is going to be around for three years or whatever, then I want to go on to something totally new – like Vince Clarke: Depeche, Yazoo, Erasure."

Simenon moved into record production considerably earlier than expected when working closely with Stockholm-born singer Neneh Cherry (stepdaughter of jazz trumpeter, Don Cherry) on her first two UK Top 10 singles, 'Buffalo Stance' (number three in December 1988) and 'Manchild' (number five in May 1989). Thanks in no small part to Simenon, Cherry went on to win the 1990 'Best New Female' award in *Rolling Stone* magazine, winning the same category at the BRIT (British Recording Industry Trust) Awards that same year.*

---

* The same year, coincidentally, that Depeche Mode scooped 'Single Of The Year' for 'Enjoy The Silence'.

Daniel Miller: "I'd known Tim even before he was a recording artist. When he was a DJ he used to come into the office, blagging records – when he was just a kid. He'd always been a massive fan [of DM]."

Tim Simenon: "I was definitely into what they [DM] did – ever since they'd released 'Photographic' on *Some Bizzare*. I was dead into what they were doing. I knew where they were coming from, and they knew where I was coming from, so I think it [was] really more of an experiment."

Martin Gore: "We all really liked the last Bomb The Bass album [*Clear*], and I particularly liked the [Tim Simenon-produced] Gavin Friday album [*Shag Tobacco*] that came out just a couple of months before we started working with Tim. I knew Tim before, and we actually met quite a lot over the years, but [I'd] never spent a lot of time with him, and he's such a lovely person. It felt like [I'd] discovered a new soul brother."

The slimmed-down Depeche Mode, Tim Simenon and his close-knit production team (including engineer 'Q' and programmer Kerry Hopwood) chose the relatively low-cost (by Depeche Mode standards) recording environs of Eastcote's Studio Two, sited in a converted Victorian factory in North Kensington (249 Kensal Road, West London) – featuring a 600 square-foot control room, large enough to accommodate the complex equipment set-up that would be involved – for a tentative recording. ("Just testing the water," to quote Gore.)

"Access to a choice of vintage analogue synths" remains one of the selling points of Eastcote's Studio Two. Not that Depeche Mode were exactly short of a vintage synth or several; according to Simenon, the 40 or so synthesisers and samplers being used by the band (and hired help) included no fewer than *four* ARP 2600s, American analogue polysynths of varying vintage from Oberheim, plus multiple modular systems from Roland – including two System 100Ms and another awesome System 700 (bought by Simenon at a knock-down price from producer Martin Rushent, who had previously put it to such good use on The Human League's *Dare*).

With Depeche Mode's recent recording and touring history in mind, Simenon was well aware of what he might be letting himself in for. "I thought I was going to be walking into a ticking time bomb," he told *Alternative Rock Fax*, in January, 1996. "The first week was tense, but from then on, my team really jelled with them, and likewise. It's a really good vibe. The songs are really classic Depeche Mode songs – I'm trying to throw in a rawer, more edgy sound."

According to *NME*, the only guidance Gore gave to Simenon during their initial pre-production meeting was that he was "interested in giving the [recordings] a hip-hop-based sonic template, a subconscious nod back to late-Eighties US groups such as 3rd Bass, whose reverence for the Mode's pioneering electro tapestries led them to sample 'Never Let Me Down Again'."

Martin Gore: "We decided, because of the way the demos had turned out, that we wanted to bring out a more rhythmic feel. Tim seemed to be a natural choice for that."

As the songwriter explained in 1997, there was another related reason as to why Simenon proved to be "a natural choice" for working with Depeche Mode. "Tim knows all about dance music trivia. He can make 69 bpm quite easily, and this is quite important to us, because we are in such slow territory. In the past, we had gone much faster than 100 bpm, but when I try writing anything faster than that, it always sounds silly to me – it just loses the atmosphere."

Before long, Gore was also singing Eastcote's praises: "Recording in a very small studio helped in some ways to create the easy-going atmosphere, because we haven't gone to the top studios all the time. It's been very low-key and it's been something that's helped us set a tone for the [recordings]."

Freshly penned, slow-moving Gore compositions worked on during those early sessions at Eastcote included 'Useless', on which Living Colour bassist Doug Wimbish was drafted in. Drummer Gota Yashiki – who had made his name working with Jazzie B's successful Soul II Soul collective (programming and performing drums and bass on 1989's chart-topping 'Back To Life'), and later Simply Red – also performed on the same song.

Other hired help included programmer Kerry Hopwood and keyboard player/programmer Dave Clayton, both of whom proved to be a revelation to the apparently revitalised Martin Gore: "We have never worked with a programmer before; we've always done it ourselves. I really enjoy having a programmer [Hopwood] there, because even though Alan did a lot of it on the last record [*Songs Of Faith And Devotion*], you still felt really involved, whereas now it's much easier to just step back and listen to what's happening. It's also a lot quicker working with somebody who knows how to work everything perfectly.

"We've never had outside musicians constantly in the studio with us before – I suppose we had Alan in the past, and Dave Clayton, the musician we're working with now, in a way fulfils Alan's role, but it's far easier to manipulate him. If Alan didn't like something, I am sure he wouldn't actually play it badly, but if we say to Dave, 'Can you try this out for us?' he'll try it, and he'll try his hardest to make it work for us."

Tim Simenon: "I think the chemistry kind of worked, and we carried on making the album."

Martin Gore: "We did those few tracks, and we all really enjoyed it, so I went away and wrote some more songs, and we decided to get together and try [to] make a whole album." So far, so good – or so it seemed.

Dave Gahan: "We went into the studio with the idea of 'Let's record a few songs and see how it feels,' but I was still using heroin, and I'd get clean for a while and then use again, so my input was really sketchy."

Andy Fletcher: "He never did what he was doing in front of us. He always did it out of our sight. So we couldn't even really be 100 per cent sure about what was happening."

Dave Gahan: "To be honest, I was what I would call a very clever kind of junkie, in that I was able to – for quite a long period of time – hide how bad I was. It was hard to hit bottom, if you like . . . a financial bottom is something that a lot of junkies come to when they have absolutely nothing left, but the problem I had was an endless supply of money."

29

From Exodus To Ultra

"The best thing that happened to Dave was his arrest. They forced him to go into rehab and told him that if he didn't come out clean, then he would be chucked out of America, and I think his love for America, and his desire to be able to work there and live there as much as he wanted – plus he suddenly realised the impact everything was having on the band – helped him through that."

– Daniel Miller, 2001

With Gahan deftly disguising his habit – Depeche Mode pushed on with their then-as-yet-untitled album project, finishing a second bout of intensive recording at Eastcote in April. As reported by *BONG: The Official Magazine Of Depeche Mode*, "They are due to start another recording period, of several weeks, later this month [April 1996], and after that they will take their summer breaks. During this period Martin will be writing some more new songs before they go back into the studio for the final period of recording."

Things did not run quite so smoothly when Depeche decamped to New York City at the insistence of Gahan, who was toying with relocating to the 'Big Apple' from the Santa Monica apartment he was renting in Los Angeles (having since sold his Hollywood home). But progress at the legendary Electric Lady studios (opened by Jimi Hendrix) at 52 West 8th Street in the heart of Greenwich Village was hampered by the singer's exploits.

Andy Fletcher: "We had a very disappointing six weeks in New York with Dave's vocals."

Daniel Miller elaborated: "One of the crises that really hit that project halfway through was [when] we all went to New York, because Dave wanted to do it in New York. He wasn't in a physical or emotional state to do vocals, and that was kind of a crisis point."

By now it was blatantly obvious that Gahan's substance abuse was far from being under control. Disappointingly, the six-week session at Electric Lady produced just one usable vocal ('Sister Of Night'), and even that was pieced together from multiple takes.

Dave Gahan: "The only vocal on the album that I recorded at Electric Lady – the only vocal that I performed high – was 'Sister Of Night'. I can hear how scared I was. I'm glad it's there to remind me." Although the vocalist claimed that this was his favourite song from Gore's latest batch, something clearly had to give if work on the album was to continue with any success.

In such times of crisis, Jonathan Kessler was usually called in. "We got to the stage where we could not make any decisions in a band meeting, because it would always end up in a fight," Martin Gore freely admitted. "We all had different agendas; nobody was prepared to listen to anybody else's point of view. It got to the stage where our manager [Kessler] would have to come to us all individually to get our opinion, then go around and tell everybody what everybody else thought, then somehow make a decision out of it!"

Kessler's keenly developed negotiating skills were put to the test. A three-month break in proceedings was agreed by all, during which Gore would write some more material. To Gahan's credit, he agreed to work with vocal coach Evelyn Halus in Los Angeles, with a view to recording further vocals with Tim Simenon at Larrabee West studios at 8811 Santa Monica Boulevard, in the general vicinity of his apartment. During an interview with Los Angeles station KCRW FM on May 22, Simenon said that Depeche Mode were on a three-month break and that seven new songs had been "worked out" so far.

Dave Gahan: "There was still the flame inside me that wanted to do [the] record, but physically I just couldn't do it. I relapsed several times, and after I knocked it on the head in New York, I went back to LA and got back to my old tricks. Before I left I said to my girlfriend in New York – I met her in detox, she's been clean [for] five years and she was instrumental in helping me admit I couldn't do what I was doing successfully anymore . . . anyway, as I left, she looked me in the eye and said, 'You're gonna get high,' and I said, 'Yup.' She says, 'You don't have to,' and I said, 'I do.' And I went to LA and had the worst binge I'd ever had."

Martin Gore: "There's not a lot you can do for someone who reaches that abyss, who's not really interested in help. It's an old cliché, but it's true that you have to want to help yourself. After all the frustrations in New York, we could easily have said, 'Why don't we just forget this?' But we didn't. We said, 'Go away; get a vocal coach; get yourself into shape, and we'll reconvene.' I don't know what else we could have done. I remember somebody said [something] about going to LA and babysitting him, but it wouldn't have worked, because Dave was just being sneaky at that stage. If I'd have moved in with him that would have probably sent him over the edge, anyway."

Like a moth to a burning flame, Gahan was drawn back to the Sunset Marquis Hotel, with results predictable in their near-fatal conclusion.

Dave Gahan: "I was using intravenously, but it hadn't been working for two years, so by this time I was mixing heroin with cocaine, and using so much I couldn't fill the rig up any fuller. The last time I did it I knew something was wrong and I asked my friend not to fill the rig up so much. It's a long story, but I had a heart attack."

News of Gahan's near-fatal overdose spread fast with the *Los Angeles Times* reporting a statement by Lieutenant Steven Weisgarber of the Los Angeles County Sheriff's Department: "Deputies and paramedics responding to a call of a drug overdose at the Sunset Marquis Hotel found Gahan passed out on the floor of a hotel room at 1.15 am [on May 28]. Authorities found syringes in the room and believe Gahan injected a 'speedball' – an intravenous brew of cocaine and heroin. The people with him who summoned help said he passed out 10 minutes after taking drugs."

Back in the UK, news of Gahan's predicament came as no shock to Andy Fletcher. "At that stage, if I'd got a phone call saying he had died, I wouldn't have been surprised."

Martin Gore: "I've only actually thought Dave was dead twice, which is not bad going. If you get a phone call and it's your manager or somebody saying, 'I need to speak to you about Dave; something really bad's happened,' the first thought you have is, 'Oh my God; this time it's the big one!' But that's par for the course with Dave."

Not only was Gahan 'speedballing', but the heroin he was using in his potentially lethal narcotic cocktail was of an extremely pure nature.

Dave Gahan: "It was a particularly strong brand of heroin called Red Rum. Of course, I just thought it referred to the racehorse, until someone pointed out that it spells 'murder' backwards."

In a scenario painfully reminiscent of his alleged suicide attempt at the same hotel in August 1995, the stricken singer was carted off to nearby Cedars-Sinai Medical Center, where he was treated for a drug overdose and released into police custody.

Dave Gahan: "I woke up in hospital hearing one of the paramedics saying, 'I think we lost him.' I sat up and said, 'No, you fuckin' haven't!' But I'd had the full cardiac arrest; my heart had stopped for two minutes. I'd been dead, basically. Later, a detective read me my rights, and I was arrested for possession of cocaine and needles. I was handcuffed to a trolley. Straight from hospital they threw me into the county jail for a couple of nights in a cell with about seven other guys – a scary experience."

Having indeed been arrested (according to Lieutenant Weisgarber) "for investigation of cocaine possession and being under the influence of heroin," Gahan was taken to the Los Angeles County Sheriff's Department's West Hollywood Station at 720 North San Vicente Boulevard where bail was set at $10,000. Although it was reported that the singer had not made bail by eight o'clock the following morning, Jonathan Kessler accompanied a dishevelled-looking Gahan from the police station where a brace of television reporters were waiting.

Silencing his protesting manager, Gahan's comments for the cameras were fragmented, ending on what appeared to be an optimistic note: "I'm a heroin addict, and I've been fighting to get off heroin for a year. I've been in rehab twice, and I don't wanna be like people like Kurt [Cobain]. I wanna be a survivor . . . I mean, I died again last night. My cat's lives are out. I just wanna say sorry to all the fans and stuff. I'm glad to be alive . . . and sorry to me mum as well. I just want them to know that it's not cool. It's not a cool thing to be an addict. You're a slave to it, and it's taken everything away from me that I love, and so I've got to rebuild my life."

Sadly, any positive actions that the singer might have been entertaining during his spell behind bars were dashed in an instant: "As soon as I was bailed, I got what I needed, checked into the [Sunset] Marquis and carried on for another couple of days until I suddenly started thinking, 'What the fuck am I doing? I died!' I went back to the house I'd rented in Santa Monica, sat on the couch and realised I was going nowhere."

Nowhere – or, oblivion, as *The Sunday Times* mercilessly depicted Gahan heading, when profiling him under the caption of 'Despair Mode' on June 9. Looking back, Andy Fletcher was bemused at a highbrow publication taking such an active interest in Depeche Mode: "We got more press over Dave's suicide [attempt] and [drug] overdose than at any time in our whole career. We got a double page in the *Sunday Times* magazine! If we tried to get into the *Sunday Times* magazine for our music, there'd be no way on this earth . . ."

Before long, the band tired of such morbid interest. "They only want to talk about drugs, especially the English press," Martin Gore moaned to Caroline Sullivan. "I get really depressed, thinking, 'It's always going to be like this. That's all they're ever going to talk about forever.'"

The Guardian journalist sympathised with the doleful songwriter's sentiment – to a degree. "Understandable," she wrote, "but not altogether fair to the press, which, presented with the spectacle of a 30-million-selling band trying its best to self-destruct could hardly ignore it."

Even KROQ's normally supportive Richard Blade didn't rate the group's chances of completing their current work-in-progress. "Since January [1996], the record company has been telling us that they've recorded four or five songs, and that the album was going to be out in June or July. But now they've pushed the release date back to February 1997, and I doubt they're even going to make that. The band is on very shaky ground. The next album is make-or-break."

In looking back, Daniel Miller also admitted to suffering some anxiety over Depeche Mode's future as a functioning musical entity: "Nobody thought they were ever going to make it through that album. Even I, for the first time, wasn't sure if they were going to make it. I felt there was a really good chance, but I started to have my doubts, because of what was going on."

Depeche Mode's own *BONG* magazine was keen to downplay the bleakness of the situation when writing: "Dave was arrested on May 28 and is due to appear in court on June 18. We don't have anything to add to the news reports, and it would be wrong of us to make any comment prior to his hearing. Some people have asked if this incident will delay the album release, and we don't see any reason why it should. The band had always planned to take a break anyway. Having said that, it now seems that there won't be any new material released before 1997."

By the time of Gahan's arrest following his drug overdose of May 28, Daniel Miller was considering whether a premature end to Depeche Mode was now in sight – "partly," he reasoned, "because of the damage that Dave was doing to himself, and also because the rest of the band was getting frustrated as well. While they were very sympathetic to Dave's problems, and understanding, they also felt it was really starting to disrupt their own lives to such an extent where if it had gone on much longer it would have been very difficult for the band to stay together."

Martin Gore: "Of course, we were worried about Dave's health. One

416

of the main considerations for me was whether it would be better for Dave if we ended the band, because the trappings – access to whatever he wanted – were obviously not doing him much good."

The time for outside intervention was upon Depeche Mode. "Our manager, Jonathan Kessler, rang and told me there was a meeting with my lawyer about the bust," recounted Dave Gahan. "But when I showed up it turned out it was a full intervention. An LA specialist called Bob Timmons was there. He's worked with a lot of addicts in the entertainment business.

"They all said, 'You're going into rehab, right now.' I said, 'No fucking way.' They said, 'You are.' I said, 'Alright, tomorrow' – thinking I could go home and cook up before I went. But they said, 'No, now.' I was like, 'What about this evening?' 'No.' I said, 'A couple of hours; I need to call my mum.' They let me go. Jonathan said he'd come and pick me up. I went home, [did] my last [drug] deal, had my last little party and checked into rehab."

On June 6, 1996, the cornered singer was dispatched to Exodus Recovery, the same Marina del Rey-based Californian psychiatric in-patient hospital where Kurt Cobain had begun drug rehabilitation treatment on March 28, 1994, before walking out and tragically committing suicide eight days later.

Cobain's addictions, discomfort with his celebrity status, domestic disputes and the personal demons of anguish that led to his demise rang true with Dave Gahan, who had been dealing (unsuccessfully) with similar issues himself. Having admitted to spending half his time in a wardrobe in his rented Santa Monica apartment with the curtains taped shut, he entered Exodus Recovery at 4644 Lincoln Boulevard, Marina del Rey, a no-nonsense facility with a prison-like reputation. According to Dave, Martin Gore's attitude didn't help matters much beforehand: "He rang me just before I went into Exodus and he was angry with me. I came off the phone in tears, because I realised, 'Fuck, they don't really give a shit about me; it's the fact that there might not be any Depeche Mode anymore.'"

While understandable, Gahan's assessment of his work colleague's standpoint oversimplified matters somewhat. "We were very compassionate for a long time," Gore told *The Independent*'s Glyn Brown a year after the singer entered Exodus Recovery.

Dave Gahan: "It all came to a grinding halt; Martin rang me up when I went back home to Los Angeles, after all the trouble and everything, and he said, 'Shall we just knock it on the head?' And I said, 'Mart, this is just *so* not important to me right now.' It just wasn't relevant to where I was [at].

"But I made a decision to give it a shot, and I took some advice from people for the first time – not just with the band, but with my personal life and stuff. I actually started listening to people who were telling me I couldn't do this anymore – people like Jonathan, my manager. I knew it was going to be a struggle; I knew it was going to be the hardest thing I ever did in my life."

Daniel Miller defended Gore's actions: "There comes a point when everybody says, 'Okay, it's come to the point: either you or the band.' But, really, the reality is that the thing that got Dave off [drugs] was the fact that he nearly killed himself, and the American legal system said he wouldn't get a Green Card or be allowed back into the country unless he went into rehab and had tests over a period of two years. In the end, his desire, first of all, not to be chucked out of America and his understanding of what he was doing to himself kind of forced the issue."

At Exodus, between seizures, Gahan gradually, painfully detoxed. Just as the 34-year-old was preparing to check out in readiness for his upcoming court hearing, another addicted celebrity was ordered into the same facility by another court – namely, 31-year-old Robert Downey, Jr. The wayward actor had wandered into the Malibu beach home of publishing magnate Bill Curtis under the impression that it was his own home, was found unconscious in one of the bedrooms, revived by paramedics and promptly arrested. Unlike Dave Gahan, Downey, Jr. would have trouble staying on the right side of the law and, arguably more importantly, staying clean, following his 'rehabilitation' at Exodus Recovery in Marina del Rey.

Fortunately for Gahan, the short, sharp, shock treatment had worked. "It changed the whole way I felt," he told Phil Sutcliffe in 1999. "I was sick of hurting everybody around me. I didn't want to lose my son. I didn't want him to grow up wondering why his dad killed himself. All that hit harder and harder. And suddenly I got it. There was hope. I could change. I could have a choice. The only thing I don't have a choice about is my feelings . . . they come and go, but they're really difficult to deal with when you've been using for a long time. You've blocked them out for so long and they come on like a freight train."

Someone once dubbed Depeche Mode's frontman, 'Garrulous Gahan'. It was a fitting description, for Gahan came under fire from some quarters for his forthrightness over his troubles.

418

Alan Wilder: "In general, I have to agree that there is something rather undignified about airing your dirty laundry in public – it's not my style – and I don't really think a lot of people want to hear rich pop stars whining about how tough it is to survive their privileged lives. However, there are cases when it's necessary to be absolutely honest about a situation and, to an extent, humble oneself in order to confront the damage that's been done. If this kind of confession has been therapeutic for Dave, then it's perhaps not such a bad thing."

Clearly, recovery would be an ongoing process, but before Gahan could begin to get to grips with his new life, he had to answer to the authorities.

After the four-week recovery period at Exodus, Gahan moved into a so-called 'sober living house' in Los Angeles which gave him more flexibility to work on upcoming musical projects – including Depeche Mode's divisive album that had been placed on hold, pending the outcome of the singer's June 18 court hearing. Matters were further complicated when the LA District Attorney's office demanded a more in-depth police probe into Gahan's alleged drug-related offences, which, according to a DA spokesperson was "not an uncommon occurrence".

Gahan's Beverly Hills court hearing was rescheduled for July 9, where the accused pleaded not guilty to charges of possession of cocaine and being under the influence of cocaine. On July 10, the Depeche Mode fanclub kept concerned fans abreast of developments via Mute Records fledgling 'Liberation Technologies' website: "His case has been continued until the end of July, for further proceedings. The court has also ordered that Dave remain in the drug treatment program he entered shortly after his release."

The fanclub also speculated as to what the future might hold for Gahan: "It is anticipated that Dave will be referred to the Probation Department at his next court appearance, for enrolment on a Diversion Program, which will involve continued drug treatment and rehabilitation for about a year. In this case, Dave would then have all charges against him dismissed, upon successful completion of the Program."

As it was, the fanclub's assessment was spot on, as they were only too happy to convey online on August 1: "Dave appeared in court again on July 30, and, as we anticipated, he has been referred to the Probation Department, who will interview him regarding his enrolment [on] a Diversion Program. As long as Dave completes his rehab, all charges against him will be dropped. Meanwhile, Dave has also been in the studio in Los Angeles, working on his vocals with Tim Simenon."

With that good news, Martin Gore was spurred on to writing more songs in readiness for the band's scheduled re-entry into the recording studio at the end of August.

Andy Fletcher: "Dave did come good in the end. He gave up drugs and drink, [and] got all his vocals done. He got himself together, basically."

Nevertheless, the troublesome album would be a drawn-out affair, spanning some 15 months from start to finish. As late as October, the Depeche Mode fanclub reported that the band was still in the studio in London and would be "recording and mixing right up until Christmas, except for a break at the end of November, when they will be making a video for the next single, which will be released in January [1997]."

Ultra, as the album would eventually be titled upon its April 1997 release, involved several London recording facilities during its final stages, including mixing sessions (presided over by producer Tim Simenon and engineer Q) at topflight producer Trevor Horn's Sarm West recording complex on West London's Basing Street, and EMI's Abbey Road Studios.

According to a spokesperson the band leapt at the chance to work in the latter's hallowed recording environs following Oasis' acrimonious departure amid reports of rows with other artists and studio management alike. "The [*Ultra*] title really fits in with our new line-up," commented Martin Gore from within Abbey Road. "We lost a member along the way, and now it's the new, improved, slimmed-down version."

Old Mode collaborator Gareth Jones was called in to engineer additional vocals for 'Home' (beautifully sung by Gore – set against a backdrop of sweeping strings arranged by programmer David Clayton, and scored and conducted by Richard Niles), 'The Love Thieves' and 'Freestate' (capably handled by a rejuvenated Gahan) at RAK Studios in St John's Wood, North West London. Jones also assisted Simenon with mixing the album's two instrumental offerings – 'Uselink' (on which Daniel Miller was credited as 'guesting' on a Roland System 700 modular system) and 'Jazz Thieves'.

Additional supporting cast members included a multitude of studio assistants (including one Paul Hickey, long-term partner of Erasure vocalist Andy Bell) and outside musicians, including drummers Gota Yashiki and Keith Le Blanc; bassist Doug Wimbish; percussionists Victor Endrizzio, Danny Cummings and Jaki Liebezeit (of German progressive rockers Can); and pedal steel guitarist, BJ Cole.

Gore was particularly complimentary about the latter two's distinctive contributions: "A track like 'The Bottom Line' is a country track. Even when the demo was finished the way the words roll have this country loop to it. So we got the idea to get this pedal steel player [BJ Cole] to enhance that, but at the same time there's other influences going on. We used Jaki Liebezeit from Can, who played percussion on that track, and there are some vibes going on that gave it this bizarre lounge feel as well. We throw all these influences – what we like – into the blender, and it comes out as this strange hybrid at the end that somehow is able to be called Depeche Mode."

However successful its songwriter might have deemed the outcome, recording *Ultra* had undoubtedly been a long haul and a testing time for all involved. "Nearly losing a singer; that's never happened to me before," Tim Simenon quipped to the *NME*. In private, the producer wasn't smiling, and confessed to feeling "fucked" by the end of the lengthy production process. "I carried on working until January and February 1997, which was the worst thing I could've done," he confessed. "I nearly collapsed. I started to feel really ill. So I took a break and had a few months off. I was just mentally and physically exhausted."

In March 1997, on the *Ultra* promotional trail, Andy Fletcher jested with Dutch journalist René Passet: "After the album, Tim suffered from what is known as PAD: Post-Album Depression!"

Both Mute Records and Depeche Mode had a lot riding on the future success of the costly project.

Daniel Miller: "*Ultra*, in terms of making the record, was a band falling to pieces, but I think the album itself is a band trying to figure out where it's going without Alan. If you listen to the album, you don't necessarily hear the problems; I mean, there's 'Barrel Of A Gun', which was done after the problems. I think Dave sort of found a new voice, which was part of his recovery."

Dave Gahan: "Instead of just singing the songs, and interpreting what Martin had done, and just [doing] something that would please him, please the producer and everyone else – apart from myself, I was able to go in and sing from my heart . . .

"The rest of the making of that album actually gave me some kind of [goal] – I wanted to rekindle the relationship with my son."

Judging from the following comments made to *Q*'s Phil Sutcliffe in 1999, it seemed that Dave Gahan, the father, finally found what he was looking for. "What's fantastic now is spending a couple of days with Jack.

Being there – really being there. Last night at the hotel I heard him kind of moaning, and I went into his bedroom, climbed into bed with him and just cuddled him, and he went back to sleep. Six months ago I wouldn't have been able to do that. I wouldn't have wanted to – because of the guilt and shame I felt about myself."

Daniel Miller: "I think the fact that they made that album was a shock to everybody who was close to the band – and to the media, who was watching the band."

Andy Fletcher: "I think for the music sometimes you do have to suffer for your art. And we *did* suffer for that period, but we learnt our lesson – to a certain extent. We [came] out with an album, *Ultra*, which we think is up there with our best albums."

As Alan Wilder had revealed, there were disagreements during his Depeche Mode tenure over the most appropriate single to release in advance of a new studio album. *Ultra* was no different in that regard, as 'It's No Good' was sidelined in favour of 'Barrel Of A Gun'. "We thought it was good to come back with a harder track," Andy Fletcher told René Passet.

Prior to its release, Dave Gahan told *BONG* magazine: "The most innovative [song], in terms of what we've ever done, is 'Barrel Of A Gun'. It's least like anything we've done; it stretched us, and me, vocally."

Andy Fletcher: "It's quite weird, because people expect it to be sort of representative of the album. But it's not a hard album; it's quite mellow."

From the moment that the song settles into its Tim Simenon-generated groove and moves into Gahan's distorted, disturbing-sounding vocal, mellow it is not.

Martin Gore deciphered Depeche Mode's 'comeback' single for the benefit of *NME*'s Keith Cameron: " 'Barrel Of A Gun' is about understanding what you're about and realising that you don't necessarily fit into somebody else's scheme of things. You can have slight diversions from your path, but I think there is something that is written for us, that is meant to be. I'm not being totally fatalistic; I think we do have a say in things, but I don't think that say is very strong."

Gore's apparent conviction that a person's fate was largely determined from birth struck a chord with the recovering Gahan: "I always liked going out for a drink, and was never able to really handle it. I wasn't much of a social drinker – I tried it for a while, but I drank to get drunk, and that was very clear to me, even when I was very young. I truly believe you're born like that – [with] that extra need for attention. I just carried on [with] all that [kind of behaviour]; I put myself in a band to be observed and judged, putting myself right out there. I think I was just looking for something that made me feel comfortable, and for a while I found that in drugs.

"But, as we all know, when that feeling stops working, it's a mess. I spent a couple of years dabbling around with drugs and then spent a good few years trying to stop. Doing that thing of stopping for a few days – it's a fucking nightmare! It's a merry-go-round that you can't get off."

Fortunately for Gahan, by 1997, he had at least succeeded in getting off that nightmarish merry-go-round, although as was apparent in his analysis of his flawed character, this was no easy task: "I think you're born with some kind of gene. There are lots of different theories about it. All I know is that I do much better in life when I just leave it alone. I don't kid myself today that I can dabble with it, and I don't miss it now. There was a time when it was a struggle – not just to even be tempted. But it takes a while once you've stopped all that stuff – for me, anyway – to really start to feel comfortable. But then I started getting those odd days where I was just totally content, and I was feeling that excitement for life again – just doing stuff, spending my time doing stuff. I spent a lot of time doing fuck all, basically, with the illusion of doing a lot."

A video for 'Barrel Of A Gun' – Depeche Mode's 30th single – had been shot at the tail end of November when Anton Corbijn set his camera controls for the heart of Marrakesh.

Dave Gahan: "The interesting thing about [that] video was that I had eyes painted over the top of my eyes. There's this wall around this old city in Morocco – this *huge* wall, which, to the Moroccans, is basically a bathroom; it's like where they go and take a shit! I had to walk all the way along this wall down one side while they were filming me, so there was this wall down the one side, and they'd be, like, 'Left, right,' because every time we came along some guy who was doing his business there I had no idea; I'm blind, so I'm walking through all this stuff – this shit, which was very amusing for Anton and [producer] Richard Bell at the time!"

Gahan actually suffered for his art when contracting salmonella during the Moroccan shoot. He was flown back to the UK where he was immediately confined to a London hospital bed for three days. Elements of Corbijn's captivating 'Barrel Of A Gun' promo were described by Dave Gahan as being "quite autobiographical" as it showed a man literally being followed by the barrel of a gun, and, as such, symbolised Gahan's recent past. "I wanted it to be like you're constantly running away from your life, avoiding life, avoiding your feelings," the reformed singer explained. "It's being a junkie, pretty much."

Having personally supported Gahan during the living nightmare of addiction and his subsequent detoxification, Corbijn's video was all the more disturbing for it. "I think he came up with the idea because he sees me today much healthier," Gahan claimed at the time.

In a press statement preceding the release of Depeche Mode's first single in three years, Mute Records announced that 'Barrel Of A Gun' was to be simultaneously released on two CDs in "special reverse jewel cases" and 12″ vinyl with a gatefold sleeve. As always, remixes would be plentiful, "by disparate dance luminaries Underworld, 3 Phase, One Inch Punch and Plastikman." All such artists, plus United, were also mentioned in eye-catching adverts placed in the mainstream music press – including a full-page in *New Musical Express*.

Andy Fletcher: "When the Underworld remix came back, it came in two mixes. Tim, who had already listened to it, said the second one was brilliant. So we listened to the '[Underworld] Soft Mix', which was the first mix; we thought, 'This is really great! The second one ['Underworld Hard Mix'] must be amazing!' But then it starts off, lasts for about 10 minutes, and there is not one recognisable bit of the song in there – and no vocals. So I went to Tim and said, 'It's really good, but it's got nothing of the song in it.' He replied, 'Well, that's the way it's done nowadays.' But we didn't think it was right, so we had a discussion. We sent the remix back and Underworld added some vocals, as a compromise. I'm still not sure about it, but I like the '[Underworld] Soft Mix'."

Martin Gore agreed: "The original version of 'Barrel Of A Gun' was about 83 beats-per-minute. When we received the '[Underworld] Hard Mix' back from them, we were sitting there thinking, 'What relevance does this speed bear to ours? Is it double the speed?' And we timed it, and it turned out to be about 148bpm! When I rang them [Underworld] up and spoke to them, I asked, 'Is there any chance you can fly some vocals in? Just so it has some relevance, because there's not one sound of the original version on there.' And they said, 'Well, we're not quite sure how that works, because the speed is different, and it's in a different key!' Different key, different speed – different song!"

Dave Gahan: "Everybody was sort of bee-lining 'It's No Good' when they heard the album as being the song that was going to be the success from it. It was like, 'Oh yeah, that sounds like Depeche Mode.' But I think the success in *Ultra* was the fact that we recorded the album – at all –

and that we managed to complete an album that we're all very happy with, and getting a hit on top of that always is very nice."

'Barrel Of A Gun' peaked at number four on the UK Singles Chart within two weeks of its release – their highest chart position since 'People Are People' some 13 years earlier.* Clearly, Depeche Mode's considerable British fanbase were pleased at seeing the band – and Dave Gahan in particular – back from the brink. Ex-Slade frontman Noddy Holder – no stranger to the UK Singles Chart himself – did the guest reviewing honours for *Melody Maker*: "I like Depeche Mode. They were my favourite band of the early Eighties. They touched a nerve with me. They've made some great singles in the past, but they've lost their way on this one. It meanders around too much. Too many drugs, methinks! Is their singer *compos mentis* again? He was in a nuthouse for a bit, wasn't he?"

When Depeche Mode appeared on *Top Of The Pops*, it was with an expanded line-up that included Anton Corbijn on drums and Tim Simenon on keyboards. Martin Gore: "Just before we got on-stage, I said to Tim, 'You realise that you're now joining the ranks of the uncool?' "

Corbijn was apparently taking his newfound musical role more seriously. "He told me he's been the happiest he's been in 10 years," Andy Fletcher told René Passet. "He's got his drum kit and he's practising. And he's drumming on-stage with us."

On March 31, a second single, 'It's No Good' preceded the UK release of *Ultra* by exactly two weeks. Once again, 'standard' and limited-edition 12″ and CD singles were simultaneously issued with several dance remixes of the title track by the likes of Andrea Parker (of Mo' Wax label notoriety), and Dutch techno artist Speedy J (a.k.a. Jochem Paap) sharing space with two versions of new song, 'Slowblow' (one of which was remixed by NovaMute – Mute Records subsidiary – artist, Darren Price). "It was a question of who had time available for our deadlines," Gore noted at the time.

One man with, to paraphrase Martin Gore's lyric, all the time in the world was Anton Corbijn, who had a drumming cameo in his latest video. "We are becoming slightly worried about our new video; we haven't seen

---

* Stateside, the single didn't fare quite so well following its slightly earlier January 18, 1996 release, managing number 47 on the *Billboard* Hot 100 Singles Chart and a reasonable nine-week showing on the Modern Rock Tracks Chart where it reached number 11.

the full script yet and we are worried that it will focus on the drummer for about 99 per cent," Gore joked.

Dave Gahan: " 'It's No Good' was one of the most fun videos I've ever made. Anton took it to the extreme, and he had me dressed up in this green lamé suit. My hair was long at the time, so we created this big Fifties Teddy Boy wig. I got to really play a role and a part – the real has-been rock'n'roll star that ends up playing these [dingy] places, but still thinks he's larger and bigger than life itself."

Andy Fletcher: " 'It's No Good' was always going to be a single. You knew it from the moment you heard the demo. I remember Martin ringing me up about 'It's No Good' and saying, 'I think I've written a number one,' and it [was] number one in many countries."

The British record-buying public lapped it up – pushing 'It's No Good' to number five by April 12, where it stood as Depeche Mode's second-highest chart ranking in their home country. The music press were equally effusive. "When it comes to such ultra-tech, yet trad toilet-seat drama, Depeche are untouchable, a fact the litany of unenlightening remixes by the likes of Speedy J and Andrea Parker only serve to emphasise," said the *NME*.

Martin Gore: "I like to make sure there is some basis to a song before they move on to a computer and electronics, because I think if you start working with a computer and banks of synthesisers, it becomes very easy to fool yourself that a song is great when the song is not great at all; it's just a few great sounds that you've got going."

30

Coming Clean

"Most of my friends that I hang out with in New York are people who are choosing not to drink or use drugs anymore, and, to be honest, most of the people I hang out with are way more creative than the people I thought were creative who I was hanging around with [before]."

— Dave Gahan, 2001

Depeche Mode were in for a pleasant surprise when *Ultra* entered the UK Albums Chart at number one, having sold a respectable 43,000 copies during its first week of release, with the added satisfaction of knocking *Spice* — the long-playing début of manufactured pop sensation The Spice Girls — off its pedestal in the process.

The reviews for *Ultra* were a predictable mixed bag. *NME*'s James Oldham awarded *Ultra* a mediocre six out of 10 rating: "Seventeen years together, 30 million albums sold, and here comes another to crank up the profit margin one notch higher. Except this time, it's not *just another* Depeche Mode album, because if it were, it wouldn't arouse such a ghoulish fascination. *Ultra* is more than that; it's the culmination of a festering melodrama that could have resulted in death, but in the end settled for a near-fatal heart attack and some lengthy cold turkey."

Melody Maker's Robin Bresnark was more caustic: "The linear tinnitus of *Ultra* makes ears ring and Depeche Mode's past success becomes overgrown with moss. Which is why David Gahan will never recover. He was away too long. Somewhere where he became a fool. Trapped into self-pity. Self-absorption. Self-delusion. Which is why Martin Gore, the broken mother, will waste the remainder of his career writing lullabies about his son's promise. Sweeping up his singer's blood-flecked detritus, sterilising the room with a mist of astringent optimism. She remembers the pain of wanting him back. But she doesn't want him back anymore."

The Guardian's long-time Mode supporter Caroline Sullivan was impressed with what she heard, skirting briefly over the obvious issue of Gahan's survival: "Gore's lyrics provide a wealth of desolation for Gahan to get his teeth into. There's less of his religious imagery than usual . . . Gore himself sings on perhaps the most austere track, 'Home'. Anyone doubting the potency of pop music should hear (the album), then pretend they're unshaken. Even an ostensible love song like the single 'It's No Good' is disturbing."

Neil McCormick, in *The Daily Telegraph*, wrote: "Although total album sales in excess of 30 million attest to Depeche Mode's worldwide popularity, British critics have regarded the group's metamorphosis from bubbly synthpop outfit to gothic electro-rockers with suspicion. Photographer Anton Corbijn's moody pictures and videos of the weedy Essex boys only emphasised their inate naffness, depicting them as a kind of cut-price U2. In this light, Dave Gahan's recent lurid confessions of heroin addiction seem less like a plea for help than a bid for credibility. Given this prevailing critical scepticism, recording songs entitled 'Useless' and 'It's No Good' might be considered a touch ill-advised. *Ultra* is certainly not useless, though the title of the group's 12th album rather begs the question: 'Ultra-what?' "

Ultra's progress was markedly slower across the Atlantic, yet it valiantly fought its way up to number five on the *Billboard* Top 200 Albums Chart, where it would remain for a total of 19 weeks. While this was a far cry from the 74-week residency enjoyed by *Violator*, it was still more than enough to considerably boost songwriter Martin Gore's coffers, and indeed that of EMI Records' gargantuan publishing empire, who had signed up Depeche Mode – effectively Martin Gore – in 1995.[*]

Robert Marlow: "Martin's got a current account that probably reads £25 million! I don't know, I've never asked, but out of everyone that I know, Martin is probably worth the most money."

Q magazine had placed the three remaining members of Depeche Mode amongst Britain's 100 richest rock stars, with Martin Gore reputedly worth £15 million (ranking at number 47), Andy Fletcher – £10 million (number 58), while Dave Gahan's £5 million pegged him at number 76

---

[*] As such, Martin Gore's latest *Ultra*-era songs were credited 'published by EMI Music Publishing Ltd, assigned by Grabbing Hands Music Ltd' except for 'Useless' which was assigned to EMI by Grabbing Hands Music Overseas Ltd.

Coming Clean

(having, presumably, blown a sizeable chunk of his fortune on feeding his former habits).

Alan Wilder: "There are thousands of other people they could (and should) have mentioned in their article, which, as with every survey I've ever seen on rock stars and their wealth, was *wildly* off the mark. Some of the figures mentioned are laughable. They are based on massive assumptions and almost pure conjecture. I used to quite like Q as a magazine, but it's rapidly gone downhill over the last few years. As for my personal wealth – that's a private matter which I don't wish to disclose."

With a new album riding high in the charts, Depeche Mode would traditionally be contemplating a mammoth tour, but certain things had changed. The *NME* revealed that Depeche Mode would be playing "a greatest hits tour" in 1998 "to promote a [forthcoming] 'Best Of' double album covering their work from 1985 to 1997."

Andy Fletcher: "I think we're gonna tour next year when we're all a bit fitter. We've released a very good album and we just want to enjoy the success of that, hopefully."

Fletcher hadn't ruled out the possibility of doing some live television performances in the meantime. "We haven't done live TV since 1982.* We had some pretty bad experiences – in those days the sound quality was pretty shit, TVs were shit and also the facilities they had were shit. Still, those things have got better now."

As it was, Depeche Mode, supplemented by session drummer Christian Eigner and David Clayton (playing a Korg Trinity workstation via a Roland A-90 mother keyboard) returned to the stage earlier than Fletcher anticipated, with a rare live set at Adrenaline Village in South London on April 10, 1997, filmed by MTV for broadcast later that year. During the first of what would become known as the 'Ultra Parties', the band performed a short set to launch the *Ultra* album, with Fletcher still using an Emax Turbo II sampling keyboard (dating back to 1990's 'World Violation Tour') while Gore played a Gretsch Anniversary guitar.†

NME's Simon Williams was there to review the invitation-only event witnessed by the likes of Nick Cave, Gary Numan and Pet Shop Boy, Neil

* Andy Fletcher was referring to *The Tube*, when all the band's equipment failed apart from Fletcher's Moog Source keyboard.
† Copied for on-stage use by Dick Knight from Gore's original Gretsch, using authentic Gretsch parts, but with more wood in its body to cut down on feedback.

Tennant. Upon discovering that a cool £50,000 had been spent on simply staging the live show, the journalist's response was scathing: "That figure enters the realms of the positively frigid when Depeche Mode eventually play *five* songs. If this is a publicity exercise to tell the world that Dave's drug problems are way behind him and he's as-fit-as-a-funky-bunny-thanks-very-much, any bozo brain can tell you that performing five tunes is hardly the most taxing of tasks in the known world. Case unresolved. If it's a 'party' for various chums, then the appearance of only one old song, 'Never Let Me Down [Again]' hardly represents great music for the masses."

Daniel Booth (of *Melody Maker*) was equally forthright: "Better than most, Depeche Mode illustrate the reversal of pop's glory, from chic to shit, from despair to nowhere . . . this isn't just some half-baked longing for groups to remain as they were when I was young. It's just that Dave Gahan has grown up to live all the rock myths that his group, and their cheap, frilly pop used to piss all over. Their self-discovery has been represented only in a hideously dark, guttural rock vocabulary and sound, which falls foul to the cliché that confessional and troubled lyricism can only be mirrored by gruesome, twisted music. Electronic music, and especially electropop, has yet to release itself fully from the grip of industrial, keyboard-trashing horror. It is *this* legacy that continues to undermine Depeche Mode; their simplistic assimilation of techno-grunge merely distorts the truth into a crass, black pantomime."

In spite of such harsh words, Depeche Mode repeated the exercise at Los Angeles' Shrine Expo Hall on May 16, during a whirlwind schedule. "We did a photo session on Monday [May 13], we had this Internet thing on Tuesday, now we've got *The Tonight Show*, tomorrow we've got the [*Ultra*] launch party, and then, hopefully, we're finished," Martin Gore noted beforehand.

On May 15, Depeche Mode made their US network television début on NBC's *The Tonight Show* with Jay Leno. "It's probably my worst nightmare going on TV with large audiences," stated Martin Gore. "I love writing songs, I love being in a band, but this isn't exactly my idea of fun. That's just one of those things I have to accept; it's part of the job."

As KNBC 4 Channel 4 News' Gordon Tukumatsu's coverage of events outside NBC's Burbank studios clearly showed, Gore's job was still an important one as far as his American following was concerned: "If there's any doubt that Depeche Mode has staying power, take a look at this — some fans overnighting, just to make sure they get a *Tonight Show* seat."

On May 13, Depeche Mode participated in the world's first live Internet chat in the RealVideo format from The House Of Blues at 8430 Sunset Boulevard, West Hollywood, to launch their www.depechemode.com website, which received a staggering half-a-million 'hits' within 24 hours of first going 'live'!

Martin Gore: "That Internet thing apparently broke records, which is nice to hear. It's just amazing, the fanaticism. We've never been able to put our finger on why our fans are so obsessive. We do seem to be the group with the most obsessive fans in this business."

Dave Gahan: "I think (the internet) is a great medium; it's really opened up a lot. I think it's cool that fans can communicate together on the hotline. It's like sending a letter and getting an instant reply."

Andy Fletcher: "My personal view is that the Internet is a bit exaggerated. The problem with the Internet is that 99 per cent of the stuff that you can get – like the Depeche Mode section – is wrong information. So there is no control and it's not very accurate, and I suppose, sooner or later, when more controls come, it might be better. But right now I think its usefulness is over-exaggerated."

Around the same time, Alan Wilder launched – and personally maintained – his own Recoil website (www.recoil.co.uk). "One should retain one's quality of life, but not at the expense of progress," Wilder stated. "Shopping is a good example. Just browsing a virtual supermarket, then sitting back and waiting for some spotty youth to deliver my weekly choice directly to my door has got to be the way forward. It's a paradox. My solo project, Recoil, takes advantage of the Net to spread the word and benefits from fans being able to exchange material (essentially bootlegging); whereas Depeche Mode, my other source of income, needs to take precautions to prevent unauthorised material flying around."

While the Internet continued to spread, 1997 saw Alan Wilder and Vince Clarke using more established promotional channels, with wildly varying degrees of commercial and critical success. Erasure's tenth album, *Cowboy*, spawned three singles, two of which – 'In My Arms' (number 14 in January 1997) and 'Don't Say Your Love Is Killing Me' (number 23 in March) – were UK hits. A 37-date tour kicked off with nine arena-sized shows in the UK before heading into Europe, and North America (having played eight club dates there earlier in the year as part of their Tiny Tour). Unfortunately, *Cowboy* bombed despite some fairly prominent advertising efforts from retailers like Tower Records.

Both album and tour were crucified by critics; Simon Williams' three out of 10 *NME* review scoffed, "*Cowboy* is more insipid humalong than inspired hump-along; obscenely inoffensive fodder from chaps once-upon-a-time not averse to strutting around on-stage showing off fake wangers, and now seemingly content to flap around living on past *Carry On*-style glories. Like the fact that Andy Bell used to be a mincer – in a meat factory! Mid-paced crisis, anyone?"

Erasure didn't fare much better on-stage, as *The Times*' Paul Sexton's review of a Wembley Arena show (April 18) confirmed: "When Erasure entered the synthpop arena in 1986, Heaven 17 were already old news. So the final night of Andy Bell and Vince Clarke's latest excursion provided an anachronistic pleasure as the earlier electronic warriors completed their first tour as the duo's special guests. In their decade-plus together, Erasure have had best-selling albums in spades, including five consecutive number ones from 1988 to 1994, and 26 Top 40 singles. But recent statistics suggest that the swing-o-meter is edging in the opposite direction. In keeping with the swift commercial demise of their tenth album, *Cowboy*, there was something humdrum in the delivery that came over as not just end-of-tour, but end-of-era. The lead singer played his usual Danny La Rue of pop while the instrumentalist tweaked the occasional knob on his synthesiser stack. Otherwise, Clarke was an unintentionally spare comic part; even dressing him up as a cactus fell strangely flat."

Meanwhile, Alan Wilder was plotting a less commercial course with *Unsound Methods*, his fourth solo outing as Recoil in October 1997.

Alan Wilder: "The album is difficult for me to comment on, though I do have something of a stock answer, which is: you can probably work out what I think about it by listening to *Unsound Methods* and then *Ultra*, because the two records tell you everything you need to know about what the musical relationship was between myself and Martin [Gore]. It's almost as if we've gone to the two extremes of what we were when we were together."

Critics were clearly confused by what they heard, including *The Independent*: "Sadly, the title of this album by the former Depeche Mode member Alan Wilder rings all too true. The dark, stream-of-conciousness-style album commits all the crimes of the unfocused artist: self-indulgence ('Drifting'), self-importance ('Incubus') and pretension, in the form of horrendous storyteller babble ('Luscious Apparatus')."

Mojo were more supportive: "Take one ex-pop star. Put him together with a handful of well-chosen guest vocalists. The result: a cleverly crafted, dark and brooding album. The songs about perverts, victims and stalkers shape themselves to fit Wilder's murky layers and expressionistic tones. Never better so than when a disembodied chorus of *'You're all I need to get by . . .'* crashes in at the end of 'Control Freak'. Remember to leave a light on."

So what did Wilder's former colleagues make of his work?

Andy Fletcher: "Very well produced; it just lacks a bit of soul."

The more mainstream record-buying public felt the same way, for all three singles lifted from the *Unsound Methods* album failed to chart. Not that Wilder appeared unduly worried: "I already had a very favourable deal with Mute – a rollover from my DM days – and a good relationship. I knew Dan Miller very well and thought that he'd support me in whatever I wanted to do – whether it was commercial or not. I like being with Mute for all these reasons, and also because they're a respected and diverse independent label. The only downside is that they don't have the funds to just throw money at projects – like the majors tend to – for advertising, et cetera, which can be frustrating when you are trying to increase awareness."

In the wake of Dave Gahan's much-publicised drug exploits, awareness of Depeche Mode was at an all-time high. The *Ultra* album spawned two more hit singles before the year's end in 'Home' and 'Useless'. The former, Martin Gore-fronted number, was released as two CD singles and a cassette single including remixes by Jedi Knights, LFO, Air Skylab and Grantby, plus live recordings of 'Barrel Of A Gun' and 'It's No Good' captured at the 'Ultra Party' on April 10; it featured a video shot in Los Angeles by Steve Green, and reached number 23 on the UK Singles Chart on June 28.

Earlier that year, Depeche Mode were asked whether they would consider releasing a CD-ROM. Dave Gahan had replied, "I believe that's something we're looking into, but we've not actually made any plans yet."

Those plans were realised, as of October 20, when 'Useless' was released on two so-called enhanced CDs (Audio/CD-ROMs), meaning its content could be played on conventional CD players while digitised versions of Anton Corbijn's videos for 'Barrel Of A Gun' and 'It's No Good' (one being featured on each disc) could be accessed by computer. As always, Depeche Mode strove to stay ahead – or at least keep abreast – of the game, and were rewarded for their efforts with another Top 30 hit in the UK, supported by a bleak, if colourful Corbijn-directed video set in a disused coalmine.

Stateside, 'Home' and 'Useless' were paired up as a joint release on 7″ and 12″ vinyl, standard and enhanced CD singles, and cassette single, which crawled to number 88 on the *Billboard* Top 100 without making any impression on the alternative Modern Rock Tracks Chart.

1997's UK chart-topping *Ultra* shifted over four-million copies world-wide. A year later, Andy Fletcher – described by *NME* as overseeing "the conception, execution and successful resolution of each 'project', as both he and Gore are wont to term official Mode activity" – was evidently encouraged by the success of the album and the band's revitalisation.

"We are enjoying ourselves again, and can't *wait* to go back into the studio again – and we've just been in there for the last three months, [where we've] recorded three new tracks. It's almost a rebirth – like it was 15 years ago."

Film footage shot in Eastcote Studios showed Dave Gahan clearly in his element, singing new song 'Only When I Lose Myself' – destined for release as a future single – while Fletcher, Gore, plus Tim Simenon and engineer Q, watched from behind the control room's expansive console. It certainly appeared that Depeche Mode had made peace with their demons.

Andy Fletcher was keen to get Depeche Mode back in the recording studio, having just finished recording and mixing three new Martin Gore-penned tracks in London's Eastcote and Abbey Road studios with *Ultra* producer Tim Simenon in March 1998. However he would have a lengthy wait ahead as the trio were planning to squeeze a lot into the latter part of that year. Indeed, it would be quite some time before Depeche Mode re-emerged when one of those three tracks, 'Only When I Lose Myself', was finally released on September 7, shadowed by new tracks 'Headstar' and 'Surrender' (plus various remixes spread across one 12″ vinyl and two CD singles).

The sleeve's distinctive, minimalist artwork was designed by Intro, who were also responsible for Recoil's *Unsound Methods* album, while old Mode sleeve photographer Brian Griffin's video was a cross between David Lynch and a slick car commercial. Not that Depeche had severed ties with long-time visual collaborator Anton Corbijn, who was busy designing the stage set and shooting video footage for the band's upcoming tour to supplement already existing material, which Alan Wilder wasn't altogether happy with: "I wasn't consulted about whether I wanted my image to be associated with a tour I wasn't involved in."

Dave Gahan: "With 'Only When I Lose Myself', it's like I went to some place with that song [that] felt good inside." *NME*'s Simon Williams: "Nowadays Depeche Mode are into beautiful packaging, beautifully pearly toothed videos and the sort of beautiful music which makes one go, 'Mmmm! Very tasteful. *Très* continental. Lovely harmonies. Smooth production. Nice teeth, too. I'm thirty-two-and-a-half years old, you know.'"

The band's champion, Stephen Dalton was nearer the mark when describing 'Only When I Lose Myself' as "Less pompous and more vulnerable than much recent Mode fare, it's a low-voltage charmer which grows on repeat hearings . . . The obligatory big-beat and old-skool hip-hop mixes are pretty rank, though."

Chart-wise, the single reached a reasonable number 17 UK placing while disappointingly taking a dive at 61 in *Billboard*.

Andy Fletcher: "I think 'Never Let Me Down Again' was one of our best tracks ever, one of our legendary tracks live, and in England, for instance, it got to number 22, which in England for us is a very poor figure because we normally tend to go Top Five. That became a legendary song, but in fact it was a flop in the single charts. And the track 'Condemnation' on the *Songs Of Faith And Devotion* album, we thought that was going to be a big hit single and that was a massive flop. Sometimes you can tell and sometimes you can't."

Five days before the single appeared in British shops, Depeche Mode began an eagerly awaited 64-date 'comeback' tour that would take in 18 countries over a four-month stretch. The Singles Tour – so named because of the forthcoming *The Singles 86>98* compilation album that *NME* had incorrectly speculated would cover the period 1985 to 1997 – kicked off at the Festival Arena in the Eastern Estonian City of Tartu on September 2, 1998.*

Estonia, it seemed, was as good a place as any for Depeche Mode to reacquaint themselves with the world stage. At a London pre-tour rehearsal, sitting astride a flightcase stencilled with 'All the way from Basildon', the short-haired, sober and sombre Dave Gahan, told *The Daily Telegraph*'s Neil McCormick, "I'm nervous – terrified, actually, but

---

* Former Soviet states were a Depeche Mode stronghold, and such is the fanatical fascination for Basildon's finest export that Tallinn, another Estonian town, boasts a Depeche Mode Bar. A visiting *Observer* journalist later noted: ". . . a corner of this foreign town will be forever Basildon . . . a shrine to Eighties Essex synthpop."

at the same time very excited. My voice is in good shape. I'm in good shape. Mentally, I feel strong. I don't know if you're ever ready for touring, but I'm as ready as I'm [ever] gonna be.

"I've had a lot of time to learn to take care of myself better. My priorities have changed. This isn't where it starts or where it ends for me anymore. Corny as it sounds, I'm excited to be able to go out on the road again, but I'm more excited about the fact that I can feel stuff now and my mood changes are not dictated by what I'm putting into my body. It's a new experience for me. For a long time I thought that being in a band you had to do everything – up 24 hours, partying, giving it 100 per cent on-stage. I really thought I had to live the words that I was singing. [But] excess doesn't mean that it's any more purposeful; it doesn't mean it's any more real. The cliché of getting fed up for your art is one that I don't want to be part of . . .

"It's about the songs and how I sing 'em. In this set it's poppy, it's rocky, it's bluesy and then we get gospelly in places. We're very adaptable."

Andy Fletcher, living up to his self-confessed role of "[saying] a few jokes, [doing] introductions to speeches at dinners," did a pretty convincing job when around 95 international journalists (the majority German) and four television crews gathered at Cologne's Hyatt Hotel on April 20, for a press call to announce The Singles Tour: "Thanks to all the reps from all the different countries, and thanks to our manager, Jonathan [Kessler], who's kept us together for the last four years – [it] must [have been] very hard. I think four years ago, when we finished the last tour, we thought maybe it might be the last Depeche Mode tour, but we've since recorded what we think is a very good album [*Ultra*].

"We've just been in the studio for the last three months, recording new material, and this next tour, which we're all very happy about . . . we think it's going to be one of the best Depeche Mode tours. We're gonna be doing all of our best tracks from the last 12 years, so it'll be a historical perspective, and we're very much looking forward to it."

Upon hearing the news that his former bandmates were touring again, Alan Wilder commented: "I think, considering everything that has occurred during the last few years, they are very brave to go out on the road again – not because of my leaving, but because the excesses of the Devotional Tour took their toll on everyone, and I doubt the remaining members will want to repeat them. That said, I've no idea what the show's going to be like."

The show was performed on considerably bigger stages with more songs, more lights, and with a slightly different personnel and instrument line-up – hired hand Peter Gordeno replacing principal keyboardist David Clayton, while Martin Gore doubled up on keyboards alongside his beloved Gretsch guitar with two Emax II Turbo samplers.

Martin Gore: "I started playing instruments when I was 13 – I started playing guitar. I didn't see a synthesiser until I was 18, so, in a way, it was unnatural for me to be a synthesiser player for the first 10 years of our history – seven years, whatever. It was a natural thing for me to progress and play guitar. If you look at [The Singles Tour set list], it's about 80 per cent songs [where] I'll be playing guitar, because 80 per cent of our songs have guitars, but there are [also] songs where I play the synthesiser."

Andy Fletcher: "We are going to use a drummer full-time on-stage – he's an Austrian guy, who's really good. He worked with us on a TV show [*The Tonight Show* with Jay Leno] – Christian Eigner."

Dave Gahan: "Using a drummer through the whole show is something we experimented with on the Devotional and Exotic tour[s]. We used backing singers there – that worked well, so we'll be [doing] that. We need a keyboard player, because Alan's not with us anymore, and he played a lot of stuff. A couple of little things that we did with the Ultra Party things really did transform the old songs quite a bit, I think. For me, it felt a lot more exciting to feel a drummer behind me."

At the Cologne press conference, Gahan addressed the question of live as opposed to pre-recorded music on-stage: "It's weird that we've never been asked a question like that before. We always got attacked for years and years and years for doing that, and [have] probably been one of the first bands to do that and openly admit to it. [But] bands have been doing that for years, whether it be Pink Floyd or Depeche Mode. For us, it's something very different to try and perform a lot of the stuff live."

Martin Gore – whose opening words at the Cologne gathering were "I'm very sorry; Alan couldn't make it!" – added: "It's still impossible for us to play absolutely everything live, because our records are too complex. It's a fact, and I think anyone with any sense will realise that."

As for the backing tracks, Wilder initially speculated, "I would think it unlikely that they would use any of the old backing tracks", later commenting, "From what I can gather, it seems that they took a view to focus their live versions very much around the original singles – make of that what you will."

Any apparent sour grapes on Wilder's part was perhaps understandable, if ungraciously taken as a jibe at his former colleagues for cashing in on his labours with what could be simply seen as being a 'Greatest Hits' cop-out. However he was far from surprised by reports of Depeche Mode's latest live successes in the Eastern Bloc.

Alan Wilder: "I don't think it's down to the kind of tour. It's simply that Depeche Mode have always had a particularly devoted fanbase, and are playing for the first time in places like Russia [Moscow and St Petersburg] and Eastern Europe [Estonia] where they're very popular. These places don't get to see their favourite bands too often, so the reaction to DM is not surprising."

The Observer's Sam Taylor joined 21,000 "Euro-goths" at Berlin's outdoor Waldstadion on September 18: "As the sun sets, the silhouetted forest looms darkly over the stage, an elegant scarlet-and-silver ensemble created by Anton Corbijn in the image of a peepshow. The air is still, the sound is perfectly clear; you can see why Hitler chose to rehearse his rallies here. At one point, the floodlights are turned on the audience, and the stadium is transformed into a pink, fleshy sea of waving arms.

"The music is suitably stern and straight-backed; you might believe this was Kraftwerk tackling Gotterdammerung, were it not for Dave Gahan baiting the crowd with his Shakin' Stevens hipshakes and yelling 'That's right' every few seconds. He is, truly, Basildon's own Michael Hutchence with half the charisma and twice the self-destructive streak; yet, somehow, he is not only alive, but a bigger star than Hutch ever was. He's certainly fortunate to be in the same band as Gore. On stage, it's clear how much they need each other. Gore alone is an anonymous wisp; Gahan alone a trite rock pastiche. Together they are oddly convincing."

Melody Maker's Carl Loben stuck the proverbial boot in; having attended the Wembley Arena show (September 29)[*]: "Depeche Mode began life as chirpy synth-poppers in the early Eighties before moving into superb clangers of scrap metal for their third album. Then they went all industrial, got *huuuuuge*, and their singer got himself a heroin habit. It's a soddin' shame they're now such 'pants' [terrible] . . . Dave Gahan's clean now, of course, although with his addiction has gone much of Depeche's latter-day appeal."

---

[*] This September 29 Wembley show was, incidentally, attended (according to *The Independent*) by Professor Stephen Hawking, awe-inspiring author of *A Brief History Of Time*, who reputedly liked the band so much that he had 'Just Can't Get Enough' programmed on his mobile phone!

Even the traditionally supportive Caroline Sullivan was more reserved: "The band get to revisit their most fertile hit-making period (though the hits have dried up a bit lately, with current single 'Only When I Lose Myself' just scraping into the Top 20), and the fans get to bask in two hours of familiar gloom. This simple arrangement is a good deal all round, except for those expecting the grandiosity that used to distinguish Mode shows. For such people, the brisk run-throughs of [hits] from their most black-clad Gothic period might have been a let-down – so, perhaps, might the stage set: blue swagged curtains flanked by a big illuminated 'DM', which was intended to convey a 'Berlin peepshow' look."

One fan found the put-downs worrying, citing a *Q* magazine review where "the closing paragraph explicitly states that Dave is a less interesting and charismatic person now that he is not a junkie."

Alan Wilder: "The only reason I would find it worrying is because it's such a cliché. It would not be the first time that it's been said [that] an artist is at their most interesting when under the influence. I can't see how the journalist can say Dave is a more or less interesting person without meeting him both before and after his drug experience. If he has done this, then he is entitled to his opinion. If he means his performance isn't as good, well, he's also entitled to his opinion."

31

Some Great Rewards

"I can't tell you how many times I get people coming up to me in the street – even at home in New York, and they're like, 'I saw you in your last show at Madison Square Garden; never seen you guys before; never really liked you, but that was amazing!' And that's really nice."

– Dave Gahan, 2001

The Singles 86>98 double-CD compilation effortlessly entered the UK Albums Top 10, topping out at number five in October 1998. It even received some glowing reviews along the way from the likes of *Melody Maker*'s David Benedict: "Whether or not you buy the theory that Depeche sewed the seeds of Detroit techno – and hence rank alongside Kraftwerk as one of the most important bands of the last 20 years – is immaterial. Either way, they've consistently produced incredibly effective pop music that has as sharp an appreciation of its demographic as any hyper-calculated boy band . . . 'Never Let Me Down Again' remains as much of a rush of tingling homoeroticism as it was 11 years ago, while last year's extraordinary, relentless 'Barrel Of A Gun' is a livid, smarting bruise of a song. Depeche Mode, once again, prove themselves essential."

Andy Fletcher: "We sort of see it as a really big achievement – the fact that we are releasing a 'best of' album, yet we're as popular now as we ever were. The piece of work – *The Singles 86>98* . . . we really see it as the best work of our career."

Alan Wilder: "The compilation is really a historical piece, which, in my opinion, correctly remains faithful to all the original 7″ releases (as did *The Singles 81>85*). I personally feel this is the right way to go even though [it doesn't] necessarily [include] the best version of 'Behind The Wheel'. The same also applies to a number of other tracks on the record, however; everybody has different opinions about their favourite versions and it

440

would have been absolutely impossible for us all to agree. I was outvoted on 'In Your Room' at the time of its original release, but since that was the decision, for this release, the correct version [Butch Vig's 'Jeep Rock Mix'] has been chosen."

Wilder was not entirely in agreement with Intro's artwork: "Intro designed all the latest artwork, which is great to see in one sense, because they did a really good job with Recoil. However, in DM's case, I think that it is a bizarre decision not to use Anton Corbijn, whose very unique style represents 10 years of DM imagery – something very closely linked to the singles themselves since 1986. In my opinion, to tie in his album artwork over the years would have been the most cohesive (not to mention loyal) thing to do. I'm not saying that his artwork would have been better, but continuity would have been there.

"As much as I like Intro's style, I think it's rather out of sync with a DM greatest hits release – with *The Singles 86>98* you're not just selling the music, you're selling the image and the memories. Intro's token rendition of some of the previous symbols – like the [*Violator*-era] rose, for example – looked a little ridiculous, but some of the main photos looked great. There is nothing wrong with change, I just feel the timing is wrong.

"Contractually, I have rights to be fully consulted about all aspects of recordings I was involved in, like which versions are used, artwork, label copy, promo items, marketing ideas, et cetera. Sometimes it is a struggle, though, for a leaving [band] member to be heard – out of sight, out of mind – and often it is assumed that because I left, I either don't care or have given up all these rights. Not so."

On that score, the so-called 'A Short Film', directed by Sven Harding, and distributed during Depeche Mode's promotional trail as an EPK rattled Wilder's cage: "For starters, I never pushed myself forward as a member of the band, and the media tends to concentrate on lead vocalists and songwriters – to a lot of people, the 'techno-nerd' in the studio isn't really that glamorous. I also haven't been to death's door and back, and, more importantly, committed the heinous crime of leaving the band – so, out of sight, out of mind.

"I can accept all of these things, but I was annoyed in particular with *The Singles 86>98* EPK, which I thought was extremely unbalanced – to have 10 years of one's hard and dedicated work represented by about 30 seconds out of a 20-minute piece is pretty insulting. I was also excluded from (and not even advised about) the interview with Anton Corbijn where the other band members discussed his videos for the singles – the same singles that I worked and performed on."

Wilder could take consolation in receiving his fair share of resulting royalties from *The Singles 86>98* album (which reached 38 on the *Billboard* Top 200 Albums Chart following its October 6 release by Reprise), and *The Videos 86>98*, the accompanying Mute Films-fronted home video released in the UK and USA by WEA. As if that wasn't enough to be getting on with, the Intro-designed repackage of the previously released *The Singles 81>85* compilation (covering all 15 singles from Vince Clarke's 1981-vintage 'Dreaming Of Me' to 1985's 'Shake The Disease') was released soon after, backed up by its *Some Great Videos 81>85* VHS visual counterpart. "I actually prefer the main (red) image, as used in the repackaging of *The Singles 81>85*," Wilder admitted.

Eye-catching artwork apart, the lavishly packaged CD additionally included the pre-Alan Wilder tracks, 'Photographic (Some Bizarre Version)' and the 12″ 'Just Can't Get Enough (Schizo Mix)' as an additional incentive.

Unlike the notorious Devotional trek, The Singles Tour rolled, trouble-free, towards its triumphant North American conclusion. Following two Southern Californian shows at Anaheim's Arrowhead Pond arena on December 20 and 22, the fully revitalised band would have performed for a grand total of 650,000 fans.

Dave Gahan: "It's music, we're musicians, we're playing . . . [we're] very grateful that we get to do this and that we've still got fans who want to come and see us. There's not that many bands who can say that after 20 years; we must be doing something right!"

On September 28, 1998, *NME*'s Victoria Segal rounded off her *The Singles 86>98* review with some clever, Gore-inspired lyrical wordplay – "Depeche Mode never really enjoyed the silence; all they ever wanted was the applause" – venomously claiming that the 'talentless' Depeche Mode had always sought credibility within rock circles.

Dave Gahan: "We've been a bit gypped in the past with that. Sometimes radio, TV and MTV, and all that, don't quite know what we're about and what to do with us. We don't really go with the Limp Bizkits of this world, so what do they do with us?"

For The Masses: An Album Of Depeche Mode Songs, as performed by the likes of The Cure ('World In My Eyes'), Smashing Pumpkins ('Never Let Me Down Again') and Apollo 440 ('I Feel You') was released on August 4.

The band themselves had touched on the then-upcoming project during The Singles Tour press conference in Cologne back on April 20.

Martin Gore: "We've got this tribute album that's coming out in the summer, which is really interesting, because a lot of contemporary bands are covering our songs. Finally, there are some good bands who've decided to cover our songs!"

Jeff Turzo, of American alternative rockers God Lives Underwater (who interpreted 'Fly On The Windscreen'), voiced his own tribute to the band's composer: "Martin Gore is an amazing songwriter; he's written so many good songs that are *great* songs – songs that we would hear, and I would think, 'Why didn't we think of that?' They're just so perfectly simple and perfectly brilliant. You could sit down at a piano and just play any Martin Gore song, and it would sound like a good song. So, it just takes a good band to do what they do with a song, and it's gonna come out cool."

Martin Gore: "The interesting thing about it [*For The Masses*] is that it's a lot of alternative rock bands, so it's not particularly electronic-based. It's coming from this American alternative angle, which we've been a great influence on."

Robert Smith of The Cure (who arguably came closest to sounding like Depeche Mode on their *Mixed Up* remix album) was happy to be involved with the project: "A lot of what Depeche do is sort of based on sounds. The songs are tied up with the sounds, but the really, really good songs, once you take all the sounds away, the song's still there. There's always about two or three songs on every Depeche album that are *very* memorable, and are really well put together.

"The reason why we did a song for this album was primarily because we were asked, and, more importantly, because I really like Depeche Mode. What makes this tribute album as good as it is, is that most of the bands aren't trying to sound like Depeche; they're actually trying to sound like themselves, doing Depeche songs, so that's why it works – judging by the quality of the album, which I think is exceptionally high, with the best collection of covers on one album which I think I've ever heard."

So what did Alan Wilder who had, ironically, once been approached to join The Cure make of their take on 'World In My Eyes'? "Not bad. I like Self's version of 'Shame'. It's just what a cover version should be – different from the original. It's got a great sense of energy. I like Veruca Salt's 'Somebody' – great atmosphere. Rabbit In The Moon also [did] an unusual version of 'Waiting For The Night'."

Dave Gahan: "I particularly like The Smashing Pumpkins' version of 'Never Let Me Down [Again]' because it's kind of like the opposite of what you'd expect The Pumpkins to do with it. I actually like their version a lot better than ours!"

Martin Gore: "Isn't it the greatest honour you can have, for a lot of contemporary bands to cover your songs and admit you are an influence? I take it as the greatest honour I could have."

On May 27, 1999, Gore was further honoured as the shell-shocked recipient of an award for 'International Achievement' by the British Academy of Composers & Songwriters at the 44th Ivor Novello Awards at London's Grosvenor House Hotel. Daniel Miller, the man who had sealed a deal with Depeche Mode with a simple handshake – no written details, no formal contracts – almost 20 years beforehand handled the presentation honours: "It's been a long time, and a lot's happened to Depeche Mode since Martin took over the songwriting role for the band from Vince Clarke in 1981. But always what's been at the core of their success and their progress has been Martin's songs. He's often, unfortunately, or sadly, been a bit underappreciated in this country, we feel, but consistently he's connected with people around the world, in every corner of the world, and helped Depeche get a huge and loyal following wherever they play.

"It's been an amazing achievement. And Martin's always extremely modest about what he's achieved, but I think – a lot of you will agree – that he's really recognised as one of the most important and gifted writers of his generation. I know I speak for Fletch and Dave from the band, and Jonathan Kessler and everybody who's worked with them over the years; we just want to say: we're proud, we love you, and congratulations, you deserve it."

Modest Martin Gore stepped up to the mic: "I was warned about this, but it's still very overwhelming, and thank you very much. It's an honour to accept this award, and I'm especially pleased to be handed it by Daniel, who's been a friend for the last 20 years."

Further indication of Depeche Mode's impact on popular music was indirectly shown when Analogue Solutions, a British manufacturer of new-generation analogue synthesisers and music accessories, named their Oberkorn analogue sequencer after the B-side, 'Oberkorn (It's A Small Town)' (the quirky instrumental flip to 'The Meaning Of Love'). Its operating manual even opens with the words "Oberkorn (It's Not A Small Sequencer)!"

According to Analogue Solutions' manager, Tom Carpenter, "The

Oberkorn is my ideal analogue sequencer. I wanted it to have a weird name. I thought it would be interesting to see how many people connected its name to Depeche Mode. They have had a huge influence on my musical tastes and career. Amongst a few other electronic bands, they are what started my interest in music and electronic instruments. 'What a fitting tribute,' I thought, 'to name one of my creations after my all-time favourite musicians!'"

In early 1999, Martin Gore, the man who had reputedly turned down an offer to write the next James Bond movie theme, resumed songwriting at his Hertfordshire studio at a leisurely pace with a view to a new Depeche Mode album.

In October, Gore enlisted the assistance of keyboard player/programmer Paul Freegard and engineer Gareth Jones, a period termed as being a 'workshop' on the latter's website. "Paul and I were there, essentially, to support our artist, Martin," Jones explained, "and, as every studio worker knows, that can cover a lot of ground.

"For whatever reason, Martin was creatively 'blocked' and we helped establish an environment where creativity could flow more easily. We experimented with the interpretations of the songs in a very relaxed, healthy and positive environment – insofar as we could. We had a good time; we did group meditations, sometimes; we listened to music; we ate well; very occasionally we went to the pub."

Gareth Jones proved especially helpful – from both an organic and electronic standpoint: "My 'equipment' included aromatherapy oils and joss sticks, organic brown rice, sardines and rice crackers, as well as tension-tamer teas!"

Gareth's 'New Age' *modus operandi* notwithstanding, the flexible engineer also put his portable Apple G3 PowerBook laptop computer-based recording equipment to good use: "From an early stage, it was clear that we wanted to be able to move seamlessly into production with this material. All in all, it was home recording-style, a style which we carried on with in bigger studios later.

"There is no point in recreating stuff again; indeed, very often it is simply impossible. So a great deal of our fantastic pre-production work came through to the finished record. Lots of guitars and Martin's lead vocals are from this session – and masses of synths and audio. Working in the virtual and tapeless world as we do, any audio is available throughout the whole production."

Come 2000, Jones' website reported himself and Freegard as being involved in "ongoing pre-production". "Dave has been over from New York and done some excellent vocals on four tunes already."

One such "tune" was 'Dream On', which made its mark as a standout in Depeche Mode's varied catalogue. "I just played it to Gareth and Paul on the guitar, and the idea was to not use a guitar at all – just to take it off in a completely different direction," Martin Gore recalled. "After we'd been working on it for about four days, we had this real kind of edgy electronic percussion going in the background, and we just cut the original guitar that I'd played [back] in, and it just sounded good, because it was so different to everything else that was going on in the track."

This latest bout of pre-production work was fronted by the band's recently founded umbrella company, Venusnote Limited – an outcome of the group having finally signed a legally binding contract with Mute Records Limited, whereby Venusnote would retain copyright of any future recordings which would, in turn, be released under exclusive licence to Mute.

"When we did the latest deal, I think they vaguely looked around to see what else might be [on offer]," Daniel Miller stated at the time. "Whether they were actually ever seriously going to go, I don't know. We're so embroiled with each other, I sometimes wonder maybe what would happen if they did do that [leave Mute], but I think if there's ever a point [where this was about to happen] it will certainly be discussed with me, anyway. I don't want to go into details too much, but hopefully we'll be working together for a few years yet."

Having resolved any external concerns of a legal kind, the band's internal dynamic also had to be assessed.

Andy Fletcher: "We did have a chat together at the start, and any problems we had with each other we sorted out. I like to think that they're nearly resolved, but I don't have to be Dave's best friend to be in a band with him. The fact is that we can argue. Martin is one of my top three [or] four friends; Dave I'd consider a brother – like a family relationship. I don't think Dave wants to spend every second of his evenings with me, but it's like my brother – I enjoy seeing my brother, but not every night. I can argue with Martin, and Martin can argue with Dave – we still have those tensions, but the band *has* to have those tensions."

Daniel Miller: "There are underlying tensions of personality differences, shall we say; not based on music, really – based on personality. They've always been there. The real mates in the band, if you like, are Martin and

Fletch, historically. That's the mate's thing – and with Vince [Clarke] as well; they all knew each other. Dave was brought in later. The others had grown up together and known each other as kids. It's Bas [Basildon], you see – different parts of Bas."

Of course, the three remaining members of Depeche Mode now lived on different sides of the Atlantic. "It's irrelevant where we live," Gore argued. "We pick a place [to work], and we usually try and keep every member of the band happy."

"When the time came for us to actually look for a producer, there weren't that many people out there who fitted the bill. [We] need somebody who is a real expert with electronics, and who is also able to fulfil an organisational role – almost a father figure," Martin Gore explained in 2001.

In the end, that someone turned out to be 29-year-old Mark Bell, who, as co-founder of Leeds-based LFO (a Warp Records signing dubbed by several American websites as being one of the most influential techno acts of the early-Nineties) had reached number 12 on the UK Singles Chart in July 1990 with 'LFO'. Bell had just completed work on Bjork's *Selmasongs* (having previously produced *Homogenic* for the Icelandic songstress in 1997). It was these critically acclaimed – and commercially successful – recordings that swayed Depeche Mode in favour of Bell.

Daniel Miller: "He's somebody I've known for years, so he came and met the band, they got on, and really that was it. And he had the right balance of understanding songs and brilliance with electronics – contemporary-sounding. We didn't want to do a genre album, like trip-hop or drum 'n' bass, or house – the songs had to live in their own world, and I think he understood that."

Mark Bell: "I had no time to think about it. They just said, 'Right, do you want to start in a week?' So I initially just concentrated on doing everything that I could for these songs – loads of rubbish ideas, but the odd good one as well! When I first heard the demos, I thought some of them sounded finished already. I think they were a bit bored with the songs, because they'd been playing with them for so long, but it was exactly what I'd been listening to – German minimalist clicks and cuts, but with real instruments. I thought, 'I'm the most qualified person in the world to do this!'"

Yet, the humble Leeds lad wore his production crown with some discomfort. "I find it so weird being called a producer, because 'producer' means so many different things to different people. It could just be

447

someone who takes artists out to parties all the time and never actually does any music at all. Or it could be someone who does *all* of the music. There are just so many variations – like the way it can cross over into programming. But I feel I'm still doing exactly the same as what I was doing 10 years ago with LFO. I saw myself [as being] more of a musician then, and now I'm still doing musical things."

Which was all part of his attraction to Martin Gore: "I don't think Tim Simenon would ever claim to be a musician at all – he'd go as far as to call himself a non-musician. Mark tries to pretend that he's less musical than he actually is. He's obviously not a trained virtuoso, but he understands more than he lets on at times."

While Warp Records played up Depeche Mode's pioneering synthpop status when announcing Bell's production coup in May 2000, Bell's recollections revealed a genuine admiration for Depeche Mode: "They were really important to me when I was 15 or 16. I liked how they always treated electronics and acoustics as one entity. Their music doesn't belong to any particular genre; it's not clichéd in any way.

"So when I got the chance to work with them I thought it would be really weird, but it didn't seem weird at all. I'd already done a remix of a track called 'Home' from their last album [*Ultra*], and they really liked how I interpreted the song. I didn't just completely change it into a hip-hop or speed garage track, or whatever was 'in' at that moment. I did it how I thought it should sound, and I think that's what they were interested in."

With nine new songs ready, on June 5, 2000, band, producer and engineer Gareth Jones commenced work at RAK Recording Studios, which boasted the only fully functional 1976-vintage API mixing consoles in the country. "We went to RAK just to see if we'd get on as people, really."

Mark Bell: "Obviously we did. We were there for three weeks, playing around with the new songs. I'd add completely new bits – nothing to do with the originals."

While Bell was technically adept, the bulk of the complex recording procedure fell on Jones' shoulders. "Valuable musical work and vocals were done at RAK," the engineer maintained, "and we started to develop an effective and comfortable way to work. It was very important to all of us that we should enjoy making the record, and our working environment was also very important to us. We wanted to be in a city; we decided to work in a commercial studio for the soundproofing, maintenance and assistant engineer support. We were not in the studio because we wanted to be recording on a large console or because we wanted access to loads of studio effects. With these priorities we were able to reassess how we used the studio space.

"Dave was very keen to spend a lot of time with the tracks, so it was very clear that he needed a space to work where he could sing, listen to music and record vocals whenever he felt he had something worth recording. I set him up in the control room, working to analogue tape at RAK, so both rooms were able to work independently if they wanted. Obviously we were wired for sound, so we could all hear what we were doing if we wanted."

Andy Fletcher: "We worked on 'Dream On' first; it was probably the first or second song Martin wrote for the album. But I think it's the real defining track – a mixture of electronic beats with acoustic blues guitar, some really good lyrics and a great, catchy chorus. It was great that we recorded that song first [as it] set the way [forward] for the album."

Next stop: New York City's Electric Lady studio complex, scene of Dave Gahan's disastrous vocal sessions for *Ultra*. The return visit was far more productive.

Gareth Jones: "After RAK, we went directly to NYC for a couple of weeks with the main intention of focusing on lead vocals. We set up more conventionally in the Penthouse at Electric Lady – vocal mics in the live room and synths in the control room. We also got a beautiful string arrangement by Knox Chandler for 'When The Body Speaks' recorded in the Neve room. Together, Dave sang and Martin played guitar for some of the takes of this song, too. So the Electric Lady sessions were very much about performance, as opposed to programming."

Indeed, solo cellist Chandler and a five-piece string section were deployed with chilling effect on the dreamy 'When The Body Speaks', perfectly complimenting Gahan's vocal and Gore's guitar without compromising the trademark Depeche Mode sound that Bell was determined to retain.

Mark Bell: "In the past I think they would have got Martin to play the guitar as perfectly as he could. Then it probably would have been edited to make it even more in time before Dave sang over the top. So I sat them in the studio and recorded them performing together. I don't think they've done that for 16 years or more – apart from live performance. Then we wanted to take the acoustic aspect further and make it sound even more like an 'Unplugged'-type thing. Dave said he'd got this friend who's a

449

string arranger, so Martin and myself put the chords together and Knox did the rest."

Both Gahan and Fletcher later attributed the remarkably up-front-and-personal vocal to 'When The Body Speaks' directly to Mark Bell. "I'm really crap at taking compliments, but a lot of that was just down to making Dave feel comfortable. I got the impression that in the past he was nervous; obviously he was performing the songs, but not necessarily how he wanted to. So I encouraged him to do what he wanted; that's why we gave him his own room, though I'd still go in there and give him directions."

Dave Gahan: "I'm not one of the most confident singers in the world. Mark was really encouraging, and he liked what I was doing. I need a pat on the back; I need that encouragement; I need to know that I'm bringing something to Martin's songs. Otherwise I wouldn't bother. I *know* I am – in my heart, but sometimes it's like, 'What am I doing here? Martin can sing this song. Why doesn't he just do it himself?' I felt like that a few times during the recording of [the] album, but Mark said, 'What you bring here *is* important; it's really valuable; it's part of Depeche Mode; and it's part of what becomes the song.' So he really encouraged me with that – and Gareth's great with that as well."

By now, Gahan had happily remarried and, furthermore, his new relationship was fulfilled further with the arrival of a baby daughter, Stella Rose (born July 29, 1999). Although Alan Wilder was invited to the wedding, it clashed with a recording commitment at his Thin Line studio that same weekend. Wilder did, however, hook up with his old bandmate when promoting the fifth Recoil album, *Liquid*, in New York.

Alan Wilder: "Hep and I did visit the Gahan household, and it was great to meet his wife, Jennifer, daughter Stella Rose, and, of course, to see Dave. He is in fantastic shape and we had a good laugh about lots of things – old and new. He is obviously besotted with Stella Rose and seems very content all round. I took a copy of *Liquid* for him."

Mark Bell picked up on the singer's joy at being a father second time around, and helped him creatively channel his joy: "I suggested he sang the album's closing track, 'Goodnight Lovers', as though he was really singing it to [his daughter], like a lullaby. And I think that comes across. It's not role-playing, but something he could really feel. Also, we tried to do all the vocals in one take, because I think your brain instinctively knows otherwise – even if it's an amazing cross-fade. That was really important to this album – and Dave. He enjoyed the support. After all, he *can* sing; he's been doing it for 20 years!"

Dave Gahan: "I [had] a lot of fun with 'Dead Of Night'. I [got] to be Dave Gahan on that, big-time – I'm in [an imaginary] gig and play out all my sort of fantasy Bowie-esque-type stuff, Iggy stuff, and the dark, gothic man."

It was while struggling with that same song, that one of the world's top jazz percussionists ended up featuring on 'I Feel Loved' and 'Freelove' – albeit accidentally.

Mark Bell: "We were having trouble with the bridge. Martin suggested using a kind of jazz/waltz sample he had, but it sounded completely shit. We were just about to take it off when in walks Airto Moriera! It was really embarrassing, as the song was at its worst, but we still ended up playing him the other songs. He came back a week later with his toys and played some brilliant stuff that sat well with some of the tracks."

Dave Gahan: " 'When The Body Speaks' was a real challenge; it has a beautiful melody – so has 'Goodnight Lovers'. I loved it; I felt like I was singing it to my baby daughter. Mark had said to me, 'You know, it's kind of got a lullaby feel about it.' "

Martin Gore: "With ['Goodnight Lovers'] I really wanted to recreate a Velvet Underground kind of feel – Velvet Underground with Nico; something like 'I'll Be Your Mirror'. It's very difficult to do that, but we got Dave to sing it really softly – almost whisper it – and I think the overall effect of the chords and the way he sung it almost recreated it, and I was quite pleased with the end result."

The production then moved over to the opposite coast at Santa Barbara Sound Design. "Martin had moved to Southern California, and the band decided to go and work on his patch for a couple of months," Gareth Jones explained. "Sound Design has two live areas and a nice vibe, so we went for that. Santa Barbara was a beautiful place to work. We stayed in hotels overlooking the ocean. Mark and I rode along the beach to the studio. Everyone had a good time, and we were free from the distractions of big cities like LA, NYC, and London, as the town shuts down at 2 am."

In November and December 2000, Jonathan Kessler dropped in on the Santa Barbara sessions, filming for Depeche Mode's website, where some of the band's synthesisers were duly displayed.

Mark Bell: "Synths are still really important to them, but it wasn't a case of us deciding this was going to be an electronic album, even though that's what I really liked about them before. Right at the beginning the songs were just written on a piano or guitar, just to get the basic chords. By the time I became involved there was just *so* many keyboards around, plus Martin's got loads of guitars. We used loads of synths on 'Dead Of Night', messing around with envelopes and pitch controls.

"Not only is Gareth a brilliant engineer – sorting out which microphones to use where, he's also so organised when it comes to the computer side of things. You could play a keyboard at any time and record it, and Gareth would instantly have it colour-coded, labelled and dated."

Jones summed up the remainder of the album's production: "We did loads of great work in Santa Barbara, as we had done already in Hertfordshire, RAK and Electric Lady! And we continued working in the live rooms of the mix studios – Sony Studio B in NYC and Sarm West Studio 1 in London – whilst Steve Fitzmaurice was mixing."

Following the Christmas break after a month mixing the album at Sony, in NYC, and two weeks at London's Sarm West, the production officially wrapped on January 20, 2001.

Gareth Jones' next task was assisting Vince Clarke at his private Chertsey recording studio, 37B, in recording *Other People's Songs*, an Erasure album of cover versions made at their own expense, that – having started life as singer Andy Bell's long-mooted solo album (comprising mainly Sixties standards) saw Erasure entering the charts again come 2003, after several years wallowing in the commercial wilderness.

As for Depeche Mode, they were once again duty-bound to step back onto the promotional treadmill in support of the new album, *Exciter*, with the touring rigmarole that this inevitably entailed.

32

Exciting Times Ahead

"We're in really good shape and we should be really embracing everything that we've created for ourselves, and going out there and doing our best to get this across to as many people as possible."

– Dave Gahan, 2001

On April 23, Depeche Mode trailered the forthcoming *Exciter* album in the UK with its first single, 'Dream On', on one 12″ and two CD singles with a selection of remixes and the obligatory Anton Corbijn video (a kind of 'mini' road movie, shot in one of his favourite Californian haunts: the Mojave desert, just outside Barstow).

Response to the record was favourable. 'Dream On' topped the charts in Spain, Italy, Denmark and Germany; it also commanded a Top 10 position in Hungary, Greece, Portugal, Finland, Austria, Norway, Sweden and the UK (number six). Despite being the most added song to North American radio playlists in advance of its April 24 release, 'Dream On' only mustered a disappointing number 85 placing on *Billboard* during its five-week run (21 on the alternative Modern Rock Tracks Chart).

Following its May 14 release, *Exciter* (with its – according to Andy Fletcher – "quite phallic" – Anton Corbijn-designed 'cactus' sleeve) topped charts in Sweden, Greece, Belgium, Poland and Hungary; attaining Top Five status in Italy, Spain, Switzerland, Finland, Iceland, Canada, Norway, Denmark, Austria; while holding Top 10 positions in the UK (number nine) and the US (number eight), spawning three hit singles in the process ('I Feel Love', 'Freelove' and 'Goodnight Lovers').

The album successfully pre-empted the 84-date Exciter Tour, opening on June 15 at Montreal's Molson Center, following three North American warm-up shows in Los Angeles, Quebec City and Ottawa (June 4, 11 and

13, respectively) – closing at Mannheim's Maimarkthalle on November 5, playing to over 1.5 million fans across 24 countries.

Anton Corbijn's minimalist stage setting, with its innovative use of an enormous state-of-the-art projection screen, dominated the entire back-drop to great effect. Gone were the backing tapes in favour of Apple G4 computer-driven backing tracks, synchronised to Corbijn's visuals.

Dave Gahan: "There's lots of songs, like songs from *Songs Of Faith And Devotion*, that would bring up all these sad emotions – lost time, and stuff like that. And I try to stay in what's going on there at the time, and often out of a lot of those sorts of songs – like 'In Your Room'. And that's kind of how it felt during those darker times for me, if you like – I was in my own little room and I felt very protected in my own little room for a while, and I was invincible. I could come out when I wanted and go back in when I wanted, and the room was a safe place.

"But now that room kind of scares me and I don't really want to go in there anymore. So when I was singing that song on the last tour it was almost like I could sing it from outside the room and go there for a little bit, and look at it and peer in. And it was a lot more fun than singing it like it was on *Songs Of Faith And Devotion*; on that tour, I really got off on the whole kind of darkness of that period of my life, but it got really boring."

Positive praise came flooding in from around the world for both album and concerts. While it's debatable if Depeche Mode ever actually went away, *The Guardian*'s Dave Simpson awarded 'Comeback CD of the week' to *Exciter*: "Central to *Exciter* is the peculiar musical relationship between songwriter Martin Gore and Gahan. Gore claims not to write with Gahan in mind, and would, no doubt, argue that *Exciter*'s themes – love, obsession, insecurity, displacement, redemption and, repeatedly, addiction – are universal, but virtually every line seems to bear some significance to the singer.

"Whatever, something has prompted Gahan into the strongest, most heartfelt vocal performance of his career, typified by the venom he puts into 'Shine's' eerily mocking line: *"You've been hanging from a rope of medi-ocrity/ Strung up by your insecurities . . ."* This is a revitalised Depeche Mode: cleansed, streamlined, and in prime condition to take on the world again."

American Terry Wickman caught a show at New York State's Jones Beach Amphitheater on July 3: "One of the things that most impressed me about the show was multi-talented Martin Gore playing guitar for 80 per cent of the show. You wouldn't think immediately of DM as a guitar band

– after all, they are considered one of the early electronically driven bands. But Gore has written a majority of the new material as well as adapting parts of older songs on guitar."

Gahan also caught the writer's attention, citing the singer as being "truly one of the better frontmen out there. His voice is very strong, many times reaching powerful deep notes. Gahan is constantly moving on the stage. His physical presence and the energy he derives from the audience is quite noticeable.

"It was appropriate [when], about halfway through the concert, a bright moon broke through the clouds. It symbolised the theme of the band's new album, *Exciter*, which is love. An emotion all of us felt watching Depeche Mode's performance."

Following one of two October 2001 Wembley Arena shows, Alexis Petridis (*The Guardian*) wrote: "Nowhere is the gulf between British and American music tastes more intriguingly highlighted than in the case of Depeche Mode. In the US, they are venerated as an influence by both the black producers who invented techno and nu-metal bands such as Slipknot and Limp Bizkit. In England, despite enormous, enduring success, Depeche Mode have always been critically derided as naff 1980s survivors – more Gary Numan than New Order. [But] Depeche Mode have founded two decades of global success on their ability to move immense crowds. For all their pantomimic qualities, it is virtually imposs- ible not to be drawn in. As the set ends, Gahan, shameless to the last, exhorts the crowds to wave their hands from side to side. Thousands of Goths and Essex boys obey."

On record and on-stage, Depeche Mode had triumphed yet again, reputedly selling £12-million worth of tickets for 34 American dates during The Exciter Tour. As Dave Gahan saw it, "We couldn't have gone out and done another tour celebrating our past. It had to be something new. There aren't that many bands that can actually say after 20 years that they're trying to be creative."

On May 27, 2002, The Exciter Tour was made available for all to see (in anamorphic 16:9 ratio) and hear (in Dolby Digital 5.1 surround sound) as *One Night In Paris*, a lavishly packaged, two-disc DVD set, filmed at the Palais Omnisport De Bercy sports stadium. "The venue itself is probably one of the best in the world," claimed Andy Fletcher. "We've played this venue many, many times, so for us it's almost like a second home in Paris."

Anton Corbijn, who had received a Grammy nomination for his

previous Depeche Mode concert film (*Devotional*), directed six camera-men, operating 13 cameras to put viewers right in the front seat, as the band and hired hands Christian Eigner (drums), Peter Gordeno (key-boards) and backing vocalists Jordan Bailey and Georgia Lewis performed for a crowd totalling some 16,000. Disc One featured the full 21-song set, including Gore's solo rendition of 'Sister Of Night', accompanied only by Gordeno's (sampled) piano, which, while not as moving as the Gahan-fronted version on *Ultra*, lent further credence to God Lives Underwater's Jeff Turzo's earlier expressed conviction that ". . . you could sit down at a piano and just play any Martin Gore song, and it would sound like a good song."

Disc Two was packed with bonus features, including an interview with a crew member (Production Manager Bill Peabody): "I think they're Britain's best-kept secrets, Depeche Mode. They've always been an inter-national rock band. I always tell people a story about when I was 19, and this is my lean on it: I'd just started to work in the music business and I went to work for Queen, and they were truly an *amazing* rock band. And I didn't rediscover that same feeling about watching four guys on-stage until I came to work for Depeche Mode. I think Depeche Mode are truly one of the great rock bands of all time."

Depeche Mode's adoption of the digital medium didn't stop there: on November 25, they released *The Videos 86>98+*, another double deluxe DVD package featuring *The Videos 86>98* DVD (first released on July 23, 2001) with a second DVD of unreleased videos and interviews from the period.

Having won the 'Best International Artist' award at the European Viva COMET Awards back on June 18, 2001 (fending off notable nominees like Destiny's Child, Madonna, Jennifer Lopez and U2), Depeche Mode's unique standing in the industry was recognised with the 'Q Innovation Award' – "which recognises creativity, invention and courage in the face of adversity" – on October 22, 2002.

In London, presenters Adam Buxton and Joe Cornish put Depeche Mode's considerable achievements into their rightful perspective: "This award honours real mavericks, people who've left an indelible mark on music, changing our perceptions forever. The winners' legacy includes their own Webring, a Site where fans do covers of their songs, and over 50 tribute albums, from orchestras through to the lovingly named Diesel Christ. They've inspired everyone from jangly Scotsmen Boa Morte through to Nine Inch Nails and Linkin Park, not to mention this year's wackiest subgenre, electroclash, and a whole host of hip-hop acts."

Indeed, Depeche Mode cover versions had recently appeared on recordings by a diversity of highly respected artists. On September 18, 2001, American songstress Tori Amos released *Strange Little Girls*, an album on which she chose to reinterpret 12 songs written by men. *The Sunday Times'* Dan Cairns wrote: "Amos gets straight to the Humbert heart of the matter on Depeche Mode's 'Enjoy The Silence', her two passing notes on the piano ratcheting up the tension with devastating economy."

Unsurprisingly, perhaps, female critic Kriste Matrische's online reading of Amos' Depeche Mode reinterpretation for www.music-critic.com probed deeper still: "In 'Enjoy the Silence,' the only way to tell the female viewpoint is from Amos' vocals. With the first listening, you hear how dull and uninspired her voice sounds. However, after listening a few times, one will learn that this is her point in an ironical sort of way. Women are often told to either shut up (not in so many words) or what they say is boring and not important. With Amos singing in the tone she does, it causes one to pay attention and wonder why she sounds so unimpressed. It's an interesting thought, nevertheless."

It's unlikely that Martin Gore would be in complete agreement with such sentiment, but – as Alan Wilder had pointed out on more than one occasion – that's the beauty of Martin Gore's lyrics: in the ear of the listener, they're nearly always left open to interpretation.

In November 2002, Depeche Mode took another leap towards universal acceptance when American country music legend Johnny Cash – the original man in black – chose to cover 'Personal Jesus' (also from 1990's *Violator* album) for the fourth instalment in his Grammy-winning 'American Recordings' series, *The Man Comes Around*, created in collaboration with respected producer Rick Rubin. In fact, it was Rubin who first brought Depeche Mode to Cash's attention; Cash responded to 'Personal Jesus' instinctively, saying, "That's probably the most evangelical song [I've] ever recorded. I don't know that the writer ever meant it to be that, but that's what it is."

Yet there was nothing evangelical about 'Personal Jesus' in the biblical sense of the word as far as songwriter Martin Gore's paean to Priscilla Beaulieu Presley's troubled time with Elvis Presley was concerned. Then again, this popular Depeche Mode lyric was only an interpretation of what its writer had read in Beaulieu Presley's book *Elvis And Me*, itself retrospectively written as seen through the eyes of one person.

Amazon.co.uk's Alannah Nash wrote: "*The Man Comes Around*, which draws on Cash's original songs as well as those by Nine Inch Nails ('Hurt'), Sting ('I Hung My Head') and Depeche Mode ('Personal Jesus'), may be one of the most autobiographical albums of the 70-year-old singer/song-writer's career. In 15 songs, Cash moves through dark, haunted medita-tions on death and destruction, poignant farewells, testaments to everlasting love, and hopeful salutes to redemption." Here the online reviewer could almost have been writing about Depeche Mode, for all are subjects that Gore has addressed during his own songwriting career (albeit a compara-tively short one to that of Johnny Cash).

At the Q Awards, DJ Shadow (a.k.a. American Josh Davis, trip-hop luminary of London's Mo' Wax label) made the presentation: "This award goes to a band that was pretty much the only band – just from a personal note – that growing up, outside of hip-hop, that I listened to. From them, I learned how to extract emotion from technology. The first 'Q Innova-tion Award' of course goes to Depeche Mode."

Dave Gahan spoke on behalf of his honoured bandmates: "I don't really know what to say. It's not something we expected. [We] probably didn't expect to be still standing here after 20 years, but we are, and we're proud of it. There's a couple of people I want to thank: Daniel Miller from Mute Records, who's constantly inspired us to try new things, and also I have to mention Anton Corbijn, who's responsible for the good [visual] stuff. So thanks a lot."

So apart from Daniel Miller's endless encouragement and Anton Corbijn's visionary visuals – what lies at the heart of Depeche Mode's success?

Alan Wilder: "Martin is most definitely an underrated songwriter. His songs have been able to touch people in a way that very few songwriters have been able to do. And it's quite clear that his songwriting capabilities have been the major part of Depeche Mode's longevity."

Daniel Miller: "I think all of the [Depeche Mode] albums are extremely good, and probably better than nearly everything else that has ever come out – certainly in the period that they [have] worked in. There's a body of work [spanning] over 20 years; I think you'd be hard pressed to find anybody whose songs have been of [such] consistent quality. Originality has been achieved.

"[*Exciter*] has proved that they're totally out on the edge again, wanting to make great experimental records. There's lots of things about some of those tracks which you could say have their roots in contemporary electronic music – electronica, if you want. They're always looking – certainly Martin [Gore] is – at the more experimental end of things and trying to adapt those ideas into the song format, and successfully doing so. That's what makes them special, I think. They have that dual life – two creative heads: one is the great, classic songwriter and the other is the experimental [musician], making it all work together. Nobody sounds like that – apart from the bands that try and copy them, and they don't really sound like that.

"I'm proud of them for keeping at it. They're so far removed from the mainstream of pop music, and that's what's so amazing."

Flood (producer): "Literally, you could say they're a pop band, but they're not. Their songs have far more depth. The way that they're perceived live is almost rock. So there's all these strange combinations that I think just give them a very unique standpoint. There's nobody else that I can think of who's anywhere near to what they're trying to do."

Gary Numan: "They became massive because, simply, they're brilliant. Sometimes that's enough . . . The Depeche Mode meeting at the Q Awards was just light-hearted and informal; it didn't strike me as particularly strange that we were still around after so many years as Tom Jones wasn't far away at the time (waiting for his photo shoot, I think) and we still seemed like newcomers compared to him!"

Almost a quarter-century after taking their first musical steps in Vince Martin's Basildon-based garage, these are truly exciting times for Depeche Mode's three remaining members.

Vince Clarke: "Maybe it was a bit more contrived back then, but in the same way that I think Depeche in the early days kind of fell onto the Futurist thing, they seemed to fall on the American thing at the same time as American rock was kind of in its heyday. Since I left, they got rockier and rockier – that's Martin's influence. I think they're more like Iggy Pop now, which is what Martin was into, and I was more into Buggles – that's why we don't work together anymore!"

During his June 2003 interrogation for Q magazine's monthly 'Cash For Questions' column, Dave Gahan coincidentally addressed the hypothetical question of whether Depeche Mode might have lasted so long had Vince Clarke not jumped ship back in 1981. "That's a good question," he responded. "I think actually no, because when Vince left we never thought for a second about not making another record. We just had to go into the studio and start working on stuff that was fairly experimental – we had no choice. Vince was fairly driven in a direction; he was clear about what he wanted and I think that he couldn't do that by playing with three other people who all have an opinion. He's had a lot of success by himself. But I'm glad that happened, because every time the band has changed – when Alan joined or when he left, for example – it's forced us to rethink. We need to do that again, to shake it up, if we're to do another album."

Asked whether he could foresee his old bandmates regrouping to record another album, Vince Clarke answered: "I know Martin's talked to some people about doing some solo projects, and as long as he does that then he'll be happy. He's got his wife and kids, so it's probably not as important for him to go out touring and do the whole rock'n'roll thing anymore. It's not as attractive as it once was. At the end of the day, you've got to ask yourself: 'Why am I doing *any* of this anymore? You don't *have* to do it.' But Fletcher will always want to do Depeche, because that's his life – more than anybody else's. I don't think it's Dave's so much, because he's been through the whole drug thing, and now he's settled. The amazing thing about Dave is the fact that he's actually got it together and pulled through, which is phenomenal."

Dave Gahan: "We're a different band now. Now, in the future, what I would like to be is kind of like a revolving door. Basically, Martin and I are what is the creative, musical [part of Depeche Mode] – what's left of it. That's become much clearer since Alan has left. Over the last couple of albums, and what I see happening in the future, if Martin is up for it, is that we leave the door open to other people – whether it's Peter Gordeno or Christian [Eigner], or other people like that . . . that they can lift and take the songs and my voice, and what we do together, to other places."

By the end of 2002, the *Exciter* 'project' and its associated spin-offs had successfully run their course. In 2003, each individual member launched his own official website: MartinGore.com, DaveGahan.com and ToastHawaii.com (in reference to Andy Fletcher's Berlin culinary passion).

Ironically it was Fletcher himself who was first in the solo stakes. The début release on his Toast Hawaii label was announced via Mute on January 22, 2003 via the following mysterious extract from *Global Music Companion* ('2132 edition'): ". . . when advances in the early twenty-first century made a revival of interest in electronic music inevitable. This coincided with the arrival of the duo Client (known only as Client: A and Client: B) who created an electronic sound simultaneously dirty and pristine, and attracted music fans bored with production line pop, super-ficial dance and tired rock. Spawning many imitators, their influence is felt even now . . ." As it was, Client's début single, a catchy slice of female vocal-fronted, synth bass line-driven electropop was released '129 years earlier' on April 7, 2003.

An energised Fletcher talked to Depeche Mode's Webmaster, Daniel 'The Brat' Barassi, about his new venture, revealing that although setting up his own independent label was something he had "always wanted to do," Depeche Mode's busy schedule had hitherto prevented him from actively doing so. "It's quite interesting, working with an act from [the] very beginning. Obviously, with Depeche Mode, I'm used to working with a band that is sort of at the top, and to go back to an earthy level is really good fun. I'm involved in every single [aspect] of the project, from the writing of the songs, to the music, to the management, to the record company – everything."

Perhaps the mysteriously monikered Client: A and Client: B of Fletcher's first signing were all part of Toast Hawaii's grand marketing plan? "This is not going to be a massive push," he told Barassi. "We're trying to promote and produce music differently to how most music is produced. That's one of the reasons [why] I've formed the record company – to do things differ-ently. We've kept our costs low. We recorded everything in Client: A's bedroom. It's going to be a slow campaign.

"At the moment, I'm fully concentrating on Client, but in the back of my mind I always know that at some point I will get the calling from above, saying that Depeche is starting again – but I don't think that will be until the end of the year, probably. Depeche Mode is the love of my life, so I have to be realistic."

Martin Gore's solo project, *Counterfeit2* was preceded by a single 'Stardust', on April 14, 2003. *Counterfeit2*, like its 1989-vintage predecessor (*Counter-feit*), featured another batch of Gore's radically reworked interpretations of a selection of other people's songs (by the likes of Lou Reed, Iggy Pop, John Lennon and Brian Eno).

This time round, Gore opted to record at his Santa Barbara home-based studio (assisted by Andrew Philpott and Paul Freegard, with Peter Gordeno guesting on Fender Rhodes on two songs). Martin Gore: "I've just got a really small studio set-up at home. It's not like a big old-fashioned recording studio. But I think it was important for me to do that, because I like the idea of working at home because it means I still can have some sort of family life. If I'd spent seven or eight months of last year [2002] in a studio, working stupid studio hours, then I wouldn't have seen my family for that whole period.

"There's a conflict of interest for me to write songs for myself while I'm still part of a band. I'm not the most prolific of songwriters; at the moment, there's usually about a three- or four-year period between Depeche Mode records, so if I wrote songs for myself and used them on an album for myself, that gap between Depeche Mode albums would grow even longer."

'Stardust' was a UK Top 10 hit for British singer/songwriter-cum-actor David Essex, at the tail end of 1974. Of his first single choice and its original creator, Gore commented, "I wasn't ever a massive fan of David Essex, but I liked a few of his tracks and 'Stardust' was one of them – and probably my favourite one. It's also from the [1974] film *Stardust*, which is a film about the demise of a rock star, and how he gets heavily involved with drugs, which, as was pointed out to me, had some kind of parallel with Depeche Mode, but that's not the reason I chose it. It does sum up, somehow, the loneliness of being a rock star at times; of course, it's a great job, but it's a very strange job; it's very weird."

One man with whom those sentiments profoundly resonate is Dave Gahan. In March 2003 Mute announced the June 2 release of the singer's eagerly awaited long-playing début, *Paper Monsters* (preceded two weeks earlier by the single, 'Dirty Sticky Floors').

"I guess the first time I really plucked up enough courage to play something to Martin was a song called 'Closer'," Gahan told Barassi on February 20. "I played him, during the *Ultra* sessions, a rough demo I made, and I could tell he liked it. For a moment there I thought it was going to be on *Ultra*. I was very excited. That lasted about three days. We had this discussion and everybody came to the conclusion that the song didn't fit with the theme that the album was heading in. At the time, I was quite hurt by that, and it knocked me back a few years, to be honest."

Gahan was used to picking himself back up again. Back home in New York City, following The Singles Tour in December 1998, he started writing songs with Knox Chandler, the musician who would go on to contribute to *Exciter* in a cello-playing and string-arranging capacity. Gahan played the promising results to Daniel Miller, who told him to write more. Gahan and Chandler worked in the latter's tiny project studio in his East Village apartment. "Put it this way – if he was playing cello in there, I'd have to be standing up in the corner," Gahan commented.

Exciter forced Gahan to again put his pet project on the "back burner" as Depeche duties called. By the time that Mute Records made the following announcement in March 2003, it was clear that his perseverance had paid off. "After 22 illustrious years with Depeche Mode, *Paper Monsters* marks Dave's début as a fully fledged songwriter. He wrote all 10 tracks with his multi-instrumentalist friend Knox Chandler. The album was produced by Ken Thomas of Sigur Ros fame. *Paper Monsters* marries the freshness of a freshman effort with the seasoned wisdom of an old soul. It was recorded, mostly in New York, in an open-ended, back-to-basics manner Dave found both liberating and exhilarating. 'What really hit me most was how happy and fulfilled it made me feel,' Dave says with a smile."

By the time of Q magazine's June 2003 'Cash For Questions' session with Gahan, it was obvious that the singer's first serious foray into songwriting had served to boost his confidence artistically – and deservedly so. "I won't be taking over from Martin, but I'd like to think that as I'm moving forward in that way I'll be contributing my own songs and exchanging ideas. I don't think I could do it any other way right now."

So what was Gore's reaction to *Paper Monsters*? According to Gahan: "[Martin] called me and said, 'I've just got back from holiday and I've got a message that there's an album at the post office which I'll pick up, but what I'm ringing about is have you got a number for a chiropractor?'"

Whatever way one views it, Depeche Mode are a musical phenomenon. Their ascendancy from Basildon to the hallowed ranks of rock aristocracy and beyond is nothing short of inspirational; not so much a black celebration as simply a cause to celebrate. If and when they choose to record and release another album, rest assured it will be worth waiting for and listening to. If they decide to tour with it, all the better.

Acknowledgements

When first approached to write an in-depth biography of Depeche Mode, I jumped at the chance; only later did a stomach-churning combination of excitement and trepidation take hold as the enormity of the task at hand truly sank in. I was excited because Depeche Mode had provided a synthesised soundtrack to a sizeable chunk of my youth.

I can still recall reading a favourable *Smash Hits* review of the group's Cabaret Futura performance of February 16, 1981 in London, back in the days when this was still a semi-serious teenage-oriented music publication; I can also clearly recall rushing out to buy their début single 'Dreaming Of Me' from the long-gone Volume Records in my home city of Newcastle-upon-Tyne. The trepidation was in no small part due to the fact that 21 years had somehow elapsed since that propitious purchase, and 21 years can easily equal several lifetimes in a capricious pop and rock world where stars come and go with alarming regularity, a fate somehow avoided by the boys from Basildon.

Then again, perhaps fate's sleight of hand determined I would one day cross paths with Depeche Mode again, albeit in a more professional capacity. For had I not (unsuccessfully) proposed another, unrelated music biography to Chris Charlesworth, editor of Omnibus Press, it's unlikely he would have instead suggested Depeche Mode for similar treatment. Nor would I have scurried around my parent's loft space in search of precious early Mode press cuttings, religiously collected during my impressionable teenage years, with no guarantee they would still be there. Having hunted high and low, I nearly gave up the ghost. My beloved wife persevered, however, coming up trumps amongst the disarray. Lo and behold, there's that aforementioned vintage Caberet Futura review, concluding "the simply wonderful 'Dreaming Of Me'/'Ice Machine' (Mute) is unreservedly recommended to absolutely everybody."

Briefly, I'm back in 1981 and the innocence of youth stops me in my tracks: I too want to be a pop star. I save my hard-earned paper round money to buy a Moog Rogue synthesiser (a fairly pointless cut-down

464

replacement for the discontinued Moog Prodigy once used by Depeche Mode's Andy Fletcher). I mime to 'New Life'! I even write some terribly twee synthpop myself (though admittedly my vocalist's younger brother did go on to find a modicum of fame and fortune, founding and fronting York's own 'Britpop sensation' Shed Seven).

But this is no nostalgia trip. It's 2002. Synthpop, Britpop, trip-hop, you name it . . . to a greater or lesser extent all have been but passing waves breaking on popular music's notoriously unstable shoreline. By remaining fashionably unfashionable with their unique blend of dark, yet somehow uplifting songscapes, Depeche Mode remain defiantly buoyant, and are indeed "utterly huge". That *Smash Hits* reviewer's off-the-cuff prediction has (long) since come to pass, as – with much excitement and trepidation – has this book . . .

So, whom do we ultimately have to thank for the weighty tome you're now holding in your hands, or even resting on your lap? It goes without saying that I'm indebted to Omnibus Press' Chris Charlesworth, and the supreme editing talents of Andy Neill for his welcome professionalism in transforming my own overenthusiastic reading of the Depeche Mode story into a tighter, more gripping read. Moreover, without Chris' belief in this book, *Stripped: The True Story Of Depeche Mode* might never have seen the light of day, and for that I'm very grateful.

In the words of French one-hit wonder FR David, words don't come easy; in the case of this music biography, there's a lengthy list of people to thank for helping them to flow more easily: special thanks – for services above and beyond the call of duty – go to Vince Martin and Rob Allen (you know who you are), Deb and Martin Mann, Jo Gahan, Rob Andrews and Gary Smith, plus the supporting cast who helped me piece together those 'Basildon Bygone Daze' and beyond; and to producers Gareth Jones and Mark Bell for their unique insight into Depeche Mode's modern – and not-so-modern – working practices. (Thanks – again – to Deb Mann and Gareth Jones for original 'Photographic' contributions.)

Thanks also to fellow writer Stephen Dalton for kindly providing me with unpublished material from his interviews with Depeche Mode members past and present (Andy Fletcher, Dave Gahan, Martin Gore and Alan Wilder), plus Mute Records main man Daniel Miller; BBC London 94.7 producer Tony Wood, for allowing me to quote from his excellent Depeche Mode documentary, as originally broadcast back in May 2001; and also former Depeche Mode member Alan Wilder for his supremely informative and superbly executed website (which is well worth a visit at: www.recoil.co.uk).

For generous donations to the 'Miller Music and Media recordings library' in the name of further background research, thanks to: Andy Fraser and Zoë Miller (Mute Records) and Sarah Watson (Virgin Music).

Thanks for beds and encouragement to my ever-supportive parents (Doris and Ken, Whitley Bay, Tyne & Wear); cousins (Joanne and Gary Sastamoinen, St Pete Beach, Florida – shame we missed the wedding, guys; the Inghams, Bury St Edmunds, Suffolk); sister (Steph – not forgetting the 'Big D', Balham, London); in-laws (Gill and Chris, Burgess Hill, East Sussex); the Watsons (Jimmy and Zoë, Beckenham, Kent – now *that's* what we call a wedding), and 'The Firs Avenue posse' (Dan Neville and friends, Muswell Hill, London).

Speaking of St Pete Beach, as I wrote in an online news update on my own Miller Music and Media website (www.millermusicandmedia.com) back on August 8, 2002: *Well, we're now reaching the home straight on our working vacation in sunny Florida – it's been a blast, that's for sure! Living the 'American dream' – even if only for a month or so – has certainly proved to be an inspirational experience for this author, both in terms of book writing and life in general. Put it this way: by the time I return to 'Blighty', it's now looking like my ongoing, in-depth music biography book project will have grown by another 30,000 words; incidentally, it took me three months to clock up that same amount before jetting off Stateside – I sure know where I'd prefer to live and work! And on that dream-like note, who knows what the future may hold? For now, it's back to reality, and that means heading home. But isn't home where the heart is?*

And my heart will always be with my wife, Emma, and daughter, Megan, to whom I dedicate this book, some 200,000 words later. Thank you for unequivocally supporting me on my Macintosh-powered writing dream journey for the last six years, a journey that has thus far taken in five abodes (and six Macs!). You've always been my safe haven in the rough sea of words – and I couldn't have done it without you both. As some guy wiser than me once said: love is the answer and you know that for sure . . .

Speaking of Apple computers, thanks are long overdue to my mother for her welcome assistance in financing my first Macintosh; 11 years and eight Macs down the line, just look at me now, mom – I'm *really* flying!

And, by that same token gesture, I must also extend my sincere gratitude to those American visionaries at Apple who, back in 1984, came up with the most straightforward operating system the home computer world had ever seen, which, might I add, in its latest OS X incarnation, remains without compare – at least in this author's humble opinion. Thanks too to their present-day star British designer, Jonathan Ives; it's cool to be a Mac user (and, no, I'm not a computer geek – nor indeed a so-called 'Apple evangelist').

On a final, positive note, I remain convinced that everything – good and bad – happens for a reason. If I hadn't taken voluntary redundancy from a (once) financially floundering magazine publishing company, then I wouldn't have had the time to propose the book which led to this one – indeed, researching/writing *Stripped: The True Story Of Depeche Mode* took something in the region of 2,000 man hours to complete (including writing these fragmented closing thoughts on what has proved to be a very exciting and rewarding last year or so), so here's hoping you enjoy reading it as much as I enjoyed working on it.

Thanks for your patronage – whoever you are. Until we meet again . . .

Jonathan Miller
(www.millermusicandmedia.com)

DEPECHE MODE

Selected Discography

(MUTE RECORDS)

SINGLES:

Note: singles marked with an asterisk (★) were issued on CD for the first time by Mute Records throughout 1991; single marked with a double asterisk (★★) was a French-only release.

'Dreaming Of Me'/'Ice Machine' (MUTE 013, February 20, 1981)
'Dreaming Of Me'/'Ice Machine' (CD MUTE 013) ★

'New Life'/'Shout!' (MUTE 014, June 13, 1981)
'New Life (Extended)'/'Shout! (Rio Mix)' (12 MUTE 014)
'New Life'/'New Life (Extended)'/'Shout! (Rio Mix)' (CD MUTE 014) ★

'Just Can't Get Enough'/'Any Second Now' (MUTE 016, September 7, 1981)
'Just Can't Get Enough (Schizo Mix)'/'Any Second Now (Altered)' (12 MUTE 016)
'Just Can't Get Enough'/'Any Second Now'/'Just Can't Get Enough (Schizo Mix)'/'Any Second Now (Altered)' (CD MUTE 016) ★

'See You'/'Now, This Is Fun' (MUTE 018, January 29, 1982)
'See You (Extended)'/'Now, This Is Fun (Extended)' (12 MUTE 018)
'See You'/'Now, This Is Fun'/'Now, This Is Fun (Extended)' (CD MUTE 018) ★

'The Meaning Of Love'/'Oberkorn (It's A Small Town)' (MUTE 020, April 26, 1982)
'The Meaning Of Love (Fairly Odd Mix)'/'Oberkorn (It's A Small Town – Development)' (12 MUTE 020)

'The Meaning Of Love'/'Oberkorn (It's A Small Town)'/'The Meaning Of Love (Fairly Odd Mix)'/'Oberkorn (It's A Small Town – Development)' (CD MUTE 020) ★

'Leave In Silence'/'Excerpt From My Secret Garden' (BONG 1, August 16, 1982)

'Leave In Silence (Longer)'/'Further Excerpts From My Secret Garden'/ 'Leave In Silence (Quieter)' (12 BONG 1)

'Leave In Silence'/'Excerpt From My Secret Garden'/'Leave In Silence (Longer)'/'Further Excerpts From My Secret Garden'/'Leave In Silence (Quieter)' (CD BONG 1) ★

'Get The Balance Right!'/'The Great Outdoors' (BONG 2, January 31, 1983)

'Get The Balance Right! (Combination Mix)'/'The Great Outdoors' (12 BONG 2)

'Get The Balance Right!'/'My Secret Garden (Live)'/'See You (Live)'/ 'Satellite (Live)'/'Tora! Tora! Tora! (Live)' (L12 BONG 2)

'Get The Balance Right!'/'The Great Outdoors'/'Get The Balance Right (Combination Mix)'/'Tora! Tora! Tora! (Live)' (CD BONG 2) ★

'Everything Counts'/'Work Hard' (BONG 3, July 11, 1983)

'Everything Counts (In Larger Amounts)'/'Work Hard (East End Mix)' (12 BONG 3)

'Everything Counts'/'New Life (Live)'/'Boys Say Go (Live)'/'Nothing To Fear (Live)'/'The Meaning Of Love (Live)' (L12 BONG 3)

'Everything Counts'/'Work Hard'/'Everything Counts (In Larger Amounts)'/'Work Hard (East End Mix)' (CD BONG 3) ★

'Love, In Itself 2'/'Fools' (BONG 4, September 19, 1983)

'Love, In Itself 3'/'Fools (Bigger)'/'Love, In Itself 4' (12 BONG 4)

'Love, In Itself'/'Just Can't Get Enough (Live)'/'Shout! (Live)'/'Photograph Of You (Live)'/'Photographic (Live)' (L12 BONG 4)

'Love, In Itself 2'/'Love, In Itself 3'/'Fools (Bigger)'/'Love, In Itself 4' (CD BONG 4) ★

'People Are People'/'In Your Memory' (BONG 5, March 12, 1983)

'People Are People (Different Mix)'/'In Your Memory (Slick Mix)' (12 BONG 5)

'People Are People (Remix)'/'In Your Memory'/'People Are People' (L12 BONG 5)

'People Are People'/'In Your Memory'/'People Are People (Different Mix)'/'In Your Memory (Slick Mix)' (CD BONG 5) ★

'Master And Servant'/'Set Me Free (Remotivate Me)' (BONG 6, August 20, 1983)

'Master And Servant (Slavery Whip Mix)'/'Set Me Free (Remotivate Me – Release Mix)'/'Master And Servant (Voxless)' (12 BONG 6)

'Master And Servant (An On-USound Sci-Fi Dancehall Classic)'/'Are People People?'/'Master And Servant' (L12 BONG 6)

'Master And Servant (Slavery Whip Mix)'/'Set Me Free (Remotivate Me – Release Mix)'/'Master And Servant (Voxless)' (CD BONG 6) ★

'Blasphemous Rumours'/'Somebody' (BONG 7, October 29, 1983)

'Blasphemous Rumours'/'Told You So (Live)'/'Somebody (Remix)'/ 'Everything Counts (Live)' (BONG 7E)

'Blasphemous Rumours'/'Somebody (Live)'/'Two-Minute Warning (Live)'/'Ice Machine (Live)'/'Everything Counts (Live)' (12 BONG 7)

'Blasphemous Rumours'/'Told You So (Live)'/'Somebody (Remix)'/ 'Everything Counts (Live)' (CD BONG 7) ★

'Shake The Disease'/'Flexible' (BONG 8, April 29, 1985)

'Shake The Disease (Remix)'/'Flexible (Remix)' (12 BONG 8)

'Shake The Disease (Edit The Shake)'/'Master And Servant (Live)'/'Flexible (Pre-Deportation Mix)'/'Something To Do (Metal Mix)' (L12 BONG 8)

'Shake The Disease'/'Flexible'/'Shake The Disease (Remix Extended)'/ 'Flexible (Remix Extended)'/'Shake The Disease (Edit The Shake)'/ 'Something To Do (Metal Mix)' (CD BONG 8) ★

'It's Called A Heart'/'Fly On The Windscreen' (BONG 9, September 16, 1985)

'It's Called A Heart (Remix)'/'Fly On The Windscreen (Remix)' (12 BONG 9)

'It's Called A Heart (Extended)'/'Fly On The Windscreen (Extended)'/ 'It's Called A Heart (Slow Mix)'/'Fly On The Windscreen (Death Mix)' (L12 BONG 9)

'It's Called A Heart'/'Fly On The Windscreen'/'It's Called A Heart (Extended)'/'Fly On The Windscreen (Extended)'/'Fly On The Windscreen (Death Mix)' (CD BONG 9) ★

'Stripped'/'But Not Tonight' (BONG 10, February 10, 1986)

'Stripped (Highland Mix)'/'But Not Tonight (Extended Mix)'/'Breathing In Fumes'/'Fly On The Windscreen (Quiet Mix)'/'Black Day' (12 BONG 10)

'Stripped'/'But Not Tonight'/'Stripped (Highland Mix)'/'But Not Tonight (Extended Mix)'/'Breathing In Fumes'/'Fly On The Windscreen (Quiet Mix)'/'Black Day' (CD BONG 10) ★

'A Question Of Lust'/'Christmas Island' (BONG 11, April 14, 1986)

'A Question Of Lust (Extended)'/'Christmas Island (Extended)'/'People Are People (Live)'/'It Doesn't Matter Two (Instrumental)'/'A Question Of Lust (Minimal)' (12 BONG 11)

'A Question Of Lust (Flood Mix)'/'If You Want (Live)'/'Shame (Live)'/'Blasphemous Rumours (Live)' (C BONG 11)

'A Question Of Lust'/'Christmas Island'/'Christmas Island (Extended)'/'People Are People (Live)'/'It Doesn't Matter Two (Instrumental)'/'A Question Of Lust (Minimal)' (CD BONG 11) ★

'A Question Of Time'/'Black Celebration (Live)' (BONG 12, August 11, 1986)

'A Question Of Time (Extended)'/'Black Celebration (Live)'/'Something To Do (Live)'/'Stripped (Live)' (12 BONG 12)

'A Question Of Time (Newtown Mix)'/'A Question Of Time (Live)'/'Black Celebration (Black Tulip Mix)'/'More Than A Party (Live)' (L12 BONG 12)

'A Question Of Time (Extended)'/'Black Celebration (Live)'/'Something To Do (Live)'/'Stripped (Live)' (CD BONG 12) ★

'Strangelove'/'Pimpf' (BONG 13, April 13, 1987)

'Strangelove (Maximix)'/'Pimpf'/'Strangelove (Midimix)' (12 BONG 13)

'Strangelove (Blind Mix)'/'Pimpf'/'Strangelove (Pain Mix)'/'Agent Orange' (L12 BONG 13)

'Strangelove (Maximix)'/'Pimpf'/'Strangelove (Midimix)'/'Agent Orange'/'Strangelove (LP Mix)' (CD BONG 13)

'Never Let Me Down Again'/'Pleasure, Little Treasure' (BONG 14, August 24, 1987)

'Never Let Me Down Again (Split Mix)'/'Pleasure, Little Treasure (Glitter Mix)'/'Never Let Me Down Again (Aggro Mix)' (12 BONG 14)

'Never Let Me Down Again (Tsangarides Mix)'/'Pimpf'/'Pleasure, Little Treasure (Join Mix)'/'To Have And To Hold (Spanish Taster)' (L12 BONG 14)

'Never Let Me Down Again (Split Mix)'/'Pleasure, Little Treasure (Glitter Mix)'/'Never Let Me Down Again (Aggro Mix)' (C BONG 14)

'Never Let Me Down Again (Split Mix)'/'Never Let Me Down Again (Aggro Mix)'/'Pleasure, Little Treasure (Remix)'/'To Have And To Hold (Spanish Taster)' (CD BONG 14)

'Behind The Wheel'/'Route 66' (BONG 15, December 28, 1987)

'Behind The Wheel (Shep Pettibone Mix)'/'Route 66 (Beatmasters Mix)' (12 BONG 15)

'Behind The Wheel (Beatmasters Mix)'/'Route 66 (Casualty Mix)' (L12 BONG 15)

'Behind The Wheel (Remix)'/'Route 66'/'Behind The Wheel (Shep Pettibone Mix)'/'Behind The Wheel (LP Mix)' (CD BONG 15)

'Little 15'/'Stjarna' (LITTLE 15, May 16, 1988) ★★

'Little 15'/'Stjarna'/'Moonlight Sonata #14' (CD LITTLE 15) ★★

'Everything Counts (Live)'/'Nothing (Live)' (BONG 16, February 13, 1989)

'Everything Counts (Live)'/'Nothing (Live)'/'Sacred (Live)'/'A Question Of Lust (Live)' (12 BONG 16)

'Everything Counts (Remix By Bomb The Bass)'/'Nothing (Remix By Justin Straus)'/'Strangelove (Remix By Bomb The Bass)' (L12 BONG 16)

'Everything Counts (Absolut Mix)'/'Everything Counts (1983 12″ Mix)'/ 'Nothing (US 7″ Mix)'/'Everything Counts (Reprise)' (10 BONG 16)

'Everything Counts (Live)'/'Nothing (Live)'/'Sacred (Live)'/'A Question Of Lust (Live)' (C BONG 16)

'Everything Counts (Live)'/'Nothing (Live)'/'Sacred (Live)'/'A Question Of Lust (Live)' (CD BONG 16)

'Everything Counts (Remix By Bomb The Bass)'/'Nothing (Remix By Justin Straus)'/'Strangelove (Remix By Bomb The Bass)' (LCD BONG 16)

'Personal Jesus'/'Dangerous' (BONG 17, August 29, 1989)

'Personal Jesus (Acoustic)'/'Dangerous (Hazchemix Edit)' (G BONG 17)

'Personal Jesus (Holier Than Thou Approach)'/'Dangerous (Sensual Mix)'/ 'Personal Jesus (Acoustic)' (12 BONG 17)

'Personal Jesus (Pump Mix)'/'Personal Jesus (Telephone Stomp Mix)'/ 'Dangerous (Hazchemix)' (L12 BONG 17)

'Personal Jesus'/'Dangerous' (C BONG 17)

'Personal Jesus (Holier Than Thou Approach)'/'Dangerous (Sensual Mix)'/
'Personal Jesus (Acoustic)' (CD BONG 17)

'Personal Jesus (Pump Mix)'/'Personal Jesus (Telephone Stomp Mix)'/
'Dangerous (Hazchemix)' (LCD BONG 17)

'Enjoy The Silence'/'Memphisto' (BONG 18, February 5, 1990)

'Enjoy The Silence (Single Mix)'/'Enjoy The Silence (Hands And Feet
Mix)'/'Enjoy The Silence (Ecstatic Dub)'/'Sibling' (12 BONG 17)

'Enjoy The Silence (Bass Line)'/'Enjoy The Silence (Harmonium)'/'Enjoy
The Silence (Ricki-Tik-Tik Mix)'/'Memphisto' (L12 BONG 17)

'Enjoy The Silence (The Quad: The Final Mix)' (XL12 BONG 17)

'Enjoy The Silence'/'Memphisto' (C BONG 18)

'Enjoy The Silence (Single Mix)'/'Enjoy The Silence (Hands And Feet
Mix)'/'Enjoy The Silence (Ecstatic Dub)'/'Sibling' (CD BONG 18)

'Enjoy The Silence (Bass Line)'/'Enjoy The Silence (Harmonium)'/'Enjoy
The Silence (Ricki-Tik-Tik Mix)'/'Memphisto' (LCD BONG 18)

'Policy Of Truth'/'Kaleid' (BONG 19, May 7, 1990)

'Policy Of Truth (Beat Box)'/'Policy Of Truth (Capitol Mix)'/'Kaleid
(When Worlds Collide Mix)' (12 BONG 19)

'Policy Of Truth (Trancentral Mix)'/'Policy Of Truth (Pavlov's Dub)'/
'Kaleid (Remix)' (L12 BONG 19)

'Policy Of Truth'/'Kaleid' (C BONG 19)

'Policy Of Truth (Beat Box)'/'Policy Of Truth (Capitol Mix)'/'Kaleid
(Remix)' (CD BONG 19)

'Policy Of Truth (Trancentral Mix)'/'Kaleid (When Worlds Collide Mix)'/
'Policy Of Truth (Pavlov's Dub)'/'Kaleid (Remix)'/'Policy Of Truth'/
'Kaleid' (LCD BONG 19)

'World In My Eyes'/'Happiest Girl' (BONG 20, September 17, 1990)

'World In My Eyes (Oil Tank Mix)'/'Happiest Girl (Kiss-A-Mix)'/'Sea Of
Sin (Sensoria)' (12 BONG 20)

'World In My Eyes (Dub In My Eyes)'/'World In My Eyes (Mode To Joy)'/
'Happiest Girl (The Pulsating Orbital Vocal Mix)' (L12 BONG 20)

'World In My Eyes (7″ Version)'/'Happiest Girl (Jack Mix)'/'Sea Of Sin
(Tonal Mix)' (C BONG 20)

'World In My Eyes (7″ Version)'/'World In My Eyes (Oil Tank Mix)'/
'Happiest Girl (Kiss-A-Mix)'/'Sea Of Sin (Tonal Mix)' (CD BONG 20)

'World In My Eyes (Dub In My Eyes)'/'World In My Eyes (Mayhem
Mode)' /'World In My Eyes (Mode To Joy)'/'Sea Of Sin (Sensoria)'/

'Happiest Girl (Jack Mix)'/'Happiest Girl (The Pulsating Orbital Vocal Mix)' (LCD BONG 20)

'I Feel You'/'One Caress' (BONG 21, February 15, 1993)

'I Feel You (7″ Mix)'/'One Caress'/'I Feel You (Throb Mix)'/'I Feel You (Babylon Mix)' (12 BONG 21)

'I Feel You (Life's Too Short Mix)'/'I Feel You (Swamp Mix)'/'I Feel You (Renegade Soundwave Afghan Surgery Mix)'/'I Feel You (Helmet At The Helm Mix)' (L12 BONG 21)

'I Feel You'/'One Caress' (C BONG 21)

'I Feel You (7″ Mix)'/'One Caress'/'I Feel You (Throb Mix)'/'I Feel You (Babylon Mix)' (CD BONG 21)

'I Feel You (Life's Too Short Mix)'/'I Feel You (Swamp Mix)'/'I Feel You (Renegade Soundwave Afghan Surgery Mix)'/'I Feel You (Helmet At The Helm Mix)' (LCD BONG 21)

'Walking In My Shoes'/'My Joy' (BONG 22, April 26, 1993)

'Walking In My Shoes (7″ Mix)'/'Walking In My Shoes (Grungy Gonads Mix)'/'My Joy (7″ Mix)'/'My Joy (Slow Slide Mix)' (12 BONG 22)

'Walking In My Shoes (Extended 12″ Mix)'/'Walking In My Shoes (Random Carpet Mix)'/'Walking In My Shoes (Anandamidic Mix)'/'Walking In My Shoes (Ambient Whale Mix)' (L12 BONG 22)

'Walking In My Shoes (7″ Mix)'/'Walking In My Shoes (Grungy Gonads Mix)'/'My Joy (7″ Mix)'/'My Joy (Slow Slide Mix)' (CD BONG 22)

'Walking In My Shoes (Extended 12″ Mix)'/'Walking In My Shoes (Random Carpet Mix)'/'Walking In My Shoes (Anandamidic Mix)'/'Walking In My Shoes (Ambient Whale Mix)' (LCD BONG 22)

'Condemnation (Paris Mix)'/'Death's Door (Jazz Mix)' (BONG 23, September 13, 1993)

'Condemnation (Paris Mix)'/'Death's Door (Jazz Mix)'/'Rush (Spiritual Guidance Mix)'/'Rush (Amylnitrate Mix)'/'Rush (Wild Planet – Vocal Mix)' (12 BONG 23)

'Condemnation (Live)'/'Personal Jesus (Live)'/'Enjoy The Silence (Live)'/'Halo (Live)' (L12 BONG 23)

'Condemnation (Live)'/'Personal Jesus (Live)'/'Enjoy The Silence (Live)'/'Halo (Live)'/'Rush (Spiritual Guidance Mix)'/'Rush (Amylnitrate Mix)'/'Rush (Wild Planet – Vocal Mix)' (C BONG 23)

'Condemnation (Paris Mix)'/'Death's Door (Jazz Mix)'/'Rush (Spiritual Guidance Mix)'/'Rush Amylnitrate Mix' (CD BONG 23)

'Condemnation (Live)'/'Personal Jesus (Live)'/'Enjoy The Silence (Live)'/
'Halo (Live)' (LCD BONG 23)

'In Your Room (Zephyr Mix)'/'In Your Room (Extended Zephyr Mix)'/'Never Let Me Down Again (Live)'/'Death's Door (Live)' (CD BONG 24, January 10, 1994)
'In Your Room (Live)'/'Policy Of Truth (Live)'/'World In My Eyes (Live)'/'Fly On The Windscreen (Live)' (LCD BONG 24)

'In Your Room (Jeep Rock Mix)'/'In Your Room (Apex Mix)'/'Higher Love (Adrenaline Mix)' (XLCD BONG 24)

'In Your Room (Zephyr Mix)'/'In Your Room (Apex Mix)'/'In Your Room (Jeep Rock Mix)'/'Higher Love (Adrenaline Mix)'/'In Your Room (Extended Zephyr Mix)' (12 BONG 24)

'In Your Room (Live)'/'Policy Of Truth (Live)'/'World In My Eyes (Live)'/'Fly On The Windscreen (Live)'/'Never Let Me Down Again (Live)'/'Death's Door (Live)' (L12 BONG 24)

'Barrel Of A Gun'/'Painkiller'/'Barrel Of A Gun (Underworld Soft Mix)'/'Barrel Of A Gun (1″ Punch Mix)' (CD BONG 25, February 3, 1997)
'Barrel Of A Gun (Underworld Hard Mix)'/'Barrel Of A Gun (United Mix)'/'Barrel Of A Gun (Plastikman Mix)' (LCD BONG 25)

'Barrel Of A Gun'/'Barrel Of A Gun (Underworld Hard Mix)'/'Barrel Of A Gun (3 Phase Mix)'/'Barrel Of A Gun (1″ Punch Mix – Version 2)'/'Barrel Of A Gun (Underworld Soft Mix)' (12 BONG 25)

'Painkiller (Plastikman Mix)'/'Painkiller'/'Barrel Of A Gun (1″ Punch Mix)'/'Barrel Of A Gun (United Mix)' (L12 BONG 25)

'It's No Good'/'Slowblow (Darren Price Mix)'/'It's No Good (Bass Bounce Mix)'/'It's No Good (Speedy J Mix)' (CD BONG 26, March 31, 1997)
'It's No Good (Hardfloor Mix)'/'Slowblow'/'It's No Good (Andrea Parker Mix)'/'It's No Good (Motor Bass Mix)' (LCD BONG 25)

'It's No Good'/'Slowblow' (C BONG 26)

'It's No Good'/'Slowblow (Darren Price Mix)'/'It's No Good (Bass Bounce Mix)'/'It's No Good (Speedy J Mix)' (12 BONG 26)

'Home'/'Home (Air Around The Golf Remix)'/'Home (LFO Meant To Be)'/'Home (The Noodles & The Damage Done)' (CD BONG 27, June 16, 1997)
'Home (Jedi Knights Remix – Drowning In Time)'/'Home (Grantby Mix)'/'Barrel Of A Gun (Live)'/'It's No Good (Live)' (LCD BONG 27)

'Home'/'Home (Air Around The Golf Remix)'/'Home (LFO Meant To Be)'/'Home (The Noodles & The Damage Done)' (12 BONG 27)

'Home (Jedi Knights Remix – Drowning In Time)'/'Home (Grantby Mix)'/'Barrel Of A Gun (Live)'/'It's No Good (Live)' (L12 BONG 27)

'Useless (Remix)'/'Useless (Escape From Wherever: Parts 1 & 2!)'/ 'Useless (Cosmic Blues Mix)'/'Barrel Of A Gun Video' (CD BONG 28, October 20, 1997)

'Useless (CJ Bolland Ultrasonar Mix)'/'Useless (The Kruder + Dorfmeister Session)'/'Useless (Live)'/'It's No Good – Video' (LCD BONG 28)

'Useless (The Kruder + Dorfmeister Session)'/'Useless (CJ Bolland Ultrasonar Mix)'/'Useless (Air 20 Mix)' (12 BONG 28)

'Only When I Lose Myself'/'Surrender'/'Headstar' (CD BONG 29, September 7, 1998)

'Only When I Lose Myself (Subsonic Legacy Remix)'/'Only When I Lose Myself (Dan The Autamator Remix)'/'Headstar (Luke Slater Remix)' (LCD BONG 29)

'Only When I Lose Myself (Subsonic Legacy Remix)'/'Only When I Lose Myself (Dan The Autamator Remix)'/'Headstar (Luke Slater Remix)' (12 BONG 29)

'Dream On (Single Version)'/'Easy Tiger (Full Version)'/'Easy Tiger (Bertrand Burgalat & A.S. Dragon Version)' (CD BONG 30, April 23, 2001)

'Dream On (Bushwacka Tough Guy Mix – CD Edit)'/'Dream On (Dave Clarke Acoustic Mix)'/'Dream On (Octagon Man Mix)'/'Dream On (Kid 606 Mix)' (LCD BONG 30)

'I Feel Loved (Single Version)'/'Dirt'/'I Feel Loved (Extended Instrumental)' (CD BONG 31, July 30, 2001)

'I Feel Loved (Danny Tenaglia's Labour Of Love Edit)'/'I Feel Loved (Thomas Brinkmann Mix)'/'I Feel Loved (Chamber's Mix)' (LCD BONG 31)

'Freelove (Flood Mix)'/'Zenstation'/'Zenstation (Atom's Stereonerd Remix)' (CD BONG 32, November 5, 2001)

'Freelove (Bertrand Burgalat Remix)'/'Freelove (Schlammpeitziger Little Rocking Suction Pump Version)'/'Freelove (DJ Muggs Mix)' (LCD BONG 32)

'Goodnight Lovers'/'When The Body Speaks (Acoustic Version)'/ 'The Dead Of Night (Electronicat Remix)'/'Goodnight Lovers (Isan Falling Leaf Mix)' (CD BONG 33, February 11, 2002)

ALBUMS:

Note: album marked with an asterisk (★) was a US-only release; album marked with a double asterisk (★★) was released in the US as Catching Up With Depeche Mode *(Sire 25346); album marked with a triple asterisk (★★★) is a re-mastered and repackaged version of* The Singles 81>85 *'best of' compilation first released in October 1985.*

***Speak & Spell* (STUMM 5, October 5, 1981):** 'New Life'/'I Sometimes Wish I Was Dead'/'Puppets'/'Boys Say Go!'/'Nodisco'/'What's Your Name?'/'Photographic'/'Tora! Tora! Tora!'/'Big Muff'/'Any Second Now (Voices)'/'Just Can't Get Enough' *Extra tracks (as featured on 1988 CD release):* 'Dreaming Of Me'/'Ice Machine'/'Shout!'/'Any Second Now'/ 'Just Can't Get Enough (Schizo Mix)'

***A Broken Frame* (STUMM 9, September 27, 1982):** 'Leave In Silence'/ 'My Secret Garden'/'Monument'/'Nothing To Fear'/'See You'/'Satellite'/ 'The Meaning Of Love'/'A Photograph Of You'/'Shouldn't Have Done That'/'The Sun & The Rainfall'

***Construction Time Again* (STUMM 13, August 22, 1983):** 'Love, In Itself'/'More Than A Party'/'Pipeline'/'Everything Counts'/'Two Minute Warning'/'Shame'/'The Landscape Is Changing'/'Told You So'/'And Then . . .'/'Everything Counts (Reprise)'

***People Are People* (Sire 25124, March 12, 1984):** 'People Are People'/ 'Now, This Is Fun'/'Love, In Itself'/'Work Hard'/'Told You So'/'Get The Balance Right!'/'Leave In Silence'/'Pipeline'/'Everything Counts' ★

***Some Great Reward* (STUMM 19, September 24, 1984):** 'Something To Do'/'Lie To Me'/'People Are People'/'It Doesn't Matter'/'Stories Of Old'/ 'Somebody'/'Master And Servant'/'If You Want'/'Blasphemous Rumours'

***The Singles 81>85* (MUTEL 1, October 15, 1985):** 'People Are People'/ 'Master And Servant'/'It's Called A Heart'/'Just Can't Get Enough'/'See You'/'Shake The Disease'/'Everything Counts'/'New Life'/'Blasphemous Rumours'/'Somebody'/'Leave In Silence'/'Get The Balance Right!'/'Love, In Itself'/'Dreaming Of Me'/'The Meaning Of Love' ★★

Black Celebration (STUMM 26, March 17, 1986): 'Black Celebration'/ 'Fly On The Windscreen (Final)'/'A Question Of Lust'/'Sometimes'/ 'It Doesn't Matter Two'/'A Question Of Time'/'Stripped'/'Here Is The House'/'World Full Of Nothing'/'Dressed In Black'/'New Dress' *Extra tracks (as featured on CD release):* 'Breathing In Fumes'/'But Not Tonight (Extended Remix)'/'Black Day'

Music For The Masses (STUMM 47, September 28, 1987): 'Never Let Me Down Again'/'The Things You Said'/'Strangelove'/'Sacred'/'Little 15'/ 'Behind The Wheel'/'I Want You Now'/'To Have And To Hold'/ 'Nothing'/'Pimpf' *Extra tracks (as featured on CD release):* 'Agent Orange'/ 'Never Let Me Down Again (Aggro Mix)'/'To Have And To Hold (Spanish Taster)'/'Pleasure, Little Treasure (Glitter Mix)'

101 (STUMM 101, March 13, 1989): 'Pimpf'/'Behind The Wheel'/ 'Strangelove'/'Sacred'/'Something To Do'/'Blasphemous Rumours'/ 'Stripped'/'Somebody'/'The Things You Said'/'Black Celebration'/'Shake The Disease'/'Nothing'/'Pleasure, Little Treasure'/'People Are People'/ 'A Question Of Time'/'Never Let Me Down Again'/'A Question Of Lust'/ 'Master And Servant'/'Just Can't Get Enough'/'Everything Counts'

Violator (STUMM 64, March 19, 1990): 'World In My Eyes'/'Sweetest Perfection'/'Personal Jesus'/'Halo'/'Waiting For The Night'/'Enjoy The Silence'/'Policy Of Truth'/'Blue Dress'/'Clean'

Songs Of Faith And Devotion (CDSTUMM 106, March 22, 1993): 'I Feel You'/'Walking In My Shoes'/'Condemnation'/'Mercy In You'/'Judas'/ 'In Your Room'/'Get Right With Me'/'Rush'/'One Caress'/'Higher Love'

Songs Of Faith And Devotion Live (LCDSTUMM 106, December 6, 1993): 'I Feel You'/'Walking In My Shoes'/'Condemnation'/'Mercy In You'/'Judas'/'In Your Room'/'Get Right With Me'/'Rush'/'One Caress'/ 'Higher Love'

Ultra (CDSTUMM 148, April 15, 1997): 'Barrel Of A Gun'/'The Love Thieves'/'Home'/'It's No Good'/'Uselink'/'Useless'/'Sister Of Night'/ 'The Jazz Thieves'/'Freestate'/'The Bottom Line'/'Insight'

The Singles 86>98 (CDMUTE 15, September 28, 1998): 'Stripped'/'A Question Of Lust'/'A Question Of Time'/'Strangelove'/'Never Let Me Down Again'/'Behind The Wheel'/'Personal Jesus'/'Enjoy The Silence'/ 'Policy Of Truth'/'World In My Eyes'/'I Feel You'/'Walking In My Shoes'/'Condemnation'/'In Your Room'/'Barrel Of A Gun'/'It's No

Good'/'Home'/'Useless'/'Only When I Lose Myself'/'Little 15'/
'Everything Counts (Live)'

The Singles 81>85 **(LCDMUTEL 1, October 26, 1988):** 'Dreaming Of
Me'/'New Life'/'Just Can't Get Enough'/'See You'/'The Meaning Of
Love'/'Leave In Silence'/'Get The Balance Right!'/'Everything Counts'/
'Love, In Itself'/'People Are People'/'Master And Servant'/'Blasphemous
Rumours'/'Somebody'/'Shake The Disease'/'It's Called A Heart'/
'Photographic (Some Bizzare Version)'/'Just Can't Get Enough (Schizo
Mix)' ★★★

Exciter **(CDSTUMM 190, May 14, 2001):** 'Dream On'/'Shine'/'The
Sweetest Condition'/'When The Body Speaks'/'The Dead Of Night'/
'Lovetheme'/'Freelove'/'Comatose'/'I Feel Loved'/'Breathe'/'Easy Tiger'/
'I Am You'/'Goodnight Lovers'

VIDEOS/DVDS:

Note: video marked with an asterisk (★) was repackaged and re-released as Some
Great Videos 81>85 *by Mute Film in 1998 (MF34).*

The World We Live In And Live In Hamburg **(Virgin Video VVD063,
1985):** 'Something To Do'/'Two Minute Warning'/'If You Want'/'People
Are People'/'Leave In Silence'/'New Life'/'Shame'/'Somebody'/'Lie To
Me'/'Blasphemous Rumours'/'Told You So'/'Master And Servant'/
'Photographic'/'Everything Counts'/'See You'/'Shout!'/'Just Can't Get
Enough'

Some Great Videos **(Virgin Video VVD103, 1986):** 'Just Can't Get
Enough'/'Everything Counts'/'Love, In Itself'/'People Are People'/'Master
And Servant'/'Blasphemous Rumours'/'Somebody'/'Shake The Disease'/
'It's Called A Heart'/'Photographic (Live)' ★

Strange **(Mute Film VVC 248, 1988):** 'A Question Of Time'/
'Strangelove'/'Never Let Me Down Again'/'Behind The Wheel'/'Pimpf'

101 **(Mute Film VVD 469, 1989):** 'Pimpf'/'Master And Servant'/'The
Things You Said'/'Blasphemous Rumours'/'People Are People'/'Stripped'/
'Black Celebration'/'Shake The Disease'/'Nothing'/'A Question Of Lust'/
'Behind The Wheel'/'Strangelove'/'Everything Counts'/'Just Can't Get
Enough'/'Never Let Me Down Again'

Strange Too **(BMG Video 790468, 1990):** 'Personal Jesus'/'Policy Of
Truth'/'Enjoy The Silence'/'Clean'/'Halo'/'World In My Eyes'

Selected Discography

***Devotional* (BMG Video BM 530, 1993):** 'Higher Love'/'World In My Eyes'/'Walking In My Shoes'/'Behind The Wheel'/'Stripped'/ 'Condemnation'/'Judas'/'Mercy In You'/'I Feel You'/'Never Let Me Down Again'/'Rush'/'In Your Room'/'Personal Jesus'/'Enjoy The Silence'/'Fly On The Windscreen'/'Everything Counts'

***The Videos 86>98* (MF33, September 28, 1998):** *Interview* 'Stripped'/ 'A Question Of Lust'/'A Question Of Time'/'Strangelove'/'Never Let Me Down Again'/'Behind The Wheel'/'Little 15'/'Everything Counts (Live)'/ 'Personal Jesus'/'Enjoy The Silence'/'Policy Of Truth'/'World In My Eyes'/'I Feel You'/'Walking In My Shoes'/'Condemnation'/'In Your Room'/'Barrel Of A Gun'/'It's No Good'/'Home'/'Useless'/'Only When I Lose Myself' *A Short Film*

***The Videos 86>98* (DVDMUTEL5, July 23, 2001):** *Interview* 'Stripped'/ 'A Question Of Lust'/'A Question Of Time'/'Strangelove'/'Never Let Me Down Again'/'Behind The Wheel'/'Little 15'/'Everything Counts (Live)'/ 'Personal Jesus'/'Enjoy The Silence'/'Policy Of Truth'/'World In My Eyes'/'I Feel You'/'Walking In My Shoes'/'Condemnation'/'In Your Room'/'Barrel Of A Gun'/'It's No Good'/'Home'/'Useless'/'Only When I Lose Myself' *A Short Film*

***One Night In Paris* (DVDSTUMM 190, May 27, 2002) – disc one:** 'Dream On (Guitar Intro)'/'The Dead Of Night'/'The Sweetest Condition'/'Halo'/'Walking In My Shoes'/'Dream On'/'When The Body Speaks'/'Waiting For The Night'/'It Doesn't Matter Two'/'Breathe'/ 'Freelove'/'Enjoy The Silence'/'I Feel You'/'In Your Room'/'It's No Good'/'Personal Jesus'/'Home'/'Condemnation'/'Black Celebration'/ 'Never Let Me Down Again' – **disc two:** *The Preparing The Photographing The Waiting The Talking The Screening Sister Of Night Bonus Track The Choosing The Subtitling*

***The Videos 86>98+* (DMDVD2, November 25, 2002) – disc one:** *Interview With Depeche Mode* 'Stripped'/'A Question Of Lust'/'A Question Of Time'/'Strangelove'/'Never Let Me Down Again'/'Behind The Wheel'/'Little 15'/'Everything Counts (Live)'/'Personal Jesus'/'Enjoy The Silence'/'Policy Of Truth'/'World In My Eyes'/'I Feel You'/'Walking In My Shoes'/'Condemnation (Live)'/'In Your Room'/'Barrel Of A Gun'/ 'It's No Good'/'Home'/'Useless'/'Only When I Lose Myself' *Depeche Mode: A Short Film* – **disc two:** 'But Not Tonight (From The Film *Modern Girls*)'/'Strangelove '88 (US Version)'/'One Caress (US Video)'/ 'Condemnation (Paris Mix)' *Violator 13/11/90 Songs Of Faith & Devotion 27/01/93 Ultra 26/02/97*

DEPECHE MODE SOLO

Selected Discography

(MUTE RECORDS)

RECOIL (ALAN WILDER) ALBUMS:

1+2 (STUMM 31, August 1986): '1'/'2'

Hydrology (STUMM 51, January 1988): 'Grain'/'Stone'/'Sermon' *Extra tracks (as featured on CD release):* '1'/'2'

Bloodline (STUMM 94, April 1992): 'Faith Healer'/'Electro Blues For Bukka White'/'The Defector'/'Edge To Life'/'Curse'/'Bloodline'/'Freeze'

Unsound Methods (STUMM 159, October 1997): 'Incubus'/'Drifting'/ 'Luscious Apparatus'/'Stalker'/'Red River Cargo'/'Control Freak'/ 'Missing Piece'/'Last Breath'/'Shunt'

Liquid (CDSTUMM 173, March 2000): 'Black Box (Part 1)'/'Want'/ 'Jezebel'/'Breath Control'/'Last Call For Liquid Courage'/'Strange Hours'/ 'Vertigen'/'Supreme'/'Chrome'/'Black Box (Part 2)'/'Strange Hours – Video'

RECOIL (ALAN WILDER) SINGLES:

'Faith Healer (LP Version)'/'Faith Healer (Healed Mix)' (MUTE 110, March 1992)

'Faith Healer (LP Version)'/'Faith Healer (Healed Mix)' (C MUTE 110, March 1992)

'Faith Healer (LP Version)'/'Faith Healer (Trance Mix)'/'Faith Healer (Conspiracy Theory)'/'Faith Healer (Disbeliever Mix)'/'Faith Healer (Deformity Mix)'/'Faith Healer (Barracuda Mix)'/'Faith Healer (Conspiracy – Double Bullet – Theory)' (12 MUTE 110)

'Faith Healer (LP Version)'/'Faith Healer (Trance Mix)'/'Faith Healer (Conspiracy Theory)'/'Faith Healer (Disbeliever Mix)'/'Faith Healer (Deformity Mix)'/'Faith Healer (Barracuda Mix)'/'Faith Healer (Conspiracy – Double Bullet – Theory)' (CD MUTE 110)

'Drifting'/'Drifting (Poison Dub)'/'Control Freak (Barry Adamson Mix)'/'Shunt (Pan Sonic Mix)' (CD MUTE 209, October 1997)
'Drifting'/'Drifting (Poison Dub)'/'Control Freak (Barry Adamson Mix)'/'Shunt (Pan Sonic Mix)' (12 MUTE 209, October 1997)

'Stalker (Punished Mix)'/'Missing Piece (Night Dissolves)'/'Red River Cargo' (CD MUTE 214, March 1998)

'Strange Hours (Edit)'/'Jezebel (Filthy Dog Mix)'/'New York Nights'/'Don't Look Back'/'Strange Hours – Video'/'Drifting – Video'/'Stalker – Video'/'Faith Healer – Video' (CD MUTE 232, April 2000)

'Jezebel (The Slick Sixty vs. RJ Remix)'/'Electro Blues For Bukka White (2000 Mix)'/'Black Box (Complete)'/'Jezebel – Video' (CD MUTE 233, September 2000)

MARTIN GORE ALBUMS:

Counterfeit E.P. **(STUMM 67, June 12, 1989):** 'Compulsion'/'In A Manner Of Speaking'/'Smile In The Crowd'/'Gone'/'Never Turn Your Back On Mother Earth'/'Motherless Child'

Counterfeit2 **(STUMM 214, April 28, 2003):** 'In My Time Of Dying'/'Stardust'/'I Cast A Lonesome Shadow'/'In My Other World'/'Loverman'/'By This River'/'Lost In The Stars'/'Oh My Love'/'Das Lied Vom Einsamen Mädchen'/'Tiny Girls'/'Candy Says'

MARTIN GORE SINGLES:

'Stardust (Album Version)'/'I Cast A Lonesome Shadow (Stewart Walker Vocal Mix)'/'Life Is Strange' (CD MUTE 296, April 14, 2003)
'Stardust (Atom Vocal Remix)'/'Stardust (Atom Instrumental Remix)'/'I Cast A Lonesome Shadow (Stewart Walker Instrumental Mix)' (12 MUTE 296)
'Left Hand Luke And The Beggar Boys – Video'/'Stardust (Album Version)'/'Stardust (Atom Vocal Remix)' (DVD MUTE 296)

DAVE GAHAN SINGLES:

'Dirty Sticky Floors (Radio Mix)'/'Stand Up'/'Maybe' (CD MUTE 294, May 26, 2003)
'Dirty Sticky Floors (Junkie XL Vocal Remix – Edit)'/'Dirty Sticky Floors (Lexicon Avenue Vocal Mix – Edit)'/'Dirty Sticky Floors (The Passengerz Dirty Club Mix – Edit)' (LCD MUTE 294)
'Dirty Sticky Floors (Junkie XL Vocal Remix)'/'Dirty Sticky Floors (Junkie XL Dub)' (12 MUTE 294)
'Dirty Sticky Floors (Lexicon Avenue Vocal Mix)'/'Dirty Sticky Floors (Silencer Remix)' (L12 MUTE 294)
'Dirty Sticky Floors – Video'/'Dirty Sticky Floors (Junkie XL Dub – Edit)'/ 'Black And Blue Again (Acoustic)' (DVD MUTE 294)

DAVE GAHAN ALBUMS:

Paper Monsters **(STUMM 216, June 2, 2003):** 'Dirty Sticky Floors'/'Hold On'/'A Little Piece'/'Bottle Living'/'Black And Blue Again'/'Stay'/'I Need You'/'Bitter Apple'/'Hidden Houses'/'Goodbye'

VINCE CLARKE

Selected Post-Depeche Mode Discography

(MUTE RECORDS)

YAZOO SINGLES:

Note: singles marked with an asterisk (★) were issued on CD for the first time by Mute Records on October 7, 1996.

'Only You'/'Situation' (MUTE 020, March 15, 1982)

'Only You'/'Situation'/'Situation (Extended Version)' (12 MUTE 020)

'Only You'/'Situation'/'Situation (Extended Version)' (CD MUTE 020) ★

'Don't Go'/'Winter Kills' (YAZ 001, July 3, 1982)

'Don't Go (Remix)'/'Don't Go (Re-remix)'/'Winter Kills' (12 YAZ 001)

'Don't Go'/'Don't Go (Remix)'/'Don't Go (Re-remix)'/'Winter Kills' (CD YAZ 001) ★

'The Other Side Of Love'/'Ode To Boy' (YAZ 002, November 1982)

'The Other Side Of Love (Remixed Extended Version)'/'Ode To Boy' (12 YAZ 002)

'The Other Side Of Love'/'Ode To Boy'/'The Other Side Of Love (Remixed Extended Version)' (CD YAZ 002) ★

'Nobody's Diary'/'State Farm' (YAZ 003, April 1983)

'Nobody's Diary (Extended Version)'/'State Farm (Extended Version)' (12 YAZ 003)

'Nobody's Diary'/'State Farm'/'Nobody's Diary (Extended Version)'/ 'State Farm (Extended Version)'/'Situation (Re-recorded Remix)' (CD YAZ 003) ★

'Situation (Deadline Mix – Edit)'/'State Farm (Madhouse Mix – Edit)' (YAZ 004, November 26, 1990)

'Situation (The Aggressive Attitude Mix)'/'Situation (Deadline Mix)'/ 'State Farm (Madhouse Mix)' (12 YAZ 004)

'Situation (Daniel Miller and Mark Saunders Remix)'/'State Farm (Madhouse Mix – Edit)'/'Situation (The Aggressive Mix)'/'Situation (Space Dub)' (CD YAZ 004)

'Situation (François Kervorkian Remix)'/'State Farm (Extended)'/ 'Situation'/'State Farm' (LCD YAZ 004)

Situation – Remixes **(CD YAZ 006, November 8, 1999):** 'Situation (Club 69 Radio Mix)'/'Situation (Club 69 Speed Mix)'/'Situation (Richard 'Humpty' Vission Visits The Dome)'/'Situation (Dave Ralph's Tea Freaks English Breakfast Mix)'/'Situation (Deadline Mix)'/'State Farm (Madhouse Mix)'/'Situation (Daniel Miller and Mark Saunders Remix)'/'State Farm (Play Doh Dub)'/'Situation (Original US Dub)'/'Situation 1990 Video'/ 'Only You 1999 Video'

'Situation (Club 69 Speed Mix)'/'Situation (Richard 'Humpty' Vission Visits The Dub)'/'Situation (Richard 'Humpty' Vission Instrumental)' (12 YAZ 006)

'Situation (Dave Ralph's Tea Freaks English Breakfast Mix)'/'Situation (Club 69 Speed Dub)' (L12 YAZ 006)

YAZOO ALBUMS:

Upstairs At Erics **(STUMM 7, August, 1982):** 'Don't Go'/'Too Pieces'/ 'Bad Connection'/'I Before E Except After C'/'Midnight'/'In My Room'/ 'Only You'/'Goodbye 70s'/'Tuesday'/'Winter Kills'/'Bring Your Love Down (Didn't I)' • *Extra tracks (as featured on 1995 CD release):* 'The Other Side Of Love'/'Situation (François Kervorkian Remix)'

You And Me Both **(STUMM 12, July 1983):** 'Nobody's Diary'/'Softly Over'/'Sweet Thing'/'Mr Blue'/'Good Times'/'Walk Away From Love'/ 'Ode To Boy'/'Unmarked'/'Anyone'/'Happy People'/'And On' • *Extra tracks (as featured on 1995 CD release):* 'Nobody's Diary (Extended Version)'/ 'State Farm (Extended Version)'

Only You – The Best Of **(CDMUTEL 6, September 6, 1999):** 'Only You'/'Ode To Boy'/'Nobody's Diary'/'Midnight'/'Goodbye 70s'/ 'Anyone'/'Don't Go'/'Mr Blue'/'Tuesday'/'Winter Kills'/'State Farm'/ 'Situation (US 12″ Mix)'/'Don't Go (Todd Terry Freeze Mix)'/'Situation (Club 69 Future Funk Mix)'/'Only You (1999 Mix)'

THE ASSEMBLY SINGLES:

Note: singles marked with an asterisk (★) were issued on CD for the first time by Mute Records on October 7, 1996.

'Never Never'/'Stop Start' (TINY 001, October 1983)

'Never Never (Extended Version)'/'Stop Start (Extended Version)' (12 TINY 001)

'Never Never'/'Stop Start'/'Never Never (Extended Version)'/'Stop Start (Extended Version)' (CD TINY 001) ★

VINCE CLARKE & PAUL QUINN SINGLES:

'One Day'/'Song For' (TAG 001, June 1985)

'One Day (Extended Version)'/'Song For (Extended Version)' (12 TAG 001)

'One Day'/'Song For'/'One Day (Extended Version)'/'Song For (Extended Version)' (CD TAG 001) ★

ERASURE SINGLES:

Note: singles marked with an asterisk (★) were issued on CD for the first time by Mute Records throughout 1993.

'Who Needs Love (Like That)'/'Push Me, Shove Me' (MUTE 040, September 2, 1985)

'Who Needs Love (Like That – Legend Mix)'/'Push Me, Shove Me (Extended As Far As Possible Mix)'/'Who Needs Love (Like That – Instrumental Work-Out Mix)' (12 MUTE 040)

'Who Needs Love (Like That – Mexican Mix)'/'Push Me, Shove Me (Tacos Mix)' (L12 MUTE 040)

'Who Needs Love (Like That – Single Mix)'/'Push Me, Shove Me'/'Who Needs Love (Like That – Legend Mix)'/'Push Me, Shove Me (Extended As Far As Possible Mix)'/'Who Needs Love (Like That – Instrumental Work-Out Mix)' (CD MUTE 040) ★

'Heavenly Action (Single Edit)'/'Don't Say No' (MUTE 042, November 11, 1985)

'Heavenly Action (Extended)'/'Don't Say No (Instrumental)'/'My Heart . . . So Blue (Incidental)' (12 MUTE 042)

'Heavenly Action (Yellow Brick Mix)'/'Don't Say No (Ruby Red Mix)'/
'My Heart . . . So Blue (Incidental)' (L12 MUTE 042)

'Heavenly Action'/'Don't Say No (Vocal)'/'Heavenly Action (Extended)'/
'Don't Say No (Instrumental)'/'My Heart . . . So Blue (Incidental)' (CD
MUTE 042) ★

'Oh L'Amour (Funky Sisters Remix – Edit)'/'March On Down The Line' (MUTE 045, April 21, 1986)

'Oh L'Amour (Remix)'/'March On Down The Line (Flood Mix)'/'Gimme!
Gimme! Gimme!' (12 MUTE 045)

'Oh L'Amour (Funky Sisters Remix)'/'Gimme! Gimme! Gimme! (Paul
Kendall Remix)'/'March On Down The Line (Flood Mix)' (L12 MUTE
045)

'Oh L'Amour'/'March On Down The Line'/'Oh L'Amour (Remix)'/
'March On Down The Line (Flood Mix)'/'Gimme! Gimme! Gimme!'
(CD MUTE 045) ★

'Sometimes'/'Sexuality' (MUTE 051, August 6, 1986)

'Sometimes (12″ Mix)'/'Sexuality (Extended Mix)'/'Say What' (12 MUTE
051)

'Sometimes'/'Sexuality'/'Who Needs Love (Like That – Single Edit)'/
'Heavenly Action (Single Edit)'/'Oh L'Amour' (C MUTE 051)

'Sometimes'/'Sexuality'/'Sometimes (12″ Mix)'/'Sexuality (Extended
Mix)'/'Say What' (CD MUTE 051) ★

'It Doesn't Have To Be (Single Edit)'/'In The Hall Of The Mountain King' (MUTE 056, February 16, 1987)

'It Doesn't Have To Be (The Boop Oopa Doo Mix)'/'Who Needs Love
(Like That – Betty Boop Mix)'/'In The Hall Of The Mountain King'
(12 MUTE 056)

'It Doesn't Have To Be (Cement Mix)'/'Heavenly Action (Holger Hiller
Mix)'/'In The Hall Of The Mountain King (New Version)' (L12 MUTE
056)

'It Doesn't Have To Be (Single Edit)'/'Sometimes'/'Oh L'Amour (Single
Edit)'/'Heavenly Action (Single Edit)'/'Who Needs Love (Like That –
Single Edit)'/'Gimme! Gimme! Gimme! (Paul Kendall Remix)'/'In The
Hall Of The Mountain King' (CD MUTE 056)

'Victim Of Love (Remix)'/'The Soldier's Return' (MUTE 061, May 18, 1987)

'Victim Of Love (Extended Remix)'/'The Soldier's Return (Return Of The
Radical Radcliffe Mix)'/'Victim Of Love (Dub Mix)' (12 MUTE 061)

'Safety In Numbers (Live)'/'Victim Of Love'/'The Soldier's Return (Return Of The Radical Radcliffe Mix)'/'Don't Dance (Live)'/'Leave Me To Bleed (Live)' (CD MUTE 061) ★

'The Circus (Remix)'/'The Circus (Decay Mix)' (MUTE 066, September 21, 1987)

'Victim Of Love (Live)'/'If I Could (Live)'/'The Circus (Live)'/'Spiralling (Live)' (1 MUTE 66T)

'It Doesn't Have To Be (Live)'/'Who Needs Love (Like That – Live)'/ 'Gimme! Gimme! Gimme! (Live)'/'The Circus (Bareback Rider Mix)' (2 MUTE 66T)

'Sometimes (Live)'/'Say What (Live)'/'Oh L'Amour (Live)'/'The Circus (Gladiator Mix)' (3 MUTE 66T)

'The Circus (Remix)'/'The Circus (Decay Mix)'/'If I Could (Live)'/'It Doesn't Have To Be (Live)'/'Say What (Live)'/'The Circus (Live)' (CD MUTE 066) ★

'Ship Of Fools'/'When I Needed You' (MUTE 074, February 22, 1988)

'Ship Of Fools (Shiver Me Timbers Mix)'/'River Deep, Mountain High (Private Dance Mix)'/'When I Needed You' (12 MUTE 074)

'Ship Of Fools (RC Mix)'/'River Deep, Mountain High (Private Dance Mix)'/'When I Needed You' (L12 MUTE 074)

'Ship Of Fools (Shiver Me Timbers Mix)'/'When I Needed You (Melancholic Mix)'/'River Deep, Mountain High (Private Dance Mix)' (CD MUTE 074)

'Chains Of Love'/'Don't Suppose' (MUTE 083, May 31, 1988)

'Chains Of Love (Foghorn Mix)'/'Don't Suppose (Country Joe Mix)'/ 'The Good, The Bad, And The Ugly' (12 MUTE 083)

'Chains Of Love (Truly In Love With The Marks Bros. Mix)'/'The Good, The Bad, And The Ugly (The Dangerous Mix)'/'Don't Suppose'

'Chains Of Love (Foghorn Mix)'/'The Good, The Bad, And The Ugly (The Dangerous Mix)'/'Don't Suppose (Country Joe Mix)' (CD MUTE 083)

'A Little Respect'/'Like Zsa Zsa Gabor' (MUTE 085, September 19, 1988)

'A Little Respect (Mark Saunders Remix)'/'Like Zsa Zsa Gabor (Mark Freegard Remix)'/'Love Is Colder Than Death' (12 MUTE 085)

'A Little Respect (Big Train Remix)'/'Like Zsa Zsa Gabor (Rico Conning Remix)'/'Love Is Colder Than Death' (L12 MUTE 085)

'A Little Respect'/'A Little Respect (Mark Saunders Remix)'/'Like Zsa Zsa Gabor (Rico Conning Remix)'/'Love Is Colder Than Death' (CD MUTE 085)

Crackers International EP (MUTE 089, November 28, 1988): 'Stop!'/ 'The Hardest Part'/'Knocking On Your Door'/'She Won't Be Home'

Crackers International EP (12 MUTE 089): 'Stop! (Cold Ending)'/'The Hardest Part (12″ Version)'/'Knocking On Your Door (12″ Version'/ 'She Won't Be Home'

Crackers International EP (L12 MUTE 089): 'Stop! (Mark Saunders Remix)'/ 'The Hardest Part (Mark Saunders Remix)'/'God Rest, Ye Merry Gentlemen'

Crackers International EP (CD MUTE 089): 'Stop! (Cold Ending)'/'The Hardest Part (12″ Version)'/'Knocking On Your Door (12″ Version'/ 'She Won't Be Home'

Crackers International EP (LCD MUTE 089): 'Stop! (Mark Saunders Remix)'/'The Hardest Part (Mark Saunders Remix)'/'God Rest, Ye Merry Gentlemen'

'Drama!'/'Sweet, Sweet Baby' (MUTE 093, September 18, 1989)

'Drama! (Act 2)'/'Sweet, Sweet Baby (Moo-Moo Mix)'/'Paradise' (12 MUTE 093)

'Drama! (Krucial Mix)'/'Sweet, Sweet Baby (Medi Mix)'/'Paradise (Lost And Found Mix)' (L12 MUTE 093)

'Drama!'/'Sweet, Sweet Baby' (C MUTE 093)

'Drama! (Act 2)'/'Sweet, Sweet Baby (Moo-Moo Mix)'/'Paradise' (CD MUTE 093)

'Drama! (Krucial Mix)'/'Sweet, Sweet Baby (Medi Mix)'/'Paradise (Lost And Found Mix)' (LCD MUTE 093)

'You Surround Me'/'91 Steps' (MUTE 099, November 27, 1989)

'You Surround Me (Syrinx Mix)'/'Supernature'/'91 Steps (Plus 24)' (12 MUTE 099)

'You Surround Me (Remix)'/'Supernature (William Orbit Mix)'/'91 Steps (6 Pianos Mix)' (L12 MUTE 099)

'Supernature (Daniel Miller and Phil Legg Mix)'/'You Surround Me (Gareth Jones Mix)'/'Supernature (Mark Saunders Mix)' (XL12 MUTE 099)

'You Surround Me'/'91 Steps' (C MUTE 099)

'You Surround Me (Syrinx Mix)'/'Supernature'/'91 Steps (Plus 24)' (CD MUTE 099)

'You Surround Me (Remix)'/'Supernature (William Orbit Mix)'/'91 Steps (6 Pianos Mix)' (LCD12 MUTE 099)

'Blue Savannah'/'Runaround On The Underground' (MUTE 109, February 26, 1990)

'Blue Savannah'/'Runaround On The Underground'/'No G.D.M.' (12 MUTE 109)

'Blue Savannah (Der Deutsche Mix II)'/'No G.D.M. (Unfinished Mix)'/ 'Runaround On The Underground (12″ Mix)' (L12 MUTE 109)

'Blue Savannah (Der Deutsche Mix II)'/'Blue Savannah (Der Deutsche Mix I)' (XL12 MUTE 109)

'Blue Savannah'/'Runaround On The Underground' (C MUTE 109)

'Blue Savannah'/'Runaround On The Underground'/'No G.D.M.' (CD MUTE 109)

'Blue Savannah (Der Deutsche Mix II)'/'No G.D.M. (Unfinished Mix)'/ 'Runaround On The Underground (12″ Mix)' (LCD MUTE 109)

'Star'/'Dreamlike State' (MUTE 111, May 21, 1990)

'Star (Trafalmadore Mix)'/'Star'/'Dreamlike State (The 24 Hour Technicolor Mix)' (12 MUTE 111)

'Star (Interstellar Mix)'/'Star (Soul Mix)'/'Dreamlike State (The 24 Hour Technicolor Mix)' (L12 MUTE 111)

'Star'/'Dreamlike State' (C MUTE 111)

'Star'/'Dreamlike State'/'Star (Trafalmadore Mix)'/'Star (Soul Mix)' (CD MUTE 111)

'Chorus (Single Mix)'/'Over The Rainbow' (MUTE 125, June 17, 1991)

'Chorus (Pure Trance Mix)'/'Chorus (Single Mix)'/'Snappy (The Spice Has Risen Mix)'/'Chorus (Transdental Trance Mix – Fade)' (12 MUTE 125)

'Chorus (Single Mix)'/'Over The Rainbow' (C MUTE 125, June 17, 1991)

'Chorus (Single Mix)'/'Chorus (Transdental Trance Mix)'/'Snappy (12″ Remix – Edit)'/'Over The Rainbow' (CD MUTE 125)

'Love To Hate You'/'Vitamin C' (MUTE 131, September 9, 1991)

'Love To Hate You (Remix by Paul Daykeyne for DMC)'/'Vitamin C (Paul Daykeyne Mix)'/'La La La' (12 MUTE 131)

'Love To Hate You'/'Vitamin C' (C MUTE 131)

'Love To Hate You (Mix by Dave Bascombe)'/'Love To Hate You (Remix by Paul Daykeyne for DMC)'/'Vitamin C (Mix by Martyn Philips)'/'La La La (Mix by George Holt)' (CD MUTE 131)

Am I Right? EP **(MUTE 134, November 25, 1991): 'Am I Right?'/ 'Carry On Clangers (Edit)'/'Let It Flow'/'Waiting For Sex (Edit)'**

Am I Right? EP (12 MUTE 134): 'Am I Right? (Dave Bascombe Mix)'/ 'Carry On Clangers (Full Version)'/'Let It Flow'/'Waiting For Sex (Full Version)'

Am I Right? EP (L12 MUTE 134): 'Am I Right? (The Grid Remix)'/'Love To Hate You (LFO Modulated Filter Mix)'/'Chorus (Vegan Mix)'/'B3'

Am I Right? EP (C MUTE 134): 'Am I Right? (Dave Bascombe Mix)'/ 'Carry On Clangers (Full Version)'/'Let It Flow'/'Waiting For Sex (Full Version)'

Am I Right? EP (CD MUTE 134): 'Am I Right?'/'Let It Flow'/'Waiting For Sex (Full Version)'/'Carry On Clangers (Full Version)'

Am I Right? EP (LCD MUTE 134): 'Am I Right? (The Grid Remix)'/'Love To Hate You (LFO Modulated Filter Mix)'/'Chorus (Vegan Mix)'/'Perfect Stranger (Acoustic Mix)'

'Breath Of Life'/'Breath Of Life (Swiss Mix)'/'Breath Of Life (Acapella Dub Mix)' (MUTE 142, March 16, 1992)

'Breath Of Life (Divine Inspiration Mix)'/'Breath Of Life (Umbilical Mix)'/ 'Breath Of Life (Swiss Mix)'/'Breath Of Life (Elixir Mix)'/'Breath Of Life (Stripped Mix)' (12 MUTE 142)

'Breath Of Life'/'Breath Of Life (Swiss Mix)'/'Breath Of Life (Acapella Dub Mix)' (C MUTE 142)

'Breath Of Life'/'Breath Of Life (Divine Inspiration Mix)'/'Breath Of Life (Stripped Mix)'/'Breath Of Life (Swiss Mix)'/'Breath Of Life (Acapella Dub Mix)' (CD MUTE 142)

ABBA-esque EP **(MUTE 144, June 1, 1992): 'Lay All Your Love On Me'/'S.O.S.'/'Take A Chance On Me'/'Voulez-Vous'**

ABBA-esque EP (12 MUTE 144): 'Lay All Your Love On Me'/'S.O.S.'/ 'Take A Chance On Me'/'Voulez-Vous'

ABBA-esque EP (L12 MUTE 144): 'Voulez-Vous (Brain Stem Death Test Mix)'/'Lay All Your Love On Me (No Panties Mix)'/'Take A Chance On Me (Take A Trance On Me Mix)'/'S.O.S. (Perimeter Mix)'

ABBA-esque EP (C MUTE 144): 'Lay All Your Love On Me'/'S.O.S.'/ 'Take A Chance On Me'/'Voulez-Vous'

ABBA-esque EP (CD MUTE 144): 'Lay All Your Love On Me'/'S.O.S.'/ 'Take A Chance On Me'/'Voulez-Vous'

ABBA-esque EP (LCD MUTE 144): 'Voulez Vous (Brain Stem Death Test Mix)'/'Lay All Your Love On Me (No Panties Mix)'/'Take A Chance On Me (Take A Trance On Me Mix)'/'S.O.S. (Perimeter Mix)'

'Who Needs Love (Like That – Hamburg Mix)'/'Who Needs Love (Like That – Single Edit)' (MUTE 150, October 26, 1992)

'Who Needs Love (Like That – Phil Kelsey Mix)'/'Ship Of Fools (Orbital Southsea Isles Of The Holy Beats Mix)'/'Sometimes (Danny Rampling Mix)' (12 MUTE 150)

'Who Needs Love (Like That – 1992 Remix)'/'Who Needs Love (Like That – Single Edit)' (C MUTE 150, October 26, 1992)

'Who Needs Love (Like That – Hamburg Mix)'/'The Soldier's Return'/ 'Don't Say No'/'The Circus (Gladiator Mix)' (CD MUTE 150)

'Who Needs Love (Like That – Phil Kelsey Mix)'/'Ship Of Fools (Orbital Southsea Isles Of The Holy Beats Mix)'/'Sometimes (Danny Rampling Mix)' (LCD MUTE 150)

'Always'/'Tragic' (MUTE 152, April 11, 1994)

'Always'/'Tragic'/'Always (Capella Club Remix)'/'Always (Microbots Trance Dance Mix)' (12 MUTE 152)

'Always'/'Tragic' (C MUTE 152)

'Always'/'Always (Extended Mix)'/'Tragic' (CD MUTE 152)

'Always (Capella Club Remix)'/'Always (Microbots Trance Dance Mix)'/ 'Always (Microbots Inside Your Brain Mix)' (LCD MUTE 152)

'Run To The Sun'/'Tenderest Moments'/'Run To The Sun (Beatmasters Intergalactic Mix – Galactic Edit)' (MUTE 153)

'Run To The Sun'/'Run To The Sun (Beatmasters Galactic Mix)'/'Run To The Sun (Amber Solaire)'/'Run To The Sun (The Simon & Diamond Bhangra Remix)'/'Run To The Sun (Set The Control For The Heart Of The Sun)'/'Run To The Sun (Diss-cuss Mix)' (12 MUTE 153)

'Run To The Sun'/'Tenderest Moments'/'Run To The Sun (Beatmasters Intergalactic Mix – Galactic Edit)' (C MUTE 153)

'Run To The Sun'/'Tenderest Moments'/'Run To The Sun (Beatmasters Intergalactic Mix)' (CD MUTE 153)

'Run To The Sun (Beatmasters Outergalactic Mix)'/'Run To The Sun (The Simon & Diamond Bhangra Remix)'/'Run To The Sun (Set The Control For The Heart Of The Sun)'/'Run To The Sun (Amber Solaire)' (LCD MUTE 153)

I Love Saturday EP (MUTE CD 166, November 21, 1994): 'I Love Saturday'/'I Love Saturday (JX Mix)'/'I Love Saturday (Beatmasters Dub Mix)'/'Dodo'

I Love Saturday EP (LCD MUTE 166): 'I Love Saturday (Beatmasters Club Mix)'/'I Love Saturday (Flower Mix)'/'I Love Saturday (303 Mix)'/'Always (X-Dub Cut)'

I Love Saturday EP (EPCD 166): 'I Love Saturday'/'Ghost'/'Truly, Madly, Deeply'/'Tragic (Live Vocal)'

I Love Saturday EP (C MUTE 166): 'I Love Saturday'/'Dodo'/'Because You're So Sweet (Mark Goodier Radio Session Version)'

I Love Saturday EP (12 MUTE 166): 'I Love Saturday'/'I Love Saturday (Beatmasters Club Mix)'/'I Love Saturday (JX Mix)'/'I Love Saturday (Flower Mix)'

'Stay With Me'/'True Love Wars'/'Stay With Me (Basic Mix)'/ 'True Love Wars (Omni)' (CD MUTE 174, September 11, 1995)

'Stay With Me (Flow Mix)'/'Stay With Me (NY Mix)'/'Stay With Me (Guitar Mix)'/'Stay With Me (Castaway Dub)' (LCD MUTE 174)

'Stay With Me (NY Mix)'/'Stay With Me (Flow Mix)'/'True Love Wars (Omni Plus)'/'Stay With Me (Guitar Mix)' (12 MUTE 174)

'Fingers & Thumbs (Cold Summer's Day – Single Mix)'/'HI NRG'/ 'Fingers & Thumbs (Cold Summer's Day – Twilight 0.2)'/'Fingers & Thumbs (Fingers In Crumbs)' (CD MUTE 178, November 27, 1995)

'Fingers & Thumbs (Cold Summer's Day – Tin Tin Out Remix)'/'Fingers & Thumbs (Cold Summer's Day – Tin Tin Out Instrumental)'/'Fingers & Thumbs (Cold Summer's Day – Dub On The Moon)'/'Fingers & Thumbs (Cold Summer's Day – Twilight Plus)' (LCD MUTE 178)

'Fingers & Thumbs (Cold Summer's Day – Single Mix)'/'HI NRG' (C MUTE 178)

'Fingers & Thumbs (Cold Summer's Day – Tin Tin Out Remix)'/'Fingers & Thumbs (Cold Summer's Day – Tin Tin Out Instrumental)'/'Fingers & Thumbs (Cold Summer's Day – Dub On The Moon)'/'Fingers & Thumbs (Cold Summer's Day – Twilight Plus)' (12 MUTE 178)

'In My Arms'/'In The Name Of The Heart'/'In My Arms (Love To Infinity Stratomaster Mix)'/'In My Arms (Crumbling Down Mix)' (CD MUTE 190, January 6, 1997)

'In My Arms (Love To Infinity Gyrator Mix)'/'Rapture (Matt Darey Mix)'/ 'Rapture' (LCD MUTE 190)

'In My Arms'/'Rapture' (C MUTE 190)

'In My Arms (Love To Infinity Gyrator Club Mix)'/'In My Arms (Love To Infinity Stratomaster Mix)'/'Rapture' (12 MUTE 190)

'Don't Say Your Love Is Killing Me'/'Heart Of Glass (Live)'/'Don't Say Your Love Is Killing Me (Jon Pleased Wimmin Flashback Vox)'/ 'Don't Say Your Love Is Killing Me (Tall Paul Mix)' (CD MUTE 195, February 24, 1997)

'Don't Say Your Love Is Killing Me (Jon Pleased Wimmin Flashback Dub)'/ 'Oh L'Amour (Matt Darey Mix)'/'Oh L'Amour (Tin Tin Out Mix)' (LCD MUTE 195)

'Don't Say Your Love Is Killing Me'/'Heart Of Glass (Live)' (C MUTE 195)

'Don't Say Your Love Is Killing Me (Tall Paul Mix)'/'Don't Say Your Love Is Killing Me (Jon Pleased Wimmin Flashback Vox)'/'Oh L'Amour (Tin Tin Out Mix)'/'Oh L'Amour (Matt Darey Mix)' (12 MUTE 195)

Rain Plus **(CDLP MUTE 208, October 13, 1997):** 'Rain (Al Stone Mix)'/'In My Arms (BBE Mix)'/'First Contact (Vocal Mix)'/'Rain (Live)'/ 'Sometimes (Live)'/'Love To Hate You (Live)'/'Rain (Jon Pleased Wimmin Vocal Mix)'/'Sometimes (John '00' Fleming's Full Vocal Club Mix)'/'In My Arms (Dekkard's Vocal Mix)'/'Rain (Blue Amazon's Twisted Circles Mix)'/ 'First Contact (Instrumental Mix)'

Rain Plus (LP MUTE 208): 'Rain (Blue Amazon's Twisted Circles Mix)'/ 'In My Arms (Dekkard's Dub Mix)'/'Sometimes (John '00' Fleming's Full Vocal Club Mix)'/'Sometimes (John Fleming Give It Some Welly Mix)'/ 'Rain (Jon Pleased Wimmin Vocal Mix)'/'Rain (Jon Pleased Wimmin Dub Mix)'/'First Contact (Instrumental Mix)'/'In My Arms (BBE Mix)'

'Freedom'/'Better'/'Freedom (Acoustic Version)' (CD MUTE 244, October 9, 2000)

'Freedom (Motiv9 Radio Mix)'/'Freedom (Jason Creasey Mix)'/'Freedom (Mark's Guitar Vocal)' (LCD MUTE 244)

'Freedom (Original Mix)'/'Better'/'Freedom (Acoustic Version)' (12 MUTE 244)

'Freedom (Motiv9 Radio Mix)'/'Freedom (Jason Creasey Mix)'/'Freedom (Mark Pichiotti Mix)' (L12 MUTE 244)

Moon And The Sky Plus **(CDLP MUTE 248, December 10, 2001):** 'Moon And The Sky (JC's Heaven Scent Radio Re-Work)'/'Moon And The Sky (The Millionaires Radio Edit)'/'Moon And The Sky (Randy Roger's Ramjet Mix)'/'Moon And The Sky (Sleaze Sisters Anthem Remix)'/'Moon And The Sky (BK Mix)'/'Baby Love (Acoustic)'/'Freedom (Acoustic)'/'Alien (Acoustic)'/'A Little Respect (Acoustic)'

'Solsbury Hill (Dave Bascombe Mix)'/'Tell It To Me'/'Searching' (CD MUTE 275, January 6, 2003)

'Solsbury Hill (37b Mix)'/'Solsbury Hill (Manhattan Clique Extended Remix)'/'Ave Maria' (LCD MUTE 275)

'Solsbury Hill (Radio Mix)'/'Video Killed The Radio Star (37b Mix)'/ 'Short Film – Dr Jeckyll And Mistress Hyde' (DVD MUTE 275)

'Make Me Smile (Come Up And See Me – Edit)'/'Oh L'Amour (Acoustic)'/'Walking In The Rain (37b Mix)' (CD MUTE 292, April 7, 2003)

'Make Me Smile (Come Up And See Me – Dan Frampton Radio Mix)'/ 'Make Me Smile (Come Up And See Me – Manhattan Clique Extended Remix)'/'When Will I See You Again (37b Mix)' (LCD MUTE 292)

'Make Me Smile (Come Up And See Me)'/'Can't Help Falling In Love (Acoustic)'/'Video – Solsbury Hill (Original Version)' (DVD MUTE 292)

ERASURE ALBUMS:

***Wonderland* (STUMM 25, June 2, 1986):** 'Who Needs Love (Like That)'/ 'Reunion'/'Cry So Easy'/'Push Me, Shove Me'/'Heavenly Action'/ 'Say What'/'Love Is A Loser'/'Senseless'/'My Heart . . . So Blue'/ 'Oh L'Amour'/'Pistol'   *Extra tracks (as featured on CD release):* 'Say What (Remix)' /'March On Down The Line (Flood Mix)'/'Senseless (Remix)'

***The Circus* (STUMM 35, March 30, 1987):** 'It Doesn't Have To Be'/ 'Hideaway'/'Don't Dance'/'If I Could'/'Sexuality'/'Victim Of Love'/ 'Leave Me To Bleed'/'Sometimes'/'The Circus'/'Spiralling'   *Extra tracks (as featured on CD release):* 'In The Hall Of The Mountain King (New Version)'/ 'Sometimes (Extended Mix)'/'It Doesn't Have To Be (The Boop Oopa Doo Mix)'

***The Two Ring Circus* (L STUMM 35, November 16, 1987):** 'Sometimes (Erasure and Flood Mix)'/'It Doesn't Have To Be (Pascal Gabriel Mix)'/ 'Victim Of Love (Little Louie Vega Mix)'/'Leave Me To Bleed (Vince Clarke/Eric Radcliffe Mix)'/'Hideaway (Little Louie Vega Mix)'/'Don't Dance (Daniel Miller/Flood Mix)'/'If I Could (Orchestral Arrangement)'/ 'Spiralling (Orchestral Arrangement)'/'My Heart . . . So Blue (Orchestral Arrangement)'   *Extra tracks (as featured on CD release):* 'Victim Of Love (Live)'/'The Circus (Live)'/'Spiralling (Live)'/'Sometimes (Live)'/'Oh L'Amour (Live)'/'Who Needs Love (Like That – Live)'/'Gimme! Gimme! Gimme! (Live)'

***The Innocents* (STUMM 55, April 18, 1988):** 'A Little Respect'/'Ship Of

Fools'/'Phantom Bride'/'Chains Of Love'/'Hallowed Ground'/'Sixty-Five Thousand'/'Heart Of Stone'/'Yahoo!'/'Imagination'/'Witch In A Ditch'/'Weight Of The World'   *Extra tracks (as featured on CD release):* 'When I Needed You (Melancholic Mix)'/'River Deep, Mountain High (Private Dance Mix)'

Wild! **(STUMM 75, October 16, 1989):** 'Piano Song (Instrumental)'/'Blue Savannah'/'Drama!'/'How Many Times!'/'Star'/'La Gloria'/'You Surround Me'/'Brother And Sister'/'2000 Miles'/'Crown Of Thorns'/'Piano Song'

Chorus **(STUMM 95, October 14, 1991):** 'Chorus'/'Waiting For The Day'/'Joan'/'Breath Of Life'/'Am I Right?'/'Love To Hate You'/'Turns The Love To Anger'/'Siren Song'/Perfect Stranger'/'Home'

Pop! The First 20 Hits **(MUTE L2, November 16, 1992):** 'Heavenly Action'/'Oh L'Amour'/'Sometimes'/'It Doesn't Have To Be'/'Victim Of Love (Remix)'/'The Circus'/'Ship Of Fools'/'Chains Of Love (Remix)'/'A Little Respect'/'Stop!'/'Drama!'/'You Surround Me'/'Blue Savannah'/'Star'/'Chorus'/'Love To Hate You'/'Am I Right?'/'Breath Of Life'/'Take A Chance On Me'/'Who Needs Love (Like That – Hamburg Mix)'

I Say I Say I Say **(CDSTUMM 115, May 16, 1994):** 'Take Me Back'/'I Love Saturday'/'Man In The Moon'/'So The Story Goes'/'Run To The Sun'/'Always'/'All Through The Years'/'Blues Away'/'Miracle'/'Because You're So Sweet'

Erasure **(CDSTUMM 145, October 24, 1995):** 'Intro: Guess I'm Into Feeling'/'Rescue Me'/'Sono Luminus'/'Fingers & Thumbs'/'Rock Me Gently'/'Grace'/'Stay With Me'/'Love The Way You Do So'/'Angel'/'I Love You'/'A Long Goodbye'

Cowboy **(CDSTUMM 155, April 22, 1997):** 'Rain'/'Worlds On Fire'/'Reach Out'/'In My Arms'/'Don't Say Your Love Is Killing Me'/'Precious'/'Treasure'/'Boy'/'How Can I Say?'/'Save Me Darling'/'Love Affair'

Loveboat **(CDSTUMM 175, October 23, 2000):** 'Freedom'/'Where In The World'/'Crying In The Rain'/'Perchance To Dream'/'Alien'/'Mad As We Are'/'Here In My Heart'/'Love Is The Rage'/'Catch 22'/'Moon And The Sky'/'Surreal'

Other People's Songs **(CDSTUMM 215, January 27, 2003):** 'Solsbury Hill'/'Everybody's Got To Learn Sometime'/'Make Me Smile (Come Up

And See Me)'/'Everyday'/'When Will I See You Again'/'Walking In The
Rain'/'True Love Ways'/'Ebb Tide'/'Can't Help Falling In Love'/'You've
Lost That Lovin' Feelin''/'Goodnight'/'Video Killed The Radio Star'

ERASURE VIDEOS/DVDS:

Live At The Seaside (**Virgin Video VVD209, 1987**): 'Safety In Numbers'/
'Victim Of Love'/'It Doesn't Have To Be'/'Don't Dance'/'Who Needs
Love (Like That)'/'Leave Me To Bleed'/'If I Could'/'Oh L'Amour'/'The
Circus'/'Say What'/'Sometimes'/'Spiralling'/'Gimme! Gimme! Gimme!'

The Innocents (**Virgin Video VVD491, 1988**): 'Chains Of Love'/'A Little
Respect'/'The Circus'/'Hardest Part'/'Push Me, Shove Me'/'Spiralling'/
'Hallowed Ground'/'Oh L'Amour'/'Who Needs Love (Like That)'/'Stop!'/
'Victim Of Love'/'Ship Of Fools'/'Knocking On Your Door'/'Sometimes'

Wild! – Live At The London Arena (**Mute Film/BMG Video 790497,
1990**): 'Piano Song'/'How Many Times?'/'You Surround Me'/'Knocking
On Your Door'/'Brother And Sister'/'Crown Of Thorns'/'Star'/'Chains Of
Love'/'Hideaway'/'Supernature'/'Who Needs Love (Like That)'/'Stop!'/
'Victim Of Love'/'La Gloria'/'Ship Of Fools'/'It Doesn't Have To Be'/
'Blue Savannah'/'Sometimes'/'The Hardest Part'/'Oh L'Amour'/'Drama!'/
'A Little Respect'/'Spiralling'

ABBA-esque Video EP (**Mute Film/BMG Video 74321-10110-3, 1992**):
'Lay All Your Love On Me'/'S.O.S.'/'Take A Chance On Me'/
'Voulez-Vous'

The Tank, The Swan, The Balloon (**Mute Film/BMG Video
74321-12250-3, August 6, 1992**): 'Siren Song'/'Ship Of Fools'/'Chorus'/
'Breath Of Life'/'Chains Of Love'/'Love To Hate You'/'Joan'/
'Voulez-Vous'/'Take A Chance On Me'/'S.O.S.'/'Lay All Your Love On
Me'/'Am I Right?'/'Oh L'Amour'/'Waiting For The Day'/'Heart Of
Stone'/'Stop!'/'The Good, The Bad, And The Ugly'/'Who Needs Love
Like That'/'Stand By Your Man'/'The Soldier's Return'/'Turns The Love
To Anger'/'Star'/'Blue Savannah'/'Over The Rainbow'/'Love Is A Loser'/
'A Little Respect'/'Home'/'Perfect Stranger'/'Sometimes'

Sanctuary: The EIS Christmas Concert 2002 (**EISDVD1, May 5, 2003**):
'Alien'/'In My Arms'/'Blue Savannah'/'Ship Of Fools'/'Can't Help Falling
In Love'/'Chains Of Love'/'Breath Of Life'/'Oh L'Amour'/'Always'/
'Love To Hate You'/'Victim Of Love'/'A Little Respect'/'True Love Ways'/
'You Surround Me'/'Piano Song'/'Everybody's Got To Learn Sometime'/

'You've Lost That Lovin' Feelin''/'Chorus'/'Goodnight'/'Solsbury Hill'/
'Sometimes'/'Stop!'

THE CLARKE & WARE EXPERIMENT ALBUMS:

Pretentious (**LCDSTUMM 181, November 27, 1999**): 'Music For
Multiple Dimensions'/'Open Your Eyes'/'Too Deep For Tears'/'I Think
I'm In Love'/'The East Is Falling'/'Wilderness'/'Turbulence'/'Disappearing
Breakthroughs'/'The Light Faraway'

VINCENT CLARKE & MARTYN WARE ALBUMS:

Spectrum Pursuit Vehicle (**CDSTUMM 194, May 28, 2001**): 'White (You
Are In Heaven)'/'Yellow (You Are On A Beach)'/'Red (You Are In The
Womb)'/'Blue (You Are Underwater)'/'Green (You Are In A Forest)'/
'White (You Are In Heaven Again)'